Columbus
Then and Now

Portrait of a Man, Said to Be Christopher Columbus. Painting by Sebastiano del Piombo. (Courtesy of the Metropolitan Museum of Art.)

COLUMBUS THEN AND NOW

A
Life
Reexamined

By
Miles H.
Davidson

University of
Oklahoma Press
Norman and London

Library of Congress Cataloging-in-Publication Data

Davidson, Miles H.
　　Columbus then and now: a life reexamined / by Miles H.
　　Davidson.
　　　　p.　　cm.
　　Includes bibliographical references and index.
　　ISBN 0-8061-2934-4
　　1. America—Discovery and exploration—Spanish—
　　Historiography.　2. Columbus, Christopher.
　　3. Explorers—Spain—Biography—History and criticism.
　　4. Explorers—America—Biography—History and
　　criticism.　I. Title.
　　E123.D38　　1997
　　970.01'5'072—dc21　　　　　　　　　　　　　　96–49447
　　　　　　　　　　　　　　　　　　　　　　　　　　CIP

Text designed by Cathy Carney Imboden. Text set in Century Schoolbook.

The paper in this book meets the guidelines for permanence and durability of the Committee on Production Guidelines for Book Longevity of the Council on Library Resources, Inc. ∞

1　2　3　4　5　6　7　8　9　10

Contents

Maps

Acknowledgments

David Henige first suggested to me that I write a critique of modern versions of the Columbus myth. He later provided me with both source materials and editorial guidance. His suggestion was taken up by my wife, who insisted that I attempt the work. At the time I was a complete unknown both to Dr. Henige and to John Drayton at the University of Oklahoma Press. With only four chapters in hand Mr. Drayton accepted for publication the as yet unwritten book. In the following years, right up until the time of publication, he continued to show his confidence and provide support for my efforts. Alice Stanton, the in-house editor, made valuable suggestions for improvement of the presentation. Teddy Diggs, who copyedited the manuscript, taught me a valuable lesson: I was in dire need of a competent and understanding editor. There is no question in my mind that she ranks among the best.

From its inception my friend Sheldon Avenius has kept a watchful eye on this work. Unfortunately, he was unable to continue providing his useful assistance in the editing of the last chapters due to his leaving the Dominican Republic for Washington, D.C. As has been the case with my other editors, I followed most of his advice. Thus any errors are truly my own.

This book is based entirely on my library. I am indebted to the many who have helped me with my collection. Foremost of these are Maggs of London, Maury Bromsen of Boston, and Don Genaro Martinez of Santo Domingo. Two friends, Jim Hingst and Bill Skilton, provided invaluable assistance for the conservation of the library.

Friends and family have been unfailing in their patience and assistance. My daughter Betsy and her husband Rich Archer helped me to solve numerous computer problems; my daughter Sandra, my son Bill, and his wife Germaine each contributed in their own ways. My friends Armando Messina and his wife Maria Martha, Manuel Pittaluga and his wife Dinorah, and Sam and Anne Houston have all provided support over the years. Finally, I recognize all that "Tuta" and "Pim" have done to help me.

The debt that I can never repay is to Virginia, my wife:

> Now boast thee death, in thy possession lies
> A lass unparallel'd.

A well-written life is almost as rare as a well-spent one.
Thomas Carlyle (1795–1881)

Introduction

In 1939 Charles Nowell commented: "The definitive biography of Columbus seems relegated to the indefinite future. Recent 'lives' of the great navigator are frankly popular in tone. The true Columbist, with a knowledge of the problems and pitfalls awaiting him, shrinks from the biographer's task and confines himself to monographs."[1]

Biographers, while sifting through the many contradictory elements in the life of Christopher Columbus as reported by his contemporaries, as well as sorting out the often inaccurate accounts of the same matters as told by Columbus himself, have made many attempts to reduce this elusive personality to an intelligible whole. When faced with the seemingly paradoxical in his life, modern-day historians frequently confound the possible with the impossible, the probable with the improbable, rarely accepting the unknowable; confrères who differ are categorized as revisionists. As a result, many writers on the subject of Columbus have simply accepted the subjective interpretations of their predecessors, whereas others have elected to avoid the more difficult issues entirely. Few have been willing to resubmit previously held opinion to the scrutiny of objective investigation.

Daniel Boorstin noted that in this repetitious process, one so often based on mutual admiration, as shown by frequent citation, "the profession itself becomes the main, sometimes the only, audience for its publications. Inevitably the language of history [not just in works on Columbus] tends to become the jargon of historians speaking to one another. The profession becomes preoccupied with its own 'classic controversies' on which members write articles and monographs, or deliver polemics."[2]

The present critique results from my discomfort with many of the Columbus biographies published over the last two decades of the twentieth century. It is restricted to works published in the United States because this group appears to form a genre in itself. As will be noted elsewhere, many of these works are not without merit, but they are, without exception, often faulty historiographically. Many of their misconstructions and even errors are shared ones, hence forming a genre. These standard modern works include studies by Samuel Eliot Morison, John Noble Wilford, William and Carla Rahn Phillips, Felipe Fernández-Armesto, Kirkpatrick Sale, and Robert H. Fuson.

There is another, more recent school of related studies, known as the New Historicism. Its primary focus is on cultural conflict and artistic perception. Other interests of postmodern historicism include interpretative dialogue, Eurocentrism, and textual deconstruction. Its principal proponents studied herein are Stephen Greenblatt, Margarita Zamora, José Rabasa, and the French critic Zvetan Todorov. Their efforts have been measured to a certain extent by reference to Michel Certeau and Arno Borst.[3] In the introduction to his *Marvelous Possessions*, Greenblatt noted, "The discourse of travel in the late Middle Ages and the Renaissance is rarely if ever interesting at the level of the sustained narrative and teleological design, but gripping at the level of the anecdote." Hence he emphasized the anecdotal. He viewed it as "shaped by a similar longing for the effect of the locally real and by a larger historicizing intention that is at once evoked and deflected." However, while "seeking intention," one must take care to avoid reshaping the evidence on which it is based.

Zamora observed that scholars have treated the Columbian "texts as evidence, and their readings are based on particular assumptions about the texts' authenticity, reliability and accuracy. . . . rather than focus on the relation between the texts and the events they refer to, I approach the texts as texts and emphasize the mediated nature of reading and writing." She duly recognized, "The result of an interpretation that treats the mediated character of a text's mode of existence as a central focus of the analysis can be unsettling to those who feel most comfortable with the positivist assumption that the past can be essentially reconstituted through the study of documentary sources."[4] This can be an intellectually stimulating approach as long as the "focus" has as its point of departure the evidence presented in the documentary sources.

Rabasa's concern was with what he termed the decolonization of subjectivity, achievable by the destabilization of factuality itself, equated with the objectivity viewed by Friedrich Nietzsche as a false "canon of all truth." Rabasa's "basic premise is this: verbal texts, maps, icons, and other cultural products should be taken as rhetorical artifices and not as depositories of data from which factual truth may be construed."[5] The problem lies not with the concept but with discourse analysis based on nonliteral representations of historical data. It remains the privilege of the scholar to interpret given facts within their extralinguistic existence; again, the point of departure—the fact—may not be willfully changed to suit the author's schema. Distortion of fact, purposeful or not, is not a legitimate form of discourse.

From the start, Todorov very properly provided his reader with his exegetical method: "In Socrates' time, an orator was accustomed to ask his audience which genre or mode of expression was preferred: myth—i.e., narrative—or logical argumentation? . . . I have chosen to narrate a history. Closer to myth than to argument, it is nonetheless to be distinguished from myth on two levels: first because it is a true story (which myth could, but need not, be), and second because my main interest is less a historian's than a moralist's; the present is more important to me than the past." The result is similar to what Raymond Burr categorized as a "dissolution of the object."

Much of the traditional account of Columbus is based on two contemporary narratives, each with strong bias toward its subject: that of Friar Bartolomé de Las Casas, in his portrayal of his divinely inspired hero, together with his personal preoccupation with his defense of the "noble" Indian; and that of Hernando Colón, who, in the work attributed to him, showed a need to find grandeur in his father, Christopher Columbus. Interpretations based primarily on these time-honored biographies are the materials on which many historians have based their own reconstructions. The suppositions of a Washington Irving, the first to popularize Columbus in English, or of a Samuel Eliot Morison, the pundit from Harvard, become, in Napoleon's definition of history, "the fable agreed on." Any subsequent discordance becomes totally abhorrent. Such subjective polemics are more evident in the United States than in Spain or Italy, where scholars have carried out much productive research over recent decades.

Those who parrot the biased opinions of their eminent predecessors contribute, by the act of repetition, to the metamorphosis of what began as personal opinion into a full-blown and neatly beautiful historical fact, albeit more often than not an incorrect one. The English historian Edward Gibbon never lost sight of such difficulties when he said that human nature is "anything but unintelligible, it remains only partly explicable." For him, "The menace to understanding was not so much ignorance as the illusion of knowledge." The American humorist Josh Billings put it in nonacademic terms: "The trouble with people is not what they don't know but that they know so much that ain't so."[6]

In the study of the life of Columbus, one replete with contradictions, the scholar must take great care to avoid interpretations based on modern historical concepts that in the long run so often turn out to be merely the scholastic fad of the moment. It is well to remember that when Columbus first arrived in the "Indies" he did not know where he was or what he had found, and he died without ever understanding where he had been. Attributing unbalanced prescience to his story only beclouds the issue. As Sir Charles Oman, a historian of the art of war, wrote, "History is a series of happenings with no inevitability about it."[7]

Perhaps Catherine Drinker Bowen summed up the matter best when she said that biographers should aim "not to startle with new material but to persuade with old."[8] Indeed, through contemporary court and naval records, manuscripts, diaries, ships' logs, and private correspondences, some published during their authors' lifetimes and others published only years or centuries later, there is a more than ample record available for the study of Columbus, his family, and his associates and an even more ample record for the times in which he lived. There are excellent compendia of such data readily available for study, obviating the need, as in the recent past, to personally research the many European archives in which the originals are stored.

In his *Luther: An Experiment in Biography*, H. G. Haile remarked on the difficult subject of biography: "Biography seeks an authentic impression of life, of the sort one receives from living men and women."[9] Bowen noted: "No one comes before us as a resumé in chronological narrative, but as an individual characterized by a particular time of life. Seen in this light 'the objects' of our investigations are not objects at all, but are themselves perceiving minds! Each has assimilated its different experiences in its own unique way. A humanist must renounce all intention of bringing them into harmony with his own mentality."[10] Recently Stephen Jay Gould, a historian of science, also dealt with this problem, commenting: "How can one possibly peel away an entire edifice of later thought to recover an embryonic state of mind unaffected by the daily intellectual struggles. . . . The timing of events becomes jumbled in retrospect, for we arrange our thoughts in a logical or psychological order that makes sense to us, not in chronological sequence."[11]

Haile added, "In this rationale for biography I found a fairly clear obligation for the biographer. He is the one who is acquainted with both worlds, that of his subject and that of his reader. It is up to him to make this community of interests apparent. This, I think, is why each generation must write history anew, including the biographies."[12] Unfortunately, many of today's rewrites are merely repetitious, providing little new insight. The objective is "insight," not hagiography or obloquy.

History and biography would be not only dull but difficult to comprehend without a judicious infusion of the human element.

This is available to the writer through the use of corroborative detail. Such detail, though necessary, must be handled with great caution. Barbara Tuchman, one of my favorite writers on history (she was careful to point out that she was a writer, not an academician), offered an excellent illustration of both the obligations and the complexities involved: "It is what Pooh-Bah, in the Mikado, meant when, telling how the victim's head stood on its neck and bowed three times to him at the execution of Nanki-Poo, he added that this was 'corroborative detail intended to give artistic verisimilitude to an otherwise bald and unconvincing narrative.' . . . Pooh-Bah's statement in the case establishes him in my estimate as a major historian, or at least, as the formulator of a major principle of historiography. True, he invented his corroborative detail, which is cheating if you are a historian and fiction if you are not; nevertheless, what counts is his recognition of its importance."[13] Unfortunately, some historians, in their attempts to provide "historical verisimilitude," do "cheat," making it often difficult to discern the difference between history and fiction.

Columbus lived at a momentous time in world history, and his personal contribution, though far from insignificant, should not be seen in any manner that takes it out of its contemporary context. In Columbus's own limited field of exploration, the voyage of Bartolomeu Dias during which he rounded the Cape of Good Hope not only preceded Columbus's but also led the way to the Orient. Columbus's own voyage of discovery, in turn, was followed by journeys to the continental Americas by others; close on his heels came Amerigo Vespucci, John Cabot (née Giovanni Caboto), Vasco da Gama, and Ferdinand Magellan—two fellow Italians and two Portuguese—each of whom opened up access to far vaster and richer territories than Columbus's Indies and Paria.

On the world political scene, the role of Queen Isabel has been romanticized, primarily by Anglo-Saxon writers who have made her name familiar in English as "Isabella," probably a case of conjunction from her Spanish title "Isabel la Católica." In fact, she spelled her name "Ysabel"; in her marriage vow to Ferdinand she added, below her coat of arms, a yoke—*yugo* in Spanish—with the "y" as a symbol of their union. Her name on the contemporary gold coins (the *excelentes*) was the Latin "Elisabet." Although she was the primary figure in the reunification of Castile, her husband, Ferdinand, was the one singled out by Niccoló Machiavelli as an example of a prince who not only could dissimulate but also proved himself capable of the utmost cruelty—in short, an effective ruler. To portray the king's treatment of Columbus as petty or worse is to misunderstand this wily king as well as the geopolitical forces at work in Spain and the world at that time. To understand Columbus in the postdiscovery period, one must understand both; they cannot be separated.

Here an attempt will be made to place Columbus and his accomplishments within two time frames. His life will be treated as a maturing process, not portrayed as frozen in time. The very times in which he lived were turbulent ones. Many important historical changes occurred during his lifetime; the Renaissance began in Europe in the fourteenth century. One may, as many do, view Columbus as a medieval man, yet he lived in times of great intellectual, artistic, and political ferment. This was his real world.

The Jews were to be expelled from Spain before Columbus set sail on his first voyage, and many of the Moors were forced out shortly afterward. The Inquisition took force in Spain at this time, and specific confiscations carried out in the name of Christ provided much of the funding for Columbus's first voyages. Pope Alexander VI (Rodrigo Borgia), the Spanish pope from Valencia, apportioned the Atlantic areas open to the discovery effort between Spain and Portugal (the latter under the terms of a prior grant made by an earlier pope). For his later voyages, Columbus had to compete for funds with the war needs generated by the Aragonese border wars with France. Columbus was not such a unique and colossal figure that he eclipsed the events of his times or the magnates with whom he dealt. They and their policies are also imprinted on the pages of history.

The study of Columbus necessarily involves three disciplines, none of them exact sciences: paleography, transcription, and translation. Unfortunately, the inherent impossibility of exactitude in these three specialties lends itself to both legitimate differences in interpretation and purposeful distortions. Differences resulting from adaptation of the facts to a particular scheme can be significant, perhaps the prime example being the distortions found in the generally incorrect presentations of the *Capitulaciónes de Santa Fé*, Columbus's initial contract for exploration. Whatever the correct reading may be of the intent in the wording of this vital document, it remains historically unpardonable that, in transcription, the wording should be willfully changed or, if correctly transcribed, that the problems should be ignored. This is historical distortion, not history. As John Gardner warned while discussing the writing of biography, "It does not mean, of course, that a biographer has license to be cavalier about historical detail, or exclude possible interpretations of the facts out of preference for others that make livelier fiction."[14]

The eminent English scholar Gilbert Murray explained his method for translations: "I have often used a more elaborate diction than Euripides did because I found that Greek, being a very simple and austere language and English an ornate one, a direct translation produced an effect of baldness which was quite unlike the original."[15] Professor Murray's views as to the difference between linguistics and meaning in the language of the "original" are not accepted by all scholars; however, the question that he raises is one that all who deal with translations from a different era must answer for themselves. The Spanish vocabulary of the fifteenth and sixteenth centuries was certainly a very limited one compared with the modern English into which it is translated. This presents an obvious difficulty to the serious translator, as well as an opportunity for the "historical novelist" or the "romantic historian," perhaps appropriate terms for many of the writers of Columbus biographies. The fact that most modern biographies use data based on translations of transcriptions made by others opens the road to yet more distortions, inadvertent as well as purposeful.

Another literary great, Goethe, warrants quotation here. He wrote: "There are two possibilities in translation, the one requires that an author be brought over to us from his alien culture in such a way that we can look upon him as one of our own. The other makes rather the demand of us that we proceed over to the foreigner and accustom ourselves to his life, ways of speech, and culture."[16] The medieval life as lived by Columbus contains much that is alien to our ways. The spirit of his era can sometimes be best imparted to us through literal translations that use the limited vocabulary and the occasionally awkward phraseology of a simpler society.

It is obvious that research is at the heart of biography. Footnotes and references can be either illuminating or thoroughly confusing. In some modern biographies of Columbus, it seems to be the norm, rather than the exception, for the author's introductory remarks to provide a caveat that a certain contemporary account cannot be accepted at face value, only to base the following text to a great extent on that very same questioned work. Using such warnings, or using cautionary citations in the back of the work, to protect the highly selective editing of the sources may reflect charlatanry rather than editorial honesty. Here one must go to the author's intent: did he seek to illuminate or obfuscate?

Research can be carried to illogical extremes. In the case of researching a complex figure such as that of Columbus, there are literally thousands of manuscripts and publications available for study. Researchers must necessarily select their own references from among those available. The important thing to be kept in mind is that references used in building the biography must be made known to the reader if the latter is to have the means to evaluate the work. Bibliographies are, unfortunately, poor guides in that authors often list, as references, works that were never personally researched.

Barbara Tuchman offered sound advice for researchers: "The most important thing about research is to know when to stop. How does one recognize the moment? When I was eighteen or thereabouts, my mother told me that when out with a young man I should always leave a half-hour before I wanted to. Although I was not sure how this might be accomplished, I recognized the advice as sound, and exactly the same rule applies to research."[17]

Each author must decide the limits to his or her own research. One scholar, commenting on Columbus's life as so often presented today, noted, "The researches of many commentators have already thrown much darkness on this subject, and it is probable that, if they continue, we shall soon know nothing at all about it."[18] It is my hope that the present work will clarify, rather than further confuse, the story of Christopher Columbus.

He who furnishes a voucher for his statements argues himself unknown.

Seneca (c. 4 B.C.–A.D. 65)

Sources

There are two basic and distinct groups of sources to be considered in the study of the life of Columbus. The first comprises the many contemporary primary sources, those published and unpublished during his lifetime, along with the secondary sources in the form of facsimiles of manuscripts and correspondence that would not otherwise be available except through personal archival research in Europe.

Most of the materials that are now readily available for study, such as the Real Cédulas, were written by court scribes. Paleographers do not always agree about the correct transcriptions for many of these. Many originals, such as Columbus's logs for all of his four voyages, have disappeared. The versions known to us today are copies made by Friar Bartolomé de Las Casas (and probably Hernando Colón) from manuscripts that are of indeterminable origin—holographs, dictation taken down by scribes, or copies of copies.[1]

Authors writing after 1989 had available to them a transcription of *El libro copiador de Cristóbal Colón*, a sixteenth-century collection of nine of Columbus's letters in which are included previously unknown letters to the Spanish sovereigns. The copybook in which these letters appear was acquired by the Spanish government in 1985, and over the years 1988–89, the Royal Academy of History published a transcription of them, together with a historical-critical study by Antonio Rumeu de Armas.[2]

A facsimile and transcription of this copybook was published by César Olmos in two volumes in Madrid, also in 1989. David Henige addressed the question of their authenticity and cited other studies in his *Finding Columbus: Implications of a Newly Discovered Text.*[3] Spanish scholars accept these sixteenth-century documents as scribal copies of letters written by Columbus.

One letter of particular value is dated March 4, 1493, at the time of Columbus's arrival in Portugal on the return trip of his first voyage. Two other letters were previously known, although with important textual differences. One of these, Columbus's 1498 letter on his trip to Cuba and Jamaica, was known through a manuscript copy made by Las Casas. The other, his letter written in 1503 in Jamaica giving his account of the fourth voyage, was also previously known through a manuscript copy, as well as through its translation into Venetian dialect as the *Lettera Rarissima*. There are now available, for the first time, summaries of Columbus's journal for his second and fourth voyages. Formerly one had to rely for information on the second voyage on Hernando's extracts from his father's log, together with the accounts written by Columbus's companions Dr. Diego Alvarez Chanca, Miguel de Cuneo, and Guillermo Coma. Columbus's own letter on the fourth voyage is also now available in a more detailed version.

In the Rumeu de Armas transcription, capital letters and accents have been added according to modern usage; punctuation has been modified, while many old spellings have been maintained. Consuelo Varela and her husband, Juan Gil, were given the opportunity to study these manuscripts in 1985 before they were acquired by the Spanish government. Gil was the first to make a comparative analysis of some words and phrasing used in *El libro copiador* with those used in the Simancas manuscript of the "first letter," the earliest known copy of Columbus's letter reporting on his first voyage. He has since provided his own transcription of these documents.[4] In a brief study, he detailed some of the errors that he found in the Rumeu de

Armas transcription, which he categorized as "chaotic."[5] In Stephen Greenblatt's *New World Encounters*, Margarita Zamora offered an English translation of the Rumeu de Armas transcription of the letter in *El libro copiador* reporting on the first voyage.[6]

These newly found letters require a study of the use of Italian, Portuguese, and Spanish words and constructions, a study similar to that made earlier by Varela of Columbus's use of such in his *Diario*.[7] The enlightenment as well as the clarifications, together with the problems, that these manuscripts present in interpreting previously known documents and publications such as the *Diario* and these letters simply cannot be ignored.

It is only recently that Oliver Dunn and James E. Kelley, Jr., provided, in their *Diario of Christopher Columbus's First Voyage*, a reliable transcription with translation into English of the Las Casas copy of Columbus's lost log for the first voyage. Earlier efforts by Samuel Eliot Morison and others have proven unsatisfactory.[8] These two scholars have performed an invaluable service by also providing a Spanish concordance, the first ever made, in any language, of this important document.[9] In my discussion of this voyage, their transcription and the facsimile of the Lascasian manuscript of the *Diario* published by Carlos Sanz[10] have been used exclusively. The English translations, however, are my own, as are all other English translations offered in this critique.

The classical works known to have been owned by Columbus and his brother Bartolomé are of equal importance to biographers. These present problems of particular difficulty in that much of the mythology of Columbus is based on what are perceived to have been the origins of and motivating forces for his discoveries. Consequently, the scholar must attempt to determine the point in time at which Columbus read the classical works that possibly inspired him. What he, and later writers on the subject, would have one believe is not necessarily factual. One important source for such studies is the register of the books in his son Hernando's library. Unfortunately for English-speaking researchers, the definitive library catalogue is not available in English.[11]

Columbus and his brother Bartolomé had the habit of writing postils in the books that they read. These provide valuable insight into their thinking. Until recently, the only published collection of these appeared in the *Raccolta di documenti e studi publicatti della R. Commissione Colombiana...*, transcribed in their original Latin, Spanish, and Italian by Cesare de Lollis.¹² Modern research has revealed that not all of the postils were included in the *Raccolta*.

Modern facsimiles, transcriptions, and translations of some of the most important of Columbus's own books in the Columbine Library (the Biblioteca Colombina) were published in Spain in 1987. More recently, in 1992, the three volumes in the *Biblioteca de Colón* (edited by Juan Gil) contributed to Columbus historiography with the publication of the translations of the texts with their postils in Columbus's copies of the *Ymago mundi*, the *Historia rerum*, the *Book of Marco Polo*, Jean Charlier de Gerson's tracts, and Pliny's *Historia Natural*.¹³

Columbus's familiarity with many Greek, Roman, and Arab cosmographic concepts, as well as biblical doctrine, is clear. The problem for biographers is the difference of opinion as to when and by whom these primary sources were read: before or after the discovery, by Columbus or his brother Bartolomé? The postils in the copies of the classics in Columbus's library seemingly provide direct evidence as to who wrote which. Unfortunately, paleographers cannot agree in their readings of these postils. Nevertheless, the editor of the *Biblioteca de Colón* indicated the authors, known and unknown, of the postils in Columbus's copy of Marco Polo's book. He provided paleographic, linguistic, grammatic, and orthographic rationales for his selections.

There are dozens of differing early versions of the Polo book; Columbus used a Depino edition. There are three basic versions of Polo's work, and they differ greatly in their content. In evaluating the work's influence on Columbus, one should be careful to use only copies or translations of the original 1485 Latin edition that Columbus owned. His postils appear only in his personal copy.

Interpretation is often based on internal evidence found in the notations. For example, the motives of those who attribute a prediscovery date to a particular work, one in which a postil alludes to compass deviation in the Western Hemisphere, are suspect because Columbus did not witness this natural phenomenon until his first transatlantic voyage. Possibly the postil in question could have been added at a later date to a book that he had acquired before the voyage. Or he could have acquired the book after the voyage. Neither assumption can be taken as conclusive.

The most difficult task for the Columbus biographers is to separate fact from myth. Their subject is a poor guide in these matters because, purposefully or accidentally, it is in his own writings that much ambiguity is found. His son Hernando added to the confusion in what appear to have been purposeful distortions, and Las Casas, further muddied the waters.[14]

The latter's motives in doing so were as complex as those of his subject. There are many excellent studies of Las Casas in English. His *Historia de las Indias* was finally translated into English by Andrée Collard in 1971, leaving pending a diplomatic translation of this all-important work. His *Apologética Historia Sumaria* remains to be translated, as do most of the tracts. Perhaps the most important one, the originator of the "Black Legend" of Spain's treatment of the Indians, is the *Brevissima relación de la destruycion de las Indias*.[15] It was first translated in 1583.[16] An excellent guide to the study of Las Casas is found in the *Bibliografía crítica*, coedited by Lewis Hanke and Manuel Giménez Fernández. This work, like so many others of equal importance, is not available in English.[17] Late-twentieth-century writers have undertaken a redefinition of the influence of Las Casas on Columbian mythology. Their works tend to center on "communications" and "discourse," key words for the postmoderns.

This is not the appropriate place to go into the question as to the authorship of the biography generally referred to by the short title *Historie*, which is generally attributed to Columbus's illegitimate son Hernando. This was first published in Italian in 1571; the definitive Spanish edition, edited by Manuel Serrano y Sanz, was published in 1932.[18] This important work was finally translated into English by Benjamin Keen in 1959, although there were earlier translations of extracts.[19] Many studies have focused on establishing both the author and the sources for this work.[20] Some biographers have used the *Historie* as their basic guide without evaluating its authenticity. In the nineteenth century, Henry Harrisse, M. D'Avezac, and others engaged in a polemic centered more on the identity of the author(s) than on the content.[21] In Spain over the past few decades, informative studies have been made of all aspects of the *Historie.*[22]

There are many similarities in wording between Hernando's *Historie* and the *Historia* of Las Casas. The latter made some thirty-odd direct quotations from the *Historie*, a work first published a decade after Las Casas finished his own *Historia*. However, some of the passages concerned directly with Columbus had been written by Las Casas several decades earlier. He copied chapters 6 and 9 of the *Historie* entirely. He included in his own work some of the details from Hernando's paraphrasing of his father's *Diario*. It is now evident that both of these biographers had access to some of the previously unknown letters in *El libro copiador.*

There are those, including Columbus himself on occasion, who ascribed the whole momentous affair of the discovery to divine intervention. Friars Gaspar Gorricio and Las Casas offered chapter and verse, from the Bible and from the saints, in support of this contention.[23] Like their contemporaries, the official chroniclers Gonzalo Fernández de Oviedo and Andrés Bernáldez also offered rationalizations based on knowledge they assumed Columbus acquired through his presumed study of Greek and Roman philosophers, as well as Arab cosmographers. Another complicated affair concerns the conflicting theory that an unknown pilot gave Columbus the route to the Indies. All three of these rationales must be evaluated, since motivation is essential to the understanding of the man.

The major work attributed to Columbus on this subject, his *Libro de las profecías*, should shed light on his motivation and intent. Valuable as it is, it only became available in English in 1991 with Delno C. West and August Kling's *en face* edition with Spanish transcription and English translation. Unfortunately, the Columbus text is preceded by introductory and analytical chapters based on the Columbian myth. Earlier, in 1984, Francisco Morales Padrón had published a facsimile edition. Many of the materials are in the hand of Columbus's young son Hernando, with others written by Gorricio and an unidentified scribe. Unfortunately, it is not always clear which man, Columbus or Gorricio, was intellectually responsible for most of its Christian exegesis. Perhaps the most important part of the book is the letter from Columbus to his sovereigns in which he explained his eschatological concepts. This letter is not universally accepted as authentic, however. The work was assembled long after the discovery, and despite pretensions to the contrary, it offers no clear indication of the author's early beliefs or of his original purpose in setting out to explore the route to the West.

Fortunately for English-speaking biographers, Henry Harrisse, John Boyd Thacher, Henry Vignaud, and Filson Young in the nineteenth and early twentieth centuries personally researched European archives; each of them was multilingual. Each provided facsimiles and transcriptions, together with English translations of the basic documents known at that time for the study of Columbus. More recently, Lewis Hanke has become perhaps the major contributor to the study of Las Casas and his many works. Most modern English-speaking biographers have been forced to rely on secondary sources such as these for their knowledge of the materials available in the primary sources.

Another source is the account of the official chronicler Fernández de Oviedo, who not only was a contemporary of Columbus's but also lived many years in the Americas. He wrote his *Historia general y natural de las Indias* while serving as governor of the fort of Santo Domingo. His name is always given as above, but his signature clearly reads "Hernandez," without the Oviedo. English-speaking authors generally refer to him as simply Oviedo. He knew many of the pilots and sailors who had sailed with Columbus and quoted many of them directly. These accounts, which would today be termed oral history, often differ from the account given in the *Diario*. However, it should be remembered that the versions of the *Diario* as first published by Martín Fernández de Navarrete and again in the *Raccolta* (neither of these basic works is available in English), as well as in the two Las Casas transcripts, do not always agree, nor, for that matter, do those in the paraphrases and direct quotations that are given in the *Historie*. The Las Casas copy of the *Diario* was made many years after the event, as evidenced by his use of postdiscovery words such as *"Lacayos."*

The many differences in the testimony given in the celebrated lawsuit known by the short title *Pleitos* should not, as is so often done, be summarily dismissed as biased. Witnesses in any court proceeding are naturally suspect, but this does not mean that they are necessarily mendacious. In dealing with historical court documents, the reader must serve as the jury. The full translation of these court records is not yet available in English; however, Thacher included both Spanish and English versions of those he considered most important.

Until recently, Columbus historians in the United States followed the advice given by Charles Nowell and generally restricted themselves to writing monographs. Some of the more recent ones have focused on the many questionable positions taken by Morison in his various works on Columbus.[24] Before Morison, the most widely acclaimed and popular work written by an American was Washington Irving's *History of the Life and Voyages of Christopher Columbus*, first published in 1828.[25] Based primarily on Fernández de Navarrete's work, this is perhaps the major source of many of the myths that today appear as facts in English-language histories of the life of Columbus. It is not surprising that in a work dealing with such a complex subject, bibliophiles disagree as to where the first edition appeared, London or New York.

Care must be taken in abstracting data from the writings of the early chroniclers. One of these, Pietro Martire d'Anghiera, was unquestionably a personal acquaintance of Columbus and of other early voyagers, undoubtedly receiving much of his information from them. The problem is whether or not he quoted them correctly. For example, in the various editions of his works, data was added to and deleted from the text. The same applies to his published copious correspondence. Thus, what he is said to have written as given in the unauthorized version of his account of the first voyage, published in 1504 in the *Libretto De Tutta La Nauigatione De Re De Spagna De Le Isole Et Terreni Nouamente Trovati*, is not exactly the same as what he says in his own first authorized published version in 1511, which was in turn modified in his 1516 and 1532 editions.

Other primary sources used in the preparation of this work include the accounts written by Dr. Chanca, one of Columbus's companions on the second voyage, by Cuneo, another companion and fellow Ligurian, and by Coma, whose account was first published around

1497. In addition, the chronicler Bernáldez knew most of the key players. On his return from the second voyage, Columbus stayed with Bernáldez, who unquestionably used information from some of Columbus's letters. Fernández de Oviedo served with Columbus's sons at court. The various contemporary historians and correspondents from Liguria also provide details of interest. Biographical data on these writers will be given in the body of the text or in the appropriate notes.

There are a few very basic documentary sources for Columbus: Fernández de Navarrete's *Colección de los viajes y descubrimientos que hicieron por mar los españoles desde fines del siglo XV* (1829–37); the *Colección de documentos inéditos* (1880); Columbus's *Autógrafos* published by the Duchess of Berwick and Alba (1892); the *Catálogo de la colección de Juan Bautista Muõz* (3 volumes, 1954–56); and of great importance for Columbus's early years, the facsimiles of civil and state documents of Genoa published by that city in 1931 (Citta di Genova, *Colombo*). The last is the only one of these essential works that is available with translations in English.

Invaluable collections by Juan Gil and his wife, Consuelo Varela, cover all known writings by Columbus, as well as the private correspondence and reports by his friends and associates. Gil served as editor of the transcriptions and translations of the principal works owned by Columbus.

Works consulted, but rarely quoted, include the following: Francisco López de Gómara's *Hispania vitrix* (1551); M. Girolamo Benzoni's *Historia del mundo nuevo* (1565); Juan de Castellanos's versified *Elegías de varones ilustres de Indias* (1589); Antonio Herrera y Tordesillas's *Historia general* (1601–15), and Juan de Solórzano Pereira's *Política Indiana* (1648). The sources for the individual letters and *cédulas* are given in the notes. References to pertinent bibliographies as well as identification of sources for facsimile copies of contemporary documents are given either in the body of the text or in the appropriate notes. All references given in the notes and bibliography are to the editions that I own. They are also listed separately in *A Catalogue of the Miles H. Davidson Reference Library* (1991) and in *A Columbus Handbook: An Annotated Bibliography of Works in the Davidson Reference Library* (1992).

In many cases I have worked from facsimiles of the contemporary books and manuscripts, providing my own transcriptions. All place-names and proper names in quotations from authors, ancient and modern, are given in the form used in the individual publication cited. On those occasions where the distortion from the modern equivalents is excessive, the usage is indicated by [*sic*]. Foreign words and expressions are italicized except for those that have become generalized through use. All translations, unless otherwise indicated, are my own. Many of these will appear structurally awkward, but no more so than they were in their original language.

Columbus
Then and Now

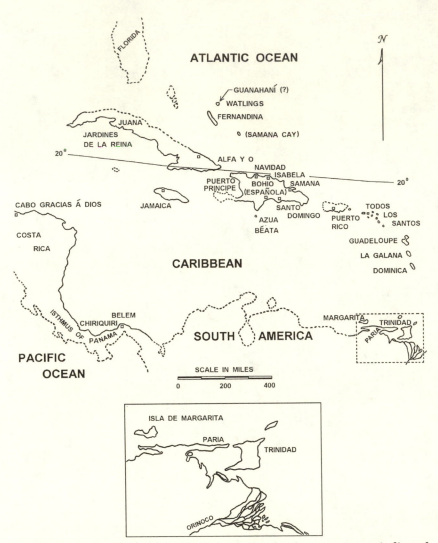

Caribbean coasts. Coasts visited by Columbus on his four voyages are indicated by solid lines.

Out of timber so crooked as that from which man is made nothing entirely straight can be built.

Immanuel Kant (1724–1804)

1
Background

Anyone attempting to write a biography of Columbus is immediately faced with a paradox regarding his origins and early years. In the case of Christopher Columbus, unlike that of so many other famous men, there is ample evidence as to just who he and his family were and where they came from. The paradox? Columbus offered contradictory versions of his background. In addition, his many biographers do not always agree on the correct interpretation of the readily available contemporary evidence, which so often contradicts both Columbus and his early biographers.

In Genoa and Savona, city-state and town on the coast of Liguria in northern Italy, there are numerous state and municipal legal records that attest to the residences and occupations of Columbus's parents as well as of him and his brothers. His father's name is given as Dominico Columbo or Colombo (as was customary in those days, all official Italian documents were in Latin). Many of the other members of his family—paternal grandfather, mother, siblings, uncles, and cousins—are named at one time or another in the numerous manuscripts still available for consultation in the city and state archives.[1]

Unfortunately for history, not all Columbists have availed themselves of these materials, and research in the archives has been carried out sporadically. One of the most important documents for the determination of his age did not come to the attention of scholars until 1904.[2] Consequently, early historians wrote their accounts of his life without having had the opportunity of reviewing all of the pertinent documents. In many cases, later archival research brought to light data unknown to them at the time that they were writing and accordingly to later historians who relied unduly on the earlier works.

There are only a few compilations of the known basic documents, and until this century these were available only in their original Spanish[3] or Italian.[4] Few of these have yet been translated into English, although British[5] and U.S. scholars have excerpted extensively from those that they consider to be of basic importance. The modern-day writer must often rely on the compiler's judgment as to what is or is not important. The Americanists Henry Vignaud and Henry Harrisse wrote their important and well-documented works in French and the latter also in Spanish. John Boyd Thacher and Justin Winsor are the major compilers who provided all documentation in English.[6]

This has often led to a habit, all too prevalent among Columbists, of relying on only one or two noted scholars, resulting in mere reworkings of the predecessors' materials. Thus, they base their hypotheses and analyses on the authority of the individual cited, rather than on personal perusal of the pertinent contemporary documents. Such practices result in unsubstantiated corroborative detail from which many of the myths surrounding Columbus derive; not surprisingly, these myths often make for better reading than do the bare facts.

Columbus's Origins and Birthplace

The evidence is clear. Columbus and his family were in the wool trade. They were listed at different times as either carders or weavers. His father enjoyed a degree of political backing, in that on two separate occasions he was appointed keeper of one of the gates of the city of Genoa.[7] His father's political association was with the local Francophile party as opposed to those supporting the pro-Aragón faction. The latter group's ascendancy to power apparently brought about the cancellation of his father's first appointment, which was then renewed a few years later. This was the first of three incidents in which either Columbus or his father appear as militants against Aragón and its King Ferdinand, Columbus's future patron. At the time that his father's appointment was canceled, the family moved back to Savona, where Columbus's father combined the carder's trade with that of tavern-keeper. On one occasion in 1470, he and his son Christopher cosigned a note for the purchase of wine.[8]

Beyond the name and residence (the valley of Fontanabuono) of his grandfather Iohannes de Columbo (in Italian, Giovanni Colombo), nothing is known of Columbus's other ancestors, although there has been no lack of unsubstantiated surmises.[9] The few known facts have been fleshed out over the years so as to portray him as a descendent of a famous early Roman consul, a member of the lesser nobility, an educated man, an intrepid commander of a corsair vessel, and a survivor of a bold and gory naval battle. All of these portrayals are either manifestly untrue or, at the very best, highly questionable.

Columbus has been said to have been a native of Spain,[10] Portugal,[11] Corsica,[12] England,[13] Denmark,[14] and Greece.[15] He was unquestionably Ligurian. His panegyrists would have it that the documentary evidence supporting his questioned allegations on matters concerning his early life has simply not yet come to light. Others say that he had to hide his humble background in order to gain social acceptance. Many simply ignore any incongruities in the written record. Most recently, partisans of the claim for Spanish nationality have asserted that the Columbus family that appears in so many contemporary documents in Genoa is a completely different family, one unrelated to the Spanish family of the Discoverer.[16]

It is important to establish the facts of his background if for no other reason than historical accuracy. Equally important, it is not otherwise possible to gauge the accuracy of those who would have him a Jewish converso, an Italian nobleman, or one of the myriad of other figures made in claims that can be at least partially evaluated through judicious use of a chronological analysis of the documented years of his life.

One of the still disputed subjects is that of the particular town in Italy in which he was born (this study accepts that he was indeed Ligurian, but it does not identify the town). Gianfrancesco Napione, an Italian historian, kicked off the debate in 1808 when he linked Columbus to a family of the minor nobility in Cuccaro.[17] He was soon followed by another Italian, Gio. Battista Spotorno, who, after a detailed study, decided for Genoa.[18] Over the years the facts have been clouded by the many legal suits for inheritance of the title of duke of Veragua, conceded to Columbus's son Diego, whose line today has passed through the distaff side on three separate occasions from the fifteenth century up to 1900.[19] Without entering into greater detail, it can be noted that in 1866 Harrisse listed twenty-eight authors[20] writing on the subject of Columbus's birthplace; in 1892 Césario Fernández Duro listed sixty-two works published between 1808 and 1891 on the same subject.[21] A *Columbus Hand-book*, published a century later, lists, in my own library, sixty-six works dealing with this ongoing debate.[22]

Two of Columbus's contemporary chroniclers, Pietro Martire d'Anghiera in 1504 and Andrés Bernáldez in 1550, both of whom knew him personally, said he was from Liguria but did not identify the town.[23] Among the earliest published reports, Paolo Interiano in 1506 clearly identified Cogoreo as Columbus's birthplace,[24] whereas Augustini Giustiniani in 1516 said Genoa.[25] Martire later identified him as "Genovese."[26] Alonso de Santa Cruz, c.1550, said he was from Nervi.[27] In a work first published in Rome in Latin in 1631, Alessandro Geraldini (first resident bishop in the Americas), who claimed to have helped Columbus get royal approval for his first voyage, reported that he was "Ligurian."[28]

Witnesses in the 1511 and 1532 hearings in the *Pleitos* agreed that Columbus was from the Ligur.[29] Pedro de Arana, a cousin of Columbus's Spanish mistress, testified that he knew Columbus was from Genoa.[30] Pedro was close enough to Columbus to have commanded a vessel on his third voyage across the Atlantic. Another witness at the same hearing placed it more precisely, testifying, "I heard it said that [he] was from the seigneury of Genoa, from the city of Savona."[31]

Of equal weight was the testimony of Diego Méndez, Columbus's *criado* (retainer), who is known to have accompanied him constantly from 1492 until his death, after which Méndez continued to serve in the entourage of Columbus's son Diego. It was Méndez who had sought help for Columbus at the time that he and the crews of the three vessels of the fourth voyage were stranded on the island of Jamaica. In testimony given in the *Pleitos*, he said that Columbus was "Genoese, a native of Savona which is a town near Genoa."[32] Those who reject this and the more than ample other contemporary evidence, given by both Italian and Spanish sources as well as by witnesses at these court hearings, are simply flying in the face of overwhelming evidence.

The answer can also be found in other contemporary documents. In a Genoese civil court document dated 1472, there is a listing for "Christopher Columbus wool worker."[33] Later, in 1479, he is described in another court document as "Christopher Columbus, citizen of Genoa."[34] He himself claimed Genoa for his home in letters, in the entail of his estate, in his will, and again in the final codicil to his will, made on his deathbed.

What is the reason behind so much futile speculation? It can be mostly attributed to parochialism. Each of the nations and cities mentioned wants to claim him for its own. Since no effort was made to locate the supporting data until the early nineteenth century, and since at that time not all of the archives had been adequately researched, there was, initially, justification for those early efforts to establish who he was and where he came from. To do so today is to fulfill Montaigne's maxim, "No one is exempt from talking nonsense; the misfortune is to do it solemnly." There are also the more recent attempts to make the facts of his background demonstrate his claimed "Jewishness." Among recent such quests is one made in 1973 by the renowned Nazi-hunter Simon Wiesenthal.[35]

Once Genoa is accepted as the town or jurisdiction where Columbus was born, the next step is to determine just who he was. This is a delicate matter, with many mutually contradictory elements that are difficult to sort out. The family's social status has been of keen interest to his biographers, beginning with his son Hernando (generally referred to by English authors as Fernando) Colón. Hernando was obviously incensed by Giustiniani's publication in 1537 that stated Columbus came from a family of "plebeians" and "wool weavers" and that later called him a "silk weaver." Both of these trades were filled by people of the artisan class. Earlier, in 1516, Giustiniani had added marginalia to his *Psalterium* in which he said, "Columbus was a native of Genoa, born to humble parents."[36] At an unidentified date in the early part of the sixteenth century, Antonio Gallo (1470?–1510), chancellor of the Bank of St. George, to which Columbus left a legacy, wrote, "He was born in Genoa of plebian ancestors."[37]

In 1551, Interiano published a history of Genoa in which he commented that Columbus's accomplishment was made yet more glorious because he had undertaken his hazardous voyage of discovery despite the fact that he was born of "most obscure parents" and that he was "ingenuous (as he was little literate)."[38] The *Historie* contains a list of twelve factual errors that Giustiniani supposedly made. These errors relate to such matters as the number of vessels Columbus took with him on his first and second voyages and the name given to the first land that he discovered. Hernando's preoccupation was not with listing these errors per se but rather with using them to demonstrate that Giustiniani was equally wrong in his appraisal of the family's social status.

The *Historie* reported that the city fathers of Genoa banned Giustiniani's *Annali* due to its author's errors in reporting on Columbus.[39] Thacher made a study of the claim and found that there is no evidence of any such ban ever having been issued. In 1887 Harrisse noted, as does the Città di Genova study, that in Columbus's letter to the nurse of Prince Juan, a copy of which was included in his *Book of Privileges*, he stated that he "came from nowhere," which has been assumed to be a reference to his family's social position. The passage reads, "The King and Queen, our sovereigns, who from nothing have given me so much honor."[40] Obviously, for Columbus, an unknown foreign sailor living in Spain, the mere fact that they showed him so much honor is notable in itself, without necessarily bearing any reference to his antecedents.

All the evidence points to one inescapable conclusion, at least at the time of Columbus: his parents, Dominico and Susanna, and his younger brothers, Bartolomé and Diego (their Spanish names), were artisans. They can also be identified as having resided over the years in various places on the Ligurian coast of the Republic of Genoa. Hernando was more concerned with Giustiniani's reference to his father as a *mecanico* than with the references to the family's admittedly poor financial condition, which he explained as their "having been reduced to necessity and poverty due to the wars and problems in Lombardy."[41]

It was while refuting Giustiniani that Hernando invented a story about Columbus: "While young in years he learned to read and write and studied in Pavia which was sufficient for him to understand the cosmographers . . . he dedicated himself also to [the study of] astrology and geometry."[42] Note that Hernando did not refer to Pavia as the University of Pavia to support his claim that his father was a man of letters, although it is part of the current mythology that Columbus did attend that institution. Neither his family's circumstances nor the very complete contemporary university records support this contention.

Hernando Colón and the *Historie*

The dispute, one that continues to this day, as to whether or not Hernando wrote all or part of the *Historie* was kicked off in 1866 by Bartolomé Gallardo, a Spanish bibliophile, who attributed the work to Hernando's library aide Juan Pérez de Oliva, who is known to have written on the subject of Columbus. To many, it has seemed inconceivable that a son, one who was a scholar in his own right, could have produced such a mishmash of fact and fiction. In 1875 Harrisse livened up the discussion by disputing the position that Hernando was the sole author of the *Historie*, a position taken by M. D'Avezac, at that time the foremost French Columbist. In yet stronger disagreement with Harrisse was another French historian, Count Roselly de Lorgues, who was a fervent believer in the uniqueness of the Colombo family. He started the movement to have the Catholic Church canonize Columbus, a move that was strongly supported at the time by Italian-American Catholics.[43]

Modern Spanish historians have attempted to determine the identity of the author(s) of the *Historie*. In 1973 Antonia Rumeu de

Armas made an in-depth study of the question. He concluded that the work is a loose patchwork put together from various sources.[44] Another Spanish scholar, Emiliano Jos Pérez, also wrote on the subject, finding the work "mainly fictitious."[45] English-speaking authors generally report the debate and then proceed to cite extensively, without reservation, from this questionable source. Modern Spanish historians lean to the view that the biographical data given in the *Historie* is of unknown origin, whereas the information on the first and fourth voyages can be unquestionably attributed to Hernando.

The avowed purpose of Hernando in writing this biography was to refute Giustiniani and Interiano. He also objected strenuously to the account of Columbus's exploits as given by Gonzalo Fernández de Oviedo in his *Historia general y natural de las Indias*. The first nineteen of this book's fifty chapters were published in 1535, the first full version in 1851. The *Historie* was first published in Venice in 1571. Hernando died in 1539, from which date it must be assumed that if he had objections to any earlier authors' works, he had to have either read the published versions or had access to the manuscripts of those that were as yet unpublished. This obvious fact is mentioned only because there are some who base their opinions as to who wrote the *Historie* on Hernando's assumed familiarity with contemporary works containing biographical data for his father, not all of which works were published during Hernando's lifetime.

Regardless of who wrote the biographic passages in the *Historie*, it remains a case of specialized pleading, as could be expected in a work written by a son about a famous parent. It was in this work that the claim was first made, incorrectly citing Tacitus, to the effect that the family was descended from a Roman named "Colon" who was awarded a consulship and praetorian eagles for having brought Mithradates, king of Pontus, as a prisoner to Rome.[46] Actually Tacitus listed the consul in question under the name "Cilon" and the eagles as having been awarded to Julius Aquila.[47] This misquotation in the *Historie* is particularly puzzling because it is one of several quotations that are made from works obviously known to Hernando. He had an annotated copy of Tacitus's book in his personal library, the famous Biblioteca Colombina (the Columbine Library), as well as copies of others that on occasion are also incorrectly quoted in the *Historie.*

The Columbine Library

It is unquestionable that whoever put together the *Historie,* this curious combination of fact and fiction, had access to some form of Columbus's journals of his first three voyages as well as to the notes of Hernando for the fourth voyage, on which he accompanied his father. Information obviously taken from Diego Méndez's account of the last voyage is also given therein. Yet, even if Hernando did not write all of the *Historie,* he did contribute greatly to what we know of Columbus: during his lifetime (1488–1539), he assembled a truly notable collection of books. Known today as the Biblioteca Colombina, it contains copies of contemporary works that are primary sources for the study of his father's life and times and, perhaps more important, preserves several books that were owned by his father and his uncle Bartolomé.

These copies of works owned by the Columbus brothers are of particular interest because Christopher and Bartolomé wrote extensive postils in many of them. Much information can be gleaned from the publication dates of the books as well as from the study of the postils. Here, as generally happens in matters dealing with Columbus, there is room for scholarly disagreement. First of all, bibliographers do not agree as to the true publishing dates of each of the individual copies, and obviously we have no way of knowing when and by whom they were acquired, although Hernando did write in some of them to whom they had belonged. For his own books, he generally gave the price and the date and place where the book had been acquired.

Since there is no way to establish aquisition dates for these books, the evidence is inconclusive as to whether or not Columbus had read any of them before embarking on his famous first voyage. There is also paleographic disagreement over the entries written in poor-to-middling Latin and Spanish (only one in Italian); many were unquestionably in the hand of his brother Bartolomé and his son Hernando. Obviously, those who see in Christopher a scientific genius read one thing into their interpretations of these disputable facts, whereas those who find his discovery to be the result of able seamanship combined with boneheaded luck draw quite different conclusions. Some historians neglect to warn the reader that their opinions on such matters are merely assumptions.

Here again the non-Spanish-reading biographer is at a disadvantage. The catalogue of Hernando's library was published in extenso by the Spanish Royal Academy in seven volumes over the years 1888 to 1971.[48] In 1905 an American bibliophile, Archer Huntington, published a facsimile of the first inventory of the library. It is difficult to read and is of possible use only to the most skilled paleographers. The definitive study of the library was published in Spain in 1970 by the Spanish scholar Tomás Marín Martínez. This study provides analysis of the existing records as well as useful critical commentary on the works of earlier studies by such eminent Columbists as Juan Loaisa, Henry Harrisse, and Simón de la Rosa.[49]

As previously noted, facsimiles and transcriptions of some of these books have been published in recent years. Consuelo Varela provided copies, with Spanish translations, of some of the most important postils that are to be found in the copies of the *Ymago mundi* by Pierre d'Ailly (known in Spanish as Pedro de Ayaco) and the *Historia rerum* by Eneas Silvio Piccolómini (Pope Pius II).[50] Although she accepted many of these as Columbus holographs, other scholars disagree with her on some of them. In her introduction to her *Textos*, she provided a study of the Columbus holographs. Juan Gil provided an analysis of both Hernando's and Columbus's orthography, their use of abbreviations, nautical terms, and syllables, their Latin and Italian spellings, and other matters in his introduction to Columbus's *Libro de Marco Polo*[51] and in the Columbine Library copy of Pliny. Francisco Socas did the same for the *Historia rerum*, as did Antonio Ramírez de Verger for the *Ymago mundi* and for works by Jean Charlier de Gerson.

Columbus and the French Corsairs

The *Historie* states that in Columbus's letter to the nurse of Prince Juan he wrote, "I am not the first admiral in my family." Some historians, such as Varela, have used in their publications the copy of this famous letter, written in 1500, as it appears in the version given by Bartolomé de Las Casas in his *Historia*.[52] Others have followed either the copy given in the first publication of this letter, made in 1823 by Spotorno in his edition of the *Codice Diplomatico*[53] and sent by Columbus to Naples for safekeeping, or the other copy, which was taken by Napoleon to Paris as war booty. A facsimile of this Paris copy was edited by B. F. Stevens in 1893, with an extensive introduction by Harrisse.[54] Many assertions to the contrary, the somewhat cryptic quotation cited above from the *Historie* does not appear in either of these earlier versions of the letter. It is of passing interest to note that the two copies that Columbus had made, and that are therefore presumably true copies, also include several paragraphs that are not found in Las Casas's shorter version of the same letter.

It would appear that Hernando (for the sake of brevity, his name will be used hereafter as the author of the *Historie*) used this possibly apocryphal statement to build a family connection with two famous fifteenth-century corsairs: the French Guillaume de Casenove, also known as Casseneuve, Casenovo, Colombo, Coullon, and Colombo the Elder; and Giorgi Bissipat, known as Colombo the Younger or "El Mozo." The latter was a native of Greece sailing under the French flag. Hernando, explaining his father's arrival in Spain, wrote: "As to the start and motive for the arrival of the Admiral in Spain, and for his having taken up seafaring, the cause was a notable man of his name and family named Colombo, very well-spoken of on the seas. . . . Marco Antonio Sabélico writes that this person was called Colombo the Mozo." He went on to say, "While in the company of the said Colombo el Mozo the Admiral navigated, which he did for a long time."[55] Hernando then described a bloody naval battle, one that never took place as it is related in the *Historie*. Even though Hernando did have in his library his own copy of Sabélico's work, his citation is inaccurate.

This is not the place to study the accuracy of this statement as regards his father and the naval battle. That will be done later. However, it is the place to point out that there is absolutely no proof for a claim for a blood relationship with either corsair. Perhaps

Hernando was more concerned here with showing up Giustiniani than with maintaining historical accuracy. He complained, "[Due to] the passion of the said Giustiniani, he made no mention of it in his history, in order that it not be known that the family of the Colombos were not as low as he said."[56] The particular Giustiniani work so objected to was not published until 1551, twelve years after Hernando's death.

The study made by the city of Genoa dealt with this matter succinctly: "No one denies today that Colón . . . created the legend of the family relationship to the French admiral. . . . What is not pardonable today is to perpetuate the error."[57]

The Family Name

Hernando was the first to recognize the importance of determining how and why the Discoverer came to use the name "Colón." English-speaking people are unique in the Western world in using the form "Columbus," one that the family never used. In Italian the name was "Colombo" or "Columbo," the use of which was abandoned by him and his siblings while they were living in Spain. Besides the tenuous linkages made by Hernando—with the Roman Cilon, with Colombo the Younger, the Greek who sailed for France but was confused by Hernando with the French corsair "Coullon," and with the Colombos, minor nobility of Placencia—Hernando sought further explanation for the adaptation of the Spanish "Colón."

He suggested the name was used "because in Greek it means member, as his proper name was Cristobal . . . that is of Christ . . . a name given in Latin, that is Christophoris Colonus," the inference here being that he was a "member" of Christ, that is, one designated to carry out Christ's mission on earth. Hernando also believed that his father saw a connection between "Colombo," the Latin word for "dove," and the significance of the dove as a sign at the baptism of John the Baptist and as the herald of land for those on Noah's ark, thereby linking these harbingers of good tidings with Columbus's own act in bringing the "True Faith" to the New World. Mystical interpretations of this and other matters relating to Columbus persist to this day.

In Spain before the discovery, Columbus was variously referred to in contemporary records as Colonus, Colom, and more generally Colono. His brother Bartolomé was first referred to as Colon in a document dated 1488; however, Christopher's name is first given this way in 1492 with the signing of his exploration contract. From that date on, the name appears in literally hundreds of documents, always as Colon, with or without the accent. These variants in name have been used in attempts to prove or disprove that a given person was or was not the same Columbus as the one referred to in the particular document in question.

Little mention has been made so far of the perhaps major source for biographic data for Columbus, the *Historia* by Bartolomé de Las Casas.[58] Las Casas shared in many of the errors found in the *Historie* while also providing firsthand knowledge of the postdiscovery events, many of which he witnessed. He did not create the myths but merely repeated many of them, generally as qualified fact. Like Fernández de Oviedo, he knew most of the key players in the pre- and postdiscovery periods. But neither of them knew Columbus personally, despite the statement to the contrary in *The Worlds of Christopher Columbus* by William D. Phillips, Jr., and Carla Rahn Phillips.[59] No adequate study of Columbus can be made without frequent reference to both of these first biographical histories of the discovery.

The beginnings of all things are small.
                                 Epictetus (c. 50 A.D.*–c. 138)*

**2
Early
Years**

Beginning with the previously established
premise that Columbus was a native of the city-
state of Genoa and that his family engaged in the
wool trade, we must next establish the date of his birth.
The year in which he was born is of particular significance
as the only real gauge available today for judging the accuracy of
some of the details of his youth as first provided by Columbus and
as since built upon by others. This may seem to be a relatively
unimportant matter, but it is precisely on such a small detail that
we can begin to reconstruct his life up until the time when he moved
to Spain. After that, the historical record provides much of the
information needed to fill out the schema for the rest of his life.

As already noted in the introduction, the historian Stephen Jay
Gould has pointed out, "We arrange our thoughts in a logical or
psychological order that makes sense to us, not in chronological
sequence." In the case of a historical figure, there is often documentary evidence available, allowing us to correct any purposeful or
inadvertent distortions of fact. For whatever reason—memory
failure or selective memory—Columbus left much conflicting data
about his life. Some of his biographers believe that he purposefully

16

told conflicting accounts in order to hide his humble beginnings. It is only natural that he should view his past from the perspective of the high point in his life; he may also have been merely careless in remembering exact details of his less exciting early years. What he did choose to remember—or, as some would have it, concoct—always fit well with the character of the future hero.

In his own accounts of his postdiscovery life, Columbus is accused of exaggeration. Thus, when he made a blanket statement such as "I have been at sea for forty years," he may have been careless with the facts. We should remember that he made this statement at a time when he felt that he had been poorly rewarded for his many years of effort. To exaggerate at such a time is only human and is not necessarily indicative of either a mendacious or an egotistical personality. Much of his discordant autobiographical data has since been put to proof through contemporary documentation.

Columbus's Birthdate

Columbus left several indications as to his birthdate. Only with difficulty can these be reconciled with other clues that he gave concerning his prediscovery life. The exact date did not become a matter of interest to historians until the nineteenth century, at which time seven different years were proposed, ranging from 1435 to 1455. Finally, at the turn of the century, the Americanist Henry Vignaud offered his considered decision in favor of 1451, which has since been generally accepted as definitive.[1] Many of the proposed dates were based on the need to reconcile a given episode in his life with his age at the time. Yet acceptance of the 1451 date makes supposed events in his youth chronologically improbable if not impossible. The solution? Move the birthdate back a few years.

The earliest mention of the Admiral's age was by the chronicler Bernáldez, who knew him well and who wrote that Columbus died when he was "around seventy years old." This would take his birthdate back to circa 1436. Neither Hernando nor Las Casas hazarded guesses. By 1730 the year had been moved up to 1441 in a widely distributed history written by the French historian Pierre-François-Xavier de Charlevoix.[2]

The most reliable approach to this problem is to seek out data in contemporary civil court records, starting with his father's age as a possible indicator of the son's. On February 21, 1429, his father, Domenico, at that time "about the age of XI" was apprenticed to a German wool carder in Genoa.[3] If one accepts the 1435 birthdate for Columbus, then his father would have been more or less seventeen when Columbus, the second son, was born. The next record of Domenico is dated 1447 in Genoa, the time of his first political appointment as gatekeeper of the Porto Dell'Olivella, at which time he would have been twenty-nine.

In 1470 Domenico appears as "a weaver of wool and tavern keeper."[4] This is important because on October 31, a promissory note for the purchase of wine was co-signed in Savona by Christopher and his father; the son is described here as "of [a majority] age of nineteen years."[5] There are those who read into this reference a legal definition of adult, one legally empowered to undertake the obligation, rather than a specific reference to Columbus's actual age in years. Many years later, on August 25, 1479, Columbus gave a sworn statement in another court case in which he was described as living in Portugal and in which he "responded that he was around twenty-seven years old."[6]

On the basis of these two documents, many historians have accepted Samuel Eliot Morison's conclusion that Columbus was born between August 25 and October 31, 1451.[7] However, the interpretation of the first document falsely assumes specificity at the time of the 1470 deposition, and the second document's date, given as only an approximation, is transposed into an exactitude. The documents simply do not justify any such unqualified assertion as to either the month or even the year of his birth. Unfortunately, many U.S. historians have repeated this unsupportable conclusion. For whatever value it may have, his father was reappointed to his post as a gatekeeper in Genoa on November 1, 1451. Like his son's birthplace, best described as somewhere in the Republic of Genoa, Columbus's birthdate, as ascertained by Vignaud, can only be said to be around 1451.

Columbus did give further clues as to his age in holographs that are preserved today. In 1503, at the time that he was marooned on the island of Jamaica, he sent Diego Méndez by canoe to Hispaniola to seek help. With Méndez, Columbus sent a letter to King Ferdinand in which he complained, "Little have I gained in the twenty years that I have served you."[8] He added, "I came to serve [you] at 28."[9] It is a simple matter of arithmetic to deduct the twenty plus twenty-eight from the year 1503, which gives a date for his birth in 1455. Yet we know, as demonstrated by Vignaud, that this is not correct.

Early Maritime Experience

Columbus's years as a sailor must be ascertained in order to evaluate his claim that he had sailed all of the known seas from Iceland to Africa and throughout the Mediterranean. This is of interest especially for those who attribute his success in crossing the Atlantic to his vast experience as a mariner. Was he as experienced as claimed? In a letter dated 1501, he wrote to the nurse of Prince Juan, "I have been at sea for forty years."[10] Las Casas quoted him verbatim as saying, "I went to the king of Portugal who understood discovery more than others, and his eyes and ears and all senses were so closed that in fourteen years he did not understand me."

By the year of this letter dated 1501, nine years had passed since the discovery, and all sources are in agreement that he was in Spain for seven years awaiting royal permission to sail. Adding all of these numbers together—fourteen plus seven plus nine—comes to only thirty years. If we accept the "forty years at sea," this leaves ten years unaccounted for. Hernando claimed that his father went to sea at the age of fourteen; therefore, if the fourteen are added to the thirty accounted for and the ten unaccounted for, the total would be fifty-four years. Yet in 1501, he would have been only fifty years old based on 1451, the year of his probable birthdate. Obviously, had he gone to sea "at fourteen"—in the words of his son—he could not have been at sea for forty years. If, in fact, he had been a sailor for forty years, then he first went to sea at the age of ten. He did say in a letter to the king, "At a very young age I went to sea navigating, which I have continued [to do] until today." In addition, during the seven years that he was at the Spanish court, as far as we know, he never "went to sea." With all of these differing years, we need to seek the facts elsewhere.

On another occasion he wrote, "Frequently navigating from
Lisbon to Guinea I observed the route with care as is usual among
naucleres—pilots—and sailors."[11] Antonio Ramírez de Verger, Varela,
and others have translated *naucleres* as "captain"; however the word
used is the plural for "pilot" in archaic Spanish.[12] In one of his postils
Columbus used *capitaneus* in Latin for "captain."[13] This gives no
clear indication of the position he held; it could as likely have been
pilot as sailor. His use of the word "navigating" could mean sailing
as well as navigating.

Several notarized documents from the archives of Genoa and
Savona indicate his presence in those cities many years after he had
supposedly gone to sea. On September 12, 1470, when he would have
been nineteen, he was most certainly in Genoa, since on that date
he signed, with his father, an agreement to abide by an arbitrator's
decision in a property dispute.[14] He was still there on September 28
when the arbitrator made his unfavorable ruling against them and
again on October 31, as reported earlier. This latter obligation, still
unpaid, was reaffirmed in the wills of both Columbus and his son
Diego, written in 1506 and 1523. This is one of the cases that
demonstrate conclusively that the "Christoforus" named in the
court records of Genoa is the same person as Christopher the
Discoverer. There is no question about the interconnection between
the debt and the two wills. The fact that he was in Genoa in 1470
for a known minimum of forty-nine days does not prove that he was
not a sailor, but it is the only documentary evidence available as to
his whereabouts in those years.

In March 1472 Columbus served in Savona as a witness to a will
in which he was described as a wool worker from Genoa. In the same
year, this time in August, he and his father co-signed a note for the
purchase of wool in Savona. It is of passing interest that this is the
only one of the many notarized documents in which the family name
is given as Columbus.[15]

It is definite that he was in Genoa and Savona at various times
between 1470 and August 1472. Of course, as a sailor, he could easily
have been in and out of port. What is less easy to explain is that in
all of these documents he is identified as being connected with
either the wool or the wine trade. Notaries and their scribes in those

days were very exacting in the details given in sworn statements. If he was indeed a mariner as well as a wool worker, in these port cities it would have been both correct and normal to so identify him. The two greatest seafaring states in the then-known world were Genoa and Venice; their sailors were highly respected worldwide.

The apparently indisputable evidence presented in the Vignaud study of the matter makes it safe to say that Columbus was born in 1451, somewhere in Liguria, of humble parents; his father was a wool carder, weaver, tavern keeper, and sometime guardian of one of the gates of the city of Genoa. The fact that Columbus's family was alluded to as plebeian did not necessarily carry any derogatory connotation. In those times the classes were rigidly separated by definition of category for legal purposes, but this did not always extend to social repudiation. Hernando became a member of the ruling minority in Spain by dint of his father's accomplishments, but as a nouveau riche, he apparently could not gracefully accept references to his humble ancestry.

At this stage in the life of Columbus, one encounters many difficulties in separating the nautical myth from the real-life prediscovery voyages. It is on his earlier voyages that those who most praise his nautical expertise base their premises. For some, his transatlantic crossing, which opened up a whole new world, is not enough; he must also appear as Morison depicted him—a boy-sailor, cruising for sport the coast of his native Liguria, and one of the most-traveled sailors of his times.[16] The first portrayal is whimsy; the latter is based only on Columbus's word—supported, inevitably, by versions of his life as given in Las Casas's *Historia* and in Hernando's *Historie*.

Voyage to Chios

Chronologically speaking, the first claimed voyage by Columbus that should be considered is one that he said he made to Chios, an island in the Aegean Sea off the western coast of today's Turkey. At that time Chios was an outpost of Genoa and of particular importance as the main source of gum mastic, a resin widely used in Europe for its curative powers, principally for headaches. It was the aspirin of its times and, as such, commercially valuable.

In the log of his first voyage, Columbus wrote of the mastic trees in the Indies: "[They] are larger . . . [than] I have seen on the Island of Xio [*sic*]. . . . [T]here is none except on the said island of Xio."[17] In a later entry he said that the mastic was collected on Chios around the month of March.[18] In a postil he highlighted the name of the island as well as the fact that "mastic grew there."[19] Yet he indicated no personal familiarity with either the island or its product. This is all that is definitely known today about Columbus and Chios.

The manner of modern reporting on this voyage is illustrative of the misuse of what Barbara Tuchman referred to as corroborative detail, admittedly more interesting than the bare facts but contrived nevertheless. Morison wrote on the subject of this trip: "His next recorded voyage was in a Genoese ship named *Roxana* in 1474, to help the city's trading factory on Chios defend itself against the Turks. . . . He may have made another voyage to Chios in 1475." On these trips Columbus supposedly learned to "hand, reef and steer, to estimate distances by eye, to make sail, let go and weigh anchors properly, and other elements of seamanship."[20] The account given in the more recent work by the Phillipses was more cautious: "Paolo Emilio Taviani suggests that Columbus went to Chios in 1474 or 1475, when two Genoese fleets are known to have made the journey . . . he may well have sailed with one of their ships in 1475."[21]

Such caution did not suit the eminent geographer John Noble Wilford when he wrote in 1991, "The family had moved in 1470 [to Savona] Columbus tells of experiencing his first long voyage four years later. This took him all the way to the Genoese colony of Chios. . . . He made a second trip to Chios the next year. . . . This may be all that will ever be known for sure about the early Columbus."[22] Neither Morison nor Wilford presented any evidence, not even a reasonable probability, for Columbus's ever having sailed on the *Roxana* or for his having made a second voyage to Chios. But by an author's very naming of the particular vessel, the reader perceives an indisputable fact! The allegation that Columbus learned his seamanship on this voyage, detailed in the account by Morison, who was an acknowledged seaman himself, gives cachet to the author's opinions, and at the same time Columbus's acquisition of his supposed nautical expertise is neatly accounted for. Columbus never said that he sailed to Chios four years after his family moved to Savona, nor did Taviani place him definitively on the *Roxana*. Wilford's closing statement—that "this may be all that will ever be known"—aptly illustrates Josh Billings's aphorism that people "know so much that ain't so."

Columbus ascribed great potential value to finding these trees in the Indies. He was so impressed with this find that he mentioned mastic in the *Diario* on thirteen separate occasions. Unfortunately, the local tree, though of the same family, is not the same as that tree found on Chios. He was to have similar bad luck with the local cinnamon bark and the false rhubarb, both of which, he boasted to his sponsors, were also abundant in the Indies. These too turned out to be of low quality for commercial purposes. There is no reason to doubt his statement that he had been to Chios; however, the claims made for the date and for his having sailed there twice are pure speculation based on unrelated documentation.

Ultima Thule (Iceland)

Without giving specifics, Columbus, on another occasion, stated that he had sailed all of the then-known seas. Only one of his voyages is dated, a trip to Ultima Thule (Iceland)—the mythical last outpost—so named by Seneca. In a possibly apocryphal 1495 letter to King Ferdinand, Columbus said, "I navigated a hundred leagues in the year 1477, in the month of February, [to] Ultima Thule."[23] He gave no indication as to "a hundred leagues" from what point. Morison extended this to mean "a hundred leagues north of Iceland" and added, "This Portuguese ship could have sailed beyond Iceland to Jan Mayen Land."[24] Morison was the first to say that this particular voyage was made on a Portuguese ship. Columbus went on to note that others were off by one hundred degrees in their locations of the longitude for that island; that Ptolemy placed it in the Western Hemisphere whereas it is in the Eastern; and that it is as large as England. Far more curious was another statement: "At the time that I went there the sea was not frozen, although there were extremely heavy tides, so much so that in some places, it rose and fell twenty five fathoms [the Genoese fathom was two feet] twice a day."[25] Tides of such a magnitude are unknown on Iceland.

In this particular case there are many disputable points, most of them leading to the conclusion that Columbus doubtfully ever went to Iceland, but the various anomalies have provided grist for the mills of the polemicists, with many resulting monographs on the subject. This same reference to the tides has provided justification for those who claim that he had reached the Bay of Fundy! As will be noted later, in discussing his arrival in Portugal, the above-mentioned voyage is dated only a few months after he supposedly washed up, wounded, on the shores of Portugal; the coincidence of times proves nothing, indicating simply another possible dichotomy.

Some of the details of this visit to Iceland, such as that of the tides, could instead indicate Bristol, an important English seaport that he mentioned in this same postil. There is no question that he could have visited Bristol, as did so many Spanish, Portuguese, and Italian vessels at that time. His fellow-Ligurian John Cabot has been identified as being in Bristol on at least two occasions; the second time Bristol was his point of departure for his voyage to Newfoundland.[26] Juanoto Berardi, a Genoan partner of Columbus's, listed a John Day of Bristol (real name Hugh Say) as one of his partners in a lawsuit in Seville in 1490.[27] This same John Day reported to Columbus in a 1497 letter on Cabot's expedition seeking the mythical island of Brazil as well as on Cabot's voyage to Newfoundland.[28]

England and Ireland

Columbus is quoted by Las Casas as referring to England three times in the *Diario*. In the first and most important reference, in 1492, he is quoted as saying, "I have been at sea twenty three years without leaving it for any time worth telling, and I have seen all of the east and west (which he says because of having taken the northern route to England), and I have traveled to Guinea."[29] In the *Historie* the version given is essentially the same but adds the following statement, which is found only in the *Historie*: "He affirmed that he began to navigate at fourteen years of age."[30] Taken together, these excerpts make Columbus thirty-seven years old at the time, indicating a birthdate of 1455. But as noted above, he wrote in a letter nine years later, in 1501, that he had been a sailor for forty years. Since twenty-three and nine amount to only thirty-two, there is obviously something wrong with all of these figures; nevertheless, they do not necessarily reflect adversely on the accuracy of the claim that he had been to England.

Columbus made two references to Ireland in his postils. One is in a copy of *Historia rerum ubique gestarum* by Eneas Silvio Piccolómini (Pope Pius II). Varela provided Columbus's postil #10 in his Latin version with a Spanish translation.[31] My literal translation differs in many ways from translations made by others. I translate from the Latin holograph: "Men of Cathay came toward the East. We saw many notable and special [things] in Iberian Galway a man and woman on two logs drawn along out of [in?] miraculous form." Here, as with so many of Columbus's writings, it is difficult to determine his exact meaning. Francisco Socas translated this postil: "Men from Catayo came towards the East. We saw many notable things, and especially in Galway, in Ireland, a man and a woman of strange visage pushed—*arrastrados*—along on two logs—*leños*."[32] The verb *arrastrar* in nautical terms means "to be urged on by wind or current." Normally *leño* means "log," although nautically it can mean "galley." The Latin version used by Columbus was *lignis* ("wood"). Socas also transformed "miraculous form" to "alien visage" (*extraña catadura*). Varela's and my translations provide a different meaning, the "admirable" or "miraculous form" relating to the manner of their arrival, not to their appearance. Varela did add the word "tempest" (which does not appear in the Latin postil). This succinct statement has been amplified so as to become the very stuff of legends. Morison wrote: "More important to him was something he saw in Galway, going or coming: two boats drifting ashore containing 'a man and a woman of extraordinary appearance,' both dead. These probably were flatfaced Lapps or Finns who escaped from a sinking ship; but Christopher and the Irish assumed that they were Chinese, 'blown across.'"[33] Do the words "two boats" make for better reading than "two logs"? More recently the Phillipses quoted from this postil: "The best evidence for an Irish landing . . . [he] said, 'a man and woman with miraculous form, pushed along by the storm on two logs.'"[34] This curious entry has a footnote that gives the source as Varela's *Textos*. These provide excellent examples of the differences so often found in transcriptions and translations made by competent scholars.

The Galway postil is sometimes cited as evidence of a rationale for Columbus's interest in finding the land that the bodies came from. There is nothing inherently implausible about his having been to Ireland, a voyage that was not uncommon in those days, or even about his having seen strange-looking remains in North Sea flotsam. However, any completely unsupported speculation that the sight of a man and a woman cast ashore motivated him to discover America is just that, speculation.

African Voyages

Columbus often stated that he had voyaged on various occasions to the fort of São Jorge da Mina, the first Portuguese outpost on the Gold Coast of Africa. In postil #22 in the *Historia rerum* Columbus wrote "which we have seen" and in postil #234 of the *Ymago mundi* he wrote "In which I was, a reference to the fort.[35] A puzzling postil notes that in the year 1485 the king of Portugal sent "magister Ihosepius" to determine the position of the fort in relation to the equator. The writer of this postil said, "He gave a report to the Most Serene King, I was present."[36] Incidentally, the sighting was taken mistakenly north of the equator. It is claimed by some authorities that this particular postil was written by Bartolomé.

In 1495 Columbus wrote a letter to the Spanish sovereigns (the letter is considered spurious by some scholars): "I was in the castle of la Mina of the king of Portugal, that is below the equator, and therefore I am a good witness to the fact that it is not uninhabitable as is said."[37] At the time that Columbus wrote this letter, both he and the king of Spain knew well that Bartolomeu Dias had already, in 1488, rounded the Cape of Good Hope, the southernmost cape of Africa and a site far below the equator.

An undated postil in the *Ymago mundi* relating to the discovery of the Cape of Good Hope raises the question as to who—Columbus, his brother Bartolomé, or neither of them—may have actually accompanied Dias on this voyage that was to open up the all-important southeastern route to the Far East. The postil flatly states, "In quibus omnibus interfui" ("In all of which I intervened").[38] Some scholars have argued that this refers either to being literally present on the voyage or to being present at the time of Dias's return to Lisbon with the news of the discovery. The postil is written in an unusual mixture of Latin and Spanish. Some contemporaries said that Bartolomé wrote a better Latin than did his brother, although Las Casas commented on this particular postil: "These are words written in the hand of Bartolomé Colón, I don't know if he wrote them of himself or in his hand for his brother Cristóbal Colón (the writing I know to be Bartolomé Colón's because I had many of his). There seems to be some bad Latin (and all of it is bad), but I put it to the letter as I found it in the said manuscript."[39] There are 24 Spanish words in Las Casas's version of this 115-word postil; 11 of the 24 are numerals spelled out. More recent biographers give these numbers in Roman numerals, making the inclusion of Spanish words far less notable. Varela followed the copy found in the Peréz de Tudela edition of Las Casas, and she has thirty-four differences in spelling from the earlier edition of Las Casas by Manuel José Quintana.[40] José María Asensio y Toledo, like Ramírez, used numerals, which he claimed to be "just as in the original."[41]

Like many other modern-day historians, Varela accepted this postil as having been written by Columbus, but at the same time she rejected the idea that he had sailed on the voyage to the cape. Asensio, on the other hand, based his theory that Bartolomé wrote the postil on the similarity between the handwriting and that of a manuscript of Bartolomé's written in 1509. Asensio also attached importance to the fact that on the last page of the copy of the *Ymago Mundi*, in which this notation of questionable provenance appears, Hernando wrote, "This book was of the Adelantado, my uncle."[42] There is also the minor question as to the manner of reporting the year of Dias's return from the cape. Portuguese and Spanish writers report the return as occurring in either 1487 or 1488, a difference due to the different customs for counting the first month of the new year as either December or January.[43] Taviani said 1487, Felipe Fernández-Armesto and Wilford 1488.[44] Obviously, had either

Columbus or his brother been on this momentous voyage, that fact would have been reported, other than by casual mention in a postil. Just what the writer, whoever he was, really meant when he wrote "I intervened" is unknowable.

Count René of Anjou

Columbus's most often questioned prediscovery claim was made in a letter that exists only in a copy written by Las Casas on a scrap of paper, found today in the Biblioteca Nacional in Madrid. To some scholars, this note is spurious. In it Columbus is quoted directly: "It happened to me, that King Reynal . . . sent me to Tunis to capture the galley Fernandina."[45] He went on to recount how, fearing enemy opposition, his crew wanted to return to the safety of Marseilles; but during the night he changed the magnetic charge of the compass card from north to south, thereby tricking them into crossing the Mediterranean to carry out their mission. This account appears in both the *Historia*[46] and the *Historie.*[47] These are the only contemporary published references to Columbus in connection with this particular raiding party.

Before exploring the historical record, we should note three conditions necessary for such a ruse to have succeeded: (1) the helmsman would have had to have been in on the operation, (2) the sails would have had to have been either trimmed or reset for the new wind direction, which would have required the assistance of deckhands, and (3) the crew would have had to have been inexperienced in order not to sense the coming about of the vessel, the changed position of the stars and moon relative to the vessel, and again, in the morning, the position of the rising sun. It must be remembered that these were not transoceanic liners but were small coasting vessels with no crew quarters; the men slept, when possible, on the deck. The holds were pestilential despite frequent dousings with vinegar. It is also noteworthy that the year 1472 is often given for this foray, since in that year Columbus was described, in a notarized document in Genoa, as being by trade a *laniere* ("wool worker"). If he had indeed captained a ship of the Republic of Genoa, a city-state known at that time as a major seafaring nation, it is incomprehensible that he would have been downgraded in a public document to the humble role of wool worker. It is equally unlikely that he would have captained a French vessel. These reasons alone make the tale highly suspect.

The House of Anjou held title to the Kingdom of Naples from 1268 until 1435, when it was dispossessed by King Ferdinand's father, Alonso of Aragón. Although René was actually count of Anjou and pretender to the throne of Naples, many English histories incorrectly list him as "King René of Anjou." There are records of Genoese assistance to the Angevins against the Aragonese. In 1459 Genoese vessels did join René's fleet and again in 1460.[48] Obviously a boy of eight or nine, as Columbus would have been in those years, could not have been captain of a marauder. Had he sailed on his own account on a later voyage, the latest year that René could have been engaged in any naval action would have had to have been sometime before the count's death in 1480.[49] It is believed that the last possible raid took place before 1470, although Benjamin Keen asserted, "The episode described by Columbus would have taken place in 1472 when he was twenty-one."[50] If the 1470 date is accepted, Columbus would have been at most nineteen at the time. In the absence of any evidence of prior naval experience, he would have been too young to command in either year.

Some modern historians follow Morison, who treated the story as true.[51] Kirkpatrick Sale rejected it as "almost laughable."[52] The Phillipses discussed the letter within the context of "assuming that it is authentic"; however, they offered no supporting evidence as to its authenticity.[53] Others vacillated, as did Fernández-Armesto, who first wondered "if it happened at all" and who then stated, "The episode is unlikely to have been a pure invention . . . the setting . . . Genoa's home waters, which he sailed so thoroughly in his youth." The route from Marseilles to Tunis does not pass through "Genoa's home waters," nor do we have evidence of his having sailed these waters "so thoroughly in his youth." These assertions are followed by a cautionary statement: "Whether strictly true or not the story should be seen as true to the man . . . a claim to a sort of natural sagacity, a deck-wise craft, which make up for his lack of formal schooling." More surprisingly, on the same page this questionable voyage becomes a key to the life of Columbus: "The tale of the voyage represents a glimpse of the first decisive shift in Columbus's life: from the weaver's shop to shipboard."[54] The point here is not only that the reasoning is circuitous but also, and equally obvious, that myths die hard.

Arrival in Portugal

The next, and by far the most famous, of the prediscovery "voyages" supposedly explains the time and manner of Columbus's first arrival in Portugal. The year can be deduced from his own statements made many years afterward, or if one accepts the story of his participation in a naval battle, as told first by Hernando, one must first determine which naval affair Hernando was referring to in order to establish the date of that particular encounter. Since Hernando is the only known source for this tale of derring-do (although Las Casas provided essentially the same story), it must be studied using his own words:

> [A] man . . . named Colombo . . . once captured four large Venetian galleys, whose size and strength could not be believed without having seen them. This one was called Colombo the Younger, as distinct from another who had been a great man of the sea. Marco Antonio Sabélico, who was another Livy of our times wrote in Book Eight of the Tenth Decade, that about the time that Maxmillian, son of the Emperor Frederick the Third, was elected King of the Romans, Jerónimo Donato was sent from Venice to Portugal as Ambassador, in order that, in the name of the seigneury, he give thanks to King John the Second, because he had clothed and helped all of the galley slaves and men of those large galleys so that they could return to Venice because it happened that returning from Flanders they were defeated near Lisbon by the famous corsair Colombo the Younger who had despoiled them and landed them . . . while the Admiral was sailing in the company of the said Colombo the Younger, which he did for a long time, it happened that they went to find four large Venetian galleys that were coming from Flanders, and they encountered them between Lisbon and Cape San Vicente, which is in Portugal, and there they fought fiercely, and they drew close so that on both sides they hooked together with great hate, wounding themselves without compassion,

the same with hand weapons as with grenades and other firearms, in
such a manner that having fought from morning to dusk, and many
people on both sides dead or wounded, the Admiral's boat and a large
Venetian boat were set on fire, and because they were locked together
with grappling hooks and iron chains, instruments that men of the
sea use for such purposes, they could not be freed either one or the
other, due to the hooks that joined them, and for terror of the fire, that
in a short time grew so much that the remedy was for those who could
to jump into the sea, in order to die that way rather than support the
flames, and the Admiral being a great swimmer, and being two
leagues or a little more from the shore, taking an oar that he found,
and helping himself at times with it, and at times swimming, it
pleased God (who had him saved for a better thing) to give him
strength to reach land, although so tired and exhausted from the
wetness of the water that he took many days to recover.[55]

It should be noted that in this passage the ambassador was sent
in regard to men that Colombo the Younger "had despoiled . . . and
landed" on shore and also that there is no mention of the Admiral's
having been wounded. The version of this same affair as given by
Las Casas reads somewhat differently: "Recovering from the
stiffness of his legs, and the great humidity of the water and from
the labors through which he had passed, and perhaps with some of
the wounds that he had received in the battle cured he went to
Lisbon, which was not far."[56] To begin with, Las Casas was the first
to mention a wound; second, the key words are *por ventura*, which
translate as "perhaps" or "perchance." This must be taken as a
supposition rather than as a positive statement.

Morison placed it more definitively: "Columbus . . . resting when
exhausted (for he had been wounded in the battle), he managed to
reach the shore."[57] Here there is no question that in this historian's
opinion, Columbus was definitely wounded, a condition that caused
him trouble even before he reached shore; this is a slightly different
story from the one told by the only contemporaries to recount this
dubious event in the Admiral's life. Hernando did not mention a
wound, and Las Casas was ambiguous on the subject. Wilford,
generally more cautious, limited himself to saying that when
Columbus came ashore, he was "exhausted and possibly wounded."[58]

There are two important reasons to verify this story. First, it could provide the date of Columbus's arrival in Portugal. If found to be true, this account also indicates an adventurous nature, one that could be expected of a renowned seaman. If the account is false, we can never know why Hernando invented this tale, nor can we readily understand its continued propagation, often with embellishments, by modern-day historians. To determine the facts, one must go to the historical record. There were two corsairs known as Colombo: the Elder and the Younger. The latter was Giorgi Bissipat, a Greek corsair in the employ of the king of France. As noted in the previous chapter, the elder Colombo's cognomen of "Coullon" led Hernando to claim a family relationship. According to Morison:

> In May 1476, Genoa organized a convoy to protect a quantity of mastic being shipped to Lisbon, England and Flanders. . . . [O]ne ship, named *Bechella* . . . took young Christopher on as foremast hand. . . . [T]he convoy was attacked by a Franco-Portuguese war fleet commanded by a famous naval hero, Guillaume de Casenove [*sic*] . . . the battle raged, by nightfall seven ships, including the *Bechella*, had gone down and the surviving vessels were glad to sheer off and seek the nearest friendly port. . . . Columbus leaped into the sea, grasped a sweep and floated free, and by pushing it ahead of him and resting when exhausted (for he was wounded in the battle), he managed to reach the shore, over six miles distant.[59]

Manuel Serrano y Sanz noted that the details given by Hernando for a battle against four Venetian galleys returning from Flanders correspond with the details of a battle that did take place under the command of Caseneuve on August 21, 1485. However, "the details that Hernando added about some vessels hooked together followed by a raging fire correspond to another earlier naval battle, where George the Greek fought against four Genoese galleys and a larger vessel on August 13, 1476." There are two versions, written by survivors, of this earlier battle. On September 20, 1476, in Genoa, Juan Francisco Pallavicini wrote that it was not easy to be saved and that all eight (not seven, as given by Morison) vessels were destroyed by fire. Another letter, written in the same year by another survivor, gives the following additional details: "Our people, not wanting that such ships fall in the hands of the said Coron [*sic*], set the said ships on fire, in which there were close to a thousand Genoese from the Riviera . . . and of which there were many from Savona."[60]

The above accounts, ancient and modern, differ in important aspects. The fleet in 1476 was Genoese, not Venetian; unlike the later Venetian vessels, which were returning from Flanders, the Genoese fleet was outward bound; the Genoese fleet was attacked by Colombo the Younger, whereas Caseneuve commanded the much later attack against the Venetian galleys. Morison offered undocumented details, not available in the contemporary accounts, down to the position that Columbus had on deck. In the *Historie* version, the Venetian fleet, while returning to Venice from Flanders, was attacked by Colombo the Younger, under whom Columbus was supposedly serving. At that time the French were supporting Afonso V of Portugal in the war of Castilian succession. Obviously, if it could be said that Columbus sailed against the Genoans, he could be judged for having fought against his own nation. If he was shown as joined in the war against Castile, then he fought against the allies of his future sponsors. None of the facts given in biographies jibe with the known historical facts of the nature of the two naval engagements.

Most historians place Columbus's arrival in Portugal between 1470 and 1473. He wrote that he had "served the king [of Portugal]" for fourteen years before coming to Spain. By one of his own calculations he had arrived in Spain around 1483; therefore he would have arrived in Portugal around 1469. There appears to be general agreement that he had been in Spain for approximately seven years before 1492, the year of the discovery. This would have had him arriving in Spain around 1485. Deducting his own claimed fourteen years in Portugal, we have him arriving there at the latest around 1471. Based on these figures, he would already have been living in Portugal at the time of the first battle and would already have left for Spain by the time of the second. The basic source for this Columbian myth is Hernando, who mixed up the naval battles, their commanders, the flags under which they sailed, and the dates of the engagements. Unfortunately, this was also one of those occasions on which Morison allowed his lively imagination to run away with his historical judgment; regrettably for the historical record, many scholars have copied uncritically Hernando's or Morison's version of these nonevents in the life of Columbus.

Trips to Madeira

On August 25, 1479, Columbus, while testifying in court in Genoa, stated that "in the month of July in the previous year," while he and "the said Paolo [Negri] were in Lisbon he was sent by the said Paolo to the island of Madeira to buy sugar . . . and at the end of his time in that island [he] contracted a vessel commanded by Ferdinando Palenciae, a Portuguese, in whose ship the said quantity of sugar was to be loaded."[61] Morison, changing Columbus's own statement, offered instead: "We find Christopher at sea again in the summer of 1478 as captain of a Portuguese ship which Centurione, his former employer, had chartered to buy sugar in Madeira."[62] Paolo Negri was at that time the Lisbon agent for the Centuriones, an important house of Genoan traders. This simple and clear instance of a commercial visit to Madeira to buy sugar and ship it by chartered vessel has here been transformed into another part of the myth of Columbus, the highly experienced sea captain!

Morison also made much of a simple statement in which Columbus is quoted as saying that at one time he had to bring two ships from Porto Santo to Lisbon; although the second vessel was delayed a day in port, he arrived with the first vessel eight days earlier because, unlike the other vessel, his had favorable winds. In this same letter, which, as previously noted, was of questionable authenticity, he said he had sailed for René of Anjou and that he had "navigated" to Iceland. In one postil in the *Historia rerum* he did say that he had often "navigated" from Lisbon to Guinea.[63] There is no contemporary evidence that he ever sailed as a ship's captain. On his four voyages of discovery, he always sailed as fleet commander.

Analysis of these disparate claims leads to several conclusions. First, it is possible but unproven that Columbus sailed to Iceland. If he did not sail to England, although it seems probable that he did, he at least had close personal contacts with Bristol. There is neither the means to confirm nor any reason to doubt that he visited Ireland during his travels. It remains probable that he once sailed to the Genoese dependency of Chios, but confirmatory details are lacking. His claim to have been to the Gold Coast of Africa sounds reasonable; but the claim, worded in the same manner, that either he or his brother Bartolomé had been with Dias on his rounding of the Cape of Good Hope either is based on a misreading of a postil of indeterminable origin or is pure fiction. The only probability for his having participated in a raid on Tunis would have been as a young sailor; the compass story is at best apocryphal. The tale of his swimming to shore after a bloody naval battle is obviously built out of whole cloth; only the more credulous among his biographers even bother to repeat it. What is important is that it is a known fact that he did live in Portugal, and there is much evidence for events in his life there that can be substantiated by contemporary documents.

It is not permitted to know all things.

Horace (65–8 B.C.)

3
Early Travels and Marriage

We know more about Columbus's life in Portugal than about his early days, but this still does not amount to much. As was the case regarding his youth, the available information is a mixture of misleading details and of conjecture—supplied by both him and his early biographers—as well as many embellishments added by later admirers. Myth and hagiography equally influence modern-day accounts of his life at this time. Thus, this important phase in his development into a man with a mission remains shrouded in mystery.

Two Visits to Portugal

In the previous chapter we attempted to determine the date of Columbus's arrival in Iberia. The tale about his swimming ashore in Portugal after a naval battle was shown to be one of those interesting myths, without historical basis, that originated in the *Historie*. The actual date for his arrival in Portugal can be placed, with any degree of certainty, only within a time frame of the two years of 1470 and 1471. Columbus stated that he lived there for fourteen years, until either 1484 or 1485. There are, however, historians who have placed his arrival in Portugal as late as 1481. It is generally agreed that Columbus and his brother Bartolomé joined forces in Lisbon; the questions remain as to when they arrived and as to who preceded whom. There is general acceptance of the notion that Bartolomé was probably, at some undefined time, established there as a mapmaker. Morison speculated, "His [Columbus's] host may have been his younger brother Bartholomew, who had already established a small chart-making business in Lisbon."[1]

As Manuel Serrano y Sanz pointed out, "The first chroniclers to write about Columbus, Gallo, Giustiniani, and Fernández de Oviedo simply say that he went to Portugal because his brother was there and in no way mention the dramatic episode of the naval battle referred to by D. Hernando."[2] Bernáldez, who knew Columbus personally, wrote that he was a "seller of books."[3] Las Casas quoted from Augustini Giustiniani, who wrote, "This Christobal Colombo, in his tender years, learnt the principles of [religious] doctrine, when he was a youth, he learnt the art of the sea and went to Lisbon, in Portugal, where he learnt matters of cosmography."[4]

There is no direct evidence that his brother was a chart maker in Portugal, but it has been often assumed, although not proven, that Bartolomé taught his brother this important craft; Las Casas, however, suggested that it was the other way around. In those early days of transoceanic exploration, navigational charts were at a premium; there is no doubt that at some point the two brothers became competent chart makers. There is, however, no proof as to when or where they learned the craft.

The account given in the *Historie* of Columbus's arrival in Lisbon is terse, saying only that he went there because "he knew that there were many of his nation of Genoa there, he went there the fastest that he could, upon being known by them, they extended him so many courtesies and such a good reception that he established a home and married."[5] As far as we know from contemporary records, he associated mostly with Florentins and Genoans during his stays both in Portugal and later in Spain. If Hernando did write this segment of the *Historie*, it would not be surprising that he failed to mention Bartolomé at that particular time, since Hernando and his uncle were never close. Las Casas mentioned the two brothers living together in Lisbon in 1487: "Cristóbal Colón and his brother Bartolomé Colón lived in those days in Portugal."[6] However, there is ample documentary evidence that in this case Las Casas was in error, because at that time Columbus unquestionably lived in Spain.

Columbus was probably visiting in Lisbon around the time that Bartolomeu Dias returned from the Cape of Good Hope (1488), since there is a letter to him at the time from João II. The king said: "We saw your letter that you wrote to us . . . and as to your coming here . . . the things that concern you will be handled in a manner that will please you. . . . And if by chance you have any problem with our justices, for any reason because of any matters that you left pending . . . we assure you . . . that you will not be imprisoned, detained, accused, cited nor demanded for any cause, be it civil or criminal of any kind."[7]

Offering an explanation for the "matters . . . left pending," Hernando noted, "With his son Diego he had left [Portugal] secretly, for fear that the king would stop him, because knowing how those that he had sent with the caravels had failed him, he wanted to ingratiate himself with the Admiral, and wanted him to come back to carry out his plan."[8] As previously noted, Columbus possibly did make this trip to Lisbon, as is stated in a *Ymago mundi* postil that is believed to have been written by him. This postil cannot mean, as might be inferred from the wording, that its writer had also sailed with Dias.

The lack of any further evidence relating to this visit, if it did take place, has inevitably led to confusion. King João's letter is clearly a response to an earlier one from Columbus; it is an acknowledgment offering a safe-conduct, not an invitation. It has been noted that similar phrases offering safe-conducts were in common usage in Portuguese correspondence with foreigners. Wilford viewed the matter differently: "Bartholomew was perhaps instrumental in securing for Columbus an invitation and safe-conduct credentials for a visit to Lisbon for John II to receive his appeal."[9] There is no way of knowing just what reason Columbus gave the king for wanting to visit Lisbon. Similar difficulty in rendering this letter intelligible is evidenced by Fernández-Armesto when he presumed the presence of the two brothers in Lisbon "in the second half of the 1480's." Yet, in a footnote discussing the postil relating to the Dias voyage, this author said, "Las Casas was convinced that Bartolomé has written many of the notations . . . but Columbus is more likely to have been in Lisbon at the relevant time than his brother."[10] Such circumlocutions and ambiguities only add to the existing confusion.

Whatever Columbus's reasons for wanting a safe-conduct to Portugal, the successful voyage of Dias would probably have caused the king to have little interest in any proposal by Columbus to find an alternate western route to India. Portugal now knew the most important part of the route to reach the spices of the East without being hampered by Turkish interdiction of the eastern Mediterranean land route resulting from the fall of Constantinople. Before the Dias voyage, many navigators believed the southernmost part of Africa to be impassable. It is important to remember that despite this much earlier Portuguese rounding of the Cape, as every English-speaking schoolchild knows it wasn't until "fourteen ninety-eight [that] Da Gama knocked at India's gate."

The Portuguese had unsuccessfully sought western Atlantic islands before Columbus's successful first voyage. It has been maintained that the Portuguese king originally turned down a proposal made by Columbus around 1484 to explore the western route because his claims for rewards and recognition in the event of success were excessive. This does not seem likely because in 1486 the Portuguese Crown signed an agreement with Fernam Dulmo to seek lands to the west, specifically mentioning the fabled Island of the Seven Cities. Dulmo had to delay his voyage until he could get financial backing, which he finally procured from Juan Alfonso de Estreito, who was to share in the command of the fleet and receive half of the benefits in the event of success.[11] (Years later the heirs of Martín Alonso Pinzón claimed that their father was chiefly responsible for putting together the fleet for Columbus's first journey and had had a similar agreement with Columbus.) Dulmo finally set sail on his unsuccessful endeavor in March 1487. Hernando confused this well-known voyage with an undocumented one that he alleged took place in 1483–84 just before his father supposedly left Spain.[12] It is important to note that Dulmo had been granted essentially the same privileges that Columbus was supposedly rejected for demanding, ones similar in many ways to those that he later received in 1492 from Ferdinand and Isabel.[13] It could even be argued that Dulmo's agreement served as a model for the *Capitulaciónes de Santa Fé*—Columbus's contract to explore.[14]

Bartolomé in England and France

Contemporary accounts differ as to when the two brothers left Portugal. The limited historical record indicates that Christopher left before, and his brother shortly after, Dias's return from the Cape of Good Hope. Hernando, Las Casas, and Bernáldez agreed that at some point, Bartolomé went to London to seek English support for the western venture. Hernando did say that Bartolomé went to London in case the proposal to Spain was rejected. Las Casas wrote, "Bartolomé Colón, who, although he was not skilled in Latin, was a practical man, knowledgeable about matters of the sea, and knew well how to make navigational charts, globes and other instruments of that profession, in which he had been instructed by the Admiral his brother . . . [l]eft for England, fortune chose to have him fall into the hands of corsairs . . . and due to his poverty and poor health, his embassy was delayed for a long time."[15]

Las Casas provided copies of two verses, written in Latin, that refer to a meeting of Bartolomé with King Henry VII of England on February 10, 1488.[16] He commented on these verses, "I found [them] written in very poor and inaccurate language, and poor hand-writing, part of them I couldn't read." Hernando reported on this visit, dating it, however, five years later, in 1493: "The king of England, having seen the mapa mundi that the Admiral offered him, happily accepted his proposal, and sent for him. But . . . the Admiral had already . . . left and returned with the success of his enterprise."[17]

Las Casas described Bartolomé as prudent and "less simple" than his brother. He reported that Bartolomé knew some Latin and was possibly even more expert in mapmaking and related fields than Columbus. He attempted to reconcile the different dates by having Bartolomé leave Portugal in 1484 at the same time as his brother, be captured by corsairs, return to Portugal in 1488 in time to possibly accompany Dias on the trip to the cape, and after their return to Portugal, proceed to England to seek the assistance of Henry VII. Las Casas quoted from the first verse: "He who wants to know will be shown on this map the lands described by Strabo, Ptolemy, Pliny and St. Isidro." The second verse noted, "Those who thought that the torrid zone was uninhabitable have been shown by experience to be notably wrong." It is in this Lascasian copy of the manuscript containing these verses that the first such reference to the ancients is actually dated by either of the Columbus brothers. Such references were to be repeated and discussed in later years ad nauseam by Columbus, Las Casas, Hernando, and Fernández de Oviedo, with the general purpose of demonstrating the "scientific" background to the discovery.

Another contemporary, Fernández de Oviedo, put the story of the offer to England quite differently: "Through his brother Bartolomé Colom he worked with King Henry VII of England . . . in order for him to favor him and provide a fleet to discover the western seas . . . he [Henry] had no confidence in this [plan], and thus seeing that his service wasn't wanted there, started to negotiate the same business with King Juan, second of that name in Portugal: neither did he believe in him although Colom was already married in that kingdom, and by marriage had become a vassal of that land."[18]

Thus Hernando had Bartolomé leaving Portugal after Dias's return, which would have been in 1488, yet in the spring of that same year delivering his message to Henry VII, despite the fact that he had supposedly been delayed due to his capture by corsairs. The king was "greatly pleased," but according to Hernando, it was not until 1493 that the English king sent for Columbus in order to give the Admiral his backing. Regardless of the internal contradictions in Hernando's version of these events, it should be noted that there is a letter from Bartolomé dated October 10, 1501, in which he stated that at the time that his brother, after returning from the first trip to the Indies, wrote him to come to Spain, he was living in the home of "Madama Borbon" in France. The lady referred to was Anne, the eldest daughter of Louis XI of France and the wife of the duke of Beaujeu. Fernández de Oviedo, on the other hand, completely reversed the sequence of events, having Columbus offer the plan to Henry VII before offering it to Portugal.[19]

A curious coincidence has been noted by Varela: in 1479–80, Amerigo Vespucci, the explorer who was to become Columbus's friend, and Francisco dei' Bardi, Columbus's future brother-in-law, were both in Paris and presumably met at that time. Francisco's brother Bernardo definitely did meet with Vespucci. Despite a difference of a decade, Varela speculated that they may also have met with Bartolomé.[20] She apparently based this possibility on the wording of instructions sent to Vespucci's brother, who at ti.e time was Florence's ambassador to the court of Louis XI. He was ordered to meet with Bernardo Bardi: "[He] will inform you of the complaints of our traders who should be compensated for their losses at the hand of Colombo that they have suffered for over a year."[21] This particular reference surely refers not to Columbus but to either of the Colombo corsairs, Caseneuve or Bissipat.

It is not impossible that Bartolomé was in Paris earlier, in 1479–80, on a mission, related or unrelated to the discovery. This raises the question of whether Bartolomé went to France before going to England and later returned, since by his own testimony he was in France in 1493. This leaves his whereabouts from 1488 to 1493 unaccounted for. His contemporaries, in mentioning this 1493 visit, refer only to his living at the home of Anne. As the daughter of Louis XI and the sister of Charles VIII, who was a minor of thirteen at the time of his father's death in 1483, Anne acted as regent for her brother until his majority in 1488. Thus the years in which the contemporary references are to Louis XI, not to Charles VIII, coincide with the years that Bartolomé has been said to have been in contact with Vespucci in Paris (Louis actually spent his declining years in his castle in Touraine, not in Paris). Fernández de Oviedo's sequence could also be more easily fitted into this pattern than the conventionally accepted one of Portugal-England-France. It should be kept in mind that all of this confusing and seemingly mutually contradictory data comes from either Bartolomé, his family, or their contemporaries.

So many contradictions, of course, open the field of speculation. Morison offered specific, but unsubstantiated, detail: "Around New

Year's 1489 the Columbus brothers decided on a plan of action. Christopher returned to Spain where he still hoped for support from the slow-moving Talavera commission, while Bartolomew sold his chart-making business and embarked on a long journey to persuade some prince to support the Great Enterprise. Henry VII of England, first to be approached, turned him down flat. Bartholomew [sic] then proceeded to France, where Anne de Beaujeu, sister to King Charles VIII, befriended him and employed him to make charts for her at Fontainbleu. Through her Bartholamew became friendly with the French king, but never obtained any real prospect of his support."[22] The Talavera Commission may or may not have been real (this will be discussed later), but the sale of the chart-making business, the friendship with the king, and other details are pure inventions.

The Phillipses speculated: "His brother Bartolomeo had been in England, trying without success to interest King Henry VII in the enterprise. It is possible that one of the Columbus brothers had already made overtures to France, and Bartolomeo was soon to travel there."[23] Wilford added yet more new details, first quoting Hernando and Fernández de Oviedo as having said: "Bartholomew secured . . . an interview with Henry VII . . . went to France, and though turned down again, at least found a patron in Anne de Beaujeu, eldest sister of Charles VIII. With a retainer from her, Bartholomew lived in France several years, making maps and sending letters to his brother."[24] No evidence has been found in England to substantiate either the meeting with or the offer to the English king. There is no evidence for a "retainer," nor are there any known letters from Bartolomé in France at that time. Paolo Emilio Taviani made a brief reference: "Bartolomeo had gone to the court of England, where he had received a good reception, then he went to France."[25] Sale correctly noted, "There is no special reason to believe the story accurate—there are no court records to support it, and Colón himself never mentions it."[26] Fernández-Armesto chose to ignore the French episode entirely. It is noteworthy that the other modern-day scholars quoted above adjusted the historical record so as to have the proper king on the throne of France in 1493: Charles VIII, not Louis XI as given by their source Hernando.

Marriage

The next step taken by Columbus, an important one in any man's life, was described by Hernando: "And because he behaved honorably and was a handsome man, and did not lack in honesty, it so happened that a lady, called Doña Felipa Muñiz, of noble blood, Comendadora [mother superior or, alternatively, internee] in All Saints monastery where the Admiral ordinarily went for mass, took up with him and became so friendly that they married. Because his father-in-law, Pedro Muñiz Perestrelo, was already dead, they stayed with his mother-in-law, who, seeing that he was so dedicated to cosmography, told him how her husband had been a great man of the sea . . . arrived at Madera and Porto Sancto, that at that time had not been discovered. . . . And because his mother-in-law saw that it pleased the Admiral greatly to know of such navigations and their history, she gave him papers and navigational charts that had belonged to her husband."[27]

Las Casas made some minor changes and added a few improvements to the story. First he changed the name of Filipa's supposed father to the partially more accurate Bartolomé Perestrello and correctly had him not discover but instead be sent by the king to occupy "Puerto Santo, that had only recently been discovered." Las Casas continued: "[He was] very excited by the attempts and success of the discoveries on the coast of Guinea [settled by the Portuguese in 1471] and of the islands that were in the Mar Oceano, and the said Bartolomé Perestrello hoped from there to discover others . . . he must have had instruments and papers and drawings suitable to navigation, which the mother-in-law gave to the said Cristóbal Colón . . . at one time he [Columbus] lived on the said island of Puerto Santo . . . (as I try to remember that his son D. Diego Colón told me . . . in 1519 in Barcelona)."[28] Note that Las Casas, generally cautious, only assumed that the father-in-law "must have had instruments." He was the first to report the unsubstantiated story of Columbus's living on Porto Santo; he even qualified this statement by saying that he wanted "to remember" what he had been told on the subject, sounding not very positive but sufficiently solid for romanticists to build on.

This matrimony was explained by Morison: "Next year [1479] Christopher, at twenty-eight years a master mariner, contracted an advantageous marriage with Dona Filipa de Perestrello e Moniz, daughter of Bartolomeu Perestrello, hereditary captain of Porto Santo in the Madeira group ... the couple shortly went to live in Porto Santo where their only son, Diego (later the second admiral and viceroy) was born, and where Dona Felipa's mother placed at Christopher's disposal the charts and journals of her seagoing husband. Not long after the birth of this, their one and only child, the Columbus couple moved to Funchal, Madeira."[29] The phrase "master mariner" apparently derives from Columbus's 1478 sugar-buying trip to Madeira; Morison stated that on this trip, Columbus was captain of a ship that Columbus said was captained by another. Thus minor errors perpetuate themselves in myth.

More recent variations on the theme include the version given by the Phillipses: "Felipa Moniz married Christopher Columbus in 1478 or 1479. Her mother gave the maps and papers accumulated by her late husband during his career ... they would have been more valuable to Columbus than any ordinary dowry. Columbus and his wife had a son in 1480 whom they named Diogo (Diego). . . . Columbus presumably had achieved some wealth and distinction of his own, or he would not have been able to make such a formidable match."[30]

Clarification and correction of all of the errors made by the authors of the above accounts is not a simple matter. There is a mishmash of fact and fiction in each account. To begin with, no one has any idea as to the year in which Columbus married. Civic records disappeared in the earthquake and fire that destroyed Lisbon in 1775. As to the name of Columbus's wife, Portuguese genealogists list her as Filipa Moniz de Mello, the latter name coming from her paternal grand-mother, a not uncommon practice in those days. Her attributed mother, Isabel, was the daughter by Filipa's grandfather's third marriage, to a grandniece of one of the discoverers of Porto Santo. Her putative father, Bartolomé Perestrello (he was neither "Pedro" nor a "Muñiz," as given by Hernando), could hardly have partici-pated in the discovery of the island of Porto Santo, since the Madeira Islands had been discovered by João Goncalves Zarco and Vaz in

1418; Perestrello would not have been of age at that time to travel. He was appointed "hereditary captain of Porto Sancto," but not by reason of discovery.

Columbus and Filipa's son Diego referred to his parents in his two wills. In the will of 1509, the reference is to both of his parents—"the Admiral and Doña Filipa Mogniz [*sic*], his wife both deceased"—as it is again in his burial instructions given in 1523: "And bring in the same way [as his father] the body of Doña Felipa Muñiz, his legitimate wife, my mother, that is in the Monastery of the Carmen in Lisbon, in a chapel that is called the Piedad, that is for the lineage of the Muñizes."[31] This presents a further complication for the Perestrello thesis in that by deed dated 1467, the chapel was reserved exclusively for the use of the heirs of Gil Ayres Mogniz.[32] The chapel of the name given by Diego in his will as his mother's burial place was not part of the Carmelite monastery, or near it.

Bartolomé Perestrello's wife, Isabel, had two brothers, Vasco and Diego Moniz; some scholars believe that one of these, not Perestrello, was Filipa's father.[33] The only one to give Diego Columbus's grand-father's name as Perestrello was Hernando, who appended the name Muñiz, which is patently false. No contemporary supplied the name of Columbus's mother-in-law. Columbus never mentioned his wife's name in any surviving record, and the only two references to her made by her son limit themselves to naming her either Mogniz or the Spanish version, Muñiz. The many today who unequivocally state that Bartolomé and Isabel were the parents of Filipa are skating on very thin ice indeed.

The speculation about Columbus's relationship to the Perestrellos derives from two sixteenth-century sources: the previously discussed passage in the *Historie* and a brief comment in the first book of *Hispaña vitrix* (the short title for *History of the Conquest of Mexico and Peru*), written by Francisco López de Gómara and first published in 1551. López de Gómara said only, "He married in that kingdom [Portugal], or as many say, on the island of Madera."[34] To validate the story of the widow's gift of her husband's charts and instruments, we need to link Columbus to the family of Perestrello, a connection accomplished here through the reference to Madeira. Unlike others of the early chroniclers, López de Gómara did not know Columbus personally: he was born after Columbus died. Since the Mognizes, unlike the Perestrellos, had no direct connection with Madeira, López de Gómara's cautious statement lent weight to the Perestrello thesis. Proof of the claim was supposedly found many years later in a sixteenth-century manuscript written by Gaspar Fructuoso, a Portuguese historian, who claimed that according to traditions on Porto Santo and in Funchal on Madeira, Columbus had married a "Filipa Bartholomeu Perestrello." For many years Columbists were told of the actual house in which the couple had lived; the cornerstone over a window was supposedly dated 1467. However, when the building was torn down in the nineteenth century, the cornerstone proved to read 1494.[35]

Wife and Children

While on the subject of Filipa, we should investigate two related matters: the number of children she and Columbus had (one, as generally reported, or three, as claimed by Harrisse); and the year of her death (before or after Columbus left Portugal). Las Casas cited Columbus's entry in the *Diario* on February 14, when he was afraid that his boat was sinking in an Atlantic storm: "He says moreover that it pained him greatly that he had two children studying in Córdoba who would be left orphans of father and mother in a foreign land."[36] Columbus's legitimate son, Diego, and his illegitimate son, Hernando, were in Córdoba at the time with Hernando's mother, a woman who was alive well into the sixteenth century. In a 1501 letter, apparently written to the Council of Castile, Columbus noted, "I came from so far to serve these princes and left wife and children, who for that reason I never saw again."[37] Some scholars have reached the tenuous conclusion that the phrase "wife and children" meant that Filipa had been pregnant and that she and the child had died in childbirth. A literal reading would indicate that he had more than the one child with her.

Columbus specified in the entail of his estate prepared in 1498 that only legitimate sons could be considered in the direct line of descent, thereby automatically excluding Hernando. Earlier, in a power of attorney executed in 1497, he described Diego and Hernando

as his "legitimate sons."[38] Again, it is Columbus who sows the seeds
of confusion. None of the surviving records show that at any time did
he say that Filipa had died, either before or after he left Portugal.
Las Casas offered a curious commentary, perhaps not unrelated to
the mystery: "Cristóbal Colón went to live in the said island of
Puerto Santo, where he had his said first-born heir D. Diego Colón,
perhaps for the sole reason of wanting to go to sea, [he] left his wife
there."[39] In the preceding sentence Las Casas had said, "I try to
remember [what] his son D. Diego Colón told me." As far as is known
with any degree of certainty today, Columbus's only "heir" was
Diego; the comment by Las Casas could be interpreted as inferring
that there were other children. In both his entail and his wills, it is
made clear that Hernando was never legitimized.

The above citations from statements made by Columbus himself,
as well as from those found in the writings of his contemporaries,
certainly leave one at the least perplexed and at the same time
inclined to believe that his wife was possibly still alive when he left
Portugal and that he and his wife may have had other children, in
addition to their son Diego. It may seem strange to modern-day
readers that a parent could "forget" his younger children. But one
of the early court documents concerning the Columbus family in
Genoa lists a "Giovanni Pellegrino" as the second child of Columbus's
parents; both Giovanni and a sister are never mentioned in any of
the other family documents known today.

Modern-day interpretations of the few known facts relating to
Filipa assume that she died sometime between 1478, the year in
which Diego was possibly born, and 1484, the year when he and his
father left Portugal. Fernández-Armesto first commented that the
marriage "was the biggest single step Columbus had taken towards
the social respectability he seems to have craved" and then added,
"Dona Felipa performed two further services for her husband: she
provided him with his only legitimate son, Diego . . . and she died
early leaving Columbus free and, it seems, unencumbered by
sentimental memories."[40] Morison believed that at the time that
Columbus left Portugal for Spain, Filipa had already died; the
Phillipses noted, "His wife Felipa had died and was buried in

Lisbon."[41] It appears that few can be satisfied with simply not knowing what really happened so long ago.

Briolanja Muñiz

Columbus did, unquestionably, have a long and close relationship with one of his wife's sisters, variously known as Brigolaga Moniz (in Diego's will) or Briolanja Muniz (in Spanish court documents). There is no contemporary mention of the name Perestrello in connection with her. She was married first to Miguel Muliar or Muliart(e). At the time of Columbus's initial arrival in Spain, the Muliarts are said to have lived in Huelva, a town near both Palos and the monastery at La Rábida. All three of these villages are located roughly three miles from each other. Ducal archives show that at one time, Briolanja leased a property from the duke of Medina-Sidonia, in whose castle Columbus possibly lived for some time before going to the Spanish court with his proposal.[42] The port of Huelva was part of the Medina-Sidonia fiefdom.

The family closeness is apparent in that shortly after Columbus's return from his famous first voyage, a Jew's confiscated property in Huelva was turned over to Miguel.[43] It is safe to assume that Columbus's newfound fame was of help to Miguel in acquiring this property. He joined with Columbus on the second voyage. The Muliarts lived on a street in Seville populated largely by Columbus's Florentin and Genoan friends and partners. Diego, and later Hernando, may have lived with the Muliarts at some point before going to court as pages for the heir apparent, although Columbus wrote that at the time Diego was appointed, his children were both in Córdoba, the home of Hernando's mother. Years later, Briolanja served as intermediary in an attempt, frustrated by the king, to marry Columbus's son Diego to a daughter of the duke of Medina-Sidonia.

Briolanja is listed as Muliart's widow in a document dated March 3, 1504, and as the wife of Francisco dei' Bardi in August 1505.[44] Bardi was a member of the prominent Bardi family of Florence, active in Portugal and Spain and linked, as were the Berardis, with the commercial affairs of the Medicis.

The Toscanelli Letters

By far the most important of the tales about Columbus in Portugal is the one concerned with a correspondence contained in three letters said to have been exchanged between Paolo dal Pozzo Toscanelli, Fernão Martins, and Columbus. The question of whether or not any such communication can be shown to have existed will be dealt with here; any possible application of knowledge that Columbus may have received from this source, and may have applied to his own cosmographic theories, will be dealt with in another chapter. Toscanelli was an eminent Florentin physician, cartographer, and mathematician. Head of his family's business dealing in hides and spices, he died at the age of eighty-five in 1482. One not insignificant point, which is rarely commented on, is that at no time did Columbus ever mention Toscanelli in any of his known correspondence.

Fernão Martins may have been a canon of the cathedral in Lisbon. No record of this person exists today, possibly a result of the loss of records in the 1775 earthquake. According to one theory, he was really "Fernando de Roriz, canonicus Ulixbonensis"—a canon of Lisbon.[45]

There are several conflicting theories connected with these three letters, the first written in Latin and addressed to Martins, the other two, in Spanish, addressed to Columbus in answer to queries supposedly made by him. There are no substantive differences between the letters. The unusual importance ascribed to these letters lies in the fact that if authentic, the letters provide a clear indication of Columbus's real objective in sailing to the west, of what he sought, and of where he expected it to be. If, however, the letters are apocryphal, one must seek the reason behind them. Of course, the matter is made even more complicated if we accept one letter and reject the others. The preponderance of scholarly thought, although not necessarily the preponderance of the evidence, favors this last conclusion: accept the first, reject the subsequent two.

If we reject any or all of the letters as false, consideration must be given to the possible rationales behind the perpetuation of such a hoax. The conceivable reasons are three. First, the letters may have been created as reinforcement to Columbus and his early biographers' efforts to explain his "Great Enterprise" as being the result of his study of the ancient cosmographers, to which now would be added the renowned Toscanelli. Second, during Columbus's lifetime the story was widely spread that he had received prior information about the route to the Indies from an "unknown pilot" who had died in his home; the letters would serve to prove that he had developed his plan independently. Third, he sought confirmation that his route was feasible and that it did lead to the Indies. The last might have been seen as necessary to refute those, such as Martire, who had openly questioned his claim that he had reached islands off the shores of India.

The existence of a letter was first made known to the public in the *Historie*. Las Casas also provided copies. These are not diplomatic copies of the Columbus copy but do contain essentially the same information. The fact is generally overlooked that the only copy known to have been used by Hernando and Las Casas was a Spanish-language translation from Latin of the so-called second letter, one generally accepted as spurious.[46]

The only known copy of the so-called first letter (in Latin) was located by Harrisse bound in with the Columbine Library copy of the *Historia rerum*, a Venice edition published in 1477.[47] Most modern-day Columbists accept this as a copy that belonged to Columbus, although some attribute its ownership to his brother Bartolomé. In support of the latter view, in 1891 the editor of the first published catalogue of the Columbine Library stated that he believed this edition of the *Historia rerum* had belonged to Bartolomé.[48]

This letter is written in very poor Latin, uses abbreviations for words and phrases that can only be surmised, and has apparent errors. Comparative translations have been made; however, all are necessarily reconstructions based on the use of a combination of paleography, linguistics, and cosmography. Since this letter was apparently written in the hand of Columbus, it seems reasonable to assume that, being an indifferent Latinist (although Fernández de Oviedo did say that he spoke a "genteel" Latin), he translated it back into Latin from a Spanish copy rather than copying from a Latin original. Surely he would have made a better copyist than translator. In that case, someone would have had to have first made the Spanish translation. This raises the possibility that the first letter was actually a translation of the second, one perhaps made to lend authenticity to the second by providing its supposed Latin source.

The first real study of these letters was conducted by Vignaud in 1902. He concluded that all three letters were apocryphal.[49] His opinion was based in part on his interpretation of translations of the original manuscripts, translations made for him by N. Sumien, a court interpreter and well-known scholar in Paris. Sumien disagreed with Vignaud and in 1927 published his own opinion that the first letter was indeed authentic, though he dismissed the others as false. Sumien explained that he had expressed his doubts to Vignaud about the latter's rejection of the first letter and that Vignaud had urged him to publish his opposing opinion; out of delicacy, however, he had preferred to wait until after Vignaud's death.[50] This gives a good indication as to the differences that can be aroused, even between close friends and collaborators, when dealing with this difficult subject.

To repeat, the copy found in the *Historia rerum* is written in very poor Latin, a language in which Toscanelli was fluent. The handwriting is Columbus's. It has been suggested that Columbus was translating back into Latin from a Spanish or Portuguese copy of the letter. Most histories quote from the Las Casas version in Spanish, presumably a translation of an unidentifiable Latin original.

The following is a literal rather than literary translation of Francisco Socas's Spanish translation of the Columbus Latin version, identified as postil #854 in the Columbine Library copy of the *Historia rerum*:

> To Fernando Martins, canon of Lisbon, the cosmographer Pablo sends you greetings. It pleased me to know of your health, your favour and treatment with your most noble [and] generous king. As on another occasion I spoke with you about a route by means of maritime navigation to the lands of the spices, more short than the one that you take by Guinea, the most serene king asks me now yet more, a visible demonstration, in order that including [even] those moderately instructed comprehend and understand that route. I for my part, although I know that it can be shown by means of a spherical figure, as the world is, nevertheless I have decided for a more easy

understanding and also for a more easy task, to show that route *** [*sic*] by the navigational charts that *** [*sic*] manifest it.

I send then to His Majesty a map made by my hands in which your coasts and islands are drawn, from those that start the voyage always to the West, and the places to which they should arrive and how much they should distance from the pole or the equatorial line and by how much space, that is, by how many miles, one should arrive at places very rich in all classes of spices and gems. And you should not be surprised if I call "occidentals" the parts where the spices are, despite the fact that generally they are called "orientals," since when one navegates always toward the west those parts are reached by means of a navigation that is made under the Earth, on the other hand, if the voyage is made by land and by the roads above, the East would always be found. Next the straight lines, shown on the length of the map, show the distance from east to west; on the other hand the transverse ones show the spaces from the midday [equator] up to the north. But I mark on the map the diverse places to which you can put into harbor, for the major information of the navigators, in order that if due to the winds or due to any other chance they reach another place than they thought; but in part so that they can show the indigenous people that they too have some information about their nation, which should be quite pleasing. But in order that they not establish themselves in the islands except the merchants. Then be assured: there is such abundance of navigators with merchandise, that in the rest of the whole world there are not as many as in one famous port called "Zaiton." For they assure that one hundred large ships of pepper reach this port every year, without counting the other ships that transport other spices. That nation is very populous, very rich due to the multitude of its provinces and kingdoms and cities without number at the orders of a single prince who is called "Gran Kan" a name which in our language means "king of kings," whose seat and residence is, at most of the times, in the province of Katay [*sic*]. His ancestors wanted [an] alliance with the Christians; 200 years ago they sent an embassy to the Pope and asked him for many wise men in order to receive instruction in the faith. But those that were sent to him, blocked in their voyage, returned. Besides in the times of [Pope] Eugene one came to Eugene who spoke of the great sympathies toward the Christians. I also had with him a long talk about many things, about the size of its palaces, the size of its rivers of a width and startling length, and about the great number of its cities on the banks of the rivers, in such a way that on one single river there are 200 cities and bridges of marble of great width and length, adorned on all sides by columns. This nation deserves that the latins go to search for it, not only because they can obtain from it great profits in gold, silver, gems of all kinds and spices that have never reached us, but because of the learned men, philosophers, and expert astronomers and those who with talent and art should govern so powerful and extraordinary a province and who conclude the wars. I put these things here in satisfaction of your request, to the extent that the shortage of time permitted and my occupations allowed, disposed in the future to satisfy farther, as much as wanted, to your Majesty the King. dated in Florence 25 June, 1474.

From the city of Lisbon by the west in direct line there are 26 spaces shown on the map, each one of which has 250 miles until the very notable and big city of Quinsay; inasmuch as it has a perimeter of one hundred miles and has ten bridges and its name means *Cità del cielo*, "City of the Sky"; and many marvels are told about her, about the multitude of artisans and moneys. This space is almost the third part of all of the sphere. This city is in the province of Mango, this is in the vicinity of Katay, seat of the royal palace of the territory. But from the Island of Antilla, that you know of, to the most famous island of Cipango there are ten spaces; then that island is very rich in gold, pearls and gems, and they cover their temples and palaces with solid gold, in such a manner that by unknown roads not very large sea distances must be crossed. Maybe many things should be explained with more clarity, but an interested and thoughtful man, based on these, could on his own understand the rest. Goodby, most affectionately.[51]

The perhaps apocryphal version offered by Hernando is prefaced by the following:

To Cristóbal Columbo, Paul, physician, greetings. I see your magnificent and great desire to be able to pass to where the spices grow, and in reply to your letter I send you a copy of another letter that some time ago I wrote in reply to another about the said matter that on orders of His Highness was written to me, before the wars with Castile, by a friend and confidant of the Most Serene King of Portugal and I send you another navigational chart, like the one I sent before, with which your request will be satisfied; the copy is the one that follows: Dated in Florence 25 June, 1474.[52]

It is singularly strange that the letter is dated June 25, 1474, in all of the three known copies—the Columbus holograph and the Hernandine and Lascasian copies—indicating a common source. This dating of the second letter cited above cannot be the date of a letter written to Columbus and including a copy of the Martins letter, since it is also dated June 25, 1474. If these letters were so dated, it would seem, at the least, an unusual oversight on the part of a man such as Toscanelli.

Interest in finding a new route to "where the spices grow" would have been appropriate at any time after 1453, the year the Ottomans captured Constantinople and thereby interdicted the Venice-controlled trade route to the Far East. At the same time the text states that the purpose of the letter is to show the way "to the lands of the spices, more short than the one that you take by Guinea." At the time of the letter, any such search would not have involved a yet-to-be-explored route via Guinea. The first crossing of the equator by the Portuguese occurred in 1473, but this was a long way from the Cape of Good Hope, which was finally rounded by Dias fifteen years later, in 1488.

By the time that Henry the Navigator died, in 1460, Portuguese explorers had sailed down the western coast of Africa as far as the Cape Verde Islands. King Afonso V made a purely commercial arrangement with Fernão Gomes for the latter to discover one hundred miles a year for five years down the African coast; his compensation was to be a monopoly on the Guinea trade. As the historian Jerry Bentley noted: "The slave trade developed with amazing rapidity: according to the Venetian mariner Cadomosto, by the mid-fifteenth century the Portuguese shipped one thousand slaves per year from their fort at Arguim in Guinea."[53] When the Gomes contract expired, he had discovered as far down as the equator. By 1481 the trading rights had reverted to the new king, João II.

Based on the record, a highly secretive one at the time, the only conclusions that can be drawn about the motivations for sailing down the African coast were exploration (Henry the Navigator) and profit from slaves and gold (Kings Alonso and João). There is no historical evidence that what the Portuguese were actually seeking at that time was a way to the "land of the spices." Their African outpost supplied slaves, not spices. As Wilford said: "It is still not certain that Prince Henry consciously sought to reach India and Cathay by circumnavigating Africa."[54] In the absence of evidence to the contrary, we can assume that Henry did not.

All of this strongly suggests that whoever wrote this part of the letters, it was not Toscanelli. If the phrase "a route . . . that you take by Guinea" referred indeed to a route to the Far East, then this segment of the letter could have been written by Toscanelli only if he had been aware of secret, and as yet unknown, Portuguese intentions in this regard. But if the Portuguese were already seeking the route in 1474, why did they wait until 1487 to send Dias to seek a way around Africa? Once he had rounded the Cape of Good Hope, why did they wait eleven more years to send Vasco da Gama on his voyage to India? Obviously there was no urgency in finding this southern route until 1498, twenty-four years after the so-called Toscanelli letter. By then it was generally accepted that, six years earlier, Columbus had already reached the fabled Indies by the transatlantic route. Even those who questioned whether he had really reached India were in agreement that he had shown the way there by sailing westward.

In the letter, the first reference to the Mongols' embassy to Rome, requesting "instruction" in the faith, relates to the time of Kublai Khan (1215?–1294). The writer of the letter stated, "Those that were sent to him, blocked in their voyage, returned." This is apparently based on Niccolò Polo's explanation that the two friars sent with him on his return trip to Cathay had deserted the party in 1272 at Giaza in Armenia.[55] This seems to be a strangely uninformed statement if it comes from Toscanelli, a humanist of repute in his day. As for the claim that the khan wanted "to receive instruction in the faith," Toscanelli would presumably also have known that a Franciscan friar, John of Plano Carpino, had reached Karakorum in July 1246. The friar returned to Italy in 1247 with a letter from the khan threatening the Christians: "In our presence, they chose Cuyuc [*sic*] as Emperor, or Chan [*sic*]. . . . The said Cuyuc Chan, together with all the princes, raised the standard to proceed against the Church of God and the Roman Empire, and against all Christian kingdoms."[56]

This brief and haughty reply hardly suggests a desire to be instructed in the Catholic faith.

Toscanelli would presumably also have known of William of Rubruck's well-publicized voyage to Karakorum in the years 1253–55. As Bentley said: "He left a rich account of the Mongol empire. At Karakorum, the Mongols' capital, he encountered not only Alans, Georgians, Armenians, Persians, Turks, and Chinese but also Slavs, Greeks, Germans, Hungarians, at least one Englishman, and French, including the Parisian sculptor Guillaume Boucher, who had fashioned a remarkable silver drinking fountain for the khan."[57] In the final paragraph at the end of his long account of his voyage (240 pages), William wrote: "It seems to me inexpedient to send another friar to the Tartars, as I went, or as the preaching friars go."[58]

There is another reference to a request for help from the pope. Rabban Sauma, a Turkish Nestorian Christian, was sent to Rome in 1287 to seek an alliance, reported by Bentley as "an alliance with the Christians that would help him [the Persian *ilkhan*] to conquer Jerusalem and crush Islam as a political force in the Middle East."[59] Yet this was a far cry from an alliance with the Mongols.

Another Franciscan, John of Montecorvino, was sent to Cathay in 1290 to serve as bishop of Khanbalik (north of today's Beijing), staying there until his death in 1328.[60] In 1342 yet another Franciscan, John of Marignolli, also left an extensive written report of his travels to Cathay.[61] He too reported encountering Venetian and Genoan traders in Cathay. These Franciscans, together with Dominican friars (there were four Dominican missions to Cathay between 1245 and 1251), served the Catholic communities in various cities including Khanbalik and Quanzou (Marco Polo and Toscanelli's "Zaiton").

There was obviously no lack of information about the situation in Cathay from the thirteenth to the fifteenth centuries. These and other travelers left detailed reports of their travels. Copies of their manuscripts were widely circulated throughout Europe in the days before printing. One of the best-known manuscripts was written by Odoric of Pordenone (c.1265–1331).[62] John Mandeville took much of his material for his fictitious *Travels* (1470) from this detailed report. Unfortunately, modern-day U.S. biographers have not studied the possible inferences to be derived from this widespread correspondence as it might relate to the Toscanelli letter.

Margarita Zamora is the only one of the authors reviewed for this critique who gave recognition to the possibility that Columbus may have been familiar with some of these works. In a footnote to her translation of the Columbus first letter in *El libro copiador* she wrote: "This is probably an allusion to the accounts of Marco Polo and the papal embassies to the Far East of the thirteenth and fourteenth centuries by John of Plano Carpini [sic], William of Rubruck, John of Monte Corvino, and Odoric of Pordenone. Columbus certainly would have known Pordenone's account, as distilled in John Mandeville's *Travels* (1470), a book Columbus knew well."[63] However, her certainty about a prediscovery reading of the *Travels* is open to serious question.

Toscanelli wrote in the letter: "Besides in the times of Eugene [Pope Eugenius IV, 1431–47] one came to Eugene who spoke of the great sympathies toward the Christians. I also had a long talk with him about many things." This is an obvious reference to Niccolò dei' Conti, who on his return from the Far East in 1444 did seek absolution for apostasy, from Eugenius IV. The pope's secretary, Poggio Bracciolini, wrote down Conti's account of his twenty-five-year sojourn in the Near and Far East.[64]

The writer of the "Toscanelli letter" should also have known, from the reports of returning missionaries who left Cathay in the mid–fourteenth century, that the Mongols (people of the khan) were being by that time driven out of the country.[65] The English historian Sir Henry Yule stated, "Khanbalik was abandoned as a royal residence on the expulsion of the Mongol dynasty in 1368."[66] Over the years the khans had addressed numerous letters to the kings of France, Spain, and England. These were of course brought by royal emissaries. It is simply not credible that Toscanelli would have been unaware of all of this available information relating to conditions in the lands of the Gran Khan.

A minor point is that of the manner in which Columbus supposedly came by a copy of this possibly apocryphal letter. Wilford surmised that it was through his wife's family connections in Lisbon.[67] Hernando[68] and Las Casas,[69] however, offered the explanation that it was through Lorenzo Giraldo (Hernando) or Lorenzo Birardo (Las Casas), a Florentin living in Lisbon[70] and better known as Lorenzo Berardi. In later years Columbus was close to the Berardi family in Spain.

There is a curious linkage among the names Berardi, Bardi, Vespucci, Columbus, and Toscanelli. Vespucci's uncle, Giorgio Antonio, was a disciple and friend of Toscanelli's.[71] As noted above, there is evidence that Vespucci and Francisco dei Bardi were both in Paris in 1479–80. Francisco's brother Bernardo definitely did meet with Vespucci. Varela suggests that Bartolomé Colón was also in Paris at that time.[72] At a later date, Columbus, Berardi, and Vespucci had business interests in common. If from no other source, Columbus would have known of Toscanelli through these close associates who shared his interest in exploration to and trade with the Indies.

As will be seen in the chapter dealing with the cosmographic concepts expressed in the letter, these too present problems. Toscanelli must have been better informed on such matters than the letter would seem to indicate. The letter remains one more of the Columbus enigmas.

It has been generally accepted that Columbus's main reason for leaving Portugal was that shortly before his departure, the king, using information supplied by Columbus, sent out a small fleet to attempt the route that he had proposed. The source for this belief is Hernando: "[The failure of the Dulmo expedition] having reached the attention of the Admiral, and his wife being already dead, he took on such a strong dislike for that city and nation that he decided to go to Castile with a young boy that his wife had left him."[73] As previously noted, at some point he did send his brother Bartolomé to England for the purpose of finding a backer. It has also been suggested that he left for fear of being caught with the purloined Toscanelli letter. With no substantiating historical data to permit us to make a judgment one way or the other on this matter, there is little point in going into it more thoroughly here.

The broad outline of Columbus's life in Portugal is reasonably well established. Columbus arrived there early in the 1470s; at some time, then or in the following years, he joined up in that country with his brother Bartolomé, and sooner or later he married a woman known to her son and contemporaries as Filipa Mogniz. They had a son, Diego, but there is no way to determine whether or not there were other progeny of this marriage. Likewise we do not know when Filipa died, though we know she was buried in a chapel in Lisbon.

There is every reason to believe that while he was in Portugal, Columbus offered the king a plan to sail to the west in search of land, an offer that was turned down. In 1487 the Portuguese king sent out a similar search, which was unsuccessful. Bartolomé was undoubtedly in London in 1488 and in France in 1493. Apparently, his reason for being in both cities was to seek support for his brother's plan for an Atlantic crossing.

While in Portugal in 1478, Columbus is known to have made a trip to Madeira to purchase sugar for the Centuriones of Genoa. At this time he probably became involved with the Bardis, a Florentin family already established in Lisbon and Spain for many years and for which there are commercial records in Seville dating back to the 1420s.[74] Another Tuscan, Columbus's future agent Juanoto Berardi, has been identified as probably being in Portugal in 1473 and as definitely being in Spain trading in slaves in 1485. Columbus thus was in touch with important traders from Genoa and Florence, who each had agents in the major ports of the then-known world. These friendships would serve him well later when he moved to Spain. There is no reason to doubt the Admiral's assertions that he made trips to the western coast of Africa, which was being extensively explored by the Portuguese during the years that he resided in that country. At some point during these years, Columbus most probably voyaged to England and Ireland, as he reported in some of his letters written in the next century.

Columbus's plan of discovery was likely conceived while he was living in Portugal, but whether these plans were based on a letter and map supplied by Paolo dal Pozzo Toscanelli, the physician from Florence, is open to debate. It has not often been noted that Toscanelli, in addition to his intellectual accomplishments, had commercial interests as head of his family's business trading in spices and hides, trade that would inevitably have brought him in contact with Portugal. Columbus and his young son Diego left for Spain around 1484–85, probably, as Fernández de Oviedo said, "[because] the King of Portugal didn't want to favor nor help the said Colom. . . . Therefore he determined to go to Castile."[75] The reason is simple, neat, not romantic, but possibly accurate. Columbus is generally accepted as having returned to Portugal for a visit in 1488, when he was living in Spain. He may have had some problem with the authorities before leaving Portugal, as may be evidenced by King João's letter to him guaranteeing him freedom from prosecution. However, Portuguese archives reveal that at that time, such safe-conducts were standard in royal correspondence with foreigners.

While residing in Portugal, Columbus experienced four very important events in his life. First, he acquired cosmographic knowledge and nautical experience that were to serve him later in the conception and execution of his plan of discovery. Second, he married and started his family, a fact that obviously meant very much to him, as was evidenced in later years by the great care that he took to establish the hereditary nature of his rewards for having discovered the islands in the Indies. Third, he made important social and commercial contacts with the principal trading families of the Ligur and Tuscany, who operated out of Portugal and Spain to most of the known Atlantic nations. Finally, he suffered royal rejection in Portugal for his plan to find a new way to the fabled riches of the East, and he steeled himself to persevere regardless of the cost. Columbus matured in Portugal.

Learned ignorance

Nicholas of Cusa, 1401–1464

4
Cosmography

Among Columbists, the matter that has perhaps created the greatest amount of controversy is that of the planning behind his great discovery. This question preoccupied Christopher's son Hernando, Las Casas, and Fernández de Oviedo, each of whom offered explications. The more closely one looks into the matter, the more confusing it becomes. Just where did he think he was headed when he set out from Palos on his presumably first transatlantic journey? What made him believe that he could accomplish what he set out to do? Why did some believe him and others not? What was the perceived wisdom at the time as to the possibility of finding land in the western Atlantic, the Ocean Sea? These questions, in turn, raise others.

In this inquiry the central theme is the Americas, and the leading character is Columbus. That he discovered the Americas is the one fact that sometimes gets buried under erudition. What the ancients knew, or what we know today, about cosmographical concepts of the time is of little significance. What is important is to attempt to determine how much Columbus himself knew or believed before he set out on his first voyage.

Cosmographic Concepts and Postils

During the half century after the Admiral's death, Fernández de Oviedo, Hernando, Las Casas, and the Portuguese chronicler João de Barros all wrote on the subject of his cosmographic concepts. Columbus's supposed enemy Cardinal Jiménez de Cisneros, archbishop of Toledo, writing around 1495, referred in his *Memorial* to the same concepts and their sources.[1]

Instead of delving into the cosmographic concepts most widely held at the time, it is far more important to determine what Columbus knew, or thought he knew, of such matters. He left ample evidence in postils in two of his books and in several letters. Unfortunately, here again problems arise, in this case major ones. Historians strongly disagree as to the ownership of one of these books, to the years in which Columbus or his brother acquired each of them, and as to who wrote many of the postils: Columbus, his son Hernando, or his brother Bartolomé.

Two of the most important postils, annotated in the margins of Pope Pius II's *Historia rerum* (postil #860) and Pierre d'Ailly's *Ymago mundi* (postil #490), are generally accepted as having been written by the same person.[2] Yet, Las Casas ascribed one to Columbus and the other to Bartolomé: "I knew his [Bartolomé's] hand well."[3] Perhaps Varela's judgment on the matter is worth keeping in mind. She observed that scholars accept or reject Columbus's authorship of many of these postils depending on the point they want to prove; she accepted both postils as having been written by Columbus.[4]

The postils most often cited as proof that he read these works prior to 1492 are #860, in the *Historia rerum*, which refers to only one event that took place in 1485, and #23, in the *Ymago mundi*, which referred merely to an event that took place in 1488. Neither infers that he owned these books in those years. The claim that he read the *Historia rerum* before 1492 is based in part on postil #858c, which reads: "From the destruction of the second temple, according to the Jews, until now, which is the year of the birth of our Lord 1481 there are 1413 years, and from the beginning of the world until this era of 1481, there are 5241 years [   ] world [   ] 5244."[5] This indicates simply that the calculation extended only to 1481. Those who use 1481 as the year in which this was supposedly written fail to note that whereas for other years the writer specifically used the word "year," in this case he wrote "era." These years were noted in an attempt to determine the age of the world in order to know how many biblical years were left before the millenium, for which Columbus claimed to be a harbinger. If we accept that the postil was written in 1481, and further accept that it was written by Columbus, this would be a good indication as to the accuracy of the assumption that he had read this book by that date. Unfortunately, Streicher, the best-known paleographer to study this matter, reached the conclusion that this postil was written by Bartolomé.

A possibly far more revealing postil relating to Columbus's prediscovery reading is found in d'Ailly's tract *On Laws and Sects*, translated by Antonio Ramírez de Verger as follows: "Note: ascending in the calendar the solar year 10 minutes, and 44 seconds every year, as was proven at the end of the tract On the Laws and the Sects and is confirmed here, we can indicate here the spring equinox in this year 1491 [was] on 11 March."[6] The two immediately preceding postils, #619 and #620, and the following one, #623, all say, "In this year of 1411." Therefore, either these are misprints or the "1491" was a misprint or a forward calculation. If these are neither transcriptional nor typographical errors, then they appear to provide clear evidence that the writer of these postils, Columbus or his brother Bartolomé, had read at least this one tract before 1492. As far as I am aware, these particular postils have not been commented on in the literature on the subject. Further study is required to determine the accuracy of these four transcriptions.

Eulogists of Columbus offer greatly expanded views of Columbus's fore-knowledge and after-knowledge. In those cases where he named one of the classical or medieval writers as holding to one or another viewpoint, these biographers assume that he was familiar with the whole body of works by the particular author cited. Actually, as will be shown, Columbus knew many if not all of these authors because he encountered them in works that were merely compendia of compendia. A case in point is the cosmographic ideas of Aristotle (384–322 B.C.), ideas passed on by the Arabian scholars Avicenna

(A.D. 980–1037) and Averroës (A.D. 1126–98), brought to the West by two Dominican saints, Albertus Magnus, a Swabian (A.D. c.1206–80), and his pupil the Italian philosopher and theologian St. Thomas Aquinas (A.D. 1225–74), and finally, continued by the English Franciscan friar Roger Bacon (A.D. 1220–92). The cosmographic data in each of these works was collated by French Cardinal d'Ailly over the years 1410–14 in his works known by the short title *Ymago mundi*. Columbus's copy is extensively annotated.

Fernández-Armesto pointed out that views such as those of Aristotle were often distorted in passage from, for example, Bacon to d'Ailly to Columbus.[7] In the literature on the subject, it is not unusual to read that Columbus is said to have found a particular theory advanced by Aristotle, as well as all of the above-named scholars, the inference being that he had read them all. The same escalation of authorities is repeated for all of the other principal "sources" for Columbus; in fact, as will be demonstrated, these authorities boil down to at the most two.

One concept that has bothered biographers concerns the perception held in ancient and medieval times as to the shape of the earth. This has fathered myths, perhaps the most ridiculous one being that Columbus had to convince those opposed to his project that the world was round. Man's understanding of the true shape of the earth dates back at least to Pythagoras around 500 B.C. Justin Winsor provided a useful thumbnail sketch of the transmission of the theory over the centuries:

> Aristotle, in his treatise "On the Heaven" . . . gives a formal summary of the grounds which necessitate the assumption of its sphericity. . . . Aristotle made the doctrine orthodox; his successors, Eratosthenes, Hipparchus, and Ptolemy, constituted it an inalienable possession of the race. Greece transmitted it to Rome, Rome impressed it upon barbaric Europe; taught by Pliny, Hyginus, Manilus, expressed in the works of Cicero, Virgil, Ovid, [the last in his *Fasti* refers to a globe said to have been constructed by Archimedes (c.287–212 B.C.)]. Plato (427?–347 B.C.1) makes Socrates (470?–399 B.C.) say that he took up the works of Anaxagoras (500?–428 B.C.), hoping to learn whether the earth was round or flat. It passed into the school books of the Middle Ages, whence, re-enforced by Arabian lore, it has come down to us."[8]

Samuel Edward Dawson found that such a belief

> was by no means general in Greek and Roman times. The Epicureans
> laughed at it as a vagary ... [and] in chapter VII of Plutarch's
> treatise, *On the Apparent Face in the Moon's Orb*, the theory is
> ridiculed by one of the speakers. No doubt in the middle ages, as in
> ancient times, the belief was common that the world was flat; but it
> was not a doctrine of the church. The passage so often cited from St.
> Augustine merely states that even "if it be supposed or scientifically
> demonstrated that the world is of a round and spherical form, it does
> not logically follow that the other side of the world is peopled, seeing
> that nobody has been there to see and that it may be all water or, if
> indeed land, may be bare of inhabitants."[9]

Saint Augustine has been quoted, at times out of context, as proof
that the opponents of Columbus at the Spanish court still believed
that the world was flat![10]

The fact is that Columbus initially believed that the earth is
round. The opening sentence in the first paragraph in chapter 1 of
the *Historia rerum* unequivocally stated that the earth is round.[11]
Columbus's postil on page 1 of chapter 1 of the *Ymago mundi* reads,
"It is called a sphere because it is a round space, it is from this that
the roundness of the world is called the sphere of the world, because
its form is round."[12] It was only late in life that he proposed that the
earth was pear-shaped, with the Terrestrial Paradise at the top.[13]
Even this concept was not original with him.[14]

The most important of the cosmographic ideas of Columbus are
those directly related to the size of the earth and the extent of its
oceans. Everything that he wrote on these subjects can be traced
directly to the *Historia rerum* and the *Ymago mundi*. In his letter
giving his account of his third voyage, Columbus wrote, "Aristotle
says that the world is small and the water is little and that one can
easily pass from Spain to the Indies." A postil in the *Ymago mundi*
states, "Aristotle: between the end of Spain and the beginning of
India there is an ocean space short and navigable in few days."[15] In
his *Georgics*, Virgil quoted Eratosthenes, who found that there was
no obstacle to passing from Iberia to India while staying on the
same parallel and that the unknown portion of this parallel was

something more than one-third of the whole circle. Strabo, also cited on occasion by Columbus, taught the spherical theory based on Homer, Eratosthenes, Polybius, and Posidonius.[16] Columbus cited all of these authors in his postils in the *Ymago mundi*.

D'Ailly noted that in order to understand the different figures given by the ancients for the girth of the world, calculated variously as 500 or 700 stades of 56 2/3 miles to a degree, one must "first define the meaning of these terms, that is to say a stade, a mile or a codo. Therefore, according to Isidore in book 15 of the *Etimologías*, the stade, the eighth part of a mile is composed of 121 paces; the mile is composed of a thousand paces, the foot has five feet and sixteen fingers." He went on to note that others assigned 125 paces to a stade and that there were different ways of measuring the codo. He conluded, "From all of this it can be deduced that the significance of the codo is ambiguous and its measure is not certain; the same can be said of the stade and the mile according to the different ways of the cited authors for expressing themselves."[17] This is essentially all that is known of Columbus's knowledge of these matters. Everything else is surmise.

Dawson explained: "The Olympic stade of 600 Greek feet (equal to 606.75 English feet) was the length of the footrace course at the Olympic games. There were eight to the mile. In the third century of our era, after the work of the geographers was over, there did come into use, in Egypt and in the Asiatic provinces of Rome, a stade of which seven and a half went to the Roman mile. This stade, called the Phileterian stade, affected the measures of the Arabs and its influence appeared in the writings of Alfragan, and passed into the works of Bacon and d'Ailly, and, through them, into the speculations of Columbus."[18] Winsor was perhaps the first to note that d'Ailly had copied verbatim the relevant passage from Bacon,[19] just as Columbus, in his postils in the *Ymago mundi*[20] and in his letter reporting on his third voyage, had copied from d'Ailly.[21]

Eratosthenes provided the first scientifically demonstrated measurement of the earth's surface.[22] He knew that at the time of the summer solstice, the sun is directly overhead at noon in the Egyptian town of Seyne. This was based on the knowledge that at a certain well in the town, at the time of the solstice every year, the sun shone perpendicularly down to the bottom of the well. Because Seyne was due south of Alexandria, he believed that it was on the same meridian (this involved a slight error) and that, furthermore, Seyne was a fifty-day camel journey from Alexandria. Since camels were estimated to travel one hundred stades per day, the two cities were presumably five thousand stades apart; he now knew the length of the arc of the meridian between these two points. On the day of the solstice, at the time that the sun would be at its maximum height over Alexandria, he measured the shadow that a perpendicular shaft of known height cast on the line of the meridian. He now had the two sides of a triangle, and with this knowledge he could measure the angle of the third side in relation to the sun. It measured about 7°12'—in other words, about one-fiftieth of a 360° circle. To his mind this figure placed the distance between Seyne and Alexandria at one-fiftieth of the earth's surface, from which figure he calculated the circumference of the earth as 250,000 stades.

In chapter 4 of his *Compendio de cosmografía II*, d'Ailly listed the different measures used by Ptolemy, Eratosthenes, and Alfragan. The earth's circumference at the equator was given by them as 31,500, 22,500, and 20,397 miles respectively, based on stades of eight to the mile. As far as we know, Columbus's only knowledge of these measurements is given in his postils. He noted in the *Historia rerum*, "This author calculates according to the teachings of Ptolemy, 500 stadia for one degree, that is worth 62 1/2 miles, at 8 stadia per mile."[23] Yet by far the majority of Columbus's postils in the *Ymago mundi* and in the *Historia rerum* stress Alfragan's shorter figure—56 2/3 miles—as the correct one.

In the *Ymago mundi*, he noted that, based on Alfragan, "each degree has 56 and 2/3 miles, and, therefore, the circumference of the earth has 20,400 miles."[24] He repeated this figure in numerous postils. Columbus did not write a postil alongside d'Ailly's conclusion in which he noted the many different figures given for the girth of the earth. From these d'Ailly rationalized that Eratosthenes' stades and miles were smaller than those of Ptolemy and, by the same token, Alfragan's length of a degree could be the same as theirs.[25] Thus all of the different measurements could be reconciled.

In 1495 Jaime Ferrer wrote a letter to Columbus in which he set out some of his own views on how and where to find the gold and jewels of the East. Aware of the differences in distances given by the classical cosmographers, Ferrer adopted the same expedient as d'Ailly of deciding that the differences were due to the fact that the stades of Ptolemy were larger than those of Eratosthenes.[26] Perhaps Dawson summed the matter up best: "This heroic method of reconciling the ancient authors gained ground ... and was advocated ... down to the early years of the present century. Under the influence of this perennial fountain of error the subject became an arena of confusion."[27]

A dispute in the late nineteenth century over the exact location of the Tordesillas dividing line nearly brought about a war between the United States and Great Britain. The dispute, involving Venezuela and England over the boundary of the British colony of Guiana, was settled amicably; but it sparked a major Western review of all of the measurements and other methods used at the time of the signing of the 1494 treaty. Such arcana are obviously not strictly limited to interpretations of Columbus's figures; they can affect, and have affected, political decisions into modern times.

Unfortunately, the different figures provided by these early cosmographers still give scholars problems. Wilford recently calculated Eratosthenes' figure to be "about 16 percent too large."[28] However, ten years later, in 1991, Fernández-Armesto noted, "The girth of the world has been consistently over-estimated since antiquity, though the best available computation, that of Eratosthenes of Alexandria was accurate to within at least 5 per cent ... perhaps to within 2 per cent if the most favourable values are assigned to the cosmographer's units of measurement."[29] It is hardly surprising that Columbus had difficulty understanding Eratosthenes' calculation if, in the final years of the twentieth century, two such eminent geographers could be so far apart in their computations based on the same data available to Columbus.

Mariners of Columbus's day calculated distances at sea in leagues. For Columbus, as for his Iberian contemporaries, the Castilian or maritime league was believed to be made up of four miles of one thousand Roman *passuum* each.[30] However, in the letter on the second voyage, in *El libro copiador*, Columbus provided a different figure. He wrote, "The spaces of each line signify one degree which I have counted fifty-six miles and two thirds that correspond to our leagues of the sea to fourteen leagues and a sixth."[31] This calculation gives a league of 3.46 Roman miles. He thus calculated using two different leagues, one for the land and another for the sea.

The Degree

All the above figures lead to one conclusion: Columbus was confused about the measurements that he used. He found that the all-important length of a degree at the equator was 56 2/3 Roman miles. This figure he took from Alfragan, whose mile, however, was the Arabic mile.[32] Fernández-Armesto, taking note of these facts, added that Columbus's claim that he had confirmed the findings of "maestro José," the Jewish doctor sent to the equator by the Portuguese to determine the length of the degree, is "incompatible with other evidence about [José] Vizinho's opinion."[33] Despite the many affirmative statements made by Columbus and his biographers up to the present day as to the length of a degree, it is worthwhile noting that in 1524 his son Hernando, at that time Royal Cartographer, gave testimony before the Junta de Badajoz. When he was asked how many Castilian or marine miles there are in a degree, he replied, "Nobody knows for certain."[34]

Columbus did not necessarily investigate the question of degrees before setting out on his famous first voyage. He unquestionably went into the matter in his many surviving letters and postils written years after the event. As will be shown in the chapter on his first voyage, his estimates as to distances traveled appear to have been tailored to fit the islands that he did discover and that he always believed to be off the coast of India. What he *did* need to know before setting out were two things—was the Ocean Sea navigable and, if so, were the lands to the west, the so-called antipodes, habitable? Columbus was convinced, correctly, that at least the so-called torrid zones south of the equator were habitable, a supposition based partly on the Portuguese experience in Guinea as well as on Bartolomeu Dias's observations during his voyage to the Cape of Good Hope.

The Antipodes

Once it became generally accepted that the world was larger than its known parts, the question naturally turned to speculation as to what was out there: land or water, habitable or uninhabitable. Opinions on the subject go as far back as recorded memory. Columbus, Las Casas, Hernando, Fernández de Oviedo, and Cisneros each referred on these matters to Gaius Julius Solinus, a third-century epitomizer who took most of his cosmographic concepts directly from Pliny and Pomponius Mela, both of whom wrote in the first century. His *Collectanea rerum memorabilium* was revised in the sixth century with the title *Polyhistor.* This later edition has modifications from the original and is the source of most of the data that was used by writers in later centuries. Solinus repeated Plato's claim that Alexander the Great had sent a fleet to find Taprobana in the Atlantic.[35]

Columbus quoted from the biblical story that tells how King Solomon sent a fleet to India to get gold for his temple, a voyage that took three years, as well as quoting from the classics that told of how Alexander the Great had sent a fleet to find Sopora, which Columbus was later to identify with Española.[36] Columbus and his first biographers also referred to the opinions elicited on these matters by Aristotle and Plato dating back to the fourth century B.C., to Saint Augustine in the fourth century A.D., and to Saint Anselm in the eleventh century, all of whom were cited by d'Ailly in the fifteenth century.[37] Curiously, Las Casas[38] and Cisneros[39] each cited Solinus incorrectly and in a like manner.

It was popular at the time to quote Pliny regarding how the distance between the two continents could be covered in forty days of navigation.[40] Others said that with a favorable wind, one could pass from Iberia to Asia in a few days.[41] Some scholars, such as Eratosthenes, even believed that the antipodes were in a temperate zone and that people could live there. Statements to this effect were annotated in Columbus's postils in the *Yamago mundi.* All agreed that before reaching Asia, one would encounter many islands. By the Middle Ages some of these islands even had commonly known names, such as Taprobana and Cipango. The question as to just

where Columbus thought he was when he discovered the Indies—
Taprobana, Cipango—will be dealt with later, in the chapter on his
first voyage.

Passage to the East and Mythical Islands

The works of the ancients contained ample evidence that a passage
to the Far East by a westerly water route was believed to be feasible.
Columbus noted in a postil, as well as in the letter on the third
voyage, that Esdras had said that the land area of the earth was
larger than the ocean area.[42] Aristotle, Pliny, Strabo, and others
believed that the known lands of Europe and Africa took up one-
third of the globe and that Asia was larger than these two. From
these concepts came the theory that the distance between Iberia and
Asia by water was less than a third of the circumference of the globe;
therefore it encompassed approximately 129 degrees. Iberia in this
case was understood to include Africa; thereby the integer of 129
could be applied at the equator. The belief, now known to be correct,
that at one time Africa and Spain were united dates back to earliest
recorded history. Columbus wrote a postil in the *Ymago mundi*
emphasizing this theory.[43]

Gibraltar was one of the Two Pillars of Hercules, whose final labor
was to take the golden apples of the Hesperides.[44] His successful
accomplishment of this challenge provided the basis for the many
myths about the island of the Hesperides and for later attempts to
link it with such places as the fabled lands of Atlantis, Brendan's
Island, the Island of Brazil, and the Island of the Seven Cities—
stories that continue to intrigue today. Columbus knew of all of
these theories through his reading of the *Ymago mundi*. These
mythical islands were also shown on some prediscovery fifteenth-
century maps.[45]

Cisneros, writing many years before Fernández de Oviedo, told his
sovereigns that what Columbus had discovered was not India but the
Hesperides.[46] Columbus, according to his son Hernando, also came to
believe this.[47] Las Casas and Fernández de Oviedo also discussed this
mythical island.[48] The latter was accused by Hernando of having
revived the tale of an early Spanish Visigoth king whose subjects

had occupied the island, identified with the so-called Island of the Seven Cities, in order to show that Columbus, by retrieving a possession already belonging to Spain, was not entitled to the rewards that he claimed as its discoverer.[49] Las Casas, quoting mainly from Aristotle and Strabo, went to great lengths in offering his rebuttal of the account of the populating of the island by seven Spanish bishops and their flocks. Yet even more recently Morison, despite the evidence presented by both Cisneros and Las Casas, found that Fernández de Oviedo had dug up the story simply "to please his masters."[50] Wilford repeated the reason given for Fernández de Oviedo's relaying of the story as cause for suspecting his supposedly "negative attitude towards Columbus."[51] This myth, current long before as well as during the time of Columbus, to this day continues to fascinate those who seek the lost continent of Atlantis.

Scholars offer varying motivations for Columbus's first transatlantic voyage. Hernando offered three natural reasons (i.e., cosmographic), the authority of those writing on the subject, and the empirical evidence of mariners.[52] Las Casas, though attributing the reasons to Hernando, actually offered five, each of which he covered much more extensively than Hernando had: first, "natural reasons," which he found to be "very effective"; second, what Columbus knew empirically based on a combination of his knowledge from his own maritime experience and what he had heard from other navigators, together with what he had read in works on cosmography; third, what he knew from Marinus of Tyre of the distance between Europe and Asia; fourth, Columbus's belief that Marinus had overestimated these distances; and fifth, the opinion of Alfragan, who made the size of the globe smaller than had other cosmographers such as Pliny.[53] The empirical reasons will be dealt with in the next chapter.

The Toscanelli Letters

In the preceding chapter, many of the incongruities in the Toscanelli letters were discussed. Another anomalous matter concerns a letter reported by Thacher. Since this letter is not referred to in any of the modern works studied in this critique, it is perhaps worthwhile to reproduce it here:

Not only à propos of Toscanelli's study of geography, but as completely disposing of the charges made by Mr. Vignaud to the effect that Toscanelli was unknown to the Portuguese, the following note or postilla [*sic*], published by Signor Uzielli in 1898, is here given. It was among the manuscript papers of Francesco Castellani, a contemporary of Toscanelli.

> In 1459 I record that on . . . July I loaned to Andrea Bochacino, for Master Paolo of the family of Domenico da Pozo Toscanelli, my great historical mappemonde complete in every way. . . . And he was to restore it to me, except it was agreed that he should have it for several days and show it to certain ambassadors of the King of Portugal: and so the said Andrea and the said Paolo promised to restore it to me.

> Received from Master Ludovico, nephew of the said Master Paolo, February 2, 1484, the said mappemonde, somewhat damaged and worn by handling.[54]

If the map referred to in this extract is related to the famous letter, there is a wide discrepancy in years. The Castellani memorandum is dated 1459; its return was dated two years after the death of Master Paolo. The Toscanelli letters are dated 1474. João II did not become king until 1481; therefore, it is conceivable that he was unaware of both the letter and the map, which were supposedly sent to his predecessor. It seems somewhat strange that Castellani reported the loan of a map in 1459 "for several days" and acknowledged receipt for its return twenty-five years later. It is an interesting coincidence that at least this particular map was returned in the same year, 1484, that Fernam Dulmo was first authorized by João II to attempt an Atlantic crossing and that Columbus is claimed by some to have left Portugal to seek his fortune in Spain.

The cosmographic concepts outlined in the Toscanelli letters are closely linked to the estimated size of the earth. The size of the mar Oceano (the "Ocean Sea")—the Atlantic Ocean—was important to Columbus's calculations. Until the discovery of the Americas, it was thought that the mar Oceano extended to the shores of India.

Whether or not these letters are apocryphal, the fact cannot be ignored that Columbus, his son Hernando, and Las Casas knew of their contents. Whether or not Columbus or his brother made the copy located by Harrisse in the *Historia rerum*, at least one item found only in this letter was repeated in a letter that has been identified as having been written by Bartolomé while he was in Rome in 1506. While not alluding directly to Toscanelli, Bartolomé did trace a map on the back of a this letter; the map shows Veragua on the coast of Nicaragua as the Cattigara of Ptolemy and Española as Cipango. More important, the grid on the map is divided in spaces of ten degrees rather than the customary fifteen, and there are thirteen such spaces shown between Lisbon and Cattigara, providing for 130 degrees, as used by Marinus of Tyre.[55] This unusual form of dividing the degrees is also given in the Toscanelli letter, a fact that indicates simply that Bartolomé Colón was possibly aware of its content. This has provided support for those who believe Bartolomé wrote the Toscanelli letters. A second sheet of Bartolomé's letter shows both the land measurement of 225 degrees as given by Marinus of Tyre and the 180 degrees ascribed by Ptolemy. Thus, if this map is correctly attributed to Bartolomé, at this date he not only was aware of these very different estimates but also, even long after the discovery, still held to the shorter measurement. This letter is known through a manuscript appended to a copy of the *Paesi nuouamente retrovati* published in 1507 by its compiler, F. Montalboddo.

According to the Toscanelli letter, the width of the ocean was "almost the third part of all of the sphere," that is, 120 degrees. Further, there were 26 spaces of 250 miles each between Lisbon and Cathay, which would mean 6,500 miles. A question is raised by the following sentence in the Toscanelli letter: "But from the Island of Antilla, that you know of, to the most famous island of Çipango there are ten spaces [i.e., 2,500 miles]." To begin with, Antilla appears first in Greek mythology. Thus any mariner would be expected to have known of it but not necessarily where it was. Antilla, which means "island opposite Portugal," appears on all early maps, both pre- and postdiscovery.[56] It was shown as southwest of the Azores and northeast of Cipango and, on the Behaim globe, as approximately halfway between the Canary Islands and Cipango. It was placed at 28°N, whereas Cipango was shown lying across the tropic of Cancer at 24°N. Columbus equated Española with Cipango in his *Diario*. The Toscanelli Latin letter clearly states that the distance between Antilla and Cipango is 2,500 miles. The distance between Antilla and the African mainland is approximatey the same, and the distance between Lisbon and the Canary Islands is half of that, in other words approximately 1,250 miles.[57] These figures are all approximations but correspond to the locations on the early maps. On this basis the transocean voyage for Columbus—from the Canary Islands to Antilla to Cipango—would have been 3,700 miles. This is roughly the figure that he provided in his *Diario*.

Las Casas paraphrased Columbus's journal entry for September 18, when Columbus had sailed 1,462 miles: "Very soon He [The Lord] will give us land. On that morning he says that he saw a white bird that is called *rabo de Junco* which is not accustomed to sleep at sea."[58] Columbus and the crews continued to find signs of nearby land. When they had sailed 2,200 miles, Columbus and Martín Alonso decided, based on a chart that the Admiral had with him, that they were near land; Martín Alonso even claimed that he had seen it.[59] These figures show that Columbus expected to find land before Cipango, presumably Antilla. We will probably never know whether he based this estimate on the chart that he had with him, on *mappaemundi* that he says he saw before setting off on his voyage, on the Toscanelli letter, or perhaps on Behaim, the maker of the famous globe.

Cipango (Japan) had been generally known of through Marco Polo and *mappaemundi*. In antiquity it was known as "Taprobana." It was also believed that Cipango was closer to Europe than Cathay. Columbus set off to cross the ocean from the Canary Islands, the "Fortunate Islands" of antiquity. These were south of Lisbon and, on the old charts, extended over a thousand miles to the west of Lisbon, the point from which Toscanelli measured. Surely Toscanelli was too well informed to not know that the location of Antilla—if it ever existed—was a mystery then as it is today, whereas the Canary Islands, the westernmost known land, had already been discovered in 1402 by a Frenchman, Jean de Béthencourt, at the beginning of the fifteenth century. It was not until 1479 that these islands were recognized in the Treaty of Alcáçovas as being under the jurisdiction of Spain, although they were not fully conquered until 1486.

Toscanelli appears to have been giving an estimate for the distance between the Canary Islands and Japan. Ten days after his first landfall, Columbus mentioned Cipango twice in the *Diario*, anticipating that the next island, Cuba, might be Cipango. This makes it evident that he believed that he was sailing between these two locations on the map.

On his first voyage, Columbus counted approximately 4,000 miles, or 1,000 leagues, between his jumping-off point in the Canaries and his first landfall in the Bahamas. The lower figure that he showed his crews was 3,400 miles, or 860 leagues. Hernando claimed that the distance he had expected to travel to find land in the western Atlantic was 2,100 miles, or 700 leagues. If Toscanelli's Antilla is accepted as the Canary Islands, he too was short in his estimate of 2,500 miles. This has three possible explanations: Columbus took this estimate, a remarkably accurate one, from Toscanelli; the forger, knowing this estimate to be correct, inserted it after the discovery; and finally, the coincidence was just that, a coincidence.

Morison not only was certain that Columbus had the Toscanelli letter but also stated, "A copy of this 'Toscanelli Letter' in Columbus's hands became his principal exhibit when arguing for a narrow Atlantic."[60] This statement raises two more questions. First of all, there is neither a contemporary claim nor evidence that Columbus ever showed such a letter to anybody, and second, it is only a supposition that a map he showed to Martín Alonso while at sea during the first voyage may have been the map from the Toscanelli letter, one that no one else is reported as ever having seen, unless it was a copy of the one noted above by Thacher.

The second question is raised by Morison's reference here to a narrow Atlantic. As already noted, in the Toscanelli letter it is said that the width of the ocean is 120 degrees. The earlier suggestion that there were 26 spaces of 250 miles each between Lisbon and Cathay would mean 6,500 miles. This has raised a certain amount of controversy because the real-life Toscanelli was too well informed to have used this measurement, based on Marinus of Tyre's extension of Asia to the meridian of 225°;[61] an exaggeration first copied and later corrected by Ptolemy, who later adjusted the figure to 180°.[62] D'Ailly first repeated Ptolemy's original acceptance of the

Marinus estimate[63] but in a tract published later included his correction. The work known as the *Ymago mundi* is actually only the first of twelve tracts published by d'Ailly over the years 1410–14. The copy of these tracts used by the Columbus brothers was published sometime between 1480 and 1487 and included all twelve, together with one by Jean Charlier de Gerson. Columbus selected from d'Ailly those figures that indicated the shortest passage to India—the figures given by Marinus of Tyre, who was supported by Seneca rather than Ptolemy's correction. As Columbus wrote, "The cardinal [d'Ailly] gives to these great authority, more than to Ptolemy and other Greeks and Arabs."[64] Thus Columbus purposefully gave preference to Marinus over Ptolemy as his authority on this all-important point.

Fernández-Armesto is one of those who accepted the first Toscanelli letter and reserved judgment on the other two.[65] The Phillipses accepted the first letter and inferred that Columbus had received his copy through his Portuguese in-laws. They further asserted that this letter was a matter of common knowledge in Lisbon at the time, yet there is no contemporary Portuguese documentation to prove that this letter even existed, let alone was widely discussed. They also felt so convinced of their opinion that they stated, "Columbus clearly knew about Toscanelli and his theories."[66] Although Sale was less concerned with the letters, he was cautious as to the correspondence with Columbus: "Real questions still linger about the presumed correspondence between Colón and the Florentine humanist Paolo Toscanelli." He found Morison's work to be "seriously flawed" and "erroneously certain stating as facts (sometimes with disdainful dismissal of contrary views) . . . some matters about which there are now (and were then) serious doubts, or at least fair controversy. (To mention a few examples . . . about the Toscanelli letter)."[67] These comments would seem to indicate that he had doubts about all three of the letters.

Morison firmly believed that this correspondence provided the initial impetus for Columbus's plan for crossing the Atlantic.[68] It is curious that many historians have ignored the obvious fact that this letter was sent for the personal information of the then king of Portugal, Alonso V, and later would presumably have been available to his successor, João II, but seemingly was never acted on by either of them. Several conclusions may be drawn from these circumstances. First of all, if these assumptions are correct, the letter's content would not necessarily have been revealed to the king by Columbus; it was, after all, a Portuguese state document. Second, the Crown and its officers would have been fully aware of Toscanelli's ideas about the width of the Atlantic as well as about the proximity to the west of the India that the Portuguese were seeking to the south. Had João accepted the Toscanelli premise as valid, he would have sent Dulmo on his 1487 expedition (originally scheduled to sail in 1484 and specified to last forty days) based on the Toscanelli letter and not, as alleged in the *Historie*, in an attempt to steal Columbus's ideas. Third, since Toscanelli's letter is dated 1474, delaying Dulmo's voyage until 1484 is not easily explained. Fourth, since Dulmo began preparations for his voyage at about the time that Columbus left Portugal for Spain, these two events might well have been connected, and the claimed secret manner of Columbus's departure might well have been for fear of being caught with a purloined copy of the Toscanelli letter. Whatever influence this correspondence may have had on Columbus, it is doubtful that the letters were involved in any negotiations that he may have carried on with the Portuguese government.

Historians have shown interest in the fact, revealed in Columbus's log for his first voyage, that he was familiar with some of the names used in the literature of his and earlier times for cities and provinces in the lands of Kublai Khan. Attempts have been made to link his use of these names to particular sources. Martín Fernández de Navarrete was the first to point out that the references to "Quinsay" in the Spanish second Toscanelli letter were copied verbatim from chapter 98 of Marco Polo's book. In the Latin letter, the "magnus kan," "katay," "mangi," "quinsay," "zaiton," "antilia," and "cippangu" are named.[69] However, in the Spanish letter there are three more—Ireland, India, and the Island of the Seven Cities. All of the toponyms for the East given by Columbus in his logs do appear in d'Ailly's tracts, but not all appear in either the Toscanelli letters or the Marco Polo book. Therefore, Columbus's use of these toponyms cannot be offered as proof that he derived them from his reading of either of these claimed primary sources. If his use of these names was single-sourced, this source could only have been the *Ymago mundi*.

Columbus's plans of discovery were probably conceived while he was living in Portugal, but whether these were based on a letter and map supplied by Toscanelli is open to serious question. There is no independent confirmation as to its existence, nor confirmation by either Columbus or his brother Bartolomé. The copies offered by Hernando and Las Casas differ from the letter in the hand of Columbus. The only available means for determining their authenticity is by textual analysis of the letters. They contain obvious errors that seem to be incompatible with any work by this renowned humanist. The dating of the Toscanelli letter raises doubts, and the letter provides no cosmographic theory, toponym, or other data not to be found in other sources available to Columbus, sources that he did repeatedly acknowledge in later years. In short, it is not possible to state with any degree of certainty that this letter influenced Columbus in any way whatsoever.

Influence of Marco Polo and Mandeville

Many modern biographers rank Marco Polo's book with d'Ailly's *Ymago mundi* and the Toscanelli letter as one of the basic sources for Columbus's cosmographic concepts. To evaluate such claims, we need to go back to the primary sources, which are, in the case of Marco Polo, Columbus, his son Hernando, and Las Casas. Marco Polo's work was generally known by the derogatory sobriquet of *Il milione* because it supposedly contained a million lies. Based on the pen strokes and ink used, Gil determined that the Columbus postils in his copy of this work were all written at the same time. This does not necessarily mean that they were composed at the same time; since there were no erasures, it is assumed that Columbus composed them first and then copied them into the margins of the book. His rough drafts may have been the notes that, according to Hernando, he kept of matters that interested him.

The only copy of Marco Polo's book that Columbus is known to have owned is the 1485 Pipino Latin edition sent to him by John Day.

(There are two other copies registered in Hernando's library.) In a covering letter, Day explained to Columbus that he had not been able to find one requested book, but he added, "I sent you the other by Marco Polo and the copy of the land that is found."[70] The copy known today of the Day letter is not dated; however, a mention in it of Cabot's voyage to Newfoundland places it sometime in the late fall or early spring of 1497–98. Columbus made no reference to Marco Polo in any of his known letters.

Las Casas made a holograph copy of the Columbus letter written on the third voyage. In all of the three known versions of this letter, Columbus sought to encourage the Crown to continue supporting his ventures in the Indies by citing their economic potential. In both manuscript copies he wrote, "I brought you [the monarchs] sufficient sample of gold, and that there are mines and very large grains, and the same way copper; and I brought you many kinds of spices, which would be long to describe, and I told you of the large qantity of brazil[wood] and other infinite things."[71] In the text of his *Historia*, Las Casas first listed seventeen minerals that Columbus had found in the islands; he then noted the "very fine pearls and pink pearls, of those that Marco Polo says are worth more than the white."[72] This *Historia* paraphrase ends with the following sentence: "These are his words." The quotation about the pearls is not bracketed by quotation marks, however. This could easily be another example of Las Casas's editorializing. There is no mention at this point in either of the manuscript letters of pearls or Marco Polo. This mention is in the Lascasian log entry for August 16, 1498. Later in the letter, Columbus went into detail about finding pearls, color not mentioned, off the Venezuelan coast—again with no mention of Marco Polo.

Marco Polo discussed red pearls in his chapter on the island of "Ciampagu" (*sic*). Columbus marked this passage, writing beside it *perlas rojas* ("red pearls").[73] As noted earlier, the postils in this book were copied from an unidentifiable source; therefore, there is no way of knowing when the original was written. Of 366 postils, Gil ascribed 242 to Columbus. He believed the others were written by Hernando (38) and an unidentified amenuensis (86). More than half of the words highlighted by Columbus dealt with either mercantile interests or the availability of precious stones and metals.

Only twenty postils relate to geography and climate. Columbus annotated Karmay once, Singuy twice, and Cambala once and noted that Quinsay was the largest city in the world.[74] His note equating Marco Polo's Coilum with "Calicut" (*sic*) dates that particular entry as postdiscovery.[75] He made three notations to regions, naming only Mangi, Gog, and Magog. He drew attention to the fact that Marco Polo said there were 1,300 cities in Mangi.[76] Marco Polo also said that there were 7,378 islands in the Sea of Mangi, but there are no annotations by Columbus to this claim. However, Columbus's postil #662 in the *Imago mundi* notes that before Taprobana there are 1,378 islands.[77]

By far the greatest number of Columbus's Marco Polo postils are in Book Three. This book, concerned primarily with the islands in the Pacific, devotes chapters to Madagascar, Zanzibar, Ceylon, Malabar, Abyssinia, and Aden. Columbus never pretended that his Indies were connected with any of these places, yet his most numerous postils are in reference to the abundance of gold and jewels to be found in them.

Four postils in *Il milione* clearly indicate that they were inserted after Columbus's second voyage. The first, the mention of Calicut, was followed by a notation in which Marco Polo's port of Zaizen was equated with the southern tip of Cuba, named by Columbus "Alfa y O."[78] Zaizen is in one of the regions of Mangi, which is where Columbus believed himself to be when he had sailed almost to the northernmost tip of Cuba during his second voyage. Next, while mentioning the island of Jan la Grande (Cuba), he noted that the nearby waters are shallow—*mar de bajos*—and that therefore one must raise the rudder while cruising there. These shallow waters are annotated by Columbus when Marco Polo talked of the Chersonese. He also wrote that the king of this island paid tribute to no one and that the Gran Khan had not yet been able to subjugate him.[79] From the postils it is evident that Columbus found this island to be his own Juana-Cuba.

In the *Diario*, Columbus described an animal that the sailors had found, calling it a *taso* or *taxo*.[80] As Oliver Dunn pointed out, in Italian *tasso* means badger. No similar animal is known on the island; however, there is a small ratlike creature known as the

jutia.[81] Marco Polo described the fauna of Aquilón, a region peopled
by Tartars, "farther away from the North Pole—'más allá del polo
ártico,'" where he encountered "animals that are called 'rats of the
Pharoa' that are very large for their species." The log entry could
relate either to Marco Polo's *ratti Pharaonis* or to the Indian *rattes*
reported by Niccolò dei' Conti. It appears to have been a Lascasian
addition to the text of the *Diario*, in that he annotated this entry with
the word *hutias*, a Taino name used to this day for a rodent indigenous
to Española.[82] Columbus probably knew of this Taino delicacy but is
unlikely to have made the linkage with the "rats of the Pharoa" at
the time of the first voyage. At some time after the first voyage, he
did write the postil *jutias* alongside the appropriate text in his copy
of Marco Polo's book, which dates this entry postdiscovery.

Las Casas, writing in the third person in the *Diario*, paraphrased
Columbus: "He found large nuts of [the kind] of those of Yndia (I
think he says)."[83] The "large nuts" is a reference to the coconut palm
(*Cocos nucifera* L.), a tree unknown in the Atlantic regions of
America in Columbus's day.[84] Marco Polo and Conti, among other
travelers, had reported these Asian palm trees. Las Casas would
have known of them from his travels on the American continent.
Columbus could have encountered them on his fourth voyage, to the
Isthmus of Panama, but certainly not on the first.

It has often been said that the use of many of the same names in
the *Diario* and in Marco Polo's book clearly indicates that Columbus
had studied *Il milione* before his first voyage. A systematic check of
these entries and their possible other sources belies this claim.
Marco Polo made thirty-six direct mentions of the Gran Khan in his
first book alone. In Book Two, Marco Polo devoted nineteen chapters
to the khan and his court. Columbus did not personally highlight
any of these many references to the khan. There are only four
notations made by his amenuensis to the "Gran Kan" (*sic*). One of
these was the claim that he had 336 children.[85] Judging by the khan
postils alone, one cannot support the proposition that Columbus was
seeking a meeting with the Gran Khan when he first crossed the
Atlantic.

There are nine references to the "Gran Can" (*sic*) in Columbus's
Diario. The first of these was made on October 21, after the recent

finding of land. This is, to say the least, highly unrealistic.[86] In it Columbus wrote that if he found gold and spices, he would then decide what to do next, but he added that he did want to go to Quinsay to give the khan the letters sent by the king and queen. Later in the journal, in the same month, Las Casas paraphrased the Admiral's comments on pearls and the possible proximity of the land of the Gran Khan because of the reported abundance of pearls there. A few days later the captain of the *Pinta* is quoted as saying that the king of Cuba was at war with the Gran Khan; after this entry Columbus commented on the khan and the size of the city of "Cathay" (*sic*), which he knew "according to what he had been told before leaving Spain."[87]

This *Diario* reference to Quinsay is either a lapsus or a lack of familiarity with Marco Polo, who placed Kublai Khan's residence in Cambalú.[88] As previously noted, Columbus did annotate "Cambalequia" in a postil in the *Historia rerum*. Columbus's reference in the *Diaro* to Zaiton, to which Marco Polo dedicated one chapter, is unrevealing. Zaiton appeared in most of the thirteenth- to fifteenth-century travelogues, as well as on contemporary *mappaemundi* and on the famous globe constructed by Martin Behaim in 1492.[89] There are no Columbian postils whatsoever in Marco Polo's chapter in which this port city is described. The Toscanelli letter also referred to Zaiton.

In the prologue to the *Diario*, written after the voyage, Columbus stated that he set sail from Spain to go to the city of Cathay; Gil pointed out that this indicates ignorance of not only the Marco Polo work but also all texts from the tenth century on. Cathay was always given as a region, not a city.[90] Columbus wrote six postils in his *Historia rerum* marking references from Nicholas of Venice (Niccolò dei' Conti), in each of which he recognized that Cathay was a region.[91] Martín Fernández de Navarrete was the first to point out that all of the references to Quinsay in the first Toscanelli letter are copied verbatim from chapter 98 of Marco Polo's book.

Interestingly, Columbus's *Historia rerum* postils that relate to the "Gran Can," "Catayo," and "Cambalequia" apply equally to citations in the text from the travelogue of Conti. As previously noted, Conti, on his return from the Far East, met in 1444 with Pope

Eugenius IV, the pope referred to in the Toscanelli letter. He dictated the account of his journey to the pope's secretary, Poggio Bracciolini from Florence (see the note for numerous words and phrases given by Conti in common with similar ones used by Columbus).[92] If nothing else, the many geographical references indicate that by the fifteenth century, these were commonplace terms. Many of them were also used by Ruy González de Clavijo (1403); Bartholomeu Florentino (1424), who also reported to Pope Eugenius; Josafa Barbaro (1436); and of course on the Fra Mauro and Catalán maps. The same applies to William of Rubruck, as well as to the reports made by the many Catholic friars established in Cathay.

Columbus's other *Diario* comments on the khan involved either noting the economic gains to be had from these newly found lands or, in late November, equating Española with the lands of the khan due to the fact that he understood the Indians to tell him of cannibals, of people with only one eye, and of others with faces like those of dogs.[93] His last mention of the khan is to state that since there were cannibals, they must be the people of the khan. The word *cannibal* is one that came into the language only with the first voyage. These age-old tales might just as easily have come from the *Ymago mundi*, the *Historia rerum*, or *The Travels of Sir John Mandeville* (c. 1356) as from Marco Polo's *Il milione*. Mandeville, however, incorporated many of Marco Polo's tales into his own fanciful account of imaginary voyages through strange lands that he had never visited.

Scholars disagree about who wrote Mandeville's *Travels*, as well as about whether it was intended as a travel tale or a romance, but such differences do not alter the fact that in both the *Travels* and *Il milione*, the authors told (as did d'Ailly, Conti, and others) of such exotica in the East as were later noted by Columbus. These fanciful comments open up the possibility that all that he knew, at the time of his voyage, of Marco Polo was what he might have gleaned from other writers of the thirteenth through the the fifteenth centuries. One of these, Ibn Battutah, traveled even more extensively than Marco Polo and personally reported in Rome, Spain, France, and England on his voyages through these areas over the years 1325–55, which were essentially the same years as Mandville's purported voyagings (1322–56).

Like Marco Polo, Battutah was accused by his contemporaries of inventing his tales. Ibn Khaldûn, author of the *Muqaddimah* (described by Arnold Toynbee as "undoubtedly the greatest work of its kind that has ever yet been created by any mind in any time or place"), said: "People whispered to each other that he (Battutah) must be a liar. . . . It often happens that people are (incredulous) with regard to historical information, just as it also happens that they are tempted to exaggerate certain information, in order to be able to report something remarkable."[94] Khaldûn met with Battutah personally. Earlier, while describing an event attributed to Alexander the Great, he made a pertinent observation about mythical creatures: "The story of the many heads they have is intended to indicate ugliness and frightfulness. It is not meant to be taken literally."[95] Khaldûn was well known in Spain. While on a peace mission to Castile, the king, Pedro the Cruel, "honoured him highly and offered to take him into his service and restore to him his family's former property."[96] It is interesting that this Arabian historian, writing half a century before the birth of Columbus, offered this reasonable explanation for such tales as that of the two-headed men.

Bernáldez, while discussing Columbus's first voyage, referred often to the similarities between the information found in Columbus's account and the fanciful tales told by Mandeville, but he made no mention of Marco Polo.[97] Neither Bernáldez nor Las Casas said or inferred that Columbus had read either Marco Polo or Mandeville, yet they did cite by name and work other authors that they believed he had read. Now, with the finding of *El libro copiador*, it has become evident that the references to Mandeville were Bernáldez's own. He copied much of his information on the second voyage verbatim from the fourth letter in *El libro copiador*. His version included references to Mandeville, yet Columbus made no such references whatsoever in this letter.

Recently the unsupported assumptions, made by Morison and others, that Columbus derived his perceptions of the East from these two sources entered into the thesis of Stephen Greenblatt when he wrote: "In the late fifteenth century that concept depended principally on Marco Polo and Sir John Mandeville, whose books

Columbus read and quite possibly carried with him on his first voyage." Greenblatt provided a footnote for this statement: "Columbus's copy of Marco Polo, with his annotations, has survived. We know of his familiarity with *Mandeville's Travels* from Andrés Bernáldez, *Memorias del reinado de los Reyes Católicos.*" In the same footnote he went on to say: "Columbus's son Fernando also wrote that among the reasons that led his father to undertake his voyage were the works of 'Marco Polo, a Venetian, and John Mandeville.'"[98] Neither observation accords with the known facts.

Zvetan Todorov asked, "Did not Columbus himself set sail because he had read Marco Polo's narrative?"[99] A close reading of the *Historie* passage that refers to Marco Polo and Mandeville indicates that this reading was Hernando's, not his father's.[100] Earlier Todorov had written about "Columbus's great motivation . . . to spread the Christian religion throughout the world. He knew because he had read it in Marco Polo that the Great Khan—the Emperor of China— wanted to convert to Christianity."[101] What was reported was from the earlier voyage made by Marco's father, Niccolò, a voyage made before Marco was born. He had reported that the khan wanted to know "if it was true that the faith of the Christians was the best of all."[102] This interest was quite different from a desire to convert.

Later, while discussing Columbus as an interpreter, Todorov went on to explain Columbus's *Diario* quotations of what the Indians, whom he could not have possibly understood, had supposedly told him: "What he understands, then, is simply a summary of the books of Marco Polo and Pierre d'Ailly."[103] If such matters were only so simple!

Greenblatt's claim that the Mandeville romance was written by "a knight and a man of the world—but he has his own version of renunciation in the service of the Christian faith"—ignored for the moment the widespread disagreement among scholars as to who wrote this work as well as to its purpose. Was it a travelogue of wonders encountered or a romance? Greenblatt pointed out some of the sources from which Mandeville lifted many of his tales and finally revealed that the author referred to above as a "knight and a man of the world" had been "disclosed as a fiction . . . a fictive persona." His evaluation of the work—"But whether it were as it seemed, or it was but fantasy, I wot not [*sic*]"—can perhaps be applied here to his own seemingly confused opinions. Greenblatt raised an interesting point when he wrote: "For it betokens not material existence as such but a circulation of signs that makes material existence meaningful, comprehensible, resonant. *Mandeville's Travels*, and the textual phenomenon we call Mandeville himself, is stitched together out of bits and pieces that had passed like well-thumbed coins or rather like old banknotes through many hands."[104] To carry this rationalization one step further, can it not be said, as suggested above, that it might have been precisely through such oral tradition—"passed like well-thumbed coins"—that Columbus acquired the toponyms of the East and his tales of the monsters that he so vividly reported in the *Diario*?

In a footnote to her translation of the first letter in *El libro copiador*, Zamora made it clear that she accepts the prediscovery readings of Marco Polo and Mandeville. As previously noted, she stated: "Columbus certainly would have known [Odoric of] Pordenone's account, as distilled in John Mandeville's *Travels* (1470), a book Columbus knew well."

José Rabasa wrote that he set out to trace "Columbus' projections of Marco Polo into the American landscape."[105] He felt so strongly in his certitude of Mandeville's influence on Columbus that he merely noted, "Next to Marco Polo, Mandeville was the major source of information about the East for Columbus."[106] He had earlier commented, while developing his thesis, "Indeed, Columbus has to fabricate a frame of reference so that the production of information about the new makes sense to a European reader." Rabasa went on to elaborate by saying, "To be sure, such compendiums [*sic*] as Marco Polo's *Divasement dou monde* and Pierre d'Ailly's *Ymago mundi* provide Columbus with an image of the world by which to imagine his whereabouts." This observation would be valid only if it could be established that Columbus had read either of these works before becoming, as Rabasa aptly described it, "immersed in the insular world of America."[107] Unfortunately, the evidence is not conclusive, although there is some evidence for his having read the *Ymago mundi* prior to the discovery.

Like Greenblatt, Rabasa placed a great deal of reliance on his assumption that Columbus was fully conversant with Marco Polo's *Il milione*. "Columbus traces a pattern of signs derived for the most part from Marco Polo's description. . . . For Columbus and the other European imagination in general, the descriptions of Marco Polo are a primary authoritative source."[108] In a footnote[109] Rabasa indicated his reliance on Gil and other translators of Columbus's annotated copy, but he did not include references to Gil's *Mitos y utopías del descubrimiento*, in which Gil wrote: "At the present time, no serious student of the postille admits that the acquisition of the work of Marco Polo is dated before 1497."[110] Gil went on to say, "Therefore, if the books of Marco Polo, of Pliny and Pius II were annotated after 1493, the most elementary logic invites the deduction that the same applied to the other volumes."[111]

Marco Polo was not cited by d'Ailly. Columbus referred to the "gran Kan" in two postils in the *Ymago mundi*. In each case, d'Ailly's text referred to the Tartars without mention of the khan.[112] Eneas Silvio Piccolómini (Pope Pius II) referred to the khan, and Columbus annotated these mentions in his copy of the *Historia rerum* eight times. As already noted, he added no postils to the numerous khan references in his edition of Marco Polo; there are several, but they are in the hand of his son Hernando. Obviously Hernando could not have written these in 1492, since he was only about five years old at the time.

For those who accept the first letter of Toscanelli as an authentic copy of a letter known to Columbus, it can come as no surprise that in this letter, the Gran Khan, Cathay, Mangi, Quinsay, and Cipango are all mentioned. On this basis alone, relating the use of these names in the *Diario* with a direct reading of Marco Polo's travel tale would be unnecessary. Mangi was not mentioned in the *Diario*, but it did appear in the later letter on the third voyage. In the *Diario*, Cathay was mentioned once, Quinsay four times, and Cipango twice. Todorov, commenting on the European discovery of perspective in the graphic arts, noted the interesting fact that "Toscanelli, inspirer of Columbus, was the friend of Brunelleschi."[113] Inferentially, he too accepted the Toscanelli correspondence.

Fernández-Armesto speculated that through the reading of Marco Polo, Columbus developed some of his concepts as to the size of the ocean and distances to be traveled to reach the Indies. He dated the copy in Columbus's library to 1496 yet added, "His own writings show that he was well acquainted with Marco Polo's version of Oriental place names by 1492."[114] There are no historiographically confirmed samples of Columbus's writings that date before 1492, nor are there any direct references to Marco Polo in any of Columbus's known writings. Fernández-Armesto attached particular significance to the belief that the tale of an island named Cipango, referred to by Columbus in the *Diario*, was first reported in Europe by Marco Polo. However, he overlooked two simple facts: first, through Marco Polo, Europeans had known about Cipango for over 150 years before Columbus set sail for the Indies; second, Columbus wrote in the *Diario* that he knew of the island, about which "marvellous things are told and on the spheres that I saw and in the pictures in the mapamundi [*sic*]."[115]

Morison supplied a translation of a passage from João de Barros's *Decada primeira do Asia* in which "Cypango" is related to Marco Polo: "The king . . . observed this Christovào Colom to be a big talker and boastful . . . and they all considered the words of Christovao Colom as vain, simply founded on imagination, or things like that Isle Cypango of Marco Polo."[116] He concluded, "Marco Polo's story, was the foundation of Columbus's ideas regarding the accessibility of Asia."[117] As can be seen in the footnote, in the translation of this passage from Barros, the Las Casas version differs in several respects, most notably in the lack of any reference to Marco Polo.[118] As previously noted, Columbus's postils in *Il milione* related primarily to gold and spices. None of his postils concerned distances between the two continents.

The Phillipses noted, "In fact Columbus probably gleaned much of what he knew about Asia from reading Marco Polo." This is an acceptable assertion as long as it does not infer that this knowledge was acquired prior to the first voyage. However, they went on to speculate that on returning from the first voyage, "he could not face his sovereigns again without news of Cathay."[119] The term "Cathay" had been in common use for centuries.

Wilford emphasized the fact that in the *Diario*, Columbus had expressed his disappointment with the first natives that he encountered because "their nakedness set the Indians apart from the Asiatics Marco Polo had described, and this must have been another source of disappointment. Where was all the silk brocade?" Further on he reversed his position, saying, "No doubt Columbus consulted [Marco Polo and others previously listed] but probably a few years later, when he used them not in the conception of his plan but to confirm and document it."[120] Earlier, he had hedged, saying, "Nor did Columbus derive his plan from a careful reading of scholars. . . . He may have perused the accounts of Marco Polo (at least he was familiar with them and those of Sir John Mandeville)."[121] Then, he asserted that Columbus made his estimates as to distances to be crossed "on the authority of Marco Polo and others."[122] Obviously, some scholars have difficulty deciding just what they believe about this nebulous matter.

This last statement in regard to distances would appear to be based on a surmise made by Hernando, who recognized the failure of both Marco Polo and Mandeville to make any reference to the sizes of the world's oceans.[123] Therefore, from their statements about the vast size of the Orient, he rationalized that the area, separated by water, bordering on Africa and Spain must be smaller than some said.

Sale indicated his acceptance of a prediscovery familiarity with *Il milione* when he reported that on October 17, Columbus became aware of an obvious fact: "It was patent by then that he was not actually in Marco Polo's Orient of marble and gold nor the fabled islands of monsters and treasures."[124]

Many authors support their theories as to the influence exerted on Columbus by Marco Polo with the November 14 entry in the *Diario*. Taken out of context, the entry refers to those "Innumerable Islands," seen by some as a reference to Marco Polo's account of innumerable islands off the coast of Asia.[125] However, in this same journal entry Columbus went on to say that these islands were "placed in the mappamundi at the end of the Orient." There were no *mappaemundi* in the early editions of Marco Polo. In this case, it would appear that Columbus was referring to the islands on the map that he had with him. Earlier, on October 24, Columbus had written that prior to the voyage, he had consulted "globes and mappamundi [*sic*]."[126]

On the Catalán map of 1375 these innumerable islands are listed as numbering 7,548. Marco Polo wrote, and Columbus annotated, that there were 1,378 islands in India.[127] Cisneros, writing in 1495, cited Plato on these islands, giving their number as 1,328, as had been reported to Alexander the Great.[128] Obviously, the matter of the numerous islands to be encountered before reaching Asia was widely discussed many centuries before Marco Polo wrote about them. This minor yet untenable claim that Columbus referred to Marco Polo's account of many islands could be ignored were it not maintained with such tenacity.

It is evident that neither Columbus's postils in Marco Polo's book nor his log references to the khan, mythical monsters, Asian toponyms, and innumerable islands are in any way sufficient evidence in themselves to warrant saying that Columbus derived any of his prediscovery concepts of Asia from his reading of Marco Polo. His postils are necessarily dated postdiscovery because, as pointed out, he did not own the particular copy in which they appear until sometime in 1497–98. As also noted, in his copy of *Il milione* are four postils that could have been written only after the discovery. As demonstrated, the *Diario* references have other possible sources for the proper names used. As Wilford, paraphrasing Hernando Colón, put it: "He cited geographical measurements of Ptolemy and Marinus of Tyre, the descriptions of Asia by Marco Polo and Mandeville and the pronouncements of Aristotle and Seneca on the possibility of sailing west to the Indies." Wilford then added, "No doubt Columbus consulted these respected sources, but probably a few years later, when he used them not in the conception of his plan but to confirm and document it."[129] Wilford would have done well to have restricted himself to this astute commentary.

D'Ailly, Pliny, and Ptolemy

There is far more certainty as to the information that Columbus gleaned from his reading of the *Ymago mundi*. The uncertainty is at what time he read it. In the letter on the third voyage, he wrote of his activities before embarking for the Indies: "I put in this six or seven years of arduous toil, showing the best that I knew how much service could be done for Our Savior. . . . It was also necessary to speak of the climate(s), where they were shown [in the] writing(s) of so many wise men worthy of faith, who wrote histories. The which told that in these parts there were many precious objects. And the same way it was necessary to bring to this the sayings and opinion of those who wrote [about] and placed the world."[130] The *Ymago mundi* is the only book of his that included 99.9 percent of the cosmographic data and toponyms that he used in his letters and postils. It is doubtful that he had personally read Solinus, Alfragan, or other classical authors. All the citations that he made from these writers could have derived from his readings in this one book.

Columbus entered into the most detail on these matters in his letter on the third voyage. In it he named twenty-five authorities, all but one of whom (Saint Bede) appear both in the *Ymago Mundi* and in Columbus's postils in that book. At the same time he gave twenty-three toponyms in the letter, all of which are also in the *Ymago mundi*, most of them with postils. This book delves into such diverse matters as the different "climates" of the earth (i.e., zones), how the four great rivers of the world emerge from the terrestrial paradise that is at the highest point on the earth,[131] and tales of amazons, monsters, and "savages who eat human meat."[132] His postils in the *Historia rerum* also highlight the many explanations in that book about the world's climates as well as statements such as those referring to the "terrestrial paradise" which is near the equator,[133] to tales of amazons,[134] and to stories of "the bodies of humans that serve as food."[135]

Justin Winsor noted, "Solinus borrowed shamelessly from Pliny." As previously noted, d'Ailly did the same from Solinus. The Western edition of Pliny's *Historia naturalis, libri xxxvii* was first published in Venice in 1469, with thirteen more editions published before 1492. Pliny did speculate that due to the land size of Asia, its western shores might be closer to Spain than to land in the opposite direction. That the world is spherical, and that the ocean dividing Europe and Asia could be crossed in "a few days" or again in "forty days," were other opinions of Pliny cited by Columbus, Hernando, and Las Casas. Each of them repeated Pliny's speculations as to the location of the Hesperides, as did Fernández de Oviedo.

Judging from Columbus's postils in his copy of Pliny's *Historia naturalis*, none of the above concepts of Pliny were derived by Columbus from his reading of his copy of the book. He did find in Pliny confirmation of his beliefs as to the location of Taprobana. However, his postils in his *Ymago mundi* and *Historia rerum* do relate to these concepts. Columbus's references to Pliny, such as his statement in the letter on the third voyage—"Pliny writes that the sea and the land all make a sphere"—has led some, such as Varela, to look up the revelant passages in Pliny.[136] The problem here is that this and similar passages are taken from Columbus's citations of Pliny in his postils in the *Ymago mundi*, not from his copy of Pliny's history. Columbus's postils in his copy of Pliny have no cosmographic significance whatsoever.

Fernández-Armesto discussed Columbus's postils in his copy of the 1489 edition of Pliny's *Historia naturalis*, as well as mentioning that work's contribution to Columbus's theories. Out of the twenty-four postils in the book, Fernández-Armesto found only one that might indicate a pre-1492 reading of this work. Wilford did not find this work to have contributed significantly to Columbus's ideas, although he did quote several of Pliny's concepts as found in d'Ailly without indicating that their source was Pliny. In his text, Wilford made one insignificant, direct reference to Pliny. The Phillipses and Sale apparently agreed with Wilford in ignoring Pliny. Perhaps they took their lead from Morison, who did not list Pliny in the index to his biography of Columbus, although he did refer to Pliny in the text.

These modern-day historians, on the contrary, did find Ptolemy's work to have exercised a major influence on Columbus's cosmographic concepts. Thacher observed that the copy of *Geographia* in the Biblioteca Columbina is the 1478 edition published in Rome; the holograph on the recto of the first folio includes the curious monogram that Columbus used only after the discovery.[137] Gil believed that this monogram was "evidently false."[138] As previously noted, Columbus rejected Ptolemy's estimate as given in d'Ailly of the distance to the Far East, preferring instead the shorter distance projected by Marinus of Tyre. Ptolemy adapted his geocentric theory from Aristotle. This work on geography became known through an Arab translation, the *Almagest*, in A.D. 827. Ptolemy's *Geographia* became available in manuscript in Europe in 1409 and was first published in 1475, with five more editions up to 1492.

Thus, Columbus could conceivably have had access to a copy before acquiring one. Dawson drew attention to this fact: "It is difficult to realize the persistent weight of authority of Ptolemy. Not until 1569 did Gerard Mercator lead the way in revolt and all traces of the error of the length of the Mediterranean Sea did not disappear from the maps until the beginning of the last century. . . . The true circumference of the earth was not known to the Greeks and they made different estimates; from Aristotle, 400,000 stades, to Ptolemy, 180,000 stades."[139] Although Columbus, Hernando, Las Casas, and others often referred to Aristotle, no one has claimed that any of them derived their knowledge of Aristotle's theories directly.[140] The theories of both Aristotle and Ptolemy can be readily traced, through Albertus Magnus via Aquinas to d'Ailly in the first case and through the *Almagest* via Bacon to d'Ailly for Ptolemy.

One of the few matters that comes nearest to gaining general agreement is the idea that Piccolómini's *Historia rerum ubique gestarum* was one of the influential works for Columbus. There are almost the same number of postils in it (861) as in the probably much more influential *Ymago mundi* (863), many of them undoubtedly written by his brother. Due to the fact that in the *Historia rerum*, the classical Greek theories of a larger universe are those accepted by its author,[141] Vignaud went so far as to say that this work had no influence on the cosmographic ideas of Columbus.[142]

Morison, on the other hand, found that it was in these two works that Columbus "picked up . . . numerous guesses about the narrowness of the ocean";[143] this was conceivably correct for the *Ymago mundi* but incorrect for the *Historia rerum*. There are no such references in Piccolómini's work. Wilford, the Phillipses, and Sale did not discuss this matter. Differences of opinion as to the relative importance to Columbus of these two works are based on the manner in which each supposedly influenced him. Perhaps the more reasonable approach, based on the content of the two, is to accept the cosmographic influence of the *Ymago mundi* while recognizing the importance of the *Historia rerum* in portraying for him the panorama of the fabled India. Fernández-Armesto restricted himself to the observation that Piccolómini dismissed the idea of the existence of the Antipodes, "with a reminder that a Christian 'ought to prefer' the traditional view: clearly, that sort of a disclaimer was not to be taken seriously."[144]

To sum up the complex and often confusing exlanations offered over the years, beginning with those of Columbus himself, as to the physical nature of the world into which he sailed blindly, we can say only that no one, perhaps not even Columbus himself, could say how or when he developed his concepts. It seems reasonable to go along with the Phillipses, who noted, "His geographical hypotheses grew incrementally, beginning with the fairly simple idea of sailing westward to reach the Indies and later adding evidence from academic geographers to buttress his case."[145]

Like so many other matters relating to Columbus, his reported offer of his project to Portugal cannot be documented. The Portuguese chroniclers, Rui da Pina and Barros, wrote of this offer only after Columbus had returned from the discovery. The story, however, was so generally believed, even in his own day, that there is more reason to accept it than doubt it. The literature on the subject does not reveal what he offered at the time. Could he have been offering only to find the islands so often referred to by ancients and contemporaries alike? Is it possible that his plan had not yet matured to the point that it was convincing? Could the same be said of the offers made through his brother Bartolomé to Henry VII of England and at the French court? Is it not equally possible that his plan evolved into a workable project during the seven years he was at the court of Spain seeking backing? Did Columbus have concrete knowledge of lands to the west, knowledge that he did not want to divulge, for obvious reasons, but that he was forced to reveal to King Ferdinand in order to get the king to override his most recent turndown at Santa Fé? These are some of the conundrums addressed in the next chapter.

He that questioneth much shall learn much.
                                    Francis Bacon (1561–1626)

5
Prior
Discovery

Other sources, in addition to those discussed in the previous chapter, could have provided Columbus with the incentive to seek out the islands in the western ocean or, perhaps, could have served to confirm notions that he had acquired elsewhere. The most important of these sources is an actual knowledge of what was out there.

The Unknown Pilot

Columbus could have come by empirical data in various ways. The most important one concerns the story that an unknown pilot, who had miraculously returned from discovering the islands in the western Atlantic, died in Columbus's house after revealing his secret to the future admiral.

Fernández de Oviedo was the first to propagate in print what has become known as the tale of the unknown pilot. In the first chapters of his work published in 1539, he reported that "some wish to say" that a caravel en route to England from Portugal with a load of wine and general cargo was blown off course and finally reached some

islands, where naked natives were found. The ship took on water and
wood for cooking fuel and set sail for home. The whole voyage took
four or five months, and on the return trip most of the crew died. The
pilot, with four or five crew members, reached Portugal; shortly
afterward, the remaining crewmen died. The pilot, a good friend of
Columbus's, asked him to draw up a map showing where the pilot
had been. Columbus took his friend into his home, where the pilot
soon died.[1]

Fernández de Oviedo went on to say that some claimed that this
pilot was from Andalucía, whereas others said Portugal or Viscaya.[2]
He noted that the story, as sometimes told, placed Columbus in
Madeira at the time or at Cape Verde, where the pilot had begun his
journey. Fernández de Oviedo concluded: "Whether or not it happened this way, nobody can say for certain; but this tale circulates
among the common people in the manner in which I say. For me it
is false, and as [Saint] Augustine says: *Melius est dubitare de ocultis,
quam litigasre de incertis.*—It is better to doubt that which we do not
know, than to dispute the uncertain." He later added, "Columbus, a
wise, learned and daring man, was moved to undertake such a thing
as this . . . because he knew, and it is true, that these lands had been
forgotten."[3] The writer then brought up the ancient tales of the
Island of the Seven Cities, peopled by Spanish Christians from
Portugal, and of the Hesperides of Greek mythology.

Fernández de Oviedo's account is generally cited as the sole basis
in the contemporary written record for the "unknown pilot" explanation for how Columbus came to discover the Indies. Actually, in
1514 Fray Antonio de Aspa told the same tale in a manuscript that
is today in the Spanish National Academy of History. This friar left
a collection of documents, in which is included the first known copy
of the important letter of Dr. Diego Alvarez Chanca containing his
diary of the second voyage.[4]

The story next appeared in Francisco López de Gómara's *Hispañia
vitrix* (the short title for Gómara's *Historia general de las Indias*) in
1553. He repeated Fernández de Oviedo's version without any
changes of importance, yet he has ever since been accused of passing
off rumor as fact. The first to question him in this manner was
Girolamo Benzoni in *Historia del Nuevo Mundo*, published in Venice

in 1565.[5] He repeated the López de Gómara version, though he added that the latter had mixed much falsehood with some truth.[6] Then, as today, López de Gómara's account was seen as a Spanish attempt to besmirch the name of the Italian discoverer.

Another account, this one written in 1589, told the story in detail. This was written by Juan Suárez de Peralta, the son of a conquistador who had accompanied Diego Colón on his voyage to Española in 1509. The father later moved to Cuba, where he joined up with Hernán Cortés, whose first wife was his daughter. He became Cortés's right-hand man. The author of this manuscript was born in Mexico in the 1530s. He began by saying that the first discovery was made by sailors in a boat possibly blown off course and that since no one but Columbus knew of this, Columbus hid the fact in order to take lone credit for the discovery. He went on to tell the story much as have others. He also speculated that Tedisio Doria and Ugolino Vivaldi had reached the Americas in 1291.[7]

The *Historie* was the next to broach the subject, recounting the tale more or less as told by Fernández de Oviedo.[8] Interestingly, Hernando did not deny the story but merely gave a capsulated version of it. He went on to discuss the voyages of Gaspar Côrte-Real and others, noting that all of them had been unsuccessful in finding the lands they sought. He passed these efforts off as being of little consequence. This treatment differs from the one in his next chapter, in which he vehemently refuted Fernández de Oviedo's claim that the Hesperides, that is, the Indies, had been discovered by early Spanish bishops and accordingly had already belonged to the Spanish Crown for centuries.

Las Casas, while following Hernando's version, added details with his own extended commentary. He began by saying, "It was very common [knowledge] among all of us who lived at the time on this island of Española, not just those who came with the Admiral himself . . . but also those of us who came soon after to discuss and say what was the cause that moved the said Admiral to want to come to discover these Indies." Las Casas recounted the tale of the vessel blown off course, saying that he was not sure where it had sailed from or whether it had been headed for Flanders or England, but that it was blown to these islands by a violent storm, and thus the crew became the first to discover these islands. In support of this claim, he noted that when he had come to the island in 1500, the story was taken as an accepted fact; and furthermore, the account was made by those who knew the story and "perhaps even knew it from the mouth of Columbus himself" or "in all or in part by some word that they heard." The second reason he offered was that "those of us" who had been on the first voyage to Cuba found that the natives had recent memory of "other white men, bearded like us," having come to Española "before us by not many years." This he says was possible in that Cuba is only eighteen leagues distant from Española and the natives traded with each other by canoe.[9]

Las Casas then went on to discuss the probabilities of a caravel being blown across the ocean in this manner, noting that in the Caribbean seas with their strong currents, during a storm a ship running before the wind under bare sticks can make thirty to fifty leagues a day. Las Casas noted that the Admiral, on his voyage to Paria, was himself driven sixty-five leagues in one day by light winds and a strong following current. Las Casas sought further confirmation of the force of winds and currents in the writings of the ancients, citing among others Heroditus and Aristotle. He then speculated that for whatever reason, be it prior friendship or curiosity, Columbus took the pilot to his home to convalesce. Before dying, the pilot, either out of old friendship or in appreciation for the help that Columbus had given him, told Columbus everything about his trip, including the route that he had taken. Las Casas ended by repeating that this tale was generally accepted as true; however, due to the many other reasons that might have motivated Columbus, Las Casas concluded, "We can pass this by and believe it or not believe it, inasmuch as it could be that our Lord led by the hand one or the other to carry out this sovereign work."[10]

Father José de Acosta published his first account of the Americas in 1588–89 and his larger work, the *Historia natural y moral de las Indias*, in 1590. Acosta repeated the story of the unknown pilot.[11] In 1589, Juan de Castellanos, a conquistador and poet who founded the present-day city of Bogotá, Colombia, wrote a versified history of the discovery and conquest of the Americas. He said that it was Columbus himself who had survived the first discovery, noting some people gave good reasons for this claim, among others the Adelantado Jimenez de Quesada. His history enjoyed considerable popularity at the time.[12]

The theory that it was Columbus himself who had made the prior discovery gained support for some historians from a phrase in a letter dated 1494 to Columbus from the Spanish sovereigns. They wrote, "It appears to us that everything that you first told us that could be accomplished, has in the greater part proven true, as though you had seen before what you told us about."[13] Others take this to be a reference to the presumed assurance, given the Crown by Columbus, that the distance between Spain and the lands he set out to discover was a mere 800 leagues. Since there is absolutely no way of knowing what was discussed before his voyage, either assumption could be correct, or by the same token, both may be wrong.

Those finding a substance of truth in the story attach importance to the fact that both Hernando and Las Casas wrote that Columbus expected to find land 750 leagues after leaving the Canary Islands. Las Casas went even further: "Knowing that they were now near to land, for one due to such obvious signs [e.g., flotsam, land birds] or the other, due to what he knew having sailed from the Canaries to these parts, because he always had it at heart, for whatever reason or conjecture that had come to him that having sailed more or less 750 leagues from the Isla de Hierro there must be land."[14]

The Las Casas history remained in manuscript form until 1875 but is known to have been studied by many historians before that time. Antonio Herrera y Tordesillas definitely used it as the basis for his history of the discovery period in the first decade of his *Historia general de los hechos de los Castellanos en las islas y Tierra-firme de el Mar Océano*, first published in 1601.[15] It is here that the distortion of history regarding this particular subject begins. Herrera, although listing the above-mentioned works as sources for his history, made absolutely no note of the unknown pilot. Thacher pointed out that years later, Washington Irving claimed to have "put aside the history of Herrera and consulted the source of his information, the manuscript history of Las Casas." Irving then made an erroneous comment: "The other early historians who mention Columbus and were his contemporaries, viz. . . . Las Casas, Ferdinand Columbus . . . are all silent in regard to this report."[16] This is but one of the many examples of blatant misinformation to be found in the Irving work, but it is perhaps the basis on which many modern-day U.S. historians, as opposed to some of their Spanish confrères,[17] have based their almost total rejection of the story. Actually, besides the chroniclers mentioned here, Juan de Solórzano Pereira, Francisco Pizarro, and a dozen or so other early chroniclers repeated the story.[18]

Alonso Sánchez of Huelva, Pero Vásquez, and Diego de Teive

Shortly after the publication of the Herrera work, Garcilaso de la Vega ("el Inca") published in 1606 part 1 of his *Comentarios Reales*.[19] Garcilaso was very careful to give his sources, among whom he listed both López de Gómara and Acosta. Garcilaso was the first to give a name to the "unknown pilot": Alonso Sánchez from Huelva. He recounted the story as told to him by his father:

> Around 1488, more or less, a pilot from Huelva . . . named Alonso Sánchez . . . had a small boat in which he transported merchandise to the Canary Islands and from there fruits of those islands to Madera and back to Spain with sugar and conserves . . . crossing from the Canaries to Madera he was caught in a storm so strong and tempestuous, that not being able to resist it, he allowed it to drive him and he ran for twenty-eight or nine days without knowing where he was going . . . after this long time the winds subsided and they found themselves close to an island . . . of seventeen men that had sailed from Spain, only five came back to Tercera, one of whom was Alonso Sánchez. . . . They stayed in the house of the famous Cristóbal Colón, a Genoese, because they knew that he was a great pilot and cosmographer and knew how to draw navigational charts . . . and they all died in his house, leaving him the inheritance of the maps.[20]

Over the years a great deal of effort has been made to either substantiate this tale or disprove it. Hernando appears to have accepted it while at the same time discounting its importance because he did not believe that the caravel had ever reached the Indies. Las Casas was far more cautious. He is often quoted as having taken his data from Hernando; it is true that he copied perhaps four or five lines of this particular chapter, but by no means all of it, as has been alleged.[21] Las Casas not only did not deny the story but offered reasons for believing it. His final judgment reflected his attitude toward the discovery and all that passed later in the Indies: it was all divinely ordained.

Attempts have been made to relate Alonso Sánchez of Huelva with Pero Vásquez de la Frontera as well as with the Pedro Velasco, supposedly a native of Palos, who is reported in Hernando's *Historie.*[22] Pero Vásquez was mentioned three times by witnesses in the *Pleitos* as having told Columbus, while he was in Palos in 1492, that he had sailed with the Portuguese Diego de Teive (referred to by Hernando as Diego de Tiene and by Las Casas as Detienne).[23] According to Vásquez, they sailed from the Azores to find the legendary Antilla but instead discovered the Island of Flores. From there they went so far to the northeast that Point Clear in Ireland lay to their east. Although the seas were calm, the winds from the west were very strong, which made them believe that they were near land. They did not search for land, however, because they feared the oncoming winter. Some, such as the Portuguese historian Jaime Cortesão, understood this to mean that they had reached the codfish banks off Newfoundland.[24] Hernando recounted another tale of a one-eyed sailor who was en route to Ireland when he supposedly saw land to the west that he believed to be Tartary, which Hernando assumed to have been "the land of the codfish."[25]

These two tales are essentially different, but many scholars still link them as one, the differences being accounted for as normal to the growth of a myth. However, Diego de Teive was a real person who did sail under Portuguese crown charter to locate the legendary island of Antilla. And he did discover the Island of Flores.

There is no reason to doubt Las Casas's statement that the story of the unknown pilot was current on Española when he first arrived there, which was during the lifetime of Columbus. The story was retold in every history written during the rest of the sixteenth century with the sole exception of the accounts given by Martire, who took up the story of the discovery with his version of the first voyage. The tale disappeared briefly from the history books with the publication in 1601 of the history by Herrera y Tordesillas, only to reappear frequently since. Las Casas heard it in 1500, and over the next six years, up to the time of Columbus's death, the tale must inevitably have reached his ears as well as those of his enemies at court. If so, he probably needed to refute it. Strangely, none of the "debunkers" of Columbus have attempted to link this story to his many later efforts to vindicate his accomplishment by frequent citation from the classics. This story might not be unrelated to the frequency with which he quoted from Greek, Roman, and Arabian authors at the time that he had lost much of his credibility at court.

Since that time, the tale of the unknown pilot has been the subject of many studies and monographs published in Spain, France, and England. All three of the famous Americanists from the United States—Harrisse, Vignaud, and Thacher—dealt with the subject at considerable length. There are still important studies of the matter being written in Spain; however, in the United States, the subject of an unknown pilot showing the way to the Indies has now become one of little, if any, significance.

Morison retold the story as given by Fernández de Oviedo, observing, "Few later writers on Columbus took Augustine's excellent advice." He went on to comment: "Certain modern pundits . . . snap up this tale of an Ancient Mariner and swallow it, hook, line and sinker. The real objection to the story is meteorological. I challenge anyone to produce a single instance. It is impossible for a vessel to be 'blown across' the North Atlantic from east to west. She might drift across in the trades after a storm that blew all her sails to ribbons; but if she had any sails left there would have been no need to drift westward, she could have worked her way home after the storm subsided."[26] With due respect for the marine expertise of Morison, I find his statement confusing and self-contradictory. In the tale the vessel did work its way home. After making the above challenge, Morison told of just such an incident that took place in 1940, with the starting point eight hundred miles southwest-by-south of the Azores, and ending on Eleuthera in the Bahamas. The fact that the survivors "arrived half dead and could not have possibly returned unaided" proved nothing.[27] They were two teenagers with little if any experience at sea, yet they survived a seventy-day trip. The tales of the unknown pilot claim a voyage of twenty-eight or twenty-nine days. Did the boys have the same store of provisions that the unknown pilot's vessel supposedly carried? They were in a "jolly boat," which, unlike a caravel, would not have had a subdeck under which to take shelter from the elements. Besides, did not all of the crew of the fabled vessel die anyway? The term "blown across" does not necessarily imply that the starting point was close to the African coast, as was the case with Morison's two boys. Morison's hypothetical point of return under sail can just as easily be postulated as from the shores of an island as from midocean. If indeed the vessel was for a time drifting under bare sticks, at some later point the crew could have done what crews have done ever since sails and masts were invented: jury-rigged the boat, enabling them ultimately to return to Europe. While discussing the finding of a European artifact on the island of Guadeloupe, Morison appears to have reversed himself, speculating that it was brought over on the currents from Africa. The counter-case to Morison's does not prove that the mysterious voyage took place, only that the reasons he offered against it are not sufficient in themselves for rejection of the story.

In the 1560s Juan Suárez de Peralta wrote:

> I heard for very certain, that a boat going from the islands of Santo Domingo, went so far as to see Cape San Vincent; there it ran into such a great tempest that it had to put back out to sea. As with time it got worse, the captain thought that he would reach the island of Madera, because he already needed water and supplies as so often happens when one has reached the end of a voyage. He missed the island and passed by without seeing it. As he was now far out at sea and with a great deal of wind, his luck followed him and he returned from where he had set out which was San Juan in Puerto Rico. The people had sustained themselves with only cow hides and sugar.[28]

Whether or not any such event happened will never be known, but obviously tales of such misadventures were not lacking.

Wilford, apparently unaware of the numerous contemporary accounts of the story, refuted it: "The story has only one weakness: there is not a shred of evidence, other than hearsay reported by Oviedo and Las Casas."[29] He pointed out, very appropriately: "Simply reaching a new land does not in itself constitute a discovery. . . . If others besides the indigenous people themselves preceded Columbus in finding America, and they almost certainly did, their imprint on history has been negligible."[30] He mentioned the reported voyages of the Phoenicians in the Atlantic, the crossing by Teive, who was caught up in the Gulf Stream and swept north to Ireland, and two later such crossings reported by Cortesão. Mention should also be made of the discovery of Brazil by Pedro Alvars Cabral after he was blown off course while trying to work his way south to the Cape of Good Hope. In short, there are neither atmospheric nor geographical reasons to doubt that the voyage of the unknown pilot could have taken place. The only question is, did it?

Vicente Díaz

Wilford made three mentions of the tale as told by Fernández de Oviedo and one mention of Pero Vásquez de la Frontera but without in any way linking the latter with the unknown pilot.[31] He gave a very brief summary of the story, then commented, "Such stories assume a life of their own. Las Casas repeated it, and even Hernando mentions it as a 'curiosity.'"[32] To begin with, Las Casas did not merely repeat the Fernández de Oviedo account; he told of hearing it from Española residents, among whom he included participants in the first voyage. Hernando mentioned, "Oviedo refers in his *Historia* that the Admiral had in his possession a map, on which the Indies were described by one who had earlier discovered them." Hernando then went on to say "that it happened in this manner," and he described a voyage made by one Vicente Díaz, who had been blown off course on a return voyage from Guinea and "imagined that he saw an island."[33] According to Hernando, he received information about this voyage from Díaz's brother in Seville, whereas Las Casas said that it was Columbus himself who first got this information from the brother.[34]

Neither of these two early biographers claimed that Diaz actually saw these lands, only that he believed he saw them. In Hernando's version, when Diaz returned to the Azores he told his story to a Genoan merchant by the name of Lucas de Cazzana; the result was several documented later attempts by others to find the mysterious island. Wilford was apparently not familiar with this account by Hernando, since, while discussing the Fernández de Oviedo version of the unknown pilot, he noted, "A new version of the story has been suggested by Juan Manzano ... in a 1976 book ... tells a story about a ship sailing from Guinea to Iberia in the 1460s that got caught in a storm and the trade winds and was carried west to the islands now known as the West Indies."[35]

Without going into further detail, Wilford wrote in a later chapter: "In the absence of evidence, the story of the unknown pilot remains one more Columbian mystery. There could be some truth to it, though probably not, and, in all likelihood, we will never know." While discussing Columbus's initial contract, the *Capitulaciónes de Santa Fé*, he wrote: "In this context, the story of the unknown pilot again becomes a central issue. If the story is true, as Vignaud has argued, Columbus not only got his idea and instructions for the voyage from the dying pilot but had as his objective those same islands found by the pilot."[36] The reader is simply not given enough information by Wilford to either judge the unknown pilot story or evaluate the reliability of Vignaud in this or any other matter. The author does not appear to take a definitive position either way. In his bibliographical notes, Wilford listed *Toscanelli and Columbus* by Vignaud but did not list the latter's *Histoire*, the work in which Vignaud dealt in extenso with the tale of the unknown pilot.[37]

Fernández-Armesto had no doubts on the question of the unknown pilot: "The story of the unknown pilot is unacceptable as it stands; it proceeds from biased sources; it is unwarranted by any contemporary authority; and it relies on the hypothesis of a freak crossing such as is otherwise unrecorded in the latitude on which Columbus sailed (although accidental crossings have happened further south, on routes not known to have been frequented before Columbus's time). The argument that the unknown pilot must have existed because Columbus would not otherwise have known where to go reminds one of Voltaire's ironic case in favor of God: if He did not exist, it would be necessary to invent Him."[38] The rhetorical conclusion simply evades the issue.

The Phillipses noted, "For reasons not clear, many writers over the past five centuries have wanted to prove that Columbus's grand design was not a triumph of the imagination, inductive reasoning, and perseverance." They briefly mentioned the Fernández de Oviedo and Las Casas versions, concluding, "Such stories are always used to deny Columbus and his 1492 voyage the importance that history has traditionally accorded them, but the tales have little but wishful thinking and a perverse disregard of historical evidence to distinguish them."[39] Inasmuch as Columbus left no clear indication as to either the why or the how of his plan, yet contemporaries did record conjectures, it is difficult to understand how such accounts can be summarily dismissed and categorized as the result of a "perverse disregard of historical evidence." Neither Fernández de Oviedo nor Las Casas can be properly accused of bias against Columbus. The charge of perverse disregard in this case could equally be lodged against the Phillipses.

Morison mentioned Vásquez only to say that he sailed with Teive, "lived long enough to encourage Columbus," and helped Columbus persuade the sailors of Palos to sign up for the first voyage.[40] The role played by Pero Vásquez, as offered by the Phillipses, included details drawn from two statements given in the *Pleitos*, information not normally found in modern accounts. "Columbus and Pinzón met at least once in the house of an old mariner named Pedro Vásquez de la Frontera . . . he had sailed with legendary Portuguese . . . Diogo de Teive . . . had sailed southwest for about 150 leagues (560–600 miles), observed the sea grasses of the Sargasso Sea, turned back towards the Azores, there discovered the islands of Flores and Corvo, and then sailed north to the latitude of Cape Clear in Ireland. Vásquez encouraged Columbus and Pinzón to try the venture and not to fear the grasses, which were harmless if disconcerting."[41]

The allusions to sea grasses were taken from the testimony of Alonso Velez, the mayor of Palos. Testifying on behalf of Juan Martín Pinzón, Velez told how Vásquez, on his voyage with Teive, had encountered the sea grasses, at which time Teive turned back without attaining their objective.[42] Velez testified that after Columbus and Pinzón returned from the first voyage, he was told that when they had first encountered the Sargasso Sea, Columbus too had wanted to turn back, but that Pinzón, based on information Vásquez had given him, persuaded the Admiral to keep going.[43] The figure of 150 leagues came from the account as told by Hernando. The Phillipses' reference to the two explorers having met at the house of Vásquez derived from Alonso Gallego, a Crown witness in the *Pleitos*, who said that during the first voyage, when Columbus had wanted to turn back empty-handed, Pinzón reminded him that in the house of Vásquez, Columbus had promised that they would not return to Palos before finding land.[44] These statements are generally ignored by historians who assume that, coming from hostile witnesses, the statements cannot be trusted. The Phillipses, using excerpts out of context from this "tainted" testimony, composed an account, somewhat unique in several ways, of the circumstances surrounding the meeting with Vásquez.

The Teive voyage took place, according to Hernando and Las Casas, around 1452. There is a record that in 1474, Teive ceded his rights to Flores to Fernão Telles. These included an exclusive privilege, dated January 28, 1474, to explore for unknown and uninhabited islands, excluding exploration in the Seas of Guinea, as the South Atlantic below the twenty-eighth parallel was then known. In 1475 these rights were amplified to cover both inhabited and cultivated lands, expressly including "the Island of Seven Cities or other populated islands."[45] Teive, like Columbus later, was barred from sailing south of the Canaries and was initially empowered only to find unknown islands, whereas the Columbus license specified both islands and mainland. Thus, this earlier authorization had as its objective the same basic project that Columbus was to espouse many years later.

Hearsay, Rumors of Lands to the West, and Flotsam and Jetsam

By the time of Columbus, attempts had already been made to find the mythical islands to the west. Such attempts had to be authorized by the respective governments of the adventurers. The necessary documents involved were not open to the public, and any routes proposed were considered state secrets, yet obviously many mariners knew the whys and wherefores for such voyages. Knowledge of such matters was passed on by word of mouth. To these tales were added the stories of distant lands glimpsed and strange flotsam cast up on European shores, as well as the many myths perennially retold by old salts. In Columbus's time, a substantial body of lore addressed what might be out there, as well as the direction to go to find it—due west.

Hernando and Las Casas reported stories, told by people living on the Canary Islands and in the Azores, about islands seen at certain times of the year. At the time they wrote about these stories, the two authors already knew that these nearby islands did not exist. They offered the stories as evidence of the influence that such tales may have had on Columbus's plans for venturing into the western seas. Morison aptly pointed out that such sea mirages occur frequently under certain cloud and atmospheric conditions.

Columbus, however, looked on such matters differently. He is quoted as mentioning a voyage in 1476 by Antonio Leme, who told Columbus that he had seen three islands, which Columbus speculated might have been the floating islands reported by Pliny as rafts of trees torn up by their roots by tropical storms. Columbus wrote no postil on such a statement in his edition of Pliny. Las Casas said that Columbus may have believed that these islands were made up of a porous lightweight rock such as had been reported by Seneca off the coast of India.[46] Hernando also quoted Seneca as the source for this tale.[47] Columbus's was the only contemporary account of Leme's voyage.[48] In his journal entry for August 9, 1492, Columbus wrote that every year, land was seen to the west from the Canary Islands, and that the same story was told in the Azores. He recalled that in 1484 an islander had come to the Portuguese court to ask for a caravel to look for land that he had seen in the distance.[49] Vignaud identified this sailor as Fernam Domingo de Arco, who was granted by King João II, on June 30, 1484, title to an unknown island that he claimed to have seen in the Atlantic.[50]

There are several other similar mentions attributed to Columbus. Hernando and Las Casas cited them as taken from a since-lost *libro de memorias* ("book of memories") kept by Columbus. They said Columbus "kept in his memory" such stories because they agreed to a certain extent with his plan.[51] The one most often referred to today concerns his wife's cousin Pedro Correa, who was quoted by Columbus as telling him that on Porto Santo he saw flotsam of carved wood and bamboo canes so thick that, according to Hernando, one joint could be filled with nine carafes of wine; Las Casas put the figure at six.[52] Both Hernando and Las Casas said that Columbus recognized these canes as similar to ones found in India and described by Ptolemy. Such bamboo canes were also described by the twelfth- and fifteenth-century Italian missionaries sent to Cathay.

From the start, Columbus's biographers reported a story they copied from his otherwise unknown *libro de memorias*, in which he told of Martin Vicente, a Portuguese pilot who, while sailing 450 leagues west of Cape Saint Vincent, found a carved log that he knew by the wind direction to have come from the west.[53] Morison attached importance to the finding of "substantial evidence of exotic lands," reporting the carved wood picked up by Vicente and the driftwood and bamboo seen by Correa.[54] He also mentioned the "two dead bodies cast up on Flores, not like Christians but broad-faced like the 'Chinese' that Columbus had seen on Galway."[55]

If these incidents were recorded by Columbus in his notebook prior to his first transatlantic crossing, they would provide clear evidence for part of his incentive to explore the farther reaches of the Atlantic. If noted after, they merely indicate his interest, at some undefined time in his life and for whatever reason, in mariners' tales of islands to the west. That he should repeat two of them in his log for the first voyage indicates that at least those particular notebook entries did precede this voyage. In addition, the story of the unknown pilot was circulated during his lifetime; Las Casas heard it in 1500, and all of the chroniclers up until the 1600s considered it worthy of repetition. Due to these facts, it is simply not possible to study Columbus and his discovery without giving close attention to both of these possible incentives to sail to the west. These are reported legends, contemporary stories or perceptions. They must be evaluated. The meaning given to them depends on the criteria of the individual historian.

Columbus obviously gathered much of this information while living in Portugal. It is part of the intellectual baggage that he took with him to Spain. Exactly when he acquired his knowledge of cosmography and navigation as presented in the classics remains highly debatable. If he had already acquired this classical knowledge and had combined it with the empirical data in the mariners' tales before he left Portugal, then his ideas for his crossing were fully developed seven years before they were realized. If this was the case, it seems strange that any such well-thought-out plan should have taken so long to find support in two nations known to be leaders in maritime exploration. It seems more reasonable to suppose that Columbus left Portugal before he brought all of these parts of his plan together conceptually, that he was still in the process of developing the rationale for his dream.

In every affair consider what precedes and what follows.
Epictetus (c.A.D. 50–c.138)

6
Years
in Spain

We can assume that Columbus left Portugal for Spain equipped with, at the very least, a general idea for what he would later term his "Great Enterprise" of the Indies. This assumption does not necessarily presuppose that India was indeed his objective. There is no question that he had a plan, but its exact nature is not known. Where he wanted to go will be addressed in a subsequent chapter. We must first determine, if possible, when, how, and where he and his young son arrived in Spain and what they did once they got there.

Departure from Portugal and Arrival in Spain

In the *Historie*, Hernando claimed that Columbus left Portugal in disgust because King João II had secretly sent a caravel to seek the lands that Columbus had offered to discover. "His wife already dead," he decided to go to Spain to seek his fortune.[1] Las Casas quoted João de Barros that the king had turned Columbus down because royal advisers believed his proposal to be unrealistic. Las Casas, however, surmised that Barros was perhaps unaware of the

Iberian regions with towns and cities visited by Columbus.

king's duplicity in having purposefully delayed giving an answer to Columbus because he was awaiting the results of a secret voyage that he had ordered.[2] "In order to carry out the business that God had planned for the rest of his life [Columbus] needed to be free of the care and his obligations to his wife"; therefore, he left Portugal together with their "little son" Diego.[3] This does not indicate that either Hernando or Las Casas necessarily believed that the wife was dead before Columbus left Portugal.

The Portuguese historian Rui da Pina was the only chronicler who was actually a witness to the later meeting in 1493 between King João II and Columbus at the time of the latter's return from his famous first voyage.[4] (Barros, the most-often-cited Portuguese historian on the subject, was not yet born.) Pina wrote that the king was upset at his mistake of not having listened to Columbus earlier, when Columbus had offered him the project. Pina seemingly knew Columbus personally; his is one of the only two known physical descriptions of Columbus made by contemporaries. Pina served with King João in many official positions, as he had with the king's predecessor and would later with the king's successor. He was the official court chronicler and finished his history of the reign of King João in 1505, a year before the death of Columbus. It does seem surprising that he would fail to mention the by-then world-famous discoverer's family connection with well-placed members of the Portuguese court. Vignaud speculated that he may have failed to mention Columbus's earlier stay in Portugal out of respect for the Braganza family, which was in power at the time that he finished writing his history; the theory here is that the connection may have been cause more for shame than for pride.[5] Both the Moniz and the Perestrello families were of the Braganza faction. This suggestion presupposes Columbus's abandonment of his wife, a criminal record, or both. It seems equally probable that the Portuguese were not interested at that time in emphasizing their king's failure to grasp a golden opportunity.

Fernández de Oviedo wrote that Columbus left Portugal because the king would not back him. He then "decided to go to Castile, and arrived at Seville."[6] Columbus's other contemporary and personal friend, Bernáldez, mentioned the offer to Portugal and said that it was turned down because the Portuguese savants believed that "no one in the world knew better than they."[7] This was but the first of the many jingoistic claims that would becloud many Columbine issues up to the present day. Bernáldez offered no further detail other than that Columbus then went to the court of Ferdinand and Isabel.

The very manner of Columbus's arrival in Spain has become the subject more of myth than of documented fact. None of his contemporaries told by what means he and his child arrived. Palos was on the shortest land route from Lisbon to Seville, if that was his destination; however, the latter was also directly accessible by boat. Antonio Herrera y Tordesillas, in the seventeenth century, was the first to say that they came by sea. In this he was to be supported by writers in the nineteenth century, primarily by the French

Columbist D'Avezac and by Count Antoine de Roselly de Lorgues. At the same time Spanish and British historians, among them José María Asensio y Toledo and Clements R. Markham, opted for the land route. In U.S. histories, following the lead of Washington Irving, father and son arrived by boat in Palos and proceeded from there on foot to the monastery of La Rábida. As will be seen, the matter of this first visit to La Rábida is actually one of the more puzzling of the Columbian enigmas.

Hernando and Las Casas were equally confused as to the sequence of events at this time. By Hernando's account, father and son came to Palos, where he left the young boy at the monastery and proceeded "rapidly" to the court, which at that time was in Córdoba. Las Casas beieved that he went to the monastery while en route to Huelva to see his in-laws, intending to proceed from there to France, where his brother was at that time. Las Casas then brought in the story of a meeting with "fray Juan Perez," who summoned "Garcí Hernandez" to hear Columbus's proposition.[8] The only part of Hernando's statement that is unquestionably correct is the reference to Córdoba. Even this fact raises questions, however. How did Columbus, while in Portugal, know the exact whereabouts of this mobile court? The queen was in Córdoba at this particular time, but over the years given for Columbus's probable arrival in Spain, 1484–86, the king was engaged in harassing the Moors in the area between Seville and Málaga, where the queen joined him at his camp in June 1486.

Las Casas's account makes little sense in that La Rábida was not on the route to Huelva; also, Las Casas had earlier claimed that at this time, Bartolomé was in England, not France. According to Garcí Hernández in his testimony in the *Pleitos*, Columbus went to La Rábida in 1491 or early 1492 on his way to Huelva. In May 1493 the Columbus in-laws referred to by Las Casas were living in Seville, not in Huelva, where they have been assumed, possibly incorrectly, to have been living in 1485. Morison wrote a moving and imaginative account in which Columbus took passage from Lisbon to Palos, leaving Portugal "because he probably feared arrest for debt. Living expenses . . . and the cost of giving Dona Felipa a burial commensurate with her rank must have consumed all Columbus' savings . . . the little ship . . . rounded Cape St. Vincent, crossed the bar at

Saltés . . . Columbus noted on a bluff the buildings of the Franciscan friary of La Rábida. . . . The Minorites were noted for their hospitality, and often conducted schools for young boys . . . on this occasion took place the pretty incident of the alms at the monastery door. . . . No doubt this happened."[9] As previously discussed, there is no evidence that "Dona Felipa" was dead; in addition, their means of transport used to come to Spain is unknown, and Spanish historians deny that the friary was either a center of hospitality or a children's school. Finally, it is highly doubtful that Columbus and his son went to La Rábida after their arrival in Spain. Morison substantiated the "pretty incident" by citing "Fernández García" (Garcí Hernández).

In the *Pleitos*, the physician Garcí or García Hernández testified that he first met Columbus after he and his son arrived in Palos. His testimony is the first source of the story of father and son arriving on foot at the door of the convent and asking for bread and water for the boy. In this account Columbus, discouraged, came to the monastery from the court, not from Portugal, and was en route to Huelva to the home of his brother-in-law "Molyart."[10] However, the doctor went on to say that he was summoned to hear Columbus's story by Fray Juan Pérez, who had been confessor to the queen. In other words, events that presumably took place seven years apart are presented as occurring simultaneously. This dichotomy has since been explained as a result of confusion on the part of the witness, a theory first proposed by Irving; the idea was that the doctor was present when Columbus was in Palos on two occasions separated by six or seven years.[11]

Morison dated their arrival in Spain to mid-1485, when Diego was five.[12] Wilford agreed that Columbus left Portugal secretly, and he repeated some of the theories as to why.[13] He observed that according to Hernando, Columbus's wife had died a year earlier, "or did he walk out on her, as Harrisse supposes from an interlinear reading of a letter Columbus wrote in 1500?" The "interlinear reading" was of the passage in which Columbus wrote that he had left "wife and children" to come to serve the Spanish sovereigns.

As noted above, Columbus did leave Portugal for unknown reasons, by as-yet-undetermined means; Hernando said the year was 1484.[14]

Las Casas placed the trip "in 1484 or [the] beginning of the year 1485."[15] His wife was dead, according to one contemporary, yet she may have been alive, according to another. Neither of these two sources mentioned the age of the son.

Briolanja Muñiz and Miguel Muliart

The matter of Diego's age is of some importance due to the fact that historians such as Morison have interpreted the testimony given by Garcí Hernández as proving the visit to La Rábida at this time. According to Hernández's statement, when Columbus came to the friary he was accompanied by a *niñico que era niño* ("a little boy who was a child"), which to some must mean a child of under five. Over the years a great deal of effort has been spent to determine Diego's age. In a letter from Columbus written in 1504 to Diego and discussing his young half-brother, Hernando, at that time around sixteen, Columbus wrote, "Although he is a child by age, he is not so in understanding."[16] Earlier, in 1499, he wrote to the king and queen, asking that they send his son Diego to Española to assist him because he was tired and because his son, who was at court, was "growing in strength and becoming a man . . . able to come here to serve."[17] Some scholars have concluded these two sources refer to boys of at least sixteen or seventeen. Yet Columbus referred to them as *niños* ("children"). These estimates place Diego's birth in 1482 or 1483. The generally accepted birthdate for Diego is between 1480 and 1481, which, if correct and if taken together with Garcí Hernández's testimony, would indicate that the two could have been at the monastery around 1484–85. The 1482–83 birthdate would mean that Columbus arrived after 1485, perhaps in 1486, as he himself claimed; otherwise, the son would have been an infant and too young to travel.

The rest of the testimony given by Garcí Hernández clearly indicated a visit in 1491, although some have read into it references to Portugal indicative of the earlier date. The strongest such indication is found in his statement that Columbus told them that his plan had been rejected after boats had been repeatedly sent to find these lands, "and all had been air." He did not say that the king of

Portugal had sent these vessels but may have been merely alluding to the efforts made over the ages to locate lands in the western ocean.

Another often repeated justification relates to Garcí Hernández's usage, throughout his testimony, of the title *su Alteza* ("his/her Majesty") in the singular, leading some to interpret it to mean the king of Portugal when referring to the rejection of Columbus's plan and conversely to the Castilian queen when referring to later events. In all such speculations, the fact is overlooked that Palos was one of the ports of Castile. Aragón had no ports on the southern coast of Spain. When one of the subjects of the queen of Castile referred to "her highness" in the singular, it was a perfectly correct thing to do in a nation not yet united into one kingdom.

The Phillipses were yet more expansive on this phase in the life of Columbus. According to their account, Columbus left Portugal in 1485 after "the king of Portugal refused to grant his request." They offered as one "plausible reason" for his going to Spain their belief that since "Columbus had already developed some ideas about the wind patterns of the Atlantic, it would make perfect sense for him to go to Spain. The Canary Islands were controlled by Spain [they had been conquered by Alonso Lugo in 1483], and Columbus may well have determined that the Canaries were the perfect starting place for an Atlantic crossing."[18] This rationale does not seem valid, however; the data available to Columbus indicated a route farther south than the Canaries, one starting from an area forbidden to Spanish vessels by the Treaty of Alcáçovas and one therefore more appropriate for the Portuguese than for the Spaniards. On his second voyage Columbus sailed south from the Canaries in order to cross at a latitude nearer to this ideal route for catching the trade winds, and on his third voyage he sailed yet farther to the south.

These authors found that his landing at Palos was an "auspicious" one: "His wife Felipa had died and was buried in Lisbon. Columbus needed a stable home for their young son Diego, and his late wife's sister, Violante Moniz, lived in Huelva with the husband Miguel Moliart."[19] Violante Nuñez, the sister of Columbus's mistress, is sometimes confused with Briolanja Muñiz, his wife's sister.

Contemporary and modern-day chroniclers have accepted without question the belief that Columbus's sister-in-law, Briolanja, and her husband, Miguel Muliart, lived in Huelva at the time of Columbus's arrival in Spain. The only documentary support presented in the literature on the subject is based on the known fact that Briolanja rented a property in San Juan del Puerto from the duke of Medina-Sidonia; but mention is rarely made of the fact that this lease was dated 1493. Varela first stated that Columbus arrived in Spain in 1485 and went to Briolanja, who rented land in the vicinity, yet without offering clarification Varela later affirmed, "Briolanja only appears as a renter of land from the duke, in the neighborhood of San Juan del Puerto, starting in 1493."[20] In the documentary record Miguel is also listed in 1493, as a *vecino de Sevilla* ("resident of Seville"). There is no reason to doubt that on either the first or the second visit to Palos and/or La Rábida, however many visits there were, Columbus probably meant to go to the home of his in-laws, a logical place to leave the child. Just where this was, Huelva or Seville, cannot be established with any satisfactory degree of certainty.

Santa María de la Rábida

What is rarely, if ever, commented on is the fact that the monastery of La Rábida is not on the route to either Huelva or Seville, whereas Seville, where his in-laws were listed as living in 1493, is in an almost direct line to Palos, his projected embarkation port for France in 1491 when he left the royal camp before Granada after his final turndown. Nor is the monastery in a direct line when going from the direction of Palos to Huelva, if he was indeed headed there. La Rábida is to the south of Palos, and Huelva to the northwest. The two places are roughly equidistant from Palos, about two and one-half miles to the monastery and three and one-half miles to Huelva, which was directly accessible by water. Seville, Córdova, and Granada, cities important in Columbus's prediscovery itinerary, are all to the east, and the road from Huelva to all three of them runs through Palos but not through La Rábida. The path from Palos to the monastery is up a steep rocky incline and terminates in a dead end. There is no way that anybody could have gone there by accident. To go there and backtrack to Palos meant a five-mile detour, one not to

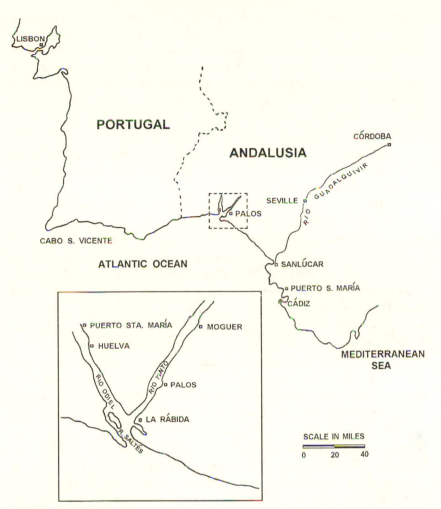

La Rábida and its environs.

be undertaken lightly when on foot and when, according to the 1485 scenario, accompanied by a very small boy. It was not exactly a logical place to go to seek bread and water. If they did indeed go there at that time, it was because that is where Columbus was headed, in which case his reason for doing so will probably never be known.

Morison maintained that they went to the monastery seeking a place to leave the boy. Wilford adhered in part to this conventional version: "This choice of destinations is easily explained. Palos was one of the closest ports across the border, and the only people he knew in Spain were his wife's relatives who lived nearby in Huelva."[21] If so, it would appear more normal to have left the child with them, not at the monastery.

Fernández-Armesto attached great importance to the fact that Fray Antonio de Marchena, whom he described as a court astronomer, was at one time the guardian of the friary; yet Fernández-Armesto did not go so far as to say that the friar was at the monastery in 1485, the year that this chronicler more or less accepted for Columbus's arrival in Spain. Fernández-Armesto did say that the location of "the friary of La Rábida, by Palos, overlooking the point where the Guadalquivir flows from Seville into the Atlantic," would, inferentially, explain its importance to Columbus.[22] This fanciful comment ignores the geographical fact that Palos is more than forty miles from the mouth of the Guadalquivir. Without venturing into the perplexing matter of the first visit to Palos, the Phillipses provided valuable background data on Palos and the nearby ports, giving thereby a number of reasons, besides the obvious one (the town owed the Crown the service of two boats), why the town should have been selected as the port of departure in 1492.[23]

Fernández-Armesto gave the date for Columbus's arrival but qualified his statement by saying this was the date "if the tradition which dates his arrival to Castile in 1485 can be trusted." He left the reason for the departure from Portugal open to speculation while repeating Columbus's own explanation, offered many years after the event, that "God had occluded the King of Portugal's vision in order to reserve the glory of the discovery for Castile."[24] Fernández-Armesto provided a historical background for Portuguese and Spanish exploration in the Atlantic and noted the maritime interests of the then count of Medina Celi and the powerful duke of Medina-Sidonia. The port of the first was close to Seville and that of the latter, to Palos.

Sale was more directly concerned with the discovery and colonization periods than with biographical detail for Columbus. He did accept Columbus's presence in Castile after 1485, and he repeated Morison's errors in the naming of Columbus's Portuguese wife and in his guessing that Columbus married her in "perhaps 1479." He gave the date of Diego's birth as "perhaps 1480" and the date of his wife's death as "perhaps 1484."[25]

This introduction to what should have been a simple matter— determining when and how Columbus came to Spain—is clear by comparison with the story of the events that followed. First of all, scholars disagree as to whether or not Columbus went to the monastery at La Rábida on arrival and, if so, whom he met there: a "gatekeeper" by the name of Juan Pérez, a "custodian" named Antonio de Marchena, or perhaps both. At what point did one or the other of these Franciscan friars come into Columbus's life, and to what extent did either of them assist him at court? To further complicate matters, one school of thought holds that the two named friars were actually the same person.

The account given by Hernando is limited to two lines in which he wrote that Columbus came to Castile, and "having left the boy in the monastery known as La Rábida at Palos, he promptly went to the court of the Catholic Kings." Las Casas was more explicit, saying they went to Palos and speculating that it might have been because Columbus knew some sailors in that town or perchance some of the friars at the monastery, where he may have left his son Diego.[26] Some of the early confusion may have arisen from the name "Santa María," equally applicable to either the monastery at Palos or the Andalucian Puerto de Santa María facing Cádiz. The port of that name was owned by the shipowner Luis de la Cerda, the fifth count of Medina Celi, whose backing Columbus is known to have sought.

Varela has pointed out that Columbus's Florentin friends in Lisbon did have business in both Palos and nearby Moguer.[27] One of the Berardis sold slaves in these port towns. He and his fellow Florentin Francisco de Riberol had each been involved in the finance of the conquest by Lugo of the Canary Islands, in association with the duke of Medina-Sidonia, who controlled the nearby ports.

The duke of Medina-Sidonia leased to the friars the Island of Saltés, which is at the conjunction of the Rivers Odiel, Tinto, and Saltés directly in front of the monastery. The proximity of all of these locations as well as of the duke's port of San Juan del Puerto, where, as previously noted, Briolanja rented some land, is not always given due attention. Medina-Sidonia, like Medina Celi, was an important shipowner, trading with the Canaries and Portugal. There is no evidence that Columbus took these factors into consideration when selecting Palos as his first stop in Spain, but they do provide a reasonable alternative explanation to the one that the choice was accidental.

All contemporary sources agree that at some point, Columbus did seek out the aid of each of the two noblemen. Note is not always taken of the fact that Medina-Sidonia had a son, who, after his father's death, contributed to the financing of Columbus's second voyage. Many years later the proposed marriage of Diego to the duke's daughter was blocked by King Ferdinand. There is justifiable reason to suggest that Columbus may have come to Spain with the express purpose of enlisting the aid of Medina-Sidonia in his "Great Enterprise."

Las Casas said Columbus went directly from La Rábida to the court, which was at that time in Córdoba. Las Casas's claim that he "arrived at the court on 20 January 1485" is based on a reconstruction of Columbus's own statement that his arrival was on that day, but in 1486. In a later entry Las Casas recognized the existance of confusing information and stated that Columbus returned to Palos in 1491 "with his son, *or* [emphasis added] to pick up his son, the child Diego."[28] In this later entry he did mention the fact that Columbus's brother-in-law lived in nearby Huelva; yet, Columbus wrote in the *Diario* that at this particular time, his young son was living in Córdoba, not in Palos or Huelva.[29] Surely on this point Columbus must have been better-informed than his biographer.

At the Spanish Court

In a previously mentioned postil in the *Historia rerum*, the writer, presumed by many to be Columbus, stated that he, the writer, was present in Lisbon in May 1485 at the time that "Master Joseph" returned from measuring the latitude at the equator. Regarding Columbus's arrival at the Spanish court, the first seemingly concrete evidence as to the exact date was supplied by Columbus himself when he wrote in his journal on January 14, 1493, "I came to serve you, which now is seven years ago on January 20."[30] This is not the clear indication that so many historians take it to be. The "I came to serve you" could mean either "I came to Spain to serve you" or "I came to your court to serve you." Much later, in a letter written near the end of the century, he did write, "I passed seven years at your court." There could have been a gap in time between the two possible meanings, arrival in Spain and arrival at court, and his later expression on the subject merely a lapsus.

Another statement made by Columbus, this one in his account of his third voyage, is less precise on the matter: "I put into this [presentation at court] six or seven years."[31] As for the seven years, obviously the year 1493 minus seven indicates the year 1486, yet in the margin on the page where this entry appears, Las Casas wrote, "The Admiral came to court to propose the discovery on 20 January 1489."[32] This must be a misprint. More recently Varela interpreted these figures to mean that Columbus came to the court in 1485.[33] It is an interesting coincidence that Fernam Arco's authorization for a voyage of discovery and the return to Lisbon of "Master Joseph" should both be dated midyear 1485.

The first official court record that has been found that refers to Columbus and his affairs in Spain is dated May 5, 1487; it recorded the amount of three thousand maravedis given to Cristobal Colombo by Alonso de Quintanilla on orders "of the bishop."[34] At that time Fray Hernando de Talavera, prior of Prado, was bishop of Avila. He has been identified by some as the bishop ordering the subsidy.[35] However, as noted below, Fernández de Oviedo wrote that it was the bishop of Toledo, Pedro González de Mendoza, later cardinal and chief minister of the Crown for many years, who issued the orders for this subsidy.[36] There are records for four more subsidies in that year totaling ten thousand maravedis, all of them "on orders of the bishop."

Taking the date of this first subsidy paid to Columbus, together with the fact that Spanish court records were maintained assiduously and therefore can be expected to have reflected any earlier subsidies, we have strong reason to believe that Columbus came to court for the first time in 1487. He may have arrived there in January 1486, as he himself indicated if one accepts his "seven years," or in 1487, if one accepts the lower figure of his "six or seven years." Considering that he may have arrived in Spain around June-July 1485, the time lapse between these dates and the above-mentioned record of his first subsidy is a long time for a person without a known means of support.

Those who argue for the 1484 arrival date should consider the fact that in April 1484, Medina Celi set off from Córdoba with the king for a protracted campaign directed toward Málaga, making a meeting with Columbus in midyear unlikely. The time lapse between the more probable mid-1485 arrival date and the date when Columbus claimed to have come "to serve your majesties" appears to be somewhat short to justify the following statement by Medina Celi: "For a long time I had in my house Cristobal Colomo." To the contrary, a stay from sometime after June-July 1485 until May 1487, the time of the first confirmed presence of Columbus at court, would give a more acceptable meaning to the duke's further claim that Columbus was in his home for two years. In which case, this would have been only a slight exaggeration.

At the time Columbus came to Spain, Luis de la Cerda was count of Medina Celi; he was soon to become the first duke. On March 19, 1493, after Columbus had returned from making his discovery, the by-then duke asked to be allowed to share in future ventures in the Indies. The duke noted, "For a long time I had in my house Cristobal Colomo, who came from Portugal and desired to go to the King of France in order that by his favour and aid he might undertake to go and search for the Indies. . . . I wrote to her Highness about it from Rota and she replied telling me to send him to her. . . . Her Majesty received him and gave him in charge to Alonso de Quintanilla."[37]

There has been a great deal of speculation by Columbists as to which court official first supported Columbus in his venture. Medina Celi said Quintanilla was the first. Quintanilla, an able Crown officer, served Isabel, as he had her predecessor. He is sometimes given credit for having introduced the Inquisition into that kingdom, and there is no question that in 1476 he supported, against strong opposition, the establishment of the Santa Hermandad, a communal policing institution controlled by the state. As will be seen later, the funds of this institution may have been the source of financing for Columbus's first two voyages. Fernández de Oviedo believed that it was through both Cardinal Mendoza and Quint-anilla that Columbus first gained access to the monarchs.

Fernández-Armesto correctly credited Quintanilla with having helped to arrange the finances for the conquest and settlement of the Canary islands, as well as with maintaining close contact with many of those who afterward financially supported Columbus's other voyages. Morison and Sale ignored the part that Quintanilla seems to have played in the affairs of Columbus. The Phillipses mentioned him only en passant. Wilford, commenting on a visit by Columbus to Jaén in 1489, remarked: "On this visit, if not before, Columbus gained another influential friend. According to Oviedo, Alonso de Quintanilla, the court treasurer, 'ordered that [Columbus] be given goods, and all that was necessary to alleviate him from poverty.'"[38] Actually what Fernández de Oviedo said was that Columbus went to the court while it was in Córdoba (not in Jaén) shortly after he first arrived in Spain, as well as that the help offered by Quintanilla was made out of "compassion." These are minor changes but ones lending different nuances.

Medina Celi indicated, as have others, that when Columbus first came to Spain, he was en route to France. Accordingly, he stopped first at Palos, perhaps to leave the boy with his sister-in-law in either nearby Huelva or Seville so that Columbus would be free to travel unencumbered by a young child. If Columbus's destination was Seville, then Medina Celi's port of Santa María would have been a more logical port of arrival than Palos.

As previously noted, the early writers on the subject, knowing of his well-substantiated visit to the monastery of Santa María de la Rábida in 1491, may have confused this visit with an earlier arrival at the count's Puerto Santa Mariá. Years later, when Columbus was preparing to embark on his first voyage, he entrusted the boy Diego to Juan Rodríguez Cabezudo and a cleric by the name of Martyn Sanchez.[39] Had the boy really been interned at the nearby monastery after Columbus's first arrival in Spain, it would seem to have been more natural to leave the boy there again. By the same reasoning, if his sister-in-law was indeed living in nearby Huelva, there would have been no reason to leave the boy in the care of Rodríguez Cabezudo.

The Dukes of Medina-Sidonia and Medina Celi

In their efforts to sort out the many conflicting stories as to when Columbus arrived in Spain and what he did next, some of his biographers have resorted to imaginative reconstructions. Perhaps the most popular is the one that has Columbus arriving in Palos, going directly to the monastery, leaving the boy Diego in care of the friars, proceeding to court, and when his plan was rejected in 1491, returning to Palos, stopping off first to try to get the support of either Medina-Sidonia or Medina Celi. He then returns to court, is turned down again, and goes back to Palos en route to France. This contrived agenda simply does not hold up in face of contemporary evidence. The supporters of this particular theory explain away the contrary evidence by interlinear readings of Garcí Hernández's testimony as well as by questioning the accuracy of his and Medina Celi's memories.

Las Casas placed the meeting with Medina-Sidonia "or" Medina Celi after the 1491 turndown. Thus he was not certain that Columbus had met with both dukes. If Columbus did meet with one or both of them at this time, he could have been so occupied for only a matter of days, since there is ample evidence for his comings and goings from the time that he left the court until his arrival at La Rábida and the final acceptance of his project in April 1492. Therefore, if Las Casas was correct in his assumptions, Medina Celi's statement that he had Columbus in his house "for a long time . . . two years" was pure fabrication, which would be most unlikely. Fernández de Oviedo claimed that Columbus went first to the duke of Medina-Sidonia and, failing to get his support, then went to Medina Celi.[40] Medina-Sidonia would have been a logical person for Columbus to approach first. Fernández de Oviedo repeated Medina Celi's claim that the count had wanted to finance the voyage but had first consulted with the queen, who then ordered Columbus to report to Quintanilla.

Morison completely ignored the perhaps crucial evidence involving Medina Celi's reference to Quintanilla and the latter's confirmed involvement with Columbus's first days at court. Morison further complicated the affair when he first asserted, "It is certain Columbus left his boy at La Rábida very soon after landing in Spain." Here he said Columbus met with either Fray Juan Pérez or Antonio de Marchena, the latter becoming "his advocate." Marchena advised Columbus to make application to "the very magnificent Don Enrique de Gúzman, Duke of Medina Sidonia, grandee of Spain and wealthiest subject of the Sovereigns. . . . The Duke became definitely interested, and was at the point of promising to equip a fleet for Columbus when, owing to an unseemly brawl with the Duke of Cádiz, the Sovereigns ordered him to leave Seville and the negotiations were broken off. Columbus then turned to Don Luis de la Cerda, Count of Medina Celi."[41] Morison not only appears to have mixed up the dukes but also raised the confusing issue of Pérez and Marchena, who will be discussed later in this chapter.

Wilford followed Morison fairly closely. He found it "more reasonable, however, to assume that he [Columbus] had already settled in Huelva with his sister-in-law and her husband before he decided to visit La Rábida." There Columbus met Antonio de Marchena and through him was "introduced to one of the most powerful and richest grandees." He was next introduced to Medina Celi "through either the duke or Marchena. . . . Influential friends cleared the way for his first audience with the king and queen."[42] All of this makes for very good reading but flies in the face of the available contemporary evidence.

Fernández-Armesto referred in a strictly factual manner to the relationships of Columbus with the two dukes and took it for granted that they met before Columbus first went to court. He did not go into the contradictory data offered by Las Casas. The Phillipses provided good background information on the two dukes, yet after reserving judgment as to when the dukes met with Columbus—"the available documentation does not enable us to say when"—they accepted that it was after Columbus's project had been rejected: "When Medinaceli [sic] wrote to the queen, she summoned

Columbus back to court." This is not what Medina Celi wrote in his letter. Here again, all of these modern accounts contain a great deal of speculation, with little or no reference to the fact that most of what they report is disputable but all of it offered with a degree of certitude that would indicate to the casual reader that each of these authors was fully documented on these matters.

Fray Juan Pérez

Historians disagree as to whom Columbus met at the friary at La Rábida, on either his supposed first or his confirmed 1492 visit. It has been established by contemporaries that he was in Palos in 1492 and that, while there, he was in close contact with Fray Juan Pérez. Alonso Velez, mayor of Palos, testified that Columbus stayed at the monastery while preparing for the first voyage. As will be shown, the presence in Palos of Juan Pérez, a Franciscan friar, is beyond question. The presence of a Fray Antonio de Marchena is highly questionable, although Velez did say that besides Fray Juan, there was also an "astrologer friar who was at the convent as guardian."[43]

The first mention of either of these two friars in any of the histories of the Franciscan order was in a work published in 1587 by Friar Francisco Gonzaga, who wrote that "brother Joannes Piertius" sailed with Columbus on the second voyage.[44] No such name appears in the listings known today, although these provide the names of only half of the twelve clerics known to have sailed on this voyage. Antonio Daza, the first official chronicler of the order to write a history of the Franciscans in Spain, did not mention, in his work published in 1611, either a Pérez or a Marchena. In 1731 another friar, known in English as Lucas Wadding (also Wadango and Wadingus), repeated the story as told by Gonzaga; however, he placed the friar(s) on the first, not the second, voyage.

In 1891 Fray José Coll, a Franciscan with the title of *Definador del Orden* ("Definator of the Order"), unsuccessfully sought to find evidence of either of these friars in the order's records. He mentioned the record published by Daza, as well as the account given by Friar Wadding. The lack of any concrete information in the records of the order leaves the matter of confirmation of the existence of one or the other of these friars dependent on lay records.

The first and certainly the most important source is Columbus himself. In his correspondence, he made five references to the friar, using the full name "Juan Perez"; another two references were to a "fray Juan," and once he referred merely to two friars. In none of these references was any mention made of either Palos or La Rábida. In a letter in which he reflected on the Santa Fé agreement on the first voyage, he listed Pérez and the Crown secretary, Juan Coloma, three times as having prepared the *Capitulaciónes*.[45] In a similar document he referred only once to the two men who negotiated the contract. He actually used the friar's name in full seven times, sufficient to convince most scholars that he was referring to a real person.

In a letter written before he embarked on the third voyage, Columbus suggested to the Crown that the sovereigns could get information on medications needed in the Indies from "fray Juan."[46] Another letter, unknown until the recent finding of *El libro copiador*, was written on February 3, 1500, on Española after his arrest. Columbus wrote: "I believe that you will recall that good religious man fray Juan Perez, who incited Your Highnesses to other enterprises, so like that of Granada and the Jews; that he and I came to your royal throne with this of the Indies, and appropriate for the conquest of the Holy House. He is dead."[47]

This is the first and only indication that the friar had died, and it may confirm the claim that Fray Pérez came to Española on Columbus's second voyage. Columbus here equated his voyage in importance with the defeat of the Moors and the expulsion of the Jews. In a letter of his grievances in 1501, while protesting his loyalty to the queen, he offered as two witnesses to his faithfulness "Fray Johan Perez" and the nurse of Prince Juan.[48] Later, in 1504, in regard to his offer to the Bank of St. George in Genoa, he wrote, "Father Juan says that those of St. George are very noble and will comply with [their obligation to] me."[49] These statements do not fit well with reported death of Fray Juan Pérez in 1500.

There is another reference, indirect and also curious. In the 1498 letter of the third voyage, he wrote of his offer to find the Indies and noted, "All of those who had knowledge about it, and heard these discussions, on the one hand made fun of it except for two friars who were always constant."[50] This is difficult to translate because the Spanish is so poor, but the intent is clear. Columbus often complained that over the years many at court had mocked him. In this particular case his statement that "all" had mocked him was simply hyperbole, since both Columbus and the contemporary record indicate support from many sources, most of them individuals close to King Ferdinand, not to the queen. Some historians have since taken it for granted that the two friars were Pérez and Marchena; others have assumed that he was referring to Diego de Deza and Pérez. Some have gone so far as to assert that Columbus acknowledged in these letters his unique debt to Pérez. More important than the hyperbole is the interesting parallel in wording in the brief phrase "two friars" used by Columbus and the similar wording in the testimony of Garcí Hernández. At some point, just when or where is unknowable, Columbus had the support of two friars, both of them probably Franciscans and one of them unquestionably Juan Pérez.

After Columbus himself, testimony given in the *Pleitos* in 1515 is the best source for Fray Pérez. Alonso Velez, justice of the peace and mayor of Palos, said that Columbus stayed in the monastery in 1492 and discussed his project with "fray Juan who as a youth had served the queen as an accountant."[51] The historian Nancy Rubin recently extended this with an unsupported statement: "Pérez had been in Quintanilla's service as a *contador* years before." She thereby associated Pérez with the man who years earlier had received Columbus at court.[52] As noted earlier Garcí Hernández, testifying at the same time, said that the friar had been the queen's confessor. Actually the two statements are not necessarily contradictory in that the friar could have on occasion confessed the queen while she was either on a trip to Andalucia or elsewhere. One of the Pinzóns was the only other witness to identify the friar by name: "[Martín Alsonso Pinzón] had him [Columbus] and a friar they called Juan Perez go to court, and they went, and this witness knows because he was there for everything."[53] These witnesses provided irrefutable testimony linking Columbus and Fray Juan Pérez with the monastery at La Rábida in 1491.

Hernando wrote that his father went to the friary of La Rábida to pick up his son Diego and take the boy to Córdoba. However, while Columbus was there, the "guardian of that house, named Fray Juan Pérez," persuaded him to delay leaving the country, and the two of them went to the monarchs' camp at Santa Fé.[54]

Rodríguez Cabezudo and Andrés del Corral

Two witnesses, Rodríguez Cabezudo and Andrés del Corral (testifying in 1512), both of whom claimed a certain degree of intimacy with Columbus, identified the friar at La Rábida only as a member of the Order of Franciscans.[55] Corral added that he, Corral, was present in Madrid at the time that the friar told the sovereigns that what Columbus said was true, after which they agreed to send him to discover. Corral was the first to say that the discovery plan, which he attributed to Martín Alonso Pinzón, was accepted because of the intercession of a friar from La Rábida.[56] However, caution must be exercised in evaluating this testimony. He claimed that Columbus and Pérez met with the monarchs in Madrid, an obvious error if this meeting took place before 1492. Columbus, Pérez, and the sovereigns met in Santa Fé.

Corral was in his early thirties at the time of his deposition in 1512. Since the meeting was supposed to have taken place in 1486, at which time the court was in Madrid, Corral would have been around six years old at the time. Even if he was wrong about his age, a not unusual thing in those days, or if one accepts the 1492 date for the meeting, mistakenly placed in Madrid, he still would have been at best a very young teenager and, as such, a not very likely companion for Columbus or Pérez at court. It is not possible, based on Corral alone, to place the two men in Madrid in 1486 or in Santa Fé in 1492.

Las Casas retold the story much as Garcí Hernández had.[57] This is not unusual in that Hernando, from whom Las Casas received much of his information, was the brother charged with the presentation of Diego's case in the *Pleitos*; accordingly, he was fully aware of all testimony given at those hearings. Fernández de Oviedo repeated most of the elements in the story—that Juan Pérez was a Franciscan, that he had been the queen's confessor, and that Columbus shared secrets with him—but Fernández de Oviedo added a new claim: that Pérez was "a great cosmographer."[58]

That a cosmographer was present at La Rábida when Columbus went there in 1492 was testified to in the *Pleitos*. What was new was identifying him as Pérez. This raises the question of the presence of a second friar in Columbus's affairs. Previously, Columbus mentioned "two friars" who had helped him, and Velez said that Columbus had met at the monastery with a friar who was an astrologer and guardian and also with Fray Juan, clearly designating two persons. It is here that Friar Antonio de Marchena comes into the picture.

Fray Antonio de Marchena

In a copy made by Las Casas of a fragment of a letter written by Columbus sometime between 1498 and 1500, Columbus categorically stated that in his seven years at court he received no assistance from anyone except God and "fray Antonio de Marchena."[59] This is a strong statement, but unfortunately Columbus gave no indication as to when, where, or how this assistance was provided. Las Casas wrote that he had seen copies of some of Columbus's letters, and from one of these he quoted Columbus as telling the sovereigns, "I found no one that didn't make fun [of the project] except for that father friar Antonio de Marchena." Las Casas went on to say that he had never been able to find out the order to which Marchena belonged but that he believed Marchena was a Franciscan because Columbus, "after becoming an admiral, was always devoted to that order." He ended by saying, "Neither could I find out when, nor in what nor how he helped him or what entrée he had with the king and queen."[60] Las Casas was clear that he knew nothing about Marchena other than what he had read in an otherwise unknown letter.

The Spanish monarchs wrote Columbus in September 1493 saying that in order to understand his log, they needed to know the degrees in which the islands lay. They added, "It seems that it would be well if you take with you an astrologer and that it be Fr. Antonio de Marchena or any other that you wish."[61] Fernández de Navarrete offered a different transcription; in the sentence referring to Marchena, the words "and it always seemed to us that he agrees with your viewpoint" replaced "or any other that you wish."[62] This letter placed Marchena neither in Palos nor anywhere else; nor does it give any clear indication about the relationship between the two men. However, one thing is clear from other sources: Marchena did not sail on the second voyage.

Allesandro Geraldini and Francisco López de Gómara

Bishop Allesandro Geraldini was the first person to combine the names given for the two friars into one single friar. He wrote that Columbus came to Andalucía, where the king and queen were engaged in fighting the Moors. Geraldini's brother, at that time papal nuncio, supported him in his project. After the death of the nuncio, Columbus left the court and took refuge in "a Franciscan monastery in the region of Andalucía at the end of Marchena, humbly begging that they give him the food necessary to live. There, Fray Juan de Marcena [sic] ... seeing in Columbus in all [was] learned, moved by compassion, he went to King Ferdinand and Queen Isabel."[63] This account, written sometime before Geraldini's death in Santo Domingo in 1522, raises the possibility that the toponym "Marchena" was taken by Juan Pérez after he assumed orders, a custom not uncommon at that time. Some of the modern confusion as to what Geraldini had to say on these matters arises from conjectures made by his descendent Mons. Belisario Geraldini, who in 1892 attributed to the papal nuncio statements that did not appear in his ancestor's manuscript, first published in 1631.[64]

Francisco López de Gómara's *Hispania vitrix* (published in 1553) was the first publication to link the two names together, as Juan Perez de Marchena, in modern times foreshortened by historians to Juan Pérez Marchena.[65] In English, this name is translated literally as "Juan Perez of (from) Marchena," just as the author referred to in English histories as Oviedo is correctly Fernández of Oviedo, and the name of Navarrete is really Fernández of Navarrete.

Geraldini knew Columbus personally, and both he and López de Gómara agreed that "Marchena" was merely the place-name, indicating either the hometown of Pérez or the place where he took orders. Herrera y Tordesillas, a major source for English-speaking historians, followed López de Gómara's lead in offering the single-person version. In the past century, French and German historians were particularly drawn to this interpretation. Recently Antonio Rumeu de Armas, after making a detailed study of the matter, concluded that there were two different friars involved in the affairs of Columbus.[66] The French historian Alain Milhou suggested that there were possibly two Marchenas and one Pérez involved.[67]

Based on this limited information, many theories have been developed in numerous monographs and studies. As far as the historical record is concerned, there were two friars, Juan Pérez and Antonio de Marchena, both of whom may have been at the Franciscan monastery at La Rábida in 1492. One or the other may have held the title of "guardian," but there is no evidence that either was doorkeeper, a later addition based solely on a misreading of the testimony of Garcí Hernández. The alternate solution is that the references were to Friar Juan Pérez from Marchena.

Modern Versions of Marchena's Role

Morison detailed the events of 1485: "It is certain that Columbus left his boy at La Rábida very soon after landing in Spain; but the friar who helped him then was Antonio de Marchena, *custodio* of the Franciscan sub-province of Seville, a man of spirit and intelligence, and of high repute as an *astrólogo*. Fray Juan Pérez, *guardian* or head of La Rábida helped Columbus in 1491 [*sic*]; on this first visit he perhaps sent Columbus to Seville with a letter of introduction to Fray Antonio, or the *custodio* may have been visiting the friary when it received this unexpected visit from two future admirals of the Indies."[68] Morison's certitudes are appropriately hemmed in with reservations, however.

He went on to give Marchena credit for sending Columbus to seek support from Medina-Sidonia and, after being turned down, to Medina Celi. He next mentioned Marchena in connection with the September 1493 letter mentioned above. Here, Morison referred to Marchena as Columbus's "old friend" and speculated as to his reason for not accompanying Columbus on the second voyage: "Perhaps he refused to go. . . . But I rather suspect that Columbus, like sundry other captains I have known, wanted no rival navigator on board."[69] In a later work Morison was apparently yet more convinced by his own earlier fanciful account. He now said, "Father and son made a long dusty walk from Palos to La Rábida, Christopher asked for bread and a cup of water for the boy, and then got into conversation with Antonio de Marchena, a highly intelligent Franciscan who happened to be visiting. . . . Columbus . . . convinced Marchena, an astrologer of repute . . . and Marchena gave him a letter of intro-duction to the Duke of Medina Sidonia. Columbus called at the ducal castle and was referred to a kinsman, the Count of Medina Celi."[70]

Wilford, accepting the first visit to La Rábida as fact, wrote: "Columbus' arrival at La Rábida proved to be a fortunate turn of events. He met Antonio de Marchena, an official of the Franciscan order and a man knowledgeable in cosmography." In a curious new interpretation of the single-friar theory, Wilford wrote that the confusion originated with the physician Garcí Hernández, who "left the impression that Marchena and another friar, Juan Pérez, were one and the same person. The confusion is responsible for a mistake common to many historians; Winsor, as a typical example, refers to the friar at Rábida as Juan Pérez de Marchena."[71] As shown earlier Garcí Hernánded mentioned only one friar and named him Juan Pérez. As also previously noted, Velez testified that Columbus dealt with two friars at the monastery, but he named only one of them, Fray Juan Pérez. Not a single witness in the *Pleitos* mentioned a Fray Marchena.

Wilford went on to speculate that "the two must have hit it off from the start," with Columbus "baring his soul" to the friar; the latter "probably directed the mariner's attention to the writings of scholars and church authorities that would fortify his case for the ocean crossing." Later Wilford added, "We know little about Marchena the Franciscan cosmographer." But he then backtracked: "Through Marchena, moreover, Columbus was introduced." Another innova-tion introduced by Wilford is that "at the urging of Father Marchena, Pinzón agreed to join forces with Columbus."[72] More than a dozen witnesses in the *Pleitos* linked the names of Columbus,

Pinzón, and Fray Juan Pérez, but there was not one such mention of Marchena.

Although Fernández-Armesto believed that Marchena was head of the Franciscan province of Andalucía and at one time guardian of the friary of La Rábida, he did add, "Another of its guardians, Fray Juan Pérez, was one of the Queen's confessors." Otherwise Fernández-Armesto simply cited the testimony of Garcí Hernández, the mention by Columbus of the two unnamed friars, and Columbus's reference to the aid that Marchena had given him, as well as the monarchs' suggestion that Marchena accompany him on the second voyage.[73]

The Phillipses, like Morison, presented Marchena as, in their words, "an astronomer, who studied the same heavens that guided the mariners." According to them, Columbus met the friar "soon after his arrival in Spain." They contributed another addition to the legend: "Marchena was ideally placed to help Columbus . . . he had powerful friends at court and was rising in the Franciscan hierarchy. Later he would become the overseer [*guardián*] of all the Observant Franciscan monasteries in the Sevillian region." According to their version of the sequence of events, "Columbus left for the royal court within a few weeks after arriving in Spain, he bore with him Marchena's letter of introduction to Friar Hernando de Talavera."[74] Unfortunately, these authors offered no documentation for these novel assertions.

Sale accepted this agenda, commenting on Columbus's arrival in Palos from Portugal, "It was here that he had met (or perhaps gotten an introduction to) the noted Franciscan astronomer Fray Antonio de Marchena, who gave the first sympathetic and supportive hearing to his Grand Scheme of sailing westward into the Ocean Sea." Sale found that Columbus met there Fray Juan Pérez, who by "all accounts was chiefly responsible for the court's giving a last hearing to Colón when all seemed lost at the end of 1491."[75]

Rubin repeated the whole myth as fact: La Rábida, Diego being left there, and the introduction to Medina-Sidonia through Marchena. Also, Columbus came to court with "solid recommendations, among them one from Fray Antonio de Marchena, a cosmographer-humanist known to Isabella's court and a member of La

Rábida's monastery."[76] She then added quotations from Medina Celi's letter written to the queen in 1493; however, the quotations were cited as though they had been written around the time that Columbus first came to Spain. The escalation in the attributes of Marchena is notable.

The very paucity of contemporary documentation for any of these events and people makes any strictly documented account sparse and dry. Regretfully, this circumstance has led many historians to resort to either interpretative reconstructions or deconstructions of what took place as well as of who was involved. Creating a role in a speculative encounter is a perilous undertaking for the biographer.

Columbus's contemporaries were more inclined to limit themselves to the facts as they viewed them: he left Portugal to seek support in Spain; he went to court and had to wait many years for acceptance of his proposal; in the meantime, either before or after appealing to the Crown, he looked for support from two dukes; but finally, with the aid of a friar at La Rábida named Juan Pérez, he was able to get royal approval. They then moved on to chronicle in detail the preparations for sailing, the great discovery, and its aftermath.

Unfortunately, many scholars are not satisfied with such a skeletal review of Columbus's prediscovery days in Spain. They must flesh out the few known facts. In so doing, they run the risk of—and, lamentably, generally fall into the error of—misconstruction. They have done this when they attempt to pass off their own or their modern sources' suppositions, rationalizations, and inventions as facts. Such faults, creators in themselves of historical fiction, are particularly evident in modern U.S. accounts of the event. In their pursuit of the journalistic "full story," these writers reinvent Columbus's life at the Spanish court.

Columbus at Court

As noted earlier, Columbus received financial support on four occasions while the court was at Córdoba between July and October in 1487.[77] The next such payment was made to him in June 1488. It should be recalled that those dating his arrival at court in January 1486 based this date on his statement in 1493 that seven years had passed since he came to serve the Spanish monarchs; yet in another statement he said that it was six or seven years. Those favoring the 1486 date must accept that the first meeting was at Alacalá de Henares because that is where the court was in that year. All of Columbus's contemporaries said that he first went to the court when it was in Córdoba, which was in 1485 and again in 1487.

More important than the date of his arrival at court was what happened after he got there: who helped him and who opposed him, how was his project judged, and who judged his plan? The *Historie*, without giving a date, said that Columbus went to Córdoba, where, as "an affable person and of sweet conversation," he became friends with those from whom he found the best reception and who were best positioned to persuade the king and queen; among these friends was Luis Santángel, who is known to have played a major part in the final acceptance of the project.[78] Like so many of the people closest to King Ferdinand, he was an Aragonese converso.

The *Historie* explained that since the project involved fundamental principles of doctrine, it was referred to Hernando de Talavera, prior of Prado and future archbishop of Granada, who was to consult with cosmographers. This is the basis for what has since come to be known as the Talavera Commission.

In his meetings with these experts, the Admiral, fearing that "the same thing [would] happen as had in Portugal," was unwilling to reveal his full plan. The many reasons supposedly offered against the project were enumerated, and finally, "after having wasted a great deal of time on this matter," the sovereigns stalled, saying that due to their "many wars and conquests, especially in Granada," they could not take on a new venture at this time.[79] They said that they would examine the matter at a later date. It was at this point, according to the *Historie*, that Columbus went to the duke of Medina-Sidonia to seek help. Failing to get it, he decided to go to France.

Las Casas wrote that Columbus suffered greatly at the hands of doubters but finally was able to get a hearing by the junta.[80] He said the junta was headed by Cardinal Mendoza, who—according to Las Casas—was reported in Rui da Pina's "Historia portuguesa" as the person responsible for the royal acceptance. But Las Casas added

that others accredited the success of the venture to the teacher of
Prince Juan, Diego de Deza, later to become archbishop of Seville.
Another whom he listed as responsible was Juan Cabrero, the king's
Aragonese chamberlain. The chamberlain's nephew wrote in 1515
that Cabrero had been the "principal cause" and that had it not been
for him, "there would not have been the Indies, at least for Castile."[81]
In 1504 Columbus linked Deza and Cabrero in a letter to Diego;
however, in this letter he said that it was Deza "who was the cause
that their Highnesses have the Indies."[82] Las Casas added that long
before he saw this letter from Columbus, he had heard that Deza and
Cabrero boasted that the discovery of the Indies was due to their
efforts at court.

Las Casas qualified these assertions, attributing the major contribution to Santángel. Despite the many recommendations, their
Highnesses only "heard and understood his demands superficially."
Las Casas noted, "It is a general rule that when kings are engaged
in war they understand little nor do they want to understand other
matters." Therefore, "in a benign way and with happy faces," they
referred the matter to experts, principal of whom was Deza, bishop
of Palencia. Here Las Casas gave the same version as that given by
Hernando, often word for word. He explained that Columbus was
unable to convince the court's experts because he faced the same
problem that "the famous flutist Timothy" had met: "When those
who had already studied elsewhere came to [Timothy] to teach them
the flute, he charged double, because, he said that it took him double
the effort, first to make them unlearn what they already knew which
was harder than teaching them music and flute." Finally, the
sovereigns dismissed Columbus for the reasons given by the experts
but "not in all taking from him hope that they would return to the
matter when they were less occupied."[83]

Thacher and most recently Jane Frances Amler, among others,
have provided interesting background information about the
Santángel family.[84] It was among the most powerful and wealthiest
families of Aragón. Despite this fact, as converted Jews, they
suffered greatly at the hands of the Inquisition. In 1484, shortly
after the Inquisition was established in Aragón, a Martin Santángel
was burned at the stake, and in August 1487, Mosen Luis de

Santángel, father-in-law of the king's treasurer Gabriel Sánchez, was given the same treatment. The mother of one of the Santángels was burned at the stake in 1489, and her son, Luis's cousin, died in a similar manner six years later. Luis Santángel, the king's chancellor, who was to be so important to Columbus's future, was obliged on July 17, 1491, to parade the streets with the despised *sanbeneto* on his breast.

While Ferdinand benefited financially from the confiscation of the properties of the Jews of Aragón, at the same time he offered protection to those who served as members of his council. Queen Isabel also had a number of conversos among her council members. Apparently, Spain needed their administrative and economic expertise. Three scholars who have studied these matters—Salvador de Madariaga, Cecil Roth, and M. Kayserling—all found that Bishop Hernando de Talavera, the prior of Prado, and Fray Diego de Deza were also descendants of Jewish families. It has been claimed that at least partly for this reason, Deza, who later headed the Inquisition, was bitterly opposed to marranos. It should be kept in mind that a converso was a Jew who had embraced the Catholic faith, whereas a marrano was a converso who secretly held to his original faith. It was the latter who were supposed to have been the prime targets of the Inquisition. Conversos, however, were far from free of accusation and of persecution as marranos.

Las Casas speculated that the consideration of Columbus's project took so many years because of several factors, among them the fact that because of the wars of Reconquest, the court rarely stayed for long in one place, giving the Crown officers little time to deal with matters other than those immediately connected with the war. Another reason may have been what he called the "normal tediousness with which affairs of state" were carried out, the fault of the "indolence and carelessness" of palace officials.[85] The many historians who ignore these simple explanations offered by Las Casas have probably never had to deal with modern-day bureaucrats, who may possibly be seen as open-minded compared with palace officials functioning under an absolute monarchy during a time of war.

According to Las Casas, Columbus left the court and sought out the help of Medina-Sidonia, who did not accept the proposition, "either because he didn't believe it or didn't understand it or because he was busy, like all of the grandees, mostly those from Andalucía, in the siege of Granada." Columbus went next to Medina Celi, who did accept the proposal, saying that he would put up three thousand or four thousand ducats to build three vessels and to stock them with food for a year or more. He started to build the ships in his yards in the Port of Santa María. After he wrote to the queen about the project, she then ordered Columbus back to court. Las Casas noted that the queen ordered the duke reimbursed for his expenses and ordered the three ships finished. "It is said that in these he [Columbus] made his discovery."[86] This was not precisely the version given by Medina Celi, who made no mention of reimbursement, and Las Casas was obviously misinformed about the provenance of the vessels in which Columbus sailed on his first voyage. Las Casas said he got his information about Medina Celi from Diego de Morales, who was the son of the duke's majordomo and whom Las Casas met on Española. Thus Las Casas provided an independent confirmation of Medina Celi's claim, made in his letter of 1493, that he had offered to assist Columbus.

Las Casas finished his account of these events by telling of Columbus's return to Palos, of the Garcí Hernández testimony, which he related to events that took place just before Columbus was called back to court in 1492 at the instance of the friar of La Rábida, and of how Columbus was again turned down at Santa Fé. What occurred after this last refusal will be dealt with in the next chapter, since it belongs more properly to the story of the first voyage than to this account of Columbus's peregrinations in Spain.

Fernández de Oviedo told the story in a different manner. He wrote that Columbus came to Spain, met in Seville with Medina-Sidonia, who turned him down, and then met with Medina Celi, who also turned him down, "although some say that [Medina Celi] wanted to outfit Columbus in his Port of Santa María, and the Catholic King and Queen did not want to give him the permission to do so."[87] As previously reported in discussing Columbus's arrival in Spain, Fernández de Oviedo then gave credit to Quintanilla and Cardinal Mendoza for having provided the most assistance to Columbus at court. Once there, he was given a hearing; the question was, where did it take place? Fernández de Oviedo believed the hearing was headed by Hernando de Talavera and first met in Salamanca, although this cannot be substantiated.

Talavera Commission

Historians have to deal with two versions of the so-called Talavera Commission. According to the first one, the commission met in Salamanca in 1486; according to the second, it met sporadically over a period of years, wherever the court happened to be. Salamanca was first named in 1629 by Antonio de Remesal, who claimed that it met at the convent of Saint Stephen in that city, supposedly in 1486. There is no known copy of any official document that confirms either the naming of a commission or the participation of Talavera. In two letters dated September 13, 1493, Martire praised the roles played on the commission by both Talavera and the count of Tenedilla, noting the numerous prediscovery discussions in which they took part. "As it seems, it was with your approval that it [the voyage of discovery] was carried out."[88]

At this point we should briefly review the travels of the court over these years. The king and queen spent the winter of 1485 in Alcalá de Henares. On the much-discussed day of January 20, 1486, when Columbus is supposed to "have come to serve" the court at Córdoba, the king and queen were unquestionably still in nearby Madrid. Later in 1486 the monarchs did go to Córdoba, although the king, sometimes accompanied by the queen, was usually in the field harrying the Moors.

Support for the belief that Columbus went to Córdoba in 1486 comes from what could be considered an informed source, the biographer of Cardinal Mendoza. In 1625 he wrote that he would discuss events in the cardinal's life in 1487: "[First] I should mention one in the preceding year, 1486, that is great and marvelous as will be seen. It was the arrival at the court of Cristobal Colón."[89]

Diego Colón presented Rodrigo Maldonado de Talavera as a witness at the 1515 hearings in the *Pleitos*. Without naming time or place, Maldonado testified, "This witness with the Prior of Prado and with other wise and learned men and mariners discussed with the said admiral his going to the said islands, and that all of them agreed that what the admiral said was impossible to be true; and that contrary to the opinion of most of them the said admiral persisted in going on the said voyage."⁹⁰ Maldonado was a member of the queen's council and is seen again in connection with Columbus in 1493, when he was entrusted with some of the arrangements for the second voyage. It is important to note that this witness not only failed to give time and place for the meeting but also failed to name any of the other participants except for Deza. The language he used did not indicate that all members of the commission were necessarily in agreement, nor did he say that Columbus received at that time a definite turndown.

Quintanilla apparently held similar reservations about the practicality of the enterprise, though he did not discount the possibility of a voyage eventually taking place. In his letter asking to be allowed to participate in the sailings to the Indies after the return of Columbus from his first voyage, Medina Celi wrote, "Your Majesty received him [Columbus] and gave him in charge to Quintanilla, who wrote me that for his part he held this business for not very certain, but that if it approached he would favour me and give me a part in it."

The *Historie*'s version is that the Crown committed the project to the prior of Prado "together with experts in cosmography"; however, because "in those days there weren't as many cosmographers as there are now, those that met did not understand what they should have, nor did the Admiral want to clarify so much that it would happen to him as it had in Portugal and they take away from him the profits." Hernando continued, "While this was being discussed, the Catholic Kings were not always set in one place, due to the war that they were carrying on against Granada, for which reason the decision and reply were delayed for a long time."⁹¹ Here, like Las Casas, he went on to tell how Columbus then sought the aid of Medina-Sidonia.

Bernáldez presented a capsulated version of these events, apparently referring mainly to the final agreement to support the venture. He wrote that Columbus came to the court and told his story, to which the monarchs gave little credit. But Columbus persisted and showed them a *mappamundi*, "in such a way that they wanted to know about those lands, and leaving him, called wise astrologers and astronomers and men of the court knowledgeable in matters of cosmography who were informed, and the opinion of most of those, hearing the opinion of Christobal Colon, said that it was true."[92] This final acceptance obviously referred to events that presumably took place at Santa Fé in 1492.

For Las Casas, Columbus's arrival at court in Córdoba was "on 20 January in the year 1485," that is, by this version, very soon after his arrival in Spain. As recounted above, Columbus found support from the cardinal, Deza, and Cabrero. Deza, like Las Casas a Dominican, was the one "principally charged" with calling together those people that he believed most understood matters of cosmography, "of which there were not many at that time in Castile; and it is something to marvel at how much poverty [of knowledge] and ignorance there was about this at that time in Castile." They met many times, Columbus giving them explanations, "but keeping quiet the most pressing ones in order that it not happen to him as it had with the king of Portugal." Again, the sovereigns dismissed him, but not "taking away from him all hope of returning to the matter when they were less occupied [with the war against Granada]."[93] Las Casas then repeated the explanations about the constant movements of the court and the other distractions.

What has been given here about this commission is all that is known at the present time from the writings of contemporaries. Any accretions are based on conjecture or are products of the sometimes lively imaginations of some of Columbus's biographers. Apparently, some kind of advisory commission was formed, and it probably would not have met before Columbus had first met with the king and queen to make his initial presentation. This appears to have happened sometime between 1486 and 1487. Given the presently available documentation, there is no way to ascertain where any such commission first met, although Salamanca sounds reasonable, and more important, absolutely no way to know if Columbus had been turned down before 1491. The latter phase of this story will be dealt with in the next chapter.

Many writers have tended to depict these negotiations in a light unfavorable to the Spanish court. Its members are often portrayed as ignorant and deaf to the explanations offered by Columbus. Such criticisms ignore the fact that the Admiral's first two biographers wrote that he refused to reveal to the council all that he knew for fear that they would exclude him and use his information for the sole benefit of Castile. A proposition such as the one made by Columbus, one that could not be judged by any known means at that time, can hardly have been expected then, nor would it today, to receive a rubber stamp of approval. Under the circumstances, no one can be criticized for being skeptical.

Significantly, even Columbus's contemporaries recognized the difficulty of mounting an expedition into the unknown at a time when the court was in constant motion and engaged in a war on its own territory. Much of the English-language writing about Spain's role in the discovery has been tainted by prejudice of the kind that evolved into the "Black Legend" of Spain's part in the opening and subsequent colonization of the Americas. Such a negative approach has also been reflected, conversely, by the near deification of Columbus, a tendency evidenced primarily in the United States and France. As a consequence the "noble Columbus" is often portrayed as being invariably treated badly by the "ignorant Spaniards" who owed him so much.

Morison dealt with these events rather briefly. He believed that the commission was organized by Talavera and met in Córdoba, "in the early summer of 1486, and adjourned to Salamanca where the court spent Christmas." The commission members held their "hearings in the College of St. Stephen." Morison quoted Maldonado incorrectly, in that he did not say that they had met in the college; as previously noted, Remesal said this. Morison did believe that at that time the commission postponed rendering a report but that Columbus was finally turned down, probably in 1490. He found that the rejection was probably for the five cosmographic reasons enumerated by Las Casas and added that this was not surprising, given the "geographical knowledge of Castile, a country not so far advanced in such matters as Portugal." Turned down, "Columbus waited another six or nine months, possibly at the house of Medina Celi. . . . In the summer of 1491 Columbus visited La Rábida to call for his son Diego . . . he proposed to leave the lad at Huelva . . . before departing for France."[94] This provided a concise and neat explanation for the seven years that Columbus was in Spain awaiting approval of his project; unfortunately, none of it can be substantiated by the evidence.

In a later work, *The European Discovery of America*, Morison was more specific and perhaps even less accurate. The first meeting at court was described as follows: "On May Day 1486, almost a year from the time he first set foot in Spain, Columbus was received by the Queen in the Alcazar of Cordova . . . she appointed a special commission under her confessor Hernando de Talavera to examine the Enterprise of the Indies." For the next six years, "he had to sustain a continual battle against prejudice, contumely, and sheer indifference . . . he had to endure clownish witticisms and crackpot jests by ignorant courtiers, to be treated like a beggar. . . . Hardest of all, he learned by experience the meaning of the phrase *cosas de España* the endemic procrastination of Spaniards." Morison continued: "At least one member, Diego de Deza, favored the Great Enterprise. . . . Christmas 1487 passed without any report from the Talavera commission. So, early in 1488, Columbus wrote to João II of Portugal, requesting another hearing and asking for a safe-conduct from arrest for his unpaid bills in Lisbon." The Morison account provided, for the first time, the information that "early in 1487 Columbus received a retaining fee of 12,000 a year, the pay of an able seaman, enough to support a man of his simple tastes." Morison then supplied, in quotation marks, the reason why: "Late in 1490 the Talavera commission issued an unfavourable report."[95] No such report is known today.

In both of these works Morison digressed to discuss the no-less-fanciful account concocted by Washington Irving of a hearing at the University of Salamanca. He described Irving's "gripping drama" in which "an obscure navigator, a member of no learned society, destitute of all the trappings and circumstances which sometimes give oracular authority to dullness . . . sustains his thesis of a spherical globe against the pedantic bigotry of flat-earth churchmen." Here

Morison added, very aptly: "Columbus and Talavera merely held committee hearings . . . at which neither side was able to convince the other. The sphericity of the globe was not in question." Unfortunately, Morison did not stop there, going on to state, "The issue was the width of the ocean; and therein the opposition was right."[96] This is possibly true, but we shall probably never know what really went on at the commission hearings.

Wilford was more cautious than Morison. He retold the manner of Columbus's arrival in Spain as testified to by Garcí Hernández, although he admitted, "The truth of this legend . . . is unknowable." Actually, as already noted, this was not a question of a legend but of testimony given under oath in a court hearing. Wilford did, however, categorically assert that it was at this time that Columbus "met Antonio de Marchena, an official of the Franciscan order and a man knowledgeable in cosmography." As to the first meeting of Columbus with the monarchs, Wilford dated this to 1486 and noted, "The meeting occurred at the Alcazar in Córdoba, fact for once according with legend despite a personal appearance by Marchena to endorse the plan." Nothing in the historical record supports the statements made in any of the three preceding sentences. However, Wilford was more cautious in dealing with the Talavera commission, noting: "Historians are not certain how long the commission deliberated. Taviani says six months; Morison, four years."

Fernández-Armesto treated this episode in the life of Columbus without historical exaggeration. He provided much fresh material on those people most likely to have helped Columbus over the waiting years. He was especially interesting in the manner in which, using the court of Prince Juan as the centerpiece, he showed the interconnections, real as well as possible, between many of the individuals who at a later date would definitely play significant roles in the affairs of Columbus. This is history supported by historical data.

The Phillipses also supplied some solid historical background for the understanding of Iberia, divided as it was at the time among four kingdoms. According to their version, Columbus arrived in Córdoba in 1485 backed by a letter of introduction from Marchena to Talavera, a letter that they supposed earned him a hearing before the royal council. "When the council rejected his petition, Columbus made an appeal to the monarchs for a personal audience. This apparently came about on 20 January 1486, in Alcalá de Henares."[97] They based their acceptance of this date on the previously noted account given by Bernáldez, together with the testimony given in the *Pleitos* by Andrés del Corral, who said that he had been in Madrid at this time (Alcalá de Henares is near Madrid). As previously noted, this testimony was of questionable value, and these authors did make note of the discrepancy in a footnote. It will also be recalled that Medina Celi wrote that Columbus had reported to Quintanilla; however, Fernández de Navarrete, while checking the archives in Simancas, found that Quintanilla was attached to the court in Córdoba only between 1486 and 1488. In the crucial years 1491–92, he was in Old Castile at both Burgos and Valladolid.

The Phillipses attempted to demonstrate a possible connection between Columbus, Portuguese exiles, Portuguese members of Queen Isabel's childhood household, and Columbus's father-in-law, "Bartolomeu Perestrelo." They presented interesting, but unverifiable, possibilities. As has been previously demonstrated, the claim that this Perestrello was Columbus's father-in-law is tenuous at best. They went on to speculate as to the sovereigns' possible reasons for holding Columbus off and as to what might have taken place when Columbus joined the court at Málaga.

Columbus at Málaga and Baza

King Ferdinand left Córdoba in April 1487. On May 3 he sent the Christians that he had liberated when he had captured the Moorish town of Veles to Queen Isabel in Córdoba.[98] On May 5, "Cristobal Colombo, a foreigner" who was there "doing important things at the service of Your Highnesses," received, on the orders of Quintanilla, his first known subsidy in Spain.[99] The queen arrived at the king's camp in front of Málaga sometime after May 7, and they stayed there until the siege ended with the surrender of the Moors on August 18. On the twenty-seventh of that month Columbus was provided with four thousand maravedis for him to travel to Málaga to rejoin the court.[100]

The siege of Málaga was no minor engagement, even by today's military standards. Bernáldez told how the king had with him initially ten thousand horsemen and eighty thousand foot soldiers. When these proved insufficient to maintain the circle around the town, he sent for Medina-Sidonia to join him with the duke's people. He also had with him "the Duke of Cádiz ... the Master of Alcántara, and later the Master of Santiago and other dukes, counts, marquises and great men and captains of the cities of Seville, and Córdoba, Ecija, and Jerez and of the other cities of Castile."[101]

It seems highly improbable that the monarchs, deeply engaged in such a major siege, would at that time have sent for Columbus and have subsidized him unless they, and their council, took Columbus's proposal seriously. Whatever else they were, neither Ferdinand nor Isabel were capricious rulers. The Phillipses believed that at this time, "whatever arguments Columbus put forth, the commission rejected them totally during its meetings in November and December of 1486 and January of 1487."[102] If he was indeed turned down at this time—although there is absolutely no contemporary evidence for such meetings—then the monarchs' recall of Columbus in August of that year, and again before Granada, indicated a major change of policy on their part.

Whatever happened at Córdoba and Málaga in 1487 and 1488, it cannot be said that Columbus's plan had been rejected. At the beginning of May 1489, King Ferdinand began the siege of Baza, which was to last until December of that year. The queen held court in Jaén until November, when she joined her husband.[103] On May 13 an order was sent from Córdoba to Columbus in Seville authorizing assistance for a trip to join the court at Baza. Zuniga, writing in the sixteenth century, said that Columbus was present at the siege, "giving examples of distinguished valor that corresponded to [a man of] his prudence and high ambition." This comment has spawned a legend about Columbus's military prowess at Baza. The Royal Armory in Madrid displays a coat of armor often depicted in histories of Columbus and claimed by modern romancers to have been worn by him at the siege. No contemporary evidence indicates whether Columbus made the trip to Baza, let alone how long he stayed there or what he did or did not do even if he did join the court there. Given the high cost of a full suit of armor in those days, it is extremely unlikely that Columbus owned such a suit at this stage in his career.

As has been shown, little is known about Columbus's activities in 1489, but several major events occurred in the preceding year, 1488, an important date in the Columbus saga. The first event was his correspondence with King João II of Portugal in regard to a return visit to that country. The purpose of this visit is unknowable but, as previously indicated, was presumed by many to have been to offer the "Great Enterprise" again to Portugal. The only known copy of the king's reply is dated March 20, 1488, and was addressed "To Cristovam Colon our special Friend, in Sevilha."[104] It is generally accepted today that by this time, Columbus had fixed his residence in Seville. This year, 1488, was also the year of the previously discussed voyage by Bartolomeu Dias to the Cape of Good Hope, a trip with which one or both of the Columbus brothers appear to have been marginally involved. And it is probably the year in which Columbus entered into his relationship with Beatriz Enríquez de Arana.

Beatriz Enríquez de Arana

The whole story of Columbus's relationship in Córdoba with Beatriz is a curious one. It has been romanticized by some of his biographers, ignored by others, such as her own son Hernando, and presented in a manner unfavorable to her by many. The problem that his biographers have had with this episode is that they have felt the need to present it in a manner coherent with the rest of his heroic life as portrayed by them. Some, showing a puritanical difficulty in accepting the fact of a mistress, ignore its common acceptance then and today in most Latin nations.

It is only logical to start any inquiry into this relationship with a look at what Columbus had to say on the subject. Before leaving on his fourth voyage, Columbus wrote a letter of instructions to his son Diego; among other things, he commended Beatriz to him: "Beatriz Enríquez is entrusted to you, for the love of me, to care for her as much as you would for your mother; provide for her 10,000 maravedis each year besides the others that she has from the butcher shops of Córdoba."[105] This last comment is a reference to the ten thousand maravedis a year that the king had promised to whoever first sighted land on the first voyage. Columbus claimed, probably unjustifiably, this right for himself and assigned the proceeds to Beatriz. The Crown decreed that this grant be funded by a levy on the butchershops in the city of Córdoba. In his will, Columbus provided again for ten thousand maravedis annually for Beatriz and an equal yearly stipend for his mistress's sister, Violanta Nuñez. Beatriz's birth name was Nuñez; she adopted the name of Enríquez de Arana from a relative who took her in when her parents died.

On his deathbed, Columbus again entrusted Beatriz's care to Diego: "And I order that Beatriz Enríquez, mother of Don Fernando my son, be entrusted to him [Diego], that he provide for her so that she may live honestly, as a person to whom I am so indebted. And that this be done to relieve my conscience because this weighs heavily on my soul. It is not correct to write the reason for it here."[106] This was the final paragraph of the codicil to his last will.

Diego Colón wrote two wills, one in 1509 and another in 1523. Copies of both are preserved today. From the latter one it appears that Diego was not certain whether Beatriz was still alive, and on this basis it is generally assumed that she died sometime between 1516, in which year she is known to have sold a house in Córdoba, and 1523, when Diego wrote his last will. In both wills he admitted that there had been delays in making the payments to her, the last delay, "in so far as he could remember," was of some four or five years. An explanation for what apparently happened to this money is found in Las Casas's account. He wrote that Vireina Doña María de Toledo, wife of Diego, told him: "These 10,000 maravedis were by law for life. . . . [T]hey were always paid to me from the butcher shops of Sevile [sic]."[107] The "generous bequests" that Morison claimed were paid by María de Toledo to Beatriz's heirs may in reality have been nothing other than the payment of the annuity that her husband had acknowledged in his wills but that she had apparently usurped.[108]

Any discussion of the Columbus family's attitudes toward love affairs and marriage must also look to the record established by

Columbus's son Diego and grandson Luis. The following self-explanatory data is excerpted from Thacher's *Christopher Columbus*:

> In Diego's second will dated May 2, 1523, Diego recognized that he too
> had an affair, providing for his possible paternity if it be shown that
> the child "in consideration of the time at which I had relations with
> this woman and the time at which I left her, such infant should have
> been born in the month of June or July, 1508." In regard to another
> of Diego's affairs, this one with the wife of a man named Pitisalazan
> and, "inasmuch as she gave birth to a son, I direct that when the suit
> which was brought against me unjustly and in defiance of the truth,
> is finished, such son shall be received by my heir." Again, "what shall
> remain of the fifth of my estate . . . to be vested in Don Christopher
> Columbus, my natural son, who is in Castile and who is now fifteen
> years of age."

Diego's legitimate son Luis was yet more careless than his father
and grandfather in his love affairs, as can be seen from the following:

> In 1541 there was born to Don Luis an illegitimate daughter . . . the
> following year he married María de Orozco . . . notwithstanding María
> de Orozco was still living in 1547, Don Luis was married in Santo
> Domingo to María de Mosquera. . . . It was about this time [1551] that
> Don Luis, notwithstanding that María de Orozco and María de
> Mosquera were both still living married . . . Anna de Castro Ossorio,
> daughter of Beatriz, Countess de Lemos, to whom he had long been
> affianced . . . judicial notice was taken of this delinquency, as he was
> arrested early in the year 1559 . . . before the sentence was carried
> into execution, however, he managed in some way to marry a fourth
> time . . . on May 26, 1565, Luisa de Carvajal, who on the same day
> bore him a son.[109]

Hernando, the illegitimate son of Columbus and Beatriz, could be
expected to shed some light on the relationship between his mother
and father. He too left a will, but it was prepared in 1539, many
years after his mother's death, so there was no reason for her name
to appear in it. There are several references to his mother's cousin
Pedro de Arana. Hernando's instructions for the inscriptions on his
tomb included references to his father but none to his mother. He left
home at an early age to go to court as a page for Prince Juan, and

there is no evidence that he ever again lived in his mother's home-town of Córdoba. There is only one contemporary document linking him to that town; he received notification there that his appointment as royal cartographer had been canceled. His residence, like his father's for several years, was in Seville.

There is a certain amount of confusion about his exact day of birth, but it was definitely in the month of August and in the year 1488. In 1503 Columbus wrote that his son was then thirteen years old, which would have placed his birth in 1490. This is but another of Columbus's inexactitudes. Beatriz was never referred to directly in the *Historie*. The close connections between Columbus and her brother Diego de Arana and her cousin Pedro were glossed over. In all fairness, it should be noted that the *Historie* was also less informative than Las Casas's *Historia* about Columbus's own brothers Bartolomé and Diego. Presumably, based on the similarity of content, both the writer of the *Historie* and Las Casas had available to them either the original or copies of Columbus's log for his third journey, which is the source for Columbus's own references to the Arana cousins. In the *Historie* no mention is made of Pedro, who was captain of one of the vessels on the third voyage, or of the fact that Diego de Arana had been killed at Navidad, but these facts are noted in the *Historia*. Las Casas, referring to Pedro, said that he was "very honest and of very sound judgment." He added, "I knew him well."

Contemporary city records of Córdoba contain many references to the Arana family. These indicate people of property, and in one sixteenth-century manuscript the family is listed as of the nobility. There are several records of real estate transactions carried out by Beatriz. In the sixteenth century she and other members of the family were reported as having supported the Pinzóns in their claim that Martín Alonso had helped to finance the first voyage, a claim always stoutly denied by Columbus's heirs. Other records show that she had trouble collecting the proceeds from the tax on the city's butchershops. The very facts that the Crown appointed her brother Diego justice of the peace for the fleet on the first voyage and that later Columbus named her cousin Pedro captain of one of the vessels in the fleet for the third voyage indicate that they were individuals of some competence. Anything beyond this is pure speculation.

There is evidence that Beatríz could read and write, not a common accomplishment among peasants in Spain, male or female, in those days. Morison explained Columbus's failure to marry her: "A peasant's daughter, unpresentable at court, would have been a bar to his ambition when still a suppliant, and an unsuitable match for an admiral and viceroy."[110] Illegitimate children were socially acceptable in those days; King Ferdinand had one of his own in his suite and made another a bishop. In the fifteenth century the Aragonese dynasty in Naples was ruled by Ferrante, the illegitimate son of the founder. His mother was either a Spanish lady or a half-caste Moor from Valencia—no one was sure which. His own son, as a cardinal, played an important role in the tainted election of Pope Innocent VIII (1484); not to be outdone by the Aragonese faction, Lorenzo the Magnificent married his daughter to a son of the new pope.

Innocent VIII was the first pope to publicly acknowledge his bastard children. In another case, the succession to Naples was disputed between the son of a servant and the son of a lady of the royal household; in this case the latter was held to have preference by virtue of the higher social status of the mother. And Pope Alexander VI, the Spanish pope who issued the famous bulls supposedly allocating the unexplored world between Spain and Portugal, was the publicly acknowledged father of the infamous pair Cesare and Lucrezia Borgia, as well as of six other children.

Morison did make the point that it was an era in which such liaisons were the accepted thing, but he added that this acceptance did not extend to marrying the mistress. However, marriage in almost all of such cases would have involved bigamy, a matter that was frowned on by the church. Columbus's grandson Luis went first to jail and then into forced exile for marrying four women while not divorced from any of them.

There is no evidence that Columbus's Portuguese wife was dead at the time that he sired Hernando. The fact that both his first wife's sister and his mistress's kin were close to Columbus in later years indicates that whatever the arrangement, it was acceptable to all parties.

Morison contributed to a myth about an apothecary shop, a place frequented by Columbus's Florentin friends and a place where neighbors customarily met to talk. According to Morison, Columbus met there with "Diego Harana" and through him was introduced into the home where the young orphan Beatríz lived.[111] Wilford followed the Morison account, sometimes verbatim.[112] Such a shop did exist, and many Florentin friends of Columbus's did live on the same street, but the rest is unsupported speculation.

The Phillipses related as unconfirmed this story as it has been told by Morison and others. Although they did assume that Columbus was a widower at the time, they commented on his failure to marry Beatriz: "The reason is not clear, but we can assume it related to Columbus's lofty ambitions. Marriage to a low-born orphan would do nothing to enhance his prestige and surely would impede his search for noble status."[113] Fernández-Armesto avoided the speculation as to how the couple met while accepting the idea that there was no marriage because "her family connections, which included such lowly artisans as carpenters and butchers, were not what Columbus demanded in a potential wife."[114] Incidentally, this biographer added that "Columbus formally legitimated" Hernando. This claim is based solely on Columbus's statement, made in 1497 when naming a guardian for his children, that the guardian was to care for "Don Diego and Don Fernando Colon, his legitimate sons."[115] The document in which he established the entail for his estate and his two wills make it abundantly clear, however, that Hernando was never legally recognized.

Over the years many writers have tried to legitimate Columbus's relationship with Beatríz. The first attempt was by Andrés Morales, in an early-sixteenth-century manuscript history of Córdoba and its noble families. The author included the Aranas among the nobility, and he listed Columbus as married to Beatriz.[116] In 1626 a book by Pedro Simón made the same claim.[117] In the nineteenth century, the story was taken up by French historians who were active in promoting the canonization of Columbus and who felt that an illicit relationship would hinder chances for approval. In 1938 a Franciscan friar conducted a study in which he set out to reinterpret Las

Casas's remark that Hernando was a "hijo natural."[118] Apparently it has not occurred to the modern-day biographers studied here that in those days, just as today, many people simply did not feel that marriage was necessarily an adjunct to paternity.

There are sufficient facts to provide an outline for Columbus's prediscovery life. He left Portugal dissatisfied with the king's consideration of his project, the exact nature of which is as yet unknowable. He first came to Spain accompanied by his young son Diego, probably by sea, sometime between late 1485 and mid-1486. They landed in either Palos or Seville, possibly seeking his sister-in-law in either Huelva or Seville. It is highly improbable that they went to the friary at La Rábida at that time. After his arrival he first sought the aid of the duke of Medina-Sidonia and then of the count of Medina Celi, who did seriously consider his project. Through the latter he was summoned to court and met with the Spanish monarchs in Córdoba in the early part of 1487. Hearings by the so-called Junta de Salamanca for his proposal to seek lands in the western Atlantic were ordered. The members met but reached no conclusion. Many of them considered his proposal impractical, but he did gain supporters among people close to the Crown: Quintanilla, Mendoza, Maldonado Talavera, Deza, Cabrero, and at some indeterminable point, friars named Juan Pérez and Antonio de Marchena. He rejoined the court at Málaga. At about this time he took up with a young woman in Córdoba. She gave him a son, Hernando.

Columbus probably met again with the monarchs in the next year at Baza, where his project was put on hold, and again, after an interlude, in 1491 at Santa Fé. There he was turned down. Impatient at so many years of procrastination and discouraged by what appeared to have been a final rejection of his proposal, he decided to pursue his dream in France. En route he stopped off at the friary at La Rábida, where he met with the friar Juan Pérez, who apparently had once served in some undeterminable capacity with Queen Isabel. The good friar convinced him that he should make one last appeal through Pérez to the queen. The result made history.

7
Preparations
for the
First Voyage

The life of Columbus is amply documented from the year 1491 until his death in 1506. He supplied much of the available information himself. There are also hundreds of court documents available for study, as well as accounts written by chroniclers, some of whom were witnesses to the events they recounted. Columbus's companions on some of his voyages, as well as his partners, left manuscripts that tell of their associations with him. The majority of these records have been available in print for almost two hundred years, thanks to the efforts of Juan Bautista Muñoz and Fernández de Navarrete. Historiographically, there is no justification for error in the treatment of substantive matters relating to Columbus in these last years of his life.

As noted earlier, no official record exists of the meetings of the so-called Talavera Commission. Some modern-day chroniclers agree with Morison, who noted, "Late in 1490 the Talavera commission issued an unfavourable report."[1] Hernando wrote that Columbus went to La Rábida to pick up his son, whom he had left there. Strangely, Hernando added that Columbus was willing to listen to Fray Juan Pérez's suggestion that he not leave Spain yet because "it

159

seemed to him that he was already a native of Spain . . . for having had sons there."[2]

The language used would normally indicate that the referred-to sons had been born in Spain. In the *Diario*, Columbus wrote that if he died at sea, he would leave sons who would become "orphans of father and mother"—a statement written at a time when Hernando's mother was very much alive. Las Casas, in his account of these same matters, did not give a date when he repeated "what people said": that Columbus left the court discontented and "went to the town of Palos with his son, *or* [emphasis added] to pick up his young son." Las Casas added here, "[This] is what I believe."[3] These reservations made by Las Casas rarely, if ever, appear in modern biographies. The claim that the boy was interned at the friary at La Rábida is based solely on the generally unreliable biographical data in the *Historie*.

Columbus at Santa Fé

There is confusion about the timing of Columbus's visits to Santa Fé, the siege camp in front of Granada. The queen was there sometime before her encampment burned down on July 14, 1491. Columbus said that he was there on January 2, 1492, the day Granada surrendered.[4] Hernando wrote this was the day that Columbus left Santa Fé for Palos.[5] In the interim—July 14, 1491, to January 2, 1492—Columbus may have been, at some undetermined time, in the queen's camp. He did not make it clear whether he was there for the first time in January or whether this was his second visit to the camp. It would appear, however, that he was there on his first visit.

Perhaps some light can be shed on the matter by working backward from the date of the signing of the agreement for his voyage—April 17, 1493. Initially, he left the court to go to Palos by way of Córdoba, met in Palos with Fray Juan Pérez, who sent Sebastián Rodríquez, a pilot from Lepe, with a letter to the queen. She replied in fourteen days, ordering Fray Pérez to come to court and Columbus to stay where he was until she wrote to him. The friar went by mule to Santa Fé. The queen then sent Columbus 20,000 marevedis so that he could "dress himself honestly and buy a mount so that he could appear before Her Highness."[6] He was recalled to Santa Fé, presented his case again, was rejected, departed, went back to Palos, was recalled once more, and then finally received his contract to explore.[7]

The first trip, from Santa Fé to Córdoba to Palos, was on foot, a matter of at least two weeks without accounting for any layover in Córdoba. Columbus would then have needed at least a couple of days of discussion to persuade Fray Pérez to assist him. Sending the letter to the queen and receiving the reply took at least another two weeks. Columbus and Pérez left for Santa Fé at different times; each would have needed a week for the trip. Thus, approximately six weeks are accounted for; the negotiations and conversations in Córdoba, Palos, and Santa Fé may have taken an equal amount of time. If these estimates are accurate, three months could have elapsed from the time of his first visit to Santa Fé until the signing of the *Capitulaciónes de Santa Fé* in April. These numbers indicate an initial rejection of Columbus's proposal after January 2, 1492.

As discussed earlier, some chroniclers still believe that Columbus, after being rejected at this time, appealed to the duke of Medina-Sidonia for backing. This claim is based on a highly qualified statement by Las Casas. After first presenting differing scenarios based on both Columbus's own testimony and that given in the *Pleitos*, Las Casas wrote, "If one makes out of all, one ... if the probability is able to harmonize [with the facts] or that, dismissed by the duke of Medina Sidonia, he left for Palos."[8] As has been noted before in this study, many of Las Casas's statements, ones that he so often hedged with reservations, have since been frequently cited as certainties. The above scenario would make a visit to the duke impossible at that time; there would simply not have been enough time between leaving Santa Fé and being recalled by the queen for Columbus to have had any meaningful meeting with the duke. The claim that Columbus next went to La Rábida to pick up his son has never been substantiated, nor does it fit into the scheme of events as we know them.

Morison wrote: "He waited almost another year.... The Royal Council reviewed [1491] the findings of a new commission ... it seems probable that the commission, reading the Queen's mind, recommended that Columbus be allowed to try, but the Council rejected it because of the price he asked."[9] This is simply unfounded speculation.

Wilford painted a somewhat different and more imaginative picture: "Columbus, his patience running out, was disheartened when, in 1491, he made another journey to La Rábida. He wanted to see his son Diego. He needed the comfort and advice of the friars. He found there a new ally, Juan de Pérez [this is perhaps the only place where the friar's name is given in this manner], who was a former confessor to the queen." Wilford dated Columbus's first visit in August, at which time "the proposal was again submitted to a committee for review . . . the proposal was rejected by the court. . . . For several months, through the surrender of Granada on January 2, 1492, Columbus remained with the court, entreating and negotiating."[10] The Phillipses followed this version, with minor differences; in their account, the first visit was in early fall 1491 instead of August, and Columbus arrived at La Rábida alone, without Diego.[11] Fernández-Armesto glossed over the preliminaries but did set two dates: first, summer 1491 for the arrival at La Rábida, and second, January 2 as the day that Columbus, discouraged, decided to finally head for France.[12]

The next question is, from whom did Columbus get help in Palos? Hernando, Fernández de Oviedo,[13] and Las Casas,[14] as well as witnesses in the *Pleitos*, all agreed that this person was a friar, Juan Pérez. The friar was identified by Garcí Hernández only as a Franciscan and former confessor of Queen Isabel. Others said he was the *guardian* (supervisor of the friary) and had been, in his youth, the queen's accountant.[15] Some modern writers have Pérez as an astrologer, although Garcí Hernández testified that the friar had sent for him because he, Garcí, was knowledgeable in astronomy.[16]

Finances for the First Voyage

Hernando, the first to write about the finances for the voyage, wrote that the queen, eager that the voyage go forward, offered to pawn the Crown jewels. According to Hernando, Luis Santángel intervened, offering instead to lend the necessary funds himself.[17] Antonio

Herrera y Tordesillas perpetuated this story.[18] In 1916 Francisco Martínez y Martínez carried out research in the archives of Seville and Aragón. He established that in 1492 the queen's jewels were already serving as surety for a loan taken out to finance the siege of Baza. He also reproduced a copy, from the Aragonese archives, of the repayment to Santángel.[19]

A seldom-noted fact is that although Santángel did arrange for the initial funding for the voyage, this was probably not before the April 17 signing of the *Capitulaciónes de Santa Fé*, yet the loan was repaid on the fifth of the following month. There are two references to this repayment in contemporary manuscripts, both of which are today in the state archives in Simancas.[20] One of these documents stipulates that repayment be made in two installments in May.

The manner of financing the first voyage is a perplexing one. There is no record as to the exact date on which Santángel made the funds available. Their provenance is also not clear; the repayment orders do not show whether the loans were from personal funds or from the treasury of the Santa Hermandad. They certainly would not have been needed before the April 17 signing of the *Capitulaciónes*. The negotiations with Columbus continued until April 30, when his agreement with the Crown was finalized. On this later day several *cédulas* and orders were issued for the provisioning of the three vessels that were to make the journey. Two of the vessels did not require immediate payment, since they were to be manned and supplied for two months by the town of Palos, and the third vessel had not yet been chartered. A later *cédula* ordered Palos to pay the sailors for four months in advance.

The most puzzling thing is that the money advanced by Santángel was listed as having been repaid on May 5, 1492.[21] What could have been the purpose for making the funds available for such a brief period of time, at the most from April 17 to May 5, what would today be termed bridge loan? Certainly the money was not used to pay for the vessels and crews, which were not contracted for until late May and early June. The first royal orders for providing materials and supplies for the voyage were not issued until April 30. This repayment of May 5 is listed in the accounts of the bishop of Palencia in Aragón (some have said that Diego de Deza was the alluded-to bishop, but he did not become bishop of Palencia until 1500). The loan was repaid with funds provided by Alonso de Cabezas, treasurer of the Cruzada, on orders of Hernando de Talavera, listed in the document as archbishop of Granada. The Cruzada was the organization charged with the recovery of the Spanish lands occupied by the Moors. Talavera was named to the see of Granada by a papal bull of January 23, 1493. The bishop of Palencia had earlier transmitted the orders to give a subsidy to Columbus on May 5 in 1487, at a time when Deza, not yet a bishop, was teaching theology at Salamanca.

Cabezas was the treasurer of the Crusada at Bajadoz, not of the Hermandad. Therefore it is not evident from this entry that the funds were necessarily provided by the Santa Hermandad, as has generally been claimed. In May 1492 he could not have been referred to as "Archbishop of Granada," for there was no such title at that time.[22] Las Casas said, "He [Deza] insisted often with the queen for her to accept the enterprise [of Columbus]."[23] Deza became bishop of Zamora in 1494, of Salamanca in 1497, of Palencia in 1500, and finally of Seville in 1504. He did not take over in Seville until 1505, although Juan de Fonseca had already been named as his replacement at Palencia.[24] Earlier he had been professor of theology at Salamanca, tutor of Prince Juan, and Grand Inquisitor and Chancellor of Seville.

Another indication of the time at which this notice of repayment was actually written is the use of the word "yndias." If we accept the notice as dating from May 1492, this would be the only known use of this word in any prediscovery document. This fact, taken together with the use of the title "Archbishop of Granada," justifies questioning the date of 1492, although one cannot discount the possibility that this was a copy made much later of an earlier journal entry.

A May 2, 1492, *cédula* also referred to this repayment.[25] It introduced a new name, Francisco Pinelo. He was listed as either colender or fellow official with Santángel in the Hermandad. Pinelo was Genoan. The reading of the order of repayment implies no position for him as co-treasurer. Thacher held that he was treasurer of that organization from 1491 to 1493 and was earlier supervisor of weights and measures for the city of Seville. Perhaps of greater interest are two later Pinelo connections with Columbus. On the second voyage he appeared as guarantor for the duke of Medina-Sidonia for the latter's share of the costs, and many years later when Columbus, ill, wanted to borrow Cardinal Pedro González de Mendoza's catafalque to take him to court, Pinelo put up the guarantee for its return.[26]

There is an order on the city of Seville in February 1492 to pay Melchior Maldonado (who accompanied Columbus on the second voyage) and Pinelo a per diem for their mission to court in regard to some customs duties that the city fathers apparently wanted changed. On other occasions Columbus appears in default on payment of money lent to him by a Bernardo Pinelo. Years later a Francisco Pinelo appeared as proxy in the affairs of Amerigo Vespucci.[27] Varela located him again as a partner with Florentin traders in the sugar business.[28] A "Pinelo" appears in an affair involving contraband slaves in 1485, and a Luco Pinelo, money changer, purchased a slave in 1506. In 1510 a Lorenzo Pinelo delivered to the court *guanin* (copper-gold alloy) from the Indies. Notably, all of the Pinelos appear to have been involved in financial matters but never as officials of the court. In the absence of evidence to the contrary, it is more likely that the name of Pinelo was linked with that of Santángel in the repayment order for the simple reason that Pinelo had been involved in the financing of the loan as an individual representing himself or, perhaps, partners such as Columbus's future agent Juanoto Berardi.

The amount first secured through Santángel was insufficient to cover the costs of the voyage. Twice Columbus referred to the insufficiency of the funds provided by the monarchs. The first time was in his "Memorandum of Complaints," addressed to the king and queen in 1501. He pointed out that at the time of the first voyage, "it was necessary for him [Columbus] to put half of the costs himself, because Your Highnesses didn't want to give for this project more than one *cuento*, and it was necessary for him to provide the half, because there was not enough."[29] The "half" refers to the fact that by the terms of the April 30 agreement, he was to put up one-eighth of the costs, which would have amounted to 250,000 marevedis, not 500,000. Columbus made a similar reference to these amounts of money in his will.

Chroniclers have long disagreed over who provided Columbus's half-*cuento*. It was obvious from the start that Columbus did not have the funds himself. There are strong indications that he either borrowed the money from his Italian friends or took some of them into partnership. Fray Antonio de Aspa offered the names of four of Columbus's compatriots, but there is no other evidence that he had direct dealings with any of these men.[30] Juanoto Berardi may have produced at least some of the funding. On his deathbed in 1495, Berardi wrote that he had been working with Columbus for three years and that the latter still owed him 180,000 marevedis.[31] It may be just a coincidence, but this is the amount that the charter of a caravel would have cost for two months, conceivably the payment for the *Santa María*. Vespucci was responsible for the collection of this debt.[32] The mere fact that Columbus owed a considerable sum of money to Berardi is not proof that this debt dated from the time of the preparations for the first voyage. It is, however, the nearest indicator in the record as to a possible source of funding for Columbus.

The cost of the voyage has been estimated at 2 million marevedis, based on Columbus's statement that by contributing 500,000 marevedis, he had paid double his one-eighth required if he was to share in one-eighth of the profits. All contemporary sources agree that the Crown put up 1 million marevedis. Another 140,000 marevedis listed in the Santángel repayment has been said to have been for a year's pay for Columbus as captain-general of the fleet; however, Césario Fernández Duro listed a like sum paid in 1492 to "pay for the caravels with which Columbus made the first voyage."[33] Some Spanish historians, Juan Manzano Manzano and Varela included, assumed that the remaining 360,000 was the value of the two caravels owed by the people of Palos, calculated at 3,000 maravedis per tun for two sixty-tun caravels. The custom was for prepayment of charters, and Columbus and the owners of the vessels obviously knew that his voyage would last longer than two months.

There is no information available as to how much Columbus paid Juan de la Cosa for the charter of his larger boat, the *Gallega*, renamed by Columbus the *Santa María*. These figures make no provision for crew and boats for the time at sea after the Paleños had complied with the two months owed to the Crown. Both Hernando and Las Casas believed, incorrectly, that the town's obligation was for three months. Hernando ignored the question of finance for the voyage. Las Casas listed the *cuento* of Santángel and the half-*cuento* of Columbus, which he said was provided by "Martín Alonso [Pinzón], either he or his brothers, a thing that is believable and close to the truth."[34] Herrera believed that it was Martín's brother Vicente Yáñez Pinzón who "put up the half a *cuento* for the eighth part of the costs."[35]

The *cédula* ordering the town of Palos to provide the two caravels read: "You well know that for some things done and committed by you in our disservice for which you were condemned by our Council and obligated to serve us for two months with two caravels readied at your expense." This *cédula* was issued in Granada on April 30, but Columbus did not present it to a town meeting in Palos until May 23.[36]

This *cédula* is obviously the source of early, and continuing, confusion: was Palos to supply two or three boats? Clearly the town owed the Crown the service of two boats for two months, but Columbus was scheduled to sail with three. Hernando was the first to confuse the two boats owed by Palos with the three authorized for the voyage. This was perhaps due to a later *cédula* that did state three vessels and mentioned a fourth one. Most recently, Varela believed the Paleño contribution was extended to three. The *Colección de documentos inéditos* and Fernández de Navarrete both give the following version: "the two caravels that by sentence you are obliged to make available."

There is much contemporary documentation on the financial aspect of the first voyage, most of it seemingly conflicting and none of it definitive. No one can say categorically how the state and Columbus raised their respective shares of the costs. The claim that Martín Alonso Pinzón supplied all or part of the required money was supported by the state in the *Pleitos*. In the absence of any firm evidence showing where Columbus found the funds, the Pinzóns, wealthy shipowners, are as good a guess as any other, with the possible exception of Juanoto Berardi.

Modern Versions of the Financing of the First Voyage

Morison had no doubts about how these financial matters were arranged:

> Isabella had proposed to raise the money on her crown jewels, but this was not necessary; the fable that she actually pawned them for Columbus dates from the seventeenth century. Santangel and Francisco Pinelo, who were joint treasurers of the Santa Hermandad, an efficient police force that had its own endowment, borrowed from the treasury 1,400,000 [*sic*] marevedies, which was eventually repaid by the crown. Columbus himself invested 250,000 marevedis in the enterprise, which he must have borrowed from his friends and supporters, such as Juanoto Berardi, or the Duke of Medina Celi. The balance was probably advanced by Santángel on his own account, or from the treasury of Aragon. This sum of two million marevedis did not include the payroll, which came to a quarter of a million monthly.[37]

Morison here makes an unsupported assumption in every sentence.

The story of the queen's jewels inspired Wilford to comment on this "endearing legend": "But there is some truthful basis to the story. With the royal treasury largely depleted, owing to the long campaign to re-conquer the land from the Moors, Isabel despaired of financing Columbus and suggested she might put up the crown jewels as collateral on a loan." He went on to discuss the roles played by Santángel and "Pinello," commenting, "The loan was eventually repaid." He found that the Columbus funding was "apparently borrowed from another Italian financier in Seville, the Florentine Berardi." This latter statement he based on Varela, whom he incorrectly quoted: "Berardi so overextended himself in backing the venture that he was driven to bankruptcy."[38] Varela gave a detailed explanation of the many business relations between Columbus and Berardi, beginning in 1492 and continued until Berardi's death in 1495. She concluded that he died impoverished due to losses sustained in his many ventures in the Indies.[39]

The Phillipses speculated: "Even though Palos proved very important for his enterprise, we are not sure why that particular town had been selected, rather than some other Andalusian port. . . . When some tuna fishers from Palos violated the royal prohibition on venturing south of Cape Bojador in 1491, the town's penalty was to pay for two caravels for the crown's use. Fernando and Isabel assigned those caravels to Columbus's expedition, making Palos a logical choice for the embarkation point."[40] This is a somewhat contradictory statement. They pointed out, correctly, that Palos was the only Andalusian port in which the Crown then held an interest; in this case Castile owned half the town, including the port. However, Isabel bought the half-interest in the town of Palos, including the port, in June 1492, paying 16 million maravedis for it. This is hardly an indication that Castile was unable to raise the 2 million marevedis for the voyage. This purchase took place a month after the town was ordered to provide the two vessels. The Phillipses also suggested, as have others, that the other southern ports were congested with vessels carrying the expelled Jews.

Fernández-Armesto offered a different perspective. Noting that Santángel "had acquired some financial responsibilities within the Kingdom of Castile, especially in managing the affairs of the local militias and in connection with the sale of indulgences . . . Santángel's importance for Columbus seems to have been in his role as a financial fixer, bringing together the sources of investment and means of raising cash." Farther along he noted, "The entire sum was advanced by Santángel and Pinelli [*sic*] against expectations from the sale of indulgences, and, in fact, it was all recovered in due course from the proceeds of sales in a poor diocese of Extremadura." He did not provide references for this assertion. In conclusion he wrote, "By January 1492 the financial obstacles to Columbus's departure—which in the final analysis, were the only obstacles that mattered—had disappeared."[41] Santángel was King Ferdinand's financial manager, not the Castilian queen's.

Sale relegated the whole matter to a footnote, in which he found the story of the jewels to be "pure fiction. . . . The main source of funds was rather Luis de Santangel, *escribano de ración* (in effect, treasurer of the royal household) for King Ferdinand . . . who may have put up some of his own money but was also responsible for securing a loan from the coffers of Santa Hermandad. . . . (The Santa Hermandad's primary banker seems to have been Abraham Senior [*sic*], a Jew, but its dealings with the crown were handled by

Santángel, a *converso*, and Francisco Pinelo, or Pinelli, a Genoese banker and friend of Colón's)."[42]

Abraham Seneor (Senior) was both a rabbi and Isabel's chief tax collector. He and Alonso de Cabrera (a converso) had been instrumental in arranging for the secret marriage of Ferdinand and Isabel, a marriage strongly opposed at the time by her brother King Enrique IV. Seneor was treasurer of the Hermandad and Ferdinand's chief source of funds. He was closely associated with Isaac Abravenal, a Jew who was repaid 1.5 million marevedis (which he had lent the Crown for the war with the Moors) in the previously discussed order of May 5 for repayment to Santángel. This is important because it establishes the repayment date as 1492, since Abravenal was expelled with the rest of the Jews later that year. The repayment of his loan at this time was perhaps connected with the effort made by the monarchs to persuade their two Jewish financial advisers to convert, thereby enabling the two to remain in Spain, like Santángel, Cabrera, and the numerous other conversos in their entourages. Seneor converted, but Abravenal led the exodus.

The "Edict of Expulsion" was issued on March 30. However, the Jews, led by Seneor and Abravenal, continued to negotiate with Ferdinand for payment of a tribute in lieu of expulsion. These negotiations were halted by Tomás de Torquemada, Isabel's childhood confessor. As J. Frances Amler has pointed out, after April 30, the day the expulsion was publicly promulgated, the monarchs did not need loans. In one town alone, the confiscations yielded 7 million marevedis.[43] All of the possessions of the estimated 300,000 Jews in Spain had been redistributed or expropriated within ninety days after April 30. This fact alone could account for the availability of funds to repay Santángel so soon after he had made the loan. By the same token, the large amount of money that the monarchs paid Boabdil (Sultan Muhammad XI) to surrender Granada, as well as the 24 million marevedis they paid for the repatriation of some of the Moors, derived from this seemingly inexhaustible source. By the time that Columbus set sail on August 3, money was not an immediate problem for Ferdinand and Isabel.

The First Documents in the Genesis of America

The enabling act for the first voyage, the *Capitulaciónes de Santa Fé*, was signed for the Spanish monarchs by Ferdinand's secretary Johan de Coloma on April 17, 1492. Each of its provisions carried the royal validation: "plaze a sus altezas" ("it pleases their highnesses"). A capitulation—section or chapter—can be defined as the chief written instrument of royal authority. This was the first document to deal explicitly with the operative phase of the discovery of the Americas.

Whereas the published version of the first letter remained the unquestioned discovery-related printed source until the recent finding of *El libro copiador*, the *Capitulaciónes de Santa Fé* was incontestably the prime document. Perhaps biographers and historians have given more attention to the two letters known collectively as the first letter because this source has been generally accepted as dealing with concrete and known matters, whereas the *Capitulaciónes* invokes questions of intent and motivation, issues difficult to resolve so many centuries after the fact. Yet the famous letter too is not immune from its fair share of as yet unresolved historical controversy.[44]

The *Capitulaciónes* consists of a preamble followed by five paragraphs in which the sovereigns acknowledged each of the provisions that had been previously agreed to by Coloma and by Columbus's representative, Fray Juan Pérez. The agreement detailed the object of Columbus's mission as well as the honors and awards, both Aragonese and Castilian, that would accrue to him if and when he should discover or occupy the islands and mainland described in the first paragraph as being located in the "mares Océanas" (Ocean Seas). Luis Arranz Marquéz described this document as "a contract in every principle of law, one that obliged both parties."[45] Francisco Morales Padrón, however, considered it to be "a simple unilateral letter of concession by their Highnesses to Cristóbal Colón, but not necessarily a contract."[46] He went on to say that although a capitulation might be considered a contract by a vassal, for the Crown it was only a promise of rewards for acts to be committed in the future.

The first *Capitulaciónes* was followed on April 30 by a royal letter of grant—*Real Carta merced*—which is by definition a royal concession, not an agreement between parties. This letter was confirmed in its provisions in 1493 after the Admiral's return from his successful voyage. Morales Padrón correctly pointed out that all the rights, including the hereditary ones ceded in this grant, were revocable. The first *Capitulaciónes* was initially confirmed at the request of Columbus on April 23, 1497, when he foresaw difficulties with the Spanish monarchs in the carrying out of what he perceived to be their contractual obligations to both him and his heirs. Disagreement over the meaning of the document began only a few years after the discovery, with the government insisting on a loosening of its legal bonds.

The perusal of these documents is essential to any study of the discovery, especially since the wording of the first document has been changed over the years in many of the transcriptions and translations made by different paleographers and historians. The preamble, the lead or introductory paragraph to the April 17 *Capitulaciónes*, is transcribed and translated as follows: "The things requested, and that Your Highnesses give and grant to Christobal Colon in satisfaction for what he has discovered in the mares Océanas and for the voyage that now, with the help of God, he is to make to them in the service of your Highnesses, are those that follow."[47] The succeeding paragraphs—the contractual paragraphs—designated the honors and other forms of compensation to be awarded to Columbus should he be successful in his search for these new lands. These paragraphs were written in the future tense. The first reads, "se descubriran o ganaran" ("that will be discovered or will be won"). This is sometimes given as "se descubrieren o ganaren" ("that would be discovered or would be won"). The later April 30 *merced* referred only to islands and mainlands that were to be discovered during his projected voyage.

In a strictly legal sense, there is no conflict in the wording of these documents; they can clearly be read so as to refer to distinct matters: the first defines what he is to do on this voyage; the second stipulates what will occur afterward. The April 17 document set out the political rewards, the manner of their determination, and the mercantile rules that would apply to the discovery or occupation of lands already discovered. The *merced* of April 30 added provisions for hereditary rights as well as mercantile provisions for lands expected to be attained for Spain on this voyage. It also omitted the important guideline that Columbus's future privileges should be equal to those of the Admiral of Castile. This second document looked more to the future than to the projected voyage of discovery.

Over the years, transcriptions of the perhaps key phrase have repeatedly been changed from "what he has discovered" to read instead "that he is to discover." In his *Crónica de los Reyes Católicos*, published circa 1550, Alonzo de Santa Cruz made the first published reference to these *Capitulaciónes*. He gave this perhaps critical paragraph as "lo que aves de descubrir" ("that you are to discover"). Las Casas used the phrase "lo que ha de descubrir ("that are to be discovered").[48] Since Las Casas had full access to the Columbus archives stored with the Carthusians in their monastery of Las Cuevas, it would be assumed that he worked from one of Columbus's own copies of these documents, both of which are known to have been inventoried as late as 1560 in the monastery library. These copies have since disappeared, although Francis G. Davenport stated that the copy in the Library of Congress is one of these originals.[49] Las Casas did not make a true copy if he did indeed use one of the copies in the monastery. This would not be the only instance in which Las Casas chose to edit or rewrite parts of the history of Columbus. Hernando offered only an extract of the April 30 *merced*, and even in this there is error: he ascribed to the Admiral a privilege that was not granted at that time.[50]

Fernández de Navarrete established the modern custom of transcribing this document incorrectly. He explained that he was working from "authentic testimony from the archive of His Excellency the Duke of Veragua."[51] He transcribed the *Capitulaciónes* correctly in his documentation; but in his text he changed the wording to have it conform to what he assumed must have been originally intended by its composers. He transcribed the wording in the key phrase in the preamble as "in satisfaction for what you are to discover in the mares Océanas."[52] This change in tense allowed the transcriber to avoid having to explain why the past tense was used in the first place. Demetrio Ramos Pérez suggested that Fernández de Navarrete never saw the Simancas copy himself but worked from a transcription made for him. Ramos is only one of those who have failed to note that this author provided both versions of the transcription. Washington Irving followed the practice established by Fernández de Navarrete, who used the future tense.[53]

The use of the past tense taken together with the rewards to be given "in satisfaction" indicates two rewards, one for lands already discovered and the second for lands to be discovered or occupied in the future. If Columbus really had foreknowledge, or even strong conviction, about the location of the lands that he was offering to find for Ferdinand, it is unlikely that he would have divulged this knowledge without assurance of compensation. As already noted, contemporaries repeatedly said that in the many fruitless preagreement meetings, he had withheld information "in order that he not be cheated."

In modern times some have found the whole question as to intent in the meaning of these words to be a matter of little or no consequence. Salvador de Madariaga dismissed the use of the past tense as being merely evidence of "a Quixotic idiosyncrasy" on the part of Columbus.[54] Morison likewise passed over the matter: "The past tense has aroused no end of conjecture; but as it did not trouble contemporaries it need not trouble us."[55]

The Wilford version—"grant to Don Cristóbal Colón as some recompense for what he is to discover in the Oceans"—is manifestly incorrect; in addition, with the use of "Oceans" instead of "mares Océanas," he ignored the specificity of the ocean referred to. In this same chapter he wrote, "The five articles of the agreement are written with extreme care in seemingly airtight legalese."[56] Wilford made no mention of the anomaly in the use of the past tense in the preamble, incorrectly given by him in the future tense.

The Phillipses showed the most interest in the rights granted to Columbus and in what they found to be the lack of mention of the objective of the voyage—for them, Asia. They simply did not mention the preamble, one way or the other. Fernández-Armesto indicated that there was an agreement prepared between the Crown and Columbus, but he gave neither date nor content. He did discuss the grants and titles: "[Columbus's] contract was recast in the form of a letter of privilege—a royal grant and therefore revocable—of 30 April 1492."[57] There is no listing for either "*Capitulaciónes*" or "Santa Fé" in the index to his work. Despite the fact that Sale gave six listings under "capitulations" in his index, he too omitted any mention of the preamble.[58] Were it not for the fact that these authors offered as references on other matters works that did discuss this anomaly at length, one could easily assume that they were unaware of the problems presented by the first capitulation.

Copies of the originals were known to those chroniclers who had access to the various codices prepared for Columbus, as well as later by those who had access to the evidence presented by the state and the Colón family in the court case known as the *Pleitos Colombinos*. Fernández de Oviedo mentioned the *Capitulaciónes* only as having been signed on April 18 (*sic*) and went on to say that on April 30, "he had the said capitulation confirmed by a royal grant—*privilegio*."[59] Columbus's friend Bernáldez did not mention either document. The general terms of the *merced* of April 30 became available, although with errors, to a wider public in 1571 with the publication of the *Historie*.[60]

The intense interest in the wording of the *Capitulaciónes* did not begin until 1823, with the publication, again in Italian, by Gio. Battista Spotorno of this and other correctly transcribed documents.[61] Morison's historically inexact comment is without merit; contemporaries could not have commented on a matter of which they were unaware. In 1893 Henry Harrisse and B. F. Stevens published a facsimile of the Paris Codex, with new transcriptions and English translations together with appropriate studies. Copies of the *Pleitos* documents were included in the *Raccolta* in 1894; however, the authoritative transcription of the *Pleitos* copy was published in 1950 edited by Federico Udina Martorell.[62] The Veragua Codex was first transcribed and published in modern Spanish by Ciriaco Pérez-Bustamante in 1951 under the auspices of the Spanish Royal Academy.[63]

Columbus attached a great deal of importance to the initial agreements with the Crown. In 1493 he began to collect notarized copies of these and related documents. Authorities on Columbus display a certain amount of confusion over these documents, as evidenced by the manner of their reporting on this stage of his discovery. A modern example is found in the eminent Argentinean historian Ricardo Levene's *Las indias no eran colonias.* He wrote of "the cited capitulation of Granada" and proceeded to give the preamble to the *carta merced* of April 30.[64] Morison referred to the *Capitulaciónes* as an "Articles of Agreement" (which it is not, at least in the sense of an agreement made between two parties) and to the *merced* as a "Title" or "Commission."[65] Such differences may seem insignificant, yet they have entirely different connotations from those of the the the actual Spanish words used.

Columbus may himself have contributed to the confusion over the legal nature of these two documents. He once listed the April 30 agreement as the prime document of the discovery, listing it as "the capitulation made before going to discover the Indies."[66] Even in his own copies of this particular document, it is not referred to as a "capitulation." Incidentally the word "Indies" does not appear anywhere in the 1492, 1493, or 1497 copies of these documents—a fact that interested Madariaga far more than the phrase "he has discovered." In 1493 Columbus may have been more concerned with the royal *merced* of April 30 than with his earlier *Capitulaciónes* for the simple reason that it was in the former document that the lifetime titles of governor and viceroy, provisionally granted to him on April 17, were transformed into hereditary ones.

The only known copy of the original *Capitulaciónes* retained by either of the Spanish monarchies was made for the Chancellery of Aragón and is today in the Crown archives in Barcelona.[67] There is no evidence today as to whether or not a copy was made for Castile, although according to the custom of the times, we can safely assume that such a copy was made.

Various copies, dated 1511, of the *Capitulaciónes* and the *merced* are in the files for the *Pleitos.* The copy of the April 30 document is listed in these *Pleitos* files as "a privilege conceded by the Kings . . . in which is included the royal letter of *merced* dated at Granada April 30, 1492 and its confirmation in Barcelona on May 28, 1493. [Prepared at] Burgos, April 23, 1497." This is tacit acknowledgment of the fact that the April 30 document was in the nature of a *merced* and not a *capitulación*. These *Pleitos* copies have the singular advantage of having been accepted by both Columbus's heirs and the court as being authentic copies of these contracts or concessions, their true legal nature in each instance depending on the point of view of the individual litigant.

Significantly, in all of the copies of the first capitulation that are found in the above-noted Columbian codices, the preamble incorporates the phrase "that you have discovered." This is important because, as has been noted, many early and some modern-day historians have quoted from these same documents, inaccurately placing the reference to the discovery in the future. There can be no question as to wording—the only legitimate question concerns meaning.

The problem with this capitulation lies in finding an acceptable explanation for this use of the past tense in the preamble. Just how did the Spanish monarchs and Columbus understand these words, or perhaps more important, what was their intent in this use of the past tense? The wording may have come from Columbus or his representative, Fray Juan Pérez, since the preamble begins by saying, "The things requested . . ." The simplest explanation, and the one apparently adopted by Santa Cruz, by Las Casas, and more recently by Fernández de Navarrete, was that rather than being intentional, the change in tense was simply a copyist's error. Most modern paleographers find this explanation to be totally unacceptable. In fact, the chancelleries of that era are said to have been very painstaking in their efforts.

The first capitulation is the cornerstone on which the foundation for the projected voyage of discovery of the Americas was built. Thus it is not unreasonable to judge historians by the manner in which they deal with its genesis. The opening up of the New World cannot be discussed logically while evading the existence, and possible inner meanings, of anomalies in the very document that made possible its discovery by Columbus for Spain in 1492.

One theory that would explain the wording has already been suggested: a copyist's error. Another relatively simple explanation is that Fernández de Navarrete and others who based their hypotheses on the phrase "that will be discovered or occupied" took this phrase as it appears in the second paragraph of the manuscript, in which case they either could have been unaware of or could have chosen to ignore the lead paragraph, which clearly states, ". . . that you have discovered."

It has also been suggested that those accepting only the version with the future tense based their options on copies of the document of April 30. This position would seem to fall apart before the fact that some of these same historians categorically state that they worked from copies of the April 17 *Capitulaciónes*, in some cases even naming their source for the specific copy, for example, the Veragua Codex or the Aragón manuscript.

There are other explanations, some of them ingenious, such as the one that proposes a proper application of semantics in the use of the word "discover," understood in the modern legal sense of "bringing to light a known or surmised fact."[68] Such a fact could, by inference, be the knowledge imparted by the "unknown sailor," the descriptions given by Marco Polo, the conjectures made by Greek and Roman writers as to the existence of islands and lands to the west of the Pillars of Hercules (Gibraltar), the idea that the world is demonstrably of a global shape, and almost as many other surmises as there are writers on the subject.

According to one school of thought, this seemingly careless use of tenses was in reality part of a purposeful plan of disinformation intended to permit the king, in case the mission failed, to say that he had been deceived by one who had claimed to know the exact location of these lands.[69] Another suggestion is that the king accepted Columbus's assurance that he had already discovered these lands; therefore, this wording was precautionary in case the king should have to defend himself later against any possible Portuguese counterclaim based on that nation's earlier papal concessions of rights of discovery in African waters.[70] The truth of the matter is that there is insufficient information available today to fully explain this enigmatic use of tense in such a vital document.

Meaning in the *Capitulaciónes*

Lewis Hanke asserted that this agreement was reached only after the monarchs "consulted the most eminent jurists and ecclesiastics of

Spain as to the most convenient means for taking possession."[71] There is no question that the Spanish monarchs did have the matter of possession studied exhaustively; the only question is whether this was also done before or after the discovery or, perhaps, at both times. If this matter was considered before the discovery, one may assume that the language used in this initial authorization to Columbus had been carefully worked out so as to protect the best interests of the state.

After the first voyage, the Spanish monarchs gave serious attention to the legal basis on which to base their rights to these new lands. This aspect of the opening of the Americas has been fully documented and studied, perhaps more so than any other single legal matter in Spain's long history. The question was also publicly debated in the celebrated Las Casas-Sepúlveda debates.[72] Sixteenth-through eighteenth-century jurists, ecclesiastics, and chroniclers such as Las Casas, Francisco de Vitoria,[73] Fray Pedro de Córdoba,[74] and López de Palacios Rubios[75] wrote on the subject. Las Casas maintained, "No State, nor king, nor emperor can alienate territories, nor change their political order without the express consent of its inhabitants."[76]

Any title to newly found lands had to depend initially on legally recognized rights such as the one cited by Juan de Solórzano Pereira as the first justification (of nine offered) for Spain's title to the Indies: the discovery and the occupation.[77] These provisions can be traced back to Roman Justinian law current in Spain in the Middle Ages as well as to Germanic law introduced by the Visigoths.[78]

The wording in the *Capitulaciónes* invoked one new concept as far as Spain was concerned, one in which the Spanish kings are seen as "rulers of the said mares Océanas," a claim that hitherto had been implicitly reserved to the kings of Portugal and had been so understood in the Treaty of Alcaçovas-Toledo signed in 1479. In this treaty, Portuguese rights of occupation and discovery in the *mares africanos* (African seas) were recognized, whereas those of the Kingdom of Castile were limited to the territorial claims on the Canary Islands, already discovered and to be discovered, with no mention made of the seas in which they lay.[79]

Differing interpretations have been given to the wording found in two *cédulas*, dated May and November 1477. At that time the Crown was giving instructions regarding an evangelizing mission ordered by Pope Sixtus IV for "conversion of the infidels that are in the parts of the Canaries and Africa and in all of the mar Oceano." Manzano found that this can be read to mean that the mar Oceano is independent of Africa and the Canary Islands and that, at least at this time, the Spanish monarchs were not claiming it for their own.[80]

The use of this expression in the 1492 document is particularly puzzling because Spain had previously maintained, in its disputes with Portugal over discoveries, that the seas were "free seas" and that title to lands in them could be acquired only by both discovery and possession. The Spanish monarchs, by their own terms at the time of the signing of the *Capitulaciónes* with Columbus, had not yet fulfilled these requisites, yet the sovereigns claimed them in this document. To be consistent, they would have had to have known about the islands "that you have discovered." The Spanish sovereigns further expressed this legal concept in their argument with João II over Columbus's discoveries, when they instructed their ambassadors to remind the Portuguese king: "As he well knows, his predecessors had no other right to possess and hold as theirs that which he now has and possesses and tries to discover, except by having been the first to discover in those parts."[81]

The second of the anomalies to be found in the *Capitulaciónes*, and one that has not been generally commented on, is that the preamble is distinct from the terms of the agreement that followed in that the opening paragraph in which it appears is not signed by Coloma, Ferdinand's secretary, whereas each of the five paragraphs is so signed. This clearly indicates that the materials dealt with in the five following paragraphs are based on the conditions established by the first. The use of the past tense in the preamble should therefore establish the rationale for the remaining paragraphs in the document. It is in this preamble that, for the first time, the Spanish monarchs assert their previously unclaimed rights in the "mares Océanas." As Manzano pointed out, the Spanish monarchs did not in this particular case, as was customary in those days, first seek pontifical authorization for the projected voyage.[82] This may have been because, under the terms of the Treaty of Alcáçovas-Toledo and confirmed in the papal bull *Aeterni Regis*, any lands in the "mares

Océanas" could be construed as lying within the jurisdiction of the Portuguese *mares africanos*.

It may be significant that by naming Columbus "Admiral" of all the lands and islands "in the said mares Oceánas," the Spanish monarchs were assigning to him a specific geographical area. Those parts of the ocean around the Canary Islands belonging to Castile already had their admiral (King Ferdinand's cousin Fadrique Enríquez); Columbus's rights were even modeled on his. There could not have been any question in the minds of the monarchs as to the separation of the Atlantic into three distinct parts.

After the discovery, the Spanish monarchs promptly shifted their claim to legitimacy from rights of discovery and occupation to a right founded also on papal donation.[83] In 1493 the four Alexandrian Bulls were issued by the Spanish pope,[84] apparently to aid the sovereigns in their intent to pin down their rights as opposed to those of Portugal. However, in a 1504 codicil to her will, Queen Isabel said that her only reason for asking for the first bull of 1493 was for the propagation of the faith.[85] She always strongly resisted papal interference in the temporal affairs of her kingdom.

These papal allocations in the New World were later taken by the Crown to supersede any earlier agreement made with the Discoverer. It was maintained in the *Pleitos* that Columbus could not claim right by discovery over divine right. These bulls obviously served for mixed purposes of state. The views of other European maritime nations were the same as Spain's when it came to questions of the temporal authority of the pope. Henry VII of England sent John Cabot in 1497 to discover the mainland of North America, an area excluded by papal bull to all nations except Spain.

The question as to the respective rights in the Atlantic of the two Iberian nations was finally settled with the establishment of the Line of Demarcation as set out in 1494 in the Treaty of Tordesillas.[86] In practice, this turned out to be an informal settlement, their respective rights being recognized in those areas that each had discovered. This bilateral treaty was not dependent on the earlier papal bulls, so it can be assumed that this reliance on a new pact between sovereign nations rather than on papal donation was based on what some Spanish commentators have referred to as the realities of the situation. In other words, occupation rights, in contrast to the need for evangelization, were now seen as purely pragmatic and, therefore, temporal matters. This treaty theoretically required, as did all treaties between Christian princes, papal confirmation, which in this case was finally extended by Pope Julius II in January 1513. By that time the concern of the signatory nations was no longer with the Indies but with the Spice Islands in the Pacific.

In Columbus's description—in the codicil to his will—of the Indies as being "as something of his own," Manzano read evidence of his belief that he had personally acquired a legal right over them, a *jus ad rem* (temporary legal jurisdiction).[87] Another opinion is that a discoverer who locates lands by dint of his own effort and ability acquires by that same act a preferential position in regard to future comers. Under this opinion, discovery alone gives only an imperfect title—a jus ad ocupacionem—one that must be completed by effective occupation. In the dream sequence in the *Lettera rarissima* version of Columbus's letter reporting on his fourth voyage, a voice tells Columbus: "The Indies, that are so rich a part of the world, I [God] gave you for your own, you distributed them as it pleased you, and I gave you the power to do so."[88] This misguided sense of divine grant, however arrived at, was the source for many of his post-discovery problems with the Catholic Kings.

Use of the Conjunction "Or"

There is a third anomaly, found in the manner of phrasing in the second paragraph (and repeated in the third and fourth paragraphs), which reads, "se descubriran o ganaran." It is a simple matter to translate this phrase with its clear meaning, which is, "that are to be discovered or gained (won)." However, with the use of the conjunction "o" ("or") instead of "y" ("and"), interesting possibilities arise, specifically those of prior knowledge and/or prior discovery. Here the phrase "as the Lords they are of the said mares Oceánas" is reiterated, possibly to place emphasis on their self-assumed jurisdictional rights. Although Las Casas changed the tense in the preamble, he correctly copied the first paragraph, where it said that

Columbus would be rewarded for "what he discovers or gains."[89] Most U.S. historians have avoided the matter by following the precedent set in the *Pleitos* and later by Herrera: the conjunction "or" was simply transformed into "and," a more readily understandable conjunction in this context.[90]

The dangers inherent in such silent emendation can be seen in two works published in 1993. José Rabasa, in his *Inventing America*, wrote of the "Admiral of the Ocean Sea and a viceroy of all territories that he would discover *and* [emphasis added] gain for the crown."[91] Stephen Greenblatt wrote in his *Marvelous Possessions*:

> At the same time, the grant that Columbus received from Ferdinand and Isabella speaks of Columbus as "going by our command with certain vessels of ours and with our subject, to discover *and* [emphasis added] to gain certain islands and mainland in the Ocean Sea." This language—"descobrir *é* [emphasis added] ganar"—suggests something more than a diplomatic or commercial voyage, but neither the sailors nor the ships of the first expedition were appropriate for a serious military campaign, so that it is difficult to envisage what kind of "gaining" the monarchs had in mind but I propose that we look carefully at the action Columbus reports and that we consider the extraordinary extent to which the action is *discursive.*[92]

Regardless of the import that these misquotes had for their theses, both of these authors start from false premises. It is not difficult to envisage the kind of "gaining" if one accepts either of two alternative solutions to the enigma: either prior discovery or a plan to reach the outer extremities of the East, the "innumerable islands" reported since antiquity but never visited.

In this particular document, Ferdinand and Isabel appear to be authorizing Columbus to seek out "lo que ha descubierto" ("that which you have discovered") in "our mares Océanas" ("our Ocean seas"). When he returned they would reward him with the stated honors if he had found any new lands **or** had conquered the ones already known. Normally speaking, for precise meaning in a legal document of this nature, the phrase used would be expected to read "that you discover and conquer," meaning, "It will not be sufficient that you find these lands; you must also attain them for the Crown." Pérez-Bustamante, in his edition of the *Libro de los privilegios*, changed the sense of the phrase to read, "As the Sovereigns that they are of the said mares Océanas . . . they send Christobal Colón to discover *and* [emphasis added] occupy . . . islands and mainlands in the said mares Océanas."[93] This was silent emendation similar to that made by Fernández de Navarrete and others in the preamble when they changed "you have discovered" to "you are to discover." This change from "or" to "and" would be understandable if the lands had not yet been known or discovered; under such circumstances, Columbus could not have been expected to conquer them if they had not yet been discovered. It is therefore a simple matter to avoid controversy by simply substituting the conjunction "and" for "or," thereby giving readily understandable meaning to the phrase. However, the opposite is equally true. If the lands were already known or had already been discovered, they must now necessarily be occupied or conquered in order for them to belong to Spain.

Morison gave the conjunction "or" in his translation of the document as it appears in the *Capitulaciónes* but failed to address any possible problems arising from its use. In a later work, however, he wrote that Columbus's mission was "to discover *and* [emphasis added] acquire certain islands and mainlands in the ocean sea."[94] Wilford used the phrase correctly without comment. Sale, however, first stated, "The royal order to this little fleet was to 'discover and acquire all the new lands it was to come upon.'"[95] Later, he expanded on the subject: "All that is said [in the *Capitulaciónes*], and it is said no fewer than nine times, is that Colón was authorized to 'discover and acquire' certain 'Islands and Mainlands' in the Ocean Sea. That reference to 'discover and acquire' is also troubling, since it would be hard to imagine the Sovereigns sending Colón to discover and occupy what was already owned by the sovereign power of the Grand Khan or some other Eastern potentate."[96] The Phillipses and Fernández-Armesto were more cautious; they simply ignored the April 17 capitulation entirely. Spanish scholars have given a very great deal of attention to this basic document.

If, perchance, the contracting parties already knew (as a growing number of historians believe)[97] of the existence of some of the islands being sought, it would have been to the point to add the cautionary "or conquer." In other words, this could be extended to mean, "Find new ones if you can but acquire (gain, conquer, settle) any lands that are already known (by you/us) to exist."

It is strange that in the many works that have been written in attempts to demonstrate a prior discovery, this particular use of a conjunction has not been the subject of comment. Perhaps even stranger, this conjunction is inappropriate or misplaced in any other reading of the phrase; therefore, it should necessarily have drawn the attention of paleographers and historians alike.

The *Capitulaciónes* and Prior Discovery

Thus it can be postulated that there are three clear indications of, or possible references to, prior discovery in the *Capitulaciónes*. This raises the question of intent. There have been numerous attempts to rationalize the "you have discovered" phrase; the matter of title to the mares Océanas has been widely studied; but no such recognition has been given to the need for study of the use of the phrase "or occupy" rather than the seemingly more appropriate "and occupy" in this same document.

Some chroniclers believe that sailors, not excluding Columbus and possibly including either Sánchez of Huelva[98] or the "unknown pilot" first reported by Aspa in 1514 (and first noted in a published account in 1535 by Fernández de Oviedo),[99] may actually have crossed the Atlantic and reached the West Indies. Consequently, the king may have felt it necessary to put evidence, in writing, that his people had already acquired rights by first discovery. The monarchs now needed only to validate their claim by occupation in order to effectively counter any possible future Portuguese claims.[100]

Consideration should also be given to the evidence presented in the *Pleitos Colombinos*. Sailors who had gone on the first voyage, as well as citizens of Palos and nearby villages, gave both direct and hearsay evidence. Some historians have been reluctant to rely on these court documents, which can be said to primarily reflect the views of the parties at interest. Whatever the merits of this cautious approach, some items reflect directly on the questions raised above.

New transcriptions of the *Pleitos* were edited by Antonio Muro Orejón, Florentino Pérez-Embid, and Francisco Morales Padrón in

1964 and 1967. One volume covers the period up until the time of the sentence of Seville in 1511, and another provides copies of the documents presented in the final appeal heard in Dueñas over the years 1534–36. In both volumes, certified copies of relevant documents were presented; however, they did not always coincide in their wording. For example, in the 1511 copies of the *Capitulaciónes*, the phrase in the second paragraph that should read "will be discovered or occupied" is given correctly in the copy submitted in evidence by the Colóns; but the interpretation given by the Crown's attorney was that Columbus was to be rewarded for islands and lands that he might "gain and hold for the service of their Highnesses." The Crown's copy of the *merced* of Toledo granted to Columbus referred to the "lands of the infidels that are acquired and won." The certified copy presented by the Crown in 1535 referred first to the islands "that you have discovered," but the phrase in the second paragraph is given incorrectly as "that will be discovered and won."[101] It was also given this way in the copy, submitted by the Crown, of the April 23, 1497, first confirmation of the original capitulation.[102] The copy in the archives of the House of Alba uses the past tense, as in the original, and also the conjunction "or" correctly.[103]

The witnesses in these hearings were presented with a list of questions that each had to answer. One of the Crown's questions, after first asserting that both the voyage and the discovery were works of Martín Alonso Pinzón rather than of the "usurper" Columbus, asked each witness if he knew that "for what the said Admiral did he won the said islands and there died many of the kindred and friends of the said Martin Alonso in order to take title to the land." This would indicate that the witnesses were being asked to state that the purpose for the settlement at Navidad, on Española, was to *enseñorear la tierra*, which is defined as "make oneself seigneur of the land." The witnesses' answers were all in the affirmative. It may be significant that no allusion was made to the claim that settlement was established only due to the sinking of the *Santa María*. Thus the *Pleitos* contains abundant evidence that the Crown relied heavily on concrete proof of occupation of the discovered lands.

Interestingly, in 1534 the reply to Luis Colón's appeal introduced another new interpretation, one in which the Crown's attorney alleged, "In the capitulation that your Highness made with him it is admitted in the first paragraph that the said ocean seas belonged to your Highness and as such could not be alienated." The word used here was *enagenar*, defined as "to pass ownership to another." Here the state took the position that Columbus had acknowledged, in the preamble to the *Capitulaciónes*, that he was sailing in the kingdom's territorial waters; therefore, any lands found therein were legally inalienable parts of the kingdom. This raises the intriguing possibility that the prologue was intended from the start to counter any future claims that might be made not only by Portugal but even by Columbus himself.

The Crown's position in 1534 raised a complex legal question as to the rights of the monarchs of Castile and Aragón (their laws were quite different concerning such matters) to transfer Crown prerogatives to individuals. The point is that the Crown had no legal right to delegate in Columbus either the administrative or the legal jurisdiction over these Crown lands as provided for in the *Capitulaciónes*. Harrisse explained:

> Especially by the law of the Ordinance of Alcalá, . . . if the King makes the grant in favor of one of his subjects and vassals, and a denizen in his kingdom, then the grant is valid to the full extent of the wording of the charter or privilege; but if the grant or alienation, be made in favour of one who is neither a subject or denizen of the realm, or an alien, in such case the donation or alienation is not valid, and ought not to be observed. Consequently, as the said Don Christopher Columbus was a foreigner and not a native or denizen, and besides possesses no domicile in the kingdom, according to the terms of said law, this grant, although made to him and his heirs for ever, is not valid, and should not be observed.[104]

More recently Pérez-Bustamante addressed the problem, noting that the Cortes of 1480 declared that all public offices charged with the administration of justice and governance of a town or province were inalienable from the Crown regardless of any royal concessions to the contrary. He went on to point out that even supposing that the Crown could make such concessions, they were even more strongly prohibited by the ban against such concessions being given to foreigners.[105] The extract of the April 30 *merced* (described erroneously

in the *Historie* as a *capitulación*) claimed, "The positions of administration and justice in the said islands and mainland were provided
absolutely or removed according to his [Columbus's] arbitrary
wishes."[106]

This is also the only circumstance in the Crown's evidence in
which the mares Océanas are referred to as being in the Crown's
domain. In the *Pleitos* copy of the confirmation of Columbus's awards
dated November 1493, references were restricted to noting that he
was sent to "the Indies that are in the Mar Oçeano to discover the
islands and mainland that has been discovered in the said Mar
Oçeano." It is notable that so soon after the discovery, they refrained
from alluding to "our *Mares Oçeanas*." The Catholic monarchs'
claims to the newly found lands from this time onward were based
less on territorial rights by discovery than on a combination of what
were seen as the morally and legally defensible rights acquired by
discovery, occupation, papal donation, and evangelization.

These are some of the possible indications as to what both the
Crown representatives and Columbus's representatives meant to say
in the wording for the *Capitulaciónes*. There remains the nagging
question concerning Columbus's apparent certainty of what he
would find on his first voyage, as well as concerning the importance
that both the monarchs and he attached to the need to occupy. On
this voyage he first discovered Cuba, an island larger than Española,
and he even believed for a long time that it was the mainland.
Presumably this mainland, the imagined land of the Gran Khan,
was more important to this venture than unknown islands. Yet, both
Columbus and Martín Alonso Pinzón pressed on separately to
Española, where they both believed, correctly, that they would find
gold.

The anomalies referred to provide only inconclusive suggestions of
prior discovery; but they do strongly indicate that consideration had
been given to conceptions of islands expected to be found in the
Western Atlantic. Columbus proved himself to be notoriously inaccurate in his estimates of the distance between Europe and Asia; but
he was surprisingly close in his estimation of the distance to the
West Indies islands that he did discover. These are among the many
puzzling questions raised regarding the discovery of the Americas.

In the particular case of the *Capitulaciónes de Santa Fé*, interpretations of the given facts can vary. The solutions to these enigmas are not to be found in silent emendation or in the simple expedient of ignoring the historical record.

Preparations for the First Voyage

A flurry of activity began at the court once the voyage had been approved. On April 30 the citizens of Palos were ordered to provide two caravels for twelve months with the sailors to be paid for four months.[107] At the bottom of the copy of this order used by Fernández de Navarrete is a notation that on May 23, with Friar Juan Pérez present, Columbus delivered this letter to the town's mayor and councilmen. Pedro de Arana testified to this effect in the *Pleitos*.[108] This brings up the interesting point that Pedro de Arana, cousin of Columbus's mistress, was already involved with Columbus's project at this early stage, although his cousin Diego was the one who sailed on this particular voyage.

On this same date, all communities were advised of the imminent voyage and were ordered to cooperate by supplying lumber, carpenters, and supplies at reasonable prices.[109] A provision was issued delaying criminal hearings against any of Columbus's crew members until after their return. Three citizens of Palos took advantage of this inducement to sign up for the voyage. Another order exempted Columbus from payment of export duties on all materials required for this voyage.[110] A week later, on May 8, any problem that Columbus may have had over what he should do with his son Diego was solved when the queen named the boy a page to Prince Juan.[111]

Many years later, the claims were advanced that Martín Alonso Pinzón had not only financed Columbus but was solely responsible for obtaining crews for the vessels and, more important, had originally suggested the project to Columbus. In the *Pleitos*, Martín's son testified that his father had obtained papers in Rome indicating the route to the west. He also testified that it was his father, not Fray Juan Pérez, who had arranged for Columbus's return to court after the first rejection. Las Casas repeated these allegations, classifying them as impertinent. He did, however, accept that Martín had been of assistance in signing up the crews.[112] Hernando passed over these events. Testimony given in the *Pleitos* indicated that Columbus had difficulty finding crews, either because the sailors did not believe in his project or simply because they did not know him; in addition, they mistrusted him because he was a foreigner.[113] According to a letter from Columbus in 1498, some of the crew members were paid in Barcelona after the return from the first voyage, whereas others were still owed their pay at the time of this letter.[114]

Columbus complained that the nao—a cargo vessel—on which he sailed was too large for the purpose of discovery; it could not get in close enough to the shoreline. In this regard he wrote in *El libro copiador*:

> These vessels, that I brought were very large and heavy for such a purpose [coastal exploration], especially the nao I brought; about which I was very fearful before leaving Castile; I would have wanted to take small caravels, more, as this was the first voyage and the people on it were afraid of running into high seas and uncertain about the voyage, and there were and had been so many obstacles, and anybody dared to contradict this route and put in it a thousand dangers without any reason that they could give me, they caused me to act against my will; and do everything that those who were to go with me wanted, and in order to make the voyage at once and find the land.[115]

From the above it is apparent that while in Palos, Columbus was fully conscious of opposition to his project and was accordingly anxious, even against his better judgment, to avoid any further local opposition in case it might jeopardize the voyage. In an earlier passage in this letter he commented, "[The Caribbean] is the sweetest [sea] in the world to navigate and with less danger for naos and navios [large cargo ships of the time] of all kinds; moreover, for discovering, the small caravels are better, because it is necessary [when] traveling along land and rivers, in order to discover a lot, to have [vessels] with little draft and that help themselves with oars [sweeps]."[116]

Over the years many scholars have attempted to determine how many men went on this famous voyage. There is no exact figure available today. All contemporaries—Hernando, Las Casas, and

Fernández de Oviedo (Bernáldez made no mention of the preparations for the trip)—agreed that Columbus had with him the three Pinzón brothers. Hernando wrote of "the three [vessels] being provided with all the necessary things, with ninety men."[117] Las Casas believed that the flagship carried "sailors and landsmen, because he took with him some retainers of the king who fancied going with him out of curiosity, and other retainers and people known to him, in all ninety men of the sea went."[118] The total number was obviously greater than ninety, since these figures were for sailors only. Fernández de Oviedo agreed with Las Casas that the sailors were all from Palos, although the records indicate that this was not so. He placed the total complement at 120,[119] as did Martire and Augustini Giustiniani.

A curious document, dated 1523, was written by Yosef ben Halevi, the Jew known in Spanish as Luis Torres. He was taken on the first voyage as interpreter. In 1523 he wrote in his diary: "My father was a scribe who was privileged to write a Torah scroll during his lifetime. I was also educated to be a scribe . . . I was fluent in the Hebrew language and therefore, I was invited to accompany Christopher Columbus as an interpreter on his voyage of discovery." He claimed that with him were seven other Jews, one of whom was Rodrigo de Triana, the first to sight land. These men also included Rodrigo Sánchez, the fleet comptroller, and two doctors, Birena and Marko.[120] Many years later Torres was given land in Cuba by the king as a reward for having sailed with the first ships to discover America. Gil, without explanation, indicated in his index that Torres had died in 1494.[121] The matter of this and the other Jews on this voyage has not been dealt with by the historians critiqued in the present work.

Morison gave a fair and accurate account of the dispute over Pinzón's real or imagined role in the conception of and preparation for the voyage. However, he accepted the incorrect figure of ninety as being the total complement of the three vessels, not just the number of sailors. Wilford quite properly pointed out that Alice Bache Gould contributed more than any other writer to clarifying this issue. She was able, after over two decades of research, to authenticate from contemporary records the names of 87 persons who definitely sailed on this voyage. At the time of her death she left an unpublished account, in which the total was brought up to 118. Wilford concluded, quite correctly, "Clearly, the true number remains unknown."[122]

The Phillipses believed Martín Alonso was in Rome at the time that Columbus first started signing up his crews. They accepted that he was eventually "the chief recruiter." They assigned to the *Santa María* 40 men (32 seamen, counting the Admiral); the *Niña*, 24 (21 seamen); and finally the *Pinta*, a crew of 26, all seamen. This gave a total complement of 90 for the three ships.[123] Sale also accepted the figure of 90.[124] Robert Fuson, however, stated the appropriate reservation, "Not only is the total count uncertain, but the roster for each ship within that count is indefinite."[125]

The beginning of this chapter pointed out that there is ample documentary evidence for substantive matters relating to Columbus's life from the time of the discovery on. Obviously, however, even though there is abundant information on minor details, much of it is conflicting. Important matters—such as Columbus's agreement with the Crown for the discovery voyage, the preparations made, the vessels selected, and the captains appointed—are among those items that have been incontestably established. The how and the why of most of these remain open to conjecture. Many writers on the subject find it difficult to accept the numerous incertitudes, finding it more satisfying to transform these into certitudes. Unfortunately, the events in the life of Columbus do not conform to a neat pattern.

The best witness is a written paper.
Carl Sandburg (1878–1967)

8
The
First
Voyage

The primary sources for the first voyage to the Americas are few but sufficient. Columbus maintained a daily log, his *Diario*. In the spring of 1493 he delivered the presumably original version to the monarchs in Barcelona. They made him a copy, which was retained by the family at least until 1554, when his grandson Luis was granted permission to publish it. For unknown reasons, Luis did not make use of this authorization. Both Colón and Las Casas had access to either the original or an as-yet-unidentified copy. Hernando provided a condensed version in the *Historie*. Las Casas first made a holographic copy, in which he intermingled direct quotations given in the first-person singular with his own paraphrases. He later used this copy as the basis for the extracts that he incorporated into his *Historia*. The early *chronistas*—Martire, Bernáldez, and Fernández de Oviedo—gleaned their information from some of Columbus's letters, from secondary sources, and from oral tradition. In addition, there is now available in *El libro copiador* a letter written by Columbus on this voyage.

The *Diario de Colón*

The *Diario* opens with a prologue in which the voyage is reviewed. This was written after the voyage, not before as would normally be inferred. Also, after the return, Columbus wrote two letters to two members of the Spanish court, Luis Santángel and Gabriel Sánchez, giving brief accounts of the successful voyage. The originals are no longer available, but the letters are known through contemporary published copies. Some scholars have suggested that these letters were composed at the Spanish court for propaganda purposes. Whereas the *Diario* was essentially a private record, in those days a state document, there was a clearly political purpose in the prompt publication of the letters. Through them, the world was notified of the discovery and at the same time indirectly apprised of the fact that these newly found lands now belonged to Spain. The publication of the letters was the first known use of the recently discovered printing press for the promulgation of political propaganda.

David Henige is foremost among those who have made detailed studies of the *Diario*, of its provenance as well as of some of its passages. He observed: "Las Casas's transcription of the diario stands outside any manuscript tradition, having no known predecessors and no other contemporaneous versions. Even so, we know that it had more than one textual ancestor and has had descendants in the form of various modern editions."[1] Later, he also noted, "Las Casas added numerous marginal notes but not a single word that could provide a clue as to the circumstances surrounding the creation of the diario's text."[2] In fact nothing can be known about an as yet unknown original text, or about the also as yet unknown copies made for the Crown and Columbus, or about what source text of the *Diario* Las Casas used for copying and paraphrasing. The result is what Henige aptly described as a hybrid text.

Henige assumed that Las Casas worked from one of the scribal copies: "We can assume that their work was calligraphically superior both to Columbus's shipboard log and to the diario." However, he went on to note: "Las Casas's own complaints about the frequently difficult handwriting that confronted him, interjected as obiter dicta into the diario, indicate that, whatever he used, it was not the first copy made, which must at least have been presentable in its penmanship." Would such a statement by Las Casas not equally well indicate that he may have been working from the original, a document probably written on a caravel tossed about on the open ocean?

Most of the published versions available today are emended, not diplomatic copies of the Lascasian holograph. As Henige pointed out, "Authorial intent is a protean and controversial concept, and it is not unusual for there to be many variants of a given text, from which editors must choose and then defend their choice."[3] Editors of this particular document tend to modify the text without presenting the requisite defense for the measures taken. This gives a false sense of a diplomatic text while at the same time denying the reader the opportunity to exercise the interpretative responsibility that such editors evidently consider their readers incapable of exercising. Is such unadvised textual transformation not only historiographically unethical but also deprecatory of the reader? Henige went on to observe: "Jenkinson did not exaggerate when she characterized silent emendation as an 'insidious vice' and a 'scholarly crime.' . . . Silent emendation is a pernicious form of arrogance on the part of editors who, in doing so, assume time and again that they know better than both their texts and their presumed audience."[3]

It is not part of the objective of this critique to analyze the available versions of the *Diario*. It is my opinion that the best version available today in English is the transcription by Oliver Dunn and James E. Kelley, Jr. However, since I do not always agree with the editors' translations, all English translations given in this study are my own. Carlos Sanz's edition of the *Diario* is useful for its easily readable facsimile of the Lascasian holograph, but it is seriously flawed in its *en face* Spanish transcription. Henige, who made a comparative textual study of the Sanz version, concluded: "[Sanz] took no steps to make the transcription resemble the holograph except incidentally. In comparing only the 220 lines that cover the three days at Guanahaní, we find between 1,200 and 1,500 differences, depending on how one counts."[5] This is silent emendation.

Morison, in the bibliography and notes for *The European Discovery of America: The Southern Voyages*, gave his evaluation of the Sanz translation: "For the unique *Diario* or Journal of the First Voyage there are many editions and translations, most of them bad. There is no further excuse for using these defective sources, since the distinguished Spanish historian and bibliographer Carlos Sanz has published a facsimile of Las Casas's original manuscript in the Biblioteca Nacional in Madrid, and also a printed edition following the ms. line by line, with the same title and a learned introduction."[6] Obviously Morison had not studied the Sanz edition. Robert H. Fuson shared in part in this faulty evaluation: "In 1962 Carlos Sanz published a truly innovative transcription that includes a facsimile of the original document, providing the opportunity to make a line-by-line comparison of the printed and manuscript versions."[7] This edition is indeed innovative, but inaccurate.

The Santángel/Sánchez Letters and *El libro copiador*

The most useful studies, in which the Santángel and Sánchez letters are treated as separate letters rather than two versions of one, are in Sanz's *La carta de Colón sobre el descubrimiento* and in his *Bibliografía general de la carta de Colón*. He also reproduced and expanded Harrisse's studies published in 1866 and 1872.[8] Efforts to determine the *editio princeps* of these two letters have caused heated disputes, resulting in innumerable monographs on the subject. Eminent historians and bibliographers such as Wilberforce Eames of the Lenox Library, Frank E. Robbins of the Clements Library, R. H. Major, a Keeper of the British Museum, the diplomatist Francisco Adolfo Varnhagen, the bibliophile Thacher, the Harvard historian Morison, and the Spanish scholar Demetrio Ramos Pérez are among the many who have written extensively on this subject.[9]

The two versions of the so-called first letter were first published in 1493. As long as they remained the only known copies of the first announcements of the discovery, they excited considerable interest among bibliographers and historians alike. In the first two decades after the discovery, some twenty editions were printed in five languages. For another decade, these were the sole published accounts of the first voyage.

Now, with the finding of *El libro copiador*, there is a new "first" account of the first voyage. In it are details not found in the other two letters; at the same time, not all the information in the first two letters is given in the third. This newly found letter may take precedence in point of time over the Santángel letter, dated February 15 with a codicil dated March 4, and over the Sánchez letter, dated March 14. The information given in the manuscript in *El libro copiador*, also dated March 4, must be compared with the relevant information in the *Diario* and in the letters to Santángel and Sánchez.

First, we should determine whether anything was known about the existence of any other letters written at this time by Columbus. Some historians felt that Columbus would have naturally written first to his sponsors, the Spanish king and queen. Others have excused the seeming lack of any such letter as a question of protocol; they assumed Columbus would not have addressed the sovereigns directly. This is certainly not true of either his letter in *El libro copiador* or his postdiscovery correspondence with his sovereigns. Incidentally, the first published Latin version of the Santángel letter refers only to the king; the Sánchez letter and the second Latin edition of the Santángel letter refer to both the king and the queen. Neither salutation appears in the body of the text of either of the letters.

In 1502 Columbus wrote a letter to Pope Alexander VI: "After I went on it [the voyage] and saw land [Portugal] I wrote to the King and Queen, my sovereigns."[10] Hernando wrote, "Entering the estuary of Lisbon, Monday, on the 4th of March, he anchored next to the Rastello, and very quickly sent a courier to the Catholic Kings, with news of his arrival."[11] In a codicil to the Santángel letter is the following notation: "This letter Colom sent to the *escrivano de ración*. It contained another for Their Majesties."[12]

There can be no doubt that Columbus sent from Portugal an account of his voyage, in a letter addressed to Ferdinand and Isabel. There are also contemporary references to another letter, sent from either Palos or Seville, in which Columbus made suggestions for a second voyage and for colonization of Española.[13] The monarchs replied on March 30, "We saw your letters, and we took great pleasure in knowing what you wrote in them."[14] One of the letters referred to has been surmised to be the letter from Palos or Seville. The second is assumed to be the missing letter to "my sovereigns."

In a letter dated March 9, Aníbal de Zennaro (sometimes given in the Latin form of Hanibal Januarius) reported the discovery to the duke of Ferrara in Milan. He wrote, "The said Columbus has made the trip back and has landed in Lisbon, and he wrote this to the king. . . . I believe that I will get a copy of the letter that was written, and will send it to you . . . and as I said, I have seen the letter."[15] This Zennaro letter has caused no end of problems; some claim that it would not have been possible for a courier to make the trip from Lisbon to Barcelona in five days; others accept the idea. It will be recalled that by March 19, Medina Celi was already informed about Columbus's return. If this news came to him from Palos, after Columbus's return there on March 15, it would have made the trip to the duke's home north of Madrid in an equally short time of four days; however, Madrid was nearer than Barcelona to both Lisbon and Palos.

The entry in the *Diario* for February 14, 1493, has been the subject of a great deal of speculation. It gives an account of a storm through which the *Niña* and the *Pinta* were passing. After much soul-searching to find the Lord's will in this matter, Columbus decided that due to the possibility that he and the *Niña* might be lost in the storm, he should write his sponsors. "So that the *reyes* [kings] would have notice of his voyage, he took a parchment and wrote on it all that he could about all that he had found, praying greatly that whoever found it, that he take it to the kings. This parchment he wrapped up in a well-tied and waxed cloth, and he ordered that a large wooden barrel be brought, and he put [the parchment] in it without anyone knowing what it was. Instead they believed that it was a prayer and that way he ordered it be thrown into the sea."[16]

The *Historie* told of the letter in the barrel thrown overboard and of a second one left in a barrel on the stern of the *Niña*.[17] Varela and others equated the letter written on the fourteenth with the published first letter that is dated February 15. Morison reported only the one, although he provided an imaginative account of its writing:

"So, in his cabin on that pitching and rolling vessel the Admiral got out vellum, quill and inkhorn, wrote a brief account of the voyage and his discoveries, wrapped the parchment in a waxed cloth, ordered it to be headed up in a great wooden barrel, and cast into the sea."[18]

Wilford followed Morison almost verbatim.[19] Varela believed that Columbus also wrote a letter to Medina Celi at this time and that, based on this letter, the duke wrote to the court about Columbus's return. Varela found that the duke's letter, dated March 19, would probably have been based on news that the duke received directly from Lisbon, where Columbus had made port on March 4, rather than from Palos, where he did not arrive until the fifteenth. Morison noted, "The duke must have received word from Lisbon, where Columbus arrived March 6."[20] However, Columbus anchored in the Tagus on the fourth, and according to the *Diario*, "then the Admiral wrote to the King of Portugal who was nine leagues from there."[21] Based on what we know about Columbus, it is safe to assume that he was in as great a hurry to notify the Spanish monarchs as João II of the success of his journey. The *Diario* entry for March 6 has Columbus still downriver from Lisbon: "It being known that the Admiral came from the Indies today so many people came from the city of Lisbon to see him and to see the Indians that it was a thing of wonderment."[22]

The Phillipses were more in accord with the *Diario*. They mentioned only the one letter in the barrel "dropped in the water off the Azores. . . . Once he had safely come to shore, his biographers tell us that he dispatched other letters from Lisbon. Presumably he sent one letter to Ferdinand and Isabel, but if so it has been lost, along with other letters that he may have written. . . . The only report available is the so-called letter to Luis de Santángel."[23] This last assertion is obviously a lapsus, since we have also known about the Sánchez letter for centuries.

In the postscript to the Santángel letter is a mention of the stormy weather encountered on the return trip: "The people here say that all of the men of the sea [say] that there never has been such a bad winter, nor so many losses of boats."[24] Morison engaged in a lengthy discussion of this storm, giving the daily movements of a cold front, changes in wind direction, and other conditions, all of which he worked out from the sparse details given in the *Diario*.[25] After a discussion of the storm on the fourteenth, Fernández-Armesto wrote, "In a letter apparently written aboard the ship the following day— but perhaps touched up by an editor with a view to publication— Columbus summed up his achievement."[26] Thus, for this biographer, Columbus wrote the Santángel letter "apparently" on the fifteenth. Sale wrote, "Before the weather turned bad, Colón started writing a summary letter to the Sovereigns to tell them of his great discoveries; he completed it off the Azores on February 15 and mailed it, probably from Lisbon on March 4."[27] This letter from Lisbon (Columbus did not arrive there until March 8), addressed to "the Sovereigns," is a reference to data taken from the Cosco Latin translation of the Santángel letter and not from the entry in the *Diario*.[28]

The question as to dates, February 14 or 15 for a first letter, depends entirely on which of the first letters known today is being cited. The *Diario* entry listed a letter written on February 14; Hernando listed two, an original and a copy. The modern-day biographers quoted above have assumed that the letter referred to in the *Diario* is the lost original of the Santángel letter, known today only through differing printed editions. The Sánchez letter is dated: "Lisbon, the day before the ides of March—March 14."[29]

In all the known versions of the Santángel letter, this Columbus letter is given as written on February 15, "aboard the caravel off the island of Canaria." To begin with, at this point on the return voyage, Columbus was off the Azores, far to the north of the Canaries. An explanation has been offered for this discrepancy: the court wanted the published version to reflect that he was in Spanish waters, not in the Azores of Portugal. *El libro copiador*'s first letter is headed "Mar de España" (Sea of Spain), which would presumably refer to the sea around the Canary Islands, not the Azores. This entry appears to negate the theory of the court's role in naming the location of the returning caravels at this time.

It seems inconceivable that Columbus would have written his letters to the court counselors on February 14 and waited until March 4 (*El libro copiador*) or March 14 (Sánchez letter) to write to the "Most Christian and very high and very powerful princes." It is not unlikely that Columbus summarized his journey on February 14 and sent extracts to court on March 4 and again on March 14. No mention is made in the contemporary literature of the Santángel and Sánchez letters arriving in Barcelona at different times. We can assume that they arrived together and were both dispatched from Portugal on March 14. On this basis, Medina-Celi and the monarchs would have received their letters on about March 19.

The first letter in *El libro copiador* raises many questions. The most important one is that of its authenticity. All nine letters have been accepted by Spanish scholars as scribal copies of genuine Columbus letters. U.S. scholars have yet to fully address the question. I accept as authentic all of the letters in *El libro copiador.* If the first letter in *El libro copiador* is indeed a copy of the missing letter so often referred to by contemporaries as having been written to the Spanish monarchs, then it may have been written before the Santángel and Sánchez letters and dated on the day that it was sent by courier to Spain. In that case, the Santángel/Sánchez letters would have been based on either extracts from the letter or independent résumés of the same information.

Another fact that must be taken into consideration when reading these letters is that those biographers who refer to a letter addressed to the king alone can be referring only to the first Plannck edition of the Cosco Latin translation of the Sánchez letter, the "Pictorial Edition."[30] The second Latin edition, or the Silber edition, is addressed to both monarchs—"the most invincible Ferdinand and Isabel."[31] The first and second Plannck editions were both published in 1493, the first in April and the second in May. For those interested in the possible priority of the first Spanish edition, available both in manuscript and in a published version by Pedro Posa, also in 1493, Sanz provided a facsimile with Spanish transcription and English translation.[32] Eames accepted this Posa or Barcelona edition as "probably the oldest edition extant."[33] Modern American biographers, citing only the Plannck or Cosco Latin editions, follow in the footsteps of their eminent predecessor Harrisse, who placed the April edition as the *editio princeps* of these letters. The May edition, with the double salutation, he placed fourth. Suffice it to say that even before the appearance of *El libro copiador*, Columbists widely disagreed as to when, where, and to whom Columbus wrote on arriving in Portugal.

Proposed Destination

The previous chapter addressed many of the details connected with the preparations for the first trip. It is the popular belief, accepted by most of the biographers under study, that Columbus set sail in quest of Cathay/India and the Gran Khan. According to them, he was given by the monarchs for this purpose letters of presentation and a safe-conduct.

The *Historie* did not mention letters given to Columbus, be they credentials or requests for free passage. In his *Historia*, Las Casas copied parts of Columbus's prologue to the *Diario* in which Columbus mentioned the Gran Khan, who was eager for information about Christianity. Farther along in the prologue Columbus wrote, "Your Highnesses ordered, that with a sufficient fleet, I go to the said parts of India." In a later passage Columbus noted that when he left the Canaries, he was en route to "take the embassy of your Highnesses to those princes."[34] In the *Diario* entry for October 21, Columbus reported, "Moreover I am still determined to go to the mainland and the city of Quinsay and to give the letters of Your Highnesses to the gran Can and ask for a reply and to come with it."[35] It must be noted *en passant* that Quinsay was a region, not a city. These references, taken together, provide a misleadingly clear description of his destination.

Bernáldez made no mention of the khan in his extensive excerpts from the Santángel letter. There is, however, a copy of a royal letter—dated April 17, 1492, and addressed to all heads of state and nobility—in which Ferdinand and Isabel announced that they had sent the "noble xpoforum [*sic*] colon with three armed caravels through the ocean sea toward the regions of India."[36] First of all, note that there is no mention in this official document of the Gran Khan. Second, Columbus's mission, as given in this letter, is not to India as might be inferred from his *Diario* prologue but to "the regions of India" (*ad partes Indie*). The phrase "regions of" does not necessarily imply a voyage to the mainland; "India" in this case meant Asia in the broad sense—the Far East as we know it today— not a specific country. In the letter of credence given to him at the same time as the safe-conduct for presentation to any heads of state or governors that he might encounter, the name of the addressee was left blank. The Santángel/Sánchez letters contain only one mention of the Gran Khan, in a reference to Española and the possibility of finding nearby the mainland of the khan.[37] There was no mention of the khan in *El libro copiador*'s first letter. This earliest documenta- tion, together with the evidence in the *Capitulaciónes*, does not sustain the theory that Columbus's primary mission was to go to the lands of the Gran Khan.

The claim that the credential was addressed to the Gran Khan originated with Las Casas, who wrote in his *Historia* that Columbus carried "letters of recommendation for the Grand Khan." This can be construed as more or less correct if one accepts that he meant that Columbus would write in the khan's name, if appropriate, in the blank space provided. Morison first reported the credential correctly in his *Admiral of the Ocean Sea* but unfortunately changed his mind in *The European Discovery of America*. He then wrote that Columbus had "three identical letters of introduction, one to the 'Grand Khan' (the Chinese emperor) and the other two with a blank space so that the proper title of any prince could be inserted."[38] By Columbus's time it was well known in Europe that the Mongols had been driven out of China and that the Gran Khan was no longer emperor.

Wilford accepted, without explanation, the Lascasian assertion: "He carried with him a letter from Ferdinand and Isabella to the Great Khan."[39] The Phillipses interpreted the above two references in the *Diario* prologue differently and added a new factor: "In the prologue to his diary of the first voyage, he mentioned the Great Khan as a possible ally."[40] Later they noted, "Among the documents Fernando and Isabel gave Columbus for the voyage, however, was a letter of introduction to the Great Khan."[41] Neither statement is in strict accord with the known facts.

Fernández-Armesto departed yet further from the documentation. He noted of the prologue, "At a superficial level, it proclaims the objective of reaching 'the lands of India and of a prince called Gran

Khan.'"⁴² The particular phrase apparently referred to reads quite differently, however: "Because of the information that I had given to Your Highnesses about the lands of India and about a prince who is called gran Can . . . you thought of sending me to the said regions of India."⁴³ Again, "regions of India" referred to Asia, and the khan was never linked with India in the travelers' tales but with Cathay (China). Sale did not go into this particular use of the term "Gran Khan," but he offered a thoughtful study of the intent in the use of this term as well as of India in the plans of Columbus and the sovereigns. The exact wording of the letter of credence did not require speculation by either contemporary or modern historians because copies of the original document were, and are, maintained in Spanish state archives.

Morison was the foremost American proponent of the theory that Columbus sailed with the intent of reaching India/Asia. Over the years others have questioned this assumption. The simplest, and perhaps most valid, objection is that neither the Spanish sovereigns nor Columbus was so naive as to believe that three caravels could take over the vast empire of China, the land of the Gran Khan. The trinkets that Columbus took with him on the first voyage could hardly have been expected to appeal to citizens of a country where "the roofs were paved with gold." All early mentions of India were in the context of evangelization, conversion to Christianity, yet as far as we know, there was no priest on the first voyage. For such purposes there would have been no need for the *Capitulaciónes* to instruct Columbus to "discover or acquire."

The eastern land route to Asia had been known for millennia; it is not conceivable that Ferdinand and Isabel intended to conquer these vast lands. In short, both logic and contemporary references make it highly doubtful that Columbus set out on August 3 to reach the eastern shores of Asia. If China was indeed the destination, all mention of it in Columbiana and state documents was soon dropped. The same was the case with Cipango/Japan. As already noted, even Columbus's references to Chinese cities and provinces in the *Diario* were scrambled. Practically all biographies go into this nebulous matter at length. The letter in *El libro copiador*, written "in the sea of Spain on the fourth day of March," offers a possible clue. In it

Columbus repeatedly referred to "these islands" and on four occasions located them in the Indies (*Las Indias*). The only time he used "India" in the singular was in a reference to "the other islands of India."[44] Barring the finding of new documentation, we can say that Columbus set sail for the west, where he expected to find islands nearer to Spain than was the Indian mainland of the Far East.

Several other matters connected with the voyage require clarification. First, what system of navigation did Columbus employ? Second, did he falsify the daily log and, if so, for what purpose? Third, was there a mutiny on the outbound voyage? Fourth, where did he first make landfall, in the Bahamas or below? Fifth, what were the problems, if any, between Columbus and Martín Alonso Pinzón? And sixth, who was Juan de la Cosa, who has been said to have sailed as master of the *Santa María*? The last question raises another one, not touched on by Columbus's U.S. biographers: was the *Santa María* sunk by accident, run aground on purpose, or simply abandoned?

Columbus's Navigational Methods

There are several schools of thought on the question of Columbus's method of navigation: he used latitudinal sailing, he used dead reckoning, he used celestial navigation, or he used a combination of any of these three.

In the *Diario*, Las Casas showed Columbus supplying three positions by latitude and none by longitude. Each of the three was incorrect. The most frequently expressed theory is that he sailed across the Atlantic by dead reckoning; the simplest description of this method is to lay down a course with a compass. Speed can then be calculated by counting the time it takes the vessel to pass by two measured distances on deck by using a floating object in the sea as a marker. The compass gives direction; the count, together with the visual estimate, gives speed. Morison is the foremost proponent of the theory that Columbus used the dead-reckoning method.[45] Wilford was in basic agreement with Morison.[46]

Zvetan Todorov, while fitting Columbus's "knowledge of the stars" into his communications ability with the Taino Indians, noted, "Columbus performs, with regard to navigation, veritable exploits . . .

he initiates sidereal navigation and discovers magnetic deviation."[47] The use of "initiates" is perplexing in that such navigational methods date back to earliest recorded time; likewise, easterly magnetic deviation was also known. What was new that Columbus has been said to have encountered was the westerly deviation of the compass. Kelley noted: "What Columbus observed [September 15] was not magnetic variation but rather the circular movement of Polaris around the celestial pole. In the late fifteenth century the radius of this circle was almost 3.5 degrees."[48] On two other occasions in the *Diario*, Columbus made observations that have also been often misconstrued as referring to magnetic deviation.

Latitude sailing used by the Portuguese was termed "running down the latitude." As for the accuracy attained by the use of this method in the sixteenth century, Bernáldez stated, "No one is regarded as a good pilot and master who, although he has to pass from one land to another far distant without seeing any sign of other land, makes an error of ten leagues, even if the crossing be one of 1000 leagues." In more recent times Nathaniel Bowditch noted: "Several hundred years ago . . . the finding of latitude furnished the only reliable navigation available on long sea voyages. Since most of these were in a generally easterly or westerly direction, it became common practice to sail first to the latitude of destination ('run down the latitude') and then follow this parallel until landfall was made."

Latitude can be devised directly from the heavens, but not necessarily through the use of the quadrant. Much earlier than when the quadrant came into use, Norse and Mediterranean sailors used notched sticks and other devices for making calculations of their relative position to certain stars. This was much the same as when modern soldiers use the finger of an extended hand positioned from a known location on the trousers for approximating distances for light mortars and traverse for machine-gun fire.

Las Casas wrote in the journal entry for November 21 on the first voyage: "Here the Admiral found himself at 42 degrees from the equinoctial line . . . but he says he has the quadrant hung up until reaching land that it be repaired."[49] The latter part of this statement makes no sense in that Columbus at the least, if not Las Casas, knew that there is nothing to repair on a wood quadrant. Of the second voyage Hernando wrote, "On April 20 he set sail and left the island of Guadalupe . . . [and] continued his voyage by twenty-two degrees."[50] This information came, presumably, from the ship's log for this voyage. Besides indicating latitudinal sailing, this passage shows that by the end of the second voyage, Columbus was placing Guadalupe, not Española, on the twenty-second parallel.

Another method often used for shipboard readings was to measure the angle of the Pole star based at the man's navel relative to other parts of the body of a man standing with his forearms on his hips. In his letter on the third voyage, Columbus indicated his use of this method: "I found there, as night fell . . . the Guards were above the head." Later, on this same voyage, he wrote, "When I was there, I found that the north star described a circle which was five degrees in diameter, and when the guards are in the right arm, the star is at its lowest point, and it continues to rise until they are in the left arm, and then it is five degrees, and from that point it sinks until they again reach the right arm."[51] This common method for measuring time at sea in the Middle Ages was one that Columbus obviously used.

In numerous postils, Columbus showed his interest in the classical division of the earth into five climates, or time zones. Tables were provided in both the *Ymago mundi* and the *Historia rerum* in which the different zones are indicated by their hours of daylight.

Whatever the method used, Columbus, by sailing with the trade winds, stayed on or near latitude 28°N effortlessly until October 7, when, for whichever reason—Pinzón's suggestion or Portuguese discovery experience based on interpreting the direction of birds' flight—he opted to change course and followed the path of a large flock of birds flying to the southwest. This decision later caused problems for his family, since it provided the basis for the Crown's claim that the discovery was the result of Pinzón's nautical knowledge, not Columbus's.

This change in course may also have been due to the fact that, as indicated in the *Diario*, he now believed he had reached a point at which a more southerly course was indicated in order to reach Cipango. Here again the important question is not so much the means of reckoning he used to reach this stage in his voyage but the motivation that caused him to seek his destination at this point. Had he correctly estimated first landfall through the use of a combination of ancient texts (distance) and fourteenth- and fifteenth-century *mappaemundi* (latitude)? Was his decision based on empirical or theoretical knowledge or, perhaps, a combination of the two? Some scholars ascribe his initial decision to select 28°N as his latitudinal course to his past experience sailing to the Portuguese trading post of São Jorge da Mina in West Africa. These voyages may have made him familiar with the wind patterns of the northernmost limits of the trade winds, that is, the only practicable way for sailing west with a following wind at those latitudes.

In a similar manner, he could have known, from his experience sailing to England, of the westerlies that ultimately returned him to Iberia by way of the Azores. On leaving Española at the end of the outward leg of his first journey, he headed directly for the latitude where he could catch these essential winds for an easterly course across the Atlantic at that latitude. On February 3 he wrote in the *Diario*, "It seemed . . . that the North Star was very high as [it would be] at Cabo de San Vicente."[52] This is an indication of his use of celestial navigation. If he was heading for his home port in Spain, he would at this point have changed course from east-northeast to due east or even east-southeast. The next day he did change to a more easterly course. Actually, at this point he was farther to the north than he had estimated; he was now headed straight for the Azores. The prevailing winds drove the *Pinta* much farther north; the ship made land at Bayona on the northern coast of Spain.

On the first voyage, Columbus sailed an outbound course that was farther to the north than was ideal for catching the trade winds. Several entries in the *Diario* report changes in course to a south-westerly direction. He was perhaps fortunate in that had he traveled that particular course later in the season, he might have run into one of the storm centers that build up in that area into the hurricanes that so often ravage the West Indies and the Caribbean. However, on the second voyage, by sailing from Hierro to Dominica, west by southwest, he was sailing a near optimum course, one that he repeated on the third voyage when he divided the fleet and directed the pilots of the colony's resupply vessels to take the same course while he sailed farther to the south in search of what turned out to be the South American continent.

The day after his landfall on Guanahaní, the *Diario* entry notes, "None of them [the natives] are black, but the color of the people of the Canaries, nor should one expect anything else as it is on an East-West line with the Island of Hierro in the Canaries."[53] This statement is indicative of his use of latitudinal sailing. Guanahaní was probably somewhere around three degrees south of Hierro.

The Phillipses gave the most attention to the methods used in those days for dead reckoning, but they did also recognize the need for knowing the latitude: "Columbus and other Europeans, as well as mariners in the Indian Ocean at the same time, sailed east or west by following the latitudes of known places."[54] Fernández-Armesto believed in the primacy of dead reckoning, but at the same time he noted: "Dead reckoning could be enhanced or replaced by what maritime historians call 'primitive celestial navigation.' . . . Columbus's task in keeping a straight course could easily have been accomplished by the unaided eye of a practiced celestial navigator: it would have been necessary only to keep the sun, by day, and the pole Star, by night, at a constant angle of elevation."[55]

Nancy Rubin, basing her account on Morison, Hernando, and Gianni Granzotto, provided a condensed version of the Columbian myth. In the process, she introduced a few new elements, one of which was the manner by which Columbus supposedly came to know of dead reckoning. This occurred, she said, while he was sailing to Chios in 1473. "Onboard a three-master called the *Roxanna*, the helmsman did something Columbus had never before witnessed: He abandoned the traditional short voyages from port to port and ventured into the open seas. Once surrounded by an endless azure horizon, the helmsman steered by dead reckoning, that is by mathematically computing a ship's position from one point to another without visual aids. This navigational feat left a deep impression on Columbus, who, nearly twenty years later, would use it to plot his course to the unknown half of the globe."[56] This is inventive, though misleading, corroborative detail.

The reader may wonder why so much importance has been attached to Columbus's navigational methods. It is because we need to understand them in order to trace his course across the Atlantic and thereby to establish the exact point of his first landfall on an island that he said the Indians called Guanahaní. Perhaps the popularity of the dead-reckoning method as the one used by Columbus is because it is by this means that the Watlings Island landfall can be most readily justified. This may be a case of resolving ambiguity in favor of an individual theory. With the finding of *El libro copiador*, much of the ambiguity has been cleared up. As will be seen in the chapter on the second voyage, Columbus gave, in the second letter, a clear explanation of his navigational methods.

Double Entries in the *Diario*

According to the *Diario* entry for September 9, as paraphrased by Las Casas: "He went that day 15 leagues and he decided to record less than those traveled in case the way was long the men would not become frightened and become disheartened."[57] This outright statement that Columbus intended from the start to make false entries daily in the ship's log has been accepted at face value by most historians and biographers alike. However, the matter is not that simple. There is no question that Las Casas cited double entries for many days of the voyage. These were always given in the third person. If one accepts that perhaps Las Casas misunderstood these entries, then he may have accordingly invented their explanation.

Hernando too had access to a copy of the *Diario*, and he repeated the claim in yet greater detail. He wrote that no sooner had the ships lost sight of land than the crews became afraid that they would not see it again for a long time: "They sighed and cried." He went on to say that although that day (Sunday, September 9) they traveled eighteen leagues, his father counted only fifteen, "having decided to lessen, in his account of the voyage, part of the count, in order that the men not know that they were as far from Spain as they actually were."[58] The *Historia* and the *Historie* are three leagues apart for Sunday's travel. It would seem that at least in this instance, either the authors were not using the same text, or someone made an error in copying.

It has been suggested that Columbus was keeping figures for himself in Spanish leagues and for the men in Portuguese leagues, which they could more readily understand. This ignores the fact that there is no consistency in the ratios between the one and the other. As noted above, another suggestion is that the figures were copied incorrectly by scribes. This could be so, but it does not give license to students of the voyage to readjust the figures to their liking. Morison took comfort from the fact that the so-called phony distances recorded were actually closer to reality than the presumably real ones.[59]

In *El libro copiador*, Columbus did frequently refer to a "big sea league" while giving land measurements. In the log he could have been using the big sea league while using a shorter league for the men. In the Las Casas *Diario* holograph, the figures were given sometimes in Roman numerals, other times in either Arabic numerals or spelled out. Dunn and Kelly, for example, emended their translation, using only Arabic numerals.

It has been suggested that Las Casas, by dividing league entries, was able to record his speed calculations as integers. Another suggestion is that Columbus was using for his own purposes a league measurement different from that used by the captains and pilots of the other two vessels. There were five captains and five pilots on the first voyage, each of whom maintained his own log. This alone brings into question the claim, made only by Hernando and Las Casas, that Columbus falsified the record in order to fool the crews into believing that they were not as far from home as they actually were. Was he supposedly misleading only the sailors and grummets? One interesting explanation compares the two daily listings made by Columbus and modern-day modes of measurement. Under this reasoning, it always sounds better to tell someone that he is only fifty miles from home rather than the larger-sounding eighty kilometers.

Twice during the outbound voyage Columbus and the pilots of the three vessels paused to exchange information on their estimates as to distances traveled. The first time was on September 18, when the pilot of the *Niña* estimated twenty-eight leagues more, the *Pinta's* eight more, and the pilot of Columbus's flagship twelve fewer than the lower estimate in the *Diario*.[60] This provided a maximum difference of less than 7 percent, whereas Columbus's double figures varied by 20 percent. On October 2 both the pilots of the other two boats estimated the distance run as less than that shown in the *Diario*. On this basis Columbus would have accomplished nothing by trying to confuse the three pilots; their lower figures would have better suited his avowed purpose. He probably simply overestimated. It is of interest to note that Las Casas (repeated later by Antonio Herrera y Tordesillas)[61] reported that on October 1, Columbus's pilot told him that they had traveled 588 leagues, the pilot of the *Niña* said 650 (on the next day), and the *Pinta*'s pilot reported 634. Only the figures of Columbus and his pilot were given in the *Diario*.[62] As will be seen, on the second voyage the pilots reported the distance from the island of Hierro to Dominica with remarkable accuracy.

This use of double entries has provided fuel for the postmodern social historians. José Rabasa found that with this "eerie stoppage of the flow of time, Columbus manipulates time by keeping two records of the crossing; . . . this duplicitous distortion of time alleviate[d] the crew's anxiety before the sighting of land."[63] At the same time that this author accepted as fact the problematical in the record, he overlooked the repeated statements made in the *Diario*, "before the sighting of land," that the crews were very anxious indeed, to the point, Columbus said, of open mutiny.

So far no detailed analysis of the daily figures has provided a satisfactory explanation for these discrepancies in the written record. Recently Henige studied the figures and concluded: "The examples adduced here can only suggest any number of unpleasant—and not mutually exclusive—possibilities: that Columbus was not as adept at estimating distances as we would prefer; that he could not count, or at least add; or that some numbers were changed or omitted at a later stage either intentionally or unintentionally."[64] What is evident in the historiography of the first voyage is that few have been willing to accept that the figures given in the *Diario* simply do not make sense when studied either individually or collectively. Columbus's hagiographers have developed theories and explanations, most of them highly selective but none of them convincing. Barring the discovery of additional sources, the true meaning of these numbers will remain an enigma.

Shipboard Morale and Mutiny or Near-Mutiny

Another area for disagreement among historians is one that concerns what has been termed either mutiny, or near-mutiny, on the first voyage. The first crossing was not without its problems. Before arriving at the jumping-off point in the Canaries, one of the vessels shipped its rudder. Columbus believed that this was a result of sabotage by the owner, who had not wanted his boat to take part in the expedition. On this date, August 6, the Las Casas paraphrase has an entry, which includes a direct quotation, that is difficult to translate. A literal translation is as follows: "The rudder of the caravel Pinta in which Martín Alonso Pinzón went, jumped or came loose, which was believed or suspected to have been the work of one Gomez Rascon and Christobal Quintero whose caravel it was, because it bothered him to go on that voyage. And the Admiral says that before they left they [Gomez and Quintero] had been found [causing?] certain setbacks and heated arguments as the said are called."[65]

Significantly, this passage expresses a negative attitude displayed by only the men suspected of damaging the rudder, not by the crew. In this case, as later with Juan de la Cosa, the Admiral showed no hard feelings toward Quintero, whom he made captain of his flagship on the third voyage. Such being the case, it is difficult to take the present complaint of sabotage seriously.

The immediate problem was resolved, despite difficulties, by Martín Alonso Pinzón, the captain of the *Pinta*. The version given in the *Diario* of this minor setback was somewhat different from that in the *Historie*. At this point, in the *Diario* at least, Pinzón still found favor with the Admiral: "[The Admiral] says that he felt less upset in knowing that Martín Alonso Pinon was an enterprising person, and with good talent."[66] Hernando first gave Pinzón credit for being a "practical man and skillful sailor," then commented that the rudder had slipped twice, which would have made a superstitious person "conjecture the disobedience and contumacy" of Pinzón later in the voyage.[67]

The so-called double entries found in the *Diario* perhaps presaged things to come. Both Las Casas and Hernando said the entries were made in anticipation of trouble. On September 16 the fleet encountered the edges of the Sargasso Sea. In the *Pleitos*, testimony about this sea was contradictory; however, at least one witness testified that Columbus at this point required Pinzón's reassurance that it was safe to sail through these floating grasses. No suggestion was made in either the *Diario* or the *Pleitos* that this unusual sight upset the mariners; on the contrary, they apparently saw the grasses as evidence of nearby land.

On the next day they observed another potentially disturbing phenomenon: the apparent westerly deviation of the compass. This did grab the attention of the sailors: "And the sailors were afraid and did not say why." Dunn and Kelley translated this passage, adding: "The sailors were fearful and *depressed*" (emphasis added).[68] On this same day the crews were apparently encouraged when they saw a crab floating on the grasses, together with "the sea water less salty since leaving the Canaries and the breezes always softer," indications to them of nearby land. This was followed by the observation that "everyone went along very happy, and the boats as fast as they could go in order to see land first."[69] Thus the earlier brief mention of fear is turned around, in the same day's entry, into a feeling of joy.

The log entries for the next few days report numerous supposedly sure signs of land. Twice the captains of the three vessels conferred. They differed in their distance estimates for the ten-day journey—by 80 to 160 miles, a difference of from one-third to two-thirds of a mile per hour traveled. These differences can be explained by the primitive methods for estimating speed and leeway. The atmosphere at this time was one of expectation. Up until then they had been sailing with following winds. On September 20, and for the next three days, the fleet faced head winds for the first time and was forced to tack. Columbus lacked the means for calculating distances while tacking. On the twenty-second he commented, "This contrary wind was very necessary for me, because my people were very excited, they thought that the winds in these seas did not blow to return to Spain."[70] Las Casas added in the margin alongside this last entry, "Here the people begin to talk about the long voyage, etc."[71]

On September 23 the subject of winds for the return voyage was again brought up. After first describing numerous presumed signs of land, the paraphrase then stated: "The sea was calm and smooth. The people muttered saying that in that region there was no high sea and that [it] never blew in order to return to Spain but later the sea rose greatly and without wind which frightened them."[72] Las Casas made another marginal notation here: "The people murmured."[73] This added emphasis was probably intended to indicate his belief in a buildup in tension. Two days later, on the twenty-fifth, Pinzón made a premature claim that he saw land. At this news the crews were overjoyed. The fleet detoured for a day until they realized that he was mistaken. Herrera reported this event; however, he added detail not found elsewhere: "Vicente Yañez [*sic*] cried out loudly Land, Land . . . this was judged to have been by contrivance agreed to between the two of them."[74] Herrera is one of the early chroniclers frequently cited today, probably because he not only gives a full account of all of these events but also is judged to have been highly favorable in his treatment of Columbus. Yet a close reading of his text reveals many questionable asides such as this one.

From the twenty-fifth through the thirtieth the winds were very light, but on October 3 the fleet picked up speed again. Columbus held to his westerly course, although he said that he believed that by doing so he was bypassing islands. On October 6 Pinzón suggested a change of course. Columbus held to his course. By now the crews' expectations were high; on the seventh the *Niña*, fastest of the three vessels, ran ahead in hope of being the first to sight land. The *Niña*'s crew raised a flag and fired a lombard as a signal that they had done so. This was another false alarm. Later that day they saw flocks of birds flying in a southwesterly direction. At this crucial point in the voyage, "the Admiral agreed to leave the route to the west, he puts the prow to the west-southwest with the determination to go that route for two days."[75] The use of the word "agreed" confirms that the change in direction had been suggested to Columbus.

The critical day as far as a near-mutiny is concerned was October 10. On this day Las Casas wrote: "Here the men could now endure it no longer. They complained of the long voyage, but the Admiral encouraged them as much as he could, giving them good expectation for the benefits they would have."[76] As Henige pointed out, the use of "no longer" implied "discontent now in the open."[77]

It was not until the return voyage that Columbus introduced into the *Diario* the first real indication of problems on the outbound leg of the journey. Worried about the storm raging on February 10, he wrote a long, soul-searching entry in which he questioned the fate that divine providence had in store for him; God, having taken him so far, would surely ensure that he could report his discovery, "mainly because he had saved him on the going (+ [*sic*] when he had more reason to fear)[78] from the troubles [of navigating] than with the sailors and people that he took with him, who of one voice were determined to return and rise up against him, making protestations, and the Eternal God gave him strength and valor against all." The notation "when he had more reason to fear" appears in the right margin, with the "+" sign to indicate its place in the text. In the left margin Las Casas noted "the anguish and disturbances that he suffered on the going from the people that he took with him."[79] This passage is most often interpreted so as to link the "troubles" with the "sailors and people." The translation offered here, as interpreted literally, would seem to say that Columbus had troubles of his own on the outgoing voyage as well as problems with the crews, perhaps referring to uncertainty about the route and worry over the distance already traveled—in short, a commander's problems.

Henige summed up the situation well when he wrote: "All in all, these differences are many and varied. Most of them are probably interpolations that appeared later than the shipboard log but earlier than the Diario. . . . But however the modern historian chooses to deal with them, they need to be addressed as they occur. It is by no means enough to accept Morison's refrain that this day's record in the *Historie* 'adds nothing but a few pious reflections, and again proves the honesty of this abstract by Las Casas.'"[80]

In his *Historia*, Las Casas offered a much-embellished version of these events; Hernando either innovated or repeated them. Before studying these versions in detail, we should recall that both of these authors wrote many years after the Colón family instituted legal proceedings in an attempt to regain their lost privileges. Although

Diego began the suit, it was Hernando who handled the details. The principal points in the dispute centered on what occurred between Columbus and Pinzón, both before and during the first voyage. The Crown's defense was based largely on the superior part supposedly played by Pinzón, with emphasis on his supposed perseverance at sea in the face of Columbus's claimed vacillation. Surely it would have been to the advantage of the Colóns to have proven that the Admiral had sailed with an unruly mob and that only by dint of personal leadership had he been able to overcome their insubordination as well as other obstacles to the continuance of the voyage. Yet no witness in the *Pleitos* referred to a mutiny.

Las Casas first mentioned the men "murmuring," though he did not give a date. Next he noted that, after one of the midocean conferences with the other captains, Columbus, surrounded by "so much bitterness" and among "so many undisciplined people . . . and most insolent . . . with sweet and loving words . . . encouraged and animated them." This approach apparently did not work. Earlier, on September 23, "the sea rose greatly, so much so that they were afraid that as there were always breezes and winds to the other parts, and, because the sea was flat and quiet, they did not believe they could return to Spain, they now trembled with so much wind against them and with the anger of the sea." On September 24: "When God had most shown them manifest signs that it was impossible that they be far from land, all the more grew their impatience and lack of constancy, and the more they got angry at Colon." Las Casas wrote of the men "making cliques" and meeting in little groups to discuss how they could turn around. They said that it was "self homicide to follow the insanity of a foreign man . . . and that they were not obliged to go to the end of the world." On October 10 the men started complaining again, "insisting in their imprudent petitions, demanding the shameful return, these Columbus overcame with 'gracious and sweet words.' "[81]

According to the *Historie*, the murmuring was at first caused by the fact that none of them had ever before sailed so far from land. Then, on reaching the Sargasso Sea, "it caused great fear . . . and as fear leads the imagination to worse things, they were afraid that it [the sea] would be so thick" as to make it impossible to move. Then, on September 22, when they faced head winds that continued to blow for three days out of the southwest, the Admiral thought that this would reassure them that they would have favorable winds for the return journey, because "while the people grumbled, among other things that they said to increase their fear, was that, as they always had wind on the stern, that in those seas they would never have a favourable wind for returning to Spain."[82] The *Historie* further reported:

> The more vain the mentioned signs [of land] the more their fear grew, they withdrew below decks, saying that the Admiral wanted to be a great man at the cost of their lives, that they had already complied with their obligations, going farther from land than anybody had before, and that they should not be made the authors of their own ruin. . . . Those were not lacking who proposed they stop the discussions, and if he did not want to give up his plan, they could resolve matters by throwing him in the ocean, reporting later that the admiral, while observing the stars, had fallen without wanting to, and that nobody would go around investigating the truth of it.[83]

Bernáldez merely noted that the men had at one time insisted on returning to Spain. His account parallels in many ways the version given in the *Diario* entry for October 10, with one perhaps-not-insignificant exception. He wrote that the upset sailors were calmed by "Colon and the other captains" rather than by Columbus alone.[84] In his *Pleitos* testimony, Columbus's black *criado* Juan Portugués, who was present on the first voyage, testified that Columbus had promised the crew to consult with Pinzón at the time that they wanted to return to Spain. According to Portugués, "The said Martín Alonso answered him that his opinion was the same [as Columbus's] and that they should continue on their route."[85] This first black to reach the Americas later lived with Columbus in Seville and, after the Admiral's death, was identified in Darien.

Martire also referred to the "murmuring" of the crews, though he reported this *not* in the first versions of his *Decadas* but only in the editions published in 1516 and after. These later editions were post-*Pleitos* versions of the story. He began his short account of his fellow Italian's vicissitudes with an indirect criticism: "His Spanish companions were first to murmur in low voices, then to increase them with insults to his face, etc."[86] With minor changes, this is the same account as given by Las Casas and Hernando.

Fernández de Oviedo dealt at great length with the discontent. In this case it was the officers and men who began by "murmuring . . . and the people and the captains mutinied, [saying that] the King and Queen had used them badly and with much cruelty trusting in such a man, and giving credit to a foreigner who didn't know what he was saying. And the thing got to the point that they assured him that if he didn't turn around, they would make him do so against his wishes, or they would throw him in the sea."[87] This was the first published work to use the word "mutiny." A few years later Alonso de Santa Cruz, writing in the mid–sixteenth century, also used it, and the word then appeared in the first edition of the *Historie*. In 1537 Paolo Interiano wrote that Columbus's people despaired and wanted to turn back.[88] The story of a mutiny was presented as historical fact by Herrera at the beginning of the seventeenth century. Strangely, Columbus, who often appeared almost paranoiac, failed to use this incident in any of his writings—an incident that would have received as sympathetic a reception in his own day as it does today, when firmly embedded in the Columbian myth.

The accounts of this incident are handled in the works under review in a uniform manner. Morison wrote: "On October 10 . . . all the smoldering discontent of the men flared up into open mutiny. . . . This mutiny, so far as we have any record, was confined to the flagship."[89] A few pages earlier he discussed tensions on board the three vessels: "Columbus and the Pinzons needed all their moral force and prestige to prevent outbreaks or even mutiny."[90] Morison, perhaps wisely, avoided mentioning mutinies in his later works. Wilford bypassed the issue entirely.

The Phillipses reconstructed the chain of events from several sources. They wrote that on October 6, "Columbus faced his first near-mutiny." They repeated a tale, often told: "Many times Columbus had told his crew they should start looking for land at 700 leagues." It may be purely coincidental, but Columbus wrote in his letters in *El libro copiador* on the second voyage that he expected land not long before he had traveled 800 leagues, where in fact he did find land. In the third letter he gave the figure of 700 leagues as the distance between Cuba and Cádiz. For those favoring prior discovery, these figures could be taken as demonstrating that on the first voyage he was seeking the route that he did take on the second. He did warn the crews on the first voyage to keep a sharp lookout at the time they had traveled approximately this distance, but the figure of 700 leagues was not mentioned in the *Diario*. However, these authors now noted the crews' reaction after sailing 800 leagues: "In response to the complaints of his crew, Columbus decided to consult the other captains. . . . Columbus told the other captains about his crew's desire to return and asked their opinions."[91] As has already been shown, none of this comes from the *Diario*, the nearest thing to a primary source available today. The Phillipses followed with excerpts from testimony given in the *Pleitos*, testimony in which the Pinzón brothers were portrayed as having insisted on continuing the journey. Farther along the Phillipses reported, "from other accounts," a version in which the captains of all three ships joined with the crews on October 10 and "expressed their fear that the nearly continuous winds blowing from east to west might make it impossible to return home at that latitude. . . . Unconvinced that the matter should be left entirely in God's hands, the mutinous crewmen began to rattle their weapons."[92] Thus these authors provided both a near-mutiny and a mutiny, supported by details not to be found elsewhere.

Fernández-Armesto treated the dissatisfaction of the crews within the context of other matters. His quotations were taken from La Casas's second version of these events in his *Historia*, such as the statement that after throwing Columbus overboard, they were to say that he had fallen in while "trying to make a reading of the Pole Star with his quadrant or astrolabe." This quotation is footnoted as from Las Casas; yet it in no way resembles the account in Manuel Serrano y Sanz's transcription of the *Historia*. The only mention in the *Diario* of an astrolabe is in the much later entry for February 3, 1493. However, by use of this free interpretation, Fernández-Armesto was able to state: "The story that the mutineers are alleged to have concocted has an irresistible grim humour. It brilliantly evokes the figure of the outlandish boffin, practicing in ungainly isolation his new-fangled techniques, while struggling on a rolling deck with an unmanageable gadget. This image . . . conveys a good deal of truth."[93] How entertaining, as fiction should be!

Sale showed more interest in the effects of the discovery on the native populations of the discovered lands than in the details of the voyages. Fuson's opinions are in a class of their own. Fuson advised that his translation "is unique, though no less accurate than the other good translations. It has, however, been edited and modernized."[94] His changes include the following: "Some of the missing elements have been reassembled from the *Historia* of Las Casas and the *Historie* of Fernando to form a more complete narrative." "Redundancies" were removed; the first person was "restored" throughout; sentences were "re-ordered"; "archaic language" was avoided; and "Spanish miles and leagues" were converted to "nautical miles." Finally, he noted, "The last example of modernization is the matching of Columbus's locations with those on today's nautical charts."[95] This book, *The Log of Christopher Columbus*, should more properly be titled *The Fuson Log*. John Cummins followed essentially the same methods in rewriting the *Diario*.[96] These are the ultimate rewrites.

The above is all that we know today on this subject. The only source from which one can perhaps infer that a near-mutiny of some sort took place is an account written by Columbus at least four months after the event. It is not unreasonable to suppose that in retrospect, Columbus may have been interested in magnifying his problems, in order to enhance the glory of his unique accomplishment. Later, his contemporaries built on his brief remarks, and some modern-day writers have since embellished the story beyond recognition.

The log that Columbus maintained is the nearest thing to a primary source for his first voyage, on which he discovered the West Indies. Unfortunately, it is known to us only through a paraphrase made by Las Casas. In it there are confusing double entries for distances traveled. Many explanations for these entries have been offered, first by Las Casas and Hernando, who believed that they were part of a ruse intended to mislead the crews as to distances traveled: the shorter the distances, the less fearful the crews woud be of not being able to return to Spain. Close analysis has led only to the conclusion that the purpose of these entries is unknowable with the information that we have today. Many writers have presumed that Columbus's destination, when he set out to cross the Atlantic, was India. The only certainty is that he expected he would find islands and he found them. Scholars have speculated for years about Columbus's navigational methods. Much of the controversy has now been resolved with the finding of Columbus's copybook, *El libro copiador.* He used all of the methods known in his day—latitudinal sailing, sidereal navigation, and dead reckoning. The small fleet's crossing was unusual for the times; instead of hugging shorelines, it went cross-ocean. The crews were understandably worried, since no one, not even Columbus, really knew where they were going. The *Diario,* our prime source, reported a problem with the crews on the outbound voyage. Contemporaries and later writers have built on this scant reference; today Columbus is seen as having put down a mutiny. Scholarly disputes over some of these anomalies provide no answers. What often seems to get lost in the debates is the one important thing: the Indies were about to be discovered.

The beginnings of all things are small.

Cicero (106–43 B.C.)

9

The

Discovery

Columbus's landfall in the Indies is the subject on which probably more time and effort has been spent than on any other aspect of his voyages. Columbus described his first landfall as being on a "small island" and later as on an island that was "good and big" (*Bien grand*).[1] The rest of his description is equally confusing, giving opportunity to pundits and aficionados alike to identify half a dozen different islands with the one that the natives called Guanahaní. Antonio Herrera y Tordesillas offered clues from Juan Ponce de León's account of his voyage from Puerto Rico to Bimini. In 1731, Catesby, in his *Natural History of Carolinas*, was the first to identify the island in print as Cat Island in the Bahamas. This identification was generally accepted; its principal proponents were, in the United States, Washington Irving and, in Europe, Humboldt. In this instance Irving did not follow Fernández de Navarrete, who opted for Grand Turk Island. Juan Bautista Muñoz in 1793 was the first to suggest Watlings Island.[2] There are approximately 29 islands and 661 islets in the Bahamas group. Rudolph Cronau was the first to make a study based on a personal visit to the islands in question.[3] He also studied the Ponce de León voyage and, as had others before him, the 1500 La Cosa map. He opted for Watlings Island.

A recent example of an intensive, yet inconclusive, study was the corporate-funded computerized effort undertaken by the National Geographic Society.[4] In a multidisciplinary round-robin recorded on microfilm, hundreds of letters were exchanged among a representative group of specialists in an effort to pinpoint Guanahaní. The result was total disagreement, often punctuated by acerbic *argumentum ad hominem*. Each of the biographies herein mentioned professed knowledge of a definite location for Guanahaní. For the record, most follow Morison's predilection for Watlings Island, recently renamed San Salvador. There is no point in listing these opinions, because each is based on unprovable assumptions. Perhaps the complexity of the matter is unnecessarily accentuated by the fact that the proponents of opposing theories tend to start from different sources, making it inevitable that their conclusions will be irreconcilable. To an outsider, the polemic appears to have been created more for its own sake than for an answer to the elusive question.

Columbus and Pinzón

The first reference made by Columbus to Martín Alonso Pinzón was in the *Diario* entry for August 6, in connection with the previously discussed problem with the *Pinta*'s rudder. There are thirty-nine references to Pinzón in the *Diario* text, not counting cross-outs or marginal notations by Las Casas. These should be sufficient to provide a fair idea as to how Columbus regarded this companion on the first voyage. Twenty-eight are direct references, of which nineteen deal with routine matters relating to the voyage; two others are flattering and seven, negative. The two men set sail together on August 3, and the first negative comment was made on November 21, the day the boats of Columbus and Pinzón lost sight of each other off the coast of Cuba. This separation came at a time when they were both racing toward Española in search of gold. Pinzón found it first.

What occurred between the two while they were in Palos preparing for the journey was testified to at length in the *Pleitos*. The Crown's witnesses contended that Columbus would not have been able to enroll crews for the three vessels without the aid of the Pinzón family, Martín Alonso in particular. Given the prominence of this seafaring family in this small port, it is perfectly reasonable to accept the proposition that its members were of great assistance to Columbus. The court order to supply Columbus with the two ships owed by the town specified that the vessels were to be made ready within ten days. This order was read to the assembled townspeople on May 23, yet the small fleet did not sail for another sixty-six days. Activities such as the assembling of supplies may have accounted for part of this delay, but the *Pleitos* witnesses generally agreed that there were difficulties in finding crews. Taken alone, the question as to who recruited these crews is of little importance; however, the idea that it was Pinzón who had arranged for them became part of the Crown's strategy to denigrate the position of Columbus in important matters relating to the voyage.

Another piece of evidence used against Columbus's family in this lawsuit was the claim that Pinzón had provided all or part of Columbus's share of the expenses for the journey. As best as we can determine today, it is equally likely that Columbus's Florentin and Genoan friends supplied the greater part of the necessary funds. For the people of Palos, it remained an article of faith that Pinzón entered into this venture on a share basis with Columbus. In the sixteenth century some even claimed that Beatriz, Columbus's mistress, supported this belief. However that may be, her cousin Pedro de Arana and the Columbus family's faithful servitor Diego Méndez, in charge of presenting the Colón evidence in the final *Pleitos* hearings, each gave full credit to Columbus in such matters. Perhaps the Crown's version of what happened at that time is the reason the only statue in Palos today is of Pinzón, the port's favorite son. In August 1535 the prosecutor offered the following introduction to the Crown's case:

> The letters and privileges that the opposing party now present, saying that by these the Catholic kings, now in glory, admit that don Cristoval Colon, by his hand and industry was the first who invented and discovered, the Indies and was the first who with his own eyes saw them and for that reason they gave him an annuity of ten thousand

[maravedis] for life, those letters and privileges, and all of the rest that they mention in their petition. These do not prejudice the right of your prosecutor, and they were obtained with lack of deference caused by the said Cristoval Colon as when he returned from the first voyage to the Indies he affirmed to the Catholic Kings that he had discovered it and as he brought with him the account of the land and at the time as there was no one who contradicted him the Catholic Kings believed that he had discovered it as he said, and, for this reason believing that it was so, they gave him the said letters and privileges as are [presented]. If it had not been so before your Highness will find that another put more effort and work and costs than the said Colon and he invented and gave the start and first tried to make the said discovery and was skilled in navigation and boats and [had] wealth, and more than the said don Cristoval Colon who met with him and he gave him money so that he could go in the name of the two of them to reach an agreement with the Catholic Kings in regard to the said discovery. In the meanwhile he rigged his ships to go, and with the said capitulation they went to make the said discovery. The other companion who was called Martín Alonso Pinçon going as the leader to whom the said Cristoval Colon promised to give and share with him the half of all that the Catholic kings conceded to him for which reason the said Pinçon put three of his boats and three brothers and other relations and friends of his who followed him for the said voyage and he was the one who really discovered the said Indies.[5]

The prosecutor added that Pinzón had died shortly after returning from the first voyage, which was why Columbus had been able to go to the court and claim for himself the glory of the discovery. Question number 8 of the interrogatory asked, "[Do] you know that before the said don Christoval Colon began to make the discovery . . . the said Martin Alonso Pinçon of Palos had information and news of the said islands of the Indies in the *mar oçeano* through a document that he had brought from Rome from the library of Innocent VIII and that by virtue of the said document the said Martin Alonso Pinçon had discussed and tried to make ready to go and make the said discovery . . . at his own expense?"[6]

Martín Alonso Pinzón Jr. testified that he had heard his father discuss this document but that he did not know whether Columbus also knew about it before they sailed together from Palos.[7] Ten witnesses testified about Pinzón's trip to Rome. Four said that they knew of a trip (one witness mentioned two trips), and three of these said that Pinzón had found a *mappamundi* there; the fourth said that he knew of the map only by hearsay. Five witnesses knew only that Pinzón had gone to Rome, two of them mentioning that he made the trip one or two times carrying cargoes of sardines.

Morison, in dealing with this matter, concluded, "[The] substratum of truth . . . seems to be that Martín Alonso picked up a yarn of some mythical transatlantic voyage . . . no doubt his example and influence were useful in recruiting men." Unfortunately, this possibly realistic appraisal of the contention is marred by a following quotation from Jean Chacot, "who had plenty of experience of that sort of thing," in regard to a supposed tendency "common to Latin countries to depreciate a great leader who wins popular applause. 'Subordinates often feel this jealousy; if they do not attack openly, their still more eloquent insinuations and reticences are quickly picked up and interpreted by those who hope to inflate themselves by diminishing others.' By no means confined to Latin countries!"[8]

It was Wilford's opinion that Pinzón was "influential in advancing Columbus's cause with the people of Palos," citing Vignaud's opinion that without Pinzón, "it is conceivable that the enterprise would not have been carried out." This sounds reasonable today too, but Wilford's statement that Pinzón, "at the urging of Father Marchena," agreed "to join forces with Columbus" is opinion unsupported by any contemporary evidence. He cited Granzotto's claim that the differences between Columbus and Pinzón were irreconcilable.[9] Wilford went on to review some of the evidence presented in the *Pleitos*, commenting that Columbus "could be ungenerous towards those who shared the risks and contributed to the success." He added, "Although Pinzón's role is still debated, most historians tend to dismiss the larger claims [the *mappamundi* from Rome] as another of the myths that cling to Columbus."

The Phillipses accepted, as fact, the probability that Columbus had difficulty assembling a crew: "Only after he struck a deal with a prominent local ship owner named Martín Alonso Pinzón did the crew begin to take shape." This enabled them to state, "It seems clear from the documents that Columbus made his agreements with the Pinzón brothers only after concluding negotiations with the Spanish monarchs."[10] Some of their earlier assessments are based on data taken from *Pleitos* testimony. The same sources contradict the Phillipses, however, in testimony that Pinzón had lent the money to hire the mule that took Fray Pérez to court to negotiate a second hearing for Columbus. This appears to derive from these authors' intepretation of Arias Pérez's testimony in the *Pleitos*.

Fernández-Armesto believed that Columbus met with Pinzón at the friary at La Rábida in 1491. He noted, "The task of recruitment had been eased by a royal pardon to any condemned man who shipped on the voyage but in practice little recourse was had to any such dubious source of manpower." This pardon, actually a waiver, has been the source of many misunderstandings. The waivers were limited to a narrow number of criminal activities. The only people to sign on for this purpose were a condemned murderer, who was a citizen of Palos, and his two friends who had aided in his escape from prison. Of far more interest is Fernández-Armesto's observation that the effect of Pinzón's "responsibility for recruitment" was "to crew all the ships with his creatures so that when he and Columbus fell out the commander was fearful, exposed and almost isolated."[11] This belief originated with the account in the *Historie* for January 6, which said that Columbus, knowing of the "bad intention of that man [Pinzón,] . . . nevertheless dissimulated with him, and accepted him in order to not unravel the project of his enterprise, which could easily happen because the greater part of the people that he had with him were from the land [town] of Martín Alonso and even, many were relatives of his."[12] The *Diario* account of these same circumstances stated: "Martín Alonso . . . excused himself that he had left [off Cuba] against his wishes, giving reasons for it, but the Admiral says that they were all false and that he had left that night with great arrogance [*sobervia*] and greediness [*codiçia*], and the Admiral says that he did not know where these arrogances and dishonesty that he had shown on this voyage had come from, which the Admiral wanted to dissimulate in order to not give cause for the bad works of Satan."[13]

Yet, later in the *Diario*, after complaining about Pinzón, Columbus attributed his own problems to Satan, "who desired to impede the voyage as up until now he had done," and explained the shipwreck by the fact that "Our Lord had miraculously ordered that the ship remain there."[14] Columbus added, two days later, that "Martín Alonso and Vicente Anes [*sic*] and others who followed them with arrogance and greed" were not punished at the time, "although he said *he had with him many men who did their duty*" (emphasis added). He did, on a later date, January 4, worry that Pinzón, who "now was on his way . . . could inform the kings with lies so that they not order that he be given the punishment he deserved for one who so much harm has done and was doing in having gone without permission and to hinder the good things that could have been done and learned."[15] In this case the "many men" were obviously Columbus's own, not Pinzón's. Besides the inconsistencies in these excerpts, it should be remembered that years later Vicente Yáñez ("Vicente Anes") Pinzón again accompanied the Admiral as captain of one of his ships.

Columbus at this time was particularly preoccupied with the gold that Pinzón had supposedly been collecting. Columbus had first lost contact with the *Pinta* on November 22, when he said, "Martín Alonso followed the route to the east to go to the island of Babeque where the Indians say there is a great deal of gold."[16] No explanation was offered as to how Columbus knew Pinzón's destination. The Admiral reached the environs of Babeque on December 19, having first stopped over in Haiti. Since the *Pinta* was faster than the *Santa María*, it can be assumed that the former reached Española many days earlier.

Columbus received news at Navidad, on Española, on December 27 that the *Pinta* was at that time approximately fifteen leagues to the east of him. According to the *Diario* entry for January 6, Pinzón had arrived there "more than twenty days ago," that is, on or before December 7. This does not show where he was from November 22 until December 7. In the *Historia*, Las Casas wrote that the men on the *Pinta* told the Admiral that Pinzón had attempted to make the crew members swear that he had been there for only six days.[17] Las Casas went on to claim instead that Pinzón had "been there sixteen days collecting much gold."[18]

All chroniclers were interested in establishing how long Pinzón and his crew were there because Columbus believed that they had been there for a considerable time trading for gold illegally. In his *Historia*, Las Casas repeated the *Diario* entry verbatim; however, he first wrote that Columbus had sent a friendly letter to Pinzón on December 28, after the Taino Indians brought him news that Pinzón and the *Pinta* were nearby. No mention was made of any need for help due to the loss of the *Santa María*. Fernández de Oviedo believed that Pinzón's two brothers, who were still with the Admiral at that time, reconciled Martín Alonso and Columbus, who ended up pardoning the captain. Fernández de Oviedo said that the Admiral did this because many of the crew members were friends of the Pinzóns.[19]

Several of the witnesses in the *Pleitos* claimed that Pinzón had returned to Navidad to look for Columbus. Fernández de Oviedo wrote that Pinzón had protested against leaving "Christians so far from Spain, being so few . . . and they would be lost. . . . And on this matter he said other words, about which the Admiral became vicious and he suspected that he would try to take him [prisoner] . . . and Martín Alonso with the fear that he had from this suspicion went to sea in his caravel Pinta."[20] One of the rare cases in which a modern history has mentioned this reported disagreement with Columbus is John Dyson's *Columbus: For Gold, God, and Glory*.[21]

Columbus complained again of the *Pinta*'s captain when they again became separated, this time during a storm on January 23. He wrote that the caravel was sailing badly because of a problem with the mast, adding that this would not have happened had the captain replaced the mast on Española instead of being "greedy . . . to get way from him, thinking of stuffing the boat with gold."[22] It is perfectly obvious that what most rankled Columbus was the gold. He was also extremely anxious, probably with good reason, that Pinzón not get back to Spain before him. At this time Columbus cannot be expected to have looked on Pinzón dispassionately.

This brings up a story for which the only source is again the *Historie*: "At the same time that the admiral arrived in Palos, Pinzón arrived in Galicia, and wanted to go, alone, to Barcelona to give an account of the event to the Catholic Kings; but these told him not to go except with the admiral, with whom he had gone on the discovery; this caused him so much pain and anger that he returned to his town, ill, and in few days died of sorrow; before he came back to Palos the Admiral had gone by land to Seville."[23] The *Diario* did not mention this supposed incident at the end of the journey. Fernández de Oviedo wrote that both vessels entered the port of Palos on the same day: "Because [Pinzón] suspected that the Admiral would have him taken prisoner he left in the ship's boat, where they came by sail [i.e., at the mouth of the river] and he went where he stayed in secret. Afterwards the Admiral left for the court with the great news of the discovery, and as Martín Alonso knew he had gone, he went to house. He died after a few days because he was ill."[24]

Morison gave his interpretation of these events: "Without waiting for Pinta's sail to be furled, without reporting to the flagship, or as much as hailing Vicente Yañez, Martín Alonso Pinzón had himself rowed ashore, went to his country house near Palos, crawled into bed and died."[25] In a later version of these events, Morison added dramatic effect: "Pinta followed on the same tide. The sight of Niña already there, snugged down as if she had been at home a month, finished Martín Alonso Pinzón. Older than Columbus, ill from the hardships of the voyage, mortified by the snub from the Sovereigns, he could bear no more. He went directly to his country house near Palos, took to his bed, and died within the month."[26]

As far as future generations were concerned, the most important single problem in the Columbus-Pinzón relationship concerned which of the two selected the final course that took them to Guanahaní. The Crown's witnesses testified that when Columbus became discouraged, Pinzón pressed him on, saying, *"Adelante! Adelante!"* (Forward! Forward!) Fernández de Oviedo, who got his information from the pilot of Columbus's flagship, said that it was Columbus who had to convince the Pinzóns and the crew that they should continue the voyage. There is also the matter, duly recorded in the *Diario*, of Pinzón's insistence that they were headed in too northerly a direction and should veer off toward the southwest. Not immediately, but shortly thereafter, Columbus did precisely this and soon afterward discovered Guanahaní.

There is little to be gained by going into the dates on which these events occurred or into which witnesses testified to what. What one must do is look at the two facts objectively. Assuming that both of these events occurred in the manner given above, what real effect would they have had on the discovery? Obviously, had Columbus turned back, regardless of whose suggestion it was, we would not be discussing the matter today. The important fact is that as fleet commander, he made the final decision to go forward. His reasons for doing so may reflect on his character, on his expertise as a navigator, and on his dedication as a discoverer, but they do not in any way alter the reality that he made the decision. By the same token, his fortunate decision to change course at the time that he did undoubtedly brought him into contact with land sooner than he would have otherwise. Why did he change course? Again, he did so because, as fleet commander, he decided to do so. Others may have urged him on, may even have insisted that he change course, but the final decisions were his, not theirs.

Morison and Wilford presented accurate résumés of the pros and cons of these matters, based primarily on the *Pleitos* testimony. The other authors reviewed here paid less attention to these disputes while accepting those versions most favorable to Columbus. Most writers, ever since the existence of Las Casas's copy of the *Diario* was made public, have been more preoccupied with attempting to trace Columbus's course through the islands than with studying any single event that may have occurred during the crossing. These chroniclers are what might be termed geographical gunkholers; they visit every bay, round every cape, and show their coastal expertise by identifying each location with today's place-name.

They have been followed by the new wave of subjective interpreters such as Stephen Greenblatt, Zvetan Todorov, and Margarita Zamora. The names given by Columbus to islands and points are analyzed for hidden meanings, for inferences of European cultural influences on such choices, and for psychological implications. The same, often esoteric criteria are applied to Columbus's descriptions of flora and fauna. These writers would do well to check first with Varela and others who have identified some of the errors made by paleographers in assigning place-names that are different from the ones Columbus used. These postmodern interpretations are often part of their authors' own "discovery of America" rather than Columbus's.

Columbus's heirs were unsuccessful in the prolonged *Pleitos* hearings, which dragged on for a quarter of a century. They failed, however, not because of the Crown witnesses' testimony that Pinzón had prior information from Rome, that he financed the civil portion of the journey, that the crews signed on only because of his influence, that he abated the near-mutiny, that he insisted on persevering at a time when Columbus wavered, or that he had indicated the course to Guanahaní. None of these claims, true or not, had any bearing on the refusal of the king to restore the rights granted the Colóns in perpetuity as provided for under the terms of Columbus's privileges. The decision was made for the sole purpose of maintaining the state's total control over all the colonies that had been discovered in the Americas. Columbus's son Diego was allowed to return to Española as a governor with strictly limited powers. He proved as inept an administrator as his father, whereas his successor, his son Luis, ended up in jail as a multiple bigamist. From that time on, all the titles such as "Viceroy" and "Admiral of the Ocean Sea" either have been withdrawn or remain politically honorific, albeit financially remunerative.

Juan de la Cosa

Columbus had with him on his first two voyages to the Indies a man (or men) called Juan de la Cosa. Edward Channing in 1886 was one of the first to infer, in a footnote listing the mapmaker's voyages, that the La Cosa who sailed with Columbus on the first voyage was not the same person as the pilot, mapmaker, and explorer who sailed with him on the second voyage.[27] In 1892 Antonio Vascano countered with the claim that they were one and the same person.[28] At no time did Columbus name La Cosa as having sailed with him on the first voyage. This raised the question as to what justification there was in the written record to sustain the claim that Juan de la Cosa, owner of the *Gallega*, renamed the *Santa María*, sailed with his ship on the first voyage.

Juan de la Cosa was born in 1449 in the town of Santa María del Puerto, known today as Santoñia, located in the northern province of Santander. He has often been referred to as a Biscayan, but in those days everyone from the Cantábrico was known as a Biscayan. That he was not from the Santa María del Puerto near Cádiz is made evident by a letter, dated August 25, 1496, from Queen Isabel to the bishop of Badajoz, in which she referred to "Juan de la Cosa, a resident [*vecino*] of Puerto de Santoñia."[29] Those who insist on the two-men theory are perhaps in part confused by the fact that two seaports, at opposite ends of the peninsula, bore the same name.

There is ample evidence that Juan de la Cosa was the owner of the *Santa María*. He received a contract to transport grain on February 28, 1494, on which date Columbus and La Cosa were both in Isabel on Española. This contract stipulated: "Inasmuch as thou didst proceed as master in one of our ships on the High seas where, during said voyage, were discovered the lands and Islands of the Indies, and inasmuch as thou didst lose the said ship, We repay and satisfy thee."[30] This alone establishes beyond question that the owner of the sunken vessel was indeed on board at the time the vessel was lost. Since the monarchs, in later years, frequently used La Cosa on state business as well as licensed him to explore, there can be no question that they were fully aware of whom they were dealing with.[31] The many references to him in the *Pleitos* are solely concerned with his post-1493 activities, for the simple reason that the testimony was directly related to the Crown's efforts to prove that Columbus was not the first to discover the South American mainland.

In the *Diario*, Columbus made the first reference to the ship's *maestre*, who has since been assumed, but who was not said at the time, to have been also the ship's owner. After describing the grounding of the *Santa María*, the entry reads, "Then the *maestre*, who was on watch, came out."[32] Columbus's letter in *El libro copiador* made no mention of the loss of his flagship. Las Casas, in his account of this Columbian voyage, made no direct reference to La Cosa. He wrote that at the time of the sinking of the *Santa María* on the coast of Española, "the Admiral awoke first . . . then the *maestre* of the ship came out."[33] This ship's officer remained otherwise unidentified.

Like so many of the anomalies found in descriptions of these events, this one had its roots in the *Historie*. Hernando recounted the story as told in the first person: "Then the boy felt the rudder drag, and heard the noise, started to yell loudly, and hearing it I got up quickly. . . . Very soon after, the *patrón* of the ship, whose watch it was came out." These uses of *maestre* in the *Diario* and *patrón* in the *Historie* pose the question as to the meanings of these words. Do they identify the one or the other with the owner, captain, or first officer? Perhaps the best way to discover what these words meant as used in the *Diario* is to seek out all examples of their use in that document.

On November 4 Columbus was approached by the *contramaestre of the Niña*. This rank would be equivalent today to a boatswain. Columbus then sent "*maestre* Diego" on an errand.[34] The owner of the *Niña* was Juan Niño, who sailed on this voyage as pilot-owner, not *maestre*. The day after the grounding of the *Santa María*, Columbus again referred to the officer who had slept on his watch as the *maestre*.[35] The last and most revealing references were made on March 5, the day after anchoring in the Tagus River. Columbus told how the "*patrón* . . . of the largest ship of the king of Portugal . . . [came to the caravel]."[36] Bartolomeu Dias then ordered Columbus to send "the *maestre* of the caravel" to report to the Portuguese battleship, to which Columbus replied that he would do so only if forced. In these two cases the meaning is clear: *patrón* meant ship's master or captain, whereas the *maestre* was a lesser figure, a first officer. It should be kept in mind that words such as *patrón* used in the *Historie* originated in a long-lost Spanish manuscript that was first translated into Italian, then back into Spanish, and now into English. There is no way of telling what word Hernando used or what meaning he gave to it.

Patrón normally referred to a master, as in the relationship between a master and a slave. It did have the secondary meaning of skipper or master of a boat. *Maestre*, in turn, denoted a professional rather than proprietary relationship. The use of either of these two words does not justify the claim that the *maestre* who was asleep on his watch on the *Santa María* was its owner, Juan de la Cosa. Alice Bache Gould located a record in which there was a listing for a "Maestre Juan" on the *Santa María*. She was the first to note that La Cosa, the owner of the *Santa María*, had been granted the mentioned state contract to transport grain in 1494. This led her to believe that there were two individuals of that name, sailing at different times with Columbus. She has been followed in this by Morison.[37] He believed that on the second voyage was a "Juan de la Cosa, second of that name, a chart maker of Puerto Santa María who shipped as a mariner aboard Niña."[38] The sole fact that La Cosa received a contract does not necessarily prove that he was in Spain at the time.

Another contemporary document gives his salary for the second expedition: "Juan de la Cosa, seaman; To his credit 1,000 maravedis each month, on board the ship *Colina*." Masters and pilots received two thousand per month. The salary level indicates that at this time, La Cosa was not yet receiving pilot's pay. As will be seen, he did receive special distinction on the second voyage, differentiating him from the other crew members. Contemporaries often said that not only did Columbus teach him everything he knew about navigation but in later years he claimed to know more than the Admiral himself!

Nicolás Pérez, a captain in the Spanish navy, described La Cosa as follows: "A great seaman in the opinion of all, and in his own, not inferior to the Admiral himself, whose companion and pupil he was in the voyages to Cuba and Jamaica."[39] Although this statement does not identify La Cosa with the first voyage, it later clearly identifies the seaman on the second voyage with the pilot that sailed in 1499 with Alonso de Ojeda. Herrera ascribed the finding of continental America to this voyage and also believed that either Ojeda's name as leader or La Cosa's name as chief pilot should have been given to these lands, since Amerigo Vespucci held only the post of cosmographer for the voyage. Herrera even credited La Cosa with solving the impasse between Ojeda and Francisco Roldán on Española over the illegal cutting of brazilwood by Ojeda at the time of the Roldán mutiny.

On yet another occasion Herrera described Rodrigo de Bastidas's 1501 voyage: "He entered into arrangements with several persons, and particularly with Juan de la Cosa, who was the best pilot in existence for those seas, and who had been trained by the Admiral."[40] The monarchs sent La Cosa to Portugal in 1503 to investigate a report that the Portuguese had sent four ships to the Pearl Coast, a claim that he verified. Then, in February 1504, they named him captain-general of four ships that they sent to further the discoveries in that area. His last voyage was as the king's lieutenant on the Ojeda expedition of 1509. He was killed in February 1510 in a battle with the Indians.

The evidence indicates that the Juan de la Cosa on both the first and the second voyages was one and the same person. This raises two very important questions. Was La Cosa captain of his own vessel (*maestre*) at the time of the sinking of the *Santa María* or was he a supernumerary? If La Cosa was the *maestre* referred to by Columbus, would Columbus, notably suspicious and jealous, have so completely forgiven the man who presumably caused him to lose his flagship on the first voyage, not only taking that man along on the second voyage but also training La Cosa as a navigator, as a rival? It doesn't make sense. If, as will be suggested below, the *Santa María* was abandoned unnecessarily, such an act surely would have required the connivance of the owner. Interestingly, not only did La Cosa sail with Columbus on the second voyage but one of the naos was named the *Gallega*, also the original name of the *Santa María*. Much about the story of the loss of the flagship is unconvincing. What really happened to the *Santa María*?

The Loss of the *Santa María*

Detailed accounts of what happened to the *Santa María* appear only in the two Las Casas versions of the *Diario* and in Hernando's *Historie*. The stranding was referred to briefly (without mention of the crew's supposed treachery) on two occasions in the testimony given many years later in the *Pleitos*. The parts played by both Columbus and the *maestre* must be closely investigated. It simply does not make sense that such a skilled sailor as Columbus was said to be, as well as the ship's owner, could have been so inept in the efforts to re-float the vessel.

The loss of the *Santa María* was first described by Las Casas in his paraphrase of Columbus's log for December 25. This entry will be used as the basis for the study of these events:

Sailing with little wind yesterday from the sea of Santo Tomás toward Cape Santa he was about one league away until the first watch had passed that would have been at eleven o'clock at night. [The Admiral] decided to go to sleep because there had been two days and a night that he had not slept. As it was calm, the sailor who steered the ship decided to go to sleep and left the tiller to a young grummet, something that the Admiral had always strictly forbidden on the whole voyage, whether there was wind or there was calm. It is important to know that the grummets were not allowed to steer. The Admiral was safe from the *bancos* [banks] and the *peñas* [rocks] because on Sunday when he sent the ship's boats to that king they had passed to the East of the said Cape Santa for a good three leagues and a half, and the sailors had seen all of the coast and the [   ] shallows that are between the said Cape Santa to the east-southeast for a good three leagues, and they saw where one could pass, something that in all the voyage had not been done. It pleased Our Lord that at the twelfth hour of the night, as they had seen the Admiral lie down and rest, and they saw that it was dead calm and the sea was as in a bowl they all lay down to sleep, and the tiller stayed in the hands of that boy. And the waters that were running took the ship onto one of those banks, which, although it was night, sounded so [loud] that they could be heard and seen from a good league [away]. And she went up on it so gently that it was almost not felt. The boy, who felt the tiller and heard the noise of the sea gave the alarm, at which the Admiral came out, and he was so quick that still none [of the others] had felt that they were run aground. Then the *maestre* of the vessel who was on watch came out, and the Admiral told him and the others to haul in the ship's boat that they towed to the stern, and to take an anchor and set it to stern and he with many more jumped into the ship's boat and the Admiral thought that they were doing as he ordered, they only cared to flee to the caravel that was upwind about a half a league. The caravel, virtuously, did not want to receive them and for this reason they returned to the ship, but the boat of the caravel was first. When the Admiral saw that they fled and that they were his people, and the waters were ebbing and the ship was now broadside to the sea, seeing no other remedy he ordered that the mast be cut and to lighten the ship as much as could be to see if he could get her out, and as the waters still ebbed it couldn't be remedied, and she listed toward the cross sea even though the seas were little or nothing, and then the ship's planking opened up, but not the ship. The

Admiral went to the caravel to put the men from the ship in safety in the caravel, and as the off-shore breeze was now blowing, and there remained much of the night, and as they didn't know how far the banks extended, he jogged until day. And he then went to the ship from inside of the reef of the [sand]bank [*restringa del banco*].[41]

The story in the *Historie* is basically the same. It is given in the first person, and Columbus is quoted as saying that the ship ran up on some rocks (*unos peñas*). Explaining why he felt safe at this time, Columbus said that he knew of the locations of the sandbanks and reefs (*bancos y escollos*). Later he returned to the ship from the inside of the reef (*restringa*).[42] It is one thing to run a ship on a reef and quite another on a sandbank. To say that it was a reef is to accentuate the difficulty in which the Admiral found himself. Incidentally, the boy's hearing of the sound of the waves on the reefs in no way indicates proximity of the vessel to those reefs. On a quiet tropical night the sound of groundswell on a barrier reef can be heard from a great distance.

In his letter to Santángel, Columbus cryptically reported: "So I went on in this fashion until the 16 of January, when I determined to return to Your Highnesses, as much because I had already found most of what I sought as because I had only one caravel left, because the nao that I brought I had left in Your Highnesses' village of La Navidad, with the men there using it for fortification." He gave no hint of a sinking!

Bernáldez speculated, "It was necessary, as it appeared, to leave them [part of the crews] because, as the ship had been lost, there was not in which they could return."[43] Fernández de Oviedo offered information rarely commented on. He wrote of Columbus's arrival at Española: "In the entrance to the port, the flagship, called the *Gallega*, touched ground and opened up, but no man was endangered: many people believed that she had been trickily made to touch [bottom], in order to leave on the land part of the people, as was done."[44] The Zennaro letter merely announced that Columbus had left some of his men at Navidad and that before departing, he had started a fort and left them supplies and artillery.[45] Martire mentioned only the loss of the boat. He was, however, the first to report in a published work that the boat had foundered on a reef.[46]

Some of the modern accounts have improved on the matter, making it clear that Columbus was in a very perilous position indeed. The Morison version of this incident is replete with details not to be found in any contemporary account:

> [The] *Santa María* slid onto a shelving coral reef in Caracol Bay, so gently that nobody was awakened. . . . Columbus promptly sized up the situation. *Santa María* had grounded gently, bow on; and as she drew more water aft than forward, the best chance to float her was to warp an anchor out into deep water, lead the cable through the tiller-port to the big windlass forward and kedge her off stern first. . . . Instead of executing this proper seamanlike order, Juan de la Cosa with some of his Basque pals piled into the boat and pulled away to *Niña.* . . . In the meanwhile, *Santa María* was being driven higher and higher on the reef by the long swells that came in from seaward, her stern swung around so that she lay athwart the seas, each surge lifted her up and let her down with a thump on the rock; and coral rock can punch holes in a wooden ship faster than any other kind.

At this point Morison made an interesting, yet equally questionable, observation: "Since this was one of the notable shipwrecks of history, we may pause a moment to comment. There is no allusion to it in the prolonged lawsuit [an inaccurate assertion by Morison] between the heirs of Columbus and the crown, in which every effort was made to cast dirt on the departed Admiral. Hence it is natural to conclude that his own account of it is correct." Here it was the Basques, not the Paleños, who were to blame. More important is the apparent fact that Morison, a competent seaman himself, implicitly recognized that the *Diario* version makes little sense and justified it with the simplistic explanation that if the Admiral said so, the account is true. Accordingly, he concluded, "So singular an action on the part of a shipmaster and ship owner can hardly be explained except by some grave defect in his character."[47] This is a questionable conclusion, based on unsupportable assumptions.

Morrison believed that at the time of the grounding, the vessel was seaward of the reef, with the swell driving it ever higher onto the reef as well as accounting for the broadsiding. If, instead, the ship was inside of the reef, as reported by Columbus, throwing out a stern anchor would have avoided broadsiding on an ebb tide. Columbus's later statement that he had meant to bypass this bay with its village confirms that at the time the ill-fated *Santa María* was inside, not outside, the reef and sandbank.

As for Morison's later statement "holes . . . in her bottom," the *Diario* told it quite differently: "And then the seams opened up but not the ship."[48] Sale wrote, with greater disregard for the facts, how "the whole beam drove against the coral and each wave lifted her up and down on the hard, sharp extrusions of the rock."[49] For Wilford, "The current had carried Santa María onto a shallow coral reef."[50] According to the Phillipses, "The tide was running out, and as the ship stood higher and higher out of water her planking opened and broke apart."[51] These fanciful tales ignore the next day's entry in the *Diario*, in which Columbus reported that the vessel was "in as good condition as she was when left Spain except that in order to take out the casks and the merchandise she was cut and opened up somewhat."[52]

Fernández-Armesto made a brief reference, based on the *Historia*, to "the treachery of the 'men of Palos' who had begun by providing a dud ship and ended by failing to ease it off the rocks."[53] This accusation has been current over the years. It is based on the following sentence in the *Diario*: "The Admiral saw that they fled and that they were his people," the "his" being taken to be a reference to the earlier mention of the "*maestre* of the vessel . . . and the Admiral told him and the others." In the awkward Spanish in which this passage is written, it is equally possible to read the "his" as referring to either the *maestre* or even the Admiral himself. Whichever way one takes it, the reference made by Fernández-Armesto to the "dud ship" provided by the "men of Palos" ignores the fact that Palos was ordered to supply two caravels, not a nao. Actually only one of the caravels was from Palos; the *Niña* was from the nearby town of Moguer.

A ready explanation is found in the *Diario* for the modern-day confusion between reefs and sandbanks. Outside of the bay in question there was a barrier reef. In the passages for these days Columbus used the word *restringa* alone for a reef. On the day before the ship was lost, the *Diario* gave sailing directions for entering this bay: "Another *restringa* [reef] and shoals . . . go far out to sea and reach toward the cape for almost two leagues."[54] Inside of these his men found a channel, seven fathoms deep with a gravelly bottom. Columbus wrote that on the day after the grounding, he approached the stricken ship "from inside of the reef of the *restringa del banco* [sandbank]."[55] On the very next day Columbus completely changed his version of the story. The *Diario* gave the account in the first person: "It is certain (he says) that if I had not run aground that I would have passed by without anchoring in this place, because it is located inside a large bay and there are in it two or three *restingas de bajas* [shoals] nor would I have left people here on this trip."[56] This indicated that Columbus had no intention of visiting the king's village one and a half leagues inside the bay; instead he had intended to sail past it from outside of the barrier reef. Despite this, his two boats were completely off course and inside "this place" when the grounding occurred. Were both caravels off course unintentionally? The change cannot be attributed to current alone, since the *Niña* was ahead of the *Santa María* by half a league, and both vessels were inside of, instead of outside of, the barrier reef at the time of the grounding of the *Santa María*. How long could it have taken for the ship's boat to row half a league? Was it not possible for the two ships' boats to return in time, given the slow ebb flow, to at least set out the stern anchor?

The lack of seamanship makes it difficult to accept the *Diario* version of the stranding of the vessel. At this time Columbus had two options: kedge the ship off or hold the stern to shore with an anchor as the vessel was on the land side of the bank. The objective would be to hold it perpendicular to the area that the ship was grounded on, in order to avoid being broadsided. The incoming tide alone would then have probably been sufficient to allow the crew to ease it off without trouble, a wait of only a few hours. The tides on the northern coast of Española are on the order of two feet maximum—that is, at the most two inches per hour.

There were no contemporary accounts of Morison's "holes punched in her bottom," which would have been at the very least highly unusual if such had happened in the dead calm reported by Columbus. The groundswell on an ebb tide could not alone have done this, even if the ship had been on a corral reef, which it was not.

Furthermore, Las Casas explained in the *Historia* that only the planking "between the ribs" opened up. It is not hard to see why Morison had problems with Columbus's log entries. Sale viewed the grounding even more inaccurately: "The Admiral ordered the flagship abandoned and watched in the light of the dawn as she began to break up and sink."[57] The ship neither broke up nor sank.

Robert Fuson stayed close to the facts as we know them through the *Diario*. He wrote, "The ship went on the bank so quietly that it was hardly noticeable. . . . Columbus used the word *banco* (bank) where the *Santa María* was grounded not his term for coral reef (*restringa de piedras*). The ship appears to have missed the reef, here the waves made the noise Columbus heard, and gently eased into a sandbank. The ship was not really damaged very much, merely hopelessly stuck."[58] Was it?

Sank or Scuttled?

In Columbus's letter reporting on his second voyage as given in *El libro copiador*, he (with La Cosa also on board) coped with similar yet even worse problems without trouble. Bernáldez reported that while off Jamaica, "they found themselves obstructed by many islands and in very little depth, in such a fashion that they couldn't find a channel that would allow them to go forward, and finally at the end of a day and a half, by force of anchors and capstan, they were able to pass the vessels almost a fathom over dry land."[59] Hernando and Las Casas each reported that on this occasion he was unable to extricate the ships by use of anchors and cables but hauled them over the shallows bow first, which caused a great deal of damage to the vessels.[60] This was a far more difficult feat than the one required for hauling off a sandbank on an incoming tide.

Columbus's fourth letter in *El libro copiador* was apparently the source for Bernáldez and the others who noted that he had trouble navigating in some of these waters. He wrote:

> Due to the little depth with big boats, and [it was] very dangerous to navigate through so many channels, where many times all three of my boats were stranded on dry ground, so that one couldn't help the other,

and other times there was less than one codo[61] of water, and [it] was hauled forward by force of capstan and anchors . . . I lost many of my supplies that had been soaked in water when the boats were stranded, that at times they were ready to open up completely; moreover I had maestros and all equipment to repair and make them new, if it was necessary, and I traveled well supplied with everything.[62]

The length of a *codo* ("cubit") was approximately 1.25 feet, and Columbus's smaller vessels drew 5–7 feet. As will be seen, he had, as was his custom, a ship's carpenter and a caulker, on his first voyage as well as this one. Those biographers who have traditionally chosen to ignore the information on this subject provided by the early chroniclers must now, with this information supplied by Columbus, reevaluate their earlier opinions on the sinking of the *Santa María*.

Undoubtedly, the strangest part of this story is the part supposedly played by La Cosa. Regardless of the fact that he was the owner of the vessel, if he was indeed also its master, could he have been so incompetent, so cowardly, or both as to have deserted his companions on a ship run aground in a "dead calm"? There was certainly no immediate danger to anybody. If Columbus was really seeking help from the *Niña*, he would normally have used the agreed-on signaling device for that voyage—a lombard shot. La Cosa, as has been demonstrated, was highly regarded later in life, as both an outstanding seaman and a reliable Crown officer. His record on Urabá indicated an unusually valorous man. Thus his personal qualities can hardly be doubted. The fact that Columbus took him on the second voyage indicated either an unusually forgiving nature or one with some other agenda. Columbus imagined injuries and rarely, if ever, forgave them. The accounts of the loss of this ship and of La Cosa's supposed involvement simply do not make sense.

This brings us to the rumor of a scuttling, a story repeated by Fernández de Oviedo, who not only was a contemporary of Columbus's but also claimed friendship with Columbus's pilot on the first voyage, quoting him on several occasions. Without considering the reasons expressed above for doubting the Columbus story, why have so many English-speaking historians ignored what

Fernández de Oviedo wrote on this matter? The same authors who have ignored this rumor recounted, sometimes at length, his version of the unknown pilot and quoted his remark that the Antilles may have been the Hesperides and, if so, had belonged to Spain for centuries before Columbus rediscovered them. What made this particular rumor exceptional?

It must be recalled that La Cosa was later compensated by the Crown for the loss of the *Santa María* on this voyage. The *Diario* was a confidential document, one not for general distribution. If Columbus and La Cosa had connived in this mishap, proof that it was an accident would have been necessary. What better source than the ship's log? If, as is not inconceivable, Ferdinand knew the truth of the scuttling, perhaps even ordered it, everyone concerned would have kept his silence to protect the official story. The king would have played along with the charade and would have allowed the owner to be compensated for the ship that had been sacrificed to the Crown's cause.

In the fourth letter Columbus explained that his two large naos, the *Gallega* and his flagship the *Marigalante*, had been brought to Española with the express purpose of using them for building forts in the interior. He proposed to do the same again on his fourth voyage. This is direct evidence that ships were used by Columbus on more than this one occasion for supplying building materials with which to carry out colonization plans.

Some historians have found it to be highly unusual that no punishment was meted out to either the officer of the watch or the sailor in charge of the tiller. Ferdinand was a stern ruler. He received what has been assumed to be the original of the ship's log for this journey. If the account of the sinking was told there in the same way as in the versions known to us, it is highly doubtful that under normal circumstances he would later have compensated La Cosa for the loss. In the same way, there is no question that Columbus was normally a severe taskmaster. One need only recall the penalties to be imposed on anyone on the second voyage who denied the Admiral's claim that Cuba was a mainland: his tongue would be cut out, and if a ship's boy, he would receive a hundred lashes as well.

The Founding of Navidad

Historians have long claimed that Columbus established a fort at Navidad because there was not enough room on the *Niña* to carry the crews from the two ships. Recently Wilford put it clearly: "Columbus decided that he had little choice—all the men could not possibly return to Spain on the two remaining ships—but to establish a garrison there among these friendly Tainos."[63] The Phillipses were equally certain that such was the case: "Her planking opened and broke apart.... There was no choice but to leave a portion of the fleet's crew on Española, because they could not all travel home on the *Niña*."[64]

At the time of the sinking of the *Santa María*, the remaining two vessels, the *Niña* and the *Pinta*, were separated. The *Historie*'s account said that Columbus found out from the Indians on December 27 that Pinzón with the *Pinta* was nearby.[65] If so, he could easily have been summoned to help. According to the *Diario*, the two vessels were shortly afterward reunited at nearby Montecristi, at which time, had Columbus so desired, they could have readily returned and picked up the men left behind a few miles back at Navidad. Witnesses in the *Pleitos* testified that Pinzón did go all the way back to Navidad for Columbus and had protested at the time against leaving his "friends and relatives there."[66] Nothing prevented the two caravels from being reunited, in which case there would have been more than enough room for both crews.

The capacity of a caravel to carry extra passengers is the best clue available today for what really happened. This number can be determined by checking how many men Columbus carried in one caravel in analogous situations. When Columbus sailed from Navidad to begin his homeward journey, he left behind 39 men out of a possible complement of 66 for the *Santa María* and the *Niña*. These figures are the generally accepted ones today. Gould's higher estimate of 118 for all three ships was not used by any of the authors under review. Fernández de Oviedo[67] and Paolo Interiano[68] also estimated the number at about 120. If correct in whole or part and if, improbably, all of the additional 28–30 men reported by Gould and these Columbus contemporaries were carried on just these two vessels involved at Navidad, there would have been at the most 96 men to carry on the *Niña*. This vessel is believed to have had a crew of 26 men; Gould listed 41 for the *Santa María*. Yet all of the modern authors assumed a total of only 90 men on all three ships on the first voyage. This would have left at most 66 to return on the *Niña*. None of these authors availed themselves of Gould's and the early chroniclers' higher figures in order to lend more credence to their claims that there was insufficient room on the *Niña* for the combined crews.

Hernando wrote that at the time Columbus set sail for Spain in March 1496, he was worried about tales that earlier returnees may have told the court. "For which reason, with two hundred and twenty five Christians and thirty Indians, on Thursday the 10th of March of the year 1496, he embarked . . . with two caravels named the *Santa Cruz* and the *Niña* which were the same boats that he had taken to discover Cuba."[69] If the ships' complements were equally divided, the *Niña* on this voyage carried 127 people. This was 30 more than the maximum that it would have possibly carried if the ship had taken on board all of the crew and passengers listed by Gould and others. As for the effects of crowding, this crossing in 1496 was Columbus's longest due to the error that he made in trying to first work his way home by sailing down the Leeward Islands, yet he made it to port in Spain without major problems.

Contemporary accounts of Columbus's second voyage listed from 1,200 to 1,500 men on seventeen ships of various sizes: three naos, twelve caravels, and two barques. It has never been specified whether these figures included the crews. Columbus wrote that he had 1,000 men with him, a figure that would not have included the crews. The figure of 1,200 makes for an average of 70 men to a ship; on some ships the number would have been higher, since many of the vessels were purposefully very small and were therefore unable to take on board many supernumeraries. The fleet also carried supplies for the men left at Navidad, for the new colonizers, and for the crews' return trip to Spain. Besides the men and supplies, there were horses, mules, sheep, and hogs on board.

When Nicolás de Ovando came to take over the governorship of the island he brought with him somewhere between 3,000 men, as reported by Angelo Trivigiano, and 2,500 men, as reported by others, on board twenty-five to thirty ships. The complement of one of these vessels, the *Rábida,* is known because the ship was lost at sea with 120 persons. Whichever figure is correct, the fact remains that there were at least 100 men per vessel, without counting the crews.[70] At the end of the fourth voyage Columbus brought back from Jamaica to Cuba the complements of four vessels in one ship. No one was left behind because there was no room. The positions taken by the authors under review are obviously without historical foundation.

The accounts given in the *Diario,* the *Historia,* and the *Historie* of the loss of the *Santa María* through a grounding, and of the failure of the crew to save the vessel by normal means, are single-sourced, each of them presumably based on the same long-lost log of Columbus. Other reports are few. In 1535 Pinzón's son testified in a *Pleitos* hearing: "He heard Viçente Yañes, the uncle of this witness say . . . that going as captain of a boat, and the said Christoval Colon going together in another boat, the boat of the said don Christoval Colon hit some rocks and it was lost and that the said Viçente had picked up the said don Christoval Colon in his boat so that he would not be lost."[71]

Herrera believed that there were many reasons for "populating this place." First, if the people of Castile knew that Spaniards were already there, they would be more inclined to go there themselves. As for the overcrowding on the *Niña,* he said that to take home all the men would have required "much trouble." He ended by finding it "understandable" that the settlement was necessary to ensure authorization for colonizing.

Contemporaneous sources support Fernández de Oviedo's report that Columbus was said to have established the fort at Navidad in order to "occupy" the land. In the *Pleitos,* the witnesses were asked if they knew that "there [at Navidad] died many of the kindred and friends of the said Martin Alonso in order to take title to the land." The reply was unanimously in the affirmative. By occupying this land, Columbus not only would have established a concrete basis for his royal privileges as viceroy and governor but also, and more important, would have established title for Spain by right of occupation. Thacher noted a copy of a letter in the *Historie* in which Columbus was quoted as writing: "I informed your Highness of the customs of the inhabitants, of the fertility of the country, and of the colony which I had left there to hold possession of the lands."[72]

The need to occupy was embodied in the *Capitulaciónes de Santa Fé* as well as juridically from time immemorial. In any jurisdictional dispute with Portugal, then—as today—possession would have been nine-tenths of the law. There may also be some significance in the fact that Columbus left his mistress's brother, Diego de Arana, in charge of the men at Navidad, perhaps to protect the family interest. The land was now occupied, and his intent to make a return trip to colonize the island was clear.

Interestingly, Columbus carried with him specialists not of a kind such as one would expect to find on either an ordinary trading vessel or an armada on a diplomatic mission to the Gran Khan. Besides Arana, he left Gutierrez, a Crown representative, and Escovedo, fleet secretary, as well as perhaps the two ship's surgeons, who were Jewish. If, as reported by one of them, there were several other Jewish crew members, it would have been illegal for them to return to Spain at the end of the voyage.

Las Casas and Hernando reported, in addition to the ship's carpenter and caulker, an artillery man, a cooper, and a tailor. Thacher added to this list of men who stayed behind a lawyer and a silversmith. Gould added a goldsmith, a painter, another cooper, a joiner, a servant, and a cabin boy, for a total of fifteen or sixteen nonsailors out of the thirty-nine men left behind. The *Diario* listed only nine of these—Arana, Gutierrez, Escovedo, the caulker, a carpenter, a bombardier, the cooper, a physician, and a tailor.[73] These men were apparently all from the *Santa María*. This list indicates that there were more supernumeraries carried on board than generally believed. What was their purpose? Were these men—tailor, lawyer, silversmith, joiner, and cooper—who were left behind at Navidad part of a larger shore party originally intended to be left on any land discovered? In his log, Columbus wrote that besides leaving the men a year's supplies, he left them seeds to grow their own food and truck for trading with the natives. Was this foresight? What was the merchandise that Columbus said that he had to take out of the stranded hull? Midpoint in his voyage, he still had enough wine and supplies to leave on the island to last thirty-nine men for a year. If nothing else, these two vessels were certainly heavily stocked for the voyage. This odd assortment of skills and supplies hardly fits with what would be expected in a fleet supposedly headed for Asia, seen at the time as the source of great wealth.

The following passage, from Bernáldez, merits a closer reading than it has normally been given:

> Christobal Colon established there [*Tomó asiento*] on Española, called Haiti by the Indians, a town to which he gave the name of Navidad, and he left there forty men with artillery and arms and victuals, beginning to make a fortress, and he left master workmen to build it and he left them enough to eat for a certain time, he left there *some of the special men of experience and understanding of everything that he had brought* [emphasis added], and it was unavoidable, as it seemed, to leave them, because as they had lost a ship there was not in which to come, and this was kept secret here and it was said that they only stayed as a beginning for a settlement.[74]

In this paragraph, Bernáldez drew attention to the fact that Columbus took with him, on the voyage of exploration, "special men." More important, he acknowledged that at the time there was an effort, which he obviously did not agree with, to portray the settlement as a colonizing move and that, in order to do so, the sinking of the *Santa María* was "kept secret." Martire, who also knew Columbus personally and was a most prolific purveyor of news and gossip, wrote in his *Décades*, "He left thirty-eight men . . . to get to know the country . . . until he should return in person."[75]

In the *Diario* on the day after the grounding, Columbus speculated that the Lord had let the ship go aground so that people could be left there. Columbus's constant theme, then and later in life, was that he was in many things the agent of the Lord. There is nothing incongruous in his statement that the Lord had ordained the grounding and that he carried out the Lord's wishes. In this case, he may have given the Lord a helping hand by not re-floating the vessel after it ran aground, accidentally or on purpose. It is perhaps not unrelated that the very day after the grounding, Columbus devoted his attention in the journal to giving reasons for establishing a fort at this "excellent" sight, one peopled by such "friendly natives," as well as to discussing the gold (mentioned thirteen times just on December 26) to be found there. The moment was now opportune for the men he left behind to find the mine from which the gold came. All of these circumstances are mentioned in his journal entries for the three crucial days for the settlement of Navidad—hardly the reactions of a distraught, shipwrecked fleet commander!

If, as Columbus wrote, the *Santa María* was adrift inside a bay in which there were at least three known reefs and assorted shallows, all of them inside a barrier reef and with sufficient current to keep the vessel under way, it remains inconceivable that the fleet commander, the captain, the owner, and the pilots all would have taken this moment to go to sleep. And, for this one and only time on the whole voyage, the ship's fate was supposedly left in the hands of a boy holding a tiller located middecks, out of which he was unable to see ocean, sky, or nearby land. For that matter, the effectiveness of a tiller on a boat adrift is minimal. The pressure on the tiller of a slight sea current is too little to ensure direction. One improbable explanation is that the vessel was adrift at the time and that those in charge, underestimating the current, felt it was safe to leave the boy in charge. The question is, in charge of what? He couldn't see to steer.

The sum of the exceptions from the norm in this whole affair is simply astounding. A close look at the pretext that men were left at Navidad because there was no room for them on the *Niña* is demonstrably false. The fact that two contemporaries reported a rumor that the boat was scuttled is significant. One contemporary chronicler reported a story that the men were left there simply to colonize the island. Other contemporary sources believed that the men had been left at Navidad to establish a settlement on American soil. If so, is it not historiographically inexcusable to ignore any or all of these contemporary accounts? At the very least, they require mention and, preferably, analysis, neither of which was provided by any of the historians under study.

Return Voyage

Apparently, Columbus and Pinzón met on Española while both caravels were at sea. According to the *Diario* entry for January 6, they turned around and headed back to Montecristi to find safe anchorage. At this time Columbus noted that Pinzón had been anchored only fifteen leagues from Navidad,[76] yet according to Columbus's own estimate made on January 4 at Montecristi, they were eighteen leagues from Navidad, and the two boats had just backtracked ten leagues from where Pinzón had been staying. To a sailor such as Columbus, a difference of between fifteen and twenty-eight leagues is considerable. In the first mention he was accusing Pinzón of treacherous behavior; in the second he was giving sailing directions. In either case, had they wanted to go back to pick up the men left behind, distance would have been no barrier; Columbus wrote later that it was only a day's journey. Fernández de Oviedo reported that instead of backtracking at this time, the two caravels continued traveling to the east and landed at the site of the future town of Isabela to hold their peace meeting. In his *Historia*, Las Casas said they met at the Rio de Gracia, where Pinzón had been moored "for sixteen days." This river lies between Montecristi and Isabela.

Once reconciled, the vessels sailed along the coast to the east. They arrived on January 13 at a bay, the site of a minor incident that has sometimes been blown out of proportion. The *Diario* account is relatively simple: Columbus sent a shore party to treat with the Indians. After the Spaniards had bought two bows, the Indians

> didn't want to give more. First they prepared to rush the Christians and take them. They went running to take their bows and arrows where they had set them apart, and they returned with cords in their hands . . . to tie [up] the Christians. Seeing them come running toward them, the Christians being ready because the Admiral had always warned them of this, the Christians rushed them; and they gave one Indian a big cut on the buttocks and they wounded another in the chest with an arrow, upon which, seeing that, they set out to flee and none stayed, one leaving his arrows here and another his bow there. It is said the Christians would have killed many of them if the pilot who went with them as captain had not prevented them.[77]

The mythologies have occasionally promoted this very minor incident into a battle with the Indians. Neither Martire, Fernández de Oviedo, nor Bernáldez mentioned it, although they gave other details from this day's entry, such as the account that these Indians were different from those previously seen and that they wore their hair long like the women of Castile. Hernando wrote that when the ship's boat approached the shore, the men saw "fifty-five all nude armed Indians hidden in the trees."[78] The Indians attempted to take the Spaniards, who wounded two, as recounted in the *Diario*. Columbus did say that this encounter pleased him because the Indians would now fear the Christians; an example had been made. In his *Historia*, Las Casas concluded, "This was the first fight that there was in the Indies and where blood ran, and it can be believed that he of the arrow died and even he of the slashed buttocks would not have stayed very healthy."[79]

According to Morison, the "Indians ran back to their deposit of weapons as if to pick them up and attack."[80] Wilford described this affair as a skirmish, with the connotation of an engagement between opposing forces. The Phillipses found that the Europeans had encountered "the first hostile islanders of the voyage . . . the Europeans put them to flight after a brief skirmish."[81] Perhaps these authors meant to indicate only a small and insignificant encounter. The hostility is shown as though of the Indians against the Spaniards. For centuries to come, Native Americans were to die because of what was seen as their hostility. Sale described the incident more vividly: "It may fairly be called the first pitched battle between Europeans and Indians in the New World—the first display of armed power, and the will to use it, of the white invaders."[82] It was by no means a "pitched battle." Columbus's reaction showed a new aspect of his attitude toward the natives. He had earlier seen them as good servants and prospective slaves, but now he observed that, when out of order, they had to be severely disciplined. Todorov devoted a chapter to the ambiguity in Columbus's treatment of the Indians but did not include this first manifestation of the Admiral's magisterial attitude.

It was at this stage on the return voyage that Columbus introduced the notion of islands to the south, of an island inhabited only by women, and of their mates, the fearsome Caribs who "eat human flesh." Columbus said that he heard these tales from the Caribs he encountered at this time, although he understood only some of their words, and "the Indians that he brought with him understood more, although they found differences between the languages, because of the great distances between the lands."[83] Many modern historians believe that these comments are evidence of readings of Marco Polo and/or Sir John Mandeville. Of course, similar legends have existed since time immemorial and were repeated over the ages by numerous European travelers to the East. Columbus also understood that "on the Island of Carib and Matininó there was much copper." Las Casas added a marginal notation: "It was never determined afterwards that there were any such women."[84] Las Casas could not know then that there is also no evidence today that these Indians were cannibals, yet this yarn provided Europe with its common word—"cannibals"—for such people.

These observations by Columbus were followed by his estimate as to the geographical position of these islands. The *Diario* entry for January 14 notes: "He says that he found much grass in that bay of the kind that he found in the gulf when he came on the discovery, for which reason he believed that there were islands straight down to the east from where he started to find them because he takes it for certain that grass originates in shallow water close to land. And he says that if that is so, these Indies were very near to the Canary Islands, and for that reason he believed that they were less than four hundred leagues apart."[85] Either he was fudging his figures at this time or he soon had time to reconsider. In his letter on the second voyage, he found the distance to be what he expected it to be—eight hundred leagues.

He next set sail on the sixteenth to go to "the island of Carib . . . because it is on the way." He chose an east-northeast course, which would have taken him far to the north of Puerto Rico, not south to the islands he had been told of. The Indians told him that he should change course and head southeast, which would have taken him to Puerto Rico. However, he found that the freshening wind to the east was what he needed to head home, and accordingly he set off on that route. Later, he contradicted his earlier statement, observing that the Indians had told him he was now on the route to Matininó. "But he doubted that the Indians knew the route well. . . . The admiral says that these two islands . . . were to the southeast and that the

Indians didn't know how to show him the route."[86] This is by no means the first time that Columbus (or his copyists) contradicted an entry made on the same day. What remains puzzling is that at this particular time he headed in almost the directly opposite direction from the island that he claimed to have been seeking, yet on the second voyage, he set his route directly and correctly for those same islands that he had said earlier were nearest by sea to the Canary Islands.

Morison read into this account of the marvels to be found in the Indies a search of proof as to where Columbus supposedly was:

> From the Indians of Hispaniola, particularly four youths who boarded *Niña* at Samana and were promptly impressed, Columbus learned of an *Isla de Carib* (probably Puerto Rico), visible "from there." The Admiral was curious to see those dreadful man-eating Caribs, of whose incredible exploits he had been told by the timid Tainos, and he was even more eager to check their tale of an island named *Matinino*, "wholly inhabited by women without men." . . . Now curiously enough, the Arawaks had a very similar myth . . . just as Marco Polo had described on the Female Island in the Indian Ocean. Columbus's eagerness to see this Isle of Women . . . [was] because it would furnish that incontrovertible evidence of being in the Indies which he still lacked.[87]

The Marco Polo connection was an article of faith to Morison and his followers. Perhaps the Admiral was merely curious or was even eager to find the islands so near the Canaries, and he may even have known his Greek classics with their similar tales. The fact that on the third day out Columbus, seeing a flight of birds, "believed that there were in that direction some islands and that ESE of the island of Española he said was the Carib Island and that of Matininó and others"[88] led Morison to believe that this "gave him an idea for the Second Voyage."[89] Wilford accepted the influence of Mandeville and Marco Polo on the Admiral's imagination, Columbus finding only "humans who differed from Europeans but were less exotic than the black Africans he had seen on his Portuguese voyages. . . . Perhaps these poor, simple islanders could point him to the creatures who were part of the Asia of his expectations."[90] Such speculative accounts ignore the fact that on his first day in the Americas,

Columbus explained, without showing any surprise, that the natives were of the same color as the natives of the Canary Islands because both groups were on the same latitude. No Oriental mysteries were invoked here.

The storm that the two caravels encountered on their way home was described differently in the *Diario* and the *Historie*. As Henige pointed out, many of the differences in the two accounts are insignificant in themselves but do add up to two different stories. The *Historie* version was purportedly taken from a verbatim account by Columbus, yet the Las Casas paraphrase of some of these same events gave twice the detail. Thus one has three versions to choose from. Fuson was not the first to combine elements from several versions into one readily understandable, if not necessarily accurate, account.

After passing through various trials and tribulations in the Azores, Columbus finally entered the Tagus River in Portugal on March 4. He first saw land while in the midst of a raging storm; earlier he reported that his sails were "torn." He rode out part of the storm under bare poles until he decided that he was too near the shore and headed back out to sea using his mainsail only. This led Morison to assume that this was the only sail left to him and that he was now "with only one square sail between him and utter destruction."[91] No clues are available today as to the condition of the sail locker; however, Morison's version does provide heightened dramatic effect to the sea perils survived by his hero.

While in Portugal, Columbus met first with the king and later with the queen. The *Diario* merely related the many courtesies that the king offered him. The king is quoted as saying "moreover that he understood that in the capitulation that existed between the king and queen and himself that conquest belonged to him."[92] Columbus diplomatically replied that he knew nothing of the capitulation, only that he had been instructed by the Spanish sovereigns not to go near the Mina or Guinea. The Portuguese chronicler Rui da Pina was present at the interview. He wrote that the Portuguese king was upset that he had lost the chance to sponsor this voyage, a perfectly understandable observation. Pina also told an interesting story about how Columbus's Indians made a map out of pebbles to show the king the number of the islands. Natives of various islands in the Pacific did use pebbles (or dried beans, according to Morison) for such purposes, but this is the only contemporary record of such a use in the Caribbean. Again, there is neither reason to accept nor reason to doubt this story.

A later accretion is the claim that some of the Portuguese nobles wanted to kill Columbus so that he could not take news of his discovery back to Spain. This ignores the fact that he would have needed Portuguese authorization to send his courier to Barcelona from the place where he was anchored on March 4 or 5. Columbus did not meet with the king until the ninth, by which time we know the news had already reached Spain. Murdering him at this late date would have been not only pointless but a near certain call for war. However, there is no telling what may have gone through the minds of courtiers at this time; such a verbal threat may have been made as easily as not. Regardless of what happened at these meetings, Columbus was allowed to go back to Lisbon and embark for Spain.

Morison not only accepted the story of the assassination threat but saw a possible trap in the king's offer to send Columbus and his pilot to Spain by land. In the *Diario*, Columbus reported that the king's messenger had offered them mules and an escort. "To the pilot he ordered a favor of twenty *espadines* (Portuguese gold coins)." Morison asked, "Was this messenger endeavoring to suborn the pilot? Nobody can tell."[93] Indeed not.

As far as the discovery of America is concerned, nothing of real importance happened on the return voyage. There were minor happenings—the two caravels again became separated, they rode out a storm, they encountered problems with the Portuguese authorities in the Azores—though none were unusual occurrences in sea voyages. A matter of some interest is the fact that whereas on the outbound voyage Columbus underestimated his distances, shown in the lower of his double figures, on the return voyage he overestimated them. If, as has been often suggested, all of this tinkering with the numbers was done with the purpose of preventing others from knowing the route, then it was a waste of time. Some of the captains and pilots who accompanied him not only knew the route but plied it frequently in years to come. Just as we cannot understand the double entries, we also cannot understand his miscalculations on the return voyage. The fact is he set sail, he discovered land, and he returned. Now he had to hurry home and report to his sovereigns the discovery of their new empire.

It is natural that the first voyage and its successful conclusion should be the most-studied phase in the life of Columbus. This not only was his great personal achievement but also was to become a matter of transcendental importance for the entire world. Despite the importance of all matters concerned with these monumental events, modern historians have shown a tendency to focus more on the mechanics of the voyage than on its many incongruities. Yet the latter require understanding if the whole is to be perceived in its proper light. The basic sources—the *Diario, El libro copiador,* Hernando's *Historie,* and Las Casas's *Historia*—present sufficient differences in fact and nuance that they should not be quoted from selectively. The nearest that we can come to a basic source is the *Diario,* and it is a hybrid text. Fernández de Oviedo, Bernáldez, Martire, and the *Pleitos* also require close attention, especially when all report the same matters in a like manner.

El libro copiador is a valuable new source that has not yet been sufficiently studied. Some biographers, writing after these manuscripts appeared in print, have jeopardized their positions on some controversial matters by not first referring to it. For example, the first letter in this newfound account offers clues to the use of the word "India" as either a destination or a region. The conventional wisdom is that Columbus was headed for India/Asia. In this chapter the attempt has been made to demonstrate that he was more likely heading for the islands never before visited by Europeans but claimed for centuries to lie somewhere in the vast ocean between Europe and Asia. He may well have had the mainland as a secondary objective and did entertain hopes of reaching the land of the Gran Khan. Claims to the contrary, however, he carried no ambassadorial letter addressed to that incorrectly assumed emperor of China.

Columbus did believe that the islands he sought were in the proximity of Cipango—Japan. On current *mappaemundi* (the Catalán map and the Fra Mauro) this was the principal island of the many islands shown in Europe's far western ocean. There is no way of establishing today, with any acceptable degree of certainty, where he was headed or where he made his first landfall. Although these matters excite great controversy among modern geographers, historians, and biographers alike, they remain unknowable. The same applies to the double entries that Columbus apparently reported in his shipboard log for daily distance made. Those who study the latter entangle themselves in a conundrum without solution.

The crews' worries that they might become lost at sea or hindered from returning to Spain for lack of favorable winds are certainly understandable. The frequent false sightings of land, and the many indications that land was nearby, would have dashed the hopes and expectations of any crew sailing into the unknown. The buildup of tension as they finally approached land must have seemed almost unendurable. But did these preoccupations with never-appearing land lead to mutiny? Biographers to the contrary, beyond strong grumbling there is no evidence of anything that may have led to even near-mutiny. The fact is that Columbus, perhaps with the assistance of Pinzón and his brothers, persuaded the crews to carry on with their duties.

This leads to the parts played by the Pinzón brothers in the journey. The Crown attorneys in the *Pleitos* made much of the brothers' undoubted contribution to the success of the effort to find islands and lands in the mar Oceano. There is no question that Martín Alonso contributed greatly to the organization for the voyage. Also, as a senior officer, he undoubtedly provided leadership to the many crew members from his hometown of Palos and from the nearby town of Moguer. But were his contributions then and later at sea crucial to the success of Columbus's "Great Enterprise"? Doubtfully.

Gould was one of the first to study the matter of whether the Juan de la Cosa on Columbus's first voyage and the Juan de la Cosa on his second voyage were one and the same person. Morison was among the many who accepted her query as since proven that they were two different people. This provided a simple solution to the question of why Columbus would take with him on the second voyage a man who may have served him badly on the first. It did not answer the similar question regarding Quintero and Vicente Yáñez Pinzón, who were also accused by Columbus of attempted sabotage and rebellion, yet he took each of them with him as captains on future voyages. Other evidence, combined with logic, indicates that there was only one Juan de la Cosa who served with Columbus.

La Cosa was involved in the curious circumstances surrounding the sinking of Columbus's flagship, the *Santa María*. Again, conventional wisdom accepts the explanation as presented in all three of the basic sources: he abandoned ship. More careful scrutiny of these same texts raises serious doubts. Fernández de Oviedo, a friend of the pilot of the unfortunate vessel, reported that the *Santa María* was said to have been scuttled. Columbus's personal friend Bernáldez wrote that people believed that Columbus had left the men in Navidad in order to establish a settlement, a claim also made in testimony given in the *Pleitos*. It has since been almost universally reported that Columbus left the men because there was no room on the *Niña* to embark all of them. Yet direct evidence indicates that on other occasions, Columbus loaded even more men on a single caravel than would have gone home on the *Niña*. Pinzón was deeply disturbed at having his friends and relatives left behind. Once he and the Admiral had been rejoined, just a few miles from Navidad, it would have been a simple matter to go back and pick up the men. There was more than enough room for them on the two caravels.

There was simply no single imperative nautical reason for leaving the men behind. The purpose was probably to fulfill the legal requirements for occupation, without which Columbus would not have had his admiralcy, nor would Spain have had an iron-clad claim to sovereignty over the area. By this act, he ensured his second voyage; the thirty-nine men could not be abandoned. A study of the breakdown by professions and skills of these men is at least indicative that a colonization may have been planned from the start. Is all the evidence conclusive? Maybe not, but that does not justify modern and postmodern authors' passing over it completely as though it never existed. I conclude that Columbus had every intention of leaving men behind to occupy the lands and to await an anticipated second voyage, which did have as its stated objective the colonization of Española. Whether the *Santa María* was unsalvageable or was scuttled mattered little, for Columbus found that the Lord's will had been carried out. A settlement was established in the Americas.

What we do not understand we do not possess.

Goethe (1749–1832)

10
Occupation, Gold, and Religion

It is important to pause to look at where Columbus was headed when he set out on his journey across the ocean, where he thought he was once he arrived, and what he believed he had found. We need also to ask, what were the immediate reactions of Columbus and his sovereigns to the discovery? These reactions are linked inextricably with what preceded. What did each person believe was being sought? Once the sought-after was found, how did each interpret it? Both of these questions have been discussed in previous chapters within an anticipatory context; now they require review under the new set of circumstances, the actual discovery of previously unknown islands.

As will be seen in the chapter on his second voyage, Columbus stated clearly in his third letter in *El libro copiador* where he believed he had been on his first journey. The islands found by Columbus were now officially discovered, and one of them, Española, was now occupied by Spaniards. Columbus even chose to believe that Cuba (which he called Juana—a variation on the Jana, Tana, or Java of pre-Columbian maps and writers?) was part of the mainland. It was of great importance to him at the time to believe this, as he demonstrated on the second voyage when he made all of the crew members sign an affidavit that this land was the mainland. Was this merely an idiosyncratic action on the Admiral's part, or was he involved in a matter of state policy to lay claim to everything, especially mainland, whether it had been found or not?

What might be termed the standard approach by U.S. biographers and historians to these matters is a simple one. Columbus was headed for the land of the Gran Khan, land that he had surmised, from his readings and empirical knowledge, to be some thirty days' west of the Iberian Peninsula. Arriving in the Bahamas, he took title to these lands in the name of Spain. After an accidental foundering of his flagship, he had to leave a shore party on Española due to lack of space on the single surviving boat. He returned to Spain to proclaim the discovery of the "Indies" by the sea route. These statements all contain essential elements of fact; however, Stephen Greenblatt's cautionary remark is *à propos*: "It is important, I think, to resist the drift toward normalizing what was not normal."[1]

There was little, if anything, normal about this whole affair. It was not normal to set off across the Atlantic in search of Asia or anywhere else in the far western ocean. Traditionally the sailors of all nations stayed as close as possible to coastlines. Once land had been discovered, it was not normal to assume that such land was not already in the domain of some sovereign, one whose title could not be challenged by three boats and a handful of men. Columbus himself wrote that although stranded by a receding tide, the *Santa María* was in as good a condition as it was the day that it left Spain. He carried on board ships' carpenters and caulkers, yet he and the ship's owner abandoned the vessel. It was not normal to leave thirty-nine men on an island in uncharted seas. Yet all of these things occurred.

The Objective of the Journey

Columbus and his sovereigns indicated that from the beginning, they were seeking unknown islands and mainlands "ad Indies" ("toward India"). These they found. Any concern for an encounter with the Gran Khan of China was forgotten after Columbus's return to Spain. Columbus believed that Española was Cipango, one of the islands believed to lie in the mar Oceano between India, that is, Asia, and the coast of Spain. Although Cipango was fabled as fabulously rich, no such riches were found, then or later, on Española. Columbus claimed to have found the sought-for mainland, yet he wrote that it had only villages with no evidence of government.

After his return, the Spanish monarchs accepted his estimate as to what it was that he had found—the source of gold. They were sufficiently convinced that they promptly ordered a second voyage with over a thousand men to take possession. Further exploration in the area was ordered. The khan was never referred to by the Crown in connection with these Antillian islands.

Luis Torres was the only person other than Columbus who sailed on this voyage and left a written record. At the end of his diary entry for the day of the landing at Guanahaní, he wrote: "We disembarked on the beach of Fernandez Bay, San Salvador, and took possession of a New World for Spain. Christopher Columbus always believed that this island, and the other ones he sighted later on this voyage of discovery were the Indies, near Japan or China."[2] This only independent witness to leave a written record of the landing is not mentioned in any of the biographies under review here.

Greenblatt found a difference between earlier land-based discoveries and Columbus's: "William of Rubruck in the thirteenth century . . . wrote how 'we came across the Tartars, when I came among them it seemed indeed to me as if I were stepping into some other world.' But however strange the Tartars seemed to William, there had been a sporadic history of contact; William expected them to be there and knew roughly where to find them."[3]

William Woodville Rockhill offered a quite different translation of Rubruck's commentary, one placing a different emphasis on the matter: "We came on the third day across the Tartars, and when I found myself among them it seemed to me of a truth that I had been transported into another century."[4] The different implications in the use of the phrases "other world" and "another century" are obvious. Surely the reaction of Columbus on first finding the Indies was similar. He too had a rough idea as to where he was going; the many islands "toward India" had been discussed for centuries. Obviously to him, when he got there he was approximately where he expected to be. He too came with preconceived ideas as to what he would find there, and he stepped into a world with gold and recognizable flora but seemingly peopled by nude natives from another era.

The Discovery of America

The circumstances surrounding the discovery and first landing in the Americas are of great historical interest. Such information as is available today comes through Las Casas, Hernando, Fernández de Oviedo, and Luis Torres. The version given in the *Diario* is a paraphrase. It is flawed, mixing up times and distances and using sixteenth-century place-names such as "Lucayos" for these islands. The only one of these authors to cite a source other than Columbus was Fernández de Oviedo, who wrote, "As I heard say Vicente Yañez Pinzón and Hernán Pérez Matheos."[5] The first of these men was the captain of the *Niña* on this voyage, and the other was the pilot of Columbus's flagship.

The main points of difference between the accounts of the initial events concern the distances traveled the day and night before the discovery, who saw land first, what one of them said, and what day this was. The argument continues today over who saw land first, an argument that many writers have attempted to resolve by reconciling times and distances so as to show that Columbus deserved the credit. In both the *Diario* and his *Historia*, Las Casas wrote, as did Hernando, that on the night before sighting land, Columbus saw from the sterncastle "a light, although it was so slight that he didn't want to say that it was land . . . it was like a little wax candle that heaved and rose." In the sentence before this one Las Casas said that the first to see land was a sailor named Rodrigo de Triana. Columbus then supposedly pointed out the light to the two king's officials who were on board; one said he too saw the light, but the other was below on the deck and could not see it.[6] I suggest that what Columbus saw was a luminous variety of jellyfish.

The possibility that Columbus did see light on land depends on the distance between his ship and the island at the time of the supposed sighting. For those devoted to the study of such minutiae—the differences between the horizon as an attribute of the curvature of the earth and the range of visibility—the following may be of help. The horizon algorithm is 1.15 nautical miles for each of the square roots of heights in feet. In any attempt to judge the accuracy of the *Diario* report of Columbus's sighting of the heaving light, one must take care to differentiate between horizon and range of visibility. A suggested gauge is that a person who is standing on a deck and who has an eyeball height of 12 feet from the surface of the water can see objects that are 50 feet above the waterline from a distance of 7 to 8 miles, whereas objects with a height of 100 feet will usually be visible from 10 to 12 miles away. These figures are taken from modern guidelines for daytime sailing in the Bahamas.

In the nineteenth century, Fernández de Navarrete provided his evaluation of the *Diario* claim that a light was seen in the night from a distance of 14 leagues—56 miles. He wrote that he had calculated that from a height of 12 feet, a figure based on the size of the caravels, the land on the horizon would have to be of a height of 2,254 feet in order to be visible from that distance.[7] According to one recent estimate, from the crow's nest of the *Santa María*, again under ideal atmospheric conditions, hills 50 feet high would be visible from 10 nautical miles. The National Geographic survey postulated a figure of a maximum of 28 nautical miles for this particular sighting to have been possible. These estimates require higher hills on Guanahaní than those reported in the *Historie* and the *Historia*.

This type of supposition brings one back to the previously discussed question: where was the fleet at this time, Watlings Island, Samana Cay, Turks Island, or some other island? Morison made a pertinent comment on this matter. Based on personal observation, he wrote: "The fleet at 10:00 P.M. was at least 35 miles off shore. The 400,000 candlepower light now on San Salvador, 170 feet above sea level, is not visible nearly so far."[8] Las Casas attempted to shed light on this subject when he wrote, "As this was a land without any cold, they leave or left their grass huts that they call bohios at night with a piece of burning wood in order to do their natural necessities . . . and as it burns like a firebrand, in this manner they were able to see the light."[9] Apparently he too was bothered by such an improbable sighting.

The confusion over who first saw the land began early. Fernández de Oviedo wrote that at nightfall Columbus ordered the boats to lay to:

> Going this way, a sailor who was of those who went on the flagship, a native of Lepe, said: "light! land!" [*lumbre! tierra!*] And a retainer of Colom's, named Salcedo, replied saying: "The Admiral, my master, already said that" and at once Colon said: "It is a while ago that I said that I had seen that light that is on the land." And so it was: that on a Thursday, two hours after midnight, the Admiral called a noble called Escobedo, the Catholic King's butler, and said to him that he saw a light. And the next day, in the morning, at dawn, and at the hour that the day before Colom [*sic*] had said, from the flagship could be seen the island that the Indians call Guanahani . . . and who first saw the land, when it was already daylight, was called Rodrigo of Triana, on the 11th of October of the said year.[10]

This version seemingly solved many of problems. The sequence of events was more reasonable and avoided the matter of the timing, a matter resolved by some modern-day historians by switching the two hours before midnight in the *Diario* to two hours after midnight. Most important, this change presumably allows Columbus to have been close enough inshore to be able to see a light on land.

As noted earlier, Fernández de Oviedo said that he had his information from Columbus's pilot as well as from the captain of the *Niña*. Unfortunately this raises another question. On what day did they discover America? Not only in this quotation but also in testimony by several of the witnesses in the *Pleitos*, the date was given as October 11. Hernando also gave the date as the eleventh. The inscription on Hernando's tomb shows the date as October 11, 1492; however, this was possibly placed there when the tomb was reengraved a century later.[11] Gil suggested that Las Casas may have changed the date, due to the Christian tradition that the number eleven signified sin and to the biblical theistic implications in the use of the number twelve, the number at Christ's Last Supper.[12] All of the authors critiqued here gave the discovery date as October 12 without comment about the earlier and more numerous claims for the eleventh.

In the diary of Luis Torres, the interpreter who sailed on this voyage, the date and time are given as "Friday afternoon, two hours after mid-day, which, on the Jewish calendar was Hoshana Raba, twenty-one days in the month of Tishrei, in the year 5235 after creation." He said: "I sat all night with Rodrigo de Triana reciting Tehillim, Psalms. . . . With the first flickering light we who had been awake all night, were the first ones to see land. . . . Rodrigo ran to alert Columbus that he had sighted land."[13] Friday in the Christian calendar fell on October 12.

Fernández de Oviedo was the only one of the earliest chroniclers of this event to include the dramatic shout, given by him as "Light! Land!" In accord with modern custom, Morison had Rodrigo de Triana call out the now famous *"¡Tierra! ¡Tierra!"* ("Land! Land!"). Wilford used the same expression but named the sailor Juan Rodriguez Bermejo, in accord with Alice Gould's findings. Actually *bermejo* is the Spanish cognomen for redhead, and Rodrigo was a common rendering of Rodriguez. This sailor was one of the Jews who sailed on the voyage. Sale also repeated the legend but reduced the cry to a single *"¡Tierra!"* The Phillipses skipped over this particular pitfall, whereas Fernández-Armesto wrote of the sailor, "probably from Triana," who called out *"¡Tierra! ¡Tierra!"* Columbus had found land; now he had to take possession.

Taking Possession

Columbus landed and took possession of the island that the natives called Guanahaní. Morison and others stressed the pomp and ceremony that accompanied this first landing on western soil.[14] Greenblatt, inquiring into the significance of what took place at that time, noted that this action was accepted by the natives, according to the *Diario*, without "contradiction," which was taken to indicate the relinquishment of title by the "voluntary choice" of the natives, who had not the foggiest idea of what was going on. As Greenblatt pointed out, the act was carried out by people from a culture that "takes both ceremony and juridical formalities seriously."[15] The extent to which such formalism could be carried is evidenced only a few years later when local officials in the colonies, who were responding to instructions from the king to carry out impracticable orders coming from Spain, resorted to a peculiarly Hispanic device: they gave full recognition to authority but failed to comply. This was done by noting on the document, "Acato pero no cumplo" ("I respect [your order] but do not comply"). In this manner the face of everyone was saved; royal authority had not been ignored, yet its orders had not been carried out.

Columbus at Guanahaní was carrying out a requisite formality; he was establishing a legal claim, as required under Justinian law—the taking of possession must be with the consent of the one to be possessed. In this case, to not protest was to consent. In the first letter in *El libro copiador*, Columbus put it succinctly, "I found innumerable people and very many islands of which I took possession in the name of Your Highnesses with royal proclamation and royal standard extended and I was not contradicted."[16] The fact that he used the word "contradicted" is sufficient proof that he knew exactly what he was doing—he was ensuring legal title. Actually this act was performed only once, at Guanahaní; on each of the rest of the islands, he merely erected what he termed "a large cross." This indicated that he probably envisaged all of the islands in the archipelago as part of a single entity for seigneurial purposes—as part of the Indies. "Indies," however, does not necessarily implicate mainland India.

If Columbus foresaw a possible dispute with the khan of Cathay, he would have been able to present the pretext that the natives of Guanahaní (as well as of the other islands in the Caribbean) had voluntarily relinquished their allegiance to their former rulers. If, on the other hand, he was anticipating the claims that might—and did—come from Portugal, his position would have been yet stronger. In the latter case he had taken possession legally of what would be depicted as previously unknown lands occupied by what he later described as an almost nomadic people—that is, unoccupied lands. Besides, such people as were there had voluntarily recognized the rights of Spain, since they had not "contradicted." In Eurocentric terminology, "unknown" meant unknown to western Europeans, that is, Christians. Such sophistry was not unusual in European colonizers of the Americas.

Did Columbus reason in such a manner, or was he only carrying out orders given him by the Spanish monarchs? Was he consciously establishing his now justified right to be the Admiral of the Ocean Seas, viceroy and governor of these lands? Recently, Zvetan Todorov read into the act of taking possession something entirely different: "That this should be the very first act performed by Columbus in America tells us a great deal about the importance the ceremony of naming assumed in his eyes."[17] Todorov found that it was as much a cultural expression as a political act. Might not there also have been an element of normal human pride in the regal act, a visible manifestation of pride in accomplishment? Surely this was a practical rather than cultural matter.

At the same time, this act provided the now admiral with the means for impressing his recently rebellious crew, even cementing their personal loyalty to him. Las Casas, departing from the *Diario*, wrote in his *Historia* of how, once ashore on Guanahaní, the crew members wept with joy. He rhetorically questioned how those who had doubted Columbus could now act so differently: "What did the reverence they showed him signify? The pardon that in tears they asked from him? The offers that they made to him to serve him for all of his life?"[18]

Here was an unsophisticated Italian sailor, at the height of his glory, carrying out a traditional legal function in the name of Spanish rulers before an audience of recently rebellious run-of-the-mill Spanish sailors and a motley group of as-yet-unidentifiable natives of an appearance previously unknown to the Europeans present. Pragmatically speaking, as Greenblatt pointed out, "Why there was no objection [by the natives] is of no consequence; all that matters is that there was none."[19] By the same token, what really matters is that Columbus did take possession in the name of the Spanish sovereigns. Although by this act he may have begun the European "invention of America," as seen by José Rabasa, he was most certainly establishing both the Crown's and his own personal rights over what he had found.

Gold in Relation to the Discovery

Columbus's immediate reactions to the discovery are voiced in the *Diario*. He first noticed the "very green trees and many pools of

water and fruits of various kinds." He next commented on the fact
that "he knew that they were people who could best be freed and
converted to our Holy Faith." Oliver Dunn and James E. Kelley Jr.
translated this phrase to read "freed [from error]." Whichever way it
is read, the first is observation, whereas the latter indicates
preconception. He wrote of the goodness of the people, of what he
took to be their pacific lifestyle, as well as of the prospect that they
"should make good and intelligent servants," a dichotomy that was
to appear frequently in his later letters.

Columbus did not lose sight of one of his goals, possibly the main
one, when he wrote on this first day in the Americas, "I was attentive
and worked to know if there was gold, and I saw that some of them
had a small piece hanging from a hole that they had in their nose."
He began by looking for gold because that is precisely what he had
expected to find there. He now found out, by "signs," that there was
much of it on an island to the south. Later he said, "And so I shall
go to the southeast to look for gold and precious stones." After noting
the cotton grown on the island, he added, "And also the gold comes—
nace, is [born] here—that they carry hanging from the nose."[20]

Columbus used the word "gold" 144 times in the *Diario*, yet in the
first letter in *El libro copiador* he used it only twice, saying that the
Indians told him there was a lot of gold on Jamaica, an island that
he did not visit until his second voyage, one possible indication that
Española was his primary destination. In the Santángel/Sánchez
letters, he referred to gold three times, giving equal or greater stress
to the wonders of nature with its aloes, rhubarb, and availability of
"all of the slaves for the navy" that the monarchs could want. One
can read into his choice of words hidden meanings, as is the custom
among social-historians. However, Columbus's immediate reaction,
as well as his form of reporting it, was strictly mercantilist. The
future presaged at this time was the exploitation of these lands and
their people.

The day after the discovery, he surveyed the island of Guanahaní
for a possible port and defensive positions, although he noted, "I do
not see this to be necessary because these people are very simple
about weapons . . . unless when Your Highnesses order they all be
taken to Castile, because with fifty men you could have them all

subjugated, and you can make them do all that you would wish."[21]
At the end of the journey he would write that Spain could have in
the Indies "so many slaves that they have no number."[22] From the
time of his first landing he was preoccupied with the economic
advantages to be had from these lands. These may have been equally
in his mind when he formulated his "Great Enterprise." There is no
discovery without intent, and it is doubtful that the intent that
persuaded him and Ferdinand and Isabel was merely one of discovery
for discovery's sake. As Luis Santángel is said to have argued: so
much to be gained for so little investment.

Todorov concluded that it is wrong to assume from these many
references that Columbus's "essential motive was to get rich." He
asked: "Is it then no more than greed that sent Columbus on his
journey? It suffices to read his writings through to be convinced that
this is anything but the case. Quite simply, Columbus knows the lure
value of wealth, and of gold in particular."[23] Todorov offered a perhaps
more understandable appraisal when he commented on "the human
side of the Spaniards in their thirst for human possessions: gold from
the beginning, as we have seen, and soon their women." He went on
to note, "In practice, too, the conquest will have these two essential
aspects: the Christians are generous with their religion, which they
bring to the New World; from it they take, in exchange, gold and
wealth."[24] From some of these recent works, it is apparent that the
Black Legend of Spain's role in the Americas, rather than dying out,
has been revitalized in the current spate of ethnocentric studies.

In the *Diario* and in the letter in *El libro copiador*, Columbus made
a strong point of his belief that Española had great economic
potential through agriculture. In the letter he told how the land was
"of such fertility" that even though he "knew how to say [describe]
it, it would be no marvel that you would doubt of believing it." This
passage came before any reference to gold. Four lines after the first
mention of gold, the Admiral wrote: "All the mountains are of a
thousand forms and all of them most beautiful and most fertile and
walkable . . . there are lands for all things and to sow and plant and
for the raising of cattle."[25]

There are no such mountains in the Bahamas. These sentences
were written after Columbus saw Cuba and Española. Foreseeing a

second voyage, he hoped "to give Your Highnesses as much gold as you might need, a pepper spice, [to fill] as many boats as Your Highnesses might send to load, and mastic . . . and cotton . . . and slaves." He added, "I believe I have found rhubarb and vanilla . . . and when I return the people that I left there will have found another thousand things."[26] In this letter Columbus placed more emphasis on the agricultural benefits than on the gold; unfortunately for him, the species found on Española of pepper, mastic, rhubarb, vanilla, and cotton were of no commercial value.

With time he came to base his future hopes on gold and slaves. For the latter he had to provide justification in the nature of the Indians to be enslaved. Some of these, the Caribs, were portrayed from the very beginning of his accounts as fierce and anthropophagous, therefore as social outcasts, that is, people legally fit to be enslaved. Near the end of the first letter of *El libro copiador* he wrote, "When Your Highnesses order that I send you slaves, I hope to bring them and send you mostly of these."[27]

News of these fearsome people was included in the Santángel/ Sánchez letters, together with an account of their women, who lived alone on an island named Matininó. This island was described in all three of these first letters and in the *Diario* as "the first island of the Indies nearest to Spain." How Columbus came by this knowledge remains unknown; the natives certainly did not know of Spain. The reason for its inclusion in these brief letters may have been to stir up interest in a return journey on which men and women of these nearest islands could be legitimately taken as slaves. Columbus was in many ways a visionary, but as he showed in his numerous writings, he was throughout his postdiscovery life always deeply concerned with his and the Crown's business affairs in the Americas.

Columbus's Religious Motivation

Some modern authors attribute at least part of Columbus's motivation for seeking the western sea route to Asia to a desire to bring the Catholic faith to Cathay. These assumptions are based on his supposed knowledge of the contents of the Toscanelli letter as well as of Marco Polo's writings that said that the khan had sent to Rome to ask for priests to indoctrinate his people. In the prologue to the *Diario*, Columbus wrote that his project had been approved because of the information he had given "to Your Highnesses about the lands of India [*sic*] and of a prince who is called the Gran Khan which means in our romance language King of Kings; [and] how he and his predecessors sent to Rome many times to ask for doctors in our Holy Faith in order that they could teach them and how the Holy Father had never provided them."[28] Yet, as was known at the time, missionaries had been sent to Cathay from the twelfth century onward. Also, so far as is known today, no priest was taken on the first voyage.

Further clues as to his possible religious intent are found in his postdiscovery letters in *El libro copiador*. Columbus told the monarchs, "All of Christianity should give great *fiestas* . . . and also the Church of God should . . . provide prelates and devoted men and wise religious people . . . at the service of God and Your Highnesses."[29] This pious recommendation is also voiced in the Santángel/Sánchez letters. Another of his supposed motives was his later self-proclaimed millenarianism, a belief that the whole world had to be brought to Christianity before the second coming of Christ. By discovering these islands, he had brought that day nearer.

Columbus's request for church celebration of the discovery is followed by a most unusual passage that is found only in *El libro copiador*: "I beg you, in the letter that you write [the pope] about this victory, that you ask him for a cardinalcy for my son, and that since he is not of the ideal age, that they give it to him [anyway], as there is little difference in his age and that of the son of the *ofiçio* [head?] of [the] Medicis of Florence who was given a cardinal's hat without his having served nor had presentation [as a candidate] for so much honor from Christianity, and that you give me the favor of the letter for this because I shall send to get it."[30] The Medici referred to was the future Pope León X, who was made a cardinal at the age of thirteen. Earlier, King Ferdinand had made his own illegitimate son Alonso, at the age of six, archbishop of Saragossa.[31] As Gil pointed out, Diego at this time was around the same age as the Medici boy, and Hernando was much younger. Columbus's "I shall send to get it" appears somewhat presumptuous from an as yet unconfirmed admiral. Regardless for which child the hat was intended, this request smacks far more of religiosity than religious fervor.

Greenblatt suggested that Columbus was putting "into practice the religious rhetoric that we glimpsed in Donne and that furthermore when he recommends enslaving the cannibals ... [t]his transformation will not enfranchise them; it will only make them excellent slaves. But they will have gained their spiritual freedom."[32] This proposed "transformation" came later, when Columbus's venture was proving to be particularly unsuccessful from an economic standpoint; he needed goods to barter, in this case slaves for livestock. He feared, and rightly so, that the monarchs might reject his proposal for Indian slaves on both legal and religious grounds, as they ultimately did. His counterploy was to demonstrate how mere enslavement was a minor matter compared with the spiritual benefits for the enslaved. Under a rigorous definition of the term *religiosity*, this is precisely what was being suggested—religion for enslavement. His "ardent faith" was at the very least convenient at this difficult time in his life. The late-life rationalizations of a frustrated man provide poor clues to his thought processes in the early days of his newly found glory as the discoverer of a new world.

Columbus made his first written proposal for the recovery of Jerusalem from the infidels in the first letter of *El libro copiador*. The *Diario* paraphrase is somewhat different. On the day after the loss of the *Santa María*, he is quoted: "And he says that he hopes in God that on the return [to Española] ... they [the men he left behind] will have found the mine of gold ... and that in such quantity, that the kings, before three years have passed will have taken on and have prepared to go and conquer the Holy House, for thus (he says) I urged Your Highnesses that all profit from this enterprise be spent on the conquest of Jerusalem and Your Highnesses laughed and said that it pleased you and [even] without this [profit] they had that desire. These are the words of the Admiral."[33]

The same matter is treated differently in *El libro copiador*:

I conclude here: thanks to Divine grace, from which is the beginning of all virtuous and good things and that gives favor and victory to all those who follow in the path, that in seven years from today I will be able to pay Your Highnesses [for] five thousand cavalry and fifty thousand foot soldiers for the war and conquest of Jerusalem, for which reason this enterprise was undertaken; and then in five years, another five thousand cavalry and fifty thousand foot soldiers which will be ten thousand cavalry and a hundred thousand on foot; and this with [despite] the very little cost that Your Highnesses now make in this beginning in order that you can have all of the Indies, and what there is in them in hand, as I will later tell Your Highnesses in person; and for this I am right and do not talk of the uncertain, and you should not sleep on this as was done in the carrying out of this enterprise, for which God pardon who was the cause for it.[34]

The most notable aspects of this letter are the egocentricity of Columbus and his censorious attitude toward his sovereigns. This letter provides ammunition for those who have long claimed that his original intent was to establish a feudal fiefdom for himself on Española. It is now he, Columbus, who will finance this crusade from "his" Española. It is possible that his later recall to Spain in disgrace was due as much to the claim made by some of the colonists and clerics who opposed him—that he and his Italian friends were trying to establish an independent fiefdom on Española—as to his supposed mismanagement of the colony. Columbus was probably falsely accused in this particular case, but his high opinion of his own importance appears throughout his writings. He must have been an irritating companion on occasion.

By 1498 he put an entirely different face on this proposal. He wrote in the provisions for his *majorat*, "At the time that I started to go and discover the Indies, it was with the intention of supplicating the King and Queen, our Sovereigns, that the revenue which their Highnesses might have in the Indies they should determine to spend in the conquest of Jerusalem."[35]

The word *crusade*, as commonly used in English to mean the military expeditions to recapture the Holy Land, refers instead in Spanish to the crusade (*la crusada*) to free the Iberian Peninsula of the Moors. The papal bull of 1486 giving Ferdinand and Isabel papal rights to keep the lands that they conquered referred specifically to the "occupied territories regained by them in the enterprise to which they consecrated themselves by vow."[36] Columbus's later eschatological rationalizations for the discovery of the Indies and the finding of the "Terrestrial Paradise" were developments in his thinking that were evidenced only long after the first voyage.

The appeal for a crusade, which was called in Spain an enterprise (*empresa*), had been usefully exploited by Ferdinand and Isabel in their expulsion of the Moors from Spain. Individuals of more humble backgrounds might have seen in this Reconquest more of the professed Christian call to defeat the infidels and less of the perhaps predominant political strategy of extending the royal domain. For the success of their enterprise in Spain, the Valentian Pope Alexander VI rewarded Ferdinand and Isabel with the titular designation "Catholic Kings"—not "Defender of the Faith," a title reserved for their son-in-law, England's Henry VIII. Although Henry is best known for his rupture with Rome and his numerous wives, he was also a biblical scholar. It was surely a lapsus when Zamora wrote: "It was no coincidence that after years of advocating his project at various European courts, Columbus was successful at last with the *Catholic Monarchs* [emphasis added], the self-styled defenders of Christian ideals on the international political stage of late-medieval Europe."[37] They were not yet so named, nor were they self-styled, and not all historians, least of all their contemporary Machiavelli, would accept the view of Ferdinand as being primarily a defender of Christian ideals. As for the discovery of the Americas, by mid-century Ogier Ghiselin de Busbeq stated, "Religion supplies the pretext and gold the motive."[38]

There are other facets to Columbus's proclaimed drive for the recovery of Jerusalem. Later in life he was to relate his opening up of the unknown world to the worldwide acceptance of Christianity in a millenarian context—the second coming of Christ must await the spread of the gospel throughout the world. As the self-styled *Christo Ferens* ("the Bearer of Christ"), he was the one chosen to carry the faith to the heathen. The fact cannot be ignored that all of Columbus's known supporters at the Spanish court were, without exception, conversos. Although they may have been sincere in their Christian beliefs, their common ancestral goal was still the recovery of the sacred city. As courtesans, they would have been equally aware of the emotional appeal of such a crusade for Christians. Close contact with these important court officials may have fed his ego and helped to lead him into the fantasy that he was predestined to be the recoverer of Jerusalem.

This is not to say that there was an atmosphere of acceptance at all levels for one final crusade to the Holy Land. As Todorov noted: "Not only did contacts with God interest Columbus much more than purely human affairs, but even his form of religiosity is quite archaic (for the period): it is no accident that the project of the crusades had been abandoned since the Middle Ages."[39] Todorov, like so many others, ascribed to Columbus a medieval mentality. Would it not be perhaps equally, if not more, accurate to portray him as the self-educated artisan that he was, one who had been raised in the seafaring city of Genoa, a city that in his day was a cultural backwater in Renaissance Italy?

It is probably correct to say that Columbus was a mixture of the medieval and Renaissance man, since his motives were mixed. However, there is no question about Ferdinand; he was the epitome of the Renaissance prince in his policies. He was clear in his priorities: these were the times to reap the benefits to be had from harassing the Moors in North Africa, not in the Middle East.

Columbus, as the Bearer of Christ, materialized in his post-discovery signature—Xpo FERENS. This is first seen on a letter dated January 4, 1493, and addressed to Rodrigo de Escobedo, one of those left behind at Navidad. It is probably a forgery.[40] The next holograph is in another suspect letter dated February 20 of the same year. The first generally accepted use that was also a postdiscovery device appeared on the Torres memorandum reporting on the second voyage. This was dated January 30, 1494, and is subsigned "El Almirante" ("The Admiral"). All of Columbus's letters dating from February 1494 until February 1498, those known today, are either unsigned or signed with only the words "El Almirante." In 1498 he signed five letters with both the cryptogram and "El Almirante." There are copies of letters and fragments of letters written between September 1498 and October 1500, most of them unsigned, one with only "El Almirante," and one with the cryptogram and "El Almirante." On only one occasion, August 1499, is there a known use of

the combination with VIREY ("Viceroy"). In an undated memorandum to Ferdinand and Isabel presumably written before he
embarked on the third voyage in May 1498, he signed for the first
time with the much disputed cryptogram:

•S•

•S•A•S•

X M Y

Xpo :FERENS

In 1501 Columbus wrote six letters or notes to Father Gaspar de
Gorricio, all but two of them signed with the cryptogram and "El
Almirante." Probably in that same year he sent a memorandum to
the monarchs in which he used both the device and Xpo FERENS,
which he did again in a letter to them on February 1502. From
March 1502 until his death, he signed either Xpo FERENS alone or
in combination with the cryptogram. Thacher drew attention to a
seldom-noted fact: the thirty-three books known to have belonged to
Columbus all bear some form or variation of the device. There is no
direct evidence that Columbus owned any of these works before
1492. The use in a letter of the signature into which so many have
read allegorical significance came almost a decade after the discovery, although in his provisions for the entail of his estate in 1498
he ordered his heirs to always use the cryptogram.

Another example of his often-cited piety derives from Hernando
and Las Casas, who each claimed that he always headed his writings
with "Jesus cum Maria sit nobis in via," so well written, they
said, that he could have earned his living as a scribe. His holographs known today do not bear out this assertion; only three of
them are so headed. Gil pointed out that his letters do, however,
all have a cross at the top of the letter. A number of his letters
contain a twisted letter like an *f.* Some have read into this a sign
for Jesus. There is also a figure at the head and to the left of
many of his letters, especially in those to his son Diego. This has
been interpreted by some as the Hebraic symbol for the Jewish
phrase "bet hai" ("Praise be the Lord"), written Hebrew-fashion
from right to left. Since Columbus gave no indication as to the
meanings of these scrawls, if they indeed had any, all comments are
speculative.

Reaction in Spain to the Discovery

One of the earliest indications as to what Columbus was commonly believed to have found is in the *cédula* of May 23 awarding Columbus the pension promised to whoever first sighted land. What he saw is described as being "in the said Islands." The use of capitalization indicated the importance of the word "islands."[41] The remarks made by Martire in some of his letters written at the time are considered to be significant in this matter, since Martire was an intimate member of the court and was generally current on court gossip.

As early as September 1493 he was writing about "a new hemisphere of the earth by the western antipodes." He located it "adjacent to India."[42] Morison, while tracing the thoughts expressed by Martire in various letters, offered a free translation of this letter.[43] In another letter written on the same day, Martire expressed his wonder that finally "what has been hidden from the beginning of creation to the present is now beginning to be known."[44]

Soon Martire, and others, began to question Columbus's claim that he had reached the Indies. Martire wrote on October 1: "A certain Colón navigated towards the West until reaching the coasts of the Indies—as he believes—in the antipodes. He found many islands and it is believed that they are the ones mentioned farther away from the Eastern Ocean by the cosmographers, and adjacent to India. I do not deny it completely, although the magnitude of the world seems to indicate the opposite; anyhow those are not lacking who believe that the Indian coast (if the supposition is admitted) is very little distant from the Spanish shores."[45] Demetrio Ramos Pérez discussed the then current of criticism that already placed in doubt the claims of Columbus to have reached the Orient. The reasons given were based on the discrepancy between the distance that Columbus had traveled and estimates as to the distance to India. It was also, according to Ramos and Emiliano Jos Pérez, the same reason why Columbus's initial offers had been turned down. Jos went further: "There is no reason to defend Spain for rejecting on repeated occasions the Columbine dreams; one must instead defend her for having accepted [such] outlandish ideas."[46]

Ramos raised the question as to the authenticity of the dating and content of these Martire letters. They were first published after the death of their author and may have been retouched in order to avoid any compromising materials that might have reflected adversely on the memory of the Catholic Kings for having been too credulous in accepting the claims made by Columbus. Ramos believed that the copy of a November 1493 letter written to Cardinal Sforza provided proof of this. Martire wrote the cardinal, "That Columbus, discoverer of the New World, already named by my Kings what the Spaniards call Admiral of the Sea of the West Indies, has been sent again with an armada of eighteen boats and a thousand men."[47] The use of the phrases "New World" and "West Indies" dates from post-1493.

Ramos noted similar irregularities in chapter 4 of book 1 of the first decade and also in chapter 1, book 2, which he found to have been obviously written much later than the dates of the letters. Further evidence as to these changes can be found in Martire's description, written in October 1494, of Columbus's attempt on the second voyage to establish that in Cuba he had found the much-sought-after Indian mainland. This opinion of Columbus's had not yet reached Spain in October of that year. Martire correctly dated the knowledge to the year in which it was written even though he could not have known of this opinion at the time that his letter is dated.

In his published edition of his first decade, Martire expressed early skepticism of Columbus's claims: "He says that he found the Island of Ophis [sic], but considering diligently what the cosmographers teach, those are the islands of the Antillas and other adjacent ones."[48] As Ramos and others read into Martire's dry account of the Barcelona reception of Columbus at the time of his triumphant return from his first voyage, the title of "Admiral" alone was given intentionally, rather than "Admiral of the Indies," which would have implied acceptance of his claim to have reached India.[49]

The *Historie* recognized that there had been early criticism of the claims made by the Admiral. It referred specifically to the adverse opinion given by "master Rodrigo, the Queen's archdeacon in Seville and some of his lay followers" who "reprehended the Admiral, saying that they should not be called Indies, because they are not Indies."[50]

Furthermore, it explained that Columbus so named the lands that he had found because "they were part of India beyond the Ganges . . . and because they didn't have a name of their own, he gave them the name of the nearest country, calling them West Indies."[51] In writing on the same subject, Las Casas explained that "Master Rodrigo" had written this opinion in the Spanish-language edition of Marco Polo. If Las Casas was correct, this particular theory was advanced only after 1503, the year of the publication of Rodrigo Fernández de Santaella y Córdoba's first Spanish edition of this work.

These and other considerations have provided grist for the mills of those who have attempted, by one means or another, to explain how India fit within the concept for the first voyage. Vignaud believed that Columbus and the monarchs never intended to reach India at that time; other writers, including Marcel Bataillon, believed that mention of India was eliminated in later correspondence and *cédulas* in order to counteract any claim by the Colón family to territorial rights on the mainland. Opposition to Columbus's later claims came from those who believed in the theories expounded over the ages by the cosmographers, as well as from those with commercial interests in the important spice trade. In addition, a strong personal element also arose from a combination of reaction to Columbus's frequent arrogance and of personal jealousies exacerbated by nationalistic intrigue.

Columbus was obviously a man driven by his dream, his "Great Enterprise." Whether inspired by a sense of adventure, by greed, by religion, or by a combination of all three, he successfully carried out his dream. His perseverance, shown both over the frustrating years before the discovery and on the first crossing, marks him as a man of truly exceptional tenacity. There is nothing unusual in the fact that he showed himself, then and later, to be possessed of both religious fervor and mundane yearnings for fame and fortune. Certainly he was a complex man. But first and foremost he was the discoverer of America. Neither he nor anyone else at the time really understood what it was that he had discovered. Hernando's explanation is as good as any: Columbus named these islands "the Indies" because they did not have a name of their own. He now had to consolidate his position.

Well begun is half done.

11
Division
of the
Spoils

On his return, Columbus intended to go directly to Seville by boat. He said so himself in the *Diario* on February 19 and again in the entry for March 13, which reported, "Today at eight o'clock with the incoming tide and the wind to the NNE he raised anchor and raised sail to go to Seville."[1] Instead, on the fifteenth, he made port in Palos. His last journal entry expressed his intention to "go to Barcelona by sea, in which city he had been given the news that their Highnesses were."[2] He proceeded instead by land to Seville. Four persons—Las Casas, Fernández de Oviedo, Bernáldez, and Martire—personally witnessed the unfolding events and left us their versions of what happened. Before reaching Barcelona, Columbus exchanged letters with the monarchs.

Proposed Colonization of Española

Las Casas wrote that Columbus went as fast as he could to Seville, from which city he sent a letter to Ferdinand and Isabel in Barcelona. Las Casas provided a copy of the sovereigns' reply, dated March 30, in which they acknowledged receipt "of your letters." After thanking him, they wrote, "We want your coming [here] to be soon . . . that you give the greatest urgency that you are able to in your coming, because in time it will be seen that it is necessary; and because as you know, summer is coming, and so that the time not pass for going there, see if something can be made ready in Seville, or in other parts, for your return to the land that you have found." Las Casas went on to say that when Columbus received this letter, he "returned to write, complying with what they had ordered, sending to them a memorandum of what appeared to him was convenient to be prepared for his return for the populating of the island of Española . . . so many caravels, so many supplies, so many people, and so many of the other necessary things."[3] Las Casas also noted that the sovereigns appointed Juan de Fonseca to prepare for the second voyage.[4]

Thacher provided a facsimile with a transcription of a memorandum from Columbus on the manner in which Española should be colonized. Columbus wrote:

> What occurs to me for the settlement and also the business of the island Española . . . [is] that there go up to two thousand residents . . . in order that the said island be populated better and more rapidly no one should have the faculty to take gold there except those who take up residence and make their houses . . . that there be churches and abbots or friars . . . that none of the residents can go to collect gold except with a license of the governor or mayor of the place where he lives [this is followed by five paragraphs dealing exclusively with the means for controlling the gold] . . . that in the said island there be a treasurer who receives the gold belonging to Your Highnesses and a scribe who writes it down.[5]

The importance attached by Columbus to gold is apparent. In response to these suggestions, the sovereigns issued a *cédula* on May 7 naming a receiver for "all that there might be there of whatever kind that belongs to Us."[6] Although the *cédula* does not establish the date of Columbus's memorandum, the latter appears to be one of the letters that the Crown acknowledged on March 30, as noted above.

Columbus in Seville and Barcelona in 1493

Las Casas provided an eyewitness account of Columbus in Seville while en route to Barcelona. Las Casas remembered the Indians, parrots, and other things displayed at that time by Columbus. "They lodged near the arch known as of the *Imágines*, at Sant Nicolás." He also told of the crowds that came to watch Columbus and his entourage pass by.

Bernáldez provided essentially the same information, though differing with Las Casas as to the number of Indians. Las Casas wrote, "[Columbus] left Seville taking with him the Indians, there were seven who remained . . . the rest had died." Bernáldez gave a date for Columbus's arrival: "He entered Seville with great honor on the thirty-first day of March, Palm Sunday, his purpose well proven, where he was given a good reception; he brought ten Indians, of which he left four in Seville and took six to Barcelona to show to the Queen and the King, where he was well received, and the King and the Queen gave him great credit and they ordered him to prepare another larger armada and to return with it."[7]

Fernández de Oviedo was with the court in Barcelona when Columbus arrived. Years after the event, while serving in Santo Domingo as commander of that city's defenses, he wrote his own account of these happenings:

> And in that same year Colom discovered these Indies, and he arrived in Barcelona . . . in the month of April . . . Colom arrived at court, of which I speak as an eye witness . . . I saw the admiral Chripstóbal [*sic*] Colom come there with the first Indians that went there from these parts on the first voyage of discovery. Thus I do not talk from hearsay . . . but from sight, although I write them from here [Santo Domingo], or better said, resorting to my notes that were written at the same time [that the events happened].

> After Colom arrived in Barcelona, with the first Indians that went or were taken from these parts to Spain, with some samples of gold, many parrots and other things that the people from here used, he was very benignly and graciously received by the king and the Queen. And after he had given a very large and detailed report on everything . . . [they] made him many favors, those grateful princes, and they began to treat him as a noble man and of rank, and for the great person that he in himself well merited.[8]

Martire, also presumably present at the time, wrote a letter on May 14, 1493: "A few days ago there returned from the western antipodes a certain Colón from Liguria, who with great difficulty got from my Kings three boats, because they believed what he said to be unreal . . . he has returned bringing as proof many precious things, but principally gold, which, naturally, is produced in those regions."[9] Eighteen years later, in his *Décades*, Martire expanded his earlier remarks, writing now of the pleasure of the Spanish sovereigns in knowing that they could spread the true religion to these newfound areas: "To Colón, on his arrival, they treat him with all honors, as he deserved for such an accomplishment. They had him sit in front of them in public, a thing that among the Kings of Spain, is the maximum sign of friendship and gratitude for an outstanding service. They order that from then on Colón be called Prefect of the Sea, among the Spaniards they say 'Admiral.'" Following this brief account, Martire, like other chroniclers, provided misinformation as to the date when Bartolomé Colón was named Adelantado.[10] Fray Antonio de Aspa wrote about these same events; however, his references to the seating of Columbus and other events were taken verbatim from Martire.[11]

There is yet one more contemporary source, the daily chronicle of events—the *Dietario*—maintained by the municipality of Barcelona. In these records one encounters much trivia as well as notice of important events and the comings and goings of the court, of ambassadors, and of other notables. This record does not mention either Columbus's arrival or his stay in Barcelona. One cannot read a meaning onto a tabula rasa, but the lack thereof is worth noting. José María Asensio y Toledo located a memorandum, dated 1643 in Barcelona, which contains a copy of a record for a baptism of six Indians, sponsored by King Ferdinand and Prince Juan.[12] This baptismal record was dated April 3, 1493, which corresponds with Bernáldez's statement that Columbus arrived in Seville at the end of March.

The version of these same events given in the *Historie*, published seventy-eight years later, cannot be taken as an eyewitness account; in 1493 Hernando had probably not yet reached his fifth birthday. The *Historie* reports that Columbus did not arrive in Barcelona until "the middle of April," due to delays en route caused by the crowds eager to see him and the Indians. When he did arrive, the sovereigns showed infinite happiness and contentment, and, as to a man who had lent such great service to them, they ordered that he be solemnly received. All those who were in the city and at the court went out to receive him, and the Catholic Kings awaited him seated in public, with all majesty and greatness on a most rich throne, underneath a canopy of gold brocade, and when he went to kiss their hands they stood up, as with a great noble, they made it difficult to give him a hand [excusing a courtier from the reglementary kiss on the hands was a special mark of favor], and they made him sit down beside them. Afterwards, a few things having been said in regard to the manner and results of his voyage, they gave him permission to go to his lodgings to which he was accompanied by all of the court; he stayed there with such great favor and with so much honor from Their Highnesses, that when the King rode through the streets of Barcelona the Admiral rode on one side and the Infante Fortuna on the other, it not having been the custom before for anybody to go with him other than the Infante who was a close relative of the king.[13]

More than a century later, Antonio Herrera y Tordesillas added details, such as that the monarchs "had their thrones placed in the street, ordered him seated, and after seeing all that he had brought they knelt down, with many tears thanked the Lord while the choir sang the *Te Deum Laudamus*. And the King had him ride by his side when he rode out into Barcelona."[14]

All the above accounts, with the exceptions of those of Hernando and Herrera, are primary sources. The more imaginative later versions of what transpired have, not surprisingly, attracted more attention than the bare facts given by the eyewitnesses. The tale of these events has continued to gain embellishments over the centuries in the telling up to, and including, today.

According to Morison, Columbus left Seville "clad in the garments, and using the state, suitable to his rank." He possibly did so, although there is no record of this. Morison reported a visit to Córdoba, where "he saw his two sons Diego and Ferdinand, visited his mistress Beatriz Enríquez de Harana [*sic*] and his old friends of the apothecary shop; here too doubtless he was entertained by the municipality." Morison failed to provide a source for this otherwise unreported visit to Córdoba. He went on to give a fanciful account of Columbus's reception in Barcelona:

> Next day Columbus was publicly received in the Alcazar with great pomp and solemnity by the King and Queen. He entered the hall where the Sovereigns held court with a multitude of caballeros and nobles; and among the best blood of Spain. His fine stature and air of authority, his noble countenance and gray hair, gave him the appearance of a Roman Senator, as he advanced with a modest smile to make his obeisance. As he approached Ferdinand and Isabella [sic] they arose from their thrones, and when he knelt to kiss their hands they graciously bade him rise and be seated beside them and the Infante Don Juan. An hour or more passed quickly ... then all adjourned to the chapel royal where the *Te Deum* was chanted in honor of the Great Discovery, while tears of joy streamed from the Sovereigns' and the Admiral's eyes. At the close of the service Columbus was ceremoniously conducted as a royal guest to the lodgings that had been provided for him.[15]

Morison's sources were Hernando and Herrera, neither of whom was present at the time. He made one interesting switch: he placed the Infante Juan at the scene. At that time, as heir apparent of Castile and Aragón, Juan was always both prince and infante, and although never mentioned, he was probably present at Columbus's reception. However, the infante referred to in the *Historie* was Enrique Fortuna, one of Ferdinand's relatives who at one time had hoped to wrest the throne away from Ferdinand and Isabel. Properly speaking, an "infante" was the firstborn of a reigning count-king of Barcelona. Although Ferdinand was count of Barcelona, he is recorded as having visited Barcelona on only six occasions.[16] As previously noted, Prince Juan did serve as godfather to one of the Indians that Columbus brought back with him. Morison placed Columbus's arrival in Barcelona between April 15 and 20, ignoring the only eyewitness account and the Indians' baptismal record. He also had Columbus stay there "for five or six weeks ... taking a prominent part in the great festivals of Whitsuntide, Trinity Sunday and Corpus Christi, attending state dinners, receiving people who wished to go to the Indies, advising the Sovereigns on diplomatic matters."[17] All of this is pure conjecture—poppycock.

Wilford followed Morison in reporting Columbus's visit to Córdoba and his arrival in Barcelona, though this writer added the reservation that these events occurred between "April 15 and 20. The exact date is unknown, for there is no court record describing the events." He went on to state, "We must depend largely on the word of his son Ferdinand . . . and hence must be wary of exaggeration." He thereby ignored Fernández de Oviedo, who was present. This is followed by a selective quotation from Martire, "the Italian courtier who was there," giving only Martire's later version, which includes the phrase "caused him to sit in their presence," with no mention of Martire's less detailed contemporaneous account. Wilford now added data: the throne was covered with velvet; Columbus "made his way slowly and solemnly through a corridor in the crowd and reached the royal stand in King's Square by the cathedral[;] . . . Ferdinand, wearing a garnet crown, had to prop his back up with a cushion, favoring a painful wound inflicted by a deranged peasant[;] . . . Isabel wore a white veil."[18] What a touching and imaginative picture!

With the passage of time the story has become so stylized that Nancy Rubin could report a definite date for Columbus's arrival, April 20. Accompanied by six Indians, he was "formally greeted by the city fathers and *grandees* of Isabella [*sic*] and Ferdinand's court." This juxtaposition of names raises a minor point. As Rubin was well aware, at the beginning of the sovereigns' marriage it had been agreed in council that Ferdinand's name would always precede Isabel's; in addition, while in Barcelona, the monarchs were in his, not her, domain. Rubin believed that Columbus did not meet the sovereigns until the next day (taken from Las Casas), when he "crossed the stone-paved courtyard between Barcelona's royal palace and the Church of Santa Clara." This is followed by the staged setting, the singing of the *Te deum*, the falling on the knees, the tears of joy, and all the rest. As for the confirmation of Columbus's titles at that time, this was "meant to establish Columbus's authority over all aspects of the second voyage . . . twelve priests were named to the expedition, among them the young Bartolomé de Las Casas."[19] Las Casas's father, Pedro, and his uncle Francisco de Peñalosa (as commander of the military) did go to Española with

Columbus but on the second voyage. And nine years later Bartolomé went to the island with twelve priests, though not as one of them. They went with Nicolás de Ovando, arriving in April 1502.[20] Las Casas was not ordained until 1510. Such is the stuff of myths.

According to the Phillipses, Columbus went to Seville with seven Indians; his "stately progress from one corner of Spain to the other created a tidal wave of excitement about the lands and peoples across the ocean." This could have been true. His "arrival in Barcelona in mid-April was tumultuous . . . Ferdinand and Isabel had arranged to receive him in the impressive Gothic throne room of the counts of Barcelona. He approached the rulers, knelt, and kissed their hands. . . . They rose . . . kissing his hands and inviting him to sit on the dais . . . a solemn mass of thanksgiving concluded the welcoming ceremony."[21] Yet the monarchs of Castile and Aragón kissed no one's hands, and as already noted, they may have excused Columbus from the formality of kissing theirs. The Phillipses were quite correct, indirectly, in one aspect—Ferdinand. While king of Aragón, he was at the same time count of Barcelona.

Fernández-Armesto limited himself to the following observation: "They allowed him to sit in their presence and ride beside them at ceremonies or in procession." This writer maintained the modern practice of amplifying the record, however: Columbus now rode with both king and queen, and in "procession." Discussing the award given at this time to Columbus for being the first to sight land, Sale lacked documentation when he wrote, "Upon his petition, Ferdinand and Isabella in 1493 dutifully assigned him the legacy, raising the money either from a special tax on butcher shops in Seville, according to one source, or from an explicit confiscation of Jewish goods in the hands of suspect *conversos*."[22] As already noted, the royal *cédula* clearly specified that the pension was to be paid through a tax on the butchershops of Córdoba. Columbus never collected this reward, assigning it instead to his mistress, Beatriz; in later years Diego's wife, Doña María, usurped it. Fernández de Oviedo reported that Rodrigo de Triana, the person who should have received the award, left Spain in disgust and died in Algiers, having renounced his religion. Luis Torres said that he was a Jew, and J. Frances Amler provided other evidence that he was a Jew;

however, at that time Jews were allowed in Algiers. As a Jew in Algiers, he would not have needed to apostatize.

Nothing of substantive importance is found in the above-cited modern-day accretions to the sparse facts available in contemporary accounts. It really matters little what outward signs of appreciation the public and the sovereigns showed to the returning discoverer. These additions to the record are commented on here solely to show how this story, like so many others relating to Columbus, has grown over the centuries. What was important is that the Spanish monarchs recognized the value of what Columbus had found and entrusted him with the responsibility for returning quickly to consolidate his success. Meanwhile, they had to seek an agreement with the Portuguese.

Portuguese Reaction to the Discovery

It was evident to the rulers of Spain and Portugal that a new area for exploration had opened up. They were equally interested in defining ownership of the islands already discovered as well as of any lands that remained to be discovered in that general area. On April 5 King João II sent Ruy de Sande to Barcelona to inform the Spanish monarchs:

> Christóbal Colón, their admiral, had come to his port of Lisbon to escape from a storm, and that he was pleased to see him and ordered that he be treated as one of his own . . . he expected and took for certain that their boats having found islands or lands that belonged in some way to him they would order maintained the friendship and brotherhood that existed between them, and as he would have done in a similar case; that he was greatly pleased with the manner by which that which concerned the King of Portugal had been included in the instructions given by the King and the Queen, that he follow his route and set out to discover from the Canary Islands directly to the West without passing to the South as he had been told. And because he did not doubt that the king and Queen would again send their boats to continue the discovery of what they had found, he begged them affectionately that they order that always they follow this order; because when he sends some boats to discover, they could be assured, that he will order that they not pass to the North.[23]

Thus, as reported in the *Diario*, the king of Portugal had claimed the newly found Indies for his own. The Portuguese claimed all lands to the south and west of the Canary Islands while recognizing for Spain rights to those to the north and west. Possibly due to the inherent threat seen by Spain in an arbitrary north-south division of the mar Oceano, Ferdinand and Isabel promptly sent an embassy to officially advise Pope Alexander VI of the discovery and to request a bull of donation, one giving them title to the newly found Indies.[24] Significantly, the islands were described only as being located "toward the Indies." The first bull is dated May 3, 1493.[25] They next asked for the immediate issuance of a second bull, one that provided both for the donation and for a north-south dividing line between the areas assigned to Portugal and those to Spain. Since this second bull, like the first, failed to address the question of the evangelical mission and the consequent privileges to be enjoyed by the Spanish Crown in these lands, a third bull was promptly issued amending the second. A fourth bull was to come later.

Papal Bulls

These four bulls issued by Pope Alexander VI dealt with the areas open to exploration by Spain and Portugal. Historians disagree as to the dates on which the first three bulls were issued. There is no way to establish the dates of these three bulls, the order of their issuance, or the dates of their delivery to Spain. As Paul Gottschalk pointed out, all that is known is that the "existence of none of these bulls is mentioned anywhere before July 19 1493."[26]

The first bull, the *Inter caetera*, was dated May 3. The original is in the Archivo General de Indias. It uses much the same language as the *Romanus Pontifex* bull given to Portugal in 1455. The second bull bears the same name as the first and is dated May 4 but is generally believed to have been issued in June. It is a literal copy of the first bull with the exception that the latter one added a provision for a north-south line of demarcation one hundred leagues west of the Azores and Cabo Verde in Africa. As Francisco Morales Padrón noted, it did not divide up the world but only indicated a line on either side of which discoveries could be made.[27] The perhaps key words were that Spain could navigate to the southeast "toward [*hacia*] the Indies" and that Portugal could move to the south "up to [*hasta*] the Indies." Later disagreements would center on the intended meanings of *hacia* and *hasta*. The earlier Treaty of Alcaçovas (1479–80) had established a horizontal line as a boundary, whereas now a vertical line was added. This did not specify how far toward India the Spaniards could go. The third bull, *Eximiae devotionis sinceritas*, also dated May 3 but with notation of July, is basically the same as the first two but also concedes to Spain the same rights from discovery and evangelization as the Portuguese possessed in Africa. The original of this bull has been lost. Morales Padrón has provided, in parallel columns, a useful linear comparison of these three bulls.[28]

The fourth bull, the *Dudum siquidem*, was dated September 26, 1493, although it may not have been issued until December. It raised important questions. The first concerned its authenticity, though this issue has recently been resolved by the locating of the original in the Archivo General de Indias. This bull increased the rights of Spain, to the prejudice of Portugal. It gave Spain rights of discovery to the southwest—"that are, or were, or appear to those who navigate or travel toward the west and even to the midday, even if they are as much in the western regions as in the eastern and exist in India completely." As for prior bulls, "We totally revoke [them] and as for the lands, [and] islands not actually possessed, we want it to be understood that it was not done."[29] This last phrase applied to any lands that might have been discovered but were later abandoned, in which case they were now reopened to discovery and occupation. In later years this bull would be taken, incorrectly, as granting a carte blanche for Spain in the Pacific. The Spanish monarchs are believed to have requested this fourth concession because of rumors, circulating at the time, that there were richer lands yet to be discovered. In their letter to Columbus of September 5, the sovereigns referred to a rumor that richer lands might be found below the Portuguese line to the south and west of the line of demarcation.

Although Columbus's opinion on the matter probably could not have reached the monarchs in time to get it into the bull of the twenty-sixth, this does not mean that Ferdinand and Isabel failed to address the problem. Samuel Edward Dawson saw the need for the bull in the fact that whereas Portugal had rights to lands toward the Indies (*ad Indus*), it had not taken possession, and since Columbus was now believed to have reached the Indies, under *Dudum siquidem* any such lands now belonged to Spain. If, as again has been assumed by some historians, the line of demarcation was applicable at that time only to the Atlantic, that is, it was not hemispheric, then the possibility that Spain and Portugal might compete on the other side of the globe could foreseeably become a reality.

This new bull did open to interpretation the respective exploration rights of the two Iberian nations by papal donation in a global division that included the Far East. For centuries the only known copy of this bull was the one published by Juan de Solórzano Pereira in 1629. An earlier printing was probably made in 1530 on orders of Fonseca. Only one copy of this imprint is known today. As has been pointed out by others, this key bull had no important effect on the situation between the two countries in their Atlantic holdings; it was in the Far East where the terms of the bull were to have a decisive impact on the Portuguese, who concentrated their major efforts in that area. This contention came about long after Columbus's time.

The official copy of the first *Inter caetera* was originally made public by Juan Bautista Muñoz, who located it in the archives at Simancas. Gottschalk pointed out that the original bull had lain unknown for 350 years, which was what led Dawson to assert that it was never promulgated and therefore had never been valid.[30] Gottschalk found the notation on the bull that these lands were ceded to "their Catholic Majesties" to be clear proof that it was not registered in the archives until after the king and queen received that honorific joint title in 1494; however, there is no way of determining when this notation was added. The only somewhat similar reference in the body of the text is given in the opening "Doctrinal Title," which referred to "recognizing them as true Catholic Kings and Princes [*Reyes y Príncipes Católicos*]." The first printed copy of the *Inter caetera* was made in Spain in 1512; an English version of the second bull was published in 1555. The printed copies were probably made for the use of captains of boats traveling in unexplored waters to serve as proof of their right to be there. Gottschalk suggested that the 1512 printing was issued for the purpose of having such a copy available for a projected trip by Sebastian Cabot to the Bacallaos.[31]

Any consideration of the papal bulls requires first a determination as to the authority of Alexander VI to grant sovereignty in previously unknown lands. No one questioned his authority to promote the evangelization of infidels. The so-called temporal sovereignty of the popes was seen as a mere form, since their temporal power was supposed to derive either from the Constantine Donation, already known at the time to have been a forgery, or by reason of the popes' inherent rights as vicars of Christ. By the end of the fourteenth century, the latter claim was no longer recognized as valid in purely temporal matters by either Portugal or Spain.

Morales Padrón pointed out, "These bulls were given at a time when papal authority was in decline, and new political concepts were emerging." It may not be unrelated that for the *cognocenti*, this particular vicar of Christ "was not only Aragonese but had brought the Holy Office to its lowest moral point in its long history." Gottschalk noted that into the twentieth century, U.S. historians still mistakenly believed in the temporal authority of the popes. In a recent example, Morison went so far as to assert, incorrectly, "The public law of Europe recognized the pope's right to allot temporal sovereignty to any lands not possessed by a Christian prince."[32]

The wording in the bulls has been understood by many historians to represent the partition of the world between these two maritime powers as well as a donation to Spain. Francisco de Vitoria maintained that such was not the intention of the pope, since he could not dispossess the Indians of their property or donate property that neither he nor any Christian had ever owned. Even had he meant to do so, and believed himself entitled to do so, he would have been in error because the infallibility of the pope is concerned exclusively with dogmatic rather than temporal matters. Gottschalk commented, "Be that as it may, Grotius' statement that a donation does not make a sovereign, but the consequent delivery of a thing and the subsequent possession thereof, seems to correspond to the provision in the bulls that not the mere discovery, but the actual temporal sovereignty of the islands or lands in the aforementioned regions establishes to other Christian princes the right to keep such property and create for Spain a title to the discovered lands and islands."[33]

Another question is whether these bulls were issued within the pope's capability to function as an arbiter. If he acted at the request of the two parties to the dispute, his decision would have been binding. Modern scholars fail to find evidence of arbitration in the wording of the four bulls. Eminent sixteenth-century theologians such as Vitoria and Hugo Grotius (founders of modern international law) took the position that "Alexander VI was chosen to arbitrate between two Christian nations; that no partition of the world, but only a boundary line between these two competitors was intended and that only the fruit of their discoveries should be guaranteed." There is no doubt that the bulls were drawn up with the intent of establishing guidelines to be followed by Spain and Portugal. They resembled defining acts more than arbitration.

Another fact regarding these bulls should be kept in mind. England and France never regarded these bulls as binding on them. Beginning with Henry VII and the Cabot voyage in 1496, England showed that it felt free to search for unknown lands wherever they were. Thacher suggested that rather than any partition having taken place, what had actually occurred was a division between Spain and Portugal of the Atlantic into what he described as spheres of influence.[34] Regardless of the legal aspects of the matter, the reality was that both Spain and Portugal chose to believe that the claimed islands and oceans were within their exclusive jurisdictions.

Not only could these islands and lands not be donated by the pope, but he was believed to have been even less empowered to give away navigational rights in the seas. Grotius's first published work, *The Freedom of the Seas* (1608), defined this age-old concept, stating that nothing can become private that cannot be limited by boundary lines. "A nation can take possession of a river because it is enclosed within its boundaries, with the sea they cannot do so." By the same token, according again to Grotius, the prohibition in the bulls from buying and selling goods in these lands was invalid because he also considered that "the right of trade is free to all nations and to all men."[35]

Alexander von Humboldt was of the probably correct opinion that "the Pope actually rendered, without knowing it, an essential service to nautical astronomy and the physical science of terrestrial magnetism" by staking out a line of demarcation. This unquestionably spurred monarchs and sailors alike to seek new techniques for determining latitude and longitude. The fact remains that neither the existing knowledge nor the existing means were adequate for the purpose. As previously noted, the Junta de Badajoz, almost a half century later, was still unable to reach an agreement due to the scientific inadequacy of the time as well as the vagueness in the provisions of the regulating documents.

The Individual Bulls

The differences in wording between the first two bulls are few but important. These include the use of the phrase "through western parts in the Ocean, as it is said, towards the Indies." There was also much insistence on apostolic authority in the one but not in the other. The first bull contains the important apparent cancellation of any conflicting rights granted to Portugal in earlier bulls or concessions, a cancellation omitted in the second and addressed again in the third bull.

The second *Inter caetera* did change its significance, establishing for the first time a north-south dividing line—the Line of Demarcation—in the Atlantic. Harrisse, Humboldt, and others believed that the line was suggested by Columbus based on his observation that at a certain point the old known world and the new were divided "by a great change in the stars, in the aspect of the sea and the temperance of the atmosphere and where the compass shows no variation."[36] The second bull was probably promulgated at the end of June and may have reached Spain in mid-July after Columbus's return from the first voyage.

Although not stating that there was an observable dividing line between the east and the west, Columbus did record, in the *Diario* entry for September 16, that the compass had "northwested a full point," but he later discovered that it was the North Star that had shifted, not the compass. He added, "They found the sea water less salty since leaving the Canaries and the breezes always softer."[37] Any still unrevealed correspondence from Palos that might have suggested such a division could conceivably have reached Barcelona in time to be forwarded to Rome by early May. In their letter of May 28 the sovereigns referred to "a line" that they had "caused to be marked, which passes from the Islands of the Azores to the Islands of Cape Verde, from North to South from pole to pole." The difference between the date of the bull and the date of its promulgation may have given the Spanish monarchs and Columbus time to communicate on the subject and time for his opinions to have been reflected in the second bull.

The third bull, *Eximiae devotionis*, is dated in the Vatican Register May 3. It was probably first published by Solórzano, who dated it May 4. Internal evidence points to the latter date as being the correct one. There is no known copy of the original or any contemporary copy or imprint. This supplementary bull was intended to give to Spain all the same prerogatives that had already been granted to Portugal.

Negotiations between Spain and Portugal: The Treaty of Tordesillas

At the same time that the Spanish monarchs were occupied with getting papal sanction for their claim to the Indies, the king of Portugal was working on the theory that the dividing line between the eastern and western parts of the Atlantic would be based on the longitude of the Canary Islands. The Spanish monarchs suggested another division west of these islands. A formal Portuguese proposal was brought to Barcelona by Portugal's ambassadors Pero Diaz and Rui da Pina. On November 3 the Spanish monarchs instructed their ambassadors to reply to this proposal:

> As our brother says that part of the Mar Oceáno belongs to him, by concession and apostolic Bull, as by possession and by the terms of peace treaties; because he says that as a good measure, in order to

avoid inconveniences, that the Mar Oceáno be divided between us by a line taken from the Canaries to the West by straight line, and that all of the seas, island and lands, from that straight line to the West and to the North, are to be ours, with the exception of the islands in that area that he possesses at the present time; and that all of the other seas, islands and remaining lands that are to be found to the South, are to be of the said King, our brother, except for the said Canary Islands which are ours: say to the Serene King, my brother that . . . we hold for certain that in all of the Mar Oceáno the said King, our brother, does not own [anything] with the exception of the islands of Madera, and of the Azores, and of Flores and Cabo Verde and the other islands that he presently possesses, and those that are found and discovered from the said Canary Islands below in front of Guinea with its gold mines and trade.[38]

These differences were actually of little consequence up until the time of Ferdinand Magellan's voyage into the Pacific in 1519. A few degrees, more or less, in unexplored Brazil had little economic or political significance. This was not the case with the soon-to-be-discovered Spice Islands, however. The Line of Demarcation would then be seen as having been intended to divide the globe. Where it fell would determine whether Spain or Portugal held title to these valuable islands. A real problem lay in the fact that the farther west the line was pushed toward Brazil, the clearer became the title of Spain to the Spice Islands while at the same time the greater became the South American territory of Portugal.

The line was finally fixed by treaty in 1529, setting it in the Pacific east of the Moluccas. This line, projected on modern maps, would have excluded Portugal completely from Brazil. At the time, it merely defined a zone in the Pacific without setting its boundaries in the Atlantic.

Spain proposed a limit for all Portuguese rights to those areas that were already discovered and occupied by Portugal. Spain now added to these legal justifications the rights granted under the Alexandrian bulls. These were not state secrets; on the contrary they were matters of public knowledge. Fernández de Oviedo wrote that he had seen one of the bulls himself.[39] In one of the few letters known to have been written by Queen Isabel to Columbus, she noted, "[I send] a copy of the book that you left here, which has been delayed because it was written secretly, in order that those who are here from Portugal, nor anyone else, know about it, and because of this, in order that it be done more quickly, it goes [written] in two hands as you will see . . . the navigational map that you were to make, if it is finished send it to me soon."[40] Even at this date Isabel was still anxious to keep the route to the Indies secret. As will be seen in the next chapter, Columbus did send her the requested map.

The two countries soon came to the conclusion that this question of zones of jurisdiction involved temporal as much as spiritual matters. They accordingly agreed to work out a treaty, which was signed on June 7, 1494. Known as the Treaty of Tordesillas, it served as a working model for future exploration, although its terms were never put into effect.

There are substantial differences between the second bull *Inter caetera* of May 4, 1493, and the Treaty of Tordesillas. The former merely delineated Spain's area, whereas the latter divided the Atlantic between Spain and Portugal. The bull had set the east-west dividing line at 100 leagues from Cabo Verde and the Azores. It is not known by what means the two nations arrived at the new figure of 370 leagues in the treaty, yet the figure represents roughly the halfway point between the Cape Verde Islands and Española. The Portuguese king believed that the original figure of 100 leagues to the west of the Azores and Cape Verde endangered his coastal traffic in those areas.

Neither nation knew how to determine where this line would fall. With Torres's first turnaround voyage to Española, the monarchs sent a copy of the bull to Columbus with a letter dated August 16, 1494. They asked him to make this determination for them but added, "If there is much difficulty in your going . . . see if your brother or someone else who knows [can go], and inform them in writing and by word and even with a drawing and by all means that they can best be informed and then send them here with the first caravels that come."[41] The language used in this letter indicates that Columbus had suggested a line of demarcation based on the papal bull and that at the same time the Portuguese envoys were claiming that they believed the islands and mainland lay within their sector of the ocean from the Cape of Good Hope to "the line that you said." The monarchs asked for Columbus's opinion on the matter and, if necessary, for any suggestions for amendments to the bull.

Since the king and queen also consulted Jaime Ferrer three times on the matter, his opinion should provide some indication as to the intent at that time. They first sent for him in August 1493.[42] He wrote in 1495 that the measurement should start from the most central of the Cape Verde Islands; that each degree in that parallel (15°) comprises 20⅝ leagues; that each degree is to be counted as equal to 700 stades; that 370 leagues counted in this manner comprise westward 18 degrees. Harrisse calculated that using these figures, "Ferrer's line of demarcation would fall on our actual sphere . . . between the bays of Maracasumé and Piracaua, 85 miles west of the entrance of the Maranhao, and 120 miles east of the Para river, and on the south, about 150 miles west of Rio de Janeiro, and about 25 miles east of Santos."[43]

The Treaty of Tordesillas required that the line be established within ten months. However, on April 15, 1495,[44] the two countries agreed to postpone until July a meeting that was to be held to discuss how to go about determining the line, and then, within ten months an expedition was to set out to determine its location.[45] The monarchs did not rely solely on the two Italians, Columbus and Ferrer, for assistance in determining the line; they also told Fonseca to have "Pinon [*sic*], the one who went the first time," come to Elvas, where the representatives of the two nations were to meet.[46] This was a reference to Vicente Yáñez Pinzón, who in 1495 was the first person, after Columbus, to receive authorization to explore in the Indies.

As Harrisse pointed out, "The experts never met, the expedition was not sent, even the order given to cartographers to trace the boundary line on maps remained a dead letter, and nothing more was said about the matter for at least ten years."[47] Furthermore, he noted: "The Treaty of Tordesillas was not confirmed by the Pope until January 2, 1506 by a Bull from Julius II. Nor do we hear about any attempt to carry those stipulations into effect until January 22, 1518. Alonso de Suazo said: 'Certain pilots were sent to mark the demarcation and fix those lines and places where they ought to be.

As this was a division by longitudes of which pilots neither know nor practice anything, they could do nothing nor knew anything certain to do and therefore returned without having accomplished anything.'"[48]

In 1579 a cosmographer working for Phillip II of Spain maintained that the Portuguese had measured from Sal Island, the easternmost of the Cabo Verde islands, whereas the Castilians had measured from San Antonio, the westernmost of the islands. As Harrisse pointed out, this was a matter of importance in that the group of islands "extends in longitude nearly three degrees (22°45′–25°25′)." However, there is yet another problem, and that is the matter of the length of the league used to calculate the degree. Up until the time of the Junta of Badajoz, at which Hernando Colón testified that the true length of a degree was unknown, 14⅙, 15, 16⅔, 17½, and 21⅛ leagues had each been used on different maps to measure a degree.

No contemporary map shows the line. Juan de la Cosa's map of 1500 does not show it; however, on the copy of the Cantino *mappamundi* made in Lisbon in 1502, a line is shown as the "Line between Castile and Portugal."[49] At the time the Badajoz Junta was called, the question as to just where the line fell in Brazil was more or less an academic one, seen at that time by both Portugal and Spain as of little economic import. However, when Magellan, sailing for Spain, discovered the western route to the Spice Islands, the matter became of deep concern to both nations.

The Treaty of Tordesillas has been seen as a triumph of Lusitanian diplomacy in that it protected the vast areas explored by the Portuguese off the coast of Africa while the Spaniards received only recognition for sovereignty over an unknown area thought to be the location of Antilla. Actually, in the long run, the key turned out to be discovery and possession, regardless of where the particular lands lay under the treaty. The treaty remained theoretically in force until January 13, 1750, when it was finally annulled by the Treaty of Madrid.

Indicative of the tenacity of his unrealistic stubbornness, Columbus, in both his will and his deathbed codicil, refused to recognize that the original papal line of 100 leagues had been extended to the 370 leagues established by the treaty. He considered the treaty to be invalid because he had not agreed to it, as he believed was his right under the terms of the *Capitulaciones de Santa Fé*.

Memorial de la Mejorada

A memorandum known as the *Memorial de la Mejorada* is believed to have been written by Columbus. Not all scholars agree on this; however, if he did write it, it provides many indications as to his cosmographic concepts. At the time that Torres went back to Isabela, he took with him the previously noted request to Columbus for an opinion on the proper location of the Line of Demarcation. With the finding of *El libro copiador*, we now know that Columbus sent the Crown a map of the islands discovered the year before as well as those discovered on the second voyage.

At some time he also gave the Crown his thoughts on the Line of Demarcation. In the famous letter to the nurse of Prince Juan (1500), Columbus clearly made reference to this: "I wrote to their Highnesses with Antonio Torres, in the reply to the partition of the sea and land with the Portuguese." This provides a definite indication that Columbus had complied in 1495 with both requests from his sovereigns. Columbus went on to say that this was written in "the same manner as in regard to the negotiation from Arabia Feliz to the Meca." He added, "And then came that about Colucuti [Calcutta] just as I said and gave in writing in the monastery of the Mejorada."[50] The reference to Calcutta dates this memorandum as having been written sometime between 1497 and 1498. These two statements taken together, without considering additional internal evidence, were sufficient to convince Antonio Rumeu de Armas that the *Memorial de la Mejorada* was indeed written by Columbus, an opinion with which I concur.

Morison doubtfully knew about the *Memorial*, which was made public by Rumeu de Armas in 1972. Varela excluded it from her 1982 *Textos* but, while reserving judgment on the matter, included it in her 1992 edition of Columbus's collected writings.[51] As noted above, she apparently did not have at hand one key piece of evidence for its authenticity—the nurse's letter in the Paris Codex. Fernández-Armesto referred to it as the "*memoria* [sic] . . . recently, but riskily, attributed to Columbus."⁵² Wilford, the Phillipses, and Sale all ignored the existence of this revealing document. These later misreadings of the nurse's letter provide a good example of the need for researchers to seek the primary sources.

The monarchs are known to have visited the monastery of La Mejorada on three occasions: 1486, 1494, and 1497. Columbus could not have met with his sovereigns in 1494 due to the simple fact that at that time he was on Española. Columbus returned from the second voyage in June 1496. He spent most of the rest of that year and the next trying to get recognition for his efforts and support for his return to the Indies. He wrote, while referring to other matters cited above, that he was in La Mejorada in 1497.⁵³ In the meantime Vasco da Gama set sail in July 1497 for India, a journey that was seen by Spain as a possible threat to the Spanish control of the region. It should be kept in mind that Columbus, Spain's expert on these matters, still believed that he had reached the extremities of India.

Rumeu de Armas assumed that the famous memorandum was delivered to the Catholic Kings in mid-July 1497. Regardless of who wrote this memorandum, one denying all rights of Portugal to the Indies, its existence was obviously known to the Portuguese, and they wanted to know its content. The events that followed could have come out of a modern-day spy novel. Many years later, around 1523, a copy was sent to Portugal with a covering letter indicating that this copy had been made from a copy owned by Columbus's son Diego Colón of "a book . . . made by don Christóbal Colón, his father, of the demarcations of the seas and lands of Your Majesty with those of Castile."⁵⁴

The procurement of this memorandum by the Portuguese ambassador was achieved through the countess of Lemos. The lady either stole or was lent a copy of the memorandum by Diego Colón, and she either sold or gave it to the Portuguese ambassador. She was of noble Spanish lineage but had at one time been married to one of the Braganzas, a first cousin of King João III. Where questions of loyalty are concerned, it should be recalled that the Portuguese king was a grandson of the Catholic Kings and was married to a daughter of his aunt, the unfortunate Spanish queen "Juana la Loca." In the

Portuguese correspondence, the countess is referred to incorrectly as a cousin of Diego's. He too was once a Portuguese citizen. There may even have been a sentimental attachment between the two. His disreputable son Luis bigamously married Ana de Castro, a daughter of the countess's. His daughter Isabel married a first cousin of the countess's first husband. Whatever the rights of the matter, it did not suit the Spaniards, even at this late date, to have Portugal know their intimate thinking on such matters.

The text of the *Memorial de la Mejorada* clearly indicated that the importance of the document was due to the perceived threat to Spain from the da Gama voyage, seen here as in violation of the papal bulls because the Portuguese were "not to navigate their boats forward [to the West] of the said limit of the Cape of Good Hope, because it was understood to be included up to there in the said pontifical donation." In a later paragraph the writer found that the current king of Portugal had also violated the Treaty of Tordesillas because he had "sent to navigate in India, by way of Guinea, and by Scythia, by its western part to the Semptentrion, beyond the said limit or line."[55] The reference to "Scythia," that is, the North, is to a voyage that was commanded by João Fernández Lavrador and ordered by João II's successor, King Manuel I, presumably in 1497. On this voyage he may have reached Greenland.

The *Memorial* made special note of the fact that prior to the da Gama voyage, the Portuguese had never passed beyond the Cape of Good Hope, for to have done so would have violated both the papal bulls and the Treaty of Tordesillas. This claim presumed that any lands to be discovered in the Indies were reserved to Spain, whether reached by the eastern or the western sea route. The danger from the da Gama voyage was due to the fact that "he [King Manuel] sent his naos to navigate a very great number of leagues to the east, crossing Persian Arabia and India, until reaching almost to where the boats of the aforementioned king and queen reached while navigating to the east from the west."[56] The reference to Persian Arabia is to the route to India traveling north from the Cape of Good Hope. Although Columbus never claimed that he had reached India, he believed, and showed his belief in this *Memorial*, that he had reached its outer islands.

He herein gave his opinion on the rights of Spain in what he viewed as the Indies. These were based on the fact, as he saw it, that "the mar Oceano is between Africa, Spain and the lands of the Indies and from the eastern part of the east and the Western part of Africa, to the west."[57] This provides a clear statement as to Columbus's cosmographic concepts as late as 1497. In his transcription, Rumeu de Armas capitalized "africa, españa y las tierras de yndia"; however, in the manuscript, the second reference in this paragraph is given as "Indias," with a capital "I," unlike the lower-case "y" in the first reference. This would seem to indicate that the first was a reference to the islands discovered by Columbus and the second was to continental Asia.

The *Memorial* was the first Spanish report to detail the encounter between Columbus and King João II in 1493 at the time of the former's return from the discovery:

> And later, returning to Spain . . . with his [Columbus often used the imperial third person] victory, forced by a very dangerous storm he came into the port of the City of Lisbon where the Serene Highness Juan of Portugal was. He . . . moved with great haste to send an armada of his own to those islands and mainlands. The navigation there, and the nature of the peoples of those lands, he was able by great diligence to get to know by forms and tricks, from pilots and sailors and people who came with the said admiral, to whom he gave concessions and gifts and moneys; and besides this he sent to take off two Portuguese sailors who came with the said admiral, so that they could be pilots of the said armada and take it by the same route to the said islands and mainlands and inform them more completely about everything.[58]

This claimed Portuguese trickery does not appear in any other contemporary source. Further note is made in the *Memorial* of the fact that at the time, the Spanish sovereigns opposed this voyage by João II: "The said King and Queen, as owners of everything, opposed it [and] hinder[ed] the said navigation, by reason of the said donation and apostolic concession and due to the possession that the said Admiral had taken in their names."[59] This is perhaps the first instance in which the rights of Spain were said in writing to have been based both on the apostolic donation and on the rights of occupancy. These two justifications were often used in the future.

As previously noted, the spices found on Española were valueless. This fact, of great interest to the Venetians who controlled the spice and perfume trades, was believed by Cardenal Cisneros, the writer of the later "Zamora Memorandum," to have been the reason why Cabot developed his plan in 1495 to find the "real Indies."[60] The negative reports believed to have been brought back from Española at that time would certainly have contributed at the very least to a questioning of the economic value of the lands found so far. By all accounts at that time, the mysterious India was the land of fabulous riches. Española had offered only many hardships, little gold, and no spices. Matters could not have improved for those supporting the Columbus thesis when Pero Alonso Niño returned empty-handed from his expedition to the South American mainland in 1500.

The monarchs, Columbus, and the duke of Medina-Sidonia exchanged letters in early May 1493 regarding a Portuguese attempt to sail to the Indies.[61] On June 1 the sovereigns wrote Columbus that they had seen his letter. "In so far as what you wrote us that you knew of two boats that the King of Portugal sent, that is in agreement with what we knew here."[62] A few days later they wrote him again, telling him that the king of Portugal had said "that he had not sent and would not send any boats."[63] In late July, Columbus received an answer to a letter of his written while he was still in Córdoba. It dealt with possible Portuguese fleet action and said that the Crown was ready to put to sea double the number of any Portuguese ships. This Spanish fleet was made ready by Medina-Sidonia; however, since it was not needed against Portugal, it was used later to instead transport Boabdil, the last Moorish king of Granada, and some of his people to Africa.

Finally, in a letter dated September 5, the monarchs wrote, "The King of Portugal sent us his messengers . . . and we probably can't reach an agreement with them because they do not come informed about what is ours." Seeing no immediate prospect for a compact with Portugal, the sovereigns instructed Columbus to set sail as soon as possible, warning him not to go near either Cape San Vincent or the coast of Portugal and its islands. They told Columbus that the caravel that he had reported as having sailed from Madeira did so without the knowledge of the king of Portugal, who consequently sent three caravels to capture the first vessel. These letters confirm information given in the *Memorial de la Mejorada*.

There is overwhelming documentary evidence that Columbus was indeed the author of the *Memorial de la Mejorada*. Those who reject this fact fail to go to the basic sources.

Consequences of the First Voyage

Within less than a month of his return from his first voyage, both Columbus and his sovereigns were seeking a speedy return to the Indies. The few contemporary reports for Columbus's visit to Barcelona in 1493 provide sparse information: he was there, he was well received, and the return to the Indies was discussed. Modern biographers have added details to the additions made by seventeenth-century authors, developing a scenario fit for a Hollywood film.

The king of Portugal sent an ambassador to Spain to explain that he "took for certain that their boats [had] found islands or lands that belonged in some way to him," and he requested that in future voyages they should respect his rights. The Spanish monarchs had already sent to Rome to get papal approval of their rights over these lands. Within thirty days of the arrival of this embassy, the Valencian Pope Alexander VI granted three bulls to this effect. The second bull added a new element: a division of the areas open to exploration by the two nations, delineated by a vertical line 100 leagues to the west of the Canary Islands. Portugal's area was to the south and east of the line and Spain's to the north and west.

Morison erred on minor points regarding Alexander VI but recognized that the papal bulls in this instance were not arbitration decisions. He assessed incorrectly the rights of papal sovereignty in such matters. Wilford was somewhat mixed up in reporting these events. He believed that the pope "owed his office to the Spanish monarchs." This may have contained an element of truth, but like the traditional charge of simony, it has been greatly exagerrated. Often overlooked are the facts that Rodrigo Borgia (Alexander VI) was the nephew of the Valencian Pope Calixtus III and had been a cardinal and church administrator from an early age.[64] Wilford was inaccurate in stating, "He [João II] dared not challenge the pope."

Both before 1493 and afterward, the rulers of Portugal and Spain frequently refused to honor bulls that displeased them. Isabel was perhaps the most notable in this respect. Bulls were likewise ignored by other European rulers—who had not waited, as mistakenly claimed by Wilford, until "late in the sixteenth century" to challenge this apparent division of the world.[65]

Many important questions that were to trouble Europe for centuries were first raised by these four papal bulls. These questions involved such matters as the pope's temporal rights, the rights of Christians to absorb the lands of infidels, especially if the latter had never before had contact with Christianity, the division of South America between Spain and Portugal, the rights of enslavement of Amerindians, and the rights of Spain and Portugal in the Atlantic and the Pacific as opposed to the rights of other European nations. Although not all of these issues are necessarily germane to a biography of Columbus, they were matters being discussed during his lifetime.

By the middle of 1494 Spain and Portugal reached an amicable settlement with the signing of the Treaty of Tordesillas. It generated much the same problems as the papal bulls but settled the immediate differences between the two Iberian nations. At that time they were the world's major seafaring nations and therefore those most concerned with such matters. The rest of the European world had not yet awakened to the tremendous importance of what Columbus had accomplished.

The terms of the treaty, and its consequences, received only passing reference in the biographies under review here. As for the *Memorial de la Mejorada,* Rumeu de Armas was the first to publish (1972) a transcript of this text. Its authenticity as a memorandum written for the Catholic Kings has been generally accepted by Spanish scholars. Unfortunately, none of the biographies mentioned this memorandum even though it is given in the texts of works cited by most of them.

There is no question that the Portuguese made poorly concealed efforts to discover the route taken by Columbus. It is equally apparent that Ferdinand and Isabel were disposed to go to war over the matter if necessary. The fear of Portuguese inteference was the probable cause for the haste that Ferdinand and Isabel showed in dispatching a colonizing party. Despite their repeated efforts to speed up the preparations, it took them from April until September to dispatch the armada carrying the first acknowledged colonizers to the Americas. The appointments that they made for the officials accompanying Columbus were indicative of their intent to maintain strict control over their affairs in the Indies. Notably, all but one of these appointees proved later to be inimical to Columbus. A fact not noted elsewhere was the obvious discord in the ranks prior to the departure. In retrospect, both of these facts were portents of things to come. Yet despite delays and problems, Columbus finally set sail on his second voyage in September 1493.

The Promised Land always lies on the other side of a wilderness.

Havelock Ellis (1859–1939)

12
The
Second
Voyage

The second voyage of Columbus was undertaken to consolidate, through colonization, the discoveries of the first. At the same time, it was also intended to be a voyage of further exploration. This was evidenced from the outset. Columbus sailed on a more southwesterly route, seeking the islands in the Lesser Antilles, known also as the Leeward Islands, which he already believed to be those nearest to Europe. He went with a large flotilla carrying men, livestock, and supplies.

Like previous parts of the Columbus story, this voyage presented biographers with a problem from the start. There is no way of knowing with certainty how many vessels carried how many men or what was the makeup of the supernumeraries. The many *cédulas* issued in preparation for the voyage fail to provide the numbers sought. But *El libro copiador,* recently discovered, does provide new sources: copies of four letters written by Columbus relating to the voyage.

Hernando provided a great deal of detailed information, including dates, for this voyage. Scholars have generally assumed that he must have had at his disposal his father's ship's log. He said that his father "wrote, according to his habit, every day what happened."[1] A comparison between *El libro copiador* and the *Historie* is not necessarily revealing in that each source passed through the hands of unknown numbers of copyists, preventing the determination of when or where various changes may have been made. What does become evident is that his father's second letter was not the sole source for Hernando. Las Casas appears to have taken much of his pre-Española information from Hernando, but he too had access to some of these letters. He undoubtedly also received information about the activities on Española from his father and his uncle, both of whom accompanied Columbus on this trip. Later, while living in the islands, Las Casas came to know others who had crossed on both the first and the second voyages.

Although he did not go on this voyage either, Fernández de Oviedo was in later years intimate with many who had. His accounts of what took place after the return to Española are of special interest. Bernáldez never left Spain, but he did have Columbus staying in his home in 1496 after the Admiral returned from the second voyage. Bernáldez wrote that he had received much information from Columbus, both verbally and in "writings" left with him: "From which I extracted and compared with the others written by Dr. Anca or Chanca and other noble gentlemen who went with him on the said voyages, and who wrote what they saw, from whom I was informed, and write this about the Indies."[2] Bernáldez was the first to publish extensive extracts from the letter of Dr. Diego Alvarez Chanca, and he also copied from Columbus's own letters as we now can confirm by comparing his account of the second voyage with those in *El libro copiador*'s third and fourth letters.

Martire wrote that he had queried his friend Columbus on many of these affairs. The first to publish a report on the second voyage was a Dr. Scyllacius (given in Spanish as "Esquilache"), who published, in about 1497, a pamphlet containing what he said were the unaltered words from a letter written by Guillermo Coma, a member of the expedition. Thacher provided a facsimile together with an English translation.[3] It has not been possible over the years to determine exactly who Coma was, but there is no question that his letter influenced biographers and historians alike up to the present. Miguel de Cuneo, a fellow Ligurian, also left a written account of his adventures on this voyage. He returned to Spain in 1495, at which time he wrote of his experiences. The manuscript was first published in 1885. Thus, with the eyewitness testimony of Chanca, Coma, and Cuneo, now augmented by Columbus's own accounts in *El libro copiador,* we have far more firsthand documentation for the second voyage than for any of the other three.

A contemporary secondary source was Columbus's close friend the Florentin Simón Verde.[4] In addition, a letter written by Giovanni di Bardi, also from Florence, contains a brief account of the voyage. In this letter he wrote, "I shall send you a copy of a letter that the admiral writes and another one directed to the Prince, our master, from which you will know minute by minute and day by day what they have discovered."[5] This second reference is obviously to the missing journal. It is equally apparent that contrary to normal expectations, the journal that Columbus kept for this voyage was not reserved for the eyes of the monarchs only.

Normally, one would expect that with so many eyewitness accounts, this well-documented second voyage would present few problems for the biographer. Unfortunately, there are so many differences in the accounts that this voyage presents greater difficulties than any of the other three. Two of the most prolific sources, Columbus and Las Casas, each had a tendency to ignore chronological sequence. Las Casas often cited hearsay as though it were fact, only to disclaim the same data at a later point in his book. This has led over the years to highly selective quotations from his *Historia.*

Las Casas, Hernando, and Bernáldez each quoted extensively from Columbus's heretofore unknown letters. There were other letters in addition to those found in *El libro copiador,* of course, but unless these too are discovered, we shall never know to what extent these early biographers did, or did not, follow Columbus's accounts closely. Interestingly, the first contemporary accounts by chroniclers other than Columbus were written by two Spaniards who had accompanied him and by five Italians, only one of whom had sailed on this voyage.

Because of the many differences found in the narratives recounting the activities of Columbus and his companions on the second voyage, it is important to keep in mind the chronology of the trips from

Spain to Española and back during the years of the second voyage—1493–96. This is not an easy task, due to disagreements between the early biographers, with inaccuracies compounded by later historians. All of the data in the following paragraph is well substantiated by contemporary documentation; the relevant citations will be given in the appropriate places in the body of the text.

Columbus returned to the settlement at Navidad with seventeen ships in December 1493. Luis Torres then went back to Spain with twelve of these, leaving Española in February 1494. Columbus left Española in late April with three caravels to cruise the coasts of Cuba and Jamaica, returning on September 29, 1494. He had with him on this trip the *Niña*, one of the three vessels of the first voyage. His brother Bartolomé sailed from Cádiz sometime between June and August 1494 in command of three caravels, arriving in Isabela, Española, shortly before his brother's return from Cuba. By the time of Columbus's return, the three caravels that Bartolomé had brought had left the island to return to Spain, carrying, among others, Fray Bernal Buil and Pedro Margarite. Shortly thereafter, Torres arrived from Spain with a resupply fleet of four caravels. He again left for Spain in the following February, carrying five hundred slaves, as well as Columbus's younger brother Diego Colón and Cuneo, among others. The next fleet to arrive was Juan Aguado's, with four caravels in October 1495. He and Columbus sailed for Spain in March 1496 on the locally built *India* and the rebuilt *Niña*.

Preparations

Much of the immediate postdiscovery activity in Spain was centered around Columbus's recognition for having successfully carried out his mission. On May 8, 1493, the capitulation made at Santa Fé was confirmed, again incorporating the phrase "the said mar Oceano which is ours." On the same day, as viceroy and governor, Columbus was empowered to appoint court officers and was given jurisdiction over criminal and civil cases. He was also named captain-general of the fleet now scheduled to return to Española. His son Diego was named page to Don Juan. A few days later, on the twentieth,

Columbus was granted a coat of arms in which were included the castle of Castile and the lion of León. Fernández de Oviedo provided copies of this first blazon and of the changes that Columbus made to it in 1502. He wrote that Columbus included the motto "Por Castilla é por Leon nuevo mundo halló Colom." This was not included in the authorization. Today this motto is given in different ways, but the Fernández de Oviedo version is believed to be the correct one.[6]

There was a flurry of activity on May 23. Columbus and Juan de Fonseca, at that time archdeacon of Seville, were instructed, "Know that We have agreed to send to prepare certain armadas of some boats and vedettes to send to the said Indies, in order to take control of (*señorear*) the lands . . . you will go to Seville and Cádiz and its dioceses and wherever you wish you will buy or embargo ships and supplies."[7]

There is no indication how much of this voyage was paid for with confiscated Jewish assets, though these probably covered a major part of the costs. At the time of their expulsion, the Jews had been allowed to sell, generally for a pittance, their properties and belongings. They were not allowed to take with them valuables such as gold and jewels. Later the Crown decreed that all goods so acquired reverted to the Crown. On May 23 and 24, orders were sent out to collect some of these funds "for the armada that is going to the Indies."[8]

One curious *cédula,* dated May 23, bears many similarities to the *cédulas* that dealt with the financing for the first voyage.[9] This new *cédula* ordered that moneys owed to the Santa Hermandad be turned over to Francisco Pinelo for expenses of the armada being prepared to go to the Indies. In this instance Pinelo was to receive, not lend, the funds. They were to be repaid in two installments in June of the same year, constituting another very short-term loan, this one definitely from the Hermandad. These funds were apparently to be used only until the above-mentioned collections could be effected. If such was the case, then the monarchs were in a great hurry to get the contracts for the boats and supplies moving. To have waited at most a few weeks seems hardly a matter of such importance that an intermediary loan had to be arranged. That it was to be repaid in the following month indicates that they were certain that in the meantime they would have collected sufficient funds for the purpose.

On this same day another *cédula* ordered Juanoto Berardi to buy and prepare for sailing a boat of from 100 to 200 tuns.[10] Berardi, a Florentin, was in this instance serving as an agent of the Crown. In another *cédula* of this date, Fonseca was informed, "Juanoto is in the business in the name of the Admiral of the said islands because he has his power [proxy] for it." Thus, Berardi was representing both the Crown and Columbus at this time.

Various *cédulas* dealt with specific categories of colonists who were to go on this voyage. The most important from the standpoint of future effects on the management of the colony was the group of twenty mounted lancers. These were to be selected from members of the Hermandad in Granada, the state-controlled police militia, and were to take with them five remounts, which had to be mares. The Hermandad was also ordered to supply from Granada twenty skilled farmers and an irrigation canal builder who was "not a Moor."[11] The "men from the country" and the canal builder were to be "safe and reliable men." For these jobs, the sovereigns obviously wanted people under their direct control, that is, people from the Hermandad. It is equally apparent that the monarchs were strictly hands-on in the planning for the colony. On this day they authorized Dr. Chanca to go on the voyage, with full salary.[12] Before the armada set sail they even limited the number of personal followers that Columbus could take with him.

Although the fleet did not sail until September, the sovereigns were already pushing in May for a fast departure. Fonseca was given special powers to speed up the preparations. Later in the month Columbus was given his "instruction from the King and from the Queen . . . for the form . . . on this voyage . . . in the departure of the armada, as on the trip, and after." This began, "First: they charge the said Admiral . . . that by all means that he can he try and work to bring the residents of the said islands and mainland to convert to our Holy Catholic faith." The next seven paragraphs dealt with such issues as supplies, as well as with the strict controls to be placed over any trading goods taken on board. Columbus was to be the only one who could authorize any trade, and all trade was to be registered with the Crown officials. After providing for civil government, the instruction further specified that all future traffic with the Indies was to come through the port of Cádiz. The final paragraph dealt with the eighth (*ochava part*) and the tenth (*décima parte*) parts, Columbus's rights of participation in the profits from trade, as had previously been agreed to at Santa Fé.

A number of orders were issued on May 28 that dealt with the authority of Columbus. All officers of the fleet were ordered to accept him as captain-general. He was authorized to submit a list of three names for each post in the government of the colony, from which the Crown would select one. For the immediate future, due to the shortage of time before his expected departure, he could name such officials himself. Since he was expected to continue with his discoveries, he was authorized to name his substitute when he left Española. A separate *cédula* gave such a person authorization to act in the name of the Crown.[13] Hernando misunderstood the temporary authorization given to his father to name the colony's officials, taking it to mean instead that this authority was vested in Columbus permanently.

The next day the sovereigns issued an order that was to cause Columbus problems in the future. It provided: "In regard to the conversion of the Indians, that Father Fray [*sic*] Buil go with other clerics. That the Indians be well treated and any who offends them be severely punished."[14] The question of who this father/friar really was has caused much controversy over the years. On June 7 the monarchs wrote to their representatives in Rome asking that "Fr. Bernal Buyl" be named the "Franciscan Vicar General in the Indies."[15] On August 4 the sovereigns sent the friar a copy of the June 15 bull in which he was ordered to the Indies. They told Fonseca to see that Buil and "the others" were provided for. This letter contains a curious reference, one that perhaps presaged things to come. The sovereigns wrote Buil, "thanking him for having informed them of what had happened and instructing him to keep on doing so [both] before leaving and after arriving there. They were angered by the things that he wrote because they wanted the Admiral of the Indies to be honoured; they hope that all will be remedied. They instructed him to attend to everything under his charge."[16]

There was known trouble at this time with one of the king's men, Juan de Soria; these problems may have been what the monarchs referred to. However, at the same time, their instructions to Buil to report directly to them may have sown the seeds of trouble for the future. Fernández de Oviedo referred to him as "fray Buil of the Order of St. Benedict."[17] Césario Fernández Duro and others have spelled his name "Boil" or "Boyl."[18] The bull as given by Fernández Duro clearly states that Buil was a Minorite in the order founded by Saint Francisco of Asisi. Those who claim that he was always a Benedictine,[19] and never a Franciscan, possibly do so in part based on the fact that a friend of Buil's, Francisco de Paula, formed the order of the Mínimos. The reason for the confusion is obvious. Juan Bautista Muñoz located twenty-three letters relating to this voyage and "Bernardi Boilli." To resolve the Francisan/Benedictine confusion, some have questioned whether the friar/priest who went with Columbus was the same person as the one named by the pope.

Morison, without explanation, appears to have subscribed to the alternative theory; he simply stated, "In contrast to the First Voyage, there were a number of ecclesiastics, of whom the most important was a Benedictine called Fray Buil."[20] The Phillipses accepted both theories, noting, "The Christian mission was under the leadership of Bernardo Buil, a former Benedictine monk who had become a preaching friar."[21] After the death of Columbus, a Benedictine monk, Fray Bernardo Buil, was entrusted by King Ferdinand with important diplomatic missions; thus it is conceivable that Buil went to Española as a Franciscan and at some later date changed to the Benedictine order. It is not reasonable, however, to assume that only days before the sailing, the pope referred to him as a Franciscan and promptly gave him the requisite permission to change from one order to another. None of these biographers mentioned the pre-sailing involvement of Buil in Columbus's troubles. As will be seen later, the problem does not lie so much in who he was as in what he did once he reached the Indies.

On June 1, three individuals whose names constantly crop up in Columbus's affairs received instructions connected with the voyage. Berardi was commissioned to supply bread for the voyage, Pinelo to provide money, and Gomez Tello, a bailiff of the Inquisition, to oversee the accounting; the last was told that if not satisfied there, he could return with the first boats coming back to Spain.[22] Tello apparently did not want to go, since on the same day new orders were cut naming Melchior Maldonado in his stead. A week later Bernal Díaz de Pisa was named Comptroller of the Fleet. In early August, Sebastián de Olano was named Receiver; he was to prove useful to Columbus. All of these were Ferdinand's men.

A week later, in a curious letter in light of future events, Columbus was asked to "provide a good position" to the king's butler (*repostero*) Juan Aguado.[23] The Aguado who returned with Torres to Spain in February 1484 was the same one referred to in the letter to Columbus, who commended him in the so-called Torres Memorandum. The monarchs noted on this commendation, "As to Juan Aguado Their Highnesses will keep him in mind as he is here."[24] In 1495 Aguado was to reappear in the affairs of Columbus. Now, however, preparations were completed, and the armada was ready to sail.

Departure and the Armada

Fernández de Oviedo wrote, "He left with his armada, sailing on Wednesday the 25th day of September in the year fourteen hundred and ninety-three . . . they were in all seventeen sail in which there were in fact one thousand five hundred men . . . on the royal payroll. And in this armada came religious persons and caballeros and hidalgos and honourable men and such as were suitable to populate new lands and to cultivate them . . . many of them dependents of the royal house, and I saw and knew all the most important of them."[25] Coma supplied considerable detail, adding that the fleet was made up of "big and little boats, there were many very light ones (the ones called Cantabric barques) whose fastenings are mostly with wooden pins so that the weight of iron does not impede their speed, also many caravels, as these boats of less draft are nevertheless capable of withstanding a long and difficult voyage . . . [and] with five large boats."[26]

Bernáldez gave the number of men sailing as "one thousand two hundred fighting men."[27] Martire wrote in his *Décades*, "The Queen orders more than one thousand two hundred armed infantrymen, among which there must be included salaried officials and number-less artisans [skilled] in the mechanical arts, to the rest of the soldiers they included some cavalrymen."[28] He too gave the twenty-fifth as the sailing date, but he gave the number of ships as fifteen.

In his letter in *El libro copiador*, Columbus left the date blank but did provide the day, Wednesday. Unfortunately, he did not mention the number of ships. In his fifth letter he wrote that he had with him "over a thousand men." This figure did not include sailors. He added, "I took artisans of all kinds with all of their tools, [of] trades [whose] occupations were to build city and town, and I took the horses, mares and mules and all the other livestock and seeds of wheat and barley and all of the trees and types of fruits, all of this in very great abundance."[29] Some of the previously cited *cédulas* made it clear that at least some of the workmen were drawn from the ranks of the Hermandad. It is possible that this was the reason that some writers claimed they were soldiers and others said artisans and laborers.

Hernando provided an eyewitness account: "Wednesday, on the 25th of September of the year 1493, an hour before sunrise, my brother and I being present, the Admiral raised anchors in the Port of Cádiz."[30] He reported that his father gave sealed directions to all of the pilots in case they should become separated from the main fleet.[31] Las Casas told only of their sailing on September 25 with seventeen "naos and caravels."[32] Based on the several eyewitness accounts reporting many of the vessels as small ones, it is probably safe to assume that the figure of twelve hundred men is close to the correct number, and the crews of the vessels may have even been included in the total. Most scholars today agree that he took with him seventeen vessels.

The Crossing

Columbus began the second letter in *El libro Copiador* by saying that he arrived in the Canaries on Tuesday, October 1, where he took on supplies; he left on the following Monday, the seventh.[33] Coma was far more informative but offered a different chronology. According to his version, they arrived at Lanzarote on the seventh and then went to Gran Canaria, where they spent a day and purchased sugar. He wrote of the plague of rabbits on that island and the severe measures taken in a vain effort to control them. The next day they headed for Gomera, where they stayed six days while replenishing their supplies. Based on Coma's schedule, they reached the island of Hierro on October 13.[34]

Chanca had them arriving at Gran Canaria on September 29. He said that after fixing one of the boats that needed repairs, they left the next day, and that it took them four or five days to reach Gomera due to the lack of favorable winds. There they took on supplies, and with a day's journey to Hierro, they had now been at sea for nineteen or twenty days. He said they left Hierro on October 13.[35]

According to Cuneo, they arrived on Gran Canaria on October 2 and at Gomera on the fifth. He too dated their transatlantic departure from Hierro on the thirteenth. Thus these four accounts, by people who were there, were in agreement that they left Cádiz on September 25 and Hierro on October 13.[36] The dates in between differ greatly. Chanca, who sailed on the flagship, complained that it was too slow, forcing the others to lower sails to let the ship catch up. It will be recalled that Columbus had the same problem with the *Santa María* on the first voyage. Apparently he favored the largest and, necessarily in those days, the slowest ship in the fleet, perhaps as being commensurate with his rank.

Chanca mentioned that Gomera was under the dominion of "Bovadilla [*sic*] la Cazadora." Varela believed that this was a misreading of the manuscript: *venatrix* ("huntress") for *senatrix* ("noble lady"). Cuneo noted that it would be boring to tell of their reception and celebrations on that island, thanks to the "lady of that place, with whom at another time our Admiral was in love."[37] The lady in question, Beatriz Bobadilla de Peraza, was a cousin and namesake of Queen Isabel's best friend; court gossip had it that King Ferdinand had fallen for the lady, so the queen had her married off to the governor of the distant island of Gomera. The derivation, if correctly applied here, of the cognomen of "The Huntress" (*La Cazadora*) is obvious. Whatever the truth about Columbus's relations with this well-known person (she was now a widow), there is no question that both the king and his admiral enjoyed the ladies, nor is there any doubt as to Isabel's well-chronicled, and equally well-justified, jealousy. Regarding women, Columbus wrote a postil about a lady who had cheated on her husband: "Nor was he the first nor be the last that a woman cheat."[38]

Morison, ever credulous, wrote: "At the time of Columbus's visit [on the first voyage] this energetic widow was still under thirty, and very beautiful; and we have it on good authority that he fell in love with her. Why not?"[39] Wilford confused the lady with her namesake, unfortunately thereby linking the latter to Columbus: "He is said to have had the ardent support of the Marquise de Moya, the wife of an important adviser to the court, and that her interest was quickened by the mariner's amorous attentions."[40] The more influential member of this family was Beatriz de Moya, not her husband, although he had assisted Isabel in her ascent to the throne. The marquise was a life-long friend and counselor of Queen Isabel's. There was never the slightest contemporary suggestion of impropriety on her part. She may have helped Columbus at court, but the romantic angle is invention. Fernández-Armesto adopted a cautionary attitude toward this affair related by "the notoriously prurient Michele de Cuneo." He added, "Still, Cuneo mentions the affair in so offhand a manner as to be convincing." This is a revealing form of interlinear interpretation indeed! It was in this passage, in which he discussed Columbus's supposed propensity for the ladies, that this author incurred in historical error, claiming that Columbus had legalized Hernando, "the incontrovertible proof of his passion for Beatriz Enriquez."[41]

The point in going into so much detail on this early stage of the journey is to demonstrate some of the many, and generally minor, incongruities in the accounts given for this voyage. Once the fleet reached the Caribbean, it became engaged in an island-hopping tour until it finally reached its destination at Navidad. Again, only the more important commentary on what took place will be dealt with here. The basic version will be the Admiral's, as given in his second letter.

Landfall and the Leeward Islands

Columbus wrote that he took the route to "first come to the island of the Cannibals." He continued, "I believed that it was more to the

East and little distant from my route . . . to which I arrived . . . in twenty days . . . [on] Sunday, November 3." His companions did not agree on the date that they first sighted land. Coma placed their arrival on the eve of the day of St. Jude and Judas, which fell on Sunday, October 27. Chanca gave the same date as did Columbus, November 3. They also differed in their manner of reporting on a storm through which they had passed. Columbus did not mention it; Chanca said it lasted for only four hours; Coma reported waves, lightning, and terrible peril, whereas Cuneo said it lasted all night with all of them in fear for their lives. According to Cuneo, they even ran out of water to drink.

Columbus named the first island Dominica, "in honour of the same day."[42] Chanca made the interesting observation, "The pilots of the armada counted that day, from the island of Fierro [*sic*] to the first one that we saw, some eight hundred leagues, others seven hundred and eighty."[43] These distances given by Chanca happen to be nearly accurate; the true distance is 802 leagues. Such a degree of accuracy is remarkable in view of the conflicting information given for distances traveled on the first voyage, seemingly indicative of the pilots' inability on that voyage to accurately judge distance traveled.

An interesting sidelight in Columbus's second letter told how a pilot named Camareco "was cause of a deceit." The Admiral wrote, "He had begged the pilot that I had, to show him my navigational chart and how many leagues I noted every day; and he said that he had heard me tell fray Buil that we had [   ] so that Sunday at dawn, while I was sleeping due to the work that I had done in the night, [Camareco was the first to sight land]."[44] His claim is reminiscent of the first voyage. Herein Columbus appears to be saying that he knew where he was going as well as when he would arrive there. This is a truly remarkable difference from his own account of the first voyage as we know it today.

Due to stormy weather and the lack of a suitable roadstead, he was unwilling to attempt a landing on Dominica. Instead he went on to the next island, which he named La Galana, although Cuneo and Coma said he named it either Santa María la Galante or Mariga-lante, "for love of the boat in which he traveled, that is named *María la Galante*."[45] Columbus wrote, "I went to shore with many people, with a royal banner, and in the most suitable place, with standard and loud voice and scribes and witnesses, I came back again to take possession of it, and of all of the others and of [the] mainland in the name of Your Highnesses, repeating the sentences of the past year, of which, nevertheless, [as] newly taken calling to see if anyone contradicted it; and I named this island *La Galana.*"⁴⁶ This shows that Columbus fulfilled the requirements for taking possession; however, unlike the circumstances under which he had carried out a similar act of possession on Guanahaní, this time there were none of the prescribed members of the indigenous population present to be given the requisite opportunity to contradict him.

The next day he sailed to the north and discovered the island that he named Santa María de Guadalupe. He was impressed, as were the others, by the island's waterfall, visible from "four large leagues" out at sea. It was so remarkable that "there were many bets among the people" whether what they saw was water or a white rock cliff. He said his men later counted twenty-six rivers within six leagues; Chanca believed that they had simply crossed over the same river many times. Columbus noted, "All of these islands belonged to cannibals and [were] populated by people who eat the other." Since the native men ran away into the dense forest, the Spaniards were able to capture only women, who told the sailors "that they had been brought from other islands." Columbus wrote, "In my view they were held in servitude and for concubines, also they told me by words and signs, how they had eaten their husbands ... I also found some youths that they had brought in the same way, and cut off the genitals of all of them; I thought for jealousy of the women, also ... so they could fatten as they do in Castile with capons."⁴⁷

He found "heads hanging in each house, and a sternpost (*coaste*) from a Spanish boat." Columbus added, "I believe that it is from the one that I left here in La Navidad last year."⁴⁸ Las Casas gave this word as *quodaste*, a word that he could not have copied from the only known version of the *Historie,* and said that it was made of wood. The Spanish translations of the *Historie* refer to it as an iron pot (*cazuelo de hierro*). Hernando speculated that it could have been brought from Española by Carib raiders and that, if it didn't come from there, it "could have been from some other boat that the winds and currents had brought from our regions to the said places."[49]

This misconstruction of the words *coaste* and *cazuelo* could have resulted from a problem in the transcription and/or translation from Spanish to Italian and back into Spanish. The object could conceivably have floated there if, as some believe, it was made of wood. If made of iron, it had to have been brought, either by canoe or, as others have claimed,[50] by a European vessel, providing evidence of a prior voyage to this island. Morison was the only one of these modern writers to report this find. He suggested another alternative, saying that it was "a piece of ship timber which they supposed to have come from the wreck of *Santa María* on the First Voyage; but it must have belonged to a Portuguese caravel, and floated over from Africa in the equatorial current."[51] Here he accepted that a piece of wood could float over from Africa, whereas earlier he had categorically denied that the boat of the "unknown pilot" could have done so.

Columbus next made a revealing statement: "I did not burn their houses so that we could use them when we pass by here, because it is on the route to Spain." Columbus already knew the return route to Spain was far to the north; these islands were on the best east-west route from Spain to Española. He went on to say that their canoes were larger than those in the islands to the west: "I destroyed all of them, small and large, and the same in all the other places and I had the intention to do the same in each island, moreover I had the great desire to take all of them, and the desire to rescue these people."[52] Apparently this was less a case of wanton destruction than of curtailment of the presumed cannibals who were later to be enslaved.

Chanca reported these matters more or less in the same way—three leagues instead of four, arms and legs in the huts instead of just heads. He did enter into a great deal of detail about the eating habits of these cannibals, and as a result he, even more than Columbus, can be said to be the true father of this gory and fanciful myth about cannibals on Guadeloupe. His malignant influence on mythmaking is still noticeable. The Phillipses, after an extensive quotation, added, "Chanca's matter of fact reporting of these horrors leaves little doubt of their authenticity."[53] Matter-of-fact reporting is not necessarily conducive to accuracy. Sale, on the other hand, offered an anthropologically supported rebuttal of these charges.⁵⁴ It is questionable whether cannibals were ever on any of the Caribbean islands.

Chanca noted, "We suspected that those islands belonged to the Caribes . . . people who eat human meat, because the Admiral, by the signs that had been given him [by] the Indians of the islands that he had before discovered on his other trip, as to the site of these islands, he had set straight [on] the route to discover them, because they were closer to Spain and also because the route straight to the island of Española was through there . . . due to the bounty of God and the knowledge of the Admiral we came so straight [to Española] as if by a known road."⁵⁵ Chanca was only the first of many who have found Columbus's uncanny knowledge of this route worthy of comment.

Coma, as throughout this voyage, concentrated mainly on the flora and geography while seeking parallels for what he had seen in classical quotations rather than commenting on the human side. He did report the cannibal story with great exaggerations, but only as told to him by Pedro Margarite. His fantasies about the cannibals were further nourished by tales remembered from his readings, identified by Varela as coming from Pliny and Hesiod.⁵⁶ Cuneo offered much the same speculative data.

This second Columbus letter contains a startling piece of information, something that appears nowhere else. He told of a little boy abandoned by the fleeing Indians; the boy was also described by others, but Columbus added the more detailed information that the boy was about a year old and every day crawled down to a river, always with a handful of arrows, where "he drank the water and then returned to his dwelling and was always happy and in a good mood." Columbus added, "I ordered that he be brought to God and happiness, and I ordered that he be given to a woman who came here from Castile; now he is well here and speaks and understands all of our language." The Admiral said that he was afraid to send the boy to Spain at this time because he was so young.⁵⁷ This was the first, and only, mention of any Spanish woman on this trip. Many years later a María Fernández presented in a loan application a copy of a payroll in which she was listed as a *criada* ("servant") on the second voyage, as well as a mantilla that she said Columbus had given her.[58] Gil accepted this as indisputable proof that women were on the second voyage.[59] Morison, as far as the information that he had available accorded with general opinion, wrote, "Not a single woman was taken aboard the fleet."[60] This new information, of course, revolutionizes all previous beliefs as to the first arrival of European women in the Americas.

While on the island, a party of men became lost in the jungle; the number was given variously as between six and eleven. Columbus limited himself to a brief comment. For whatever reason, he did not go into the matter in detail, although the others did. Chanca said that the missing party was made up of a captain and six men and that they were lost for four days but found their way back by following the beach. Cuneo wrote that it was a party of eleven men and that the Admiral sent out two hundred men looking for them in search parties with trumpets. An old woman showed the lost men the way to the beach, where they lit a signal fire and were rescued by boat. They had been lost for "five or six days." He ended this account, "If it hadn't been for the old woman who showed them by signs the way, they would have been lost, in that the next day we wanted to raise sail for our voyage."[61]

The fleet went next to an island that Columbus named Santa María de Monsarrate, "very high land like Monsarrate [*sic*]." At some point in his life, Fray Buil is said to have been a monk in the Benedictine monastery at Montserrat. The Admiral soon found so many islands that he named them Todos Los Santos. He reached a "very long island," where they encountered three men with two women in a canoe. When the Spaniards tried to capture them, the Indians wounded three of the sailors with arrows. One of the Indians was killed, and the rest were captured. They told Columbus that "over there is so much gold that it is a marvel." He reported that farther along the way he counted 140 islands, some large, most of them small. He called the largest one Santa Ursula and the others the Eleven Thousand Virgins.

His Map of the Islands

Columbus offered in this letter very important and revealing information. In an earlier chapter, we discussed the question of his navigational theories. Now, in this letter, he revealed information that could only be surmised before:

> All these islands, that have now been found, I send with a drawing with the others of the past year, and all in a letter that I composed, well (*bien*) with sufficient work due to my great occupation with the settlement that is being made in the town here [Isabela] and the dispatch of the [Torres] armada so that it return [to Spain]; . . . Your Highnesses will see the land of Spain and Africa, and, in front of them, all of the islands found and discovered on this voyage and the other; the lines that go along the length show the distance from east to west, the others that run across show the difference from the North to the South. The spaces between each line signify one degree, that I have counted fifty-six miles and two thirds that correspond to fourteen and a sixth of our sea leagues; and that way it is possible to count from the west to the east, as from the north to the south the said number of leagues, and count with the account of Ptolemy, who apportioned the degrees of longitude with those of the equator, saying just as four degrees at the equator corresponds to five at the parallel [*pañuelo*, meaning "shawl," probably a scribal error for *paralelo*] of Rhodes, thirty six degrees; just as every degree that is on the said map corresponds to fourteen leagues and a sixth, the same from north to south as from east to west. And so that the distance of the route that is from Spain to the beginning or end of the Indies can be seen, so you can see what distance corresponds to the lands [discovered on the first voyage] to the others [discovered now], you will see on the said map a red line that passes from the north to the south, and passes over the top of the island Ysabela [*sic*] [Columbus frequently interchanged Ysabela with Española] over the Tin of Spain [Columbus's name for the region on Espanola known as Samana], beyond (*allende*) which are the islands discovered on the other voyage, and the others of now from here (*aca*) the line; it is understood, and I believe in God that each year we will have many to add to the drawing because [they will] be discovered continually.[62]

The above quotation clearly indicates that Columbus sent with Torres, to give to the sovereigns, a map with grids. Antonio Rumeu de Armas and Gil differed in parts of their transcriptions of this letter. Evidence of the influence of Eratosthenes by way of Ptolemy on Columbus's thinking is seen in his reference to Rhodes. As Wilford explained, "He [Eratosthenes] drew east-west lines through familiar places that he supposed were on the same latitude: one line ran from the Pillars of Hercules through Rhodes."[63] In this letter, Columbus's sea league is 3.63 miles, rather than the customary 4.

No contemporary reference reveals whether the monarchs received this map. As Gil pointed out, this settles the long-disputed question as to what system Columbus used: Ptolemic (although his later measurements indicate the influence of Alfragan). With the addition of the red line he graphically showed the monarchs the progress of his discoveries. Those on one side of the line were found in the previous year, those on the other side, in the current year. The description of the map shows that Columbus was answering the specific questions that the queen had asked him to respond to before his departure. Later on in the letter, which was written, as he said, after he had been in Isabela for thirty-one days, he added the following interesting observations on the geographical location of Española: "I already said that the lands that have been discovered on this voyage are as much and more than in the past year, and not of less value, as the map will make manifest; for which Your Highnesses will see that here in Ysabela we are twenty-six degrees more distant from the equator, that it is on a parallel with the Canary Islands, especially Gomera, and it is only thirty minutes different in latitude."[64]

It will be recalled that on the first voyage he placed Guanahaní on the same parallel with the Canary Islands, but he also said, in his November 21 entry in the *Diario,* that the southern tip of Cuba was at a latitude of 42°, although Las Casas explained that this was a misreading with the quadrant. He now lowered this to 26°, whereas the correct reading for Isabela is 19°57′. In his first decade, Martire provided a somewhat jumbled version: "This island Española, which he maintains is Ofir, which is spoken of in the third Book of Kings, has [a length of] five degrees of latitude to the west; in fact it is twenty-seven degrees above the septentrion, from the equator [i.e., north of the equator], as they themselves assure, twenty two."[65] He appears in this passage to have been correcting Columbus's earlier figure, 27 in lieu of 26, with a closer-to-reality 22°.

At the end of the third letter is another of Columbus's previously unknown explanations as to the geographical location of the Indies. He now said of this city (*esta çudad*):

> [It] is twenty-five degrees distant from the equator, and the southernmost part eighteen degrees towards the outside Arctic pole [Antarctic]. From the West of Ptolemy to the Cape of Sant Rafael [identified by Las Casas as Cape Engaño] that is the East end of the island, is distant from that parallel *** degrees . . . when I was in the port of Santa Cruz, that is twenty-nine leagues farther to the south, on 14 September of this year 1494, I saw the moon eclipse at 52 minutes past midnight . . . I don't say anything of the other eclipse that was in the past month of March . . . it didn't show itself to us because the skies were closed in . . . not like now which was very clear. From this cape to the West it is about 700 leagues to the Evangelista Cheroneso [northwestern Cuba] the last mainland that I discovered to the West this year, and the island of San Juan Bautista [Puerto Rico] is to the East . . . I was more than ten hours distant from Cáliz [*sic*] when I was navigating in the white sea [Chersonese] the sun rose in Sevilla two hours after I felt night [coming] and the sight of the sun left me.[66]

His latitude figures are for the readings for the northern and southern coasts, although the language used is difficult to understand. Columbus is known to have carried with him on the fourth voyage a copy of a table of eclipses, and this entry now shows that he also had one on this voyage. His estimate of distance in this case was based on astronomical hours; in one hour of the sun's movement over the earth, the sun was assumed to travel the distance of 15 degrees; hence ten hours would be 150 degrees (20 farther than his own estimate of the distance to the islands off Asia). The actual distance between "the white sea" off the northwestern coast of Cuba and Cádiz is around 80 degrees. Columbus obviously attached great importance to his estimates based on the timing of the eclipse. He offered a radically different and far more accurate estimate when he wrote in the *Libro de las profecías*: "In the year 1494 . . . there was an eclipse on September 14 and it was found that there was a difference from there [Saona Island] to Cape San Viçente in Portugal of five hours and more than a half."[67] The actual difference is four hours and nine minutes. Again, writing to Pope Alexander VI in 1502, he gave similar erroneous calculations and added, "There can have been no mistake, because at that time there was an eclipse of the moon on September 14."[68]

As for the 700 leagues he believed he had traveled, this measurement was apparently based on his estimated 335 leagues up the coast of Cuba, with the remaining 365 leagues being his estimate of the distance between the southern tip of Cuba and the westernmost tip of Española. He thus calculated his distance traveled as 2,800 miles, whereas the distance between these two points as the crow flies is close to 850 miles. Perhaps he reported what appears to be an excessive length for Cuba in order to support his contention that it was a continent. As Cecil Jane pointed out, the greatest length of Cuba is only 750 miles; however, due to what Jane described as the extreme indentation of the shore, the island has a total coastline of nearly 6,000 miles, and Columbus was following the coastline.

Columbus believed that the estimate found in the *Ymago mundi*— that the ocean between Asia and Europe was one-seventh of the globe's circumference, that is, 51 degrees, consisting of 56⅔ miles each, for a total of approximately 725 leagues—was accurate. On both the first and the second voyages, although on different parallels, he expected to find land at between 750 and 800 leagues from the Canary Islands. Only Hernando wrote that his father told the crews on the first voyage that they could expect land at 750 leagues. When he returned to Española at the start of the second voyage, the figure to Dominica confirmed this belief. His reported distances traveled were approximately correct for the West Indies, but not for the Far East.

Las Casas quoted from Columbus's writings in a letter that "he sent to the kings": "From the cape of Cuba (that can be seen from Española), that he called the Fin de Oriente, and by another named Alpha et Omega, he had sailed for the time of ten hours on the sphere to the West from the East, in such a manner that while he was there, when the sun went down for him, it had risen two hours earlier for those who lived in Cáliz [sic] in Spain, and he says there can't be any error, because there was then an eclipse of the moon, on September 14, and that he was well provided with instruments and the sky was very clear that night. These are all his words."⁶⁹ Apparently, despite minor differences, the above data given in the fourth letter of *El libro copiador* and the quotation by Las Casas had a common source. Columbus's "Alpha et Omega" was to his mind the point on the southern coast of Cuba where the East began and the West ended. The mention of "instruments" was probably a reference to the table of eclipses.

The knowledge that this newly revealed map existed suggests that it may have been the map on which Juan de la Cosa based his map of the Indies, which was first printed in 1500. In the *Pleitos,* four witnesses testified not only that Columbus had shown his map to La Cosa on this voyage but also that he had become angry because his servant had allowed La Cosa to copy it. More recently, attempts have been made to link a previously unknown map made by Columbus with the recently discovered Ottoman Piri Re'is map, dated 1513 by some.⁷⁰ In light of the above excerpts, all previous studies of Columbus's cosmographic concepts require reappraisal.

Columbus's Treatment of the Carib Indians

Columbus viewed the islands of the Caribs as commercially exploitable. Despite what must have been the negative reaction in Spain to the "spices" that he brought back with him from the first voyage, he persisted at this time in his belief that they were of value: "In this island of Guadalupe [*sic*] and in almost all of the others, especially on this Ysavela . . . in the trees, vanilla and a great quantity could be had except that it is bitter in taste, which I believe is due to the season . . . and mastic and incense, and wax and honey, and many resins, and aloes, and mints." He made another curious remark: "I do not err as to the abundance of all of this; the truth is that nobody bothers to gather anything, and not [even] gold, of which I know that there is more than I said nor wrote in my letter." This is one more example of Columbus's tendency to always hold back some bit of information. He never attempted to export any of the above-named products with the sole exception of brazilwood. In the *Diario* he

frequently commented on the innocence of the natives and the goodness of nature, praise repeated even more often in the first three
letters of *El libro copiador.* He constantly maintained that it was necessary to treat the natives well, "so they not be angered with us," yet
his actions, more often than not, belied his professed good intentions.

Another account contains a boastful report of the rape of an Indian
girl; written by the rapist, Cuneo, this story may seem strange to
modern readers. Cuneo, an acquaintance of Columbus's from his
Savona days, sailed on the flagship. He wrote of this incident:

> When I was on the ship's boat I captured a very lovely cannibal
> (*cambala*) who the Admiral gave to me; and having her in my bunk,
> she being nude according to [their] custom, the desire to amuse myself
> with her came over me; and, on trying to put into effect my desire, she
> resisting, scratched me with her nails in such a manner that I
> wouldn't have wanted to have started; but in view of that, to tell you
> the end [of the story] I grabbed my belt and I gave her a good beating
> with lashings, in such a manner that she screamed in [such] a way
> that, not heard, wouldn't be believed. Finally, we reached an
> agreement in such a way that I can tell you that in the act she seemed
> to have been taught in the school of whores.[71]

The rape was not mentioned in any of the other contemporaneous
accounts. Earlier, on this same day, Cuneo also told of hauling an
Indian on board after a brief fight with four men and two women and
of the chopping off of the Indian's head with an ax. Chanca said that
the Indian was first thrown two times into the sea as dead but finally
had to be killed with arrows.

Wilford wrote of the rape: "This earliest preserved account of
sexual intercourse between Europeans and Indians symbolizes the
rape, of the people and of the land, that was only the beginning. . . .
Morison writes by way of explaining his hero, though not condoning
his behavior in this regard. They were the superior people, and these
Indians were their inferiors, to be seized and used. . . . Finally, as the
ultimate insult pointed out by Todorov, Cuneo's woman 'who
violently rejected sexual solicitation finds herself identified with the
woman who makes this solicitation her profession.' "[72]

These commentaries raise two questions. First, is not such behavior
more typical than otherwise of the relationship between conqueror

and conquered, on occasion even into modern times? The Russians in Berlin, the Japanese in Korea: there is a difference of degree in that this was a peaceful takeover of another's territory. The second question is whether the rapist and his victim might not be possibly considered as atypical and not, therefore, necessarily representative of the colonists and the Indians of their day. Later accounts by Spaniards stressed the liberality of the Taino women in sexual matters. Miscegenation soon became the custom, rather than the exception, on Española.

Another, perhaps more important issue from a biographer's standpoint is that Columbus "gave" the girl to Cuneo, as well as acquiesced, at least through his silence, in the ensuing abusive behavior by his compatriot. This behavior is despicable in our eyes today, but obviously not so in his. As for those who see in this affair an early and telling example of the Spanish Black Legend, they should remember that the girl was given by one Italian to another Italian. It would be a long time before a rape of an Indian woman by a Spaniard would be reported in a contemporary document.

Columbus never returned to this chain of islands. The discovery was only of geographic interest. The islands contributed nothing to the economic future of Spain's colony on Española. The fleet had now reached the northernmost island in the Lesser Antilles. Next on the itinerary was a brief layover on the island of Puerto Rico, followed by a return to Española on its eastern coast, at approximately the point from which the two remaining ships of the first voyage had set sail for Spain.

What's past is prologue.
        William Shakespeare (1564–1616)

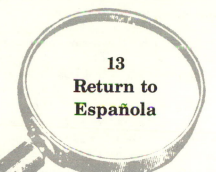

13
Return to
Española

In the second letter, Columbus wrote that after a brief layover in Puerto Rico, he touched Española first at Samana. Like the other writers, he said that he delayed only long enough to send to shore one of the Indians that he had taken with him to Spain. However, in the letter he gave a detail not reported by the others: "[He was] one of the four Indians that I had taken there the past year, who had not died from smallpox as the others had done on leaving Cáliz [*sic*], as well as others from Guanafani [*sic*] or Sant Salvador."[1] Chanca said only that five Indians had died on the trip back. This was the first mention made of smallpox, a disease that in the coming years is said to have decimated the native population of Española. It is important to note that the smallpox affected these particular Indians after they left Cádiz, a strong indication that smallpox was brought to the island with the second voyage. Some might see in this a cruel form of retribution, in that the virulent form of syphilis that was to become the scourge of sixteenth-century Europe was believed to have been introduced by the Spanish sailors returning from this island on the first voyage. Many have attributed

Martín Alonso Pinzón's death shortly after his return to this sexually transmitted disease.

All versions, by participants and chroniclers, basically agree on what happened next. Columbus wrote in the letter of events after leaving Montecristi for Navidad:

> Half way there I saw that a canoe came at great speed behind me, and I didn't want to wait for it because it would make me late to enter the port by day, and with all that I couldn't arrive in time, I had to anchor outside . . . the said canoe arrived, by which there came a messenger from a king Ocanaguari [sic] . . . and until he saw and heard me he didn't want to enter into the boat. . . . This one told me how the people that I had left in the city had disagreement among themselves and that one killed another one and Pedro, the steward of Your Highnesses, had gone with a large part of the people to another king who is called Cahonaboa [sic], who has land in which there is much gold; and a Viscayan, who is called Chacho, had gone with other Viscayans and boys; only eleven had stayed with Diego de Arana from Córdova; and that three had died of ailments, that they themselves said was caused by the great treatment of the women, saying that, those that stayed there, that each one had taken four women, and these alone weren't enough, that they took the girls. And they said that the beginning of this discord was that, after I left, each didn't want to come under orders, nor pan for gold except for himself, except Pedro, steward, and Escobedo—I had left him in charge of all the things. And that the others didn't understand except women and lived in their houses, and that Pedro and Escobedo killed one called Jacomé; and then they went with their women to this Cahonaboa; and after a certain time this Cahonaboa came and at night put fire to the village, all of which he burned so that nothing remained, for which one must have pity, because I have not seen in all of the Indies another so large a village nor such attractive houses. Upon which Ocanaguari fled with all of his people, men, women and children, and invited the Christians to go with him, and it didn't suit them, instead they went to the canal where they drowned; and eight were drowned, and three died sleeping, as later could be seen from their wounds.[2]

After landing, Columbus found that the Indian village had been destroyed, "except for the fort, that although destroyed and burned, [if it were] in the middle of Castile, [it] could [still] be defended against a lot of people." He added, "And I found eight men buried by the side of the sea and three in the country, which could be seen that they had been wounded from the front with stone[s]; and it must be so, because the fort was very full of artillery." He had the men buried and their souls prayed for. He immediately had the floor of the fort excavated to see if they had buried any gold there. The next day he went to see Guacanagarí, who told him the same story about the men that the Admiral had left at Navidad, but Columbus added an interesting piece of previously unreported information. He said the cacique told him that Pedro had a son with him.[3] This is the first report of a mestizo in the Americas. Hernando told the story in much the same manner, not mentioning the mestizo child, and with only minor variations in the timing of the sequence of events. Shortly before leaving Navidad to find a new location for a settlement, Columbus wrote in the second letter, "I believe that this Ocanaguari [*sic*] is not to blame for the death of our people."[4]

Las Casas added information, saying that Columbus at this time used as interpreter one of the Indians that he had brought back, a Diego Colon, whom Las Casas "knew sufficiently." He said that the king and some of his men showed Columbus their wounds from fighting with "Canabo [*sic*], who was seignior of the mines." He added in parentheses, "I believe that the writing is wrong, that it should have said Caonabo." These wounds "looked like the wounds from the arms that the Indians used, which were slings, like darts, with the bone of a fish for a point." He continued, in brackets, "The Admiral says furthermore here that, that father Buil, and all the others wanted him to take him [Guacanagarí], but he didn't want to do it, although he says that he could have, believing, that as the Christians were dead, that the imprisonment of Guacanagari could neither revive them nor send them to Paradise, if they weren't already there."[5] Las Casas went on to say that the Admiral reasoned that such an act would make relations between the settlers and the Indians only more difficult and that if the cacique was really innocent, such an act would cause hatred and reprisals. The foregoing is given by Las Casas as a quotation.

Chanca, who was often confused in his timing of events, wrote that they had found two dead men four days before arriving at the site of Navidad and another two, three days later. He said Indians came aboard when they anchored in the port at Navidad and that they told conflicting stories about the Christians—some were alive, some were dead, all were dead. Before Columbus went to visit "Guacamari," the men saw the destroyed fort and town: "There were between us many different opinions; some, suspecting that the same Guacamari [sic] was in the conspiracy and death of the Christians, to others it seemed not so, because his village had been burned, and therefore the matter was to be much doubted." He reported that on a visit the next day to "Guacamari," Columbus had a surgeon examine the king's leg because the cacique claimed that he had been wounded fighting Caonabo, yet the surgeon could find nothing wrong with the leg.[6]

Coma gave a much more elaborate recital, writing that Columbus went with a hundred men in formation "with the sound of trumpets and the roll of drums" to visit "Goathanario [sic] who was sick and in a hammock [from the Taino word *hamaca*]." Cuneo said that "Goacanari" told them how "Guanacaboa" had attacked the village with three thousand men. Cuneo claimed that the Spaniards found the dead men "still lying here and there on the ground without eyes, which we thought they had eaten, because, when they decapitate anyone, they immediately take out his eyes and eat them."[7]

Morison added details to Las Casas's version: "The Admiral held a council as to what should be done about the murder. Fray Buil and a number of others jumped to the conclusion that Guacanagarí was guilty, and demanded that he be seized and put to death as a warning to his countrymen. Columbus trusted human nature better than did the reverend father."[8] Fernández-Armesto decided, "The faction that demanded vengeance was led, inappropriately, by the missionary leader Fray Bernardo Boil [sic] whose evangelical charity seems sometimes to have been dimmed by natural spite."[9] Wilford also made some minor changes in the contemporary accounts. On the night of their arrival at Navidad, the Spaniards tried to attract attention: "The seamen lighted flares and fired canon." Chanca said only that the Admiral ordered two shots fired, with no mention of flares.[10]

Columbus and his companions agreed that the site of Navidad, seen on the first voyage as ideal, was marshy and unhealthy.

Another, perhaps more cogent reason for a move was Columbus's declared desire to find a place closer to the mines of the interior. Chanca maintained that when they first arrived at Montecristi they spent two days seeking a place for a suitable settlement. At this point in the account, just before the Spaniards left to find a new site, the Columbus letter supplied a revealing word—*Diurnal*—which Gil assumed to be the first time that the correct name for Columbus's *Diario* was given.[11] Columbus did not give a date for the departure, whereas Cuneo supplied December 8. Coma did not give a departure date but did state an arrival time at the place where they finally landed.

Isabela

Hernando wrote that Columbus had fallen sick at this time and for that reason failed to maintain his *Diario* from "the 11th of December until the 12th of March of 1494." The second letter twice mentions this sickness that until now has been known of only through Hernando. Columbus wrote to "Your Highnesses": "From December until today it has been very cold . . . one night I left the village of Navidad with the barques to see a port . . . and, at the time I went to sleep my right side tormented me, from the bottom of the foot up to the head, as with palsy, from which I have suffered not little pain."[12] At the end of January he wrote, "Now I am better; nor do I stop from working." In these excerpts Columbus reveals that what he suffered from was palsy. Over the years there has been much speculation about his ailments, generally accepted as Reiter's syndrome. Here we have, for the first time, Columbus's own statements on the matter. Although he may not have maintained his *Diario* while sick, he did write in the letters about what happened during this period.

Columbus wrote that the armada went first to Montecristi: "I persisted many times, with the wind against me, to come to Cape Angel . . . at which place I had seen a good landing and handsome land and water and rivers, and it seemed it was a good territory and near to the Çivao [*sic*] and the other mines." This supplies the first concrete information that Columbus had intended for some time to go to the site where he now established the settlement of Isabela. The account given in the letter for the next two days is simply confusing but finally:

> I came back here the next day, where we built the town of Ysabela, which for its merit, which I shall tell later, I beg Your Highnesses that you make it a city where there will be four leagues; it is not here an enclosed port, it is more of a large bay in which all of the boats of the world could fit. Storms never enter here, and here is an ideal place with high ground, almost an island, at the foot of which a large boat can come and discharge at the foot of the cliff. From here a lombard shot away [300–500 yards] there is a powerful river of water, better than the Guadalquevir [*sic*], from which it can be brought into the town to the plaza by canal, it passes through an extremely large plain that goes to the Southeast, to which up to today I have not been able to know [reach] the cape. The which is marvelous land without comparison to any in Castile, that now there is tall and green grass everywhere and much better than barley in Spain in the best time. From the town to the west there is a handsome beach for two big leagues, and at the cape a port that is one of the best in the world, in which would fit all of the boats there are. Together with this plain, also in the part to the west, there is a mountain from the northeast to the southeast. In it there is a port . . . in this plain there is [space] for twenty thousand settlers to plant bread [wheat] and make gardens and water buildings [i.e., mills].[13]

Las Casas believed that the original intent had been to land at Puerto Plata but that the head winds were such that Columbus backtracked only as far as Isabela.[14] Chanca wrote: "It gave us more difficulty to go back 30 leagues than it took to come from Castile. Due to contrary weather and the length of the voyage, three months had already gone by when we landed."[15] The dates given by Chanca (December 25, 1493) and Coma (January 2, 1494) for the founding of Isabela have been a source of confusion. First, it must be noted that Fernández de Navarrete in 1825 transcribed the sentence in Antonio de Aspa's sixteenth-century copy of the Chanca manuscript as, "The day that I went to sleep on land was the first day of the Lord."[16] Varela, however, transcribed it as "the first day of January."[17] Bernáldez provided the first published extract from this letter but gave no date, only the month as "Henero." Varela made a study of the similarities and differences between the Aspa copy and the Bernáldez extract, again giving the month as "Henero."[18] The evidence indicates a correct reading of "first day of the Lord," in short, Christmas Day.

Varela and others translated the Latin version of Coma's letter in Dr. Scyllacius's pamphlet of circa 1497 as, "They take land on the coast at eight days from the Nativity (*de la Navidad*) of [the] Savior," which would be January 2.[19] Columbus provided a clue for the settlement date when he wrote in the second letter, "Today it is thirty-one days since I arrived at this port."[20] The "today" would be before Torres left for Spain. The copy in Spanish archives of Columbus's memorandum that was given to Torres to take to the sovereigns is dated January 30.[21] The "thirty-one days" thus indicated December 30.

Antonio Rumeu de Armas transcribed Columbus's orders for the fleet's return to Spain as, "I have already dispatched the armada so that it may return" ("*ya e despachado* [emphasis added] del armada porque se buelva").[22] Gil's transcription places a different light on the matter: "And the dispatch of the armada so that it may return" ("*y el despach[ad]o* [emphasis added] del armada porque se buelva"). It appears that Rumeu de Armas's use of the past sense was silent emendation; later references show that Gil's transcription is the correct one.

If the Rumeu de Armas transcription is accepted, it would indicate that Torres had already left by the time that the second letter was written. However, there is no question that Torres brought the memorandum to Spain at this time. In the third letter, Columbus provided a definite date for Torres's departure: February 3.[23] Cuneo said that the Torres fleet sailed "in the month of February." Las Casas gave the date more precisely as February 2,[24] and Bernáldez reported the third.[25] If Columbus, as he said, wrote this before the departure of the homebound fleet, be that on the second or third of February, then Isabela was founded on either January 1 or 2.

Columbus earlier told that he had switched ships at Montecristi. He included the first information that the fleet had split up, some staying behind while he had gone ahead. He landed some of the horses and cattle at Montecristi, which seems to have served as a way station to Isabela. Some of his companions complained that it had taken them longer, actually a minimum of twenty-five or twenty-six days if they all left together on the eighth, to sail up the coast from Navidad to Isabela than it had taken them to cross the Atlantic, which took twenty days. It is now obvious that only some of them took longer to reach Isabela.

Basing himself, inaccurately, on Chanca, Morison wrote, "On January 2, 1494, the fleet anchored in the lee of a wooded peninsula."[26] Wilford passed up the question of the date, remarking merely, "[He] established there La Isabela, the first planned European town in the New World." The Phillipses restricted their estimate to the more general "early in January." Fernández-Armesto also offered January 2 as the date. Although all of these authors were apparently unaware of the recently recovered Columbus letter, they each arrived at near-accurate conclusions.

The Settlement at Isabela

Chanca wrote that the settlement was first named Marta.[27] The *Libretto* provided the only known instance in which the native name for the village where Isabela was established is given: "The Admiral took Locinfrone a place near a harbour, in order to build a town: and commenced to build; and construct a church: but the time was drawing near when he promised the king to inform him of his success. So he sent directly back twelve caravels."[28] Martire mentioned that one reason for selecting this site was that it was near some cliffs suitable for extracting building materials. Las Casas wrote that the huts were of straw and palm leaves but that the public buildings were of stone. Cuneo said the huts where the men lived were built like the duck blinds of Spain.[29] In his second letter Columbus described them as shacks (*chozas*).

Columbus's declared interest was to be near the unexplored land of the presumed mines. A few miles down the coast to the east is where Pinzón had anchored. He had supposedly traveled inland from there to what were called, unseen, the mines in the Cibao. Pinzón's landing place would have been a more hospitable one but would

probably have been unacceptable due to its earlier connection with
a man whom Columbus had come to regard as his enemy. Columbus
had now, on two occasions, bypassed Puerto Plata, an excellent
landlocked port with the largest roadstead on the northern coast;
although he could not have known this then, it was far more
accessible to the Cibao. The port, the beaches, and the large rivers
that he described at Isabela are nonexistent today.

It is difficult to visualize how this barren, godforsaken area must
have appeared when still covered with virgin growth. Perhaps at
that time the streams carried more water than today, but never
"better than the Guadalquivir." The nearest river, the Bahabonico,
could never have been navigable as was reported. The inlet to the
west of the settlement was completely open to winds from the north
and west, which are the prevailing winds for a good part of the year.
At that time there probably was some tilth to the soil, although by
its very geophysical nature it could never have been considered as
anything approaching prime farmland. The waterside cliff is today
a mere six to eight feet, with at no place more than two feet of water;
there is no way, as Columbus claimed, that a "large boat" could tie
up today to unload. It was even said at the time that the shallow-
draft caravels (six to eight feet) had to anchor half a mile out in open
water. The inlet to the immediate west of the settlement could
provide moorings today for at the most a dozen very small fishing
boats. Chanca and Coma gave descriptions of Isabela that simply do
not fit with the foundations that can still be seen there. I say this
as one who is personally familiar with the site and the surrounding
countryside. Interestingly, even Morison, who also visited the site,
found it unsuitable but excused the error of its selection by a lack
of colonizing experience at the time. One hardly needs to be a
colonist to pick a suitable harbor. Fernández-Armesto and Sale also
drew attention to the total unsuitability of this ill-conceived experiment in urbanization. If one was to seek Isabela today, based solely
on Columbus's glowing description, there would be absolutely no
way of locating it.

The site as it is presently laid out raises serious questions.
Regardless of any inconveniences due to location, there is the
question of space. Columbus has been variously reported as having

sailed with from 1,000 to 1,500 men. He wrote in the fifth letter that the number was "over a thousand." These men, together with the sailors, could have totaled around 1,500. As has already been discussed in the chapter dealing with the loss of the *Santa María*, this fleet of seventeen vessels—naos, caravels, and barques—may have brought close to 1,200 men in addition to the crews. However, even if one accepts the lowest figure of 1,000, there was still insufficient space in the area to house so many people. The outlines of the footings of the public buildings—the "palace," the fort, the warehouse, the public square, and the church—are each of them minute in size and bear no relation to the needs of such a large population.

A U.S. naval shore party surveyed the site and its ruins in 1891; the area was roughly 150 yards long by 100 yards wide. Based on a figure of 1,200 settlers, this would provide living space of around 12½ square feet per man. Deducting from this the "spacious" streets described by Columbus and Chanca, as well as the public buildings, there would have been no way to accommodate such a large number of people. Due to the limited space, it is obvious that the horses, mules, cattle, goats, sheep, and hogs had to be located outside the main compound, where there is evidence of dwellings. Columbus wrote that the site was an Indian village that he allowed to remain where it was. It seems doubtful that either Columbus or his men, coming from Navidad, where their compatriots had all been slaughtered, would have initially risked dividing the main body by putting any of them outside of the compound. In his second letter in *El libro copiador* he mentioned, on more than one occasion, the need for a wall around the village to protect it from the Indians, who he said had no respect for property.

Recently, archaeological studies of the site have been made, but there is no record of any that tried to reconcile the location with its stated occupational requirements. The area was bulldozed during the regime of the dictator Rafael Trujillo, preventing any effort to determine the layout. When a group of VIPs from the United States had asked to visit the site, the dictator had ordered it cleared; his minions, taking the order literally, complied by bulldozing away virtually all of the remaining traces of the buildings. Today an attempt is being made to reconstruct their outlines. Viewing the

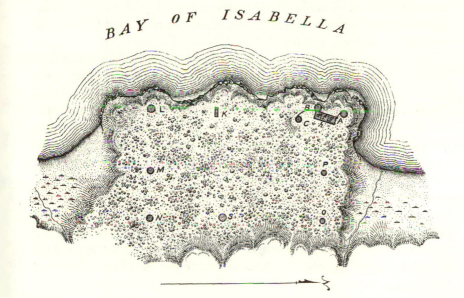

Plan of the Ruins

of

THE CITY OF ISABELLA

Santo Domingo.

1891

Scale of Yds.

Redrawn from John Boyd Thacher, *Christopher Columbus*, vol. 2 (New York: G. P. Putnam's Sons), 285.

site, the visitor can easily visualize the cramped quarters and inadequate shelter and can readily understand the resultant illness and general discontent of the settlers.

The horticultural potential at Isabela, as described by Columbus and his companions, was no more accurate than the details given for the town site. The Admiral claimed that one month after arrival, the radish and parsley seeds that they had sown were already supplying the needs of the colony; the wheat and barley were a foot high; orange trees and sugarcane had already grown. In the third letter he said that he had been unable to plant the wheat until the end of January, yet by March 29 they had a bundle with "grained spikes, and ripe, and very large, more so than those of Castile."[30] He noted that all of the sugarcane brought in the smaller boats had been spoiled by seawater, as had the sugarcane in the flagship, which he said had only arrived at Isabela the week before, that is, in late January. He did not explain the source of the cane that was growing so quickly.

Admittedly, the whole group was in this area for only a short time. Until February 2 many of the people may have at least slept on board the seventeen vessels in the harbor, and even after that date, when Torres took twelve ships back to Spain, five vessels remained anchored offshore. Columbus sent out two parties, totaling some forty men, to explore the interior. As previously noted, Columbus wrote that before he set out for the Cibao, a fire had destroyed two-thirds of Isabela. Seventy men were sent to establish a fort at Santo Tomás. A short time later he sent three hundred men to explore the interior. This dispatch of so many men to the interior could have been as much a result of the lack of living space, worsened by the fire, as of the need for men in the Cibao.

Contemporary chroniclers agreed that by the time Torres sailed in February with the twelve caravels for the return voyage to Spain, many of the settlers had already died. Martire was the first to publish an account of these events; he claimed that in "letters sent to the king and Queen [it was] reported that 12 boats had arrived from the islands . . . the head [Torres] of the boats said . . . the Admiral had stayed in Española with five boats and nine hundred men."[31] Fernández de Oviedo, writing many years later, claimed that by the time Margarite left the fort at Santo Tomás, according to him at the end of April, half of the settlers had died. Later he claimed that at the time Bartolomé was in charge at Isabela in 1494, two-thirds of the Spaniards had died.

The figures given in contemporary accounts add up to approximately 800 survivors by April 1494. These included 395 men sent to the fort at Santo Tomás, 57 who sailed to Jamaica and Cuba with Columbus, and 325 who were left at Isabela. If only 1,000 went there originally, and if these figures are realistic, then the tales of suffering and deaths have been grossly exaggerated; at the most, one-fifth of them died, not half. If 1,500 sailed originally, as claimed by Hernando, together with horses, mules, goats, and other animals, the boats would seemingly have been loaded beyond their normal capacity, but the 50 percent figure given by Fernández de Oviedo would have left around 750 alive, close to the number estimated.

In the fifth letter, Columbus wrote that at the time Torres sailed for Spain in February 1495, the colony's supplies were down to 1,200 bushels of wheat, rationed at the rate of 4½ pecks per man per month, which required 540 bushels a month. If these figures are accurate, we now have, for the first time, Columbus's own estimate as to the number of Spaniards on Española in February 1495: 500. If the higher figure of approximately 800 is correct, Columbus would have had less than two months' supply on hand, yet he wrote that he did not expect relief for four months, which would seem to lend support to the 500 figure.

Whichever of these figures is accurate, the deaths that undoubtedly occurred were probably a result of many things: the long time spent cooped up in insalubrious vessels during the crossing; the time spent exploring the Leeward Islands; a greater time wasted working up the northern coast from Navidad to Isabela; and later, the shortage of food. The fevers that Columbus himself complained of, as well as what must have been the extremely unsanitary conditions at the campsite at Isabela, would have also contributed.

Contemporary accounts also reveal that the food supplies that could be acquired from the natives were soon exhausted. Las Casas attributed this to discontent on the part of the natives; they simply stopped planting the yuca to make the cassava that had become one of the mainstays of the Spanish diet. He said they did so because they objected to the Spaniards taking over their country. Fernández de Oviedo claimed that half of the men died because of this "bad cunning" of the natives.[32] He also noted the adverse effects of syphilis, which had already seriously affected the colonists.

Of perhaps equal importantance was the large demand for food. It was calculated at the time that one Spaniard ate as much as eight natives; Las Casas said twenty. The natives, unlike the Spaniards, were not concentrated in small areas but were scattered throughout the island. Living a seminomadic life, they did not plant or harvest more than what was necessary for their immediate needs. Unlike the natives of the great indigenous nations of South America, the Tainos made no provision for storage of their crops; they literally lived off the land. The influx of Spaniards with their, comparatively speaking, voracious appetites simply overtaxed the rudimentary native food planting and gathering system. Soon after the arrival of the Spaniards, there was as much discontent among the natives as there was among the Spaniards, probably due to the one problem they soon shared: inadequate food supplies.

First Mass at Isabela

A great deal of interest has been shown in recent years in a statement given only by Martire. Reporting on the settlement at Isabela, he wrote of an event on April 29, 1494: "The Prefect [the Latin alternative form for 'Admiral' used by Martire] selected a high place near to the port to found a city . . . in a short time . . . [he raised] a little chapel, on the day that we celebrate the feast of the Three Kings the sacred mass was sung by thirteen clergymen."[33] The key word is *sacellum* ("little chapel" or "small sanctuary"). This is the word that appeared in his 1511 edition of his first decade; it was not mentioned in the earlier, but possibly unauthorized, 1504 version. None of the other contemporary chroniclers mentioned either the chapel or the mass. No way has been found for determining how many clergymen went on this voyage. Friar Ramón Pane was present, and Columbus noted in the fourth letter that on this voyage there was a Trinitarian and an abbot from Lucerne. Three other friars have been identified, bringing the total to seven including Buil.

On July 7, while on the Cuban side trip (the date is according to Hernando),[34] Columbus went on shore, reporting in his third letter, "Sunday when I said mass, I descended to land, where I had first ordered the cacique here to arrange a church (*iglesia*)—who seemed a very honourable man and seigneur of many people."[35] Hernando reported that later, on the return trip to Spain on the second voyage, Columbus reached the island of Marigalante on Saturday, April 9, 1496, and "the next day, although it was his custom to not raise anchor on a Sunday if he was in any port[, he] set sail because the crew were murmuring, saying that as they were going to look for food, the holy days should not be so rigorously observed."[36]

Juan de Quexo, a pilot from Palos who was on the third voyage, testified in the *Pleitos* that at the time Columbus took formal possession of Paria, "they made a forked prop and with sails from the ships they made awnings as a representation of an *iglesia* and a mass was given by a Franciscan friar who went there and by Juan Martinelo, a cleric, native of this town [Palos] who went with the said armada."[37] In his known letters reporting on this voyage, Columbus made no mention either of priests or of any mass. These excerpts lead one to conclude that it was Columbus's custom when at anchor to have a mass said at every appropriate opportunity. This would apply equally to the outbound and the inbound voyages. The linkage with the act of the taking of possession expands the opportunities on which masses were probably said.

Hernando, present at the time, wrote that on the fourth voyage, Columbus sent Bartolomé Colón to take possession of what he named the Costa de Oreja, "with flags and the captains, and many others of the armada, to hear mass."[38] Again, there was no earlier mention of a priest having been on board, nor is one listed in the official roster for the crews.

The use of the word *iglesia* ("church") by Columbus may provide an explanation for Martire's statement that so soon after Columbus's arrival at Isabela a mass had been said in a chapel. Certainly no permanent structure could have been built in the few days that elapsed between the arrival and the mass. The mass may have been said in a lean-to shack, under a tent, as was done later at Paria, or out in the open, as in Cuba.

The Puerto Ricans have long held that the first mass in the Americas was said on that island before Columbus reached Española on the second voyage.[30] Others have placed it on Guanahaní or Navidad on the first voyage.[40] The *Diario* entry for December 23 says, "He believed for certain that if that Christmas festival could be held in that port all the people of that island [Española] would come."[41] Obviously a celebration was to be held; whether it included the normal mass or not remains unknown. It is almost certain that a mass would have been celebrated on Christmas Day. It seems at best improbable that with many priests on board on the second voyage, Columbus and the priests would have waited until Isabela to celebrate a mass. It is more likely that this landmark event was celebrated on the first Sunday that Columbus was at anchor on a friendly coast on this second voyage.

Any analysis must take into account that only one contemporary mentioned the mass at Isabela and that this allusion was made eighteen years after the event it claimed to portray. Even this first mention did not ascribe any sense of primacy to the act. The very fact that no one else mentioned it leads one to presume that masses were such a normal part of the voyage that they were not deemed worthy of specific mention. The historical evidence simply does not support the claim that the first Catholic mass said in the Americas took place at Isabela in January 1494. Regrettably, this Columbian myth has recently been set in concrete with the erection of a commemorative church at Isabela under the auspices of local and international organizations as part of the quincentennial celebrations of the discovery. Not only historians and biographers, but also interested parties such as clerics and tourism promoters, contribute to the perpetuation of the myths.

Exploration of Española

Columbus wrote in the second letter about the abundance of "gold and spices of all kinds, more so because they have no value here among the people, because they go nude and care for no other thing except to eat and women." In an interesting forecast of things to come, he said that after they had landed, heavy rains came.

> Then they [the colonists] suffered greatly from the tertian fevers (*çiçiones*) [as] if [due to] the movement of the winds, although they are the best in the world, and they have been proven [to be], and the foods (*las biandas*) of the sea have changed (*mudado*) the blood, with the great expectation of winter for which their bodies were however accustomed. [Rumeu de Armas here used the word *esperando* ("waiting"); Gil used *empero* ("however")]; I gave the greatest blame to the treatment of [with?] the women, that are here found abundant; and, if they [the men] are dishonest and disorderly, it is no marvel that they have pain. With all, thanks to Our lord, soon [in] four or five days they are cured, that is its force, it leaves some more burdened; I have greatly benefited from the **** that Your Highnesses sent here with all the medicine.[42]

Once established at Isabela, he sent "Ojeda, a good young fellow and well enterprising, with fifteen men to explore the way and to see how far it is from here to the Cibao and if the gold mine can be found." He also sent another expedition, this one headed by a retainer of Fonseca's (Ginés de Gorbalán), to find "Cahonaboa" (Caonabo) and to see "if it is true that there is so much gold." He added that both men had instructions not to go into the Indian villages if they could avoid it, although he expected this order to be difficult to follow because the Indians who went with them never slept in the open. According to Gil's version of Coma, Alonso de Ojeda was sent "to the interior of the Sabeos [*sic*] to see king Saba."[43] (This free translation made by Gil contains many departures from the original. For those interested in the wording of this particular text, a facsimile is available in Thacher's *Christopher Columbus*.)[44]

A following reference suggesting a linkage in these words with "the Sabines" is probably an explanation by Scyllacius to explain a word that he could not understand. Apparently Coma did not know that Saba was a region, not a person. It is equally probable that Columbus too was confused by an Indian word and came to believe that he was now in the region of the island of Saba. There is no doubt, however, that Ojeda had been dispatched to the very real Cibao.

According to Ptolemy, "Zaba" was one of the islands to the east of Asia.[45] Marinus of Tyre wrote that Zaba was between the Golden Chersonese and Cattigara. Marco Polo, Friar Jordanus (1322), the Catalán map (1375), and Niccolò dei' Conti (c.1430) all placed it in the western part of the Indian Ocean.[46] Polo wrote: "In *Persia* is a citie called *Sabba*, from which the saying is, the thrée kings departed ... I Marcus Paulus was in that Citie, and asked of the people of that Countrey what they could say or knewe of the thrée Kings, to which they could say nothing, but that they were buried in the thrée Sepulchres."[47] John of Maraginolli (1342–46) reported Christians in Saba.

In the memorandum of January 30 that Columbus sent back with Torres, he complained about having been cheated in Seville on the supplies for the voyage. In the letter he repeated this complaint, especially as to the wine, which he found to be essential for the health and the good spirits of the men. He asked that those responsible for supplying these defective goods "of which Don Juan [Fonseca] was in charge," be punished.[48] Though not a direct accusation, this appears to have been what in Spanish is called an *indirecto* ("an indirect attack") against Fonseca. In later letters Columbus was highly critical of the artisans sent on this trip, as well as of the horses brought by the lancers.

The second letter indicated a break in the sequence of events: "After all the above was written, today that is the day of San Sebastián, Ojeda came."[49] Chanca wrote that Ojeda and Gorbalán "left and came, the one on January 20, and the other on the 21st."[50] He mistakenly dated their return as taking place after Torres's departure. Coma went into great detail about the trips of these two and about the fabulous mines of gold that they supposedly found. After their return, he wrote, "The Prefect writes to the Kings about these actions realized."

Cuneo provided no clues here, passing from the two parties that explored the Cibao to an account of the later trip into the interior on which he accompanied the Admiral, saying only that this later trip took place after the departure of the fleet, which is an undisputed fact. Columbus himself wrote on January 30 that Gorbalán was going back to Spain with Torres. At the same time he mentioned that Ojeda had given him a written report, together with samples of the gold: "[The] letter, with the samples of gold I send to Your Highnesses with this." Much later, in the third letter, Columbus provided the missing dates: "After the departure of the above mentioned armada, that was on the third of February . . . on the 12th day of March I left with all the people possible on foot and on horseback to go to the Çibao."[51] It is unquestionable that Torres started his journey after the return of Gorbalán and Ojeda. There is ample contemporary evidence that Torres arrived in Cádiz on or before March 19.[52] In November, before any other vessels had returned, Gorbalán was definitely in Spain, since he was rewarded at that time for his work on Española.[53]

Bernal Díaz de Pisa had been named comptroller of the colony by royal command. Apparently from the start he had created problems for Columbus. In the January 30 memorandum Columbus complained, without giving names, of the lack of cooperation from "some of the people that said there [in Spain before the voyage began] that they so wanted to be of service to Your Highnesses." In the second letter he wrote: "Vernal [*sic*] Pisa . . . I have prisoner . . . about whom I wrote and sent by public scribe [i.e., notarized] to Your Highnesses with Torres." Las Casas went into detail on this affair, one that he termed "the first rebellion attempted in the Indies." Rumeu de Armas erred in stating that Las Casas dated this event as occurring on March 12.[54]

Las Casas was the source for the story that Columbus found an accusation (the word used, *pesquisa*, means literally "investigation") written by Bernal Díaz. He wrote, "[Bernal Díaz] concealed [it] inside a buoy, and I don't know how the Admiral, who had not been two months on the ground, could have committed so many offenses in so few days."[55] This would indicate that Las Casas was privy to the nature of these accusations. He went on to say that Bernal was imprisoned on one of the five remaining ships and that, at the same time, the Admiral moved all the munitions and supplies onto the other four. Although Las Casas has now been proven correct by Columbus in saying that Bernal was imprisoned on one of the ships, he erred in the timing.

Columbus wrote in the third letter, "I intend to take Bernal with me [to Cuba/Jamaica]." He did not do so, however. When the monarchs responded to the Torres Memorandum, they sent Columbus a separate letter, dated April 13, in which they instructed him, "We have been angered by the things done there against your wishes. which we shall have remedied and punished. In the first voyage back here you are to send Bernal Diaz de Pisa."[56] The certified copy of this letter, as given in the *Pleitos*, referred to him only as Bernal de Pisa.[57] Fernández de Navarrete and Thacher used the complete name "Bernal Díaz de Pisa." The Quintana edition of Las Casas's *Historia* used the abbreviated "Bernal de Pisa."[58] The reason for so much attention given to his name is that a Bernal Díaz de Pisa was appointed to yet more important governmental posts by Ferdinand and Isabel soon after the supposed miscreant's return to Spain.

Although there is no evidence that Columbus complained about Buil or Margarite, they both are generally believed, perhaps incorrectly, to have reported unfavorably on him on their return to Spain. Both of these men later received very important appointments. Such being the case, there would have been nothing incongruous in Bernal Díaz's having been similarly honored. Either these Crown servants had fewer problems with Columbus than is generally claimed or, as is also possible, the monarchs simply chose to ignore all such bickering.

Not until Columbus recapped in his third letter many of these events did he give the information that he had sent Ojeda and Gorbalán to the Cibao with "thirty messengers." He noted, "I sent you the gold that . . . they had found."[59] Las Casas was the source for the widely held, incorrect belief that Torres had left before Ojeda returned to Isabela and after Bernal Díaz was arrested. He said, "In the meantime, when Hojeda [*sic*] went, the Admiral understood [took care] to dispatch quickly the ships that had to go to Castile." Later, in the same long paragraph, he wrote of Ojeda's return with the news of finding the source of the gold: "With this news, all, as I said, received a mixed (*mezclado*) unexpected joy; but the Admiral was the one who most enjoyed it, and determined, the ships for Castile having been dispatched, to go to see the said province of Cibao."[60]

Hernando commented at this point that his father was sick and that thus no entries were made at this time in the journal, but he did not give his source for the continuing information that he provided. He noted that the Admiral "sent Hojeda [*sic*], with fifteen men, to look for the mines of Cibao. Afterwards, on 14 February, twelve ships of the armada returned to Castile . . . with a captain called Antonio de Torres . . . he took with him a carefully written [account] of what had happened. . . . In a few days Hojeda returned."[61] Hernando also erred in his belief that Torres had left before the return of Ojeda, and he delayed the fleet's departure until the February 14 date. In this instance Las Casas was better informed than Hernando.

Columbus wrote that Gorbalán returned to Isabela after Ojeda. He also said that before Torres set sail, a caravel captained by Diego Márquez returned. It was Márquez who had become lost on Guadeloupe. In December he had been sent to round the island of Española but had disobeyed orders and made a foray inland instead. Columbus did not say that Márquez had circumnavigated the island; the impression given is that he did not. This foray, when linked with a letter that Angelo Trivigiano wrote and that was discovered by Thacher (see chapter 14), has provided the basis for the claim that continental South America was discovered during this voyage.[62] Although there is a considerable body of literature on this subject, none of it is conclusive. The generally accepted opinion is that neither Columbus nor any of his people reached the mainland of South America until the third voyage.

Writing about the Márquez foray, Columbus added that "Fojeda" had fallen sick and had sent the Admiral a letter, to ensure that Columbus was fully advised. This is obviously an unintentional linkage, in that Ojeda did not go with Márquez. Columbus wrote that he sent the log for this exploratory voyage, together with the Ojeda letter, to Ferdinand and Isabel. He added, "And as it seemed to me that Your Highnesses would want to see it with full particulars, I copy it here, at the end of this one, and it is the one that follows."[63] Unfortunately the scribe who copied this Columbus letter omitted the log as well as the Ojeda letter. Gil assumed, possibly correctly, that this missing letter was the source for Las Casas's extensive report on this particular survey trip.

After dispatching Torres with the letters for the sovereigns, Columbus noted that the gold region was only twenty leagues from

Isabela. However he noted, "I am not going there now, because many people from here are sick, and further, for this reason, I have kept some here, that I intended to send to Castile." A month and a half after Torres's departure, Columbus set out to explore the interior.

First Trip into the Interior and Pacification

In letters numbers three and four in *El libro copiador*, Columbus reported on his 1494 voyage to Cuba and Jamaica. He prefaced each letter with recaps of earlier events on Española. He said that he left Española at this time in order to be back before the anticipated return of Torres in May. Actually the first to return from Spain was a fleet captained by Columbus's brother Bartolomé, who arrived sometime between June and August (the date is disputed). Columbus mentioned at this time an otherwise unreported fire that he said had destroyed two-thirds of Isabela before he set out for the Cibao. He described the difficult path over the cordillera and the two passes, one of which he said he called the Pass of the Hidalgos, a name used to this day. He also named the plain below the Vega Real. He waxed euphoric describing a river (the Yaque) as bigger than any in Spain, comparing it to the Ebro. He went on to say "This is the river that has its mouth at Montechristo [*sic*]."[64] It is notable that Columbus realized that this was the same river that had its mouth near Montecristi. Las Casas also said that Columbus found the river to be as big as the Ebro but added that he "named it the river of the Canes, not remembering that on the first voyage when he was at its mouth he named it the River of Gold that comes out at Monte Cristi."

The exact date on which he set out for the Cibao was not known until the third letter was recovered. In earlier letters Columbus said only that he went after the twelve ships had left for Spain. The only one of his companions to write on this phase of the voyage was Cuneo, who said, "Five hundred of us went with the said Admiral to the said place of Cebao [*sic*] not well supplied with equipment; and on the said journey, between going and coming we spent thirty-eight days with the worst weather, bad food and worse drink, but the anxiety for the said gold maintained us strong and high-spirited."[65]

Hernando and Las Casas each gave the date for the day that they crossed the Yaque as March 14, which was undoubtedly correct because Columbus wrote in the third letter that he left Isabela on March 12. Columbus made clear in all of these letters that his primary interest was gold, claiming in the second that there was more gold in the Cibao than there was iron in all the mines of Viscaya. Although he wrote of sending for miners to work the mines, the only gold that he had found so far was placer gold.

Columbus made several interesting comments in his letters while discussing the Cibao and the fort that he built at Santo Tomás. He said that he left Margarite there with seventy men, including carpenters to finish the fort, which was designed for defense by twenty-five men. One observation that caused much speculation when first made by Las Casas is now confirmed by Columbus. He wrote of a discovery made while excavating a tunnel: "I found many lombard stones made and dressed [by man], the size of a large orange, and placed in threes and fours and covered with hay and straw."[66] Later writers, confused by Las Casas's reference to lombards, changed his meaning, saying instead that he found nests of stones that were prized possessions of the Indians. Silent emendation started in the early fifteenth century. The mentions made by Hernando and by Las Casas were definitely taken from this Columbus letter, since the wording is almost identical.[67] There has been speculation as to whether the shot were left there by Martín Alonso Pinzón, who is known to have traveled some distance inland during the first voyage, or whether they provide evidence of prior discovery. According to Las Casas, Columbus returned to Isabela on March 29.[68] Cuneo's dates gave a return on April 19.

Both Hernando and Las Casas worked from either the third letter or a very similar one. They added the information that after the capture of a cacique by Ojeda and his ten men, a man came by horse to Isabela to report that the villagers of the cacique had captured (according to Hernando) or trapped (according to Las Casas) five Spaniards but that he had frightened them with his horse and that the men had been freed. Columbus, without having mentioned earlier that he had established a fort at a place he named Santo Tomás, now reported that he intended to go exploring by boat but

first decided to send Ojeda as captain of the fort. He explained that
Ojeda had not gone on the trip into the interior because he had been
too sick at the time. The Admiral now sent him with three hundred
men, from among whom Margarite was to select men to go with him
to explore the rest of the "Çibao and all the island." In recounting
these same events, Las Casas frequently used the phrases "the
Admiral says" or "as he told in letters to the king." Las Casas
provided details that are not in this letter, such as that Columbus
sent aid to Margarite because the latter had written him that
Caonabo was preparing to attack the fort at Santo Tomás and that
the twenty-five men referred to by Columbus were for the purpose of
guarding the pack trains.[69] Margarite and his men were to live off
the land, and Columbus said that he sent along the treasurer
(Sebastián de Olano) with hawk's bells and other trinkets with
which to pay for the Indian's foodstuffs.

Strangest of all, Columbus wrote, "And another person I sent was
the chief accountant so that in his presence everything be bought
and gold traded in front of him; and I sent the mayor and the bailiff
and scribe because, as I said, I found our people to be so greedy that
it is a marvel, and at times they anger the Indians, it doesn't matter
what punishment I give them."[70] This would appear to be supported
by the letter that Columbus had Olano write to the monarchs: he
said that he had "not received gold in the absence of the Lieutenants
and Senior Accountants."[71] Columbus's statement appears to contradict one given shortly after the return from the Cibao because, as Gil
pointed out, the chief accountant (*contador mayor*) of the island was
Bernal Díaz de Pisa. Columbus stated:

> I shall take with me [to Cuba] Vernal de Pisa, who, since I left for the
> Cibao I have in prison in a boat, because it is not enough what he had
> done, about which I wrote and sent by public scribe [i.e., notarized] to
> Your Highnesses with Torres. Now, again he has returned to arrange
> his evils, and acted [in a way] and said things that deserved and
> deserve great punishment, which I didn't want to give him because of
> the high office that he holds; before, I let him perform them [his
> duties] from the boat, and for that purpose I give him all the favors
> and help that he demands.[72]

Olano's and Columbus's versions appear to be mutually contra-dictory. Passages such as the above provide a fresh perspective on Columbus's views on his growing administrative problems. He may not have taken Bernal Díaz with him, since the latter's name does not appear on the affidavit signed by all the crew members who went on the voyage. This alone is not necessarily conclusive: the names of Cuneo, the Trinitarian friar, and the abbot from Lucerne were also absent, although these men were definitely on this voyage.

The third letter in *El libro copiador* provides, for the first time, Columbus's own report on the administrative setup that he estab-lished for the colony during his absence while he cruised the coasts of Cuba and Jamaica. He wrote that he had appointed a council made up by his brother Diego and Fray Buil as co-presidents, Pero Fernández Coronel as chief constable, and Alonso de Carvajal, Juan de Luxán, and the "Gallego bachelor" (an academic designation) with his "power of attorney and instructions," a copy of which he sent to Spain.[73] This was the first mention by Columbus that Carvajal, his future agent, was on this voyage. The Gallego (Galician) has never been properly identified, although Las Casas designated him as a knight commander (*commendador*). Neither in this letter nor in the fourth letter, where Columbus also mentioned his appointments in the colony, is Margarite mentioned. Las Casas said that he was placed in charge of the armed men. On the trip over, Las Casas's uncle Peñalosa was in overall command of the military on this voyage.

Morison believed, incorrectly, that at this time Columbus appointed "a council consisting of his brother Don Diego as president . . . to govern the island in his absence." This error was repeated by Wilford, the Phillipses, and Sale.[74] Unfortunately, a copy of these provisions for governing the island during his absence has not yet been found.

He did write in the fourth letter that he had left these instructions, together with his report on his trip to the Cibao: "I wrote everything in a long [letter] when I left to discover, and I left the packet in Ysabela, so that, if caravels came or some of the ships that were expected, and if they were to leave before I returned, so that your Highnesses will be well informed." He added, "All of which and the transcript of the instructions I left with the same packet."[75] This is the first indication that Columbus had sent a second message to his sovereigns in 1494, one that would have gone with the three caravels on which Buil and Margarite returned, in which case the sovereigns had Columbus's own reports to compare with those of the returning officials. Fernández de Oviedo wrote that Columbus left Diego as his lieutenant "until such time as the adelantado his brother Bartolomé Colom [sic] arrived."[76]

With the third letter, Columbus's own version of the first punitive expedition is now available. He wrote that at the time that he sent Ojeda to the Cibao, some Indians acting as porters at a river crossing had run away with a sword and some of the men's clothing. Noting that it was the custom of the natives to give such items to their caciques, he explained:

> When I knew [of] it, I sent then to the said Ojeda that he send up to ten people to the said village, because if more went, they would all run away, especially if they were guilty, and I wrote him to see with great care if he could find out the truth and capture the same malefactors and punish them, because it is not good to ignore that they lower [?] (*se abezen*) themselves to do vile things, and [it does good] to honour him who does well. And the said Ojeda went in person with ten men, . . . and one of the three men who had lost clothing recognized the Indian who had taken it and another who had taken the sword and they found out that the cacique had all [of these] . . . he took the cacique and had the other two taken . . . and another brother of the cacique . . . he sent the cacique to me here, and the brother, and the nephew tied up; and the boy of the sword and the other, he took in the middle of the plaza, in front of everybody . . . tied them there and cut off their ears . . . they came through another village . . . and its cacique they say is a brother of this prisoner . . . he didn't know what else to do but take a gold necklace and come here to bring it to me . . . I made much honour of this man of the necklace because I knew that whenever our people came from or went to the Cibao he took them into his house and gave them whatever they needed, and also for me the other day, when I crossed the river, he came with all of his people with great love, even though I didn't need him to help me to cross, and so I made him much honour and dressed him very well and gave him many jewels . . . it shows them that who behaves well, that he will be

made much honour, and who should do wrong will be well punished, I ordered three poles be set here in the plaza, and had them tied to them and take out a sword to cut their heads off, and the other cacique went on his knees crying before me that I not kill them. I gave them to him and gave him his necklace of gold which I didn't want to receive from him, so that he would know that for gold justice wouldn't be stopped.[77]

Columbus showed his confidence in Margarite at this time in the instructions that he gave the latter on April 9, 1494, a few days before he left on the Jamaican-Cuban voyage. In the fourth letter Columbus recalled that he had advised the monarchs of having sent Margarite to explore the interior, specifically the region governed by Caonabo. He added, "I told him that if he couldn't reach agreement with him, that he do him all the harm that he could." These instructions present a somewhat different picture:

As to this about Cahonaboa [*sic*] I very much want that we should have him in our power, and to do this you should do it in this way as I want: send someone with ten men, that are very discreet, that they go with a present of certain things that are taken there by the aforesaid for trading, praising them and showing him that we much want his friendship, and that I will send him other things . . . and that I shall always send him things that will be brought from Castile. . . . And you shouldn't take the trouble to go now with the people to Cahonaboa, instead send Contreras who should go with the ten people, and that they return to you with the reply . . . and you could send another and another time until the said Cahonaboa is reassured and without fear that you intend to do him harm; and then have the way to capture him as best you see fit. . . . The way that you should have to take Cahonaboa . . . is this: that the said Contreras deal a lot with him, and find the form for Cahonaboa to go to talk with you, so that you can make his capture more safely; and because he goes nude and it would be hard to hold him, and if he once got free and ran away, it would not be possible to get him back due to the roughness of the land, being with him, have him given a shirt and then dress him, and a cloak and gird him with a belt and put a bonnet on him, where you can hold him and not let him loose, and you should also take his brothers who will go with him. And in case the said Cahonaboa should be indisposed to go to be with you, have an arrangement with him that he view well your going to him, and before you arrive where he is, the said Contreras should go first, saying that you go to him to see him and to get to know him and to have friendship with him, because seeing you arrive with many people it could be that he would become distrustful and decide to go to the hills, and spoil the capture, but I leave everything to your good discretion.[78]

Las Casas presented the picture somewhat differently. First of all, he believed, correctly, that it was Ojeda who actually made the capture, going to the cacique with nine men. He told how Ojeda took Caonabo a present of handcuffs, which the cacique was told were made of brass, a metal highly prized by the Tainos. Caonabo was told that this particular brass came from the sky and had secret virtues. According to Las Casas, Ojeda took the cacique aside and "put him on the rump [of the horse] and there the Christians with great pleasure and joy put the foot chains and handcuffs on him."[79]

Pedro Margarite and Fray Bernardo Buil

Pedro Margarite was a longtime dependent of the Crown. He was recognized in a *cédula* dated October 30, 1490, as "our beloved servitor." Again, on June 7, 1491, his military service in Granada was recognized by the Crown, designating him as "our illustrious Pedro Margarit [*sic*], soldier, [who] gave great and noble service in this war of Granada and others."[80] He joined the second voyage as a royal standard-bearer (*contino real*) and was named captain of one of the caravels on the outbound voyage. For some unexplained reason he returned to Spain with Buil before Columbus's return from Cuba. Perhaps Fernández de Oviedo's claim that he had contracted syphilis on the island was the reason for his premature departure.[81] There is nothing in the contemporary record to substantiate Morison's fanciful assertions: "Don Diego as president of the council wrote to Margarit [*sic*] ordering him to mend his ways . . . Margarit regarded this as a reflection on his honor as a caballero . . . marched down to Isabela in a rage . . . seized the three caravels that Bartolomé had brought out from Spain and sailed for home."[82] Wilford made the undocumented claim that Margarite, like Buil, had "been instructed by the crown to report on Columbus' activities."[83]

In part Morison's version derived from Las Casas, who has also generally been cited as the source for the stories about Margarite's "terrorizing" of the Indians. To the contrary, Fernández de Oviedo wrote that an Indian said of Margarite, "He seemed to him good and was a man who did not do violence nor anger the native Indians nor permit violence be done to them."[84] Las Casas gave a summary of the Indians' problems: the Spaniards stole their food, women, and daughters and were "intolerable, terrible, fierce, cruel, and knew no reason." He said that this was why the Indians kept away from the Spaniards and hid themselves when the Spaniards passed by. Las Casas explained:

> At this time Pedro Margarite began to [stand on?] his point of honour [dignity] and to disgust himself with those of the Council that the Admiral had left to govern, or because he didn't want to be ordered by them, or because they wanted to command him, or because they reproached him for what he did and consented be done against the Indians, or because he was quiet, not going around the island conquering it as the Admiral had left him instructions to do. This disagreement was the cause of greater harm, and to a great part, or the greatest part, for the sedition and de-populations of this island that came later; and because he had been impertinent in letters against those who governed, and perhaps shown other insolences and committed other defects worthy of reprimand, some ships having come from Castile, that I believe were those that had brought the said Adelantado [Bartolomé], in order to not wait for the Admiral, he left the people that he had with him, who were 400 men, and he came to Isabela to embark.[85]

Judging from this highly qualified quotation, one finds it hard to reach a conclusion as to the exact nature of Margarite's problems. In these few lines Las Casas used qualifiers six times; he himself did not know what had happened but merely offered several alternative speculations. From his account, and his account alone, the story of Margarite's ravaging of the island was developed. Martire limited himself to saying that Margarite left the island with others who returned to Spain with "sinister intentions against him [Columbus]."[86]

Some of the problem over the dates of these occurrences also originated with Las Casas. He was under the mistaken belief that

Bartolomé arrived in Isabela "on the fourteenth day of April of the same year 1494, before the Admiral came from discovering Cuba."[87] As is known, Columbus did not leave Isabela for Cuba until April 24, and his brother had definitely not yet arrived. Las Casas stated that Fernández de Oviedo had been mistaken when he dated Bartolomé's arrival on August 5.[88] Yet, Las Casas misconstrued the August date given by Fernández de Oviedo—it referred to the founding of the city of Santo Domingo two years later, not to the time of Bartolomé's arrival.[89] Fernández de Oviedo was also confused, however, in that he gave the year for this founding as 1494, which is manifestly incorrect; yet this is correct for the year that Bartolomé arrived in Isabela. On this flimsy basis many historians have accepted August 5 as Bartolomé's arrival date. There is no agreement on when the city of Santa Domingo was founded—sometime between the summer of 1496 and the summer of 1498.[90] Las Casas also had Bartolomé leave Spain on April 14 yet arrive in Isabela on April 29, another obvious impossibility.

Bartolomé was named captain of the resupply fleet of three vessels on April 14, a few days after the return of Torres with the twelve-vessel armada that had taken Columbus and the colonists to Española.[91] Las Casas wrote: "When the Admiral arrived at Isabela from the discovery of Cuba and Jamaica (which was on April 29 of the same year 1494) the said father Buil and mosen Pedro Margarite and others has already gone to Castile."[92] This reference to April was either a lapsus on the part of Las Casas or a scribal error; later he said correctly, "The Admiral returned from discovering, he arrived at Isabela on the 29th of September of the year '94."[93]

According to some chroniclers, Bartolomé arrived in Isabela on June 24,[94] though others said July 28.[95] His three caravels left for the return trip on an unknown date in September. As of September 11, the Crown still did not know of Buil's whereabouts, since on that day they wrote him to stay on Española. Buil's arrival in Spain was first acknowledged on December 3 in a *cédula* ordering him to come to court.[96] Ample documentary evidence shows that Buil did not arrive in Spain until sometime in late November. No mention was made at the time in court documents of Margarite, although there is evidence that he remained on the royal payroll at least up until the end of 1497.

The story that Columbus and Buil had problems began with Fernández de Oviedo. He wrote that Columbus had ordered the hanging of an Aragonese by the name of Gaspar Ferriz. In protest, the friar stopped celebrating mass, and Columbus in turn cut off the rations for him and his party.[97] Fernández de Oviedo also wrote, which is incorrect, that Columbus, Margarite, Buil, Bernal Díaz, Aguado, and others of the principal figures in the colony all returned to Spain in the same fleet. Nor is there any truth in Fernández de Oviedo's claim that in 1496 Columbus was returned to Spain as a prisoner by order of the monarchs.[98] There is no question that Margarite and Buil had left Isabela over a year before the time that Columbus and Aguado left together. The only written record today clearly indicates that Columbus left in 1496 of his own volition. Las Casas contradicted much of this:

> All of this that he [Fernández de Oviedo] says was false, many witnesses are not lacking, because, when the Admiral left to discover, as yet there had not been any man hung, in the period of five months that he was on this island after coming from Spain, . . . when the Admiral arrived from discovering Cuba and Jamaica (which was on 29 April [*sic*] of the same year of 1494) the said father Buil and mossen Pedro Margarite and others had already left for Spain, without permission of the Admiral; therefore there were no quarrels nor was there discord [between] the Admiral and father friar Buil, so that the one excommunicate nor the other deny rations and food to the father friar Buil and his group.[99]

Perhaps some of the distortion of these facts from Las Casas was the result of his repeating, with detail in an earlier chapter, the specifics of the supposed conflict between the two men, claims that he categorically refuted in this later entry. As previously noted, Buil had already sought permission to return to Spain two months before Columbus set sail for Cuba. From one of Columbus's letters at this time, we now know that Buil was sick. Buil's letter with this request had been taken to Spain by Torres.[100] Varela indicated that Buil and company set sail on September 29, a highly improbable date because it was the same day that Columbus returned from Cuba. She also noted that Gorbalán was on this voyage, whereas, as noted ealier, he had already left for Spain with Torres in February. Fernández de

Oviedo indicated, not too clearly, that Margarite was still on the island at the time of Columbus's return from Cuba, an apparent confusion with Columbus's earlier trip into the Cibao.

Buil had not arrived in Spain by mid-September 1494. As previously noted, the monarchs at that time were under the impression that he had remained in Isabela, and they wrote him at that time to stay on Española despite his complaint that he could not carry out his mission for lack of an interpreter. This complaint was seen by Gil as a veiled criticism of Columbus, who did have an excellent interpreter, the Indian he had named Diego Colón. Columbus took Diego with him on his Cuban voyage. Coincidentally, at this same time Columbus wrote in a letter to the monarchs: "These people of this land are the most tame and fearful and of good faith that there are in the world, and so I return to say, and say again, that I lack nothing else in order that they all be Christians except for not knowing how to speak nor preach in their language."[101] Could this have been, as Gil suggested, an astute cover story to protect him against Buil's implied criticism?

In his fifth letter to the sovereigns Columbus addressed what he considered to be the main problem for the conversion of the Indians in the face of what he viewed as the un-Christian behavior of the colonists. He wrote:

> I am sorry to see the loss of conscience, and more [so] for the other damage; what would one say to the Indians if they understood all of this, when one speaks to them of our holy faith, saying that it is not so strict. It would be very good if fray Buil brought some devout religious people, both to correct this, as well as for all of us who are here, because Your highnesses provided him by the hand of the Pope. Your Highnesses would do a great service to God by sending here some devout friars without greed for things of the world, so that they could give us good examples that, certainly, we sorely lack, and we suffer from malign things. . . . Your Highnesses should do it, because we have more need of who would reform us in faith than that the Indians should take it.[102]

Although Columbus made no direct accusation against Buil, there is in this paragraph a strongly implied accusation of greed against the friars who had come with him. These clerics had presumably returned to Spain with Buil before this letter was written. The assertion that the colonists were in more need of spiritual guidance than the Indians would also seem to indirectly implicate Friar Buil for failure to provide the needed spiritual guidance. The sentence immediately following the above went into the problems that Columbus had with the dishonest and incompetent ship's carpenters in the colony.

Nothing in the historical record supports Morison's claim that Buil "proceeded to court, where he circulated the most outrageous slander against the Columbus brothers."[103] Fernández-Armesto exaggerated Margarite's position in the colony: "[Columbus] left Margarit in charge of Hispaniola, nominally but ineffectually under the orders of Diego Colón."[104] He repeated this mistake when he wrote about "the terms in which he instructed Pedro Margarit, when he left him in charge of Hispaniola during the explorations in Cuba in 1494."[105] At no time was Margarite ever "in charge of Hispaniola," nor did the Admiral make "explorations in Cuba." Columbus sailed up the Cuban coast seeking its supposed continental limits, but at no time did he either explore or circumnavigate the island.

People both in the colony and in Spain were afraid that Columbus and his companions had been lost on the Cuban voyage. Columbus was away for more than four months, during which time the hard-pressed colony had received only the three resupply ships brought by Bartolomé. For over three months of that time Diego Colón and Fray Buil had been in joint command of the colony. With the arrival of Bartolomé, that responsibility fell on him. Buil had written the monarchs in Febuary that he could do nothing without an interpreter. Margarite had cruised the inland country and had found only the gold collected by the natives, an amount insufficient to even pay the salaries of those on the island. Before Columbus left for Cuba, Margarite had been too sick to accompany him into the interior. After Buil returned to Spain in November 1494, the Spanish monarchs wrote to their ambassador at the Vatican on the following February: "Fr. Bernal Buil came from the Indies sick, and because he can not return, ask His Sanctity to give the faculties that he had to another person."[106] This confirms Columbus's statement that the friar was sick.

Before Columbus set out on his voyage to seek the "mainland" of Cuba, according to Las Casas, he put three hundred of the soldiers of the colony under the command of Margarite, charging the latter with exploring the island and repressing any Indian opposition in the Cibao. Columbus had even written to Spain in February asking that the Crown provide for Margarite's family by assigning "mossen Pedro 30,000 maravedis every year." In the third letter Columbus wrote, "I left there [in charge of the fort at Santo Tomás] mosén Pedro Margarite as the most capable person."[107] This in no way implies command of all of the armed forces on the island. These are not signs of conflict or antipathy on the part of Columbus, yet as already noted, Margarite decided, for whatever reason, to leave his post during the absence of Columbus. Fernández de Oviedo's explanation that the behavior was based on discord among the colony's leaders simply does not hold up in the face of the evidence. His belief that Margarite was ill makes more sense.

No one should have been surprised that these important court officials, both of them sick, availed themselves of the first opportunity to leave the island. They had little if anything to gain by staying. They left only a few days before Columbus's return; therefore, by the time they reached Spain, they had had no personal contact with him for seven months. If they reported that the settlement at Isabel was not a viable one, however, they would have been entirely correct.

Wilford wrote: "An Indian uprising spread throughout the island late in 1494. Pedro Margarit [sic] had exacerbated relations with his marauding through the hills, terrorizing the Indians and stealing food." Morison wrote that in response, Columbus acted on "the principle that no Christian could do wrong. Instead of chastising and curbing Margarit, he rounded up hundreds of Indians and punished the victims. Unappeased and more restive than ever, Margarit seized three of the re-supply ships that had recently arrived and with his confederates, including Boyl [sic], sailed away to Spain."[108] Morison and Wilford each confused issues, times, and events.

Morison did have the timing correct for Buil's arrival in Spain—sometime in November—but he joined in the attacks on the friar: "Buil, initiator of a 'hard-boiled policy' towards the Indians, was a bad egg indeed. He and the other friars under his orders had done absolutely nothing to convert and instruct the docile Tainos who lived near Isabela. . . . This Catalan faction had sailed before the Admiral returned from Cuba."[109] All of the modern authors wrote of Buil's having been sent to the island by the Spanish sovereigns. To be precise, he was recommended by King Ferdinand but was Pope Alexander's apostolic delegate to the Indies. The papal brief naming him and giving him his instructions, dated July 25, 1493, has been available to scholars for centuries.

The names of six clerics who accompanied Buil on his evangelical mission have been identified.[110] One of these, Fray Ramón Pane, learned the local language and wrote the first ethnographic study of Amerindians. He was able to overcome the linguistic difficulties that so perturbed Buil. He stayed on the island when Buil, with an unknown number of the other clerics, returned to Spain in 1494. Many years later he baptized the first Indian confirmed on the island.

Based on the historical record, the only conclusion that one can reach is that there is no credible evidence of personal conflict between Columbus and Friar Buil or Margarite. That there was general discontent in the colony is unquestionable. According to Las Casas, Columbus attributed this mainly to the fact that the discontented "considering that the gold was not already taken out and placed in the coffers, or that it was fruit that [only] had to be taken from the trees (as the Admiral complains and with reason) but instead in mines and under the ground, and that never in any part of the world was silver, or gold, or other metals taken out without great effort, unless it was stolen from the coffers of its owners."[111]

Discontent on Española

Las Casas, puzzled by the early defections by Buil and Margarite, thought they might have left in part because all the colonists were forced to join in the building of Isabela, together with the conse-quent rationing of food as a punishment for those who failed to participate in the effort.[112] Las Casas wrote that when Columbus returned to Isabela from his March trip into the interior, he found so many of the men sick that "it was necessary that the hidalgos and people of the Palace or of the black cape, who were also suffering from hunger and misery, and the one and the other to whom it was like death to work with their hands, and especially [when] not eating; it was therefore necessary that the Admiral add to his command violence, and to give heavy penalties ... in order that such public works be done."[113] Las Casas observed that he was not certain whether Fray Buil opposed Columbus because at this time the Admiral reduced his and his men's rations or because Columbus refused to give them more rations, which they had asked for. It must be recalled that within a month after his arrival in Isabela, Buil wrote for permission to return to Spain.

As previously discussed, Fernández de Oviedo explained the disagreement between Columbus and the others over the hanging of Gaspar Ferriz, as well as over the rations for Buil and his entourage.[114] This version dated the problems with Buil as having arisen after the Admiral returned from his exploration of the other islands, an obvoious impossibility. Las Casas said that these problems arose in March, almost a month before Columbus left for Cuba. Buil and Margarite left Isabela a few days before Columbus returned from exploring the coast of Cuba; by then Bartolomé had been in charge at Isabela for only a short time. As later events were to demonstrate, Bartolomé did occasionally mete out severe punishments. The chroniclers could have been confused between the two brothers because brother Diego, who had been left as co-president with Buil, was a mild man, one said to have been incapable of harming anybody. If Buil had a problem with any of the three brothers, it would have been with Columbus and could have occurred only between January and April 24, during which time Columbus was busy setting up the camp at Isabela, exploring the Cibao, establishing a fort at Santo Tomás, and preparing for his voyage to seek the mainland. By his own account, Columbus was also sick during those first months in Isabela.

Las Casas also speculated that at least part of the cause for any discord was due to the Spanish hidalgos' resentment at being under the command of a foreigner. Wilford, among others, accepted this explanation: "For the hidalgos, manual labor was considered degrading and beneath them. They resented the foreigner Columbus's ordering them about."[115] The situation was not that simple. As Demetrio Ramos Pérez pointed, out Columbus was no more foreign at the time of the supposed defections than he had been at the start. Buil was co-president of the council that Columbus left in charge of the colony, and Margarite was named commander of the troops in the field. As such, the problems arising during the period April 24–September 29 were as much their responsibility as that of the younger Columbus brothers. Ramos, accepting Bernáldez's statement that Columbus had set out in April to find Cathay and visit the Gran Khan, wondered what could have happened to make Buil and Margarite embark for Spain without waiting to hear the results of his voyage.

Bernáldez attributed the first problems to the colonists' disappointment over the gold. He wrote that they complained that the Admiral "had deceived the King and the Queen by telling them that there was so much gold, which they said was not true, and if there was some, the expenditure made to find and extract [the gold] would be greater [than its value] . . . and there were great slanderings against the Admiral, and he, as sovereign over them, sent some of them to prison, such as Fermín Zedo [Diego de Hormicedo], a native of Seville, who had gone there to know and refine the gold."[116] Unquestionably, Columbus had, at least for the short term, badly oversold the Indies.

The reality of the situation was that Columbus had been provided with the bureaucratic infrastructure for a well-organized colony, whereas the establishment on the island was simply a miserable village of thatched shacks at Isabela and a tiny fort at Santo Tomás, both of them located in potentially hostile territory. Columbus wrote in the third letter that before he built the fort at Santo Tomás, two-thirds of the settlement at Isabela had burned down, yet this fire is not mentioned in other contemporary accounts.[117] Such a conflagration could not have eased matters in the colony. More important, perhaps, were the related facts that while sickness and shortages besieged the colony, none of the promised riches were forthcoming. The men who had come on this voyage were all salaried; they were not free to exploit whatever they found in the Indies. They probably sometimes felt that they had come on a fool's errand to a fool's paradise. The discontent must surely have gone deeper than the men at the top. Hernando claimed that Columbus had decided to "not leave on the island more than three hundred men, and send the others to Castile, because considering the quality of the country and the Indians, that number would be sufficient to keep that region tranquil."[118] Columbus's primary interest may have been to rid himself of the uncooperative Crown appointees together with any other malcontents.

The "Revolt of the Lancers"

Discontent had existed before the fleet had even left Spain. One example involved the only organized military force that went on this voyage. The royal order for twenty lancers to go with Columbus specified that they be selected from among the members of the Hermandad in Granada, that they be reliable, and that they go voluntarily. Provision was made for six months' pay in advance. These *caballeros* ("men of horses") were lancers, members of the militia—attributes that made them members of a special class, one accustomed in all things to act in unison. Coming from Granada, they had recently been engaged in the final campaign of the Reconquest, another factor that would contribute to a sense of brotherhood. In a new and untried colonial experiment, a cohesive group such as this one, as Columbus soon learned to his regret, would not be easy to control.

The mounted lancers (*lanzas jinetas*) were a Spanish innovation, a light cavalry, less heavily armed and cheaper to maintain in the field than the medieval knights in armor. The Hermandad, another innovation, provided troops of foot and mounted soldiers under the direct control of the Crown. This dependence was seen by Ramos as the reason King Ferdinand sent these men with Columbus. They were the king's men.

Apparently Columbus was not pleased with the idea of taking an independent military group with him. Aware of the difficulty that the Crown was encountering in finding funds for this armada, he wrote the monarchs that the seventeen boats authorized were full;

therefore, there was no space for the lancers' twenty-five horses. They replied by saying their financial difficulties did not permit the charter of another vessel; therefore, he should reduce the number of people in order to make room for the men and their horses.

Fonseca warned the monarchs that Columbus wanted to place on each ship a *contino*—a noble's standard-bearer (i.e., his personal representative)—with the probable intent of establishing his preeminence. This request was promptly denied, Fonseca being instructed, "For this voyage it is not necessary to take any, as those that go there on our orders have to do what he orders them in our name, and having together his and others could cause great inconvenience, but if he wishes for his convenience to be accompanied by some who bear his name, he can take up to ten shield bearers (*escuderos*) as part of the fifty that are to go." A few days later Columbus was authorized the ten *escuderos* as well as twenty "men that are his," yet, even here it was stipulated that they must be on the Crown payroll; they would be beholden to Columbus in name only. If he was already seeking complete personal domination in the Indies, the Crown was subtly maintaining the hierarchical order. In each of the first three letters in *El libro copiador*, Columbus complained about the behavior of the men sent by the sovereigns.

The orders further specified that Columbus's ten were to be "on foot" and that his other twenty servitors were to be merely servants and peons. The king and queen obviously had something in mind when they gave strict orders that the lancers were to report to Fonseca and Columbus, making it clear that Columbus was not in sole charge of these men. The monarchs went even further in their orders regarding "Villaba, supervisor of the people of the Hermandad." They stipulated, "[He is] to not separate himself from the said people until he has left them on the boats, about which we will write him, and in this put much diligence and caution." Given the circumstances, it is reasonable to read into these instructions the great care being exercised by the monarchs to retain control over these troops.

If Columbus was indeed playing politics with the matters of the lancers and the standard-bearers, he was outplayed by the wily king. Each of these two able men were, undoubtedly, fully aware of what was at stake. Even before Columbus sailed on this first colonization trip, it was clear that the interests of the Crown and those of Columbus were not necessarily the same. This latent conflict of interests must have been equally apparent to persons such as Margarite and Buil, men thoroughly familiar with the affairs of the royal court.

Ramos recently uncovered records that revealed the names of most of the lancers and the number of their horses, information gained through the study of the names of the leaders of the troops from which they were recruited. Some of them came from troops headed by important figures of the time. One had distinguished himself in engagements against the Moors. Another, the father of the poet Garcilaso de la Vega, was an important commander and grandee of Spain. Another grandee, Alvaro de Luna, had distinguished himself in the seige of Granada. One troop was led by Francisco de Bobadilla, a court official and governor of the camp at Santa Fé. Until recently he was often confused with the Francisco de Bobadilla who imprisoned Columbus, yet they were unrelated.[119] Coincidentally, Luna was married to a sister of the latter Bobadilla. Before coming to Santo Domingo to investigate the affairs of Columbus, this Bobadilla had possibly already received information about conditions there from the returned lancers. It is also possible that these particular lancers were sent with Columbus in order to keep their former leaders abreast of affairs in the Indies.

The first visible sign of trouble between Columbus and the lancers is found in the memorandum that he sent to Spain with Torres. He wrote:

> I shall tell Your highnesses how the mounted shield bearers from Granada, in the show that they put on at Seville showed good horses, and later on loading I didn't see [them], because I was slightly ill, and they loaded such as the best of them didn't seem to be worth 2,000 maravedis, because they sold the others and bought these. And this was the luck of many people, there at the display in Seville, I saw very good [things]. It seems that Juan de Soria, after having been given the money for salaries, for some interest of his own, put others in the place of those that I thought to find here, and I find people that I had never seen, in this there has been great mischief, so that I don't know if I should complain of him alone.[120]

Columbus continued to find fault with these men. He wrote, "When they were either ill or didn't feel like it they were unwilling to allow their horses to be used for Your Highnesses without themselves, and they don't see that they should do anything except on a horse, which at the present time doesn't apply, for this [reason] it seems that it would be best to buy the horses from them, as they are worth little, and not be [involved] every day in these quarrels with them; therefore, let Your Highnesses determine this as [best] serves you."[121]

The situation could not have been as bad as Columbus portrayed it in this report to the Crown because before he received their reply, he wrote Margarite on April 9, "First I send you sixteen horsemen."[122] At least that many of the twenty were obeying his orders. Ramos saw in this action—sending Margarite and the lancers to the Cibao—the precedent for the later practice adopted in colonial Peru for ridding a town of its malcontents and troublemakers by sending them on a mission of exploration. This practice became known as the "chances to be rid of" (*entradas de descarga*).[123]

According to time-honored custom, when a *caballero* lost or sold his horse he had a limited time in which to replace it; otherwise he lost his special status. Thus, with this proposed purchase of the horses, Columbus would have eliminated the privileged position of the lancers. At the same time, by passing the horses over to his own followers, he would have elevated their status, thereby putting himself, their master, on a footing with a grandee of Spain. In response to this request, the monarchs merely ordered Fonseca to investigate the charge and, as for the mounts, stated that Columbus could order that they be used by others when necessary; if any horses should be injured while mounted by others, the horses would be paid for. Thus the immediate situation was defused while the question of the lancers remained as it was. While Columbus was away, most, if not all, of the lancers returned to Spain with Buil and Margarite. They were later paid by the Crown for their horses and equipment left behind on Española.

Trip to Cuba and Jamaica

In the second letter in this series Columbus wrote, "I shall leave in the name of Our Lord on Monday, which will be the 21st of April . . .

I shall take with me a good eighty people and supplies for four months." The names of only fifty-three mariners are given in the affidavit that he later made the crew sign. He did take in addition Cuneo, the interpreter Diego, a Trinitarian friar, and an abbot from Lucerne, for a known total of fifty-seven. Cuneo wrote that there were ninety-eight men in all.[124] They were gone for five, not four, months. As previously noted, the people left behind on Española later became afraid that Columbus, and those with him, had been lost. This belief may have contributed to the decision of Margarite and Buil to leave for Spain in September, only a few days before Columbus's return.

Las Casas wrote, "He left [for Cuba] in the name of the Holy Trinity, he says, Thursday, 24th of April of the same year 1494."[125] Columbus confirmed this date in the fourth letter.

After announcing his departure, Columbus digressed, recapping some of the things already done and found earlier on this voyage. He reported his differences with Diego de Hormicedo (given as "Fermín Zedo" by Bernáldez), of whom he said, "They told me he knew more about mines and gold than any other person." Columbus maintained that the gold artifacts found on Española were of beaten gold, whereas Hormicedo said that many of them were smelted; he even claimed to have found some alloyed with brass, meaning copper. Columbus vehemently denied this, possibly because at this time he was more interested in convincing the sovereigns that they owned the "source" of the gold of the Indies.[126] Since the Taino culture had not yet advanced to the point of smelting metals, there must have been another source. And since such knowledge was indicative of an accessible higher culture, it could have suited Columbus to stress this possibility if it was true that he was only seeking mainland Asia, but he did not do so. Recent research has traced the alloyed trinkets found at this time as having probably come by a trade route running from the Gulf of Ecuador up through Central America, over to Cuba, and finally down to Española.[127]

The information sent in this letter is but one more example of Columbus's astuteness. He knew that matters such as this disagreement over the gold would be reported back to Spain, so he reported it first, together with his explanation. Columbus also ensured that Hormicedo would not be there to give his account first: the Admiral kept him against his will on Española until 1496, when the two of them went back to Spain together. There is no other evidence besides Fernández de Oviedo's that Hormicedo was imprisoned.

In the fourth letter Columbus gave a detailed description of his plans for his Cuban voyage. He recalled that on the first voyage he had believed Cuba to be continental but that the Indians had assured him that it was an island. He now explained their belief, saying that since they lived on an island and traveled little, they believed that all lands were islands; they simply did not understand about continents. He explained: "I thought to go by this way to Jamaica, and that if Juana [Cuba] should be an island, and that if I passed from its southern part until its western end, and from there navigate to the north and the west until Catayo."[128]

It is interesting that in this letter he seriously considered the possibility that Cuba was an island, albeit one that was on the way to the mainland. In both assumptions he was quite correct. His naming the island "Juana" may derive from the many reports of an island named Jana (Java) supposedly located to the west of China. Earlier in this same letter he had noted that "Mago" was next to "the most noble province of Catayo," from which he had wanted to go on the first voyage to "the city of Quinsay and to see her and the many others, and see if it is so very noble and extremely rich as is written, and if, as is now said, they have friendship for Christians."[129] "Mago" appears to be a confusion with "Mangi," the southern China reported by all early travelers.

In this phrase Columbus clearly stated that his intention on the first voyage had been to sail up the southern coast of Cuba in a west-northwesterly direction and, of even greater interest, that this was again his plan a year later on the second voyage. This seems to confirm the theory that Columbus set out on the first voyage to find islands, not to go immediately to the mainland of the Gran Khan. In this letter, he portrayed his projected trip to the mainland as a side trip, an excursion to see if everything that was said about China was true. He went on to say that on his return trip to Española, he sailed near the Chersonese islands, the fabled islands off the coast of Asia, variously identified today as the Moluccas (Spice Islands) or Malacca (Malaysia).

As we discussed in an earlier chapter, he gave in this letter a full description of the problems he had sailing in these shallow coastal waters. As was usual for him, he rhapsodized over the land and the Indians, who, as always, were too numerous to count. He added one new detail: while on Jamaica he measured one of the cacique's canoes—"ninety-six feet long and eight feet wide."

On Jamaica he decided that since the Indians were so many and the Spaniards so few, he dared not risk going among them. So instead he fired some shots to frighten them and then released one of the dogs that he had with him. "A dog that I took did them great harm: here a dog fights a good battle, so well that one [dog] is worth ten men, and we have great need for them." Although he found the land to be unparalleled by any in Spain, he decided to leave it and return to Cuba "in order to not waste time and already knowing the island and its substance and seeing that it had neither gold nor other metal."[130] Again, his main objective was gold, but he failed to explain how he knew there was none on Jamaica.

On May 15 he arrived at the many islands that he named the Queen's Garden. A few days later he wrote that the Indians gave him to understand that Magón was ahead, "in which province the people have a tail," and the people wore clothes to hide the ugliness of their tails.[131] This speculation was repeated by Hernando, Las Casas, and Bernáldez, all three of them using Columbus's words. This was one of the references that prompted Bernáldez to digress on the subject of Sir John Mandeville. As already noted, many European travelers had reported on Mangi-Magón-Magi. The story of the men with tails has since caused many historians to believe that Columbus not only had read Mandeville but also had derived many of his cosmographic concepts from the writer. As Morison correctly pointed out, "That name suggested to Bernáldez Sir John Mandeville's mythical land of Moré where the tailed people lived."[132] Margarita Zamora believed that at least by the time of the third voyage, "Mandeville's Travels [was] perhaps the most widely read travel book of the Middle Ages and one Columbus knew well."[133] José Rabasa, in turn, said, "Next to Marco Polo, Mandeville was the major source of information about the East for Columbus."[134] This theory about the supposed influence of Mandeville on Columbus was not only accepted by Stephen

Greenblatt but is one of his basic tenets. Wilford, the Phillipses, Fernández-Armesto, and Sale were all on historiographically safer ground when they relegated Mandeville to a less-than-significant role in Columbus's cosmographic perceptions.

Since so much, in recent years, has been made of the men with tails and possible sources for Columbus for this myth, it is appropriate to cite the English historian John Hale, who wrote, "The medieval notion, half superstition, half belief, that the English actually had tails rolled up inside their breeches, though it surfaced in the propaganda poem of 1513, faded after the mid-fifteenth century."[135] The practice, so common today, of building theories on stereotypes is one fraught with danger.

Still working his way up the western coast, mostly with difficulty due to the shallowness of the coastal waters, Columbus reached a point after a few days where he could finally take on water and firewood. While there, one of his men went hunting and returned with a tale of a white man who wore long white robes down to his feet. Columbus wrote that the sailor was surprised and thought that he was "the friar of the Trinity" that Columbus had brought. "Then two others came to him with white tunics, and the man in the long tunic ran after him calling, but the sailor didn't stop until he reached the boat." Columbus then sent a large shore party to try to contact these people, without success.[136]

Hernando repeated the story almost verbatim but reversed the men's clothing—one wore a knee-length tunic, and two wore tunics reaching down to their feet—and noted that the three of them were "white like us."[137] Las Casas too gave this story almost verbatim, but like Hernando, he made a slight change; in his case there was only the one man dressed in white, with no mention made of the color of his skin.[138] Bernáldez gave the story word for word as given by Columbus in the fourth letter.[139] Since then, some chroniclers have seen in this tale evidence of Europeans marooned on the island. Others have suggested that the three men might have been an optical illusion created while viewing white cranes. Hernando and Las Casas each mentioned the cranes, Hernando adding that they were "more corpulent" than those in Spain. Morison contributed: "A crossbowman who went hunting in the woods encountered a band of thirty Indians, one of whom [was] dressed in a white tunic that came down to his feet. . . . To the Admiral these apparitions meant Prester John, the legendary priest-king of Hither India or Ethiopia, whom he had hoped to meet if he missed the Grand Khan."[140] Columbus made only one comment on this strange apparition: "I understood that this man of the tunic was the seigneur or cacique of these lands."[141] Hardly Prester John!

A day later Columbus's men encountered tracks "of very large beasts with five toes, that they thought were griffins or of some other beasts, and they decided that they were lions."[142] Note that Columbus did not say that he thought they were griffins, only that his men thought so. The difference is of some importance when considering whether or not Columbus was influenced by Mandeville, who did report griffins. In the Middle Ages, griffins and other such marvelous creatures were believed to exist. Columbus's version of these two episodes constitutes flimsy support for the adherents to the theory of the important Mandevillian influence on Columbus.

At this point Columbus gave his account, one repeated by Bernáldez, about having to winch his boats over some shoals, as mentioned in an earlier chapter. Later he met some Indians who told him that there were "infinite provinces" over the mountains to the north that were governed by a king called Sancto who wore a white tunic. Bernáldez was the only one who repeated this story as it was told by Columbus. Of particular interest here is that obviously all three of the mentioned authors—Bernáldez, Hernando, and Las Casas—had access to some document with Columbus's own account of these events; each of them also supplied dates for every stage of the journey to Jamaica, Cuba, and back, yet Columbus supplied none of these dates in his fourth letter. This letter was necessarily an extract of his log, which may have contained these commentaries as well as the missing dates; however, this letter was written in 1495, some time after the events recounted. We can assume that in this letter he repeated all of the salient points found in his log.

Cuneo was the only chronicler to mention a disagreement that Columbus had with the abbot from Lucerne over the question of whether Cuba was an island or the mainland of China. Cuneo, who agreed with the abbot's idea that it was only an island, also wrote that Columbus did not allow the abbot to return to Spain when the latter wanted to because he did not want the abbot denying that Columbus had found the mainland. Manzano located *cédulas* dated June 1, 1495, ordering Columbus to allow several men to come home. These men included the abbot, Columbus's brother-in-law Miguel Muliart, and the gold assayer Hormicedo, whose name was given in the *cédula* as "Formecido."[143] The Admiral was not tolerant with those who disagreed with him.

Columbus's friend Bernáldez doubted that Columbus had found the mainland on this voyage. He said that he had told Columbus this: "By the side that the Admiral looked for Catayo, it is my belief that going another one thousand two hundred leagues, by sea and land he [still] wouldn't reach there, and I told him so, and had him understand when he came to Castile in 1496."[144] As already noted, Martire had also come to the conclusion that Columbus had not reached the Asian mainland. These differences of opinion must have been known by the court.

On his way back from Cuba, Columbus stopped off at a Cuban village, at which point he gave the earliest detailed contemporary description known today of the Tainos' gala dress, protocol, and other matters. He followed his route down the coast to the eastern end of Cuba and then sailed west back to Española. He decided to course its southern coast, which he "hadn't seen before." Arriving at Puerto Rico, he became ill. Hernando said that when he became ill this second time, he again ceased writing in his journal. In this letter, Columbus wrote that he became so sick that in eight days he slept for only an hour and a half and became half blind, "and for some hours of the day completely."[145] The fourth letter ended at this stage in the journey.

Columbus later explained that he had not gone as far to the north as he had wanted to because of the poor condition of his boats, a shortage of rations, and the sickness among the crews. As mentioned earlier, he had the crews of the three vessels sign an affidavit, prepared by a notary, in which they certified that they had run up the coast of Cuba for, three hundred and thirty-five leagues . . . and he [the Admiral] said that this was mainland, due to its shape and information that he had, and the name of the people of the provinces, especially the province of Mango . . . and having arrived here at a populated place he took some Indians, who told him that this land extended along the coast for a journey of more than twenty days, and they didn't know if that was the end or how far it went . . . he went on four more days so that all could be certain that this was mainland . . . the Admiral . . . [had the notary] go personally with witnesses to each of the said three caravels . . . to have . . . all of the other people in them say publicly if they had any doubts that this land was not the mainland at the beginning of the Indies . . . I put a penalty of ten thousand maravedis for each time that any should say later at any time the contrary to what was now said, and have his tongue cut out; and, if he was a grummet or person of that type, that he be given a hundred lashings, and have his tongue cut out.[146]

Obviously, under these conditions, all signed on. Cuneo, the friar, and the abbot were not made to sign. Interestingly, the captains, pilots, and masters of each vessel signed first, each in separate paragraphs of this document. Juan de la Cosa was selected from the crew in a like manner; he is described in the affidavit as "Johan de la Cosa, resident of the Port of Santa María, master of making charts, a sailor on the said caravel *Niña*."[147] Those who today dispute the identification of the La Cosa of the *Santa María* with this one have argued inconclusively that the owner-master of a large vessel on the first voyage would not have shipped out as a humble sailor on the second. The distinction that Columbus gave to him in this affidavit belies that contention; he was considered as more than an ordinary sailor.

It is also noticeable that Columbus's ideas for discipline were harsh, and not just with the Indians. As discussed in an earlier chapter, this document may have been prepared for political purposes and, as such, need not necessarily have reflected his beliefs. Bernáldez was the only one of the contemporary chroniclers to mention the affidavit. Morison found Cuneo's judgment that this was indeed an island to be of importance, yet Cuneo was only one of four knowledgeable contemporaries who thought this. Morison also found it significant that the La Cosa map of 1500 clearly showed Cuba as an island.[148] Yet the fact that a map drawn six years after the event showed Cuba correctly does not necessarily indicate that at the earlier time La Cosa may not have accepted, for whatever reason, the proposition that Cuba was part of the mainland.

Return to Española from Cuba

As far as we know there was a hiatus in Columbus's letter writing until October 14, 1495, on which day he took up the story again. As was usual in these letters, he first gave a recapitulation of much that had gone before. Much of the information given in this fifth letter is also found in Martire's first decade.

Before Columbus returned to Española, two important events had occurred. The first was the arrival of his brother Bartolomé; the second was the departure of Fray Buil and Margarite. There was confusion among the chroniclers as to the dates for these related events, which are also linked to Torres's return to Cádiz with the twelve-vessel armada. Obviously Ferdinand and Isabel could not have taken measures to satisfy Columbus's requirements, laid out in detail in his memorandum dated January 30, until they had received it from Torres. Martire wrote that he was present when news was received that Torres had arrived in Cádiz and when the latter came to the court on April 4; Las Casas believed that this occurred between the eighth and tenth of April. On this occasion Martire said, "I shall tell you [Antonio Sforza], in order to give you satisfaction, what they answered to my questions, as much he [Torres], as other men worthy of credit."[149]

Bartolomé could not have set sail before Torres returned. Martire first,[150] and Las Casas later, incorrectly dated Bartolomé's arrival in Isabela on April 14. As noted, he was named fleet commander in Spain on that date. His actual arrival date is uncertain but was sometime between June and September. Either Martire knew better later, or the editor of Martire's *Orbe Novo* (published in 1508) corrected his earlier figure, because in this publication the arrival date for Torres on the return trip to Spain was given as March 24, and Bartolomé had not yet sailed for the Indies.[151]

Fernández de Navarette was the first to report a letter dated March 19, 1494, and written to Fonseca from the Crown, who thanked him for "the good news of the arrival of the caravels from the Indies, and to their standard-bearer Torres, to come quickly to inform their Highnesses personally." Fernández de Navarette provided copies of letters to Fonseca and Torres.[152] On March 19, Juan Batista Strozzi, an Italian merchant living in Spain, wrote that Torres had arrived in Cádiz, bringing "vanilla that tastes like bad ginger . . . the pepper has no flavor . . . and the so-called sandalwood has white wood."[153] Columbus's friend Simón Verde wrote a letter reporting from Valladolid, dated March 20, in which he gave details on the first five months of the second voyage.[154] Apparently Torres arrived before March 19, probably around the fifteenth, in order to allow time for the sovereigns to have received a messenger from Cádiz. Morison dated his arrival on March 7, and the Phillipses gave it as "in the late spring of 1494."[155] The date is important because it helps to establish both Bartolomé's sailing date and his arrival in Isabela. This latter date, in turn, establishes the time for Buil and Margarite's departure for Spain, since they came back with the three caravels that Bartolomé had brought over.

Resupply Fleets in 1494 and 1495

To avoid confusing details in regard to the resupply ships of 1494 and 1495, one should take great care while assessing dates given in the official records. Possible confusion derives from the fact that in both years, Torres set sail for return voyages from Isabela in February. In both years, considerable time elapsed between the return of these Torres fleets and the dispatch of the next vessels. Accordingly, in both years, numerous *cédulas* were issued over the months April to July, many of them dealing with similar pre-sailing problems. There is no documentation for the sailing date for the 1494 fleet captained by Bartolomé; however, the fleet definitely sailed after Torres returned in that year.

The first documentation for a resupply fleet for Isabela was dated April 7, 1494, when a *cédula* was issued ordering Fonseca to prepare four caravels to sail with supplies for the colony, two million marevedis being provided for the purpose.[156] The sovereigns had already considered the suggestions made in Columbus's January 30 memorandum, as evidenced by their reply dated April 13 to his comments about Bernal Díaz. On the next day Bartolomé was named commander of the fleet being prepared to go to the Indies.[157]

Some of the confusion over dates is probably due to the fact that the Crown originally ordered twelve resupply ships but first dispatched Bartolomé with only three. Then the monarchs ordered that eight more be sent immediately, a number soon reduced to four. There are *cédulas* referring to all of these planned fleets. Only seven caravels left for the Indies in 1494—the three captained by Bartolomé and four by Torres. From their dates it can be seen that about one month passed from the time of Torres's arrival in March until any official reaction. It should be recalled that these were the months in 1494 during which Ferdinand and Isabel's most intense efforts were being made to come to an understanding with Portugal over title to the Indies. The two kingdoms finally reached an agreement with the signing of a capitulation on June 7. Until this agreement was reached, any fleet sailing to the Indies could have run into armed Portuguese interference.

There is no official confirmation for the day or month that Bartolomé set sail for Española. As shown, he was named commander of the fleet on April 14,[158] and on the twenty-eighth he received a substantial sum from Fonseca; therefore, he was still in Seville on the latter date.[159] Asensio gave the date of his arrival in Española as June 24,[160] a date accepted by Morison. Gil, based on Manzano, accepted the date as July 28.[161] Fernández de Oviedo believed the departure was on August 5. Bartolomé's ships probably left Isabela for the return trip to Spain in early September. The return to Spain of these three caravels was acknowledged on December 3 in two *cédulas*, thereby placing their arrival in late November.[162]

These three caravels were the only vessels known to have come to the island until Torres returned with four caravels; again the exact date of arrival is unknown. Torres could not have left Spain before the middle of September because the monarchs were still issuing *cédulas* relating to his planned voyage on September 11.[163] Cuneo wrote that Torres arrived shortly after Columbus's return to Isabela, which was on September 29.[164] Las Casas gave the date for Torres's departure from Spain as late August or early September based on a letter the monarchs wrote to Columbus on August 16. Las Casas assumed this letter to be the last record of Torres in Spain.[165]

Las Casas was apparently unaware of the previously mentioned September 11 letter to Buil, a letter that could only have gone with Torres. Also significant were three letters from the monarchs on October 8, one to the king of France and another reprimanding the count of Cifuentes for the imposition of an embargo on the vessels destined for the Indies. The city officials of Seville were ordered on the same day to lift the embargo.[166] These letters indicate that Torres did not leave Spain until early October, since his were the only vessels intended for the Indies at that time. Morison followed Las Casas, mentioning only the August 16 letter.[167]

Torres probably arrived in Isabela around the end of November or early December, with four ships loaded with supplies for the colony.[168] Columbus wrote that Torres left again for Spain in March 1495. On this second turnaround voyage, Torres took to Spain five hundred Indians, as well as the first news that Columbus had returned safely from his Cuban expedition. Earlier, Buil and Margarite, accompanied by an unknown number of friars and settlers, had also returned to Spain. Thus, by the spring of 1495 the monarchs were fully informed on the current state of affairs in their far-off colony.

Torres had definitely reached Spain again by late April 1495, since Columbus's brother Diego, who had returned to Spain with him, was authorized on May 5 to keep the gold that he had brought from Española. A little less than a month earlier, Sánchez Carvajal had been authorized to keep the gold that he too had brought back. If, as Gil and others believe,[169] Alonso Sánchez de Carvajal was sent back to Spain by Diego and Bartolomé, taking with him the gold collected on the March 1494 expedition into the interior, then he would have returned with Buil and Margarite in the fall of that year. Regardless of the timing, his return has led to speculation that the gold he brought was to serve the dual purpose of impressing the monarchs and providing funds for supplies for the colony. Some have also speculated that part of his mission was to counteract the bad news that would supposedly be spread by Buil.

Fonseca was instructed at this time to take care to please Diego so as to "erase any resentment that he might have." There is no indication as to the possible cause for such resentment. In another *cédula* Fonseca was told, "If he [Diego] doesn't want to go to Italy, that he not go, and reside wherever he wishes."[170] There must have been some unpleasantness, as well as prior thought on the subject, either on the part of Diego or the state, for this permission to have been needed.

The first news of a proposed 1495 resupply fleet was on April 7, when Fonseca was instructed to dispatch four boats to be supplied by Columbus's agent Berardi. They were to be sent as soon as possible because "those who are in the said Indies need supplies, and if they are delayed they could be hurt or even in danger." Two days later, confirmed on the twelfth, the Crown reached further agreement with Berardi for the dispatch of twelve resupply ships to the colony, to be sent at the rate of four every two months. Berardi undertook this contract at a price per vessel of 1,000 maravedis below the going price for charters; in the event that lower prices were offered, he agreed to provide the vessels at 1,000 maravedis below the group price for charters. Four of these vessels did finally sail, but only much later in the year. All four were lost at sea.

The April 7 *cédula* ordered Diego Carillo to follow with more caravels. The monarchs at this time were planning to greatly increase their colony on Española. An April 10 *cédula* provided that colonists who went without pay were to receive title to the homes they built, as well as to any properties they developed on public lands assigned to them. They were to be given supplies for one year and to receive one-third of any gold they mined or found but no compensation for gold received in trade with the Indians. Thus the monarchs were already decided on a plan to open up colonization, bypassing Columbus as well as some of his prerogatives.[171]

The April 7 *cédula* also mentioned future explorations, stipulating that on all such voyages one or two court officials be sent with each ship to report on what was discovered.[172] Now the sovereigns had Columbus's map showing the locations of his discoveries. This decree was the first evidence that they intended to open up exploration to others in addition to Columbus. Provisions such as this one infringed on Columbus's discovery rights; he would no longer enjoy a monopoly. The first capitulations for the following voyages were issued in 1499. They limited the new adventurers to lands not discovered by Columbus up until 1495, a clear indication that this was the cutoff date for his privileges.[173]

There is no doubt that the news from the colony had not been good. On May 5 the Crown reassured prospective emigrants that it was not true that in the colony "they would be mis-treated, or detained for more time than they wished to be there, or that some of the things that they brought such as cattle and Indians and fowls and other things that they brought would be taken [from them], or that they wouldn't be paid the salary that they were supposed to be paid."[174] That these complaints were first brought back by returnees with the fleet carrying Buil is unquestionable; that it was Buil who was responsible for these stories is speculative.

This mention of Indians clearly indicated that the natives counted among those things that the colonizers "brought" from Spain. This is perhaps the only indication that at least some of the five hundred Indians brought back by Torres in 1495 were given or sold to some of the prospective colonizers.

One sentence in the April 9 letter of instructions to Fonseca causes problems. The letter says that Columbus may be dead: "There is such a long time that we haven't heard from him."[175] This would presumably indicate that Torres had not yet returned by this date with the news that the Admiral was alive. Such being the case, the plans for resupply, for colonization, and for future exploration would all have been decided on before the return of Torres and, therefore, were unconnected to adverse reports received from returnees. This would seem to place an entirely different light on the generally accepted belief that these decisions were taken only after Torres returned. Yet, on this same day, the monarchs wrote letters to the Admiral and his brothers Bartolomé and Diego in which they said, "We saw your letter that you wrote to us with Alonso de Carvajal, and we listened to what he spoke to us on your part."[176] As noted, Carvajal probably had returned earlier with the fleet that had brought Buil and others. The monarchs may have been referring to letters from Bartolomé or to the letters that Columbus wrote before leaving for Cuba.

Olano, the royal receiver of the treasury, also returned to Spain with Torres on this voyage. He carried with him certification that Columbus had at all times complied with royal orders requiring the recording of all gold received on Española.[177] The fact that Columbus had him prepare a sworn statement to this effect indicates either that the Admiral's compliance in this matter may have already been questioned or that he feared that it would be.

Columbus's Treatment of the Indians on Española

From the time of Columbus's return from his Cuban trip in September 1494 until his departure for Spain in March 1496, he was occupied primarily with consolidating control over the island. Because he returned sick from Cuba, he did not set out again personally for the interior until late March 1495. Columbus said that he set out, although not yet fully recovered from his Cuban trip, "after having dispatched the said Torres in the month of March [1495]."[178] Las Casas extended this time to nine or ten months, "as he himself said in various letters to the kings and other persons."[179]

As previously noted, Torres brought back with him in March 1495 over five hundred Indians. Las Casas gave what he believed to be the reason for the capture of these Indians. He said that Columbus had fought with "the cacique or king Guatigará" to punish the chief for killing ten Christians. Columbus captured many of this cacique's subjects and sent five hundred of them to Spain to be sold as slaves. According to Las Casas, this took place after Ojeda had been sent to capture Caonabo.[180] With these explanations, Las Casas linked together Torres in March 1495, the five hundred slaves, Caonabo, and a storm that wrecked the ships in the port of Isabela as events occurring almost simultaneously. The problem lies in the fact that Las Casas also wrote that Caonabo drowned in the storm that destroyed the ships in Isabela sometime in mid-1495.

Note that Las Casas constantly asserted that it was Ojeda who had captured Caonabo, not Margarite. Margarite had left for Spain seven months earlier than the events recounted here by Las Casas. In his fifth letter Columbus presented a slightly different explanation for the detention of this important cacique: "And while I was engaged in this, I received letters from our people that I had sent to see the sierras . . . and he told me how he had come to where Cahonaboa [*sic*] lived, and they had induced and made him determine to come to Ysavela [*sic*], telling him that I would give him big celebrations, and would give him great presents."[181] Bernáldez also recorded the shipment of these slaves at this time, adding that they were "male and female Indians, all of a good age, from twelve years to thirty-five."[182]

Las Casas first wrote that Torres left on February 24 with five hundred slaves,[183] yet he was not quite sure whether the shipment of slaves coincided with the dispatch of Caonabo as a prisoner to Spain. According to Las Casas, at this time God, to avenge the "injustice of his imprisonment (and of all of those innocents) made . . . a destructive storm." He continued, "All of the vessels that were there, with all of the people that were in them (except for the Spaniards who were able to escape), and the king Caonabo loaded with chains, drowned or would have drowned; (I did not know if they had loaded that night the 600 Indians)."[184] Since the storm did not strike Isabela until July of that year, either Las Casas believed, mistakenly, that there were two different shipments of over five hundred slaves in 1495, or there were two storms, or Las Casas was simply mixed up in his dates. The only ships to return to Spain after the July 1495 storm were the two that sailed in March 1496 carrying Columbus.

Five months after his return from the Cuban voyage, Columbus decided to make a trip through the interior. "I found all of [that] part of the country very destroyed of supplies, and so much so, that innumerable Indians had died of hunger." He went on to say that after the Indians had stopped planting, in a vain attempt to make the Spaniards leave the fort at Santo Tomás by starving them out, the Indians replanted because they themselves were now dying from hunger; but a drought only made the situation worse, "and that they were so lost, and died, and are dying that it is a marvel."[185]

Either anticipating trouble or, more likely, hoping to preempt it, Columbus left for the Cibao in March. He said that he planned to reach an agreement with Guarionex: "[He] had many times sent me presents and to say that it pleased him to do everything that I ordered, and that he was an enemy of this Caonabo." Columbus made plans to assure himself of Guarionex's loyalty: "I was afraid, and for this [reason] provided in time, [for] an Indian of those that I took to Castile, although he was not of this land, to subscribe [to my plan]. I arranged [things] so that Guarionex married him to Cora, his sister, and this suited him very much."[186]

It is not clear whom this arrangement pleased: the Indian from Gaunahaní or the cacique. This sentence provides an excellent example of the difficulty in choosing between the Rumeu de Armas and the Gil transcriptions of these letters. Rumeu de Armas's transcription is given above. Gil's version states: "I had provided in time for this, I had an Indian of those that I took to Castile, and although he was not of this land, I had Guarionex marry him with one of his sisters, and this suited him very much."[187] In the first transcription Columbus arranged the marriage precisely because he "was afraid," whereas in the second he did so merely because he had acted with forethought. Rumeu de Armas also provided a name for the bride, but Gil did not, although they both worked from the same manuscript.

Martire provided a slightly different version, one in which it was "Guarionexio" who decided to establish a closer relationship through the marriage of his daughter, not his sister, to "Diego Colón, a man educated from the time when he was a child in the Prefect's house, and who had served as an interpreter while cruising Cuba."[188] Diego was one of the Indians taken from Guanhaní a year earlier during the first voyage.

Cassava was available in the region of the Cibao controlled by Guarionex, and Columbus's men, after having gone sixteen days eating only fruits and grasses, were supplied "very well" by him.[189] Martire saw this letter and gave an almost verbatim version of these events.[190] Columbus said the Indians believed that the Spaniards would ultimately leave the island because they did not have women and children with them, and they did have boats to go in. To convince them otherwise, he said that although he was in friendly country controlled by the cacique Guarionex, he built a fort there that he named "Santa María de la Conçebçion." After extolling its many advantages—proximity to the gold mines, abundant water—he noted: "This building [the fort at Concepción] and the dismantling of the naos, which were already old and not navigable, had taken from the Indians the opinion of my going to Castile; and with all of that they don't stop asking ours about it. . . . I determined to send some parties with the bread that I found in Conçebçion [*sic*] to walk and explore all of the province of [the] Cibao."[191]

He went himself on trips, on one of which he found copper and took a sample to send to Spain. He also found a gold nugget weighing twenty ounces. The Indians gave him a great deal of trouble because they did not want him looking for gold in their territory. "I dissimulated with them . . . I told them that I would stop digging mines, if they wanted to give me in the name of Your Highnesses, every four moons a half a hawk's bell half full of gold for each head [person]; and they said that it pleased them . . . I had an experiment done to see if in three days they could gather it; and I found that some people who well knew how to get it, gathered a full bell of eight castellanos [a coin worth 480 maravedis]; it is true that there are places and caciques where they don't have such good rivers and such good preparation as others."[192] As receipts for this tribute, he agreed to give to the caciques brass collection boxes and to the others sheets of brass as "big as a finger." He added, "If they get over this hunger I hope to God to keep this agreement with them and it won't be of small benefit."[193]

He sent instructions to all of the other caciques to do the same but was able to locate less than a quarter of them because the others had gone to the hills looking for "roots to eat." He counted on the Lord's help for a regrowth of the crops so that the Indians could return and provide the tribute. He said that in the other provinces where gold was not found, the tribute would be in "cotton and pepper and other things that are worth gold."[194]

Despite the famine, Columbus increased the tribute to "one full hawk's bell full of gold every four moons." He went on to explain: "The strange hunger, that there has been in all of the island especially in the Cibao continues, and has made me revise my hopes, because I had an agreement in the province with so many caciques who gathered a good fifty thousand naborías that we call vassals, and [with] most of them in writing . . . moreover the necessity and hunger has been the cause of the death of more than two thirds of them, and it is not over nor is it known when the end can be expected."[195]

Since Guarionex and the other caciques were unable to meet their commitments, Columbus pretended that they had complied, reassuring them that things would get better. He had other thoughts in mind when he wrote, "It is [necessary] to deal with them sweetly and with benevolence, so that they not leave their towns and leave the province, that is before arranging to bring in people from other parts."[196] This is the first indication that he intended to import Indians from other areas to work the gold mines, a practice that was carried out in later years by bringing Indians in from nearby islands. Martire also noted that the Tainos had been unable to meet their quotas of tribute; he explained, "The awful hunger broke all of these agreements."[197]

Columbus said that if the people of the Cibao misbehaved, they would be sorry because, citing as an example the punishment that he had already inflicted on them. He added, "It was very necessary." This was the first mention of the punishment, and it came in the sentence following his explanation of the need for treating them gently! He went on to discuss the ease with which they could be brought to baptism, even though he admitted, "I don't believe that they know or understand [this sacred mystery]." He thought that what was needed in the Indies was not masters of theology but "only [those] who were clear in speaking in their language [and] who knew how to tell the story with pictures."[198] This is but another example of Columbus's habit of commenting simultaneously on the need for a benevolent policy and for repression and subjugation, together with the need and means for the evangelization of the Indians.

Without question, Columbus was fully aware of the potential danger from so many Indians if they set out to dislodge the relatively few Spaniards from their island. He said, "Because it is certain that there are so many people here, that in a manner of speaking, that only if they did it only by blowing, they would throw [send] us without our feet touching [ground] back to Castile, nor are they lacking in ingenuity, nor strength nor in severity in fighting."[199]

Once he had established the alliance with Guarionex, Columbus returned to the matter of Caonabo. As noted earlier, before he left on the Cuban trip he had instructed Margarite to capture the cacique; however, Margarite had left for Spain without carrying out this mission. Now, almost a year later, Columbus again sought to assure himself of Guarionex's support for the final solution of the problem with Caonabo. Initially Columbus had attributed the deaths of the men at Navidad to their own bad behavior. Now he blamed Caonabo, who, he pointed out, was the most powerful cacique on the island. The chief's power is what disturbed Columbus most. He wrote that after Caonabo was taken prisoner, the cacique wanted to make a deal, asking Columbus to send men to him to help him fight his enemies. This version was repeated by Martire. Columbus believed that this request was made with "malice"; he believed that Caonabo intended to capture the Spaniards who came to help the cacique and hold them hostage for his release.

Columbus also believed at this time that the Indians were "so subjugated" that there would be no trouble with the collection of the tribute. He now said that he would send to the monarchs Caonabo, whom he held prisoner. Bernáldez believed, probably correctly, that when Columbus returned to Spain in June 1496, he brought with him "the great cacique Caonaboa [sic] and a brother of his, and a son of about ten years of age, not as in fighting [i.e., a captive of war] but after he secured him, and then he said that he would bring him to see the King and Queen so that later he would return them to their dignity and state . . . and Caonaboa died at sea of sickness or displeasure."[200] This account is of particular importance because it is, in a sense, a firsthand account in that at this time Bernáldez had as a guest in his home not only Columbus but also Caonabo's brother.

These passages raise the question as to just what kind of captivity Caonabo was suffering. He was captive yet free to negotiate. Later Columbus said that Caonabo was a prisoner at the time he was shipped to Spain. But Bernáldez added that Columbus had promised him that he would be free to return. Apparently Caonabo did attempt to make peace with Columbus. On March 10 the court receiver made an inventory entry: "[He] received three masks with 19 pieces of gold and two mirrors, their reflectors of gold sheet, and two ornaments of gold sheets, that the brother of Cahonabo [*sic*] brought on the said day."[201]

Another entry made by the royal receiver, this one dated May 6, 1495, reported various articles that were from the spoils, or plunder (*despojo*), of Caonabo.[202] This would indicate that Caonabo was taken prisoner at some time in April or early May, which would place him as being detained at that time in the fort at Concepción, not in Isabela. Columbus wrote that he thought otherwise about Caonabo's offer of peace; he said: "It would be well to go there to terrorize all of those lands and the other provinces in order that it not appear that for some reason we had not gone there, and because by doing this we would get to know much of the island. And therefore I sent there Hojeda [*sic*] with seventy men, whom a brother of Cahonaboa [*sic*] then besieged."[203] He ended his account of his activities against the Indians by saying that when the caravels arrived (the four captained by Aguado), he returned to Isabela, leaving the Indians "well punished."

The above was the first use by Columbus of the word "terrorize." He said that Caonabo's brother had with him more than 2,000 men; Martire said "some 5000 men,"[204] and Fernández de Oviedo reported "more than five or six thousand."[205] The Indians arranged themselves in five groups, but the Spaniards attacked first. Columbus described this battle as the main one, yet Fernández de Oviedo and Las Casas wrote of later battles headed by Bartolomé against 15,000 and "over a hundred thousand," respectively. Chroniclers have generally accepted that Las Casas said there were 100,000 Indians. He actually wrote, "On March 24, 1495, he left Isabela, and in two short days, that are ten leagues, as was said, he entered the Vega where many people had gathered, and they said that they believed that together there were more than 100,000 men." This qualified statement is a quite different matter from the positive "Las Casas said."[206]

Martire told the story somewhat differently: "Afterward he sent Hojeda [*sic*] as ambassador to Caunaboa [*sic*] . . . whose followers had kept Hojeda himself together with fifty soldiers encircled in the fort of Santo Tomás for thirty days . . . while Hojeda was staying in the home of Caunaboa envoys of different caciques came to try to persuade Caunaboa to not agree to the Christians establishing themselves on the island." Martire said that Ojeda threatened them with war, that Caonabo finally made a plan to kill Columbus and the Spaniards if the chance presented itself, and that, with his family and his own armed guards, Caonabo set off to see Columbus. En route he decided against leaving his homeland, but Ojeda persuaded him, with soft words and promises, to continue. He was then detained and placed in chains.[207]

Fernández de Oviedo was confused when he said that Caonabo revolted after Columbus had left for Spain. He wrote, "Finally Caonabo with a large number of his people were taken prisoners; although it was said Hojeda had not kept the guarantee that the cacique said was promised him, or Caonabo had not understood it. . . . Caonabo had a brother . . . [who] not forgetting the imprisonment of his brother, decided to go and redeem him by force of arms, going with the intent of taking all of the Christians that he could; believing that then by exchange he could have and rescue his brother Caonabo."[208]

In this fifth letter Columbus made it clear that the main problem in the colony was hunger. He stated that the Indians had been subjugated and would pay tribute if they could survive the countrywide famine. He said that Caonabo had been brought in by Ojeda, although the cacique's status was less clear. At the time that this letter was written, October 14, 1495, Caonabo had not yet been embarked for Spain. The early chronistas were confused about both the manner and the timing of his capture. So far, the colony was a dismal failure as a financial investment, and the stated mission of evangelization had not been even minimally accomplished.

Juan Aguado

Juan Aguado was among the first people in the colony whom Columbus had singled out for praise in the January 30, 1494, memorandum. He held the honorific title of king's butler, and Ferdinand had personally recommended him to Columbus, who named him captain of one of the caravels with the 1493 colonizing fleet.[209] He returned to Spain from Isabela in the following February.

In the January memorandum, Columbus recommended that favors be granted Aguado; significantly, the royal annotation in the margin of this request indicated that this would be seen to "because he is here."[210] Fernández-Armesto erred in stating that Aguado did not leave until August-September 1494 with Buil and Margarite.[211]

As has been previously noted, many feared at that time that Columbus had been lost on his Cuban trip. Accordingly, Fonseca was told to send Carillo "in case God has disposed of the Admiral." What is particularly interesting is that the instructions given to Carillo also provided for him to remedy the situation on the island: "In the absence of the Admiral attend to everything there, and *even in his presence* [emphasis added] correct the things that need to be corrected, according to the information that we have from those who came from there." Fonseca was also told to send with Carillo a "cleric of conscience and of letters."[212]

On the same day that a compact was signed with Berardi for a resupply fleet, Aguado was given his credentials for an unspecified mission to Española.[213] Whatever their sources, the monarchs had obviously received some negative reports from the island and intended to find out what the problems were. Apparently, certain matters needed remedying.

One minor matter connected with Aguado's mission has caused confusion. When Carillo was first ordered to go to the Indies to find out if Columbus was still alive, he was told to take with him a suitable person to help him. Accordingly, the name of the indicated assistant was left blank for him to fill in at such time as the assistant was named. In a matter of days this authority to select his assistant was revoked. The monarchs decided instead to name Aguado for this position, possibly because he not only had the confidence of King Ferdinand but also had already been to Española. Carillo was ordered to turn over to Aguado the letter with the blank space.[214] These instructions have led to the idea that Aguado was given instructions with blanks for him to fill in with names when he got there. This in turn has led to the mistaken belief that he traveled with some sort of carte blanche. In fact he simply carried letters that were limited to instructing the colonists to respect him as a messenger of the Crown.

Years later, after Columbus had been arrested by Bobadilla, he wrote his famous letter to the nurse of Prince Juan. Here he stated, "I made public, by word and in writing, that he [Bobadilla] could not make use of his decrees, because mine were stronger, and I showed them the decrees that Juan Aguado brought."[215] Later in this letter, he defended himself from the accusation that he had tried to take over the colony for himself. He asked rhetorically how this could be thought possible when he had received such great favors from Ferdinand and Isabel. Continuing in this vein, he wrote, "And those [the monarchs] who hold that I have served them well and maintain my privileges and concessions, and, if someone break [as in a contract] them, they increase them with advantages and order me to be shown great honor, as was seen in the case of Juan Aguado."[216] Although these decrees cannot be located today, Columbus's assertions indicate either that Aguado had brought him some kind of reconfirmation of his vice-regal powers on the island or that they were reconfirmed after Aguado rendered his report. Contrary to some opinions, it is not clear whether, in the second of these quotations, Columbus meant that it was Aguado who had tried to get the Admiral's privileges canceled or whether it was the indefinite "someone." Taken together, these quotations provide a seeming contradiction to the generally accepted supposition that Aguado had come with powers over the Admiral.

Fernández de Oviedo was also familiar with the fact that the monarchs had received, in correspondence brought by Torres, contradictory opinions on the state of affairs in the colony. He wrote that he had seen the May 5 decree ordering Aguado to the island. He noted of the accusations, "These passions responded to diverse opinions, although they were not made public; but each side found the manner to write to Spain what they felt about them."[217] The inference here is that the complaints came in letters, not necessarily by word of mouth.

At the time that Aguado left Spain in the early autumn of 1495 with the apparent mission of reporting on the affairs of the colony, the only news that the monarchs had received about Columbus had been brought to them by the three caravels that had returned to Spain in the fall of 1494 and by Torres in March-April 1495. In the fall of 1494 Buil and the others could report only that Columbus had not been heard from since his departure for Cuba in late April 1494. These returnees must have brought disquieting news about conditions in the colony, yet although Ferdinand and Isabel assumed that Columbus had possibly been "taken by the Lord," it took them nine months (December 1494 to August 1495) to mount another expedition to relieve the colony and see to its administration. In the interim Torres had returned with the news that Columbus was alive and again in command of the colony. This occured before Aguado was named to go to Española. Obviously great care must be exercised in using any of the many court orders and letters that related to these events. It is important to differentiate between what was contemplated and what was done.

Columbus wrote that while he was in Maguana, the caravels came from Spain, a reference to those commanded by Aguado. This would indicate that the latter arrived in Isabela sometime in October. If, as has so often been claimed, Aguado left Cádiz on August 5, he took an unusually long time to cross the Atlantic.

Las Casas went into considerable detail about Aguado's mission. To begin with he wrote, "[Aguado] was sent without any jurisdiction whatsoever, instead almost as a spy and pryer into all that happened ... this person started to water all of the pleasures and welfare of the Admiral." Las Casas viewed this as just retribution by the Lord for what he saw as Columbus's cruel treatment of the Tainos. He said that Aguado, by his words and actions, gave the impression that he had greater authority than he actually had. Las Casas said that many witnesses to these events told him how Aguado had interfered in matters that did not concern him, how he had corrected the Admiral's officials, and how he had showed little respect for Bartolomé. Las Casas further commented that when Aguado went into the interior to find Columbus, people mistook him for the new head of the colony.[218]

Las Casas reported that although Aguado made a general nuisance of himself, many witnesses to these events told him: "The Admiral, with all modesty and patience, put up with him and responded to him (and always treated Juan Aguado very well, as though he were a count). [Yet] Juan Aguado said that the admiral had not received the *cédulas* and letter of credence of the kings with due obeisance and reverence." Aguado later attempted to force the notaries to testify to this effect. Las Casas noted that these actions caused the people, especially those in Isabela, to be less inclined to obey Columbus and his officers.[219] These disagreements were not reported by any of the other chroniclers. Hernando did not even mention Aguado in connection with the second voyage.

A flurry of royal orders were issued on June 1, 1495. These were brought over later with Aguado. Columbus was ordered to allow those who wanted to return to Spain to do so. Apparently, the sovereigns knew that Columbus had not allowed some men to return with Torres. He was also told to distribute the supplies among the colonists according to a schedule given him and not to permit anyone to go hungry due to having committed a crime.[220] At the same time Fonseca was ordered to take the necessary steps to reduce the size of the colony to five hundred, and Aguado was notified that a Galician by the name of Loazes had died of hunger in Isabela.[221] These *cédulas* indicate that the Crown was aware of at least some of the problems in the colony.

In his letter on the third voyage Columbus said that his discoveries had come under severe criticism. However he noted, "Your Highnesses answered me, laughing and saying that I should not worry about anything, because they did not give importance nor belief to any who maligned this enterprise." Jane, like other scholars, read into this part of his general citation of his grievances an indication of "the rejection of this unfavourable report made by Juan Aguado."[222]

Morison accepted Aguado's mission as an investigation of Columbus. He incorrectly listed Aguado as a member of the queen's household. He gave the reason for the mission: "The Sovereigns could not ignore the complaints of Fray Buil and the other malcontents, several hundred in number, who had returned home." This is the first claim that so many colonists had already left the colony by the fall of 1494. He confused Fonseca's instructions for the reduction of the colony, making it instead an order to Columbus. He went on to give other specifics, also previously unknown, without giving his sources: "Yet he [Aguado] made a pompous entry into Isabela with the sound of trumpets, and at once countermanding orders of the Adelantado (who had charge in the Admiral's absence inland), hearing complaints, arresting people, and in other words assuming the functions of viceroy."[223] There is no evidence that Aguado did any of these things.

Wilford chose to ignore Aguado completely. The Phillipses believed, erroneously, that Aguado "had accompanied Columbus on his second voyage, commanding one of the caravels, and had returned to Spain with Torres in 1495." This statement is incorrect. They wrote that Aguado was charged with the responsibility for distributing the rations fairly; the official record shows that it was Columbus who was so instructed. They added an interesting commentary: "Fernando and Isabel told him [Columbus] to do nothing, for the moment, about slavery or the slave trade."[224] These same instructions are known to have been given to the bishop of Bajadóz with reference to the five hundred Indians that Torres brought to Spain, but not to Columbus. Wilford also was under the mistaken impression that in their comments on the Torres Memorandum, "the king and queen urged him not to resort to slavery."[225]

The Phillipses went on to say, "Aguado was appalled by what he found."[226] Unfortunately, there is no record as to what Aguado did or did not determine during the course of his brief second visit to Española. Fernández-Armesto also mistook the date of Aguado's first return to Spain. He believed, incorrectly, that Aguado had first returned in 1494 with Buil and Margarite. He did, however, note correctly on Aguado's second trip to Española: "What he unearthed against his former master, when he returned with every opportunity to spite him, is unknown. Columbus's own subsequent references to the episode imply satisfaction with its outcome."[227]

Return from the Second Voyage

Columbus wrote of a storm in July 1495 that sank all of the ships in the port of Isabela. When he had sailed in the previous year for Cuba, he had left two naos, the *Marigalante* and the *Gallega*, together with two smaller coastal craft in Isabela to take care of the needs of the colony. The three caravels that Bartolomé brought over later in June or July 1494 soon returned to Spain. After Columbus's return from Cuba in late September 1494, Torres arrived at Española with four caravels, returning with them to Spain in February 1495. The next fleet to arrive was Aguado's, around October 1495 with four caravels. Based on these figures, only the three navigable caravels from the Cuban expedition, two unserviceable naos, and two barques were in the harbor when a storm ravaged the colony in July 1495.

The descriptions of the storm capsulated meteorological elements from two different types of storm into a single one. In his fifth letter Columbus wrote that the storm occurred in July and that it tore up trees that had been there since the time of Adam. He noted a windstorm and an earthquake. When the storm reached Isabela, "it broke the cables of these naos and sent them to the bottom near the shore."[228] He went on to say, "A thing happened here that seems a marvel, it is that since we are here the waters of the sea have risen more than two fathoms inland, so that, where it was dry, there is now bottom."[229]

Shortly before giving the above details, Columbus told how he had repaired the caravels that he had taken to Cuba. His account of the storm would seem to indicate that it was the two large naos that had been sunk, yet he also wrote, "These naos and the ones I made sank." Las Casas admitted that he was confused as to the timing of two disasters. Columbus wrote of only the one storm in July 1495. Gil reported a document in the Archivo General de Indias reporting the loss of some of Aguado's ships in a hurricane on an unspecified date.[230]

One of the reasons that Columbus gave for not continuing his exploration in September 1494 was that the three caravels he had taken on the Cuban trip were in terrible condition, too bad to continue. Before mentioning the July storm, he said that he was repairing the caravels so that they could take Bartolomé on a voyage to find Catayo. He wrote in the fifth letter that these were not ready until October, which was around the time when Aguado arrived. Sometime after July, Columbus said that he had used the hulks of the no longer serviceable naos, the *Marigalante* and the *Gallega*, for materials with which to build the fort at Concepción and, although he did not say so, probably also for the fort at Magdalena.

Las Casas said, "The four ships brought by Aguado were lost in the port of Isabela in a great tempest that the Indians call hurricane in their language . . . and because I am doubtful if the four of Juan Aguado were among the six ships, that above, at the end of chapter 102, we said were lost in the port of Isabela, because it has gone from my memory, as since then 59 years have passed."[231] In chapter 102 he had not said how many ships had been lost, only that all of the ships that were in the port sank. He now went on to say that Columbus had two caravels built out of their wrecks, "one of which [Las Casas] saw, it was called the *India*."[232] Hernando said that his father sailed with Aguado for Spain with two of the caravels that he had used on his Cuban voyage, the *Santa Cruz* and the *Niña*. Thus, neither of Columbus's earliest biographers was able to clarify these matters.

Martire provided a detailed account of a storm. He first described the battles with the Indians in 1495, then added: "They say that in that year, in the month of January, there was a whirlwind from the east, [such as] never seen [before], that raised eddies up to the stars and tore up by the roots whatever trees that it found, no matter how large they were. This typhoon, on reaching the port of the city, sank in the depths three ships that were held only by their anchors, breaking their cables without there being a tempest or waves in the sea, after making them give a thousand and one turns. They affirm that in that year the sea rose more than usual and it grew more than a cubit."[233]

There are notable similarities in these two accounts. Although Martire gave the date as January 1495, he could have been using the Italian system for the year ending in January. The inference in the text is that the storm described by Martire occurred after the pacification of the Indians; therefore, if it happened in January, it would necessarily have been in 1496, not, as he wrote, in the same year of the pacifiction. Besides the July storm during which the naos, barques, and three caravels sank, there was obviously another storm, probably in January 1496. This second storm sank all of the vessels in the harbor including the four brought by Aguado; out of these wrecks the *Niña* was again rebuilt, and a new caravel, the *India*, was built. These were the two vessels used by Columbus and Aguado to set sail for Spain in March.

Fernández de Oviedo wrote, "This return of the Admiral to Spain was in the year ninety six; as a prisoner, inasmuch as (*puesto*) he was not ordered to be taken prisoner." He went on to say that Buil, Margarite, the Gallego, Bernal Díaz, and others returned with Columbus.[234] Obviously Fernández de Oviedo was completely confused on the subject of who returned with whom and when. Martire did not mention Aguado but incorrectly dated Columbus's return in 1495 rather than 1496.[235]

What Fernández de Oviedo was apparently trying to say was that Columbus returned voluntarily, assuming the stance of a humble prisoner. Bernáldez had Columbus as a houseguest after the Admiral returned to Spain. He described how Columbus had allowed his beard to grow and how he wore a costume similar to those worn by the lay orders of Franciscans. Las Casas saw Columbus in Seville at this time and also reported the pseudo-Franciscan habit. There is no evidence whatsoever that Columbus was ordered to return to Spain by either Aguado or the monarchs.

According to Hernando, Columbus carried home on this voyage 225 Christians and 30 Indians.[236] For some unknown reason, Columbus tried to work his way home by sailing down the Lesser Antilles, where, on finding the winds against him, he returned to the more northerly route. Since he knew from his first voyage where to find the favorable winds for an easterly crossing, he must have had some purpose in mind for attempting this less desirable route; perhaps he wanted to show Aguado the rich islands that he had discovered earlier. Although seriously delayed by this false start, he returned to Cádiz without further incident. Bernáldez described his arrival in June 1496.[237] The first official notice of his arrival back in Spain was a letter dated July 12 in which his sovereigns asked him "to come to the Court when he can do so without trouble."[238] The courteous tone of this letter belies the claim that he had returned under restraint.

Resumé

Columbus had set out on his second voyage to the Indies with the primary purpose of establishing a colony on the island of Española.

He expected that he would find his plans advanced by the men that he had left at Navidad on his first voyage. His secondary purpose was exploration. He sailed on a more southerly route this time and did discover the Leeward and Virgin Islands. From there he worked his way north and, after touching at Puerto Rico, returned to Española. At Navidad he found that all of the men he had left there were dead and the fortress had been razed. By this time he had been at sea for two months with over one thousand men together with horses, cattle, and other livestock. He wasted almost another month finding a new location for the colony. He named this site Isabela. He established a rudimentary settlement there and shortly afterward set up a small fort in the interior.

Columbus left a council in charge at Isabela and gave orders that the island be explored in search for gold. He then set out to cruise west-northwest up the slope of the southern coast of Cuba in hopes of finding Cathay—the promised mainland of China. On the two legs of this side trip he circumnavigated Jamaica, and on his return he cruised the southern coast of Española. He returned to Isabela a sick man. Columbus found that his brother Bartolomé had arrived and that most of the senior officials that he had left in charge had departed for Spain. In Spain at that time it was feared that Columbus had been lost on his Cuban trip, an assumption that provided the initial pretext for the dispatch of officials ordered to take over the colony. Aguado, one of the king's men, was finally sent to report on the conditions in the colony.

Meanwhile, Columbus was engaged in the task of subjugating the Indians. He built two more forts in the interior. Indians and Spaniards alike suffered from famine, and somewhere between one-fifth and one-third of the Spaniards died. Columbus established a crude system of tribute, promising the native chiefs that if they fulfilled their quotas, he would leave their lands undisturbed. For several reasons, the main ones being famine and scarcity of placer gold, these requirements were not met.

He had intended to send Bartolomé on another voyage in search of Cathay, but a severe storm sank his caravels. It took three months to repair the ships, and by the time they were ready, Aguado's relief fleet from Spain had arrived. Another storm, this one unrecorded in contemporary documents, probably sank all the caravels, including the four resupply ships. Columbus spent two months repairing one and building a new one out of the wreckage. Columbus then left Bartolomé in charge of the depleted colony; accompanied by Aguado, he sailed for Spain.

The amount of gold found so far was far below expectations. The other products that had held such promise, such as the many spices that Columbus believed he had found, turned out to be of no commercial value. A great deal of money had been spent with little return, and many lives had been lost. The evangelizing mission had not yet even begun. Many of the adventurers who had come on this voyage did so in the hopes of finding quick and easy riches. They found instead hard work and privation. The resulting atmosphere of discontent, which must have bordered on despair in the colony, undoubtedly caused many personality clashes. Columbus was not an easy taskmaster and was certainly a poor administrator. He now had to return to Spain, reassure Ferdinand and Isabel that the colony could become self-sufficient, and get their support for further exploration in search of the mainland.

There are more things in heaven and earth.
William Shakespeare (1564–1616)

14
The
Third
Voyage

Columbus wrote a letter known today as the letter on the third voyage. Dated October 18, 1498, it was sent from Española with a fleet that sailed in that year. Two previously unknown short letters in *El libro copiador*, letters written to the monarchs in 1500, are now also available for study. Also in 1500, in a letter written to the nurse of Prince Juan, Columbus took the story from where the 1498 letter left off up to the time of his return to Spain in 1500. This letter was translated into Italian by Gio. Battista Spotorno in 1823. The Daelli edition in 1863 listed Spotorno's copy as from the Genoa Codex.[1] B. F. Stevens provided a facsimile with translation into English of Columbus's copy of the nurse's letter in the Paris Codex. Las Casas also provided a version, which is the one that Varela used in her *Textos*. The copy in the Paris Codex is believed to be the most accurate of the three versions of the letter to the nurse of Prince Juan.

A Las Casas holograph of the 1498 letter survives. It was first translated into Spanish by Fernández de Navarrete in 1825. Earlier Juan Bautista Muñoz had located a copy, since lost, in the archives of the monastery of Las Cuevas. Las Casas also offered a slightly different version of this letter in his *Historia*. Another version, in *El libro copiador*, now provides Columbian scholars with the opportunity to compare it with the Lascasian holograph of presumably the same letter. The letter in *El libro copiador*, though substantially the same as the Lascasian holograph, is more complete; yet, it also lacks some data found in the other version. The latter has supplementary interest for the many marginal notations added by Las Casas. Carlos Sanz included these in his *en face* facsimile edition *Relación del tercer viaje*.[2] There is no way of telling at this time from what copy or copies either the Lascasian holograph or the version of the letter in *El libro copiador* was made. Antonio Rumeu de Armas and Gil have each provided transcriptions, together with comparative analyses of these two documents.[3]

Zamora, referring to the Sanz transcription, noted, "Surprisingly, even the editor of the first facsimile edition, Carlos Sanz, silently omitted many of the marginal notes in his transcription."[4] However, the *en face* facsimile clearly shows the objected-to omissions. She also noted that in both Fernández de Navarrete's *Colección* and the later *Raccolta*, the copies of the Lascasian manuscripts of both the *Diario* and the *Relación del tercer viaje* had been silently emended, leaving out corrections and marginalia.

It is of paramount interest to note that, in the Lascasian text, those sentences terminating in "*etc.*" are completed in *El libro copiador*. The most important of these is the paragraph in which Columbus gave his opinion as to the location of the Terrestrial Paradise. Las Casas closed the explanation by writing, "And all of the theologians agree that the Terrestrial Paradise is in the west, etc."[5] The more complete version in *El libro copiador* goes on to say that the West is the end of the world and that traveling in this direction, one reaches a high mountain arising in those turbulent airs to a height above that reached by the biblical flood. The water from a spring falls into the sea, making a large lake from which the Ganges, the Tigris, the Euphrates, and the Nile Rivers flow. These reach their respective sources by "passing under the ground."[6] This explanation was copied from chapter 57 in the *Ymago mundi*.[7] It is also to be found in Rodrigo Fernández de Santaella y Córdoba's Spanish translation (1503) of Marco Polo's *Il milione* but not in the

Pipino Latin edition (1487) used by Columbus.[8] The final observation was that the people who live near where the river flows into the lake are born deaf because of the great noise of the waters. Modern commentators neglect to identify Columbus's many possible sources for this theory, which originated in the Bible (Genesis 2:10–14).

Another omission also concerns the Terrestrial Paradise. Las Casas limited Columbus's final statement on the matter by writing, "And if Paradise does not come from there, it seems to be an even greater marvel, because I don't believe that a river so great and deep is known in the world."[9] The version in *El libro copiador* added that the river is "so deep in some places its bottom is so far that it cannot be reached with an eighty fathom line with a twelve pound lead weight."[10] The *Ymago mundi* also described the depth of the rivers emanating from paradise, but this observation was not made by Marco Polo and his father, who have often been assumed to have provided Columbus with much of the data that he used.

There are too many variances to cover in this critique. Suffice it to say that some of them give clearer meanings while others provide different nuances. An example of the latter is when Columbus wrote that all of the monarchs' subjects "wanted (*quisie*) a map" (Las Casas) of the Indies or "had (*ovo*) a map" (*El libro copiador*). According to the latter, in other words, copies of his map had been made available to others.

The earliest independent source known today for the third voyage is a brief account in a letter written by Columbus's friend Simón Verde; this letter is dated, in the Florentine fashion, January 2, 1498, otherwise 1499.[11] The date is of particular importance in that it shows that Verde had access to information given by Columbus in a letter to the Catholic monarchs within a few days of their receipt of it. Earlier, Verde had also written two letters reporting on the second voyage, the first of these within days of the return of Luis Torres to Spain. Data given in the second of these earlier letters indicated that Verde had apparently also had personal contact with Columbus after his return from that voyage.[12]

We now know that Martire, Bernáldez, Hernando, and Las Casas each had access to copies of Columbus's letters on the third voyage in *El libro copiador*. The first version of the complete text of the 1498 letter on the third voyage was published by Fernández de Navarrete in 1825.[13] As previously noted, the first copy of the second letter written on this third voyage, known as the letter to the nurse of Prince Juan, was published in 1823.[14]

As Thacher pointed out, the copies found in the Columbian codices had been assembled in 1502 by Columbus; accordingly, they should take precedence over Las Casas's copies, due to a presumption of their greater fidelity to the original. There are differences between all versions.[15] The differences between the copies in the codices and the Lascasian copies are rarely noted today because of the generally accepted modern practice of working only from one or the other of Las Casas's versions.

Simón Verde

The interest attached to Verde's letter is not so much for either its date or its text as for the fact that its writer derived some of his information from one of Columbus's own letters. These were directed to the Spanish monarchs and, as such, would have been normally considered secret. This rule of secrecy applied especially to all matters dealing with discovery and ocean routes. Testimony given in the *Pleitos*, repeated by Hernando and Las Casas, stated that Juan de Fonseca made available to Alonso de Ojeda either the original of or a copy of the map that Columbus had sent with the 1498 letter. These same sources reported that Ojeda and his partners, Juan de la Cosa and Amerigo Vespucci, used this map as a guide for their 1499 voyage to the Venezuelan coast, for which they have been credited with being the first to discover the South American mainland. Vespucci's self-proclaimed prior discovery of the South American continent on an earlier voyage in 1497 is seriously questioned; it was first reported in 1504 in the published versions of his letters to two of his Italian patrons.[16] Pero Alonso Niño, Columbus's pilot on the first voyage, and his associate Cristóbal Guerra are also said to have had access to this map. They sailed in one caravel for the coast of Paria two weeks after the departure of the Ojeda fleet. Niño took with him two of the pilots who had accompanied Columbus on his third voyage; therefore, a copy of

Columbus's map would not necessarily have been essential to the success of this voyage. Louis-André Vigneras discounted the claim, sometimes made, that Niño had sailed with Columbus on the third voyage.[17]

After first discussing some of the events of the third voyage, Verde wrote, "I have read a copy of a letter that the Admiral writes to the King, giving him great hope for the enterprise."[18] Martire used some of the same phrases as Verde, indicative of a common source. In his letter, Verde first referred to events that took place in connection with the second voyage; for example, he noted that five hundred slaves embarked at Isabela in 1495 but only three hundred arrived alive in Spain. He wrote that Columbus had sent at that time "some gold" but "much brazilwood." In the introduction to his own letter, Columbus wrote, "I brought them [the monarchs] sufficient samples of gold . . . and I told them of the great quantity of brazilwood and infinite other things."[19] In a direct reference to the third voyage, Verde made an interesting comment: "They discovered *new lands* [emphasis added] leaning toward the equator, where they found— and they say on a *mainland* [emphasis added]—villages in better condition than the others found up until now."[20] This was the first known reference to "new lands" and "mainland" by anyone other than Columbus.

Columbus, Verde, and Martire each referred to a wine not made from grapes, as well as to the all-important finding of pearls. Verde wrote that he could not tell "with certainty where they fished for them and in what manner and quantity." Columbus did say that he had been given pearls and was told on Paria where they came from but that, before locating the pearl coast, he had veered north to the island he named Margarita, a Spanish word for "pearls," although Vigneras believed that it was so named "in honor of the widowed Princess Margaret of Burgundy, whose wedding he had attended fifteen months before."[21] Actually Columbus did not attend the wedding but did suggest sailing directions for the wedding fleet.

Many years later, Columbus's failure to sail farther along the coast at this time provided the Crown with material in the *Pleitos* for its contention that Niño and Guerra in 1499, not Columbus, were the first to discover the continent. The Colóns' defense was that although others did sail some four hundred miles farther up the coast, they were sailing along lands already discovered by Columbus, lands that were, consequently, already in the possession of Spain. Thus they held that Paria was the mainland. When Columbus took possession at Paria, he still believed it to be an island, whereas Niño and Guerra later made an act of possession of what they conceived to be the mainland on the Pearl Coast.

There was further dispute in the *Pleitos* over whether or not Columbus had landed, and taken possession in person, on Paria. Columbus's pilot, Hernán Pérez, and Juan de Quexo each testified that he had. Andrés del Corral said that Columbus was suffering at the time from eye trouble and sent the captain of his ship to perform the act in his name. Columbus wrote in *El libro copiador* that on the first voyage, his eyes had "not broken with blood and with so many pains as now."[22] His *criado* Juan Portugués also testified that Columbus had not landed. Columbus made no mention in his letters of the act of possession having taken place. He merely noted that he sent his men ashore to get fresh water and some rest after their long sea voyage.

From Columbus's letter Verde knew that the Admiral had encountered a gulf on this voyage, one that was twenty leagues wide and where the water was always sweet, that is, not salty. He noted, "The philosophers say: that the world has a spherical form, and the Admiral has been greatly pleased and clever to have discovered the *other world* [emphasis added] opposite to ours."[23] At least for Verde, Columbus's use of the phrase "other world" was not a casual observation but a transcendental geographical discovery by Columbus, who had discovered "the other world opposite to ours." Verde's was one of the first two letters known to have advanced the idea that this was another world (*otro mundo*). The other letter was written by Columbus. Yet, neither Verde nor his letter has any place in any of the modern biographies under review here.

Martire, Trivigiano, Montalboddo

It is equally evident that Martire too had access to Columbus's letter of the third voyage. In 1504 a summary version of the letter, as paraphrased in a letter written by Martire in 1501, appeared in the *Libretto De Tutta La Nauigatione De Re De Spagna De Le Isole Et Terreni Nouamente Trovati*,[24] a work that was published from reports written by Angelo Trivigiano ("Trevisan" in English and "Trevino" in Spanish), possibly without Martire's permission. The above capitalized version of the title is as given in the Biblioteca Marciana copy of the *Libretto*. Lower-case versions are a modern emendation, although the John Carter Brown Library copy has all of the words capitalized on the title page with the exception of the word "tutta."[25] This title page is missing in the Marciana copy. There are only these two copies of this work known today. In a most unusual twist, the codex of this work still exists. For Lawrence C. Wroth, the *Libretto* should "rank in historical importance as second only to the very earliest issues of the Columbus Letter."[26] In 1903 Thacher published the first facsimile of the 1504 edition together with an English translation.[27]

In 1501 Trivigiano wrote a letter in which he said that he had a copy of what is now known to have been Martire's letter that became known as the first decade. Martire originally wrote these decades as letters, and it is evident that Trivigiano was able to copy the first of these in the same year in which it was written. Martire wrote in Latin, and Trivigiano translated the letters into the Venetian dialect. This first decade took up the story of the discoveries only until the end of Columbus's third voyage. Wroth noted that it was "the first collection of voyages ever printed, the first published relation of the third voyage and part of the second voyage of Columbus, and the first edition of the first book by the earliest historian of America."[28] This work is of far greater historiographic interest than as merely a bibliophile's rarity.

At this time Trivigiano wrote, "The author . . . comes from yonder [Martire's return from an embassy to Egypt] intending to present it to our Prince who, I think will have it printed, and then your magnificence will have a perfect copy of it."[29] Later in the same year he wrote, "At this very moment it will have passed into print."[30] These statements raise the question of whether or not the publication of Trivigiano's copy was unauthorized. Years later Martire did object strongly to someone who "extracted and stole certain writings from the first three books of [his] Decade." Thacher[31] and Wroth[32] each came to the conclusion that this comment on plagiarism was more likely to have been a reference to F. Montalboddo's *Paesi nuouamente retrovati*, published in 1507, than to the earlier *Libretto*. Martire went on to say, "Many famous men are sent to the Catholic Sovereigns from that illustrious [Venetian] Senate and I freely disclosed to them my books: and I was quick to suffer them to make a copy of them."[33]

Two of the more serious errors in the *Libretto* cannot be attributed to Trivigiano, since a comparison of the entries in his codex with those in the *Libretto* show that he had copied from Martire correctly. The Trivigiano codex identified Columbus's pilot on the *Santa María* as "Alonso Nigno"—Alonso the Younger. In the *Libretto* he became "Alonso negro"—the black—a misnomer copied in the *Paesi* and other early accounts of the first voyage. The second error was a change of Trivigiano's reference in Venetian dialect to the island of Joanna (Cuba), when it was still believed to be a part of the Asian mainland, from "Zoána, ma la" into "Zoána mela," with the result that Cuba first, and then North America, became known for a time as Joana Mela. This error was repeated for the name of the North American continent even on the important 1515 Reisch map.[34]

It is interesting to note that in one of his 1501 letters, Trivigiano said that he expected to get a copy of an "account of the voyage from Calicut," though it was "not possible to procure the map of that voyage, because the King [of Portugal] has declared a sentence of death against anyone giving it out."[35] Apparently the Portuguese were more zealous in protecting their discovery information than the Spaniards. The voyage referred to was Pedro Alvars Cabral's. He was a friend of Vasco da Gama's and had with him on this voyage Bartolomeu Dias, the captain who was the first to round the Cape of Good Hope. Cabral set out for Calcutta but en route was driven off course onto the coast of Brazil. He went on to India, where he met with armed resistance to his attempt to establish a trading post and a mission. In this same year, 1500, Vicente Yáñez Pinzón, who had sailed with Columbus on the first voyage, also reached the Brazilian coast. Although Cabral's primacy of discovery was questioned, this was another of those cases where prior discovery took precedence over legalisms, and it was accepted that this part of the Brazilian coast fell under the jurisdiction of Portugal.

Trivigiano introduced a possibility that he had sent his correspondent either a Columbus holograph or a scribal copy of Columbus's letter. He wrote: "I send with this another book of the voyage of Columbus, which being badly written, Your Magnificence will pardon me that I have not time to transcribe."[36] It would appear doubtful that a scribal copy would be badly written, although the reference may have been to the syntax rather than to the orthography. It will be recalled that Las Casas had problems with his reading of Columbus's handwriting.

The *Paesi nouamente retrovati et novo mondo da Alberico Vesputio* was published, without attribution, by Montalboddo in 1507.[37] It included a faithful copy of the *Libretto*'s materials concerning Columbus's first three voyages, errors and all. Martire's own publication of his first decade first appeared in a 1511 edition. In the *Libretto* the sailing date from Cádiz for the fleet of the second voyage was given as September 1, whereas Martire gave the correct date of the twenty-fifth. This was possibly a correction introduced into the 1511 edition. Martire or his publisher continued to correct earlier errors of his own making in both his 1516 and his 1530 editions. The date given for the court's receipt of the first news of the return of the twelve ships was March 24 in the *Décades* and March 23 in the *Libretto*. Again, the two accounts were two days apart in the dates given for the departure on the third voyage. Those who have accepted the *Libretto*'s dates as the more accurate of the two did so because this work, being the earlier version, was closer to the time of the events recounted and thus conceivably more accurate. Perhaps some of the differences can also be accounted for by the difficulties Trivigiano encountered in translating the copy from which he worked.

The *Libretto* paraphrase of the Columbus letter on the third voyage began with the above-mentioned difference as to the sailing date for the second voyage. Martire's *Décades* had the correct date for the third voyage as given in Columbus's letter—May 30, 1498. As is known, Columbus sailed with six vessels, yet Martire's letter and the *Libretto* both gave the number as eight. This confusion arose from the fact that Columbus was authorized to provision eight vessels, and he did send ahead on February 6 (Vigneras gave the date as January 23)[38] two ships with supplies for the colony on Española. Gil pointed out that Martire corrected this slight error in his 1511 edition, saying that Columbus left "after having sent before the two [caravels]."[39] The advance supply ships were the *Niña* and the *India*, in each of which Columbus owned a half interest. While waiting for permission to make the third voyage, Columbus had chartered out both of these vessels, one for a trip to Flanders, the other to Rome; he always paid close attention to the mercantile possibilities of his voyages. One of these advance caravels was commanded by Fernández Coronel.[40] Although these two served as resupply vessels for the colony as well as transport for colonizers, they had on board seventy-seven armed soldiers but only twenty-eight farm workers.[41] The revolt by Francisco Roldán had not yet occurred, but obviously Columbus must have sensed that his brother Bartolomé was in more immediate need of soldiers than of colonizers.

Notably, in all three of the earliest published accounts of the events at the beginning of the third journey, mentions of a Terrestrial Paradise, of the Orinoco River as the source of the four great rivers of the world, and of other mystical fancies repeated by Columbus are omitted. These publications had a common source—Martire. He too had a single source—Columbus, who had placed great emphasis on such observations in his letters known today. The only place-name on the island of Trinidad offered by Martire was for the sand point (*Ponta de Erena*); the island itself remained unnamed by him until "Trinidad" was given in his 1530 edition. The account of the third voyage appeared in the third book of Martire's first decade, which derived from a letter he had sent to Pope Julius II (1503–13), formerly Cardinal Giuliano della Rovere, a native of Savona, the town of Columbus's youth. This pope was better known, even in his own day, as a politician and warrior than as a spiritual leader. Apparently, while extracting this résumé, Martire edited out all of Columbus's mysticism. Another possibility is that Columbus prepared different versions of this letter and that the one seen by Martire was a despiritualized one.

In a letter dated November 1493, Martire was the first to give the title "New World" to the lands discovered by Columbus.[42] He also used the phrase "Western Hemisphere." The first publication by Martire of the first nine books of the first decade, and part of the tenth, in Seville in 1511 had the title *De Babylonica legatione*, the title being taken from his account of his embassy to Egypt. The subtitle, *Oceani decas*, applied to the narrative of the first three Columbian voyages. The first complete edition of his eight decades, generally referred to by the short title *De orbe novo*, was published in 1530.[43] An earlier, less complete 1516 edition was also given this title. Morison recognized Martire's "distinction of being the earliest historian of the New World," but he made no mention of the first published edition and the more widely distributed versions of Martires' history published by others.

The first published work to incorporate the designation of the Indies as a "New World" was the 1504 *Mundus Novus* edition of Vespucci's letter to Lorenzo di Medici.[44] This work included the account of Vespucci's first voyage, one questioned by many historians, an account also found in his letter to Soderini written in 1504.[45] The title of this little book is sometimes given as partial explanation for the naming of these continents "America," a variation on Vespucci's first name—"Amerigo" in Italian and "Americus" in Latin. As José Rabasa and others have pointed out, Vespucci wrote in the spring of 1503: "None of these countries were known to our ancestors and to all who hear about them they will be entirely new. . . . [Even if] they have affirmed that any continent is there, they have given many reasons for denying it is inhabited. . . . But this opinion is false, and entirely opposed to the truth. My last voyage has proved it, for I have found a continent in the southern part; more populous and more full of animals than our Europe, or Asia, or Africa, and even more temperate than any other region known to us."[46]

Sale was the only one of the modern biographers studied in this critique who took even minimal notice of the part played by Montalboddo in spreading news of the discoveries; at the same time, however, Sale ignored Trivigiano. Sale listed what he believed to be all of the publications in which Columbus was mentioned up to 1606, but the *Libretto* was not included. He noted nineteen editions of Martire's *Décades*, which was "the first and for a long time the most important work on the New World.... [It] became the center-piece ... for other important books on America in the first half of the century, including the versions of Montalboddo, Grynaeous, Mÿnster, and Ramusio, which collectively passed on Colón's story in fifty-seven editions."[47] There were actually seventy-six sixteenth-century editions of works by different authors, who provided much of the background for the Columbus image that persists to this day. Some of them were basic source books for his early biographers. Hernando owned two editions of the *Libretto*, and it was cited as a source by Fernández de Oviedo, Francisco López de Gómara, and Antonio Herrera y Tordesillas, among others.[48] More recently, both Arthur Helps and William Hickling Prescott attached great importance to Martire's reports. Several of the biographies studied herein mention Trivigiano solely in connection with his physical description of Columbus, the earliest one known. His role as a primary source passed unnoticed.

The Religious and Mercantile Motivations of Columbus

At the time Columbus set out on his third voyage, he left a troubled past behind him. His first two voyages had been financial failures. Regardless of whether he was indeed motivated to search for the riches of the East for the purpose of financing a crusade to recover Jerusalem or for the more prosaic reason of increasing his personal wealth and power, he had not accomplished either objective. At a time when Spain and the other western European nations were fully engaged in exerting their individual influences over the Italian states, messianism was not at the forefront of any of their goals. Even the pope was more bent on expanding the Borgia family's temporal domain than on either recovering the Holy City or spreading Christianity. Ever since the capture of Constantinople, the popes had been promoting crusades to oust the Turks, but not for the purpose of recovering the Holy City. It was of far more immediate importance to King Ferdinand to recover Perpignan from the French and keep them from conquering Naples. A great deal of caution must be exercised in distinguishing between religious expressions and religious belief.

There did still exist at that time a universal Christian belief in an earthly paradise. Scriptural prophecies were generally believed literally. It was not only natural for Columbus to believe in these things but it would have been heretical for him to think otherwise. It should be recalled that it was King Ferdinand, the consummate politician, who introduced the Inquisition into Aragón before it reached Castile. Zvetan Todorov noted, "Furthermore, Columbus believes not only in Christian dogma, but also (and he is not alone at the time) in Cyclopes and mermaids, in Amazons and men with tails, and his belief, therefore permits him to find them."[49] As has been previously noted, Columbus was more inclined to ascribe such beliefs to "others," the "men," than to himself.

In reference to Columbus's claim, made in the 1498 letter, that he had discovered the Terrestrial Paradise, Todorov wrote, "There is nothing of the modern empiricist about Columbus: the decisive argument is an argument of authority, not of experience. He knows in advance what he will find; the concrete experience is there to illustrate a truth already possessed."[50] Stephen Greenblatt viewed this identification with paradise somewhat differently. He first quoted Columbus: " 'And I say that if it [the Orinoco River] not be from the earthly paradise that this river comes, it originates from a vast land, lying to the south, of which hitherto no knowledge has been obtained.' Faced with such a staggering thought—the idea, in effect, of South America—Columbus retreats to the safer ground of the land of Eden."[51] Following the sequence of Columbus's thought as expressed in his letter, the "retreat," if any, was to "another world," that is, the Americas.

Gil proposed that what Columbus was seeking on the third voyage was Taprobana, the island recommended to him by both Cardenal Cisneros and Jaime Ferrer. Gil drew attention to the fact that both Pliny and Pomponius Mela speculated that it was "another world"; Pompinius Mela expressed large doubts whether Taprobana was "a very large island or the first part of 'another world.' "[52] This offers a simple cosmographic explanation for the use of the phrase by Columbus.

The fact should not be overlooked that after saying that he had made this supposed monumental discovery, Columbus, ever cautious, wrote that even if, as he had previously surmised, the Orinoco River did not flow from paradise, it was an "even greater marvel" to have found such an incredibly large and previously unknown river.[53] He went into great detail—which, as mentioned earlier, is found only in the copy in *El libro copiador*—in explaining the geophysical nature of this Terrestrial Paradise. He also rationalized how it was geographically possible that the source of the Orinoco could also feed the other great rivers of the world. He even offered his actual measurement of its great depth as proof of its "marvelous" nature. These offered more empirical than mystical explanations for his suppositions and, as previously noted, were probably single-sourced from the *Ymago mundi.*

Columbus went on to cite from the classics in support of his claim that he had reached the end of the world, and after naming dozens of authorities, he stated that he had indeed found an "other world." Again, as was customary with him, this prolonged discourse was interlarded with comments on both the spiritual and the material benefits that would accrue to the Catholic Kings if they would pursue these finds with further explorations.

A great deal has been made of the two reasons that Columbus gave in support of his belief that he had found land near the Terrestrial Paradise. First, his support came from the scriptural identification of the paradise as being the source for the world's great rivers—the Ganges, the Euphrates, and the Nile—to which he now added the Orinoco. The second reason was that as one approached the area that he was in, as one proceeded from south to north from the equator, the world sloped upward; conversely, it sloped downward when one traveled from Trinidad southward. Therefore he now proposed that the earth be considered as pear-shaped. If one looks at a globe and assumes the line at the equator to be static, it is obvious that Columbus was simplistically correct in his explanation of climbing— he was traveling upward to the apex of an arc. In his attempt to understand this conceptual illusion, he reached out to the basic authority of the times, the Bible, and came up with a solution—the Terrestrial Paradise, the highest point on earth. He likened it to the teat on a woman's breast. As noted above, he then hedged his bets, suggesting that perhaps this was all just part of another of the marvelous things that he had discovered.

As noted earlier Columbus wrote a postil in his copy of the *Historia rerum* referring to the authorities who had found that the earth was so shaped. He wrote another postil in the *Ymago mundi*, alongside the text in which it was reported that the Terrestrial Paradise was in the mountains near the equator.[54] Zamora, possibly unaware of these postils, found further religious symbolism in this passage: "The voyage's trajectory, described by Columbus as an ascent on the slope of the earth toward its highest point in the extreme Orient, can be read figuratively as a spiritual ascension to Paradise or the heavenly Jerusalem."[55] It can also be read literally as perceived geographical fact.

Greenblatt concluded, "Indeed the production of a sense of the marvelous in the New World is at the very center of virtually all of Columbus's writings about his discoveries, though the meaning of the sense shifts over the years." He also noted, "The marvelous stands [in the 1498 letter] for the missing caravels laden with gold; it is—like the ritual of possession itself—a word pregnant with what is imagined, desired, promised."[56] There is the simpler possibility that Columbus's frequent use of the word "marvelous" as applied to both animate and inanimate objects may have been due to what John Hale described as his "joyous spontaneity."[57] Considering Columbus's rudimentary education, perhaps he knew no other way to describe, given his very limited Spanish vocabulary, what he had encountered. His frequent use of the word "marvelous" in his postils in the *Historia rerum* was in the literal sense, for example in his comment on the custom of the people of Cathay to eat roasted snakes and red ants the size of lobsters.[58]

Columbus may well have believed everything that he wrote about providentialism, messianism, and millenarianism; however, these concepts first acquired primal place in his writings beginning with the third voyage. This was also the period in his life when he began to see himself as the victim of an unkind world. He began to collect documentation to support his claims, which he rightly believed were being ignored. He wrote of his grievances (*agravios*). He eventually came to visualize himself no longer as the erstwhile successor of King David, as on his first voyage, but instead as a humble modern-day Job.

For these reasons, one must take great care in analyzing Columbus's affairs from this time on. There is an inherent danger in any attempt to separate the divine from the mundane in Columbus's thinking at any given time, especially so if this results in attributing primacy to one drive or the other. The religious drive was there, as were the mercantile and the political motivations. Columbus was no less a complex man than any other exceptional person. His motives cannot be judged as having been the same in 1481, or in 1486, as they were in 1498 or 1500.

Zamora attempted to resolve this Columbian enigma when she wrote, "In identifying economic and spiritual goals as the great motivators of his journey, Columbus was expressing a cardinal aspect of the medieval world view: the interrelatedness of the profane and the sacred, of gold and God."[59] Zamora may be correct in this assessment, but Columbus may not necessarily have been consciously aware of any such dichotomy.

The 1498 Letter on the Third Voyage

Any evaluation of the Lascasian holograph and the third letter in *El libro copiador* must consider the previously mentioned earliest known versions of the third voyage. Each of these earlier summaries has definite dates of writing, falling between 1501 and 1511. The versions found in Las Casas's holograph copy and in his *Historia*, as well as in *El libro copiador*, date from half a century or more later. Neither in the earlier versions—the *Libretto* and the *Oceani deca*—nor in the two more complete Lascasian and *El libro copiador* copies is there any definitive indication as to their respective authors' sources. Hernando, like the others, used now unidentifiable copies of his father's letters. All that is known is that all three of them—Martire, Las Casas, and Hernando—used either Columbus holographs or scribal copies and that they all purported to report Columbus's own words. Whether one, the other, or all three had access to Columbus holographs will probably never be known. It is possible that Columbus prepared several copies himself or, more likely, that all, including the originals, were written by scribes. Unlike the other two chroniclers, Las Casas never knew Columbus personally. With so many unknowns, it is presumptuous to ascribe primacy to the Las Casas holograph. All that can be said with any degree of certainty is that he and the scribe who copied the letter found in *El libro copiador* both worked from textually similar sources.

The modern reader should keep in mind the explanation that Las Casas offered for his difficulties in deciphering Columbus's writings: "And in this and other things that are in his *Ytinerarios* ["Journals"] he seems to be native to another language, because he does not fully grasp the significance of words in the Castilian language, nor in the manner of speaking it."[60] Zamora discussed at length the editorial voice of Las Casas in his *Diario* holograph. She noted, "Indeed, Las Casas's manipulation of the Columbian discourse is so extensive and complex that it seems more accurate to describe the *Diario* as a rewriting, not a transcription, of Columbus's journal."[61] According to Las Casas, his "manipulation" was, at least in some instances, the result of difficulties in deciphering the texts.

While acknowledging that Las Casas undertook the task of transcribing the journal, Zamora overlooked his above-expressed opinion on the difficulties he encountered in both reading and comprehending the generally awkward grammatical structure, as well as the Italianization of many of Columbus's Spanish words and their meanings. With the finding of *El libro copiador*, now available for purposes of comparison, it is safe to say that the editorial voice of Las Casas did not intervene to any important degree in the transcription of the 1498 letter. However, there is no way of knowing which of these two copies was first, nor from what copy each was made. One of them could even be a copy made from the other, but which was first? One indication might be found through a study of the stylistic construction of the two, to determine which was closest to Columbus's known usage of Italian and Portuguese constructions for Spanish words and sentence structure, as well as his extensive use of Portuguese nautical terms. Comprehending some of his phrasing even requires a knowledge of Italian. Zamora was perhaps on solid ground in her analysis of the Lascasian modifications of the earlier Columbian text, but the basic textual problems inherent in the unknown originals cannot be overlooked.

In the opening sentences to Columbus's letter on the third voyage he asserted: "The Holy Trinity moved Your Highnesses to this enterprise of the Indies and . . . made me its messenger thereof." This sentence unites three recurrent Columbian themes: divine guidance, the mercantilism of the "enterprise," and Columbus's self-styled anointment by God to open up the unknown world to Christianity. This passage, like so many other similar ones, has been given perhaps undue importance by those who read into it a primarily messianic impulse behind all of Columbus's accomplishments. In evaluating such statements, one must go beyond Columbus and Las Casas and give due consideration to the universal literary use in that era of such pious expressions. In relation to Columbus, they are frequently evidenced in the writings of Fernández de Oviedo, even earlier than in Las Casas. Bernáldez too found frequent evidence of the divine hand in Columbus's affairs. The not readily comprehensible was, per se, divinely ordained.

Many of the pious notations of this nature could have been what we would term today "boilerplate." Biblical citations in works on scientific subjects were the norm in a society theoretically guided on all such matters by the written word as found in the Christian Bible. Marc Bloch discussed the question of the frequent dichotomy found between what was written and what was done in feudal times. During Columbus's years in Spain the chancelleries of the Catholic Kings were headed by churchmen. As Bloch observed: "There came to be diffused over the documents of almost the whole feudal era that veneer of ingenuousness the evidence of which is seen in the preambles of so many enfranchisements . . . made to appear as inspired by simple piety. Since for a long period the writing of history itself was also in the hands of the clergy, the conventions of thought as much the conventions of literature combined to hide the cynical reality of human motives behind a sort of veil which was only finally to be torn asunder on the threshhold of modern times, by the harsh hands of a Commynes and a Machiavelli."[62]

It should also be recalled that in the late fifteenth century, few people had access to copies of the Bible; the few available were chained to lecterns in monasteries and churches. Martin Luther, a child when Columbus discovered America, liked to marvel at how unfamiliar the Bible had been even among the learned. He had not seen one himself until his university days, and that one had been nailed down![63]

Even the literate generally took their biblical citations from compendia that were far more readily available. Therefore it is not surprising that all of these early chroniclers of Columbus's voyages used the same basic citations, probably derived as often as not from the same sources—for Columbus, the *Ymago mundi* and the *Historia rerum*—but rarely, if ever, from personal readings in the Bible. Delno West categorically stated: "Christopher Columbus was a careful student of the Bible. He studied it systematically . . . the *Libro de las profecías* dictated by Columbus and compiled under his direction, is a notebook of Bible studies, a working file of source materials intended for his continuing study of and meditation on the Bible."[64] West's assumptions are highly debatable, and he even recognized that it was rare for laymen to read the Bible in the fifteenth century.

The letter on the third voyage has been of particular interest for Columbus's biographers because it is the first of his known letters to offer so many quotations from the Scriptures, early church fathers, and classical authors, offering what Rumeu de Armas termed his "mystical exaltations." In later years, in relation to a decline in standing at court, Columbus was to become more and more dependent on religious mysticism for support of his theories and accomplishments. As Zamora phrased it, "Over the course of the four voyages, the prophetic and the miraculous came to play an ever more important role in defining Columbus' experience of space."[65] The miraculous also provided justification for what had turned out to be a financial misadventure.

Columbus's earlier reports on his discoveries interested mostly cosmographers and geographers; this report instead has served in recent years as a point of departure for linguists, ethnicists, philosophers, eulogists, detractors, and deconstructionalists in their attempts to fit Columbus into their individual schemata. Rabasa considered one aspect of this modern multidisciplinary approach: "[Jacques] Heers manifests a tendency in traditional scholarship to separate the image of a modern Columbus armed with a 'rational' or 'scientific' geography from the image of a medieval Columbus endowed with a 'mystical' or 'poetic' imagination."[66] He went on to note, "Instead of construing the typicality of the explorer by measuring his accounts against the discourse of the conqueror or the missionary, we ought to consider the specificity of Columbus' situation in which he encountered unprecedented people and natural phenomena."[67] It is precisely with such "specificity" that this critique is concerned. Neither "unprecedented people" nor "natural phenomena" were found by Columbus, but he did find much, if not all, that had been speculated about for centuries. What he provided was the actual geographical locus—the Americas.

This letter in particular recommends itself to the study of those elaborate subtleties of thought and expression that many read into Columbus's letters. It was in the letter on the third voyage that Columbus first used the words "another world."[68] Herein he also described the possible finding of the Terrestrial Paradise. The semantic possibilities are innumerable. The reader must look first to what was actually said, together with the immediate circumstances under which it was expressed. As previously noted, the 1498 letter opened with phrases of exaltation: "The Holy Trinity moved Your Highnesses to this enterprise of the Indies and through His infinite goodness made me its messenger thereof."[69] This is immediately followed by the first of his many listings of the wrongs (*agravios*) done to him over the years of waiting until "finally, Your Highnesses determined that this work be undertaken." After reciting the many marvels that he had found on his first two voyages, he returned to the subject of his complaint: "All of this was of no use, in order that some people, who had a mind to, gave a start to malign the business, nor [did they] go along with talk of the service to Our Lord of saving so many souls, nor to say that this was due to the greatness of Your Highnesses, of a better position reached until today than by any prince, because the labour and expense was for the spiritual and temporal." He went on to liken the accomplishments of his monarchs to those of Solomon, Alexander the Great, and "Nero" Caesar. After further praise of the monarchs for their conquest of the Moors, he returned to the subject of his grievances. At this point in his letter he said: "Nor was it worthwhile to say that I never read that princes of Castile had ever won land outside of their [borders], and that this here is *another world* [emphasis added] from that in which Romans and Alexander and Greeks, worked with great efforts to gain."[70]

There are slight, yet important, differences in the version of this last statement in the letter in *El libro copiador.* The word "land" was omitted, as was "this" before "here." This passage continued with an indirect criticism of the Spanish monarchs: "Not to speak of the present of the kings of Portugal, who had the heart to maintain Guinea and to discover in her, and who expended gold and many people . . . and also have dared to conquer in Africa, and maintain the effort at Ceuta, Tangiers and Arcilla, and Alcazar, and to continue making war on the Moors, and all of this at great cost, [so as] only to do princely things, serve God, and increase their dominion."[71]

In the above passages the stress is definitely on the temporal goals over the spiritual—the territorial expansions of both Spain and Portugal. This outburst was brought on by his often expressed fear that the Catholic Kings would not persevere in their efforts to explore and settle these lands unless sufficient gold was soon found to recompense them. As previously noted, the monarchs were financially overextended at this time, being engaged in wars with France on two fronts, on their common border as well as on the Italian mainland, where they were joined by their allies in the League of Venice. They were also expending great amounts of energy and money on the marriages of their son and their daughter, marriages designed to strengthen Spain's international position.

Needless to say, Columbus's use of the expression "another world" has excited a great deal of interest over the ages. It must be noted that different authors have translated *otro* alternatively as "another" and "other." Did this simply refer to an otherness as compared with the lands discovered by Alexander and others or to another previously unknown land? Or, did it mean "another world" than the one then known of three continents, therefore an acknowledgment that he had found not Asia but a new world, a fourth continent? Zamora stressed the difference between the concepts of a new world and an other world. Gil took this phrase to mean that "we should not believe that here Columbus thought he had discovered a new world, but instead a world already known by the ancients but one that they hadn't been able to conquer."[72] As noted above, Verde, a contemporary and personal friend of Columbus's, did understand the phrase empirically; it meant for him an unknown part of the world opposite to the European continent. Columbus developed his concepts through his readings, together with his experience gained over the years of discovery. The fact that he might, for example, have given one meaning to the otherness in this letter and a more clearly spiritual one in his *Libro de las profecías* does not mean that the words necessarily meant the same thing in 1498 as they came to mean to him in 1502.

The Naming of the New Lands

Columbus said that he named the first land seen on this voyage "Trinidad." He seems to have been clear as to his reason: "A sailor climbed the topmast, and saw to the West three mountains together . . . I arrived at a cape that I named Galea, after having named the island Trinidad."[73] The archaic definition of "Galea" is a Roman helmet. In his *Historia*, Las Casas reported this arrival somewhat differently: "A sailor from Huelva . . . named Alonso Pérez, climbed the topmast and saw land to the West, and it was fifteen leagues away, and what appeared to him to be three knolls and three mountains. These are his words. He gave to this land the name of the Island of Trinidad, because he had determined that the first land that he should discover would be so named."[74] Either Las Casas was emending the data now found in his holograph or this added explanation came from a copy of the journal.

Morison copied this part from Las Casas accurately, but he offered a completely different explanation for the name for the cape, which Columbus "called Cabo de la Galera [galley] from a great rock which it had, which from a distance looked like a galley under sail."[75] This passage is not in the Las Casas holograph or in Hernando's *Historie*. The holograph does give the name of the cape as "Galea." Cecil Jane also transcribed the cape's name in the letter of the third voyage as "la Galea," but in a footnote he noted the "Galera" version was given in Las Casas's *Historia*.[76] In the latter, the name given to Cape Galera is as Morison gave it.[77] Thacher had earlier accepted "Galera" while noting that both Hernando and Fernández de Navarrete used "Galea."[78] The Sanz facsimile of the Las Casas holograph shows that the word was originally written as *galera*, but the *-ra* had been overwritten, now appearing as a smudged *-a*. There is no mention of great rocks or galleys in this manuscript.[79] This is one of those cases in which paleography does not support a reading by the biographers.

Wilford claimed, "The three high mountains that he sighted inspired him to give the island the name Trinidad, for the Holy Trinity."[80] Fernández-Armesto went one step farther: "Columbus was going through a phase of particularly strong devotion to the Holy Trinity. . . . When . . . he sighted land . . . in the form of three low but distinct hills . . . he was pardonably struck by the potency of the coincidence . . . in token of which . . . he named the island Trinidad." He went on to describe this as "a nicely calculated piece of theological semiotics."[81]

The use of alternative readings of the word "Trinidad" ("Trinity") presents a good example of allegorical interpretation or "theological semiotics." Scholars in this field are well within literary bounds as long as they advise their readers at some point that Columbus had probably named the island Trinidad because from the sea it was first seen as three mountain peaks. The fact that the next ten toponyms given by Columbus were each physically descriptive should not be ignored in favor of only one name with possible religious significance. As previously pointed out, the first accounts of the third voyage by writers other than Columbus never even mentioned the name of this island, although each made note of the three mountains. In a similar manner a semiotic relation to the Garden of Eden has been discovered today in his later choice of the word "Gardens," equated to Eden.

A strict reading of Columbus's own letter indicates that Columbus named these two geographical features by words descriptive of their physical appearances—a triad of mountain peaks and a helmet-shaped cape. The next name that he gave was to a point that he named Punta Arenal ("Sandy Point"). He then stated, "From this point of the Arenal there is a large mouth two leagues wide from West to East, the Island of Trinidad with the land of the Gracia." This reference is the first made in this letter to the island of Gracia, in reality the Venezuelan mainland. He came to believe it to be an island because of the extent of the Gulf of Paria. According to Las Casas, Columbus first named the island "Santa," then changed the name to "Gracia" before finally naming it by its Indian name, "Paria." The next point of land that he named was the Aguja ("Needle"). His following toponyms were Jardines ("Gardens"); Ballena Bay ("Whale Bay"); a strait, Boca de la Sierpe ("Mouth of the Serpent"); "Cape Boto because it was bulky and blunt" ("Cape Wineskin"); the islands of Caracol ("Shell"), Delfín ("Dolphin"), Dragón Boca ("Dragon Mouth"), and Bellaforma ("Beautiful Shape"); and Cape Lapa ("Cape Barnacle").[82]

Zamora found that Columbus's ultimate goal was "marked by such spiritually charged names as Isla de la Trinidad, Tierra de Gracia, and Paraíso Terrenal." She noted what she believed was "a similar textual cartography . . . found in Mandeville's Travels, perhaps the most widely read travel book of the Middle Ages and one Columbus knew well."[83] In a discussion of what she termed a medieval "correspondence of sexual desire and the paradise image as an inaccessible ideal," Zamora found that Columbus instead treated the "paradise theme in the context of mercantile and conquest literature. Closer to Columbus's own ambitions and dearer to what we know of his reading tastes was the account of Marco Polo's travels in the far East, a keystone text for Columbus during the period in which he formulated the nature and goals of the enterprise of the Indies."[84] Unfortunately for Zamora's proposition, Columbus's prediscovery reading taste not only is not known today but also is extremely unlikely to have included either Sir John Mandeville's *Travels* or Marco Polo's *Millione*. His source in the *Ymago mundi* is indisputable.

Columbus's use of the prefixes "de la" before "Trinidad" might have been seen as expressly indicative of a spiritual connection were it not for the fact that it was his custom to use these prefixes, as in the earlier designation of the "*cabo a que dije de la Galea*." Unlike Sanz's transcription and the above Zamora version, the holograph did not capitalize either "isla" or "trinidad." The words in the Lascasian holograph, transcribed by Sanz as "Trinidad" and "tierra de Gracia" and given by Zamora as "Tierra de Gracia," warrant careful paleographic study, since their initial appearance in folio 3 does not clearly indicate "tierra," and the word transcribed as "Gracia" has seven and possibly eight letters. These same words—"Trinidad," "tierra," and "gracia"—are, however, clearly legible as they appear in the following folio of the manuscript. The capitalizations of "tierra" and "paraiso terrenal" are emendations of the original text; they project a perhaps false sense of speciality to the use of these words.

Religious Symbolism in the 1498 Letter on the Third Voyage

Zamora noted, "The profoundly religious symbolism of such names suggests that the phrase 'otro mundo,' which has so exercised scholars of the Discovery, has strong mystical connotations, as it does in the discourses of pilgrimage."[85] Rabasa was presumably referring to Columbus's use of the phrase *otro mundo* rather than to a new world when he wrote, in agreement with Zamora, "Columbus's use of the term *new world* does not refer any longer to one more discovery among others, as in the literature of the exploration of Africa and the Canary Islands, but to a notion with aesthetic, historical, and mystical dimensions."[86] Todorov noted, "At sea, all the signs indicate land's proximity, since that is Columbus' desire. On land, all the signs reveal the presence of gold: here, too, his conviction is determined in advance." He emphasized this further by adding: "Las Casas remarks with some justice apropos of another such example: 'It is a wonder to see how, when a man greatly desires something and strongly attaches himself to it in his imagination, he has the impression at every moment that whatever he hears and sees argues in favor of that thing.'"[87] This statment is very much to the point for some scholars!

The context in which *otro mundo* was used by Columbus indicates a possibly different interpretation than that given by Zamora. In one

passage Columbus made the more prosaic point that it was unfair
to judge him by how he would have acted had he been sent "to Sicily
or to a city or two under settled government" when in fact he went
"to the Indies to conquer a people, warlike and numerous, and with
customs and beliefs very different from ours . . . I have brought
under the dominion of the king and queen, our sovereigns, *another
world* [emphasis added], whereby Spain, which was called poor, is
now most rich."[88] First of all, this letter, written in 1500, cannot be
said to imply that the "warlike and numerous people" were those of
the Gran Khan, whose reputedly great empire was not a suitable
target for the puny forces at Columbus's command. On the other
hand, the making of Spain "now most rich" is a far cry from any
mystical discourse on the subject of the earthly paradise, unless one
relates anagogically "most rich" with "earthly paradise." Such a
connection would probably have required a more imaginative mind
than Columbus's.

The works of Columbus, like all other works from the time of
Homer on, have been read variously on one or more of the four
classic levels. The first is the historical or literal level, which in
Columbus's case is one in which it is often difficult to determine
exactly what he meant in many given instances. Many of the
Columbian studies of today prefer interpretations based on the
second level, the allegorical or spiritual level, sometimes alone and
other times in combination with the third level, the anagogic or
mystical. The fourth level, the tropological or figurative, is discerned
by some of today's scholars in the underlying moral tones of many
of his more pious writings. The last three levels are popular among
current readings of Columbus, which generally follow faithfully one
or more of these classic forms but often at the expense of the first—
the historical.

The *Libro de las profecías* presents in its introductory paragraphs
this fourfold manner of interpreting the Bible as taught by Saint
Thomas Aquinas (his *Quadriga*) and as explained in verse by Jean
Charlier de Gerson (1363–1429) in his *Decretis*.[89] Columbus did not
annotate this passage in his copy of Gerson's work. The problem
with accepting these as explaining Columbian exegesis is that the
appropriate quotations are in paragraphs written in the hand of

Columbus's friend and mentor Father Gaspar Gorricio, not in Columbus's handwriting. Later, Nicholas of Lyra is invoked in support of the book's hermeneutics. Even if Columbus had composed these entries, which is questionable, his knowledge of such figures as Nicholas de Lyra would have most likely come from his readings of compendia rather than from any familiarity with the works of the cited authors. Unlike West and August Kling, most other historians have carefully steered clear of the *Libro de las profecías* for the obvious reason that it is next to impossible to determine who wrote or dictated the various parts. Evaluating fairly West and Kling's ambitious study of this work is difficult, since their extensive introduction is based primarily on the authors' ready acceptance of most of the Columbian myths as factual.

John Gardner pointed out: "In the Middle Ages people took it for granted that the very best poetry is metaphysical; that is, the poet sought to understand and express man's nature, his place in the universe, his meaning. As in medieval philosophy and political theory—as in metaphysical speculation in any age, and as in all great poetry—this meant what is now sometimes casually dismissed as 'argument by analogy.' If we understand the exact relationship between gold and lead, between Christ and the Virgin, so this argument runs, we can determine the proper relationship between, say, a king and his subjects."[90] The problem for today's biographer lies in making a plausible determination of the intellectual dimensions of Columbus so as to situate his metaphysical conceptions within the context of the times in which he lived. To paraphrase Goethe, Columbus's virtues were his own attainment, whereas his delusions were infections from the age.

What makes such differences interesting is that the words and phrases in question were used at the very beginning of the discovery of the South American continent. They have provided the grounds for the many differing interpretations of the remaining data, not only in this important letter but for the total image of Columbus. As has already been noted, as the years went by, Columbus himself lapsed more and more into mystical interpretations of the major events in his life. His letters show that Columbus's mysticism increased in direct proportion to the steady decline in his position at court. The careful study of his use of such expressions undoubtedly provides guidelines to the evolution of the persona of Columbus. Reading too much into them at any given point in his life, however, may be misleading.

Preparations for the Third Voyage

There is a certain amount of confusion as to the makeup of, as well as the avowed purpose for, the fleet that Columbus took with him on this third journey. As previously noted, two supply ships had been sent ahead to the colony in the month before Columbus sailed. He originally intended to go with five more vessels, but at the last minute he purchased a sixth vessel, one that happened to be half-owned by the Spanish monarchs. Reluctance on the part of the Spaniards to migrate was seen by Morison and others as the reason for the pardoning of certain classes of criminals if they signed on for the colony, yet the same offer had been made on the first voyage and would be repeated in 1503.[91] It was to become the custom for some of the later colonial powers to use what became known in English as "colonial transportation" in order to empty their local jails. The rosters for the third voyage list ten criminals convicted for homicides, four of whom were gypsies—"Egyptians"—two of them women.[92]

Columbus was authorized in June 1497 to make this voyage, yet it took him until May 1498 to ready for sailing. It seems strange that after so long a time there should have been a last-minute need to purchase another vessel. Although Columbus was authorized to take 300 settlers, the rosters for seven of the eight ships that sailed that year listed only 226, of which 77 were soldiers.[93] Early on the outbound voyage Columbus dispatched three of the caravels directly to Española while he continued with the other three on a more southerly course to seek lands closer to the equator. One of the three headed for Española was captained by Pedro de Arana, cousin of Columbus's mistress; the second was captained by Columbus's agent Alonso Sánchez de Carvajal and the third by the Admiral's cousin Juan Antonio Columbo.

Strangely, Columbus had divided up the supplies being carried to the colony between the five originally provisioned vessels, with the result that the supplies he carried were spoiled due to his delay in reaching his final destination. Since the original five vessels of this fleet were provisioned before the sixth vessel was purchased, only two of the vessels that went with Columbus were carrying supplies for the colony. Hernando identified the sixth boat by the Italian name *Vacchina*.[94] For some reason most historians have given the Spanish translation as *Vacqueños*, in the plural.[95] This was the largest of the three vessels that went with Columbus to the south.

The two squadrons separated off Gomara. It appears likely that had Columbus's plans for exploration been known before sailing, the three vessels destined for Española could have sailed there independently. It would also have been logical to have had these three carry all of the supplies as well as all of the colonists headed for that island. This could have been done by sending the largest of the vessels ahead while keeping the three smaller ones for exploration. Columbus repeatedly said that only small vessels were effective for this kind of coastal work.

The actual division of the fleet was typical of the incongruities to be found in so many of Columbus's actions. As Sale pointed out, the Las Casas abstract of the log for this voyage noted that he "had lied to his crew about where he was going, not daring 'to tell them in Castile that he was setting out with the intention of discovering, lest they set up obstacles and ask more pay than he could give.'"[96] Dissimulation was a Columbus trait.

Before news from Columbus's voyage had reached Spain, the Spanish ambassador in London wrote in July 1498 in regard to Cabot's projected return voyage to the Americas, "The route they are following leads to the possessions of your highness."[97] Columbus had already received, from his English friend John Day, information about Cabot's first voyage during which the latter claimed he had discovered a continent. Cabot had been back in England for almost a year by the time Columbus set sail in 1498 on his own voyage to discover a continent. England authorized Cabot to sail again in February 1498 with six ships, the same number that Columbus, with similar purpose, sailed with in May of that year. In addition, Portugal sent out Gaspar Côrte-Real in 1498 on a voyage of exploration that reached Newfoundland, discovered the year before by

Cabot. On these later voyages, Côrte-Real was sent on the northern route, whereas Cabral followed a southern route that took him inadvertently to the Brazilian mainland. The race was now on.

There is the question as to whether Cabot was merely imitating Columbus or whether Columbus's third voyage came to be viewed as imperative by the Catholic Kings because of the competition from England with Cabot and from Portugal with Côrte-Real. Morison was chronologically correct when he stated that Cabot sailed after Columbus had traversed the Atlantic twice. However, Cabot had been authorized by Henry VII in March 1496 to seek islands and lands in the western Atlantic, and he did sail before Columbus returned from his second voyage. That the Spanish monarchs were concerned was evidenced by a letter to their ambassador in London; dated March 28, 1496, this letter asked him for news about Cabot's projected first voyage.[98] The interest shown in Cabot's plans indicates that both the monarchs and Columbus very likely took these voyages into consideration when making their own plans to conserve and expand their newly found territories in the Indies.

Columbus had more than a passing interest in Cabot's first voyage. In the fall of 1497 John Day had responded as best he could to an inquiry by Columbus about Cabot's voyage to Newfoundland. The letter clearly states that Columbus had asked for a copy of Cabot's chart, which Day had been unable to get. He did, however, manage to send Columbus place-names from the chart, distances traveled, and other information.[99] Fernández-Armesto saw this inquiry as having been merely "to supplement his reading" about "cosmographic tradition."[100] The Phillipses were apparently unaware of the Catholic Kings' letter to the ambassador in London when they wrote, "The Spanish monarchs may not have known about Cabot's voyages."[101] They did recognize the fact that at least Columbus knew about the first voyage of "Jacobo Caboto." Sale held a different opinion: "In the two years of his wait, though Colón almost certainly didn't know it . . . [o]n June 24, 1497 . . . Giovanni Cabotto [sic], sailing for King Henry VII of England . . . sighted the coast of what we may assume to be northern New England."[102] James Williamson's study of the Cabot family noted, "In all contemporary references in Italian his Christian name appears as Zuan or one of its variants."[103]

As shown, Columbus did know of Cabot's first voyage, and the monarchs knew of both his first and his second voyages.

Las Casas noted that when the monarchs agreed to Columbus's proposal for a third voyage, they specified that there should be 330 salaried subjects of the Crown on Española, among whom were to be 20 government officials as well as 30 Spanish women. Las Casas confused some of the details in these decrees with the earlier decree of April 10, 1495, authorizing the first colonists to go to Española.[104] Columbus intended to have the state finance storekeepers who would be controlled by price regulation. Priests were also to be sent to provide religious services for both the colonists and the Indians. Four women and two priests are on the rosters known today. Donkeys were included for the first time. Columbus was authorized to raise the number of salaried colonists to 500 if he thought it necessary. At the same time, a decree was issued permitting those who wanted to go without pay to do so.

Las Casas said that it was at the request of Columbus that a decree was issued granting a general pardon for prisoners, male and female, who wanted to go to the colony. Those condemned to death were to serve without pay for two years and others for one year. Another decree ordered all of the nation's justices to send to the colonies all delinquents who had been condemned either to exile or to work in the mines. This was not done but has contributed to the myth that Española was peopled by criminals. Las Casas said that these last two decrees were issued on June 22, 1497. Those taking advantage of these colonization decrees were to receive title to state lands and improvements after living for four years on the land. This applied only to fenced-in properties; all other land was to be held in common. At this time the Crown was definitely promoting the colonization of the Indies.

Columbus's Return to Española in 1498

Sailing north from the island of Margarita, Columbus sighted the islands of Beata and Alta Vela off the southern coast of Española on August 19. He sent the ships' boats to the mainland to contact Indians to carry a message to his brother Bartolomé, who then came to Beata. This explains how Columbus was able to find Santo Domingo, the new island capital that had been founded during his absence. At this time Roldán was in open revolt against the younger Columbus brothers. Las Casas and Hernando are the primary sources for the events that transpired on the island during the Admiral's absence. Fernández de Oviedo provided additional information, mostly received from oral tradition. These three supplied the only independent versions of Bartolomé's and Diego's problems with the Taino Indians as well as with the settlers. Columbus, of course, had no direct influence on what happened during his absence. Columbus's letter to the nurse of Prince Juan is the primary source for what occurred after his return.

Columbus's correspondence at this time began with the letter, discussed earlier in this chapter, that he wrote shortly after his arrival in Santo Domingo in August but was only able to send to Spain in October. Las Casas provided copies of fragments of several other letters written at unspecified times between 1498 and 1500. Later, after his arrest by Francisco de Bobadilla, Columbus wrote two letters that are now known from their copies in *El libro copiador.* Las Casas has also supplied copies of Columbus's exchange of letters with Roldán; these trace the course of their negotiations to end the revolt.

The key letter for the second phase of the third voyage, however, is the one Columbus wrote to the nurse of Prince Juan. Of the various copies known, the one most generally cited is the Las Casas copy, although another one, in the Paris Codex, antedates the former by half a century. This latter copy was placed in Columbus's *Book of Privileges* in 1502 and was first published by Stevens. As Thacher pointed out, "[It] contains an important passage omitted in them [the Las Casas and Fernández de Navarrete versions], and a careful rendering of other passages which in Las Casas and Navarrete are more or less obscure."[105] The other copies lack the introductory paragraph: "Copy of a letter that the Admiral of the indies sent to the nurse (*alma*) of Prince Juan of Castile, in the year MD, coming a prisoner from the Indies." Spotorno published a copy in 1823 from a manuscript that has since been lost. Fernández de Navarrete worked from the Spotorno text. Modern-day U.S. biographers rely almost exclusively on the Lascasian versions.

There are more omissions than Thacher's statement would indicate. The first sixty lines of the Paris Codex copy of the letter contain eleven additional words or phrases, as well as one paragraph not in the Lascasian copy. These same lines, depending on how one counts, contain over seventy differences with the Las Casas copy used by Consuelo Varela. Some of the differences, seemingly insignificant in themselves, either change the meaning or make the content more intelligible.

One example involves the pearls that Columbus had located off the coast of today's Venezuela. It is claimed that at the time, he was accused of hiding these from the monarchs, the inference being that he was keeping them for himself. The Las Casas version of the letter merely stated that after arranging to have more collected, "this came out as many other things."[106] However, in the Codex this last sentence is prefaced with, "If I did not write about it to Their Highnesses it was because I wished to have done [so] first about the gold."[107] In other words, he was withholding the information until after he could give them the far more important news about the recent finding of important gold deposits on Española.

In the Las Casas version Columbus wrote, "When I went to Paria, I found almost half of the people of Española in revolt." The Codex more logically gives this as, "When I came from Paria . . ." Columbus went on to write that there "were [on Paria] disturbance[s] and suspicion, [but] no more damage." Las Casas followed this last sentence with the statement: "The Indians said later the news of six other caravels." According to the Codex: "The Indians told about many others against the cannibals, and in Paria, and then the news of six other caravels." This is an obvious reference to Columbus's repeated complaint that the crews of the ships of the Andalusian voyages that followed his to the South American continent had made implacable enemies of the natives.

There is one seemingly insignificant difference that perhaps casts a different light on Columbus's supposed mystical discovery and his concept of a new world. The Lascasian manuscript provides a sentence that can be, and has been, read as a metaphorical reference to the Terrestrial Paradise: "I made a new voyage to the skies and world that until then was hidden; and if it is not held there [Spain] in esteem such as the others [lands] of the Indies, it is no marvel, because it appears that it was a result of my effort."[108] The "skies" have been seen as paradise, and the "world" as the lands of Paria. The Codex copy presents a quite different slant: "I made a new voyage to the *new sky* [emphasis added] and world that until then was hidden and if it is not held etc."[109] The "new sky" and the "world" were one—his mainland discovery. Note that whereas a semicolon has been interjected in the first version, in the second the sentence runs together. It was not the thought of a Terrestrial Paradise that was being rejected but the value of the newly discovered "other" lands as compared with Española.

It is not the purpose of this critique to analyze the many differences between these letters. The above examples are sufficient to indicate that Columbus's own copy, which he had purposefully placed in his *Book of Privileges*, is not only chronologically but also probably textually the closest to the original and, as such, should take precedence over the Lascasian versions in studies of the third voyage.

Morison, in his account of the third voyage, drew heavily on Las Casas and Hernando. His greatest interest was in the course of events after the Admiral's return to Española. All of the early accounts differ greatly as to the timing of many of the more important of these, making it difficult to sort them out, especially so because none of the participants left their own accounts. Columbus did deal with the opposition by Roldán and others but was more concerned with self-justification than with providing a chronological report.

The only direct quotations given by Wilford were emended to the point that it is not possible to determine which version of the letter he used for his source.[110] The Phillipses used the Jane translation, which is a more free than literal one and which was apparently made from the de Lollis transcription in the *Raccolta*. Fernández-Armesto wrote of the third voyage in a generalized manner that required no identification of his sources. Sale, more specific, drew information from both Las Casas and Hernando. He attached greater importance than the others to the significance to Columbus and Spain of finding substantial gold deposits in the Cordillera

Central. While doing so, he drew attention to what he viewed as Morison's downplaying, or misunderstanding, of its significance.

The important events that took place over the years that Bartolomé was in charge of the colony included further pacifying the Indians, discovering important gold deposits, finding the means to exploit those deposits, and handling the colonists' discontent, which grew into open mutiny. As far as Columbus was concerned, the gold and the revolt where of most importance; he said, "When I came from Paria I found almost half of the people of Española in revolt." According to Columbus, at this time the settlers were afraid that the monarchs would not send any more ships to their aid.

Ojeda had stopped off at Española on his way back to Spain from his voyage to the Venezuelan coast. He had been with Columbus on the second voyage, and now he was accompanied by La Cosa and Vespucci. All three of these men were to receive substantial royal favor over the years to come. Ojeda claimed at this time that he had been sent by the monarchs with "promises and gifts." He also brought the disquieting, albeit incorrect, news that Queen Isabel was near death. When Columbus forced him to leave, he threatened to return with "more ships and men." The Admiral reported that further complications arose with Vicente Yáñez Pinzón, who arrived at this time with four ships.

Columbus compressed the timing for these events, which he reported as occuring simultaneously. However, Ojeda reached Española on September 5, 1499, over a year after Columbus's own return to the island. Yáñez did not arrive until June 23, 1500. From other accounts it appears that whereas Ojeda did cause Columbus considerable trouble, there were no such problems with Yáñez. It is possible that Ojeda's troublemaking was at least in part a result of his knowlege that the monarchs had already decided to replace Columbus as governor. Perhaps he was also influenced by the fact that Columbus had opposed his taking a load of brazilwood to sell in Spain. It appears unusual, considering the reported troubles, that Columbus should write, on two previously unknown letters, dated February 3, 1500, "It was written to send with the ships of Hojeda."[111]

Ojeda had left Spain for the Indies only eight days before Bobadilla was instructed, on May 26, to go to Española to replace Columbus, although Bobadilla did not sail for another fourteen months. As Vigneras pointed out, Bobadilla sailed one month after Ojeda's return to Spain, which caused Vigneras to ask: "Was this part of a preconceived plan? Was it decided to wait for Hojeda's [*sic*] arrival and find from him the true state of affairs in Española. . . . Did it really take Bobadilla fourteen months to prepare for his mission?"[112] Ojeda's own behavior while on Española would seem to support the theory that Bobadilla was waiting on Ojeda's return.

All early sources agree that after the problems with Roldán had been settled, Adrián de Múgica started another revolt, this one put down by Roldán. A document giving a partial roster of the crews accompanying Ojeda lists Don Fernando Ladrón de Guevara, a member of a prominent family.[113] He had been entrusted to Ojeda for training. He is listed as captain of a caravel captured off the coast of Africa on the outbound journey from Spain. Las Casas and others were not able to reconcile acts attributed to him with other acts reported on Española after Ojeda's departure, the assumption being that this scion of a noble house would not have been left behind. In the Codex copy of the letter to the nurse, Columbus included a paragraph not found in the Lascasian copy: "This Adrian as is shown had sent Don Fernando [Ladrón] to Xaragua to join some of his followers and there there was a battle with the justice of the peace [Roldán], where there arose discord to death, it didn't in effect go farther; the justice of the peace took him and part of his group, and the case was such that he would have condemned him if I had not prevented it."[114]

Columbus later wrote of Adrián, "I had intended to never touch the hair of anybody, and with tears that couldn't be held back to this one I could not keep it as I had thought due to his ingratitude: I wouldn't have done less to my brother if he had wanted to kill me and rob the dominion that my king and queen had given me to guard." Las Casas said that the day Bobadilla arrived, the news was brought to his ship, as he lay to offshore waiting for the morning breeze to enter the port, that during that week "seven Spanish men had been hung" and that in the fort of Santo Domingo were five more waiting to be hung.[115] Las Casas named "Fernando Guevara" as one of the latter. Morison offered a more melodramatic picture: "As Bobadilla entered the harbor his eyes were affronted by the spectacle of a gallows on which were hanging the corpses of seven rebel Spaniards."[116]

Referring to another of the unusual happenings at this time, Columbus wrote, after the arrival of Bobadilla, "It softened me to know of the friars that your Highnesses had certainly sent." In this and other letters he referred to the fact that he had frequently asked both for a person to take charge of justice on the island and for friars to serve the disorderly settlers. Yet, in this case, the friars were three Franciscans who wrote Cisneros and accused Columbus of trying to become the "Pharoah of the Indies"; they asked that neither he nor any other Italians be allowed back on the island.[117] Having arrived with Bobadilla, they had had little time in which to develop such a strong objection to the Admiral. It seems more likely that they arrived with either prejudices or even instructions to find fault with Columbus.

Columbus wrote that Bobadilla was sworn in as governor on the day after his arrival: "[He] made officers and executions and proclaimed gold franchises . . . and all sorts of other things for twenty years . . . and published that I and my brothers had to be sent in irons. . . . This was all on the second day after he arrived, as I said, and [while] I was absent far away [in Vega], without knowing about him or his arrival."[118] Columbus went on to explain that he took these threats to be more like the vain ones made by Ojeda or some "of the others" and that therefore, in order to stall for time, he protested that his royal orders took precedence over those of Bobadilla. These initial measures taken by Bobadilla concerning the gold and division of Indian labor were later rescinded by the Crown.

Las Casas was never sure whether it was Columbus in 1496 or his brother Bartolomé during the Admiral's absence who had started the system of *repartamientos*, the assignment of Indians to individual Spaniards to serve them as farm laborers. This measure was originally intended to be an alternative to the Indians' payment of tribute, which had not been forthcoming. In a letter to the Crown, Columbus blamed the later abuses of the system on Bobadilla. Morison claimed that Columbus established the system as a means of placating the rebellious Roldán.[119] This is inaccurate.

The words *repartamiento* and *encomienda* have become confused with slavery in the minds of many of Columbus's biographers. The system of *repartamientos* was developed in the Middle Ages in Spain during the Reconquest. As Ots Capdequí pointed out, this system encompassed three important elements: the historic, the economic, and the juridic. Originally, during the Reconquest, it required two stages. First was the right granted by the Crown to its servitors to acquire the right to occupy specified lands. However, only when "the land was populated, was the juridical relation of domain, the seigneurial, consolidated with respect to the land so occupied."[120]

As has been previously pointed out, in 1495 and again in 1497 the Crown specified for Española that on lands assigned to individuals by the Crown, the lands to become hereditary were only those on which there were "the houses that they made, and the lands that they worked, and the properties that they planted." In other words, the title did not give the ownership; the land's use and occupation did so. Again, following the custom dating from the Middle Ages, once such ownership was established, be it in Spain on lands formerly occupied by the Moors or on Española, the occupants of the lands automatically became vassals of the occupiers.

The *encomienda*—"commend," historically, the entrusting of oneself to a protector—now came into play. This transfer of legal attributes could be personal only or could include the land of both freedmen and boundmen. Over the centuries, these practices assumed complexities of law; customs varied greatly from one region to another. These could include permanent servitude, part-time labor, and/or payment in kind or money.[121] Since the Indians were seminomadic, the only means for assuring the landholder of labor to work his lands was to have the caciques provide tribal members in lieu of the earlier agreed-upon tribute in gold.

It is perhaps overly facile to see the development and evolution of this system on Española as merely the assignment of servitors, who became essentially slaves. The Spanish monarchs did specify both the labors to be performed by and the compensation to be made to the Indians. Duties required in Spain—of military service and farm labor—were modified to meet the needs of the new colony for laborers in the mines. The principal of primary attachment to the land and its use applied also to the colonists. In 1526 a royal decree ordered the authorities on the island to prohibit "the married settlers there to abandon them for the attraction of the new discoveries [New Spain], under the penalty of death and loss of property." Failure to understand the internationally institutionalized commend system has contributed to the growth over the centuries of the "Black Legend" of Spain.

The manner of populating the newly acquired territories also has revelance for the question of slavery of the Indians. It is today politically correct to see Columbus as the one who instituted this practice and the saintly Queen Isabel as the one who opposed it. Actually, as Columbus wrote in detail in his letters, he was only suggesting the then legally correct enslavement of hostile natives and, in doing so, was closely following the patterns established by the Portuguese in Africa and the Spaniards in the Canary Islands.

The queen came down hard on the practice when Columbus gave some three hundred slaves to Roldán and his followers as part of his peace agreement with them. These slaves returned with their new masters to Spain in 1499. The queen became angered and is quoted as saying that the Admiral had no right to give her vassals to anybody. On June 20, 1500, she ordered them returned to Española, but by then it was too late: they had already been absorbed into the community. Three days later the person ordered to send them back was able to locate only twenty-one of them; one was too sick to send back, and another, a young girl, asked to stay in Spain. In this case the queen's objection was to Columbus's usurpation of authority, not to slavery per se.

Las Casas blamed Columbus for having initiated the practice of sending Indians to be sold "in the Canaries, the Azores and Cabo Verde and wherever they could be well sold." There is no question that he sent five hundred in 1495 and three hundred in 1496 to Spain and later gave Roldán and his followers three hundred to take back with them. There is no other report of such shipments. Far more people had been enslaved already by the Spaniards on the Canary Islands, which were under the jurisdiction of Castile—that is, Isabel.

The real problem with the Indian slaves as far as Spain was concerned was not the country's violation of human rights, as this would be termed today, but its inability to absorb the slaves. They were useful only in the colonies themselves. Slave-owning was almost a novelty in Spain; the supply of peasants to work the landed estates was, if anything, overabundant at that time. The Moors, who provided the supply of artisans and much of the farm labor, were not finally expelled from Spain until 1614.[122] A corollary was the constant opposition to the emigration to the Americas expressed by the grandees, who feared an artificially created labor shortage. The Church was a major beneficiary of the commend system in Europe and Española. Las Casas and Fray Antonio Montesinos drew the attention of the Spanish body politic to the often inhuman abuses committed against the native population of Española, but even they never questioned the legal and, to them, the morally justifiable right to enslave certain categories of people and make vassals of others. The Church did not condone excesses but did accept slavery.

The third voyage, with its discovery of the South American continent, should have been one of utmost satisfaction for Columbus. On his return to Española he found the long-sought gold deposits. The Crown's investment in the discovery and colonization of the Indies was now fully justified in his eyes. Yet, unknown to him, the monarchs had already determined on a change in administrative policy. The problems with Roldán may well have aggravated their discontent with the manner in which Columbus and his brothers were administering the colony, but it is more likely that they felt the time had come to assume direct control of the enterprise. Whether Bobadilla exceeded his instructions in sending the Columbus brothers home in chains will probably never be known, but the effect of this act was no less shattering on the prisoners. It was a perfect way to demonstrate to all concerned that the break was clean. Regardless of the terms of the *Capitulaciones de Santa Fé*, the Crown had now assumed direct control of the island.

From this time forward, Columbus's every effort would be to preserve as many as possible of his and his family's privileges. Even his fourth and last voyage was probably conceived more as a justificatory measure than as a voyage of new discovery. If he could prove that he had indeed found a direct western route to the riches of the Indies, this would justify all that had gone before. His primary concern was no longer discovery or administration but the preservation of his political, social, and economic status.

'Tis a consummation devoutly to be wished.
William Shakespeare (1564–1616)

15
The
Fourth
Voyage

Columbus was returned to Spain in chains, arriving in Cadiz at the end of October 1500. Whatever the reason for his forced return, he was immediately pardoned, and orders were issued to Francisco de Bobadilla for the restitution of his confiscated property. He was delayed in getting royal approval for another voyage, however. He finally set out, accompanied by his brother Bartolomé and his son Hernando, in May 1503.

Columbus left on his fourth voyage with the intent of finding the passage to India via the western approach. This was to have been the consummation of his dream, of his "Great Enterprise." He was convinced that Cuba was either part of the Chinese mainland or near to it; therefore, there must be a passage or strait to the northwest of Cuba that would lead to India. There are a number of firsthand accounts of this, his final voyage. Columbus wrote a letter from Jamaica on July 7, 1503, a copy of which is preserved in the Royal Library in Madrid. Generally refered to as the Salamanca Manuscript, this is one copy of the only known letter written by Columbus for this voyage, although he indicated that he had written several letters to the monarchs. A transcription of the Salamanca

448

Manuscript was first published in Spanish by Fernández de Navarrete in 1825. An Italian version, published in Venice in 1505 during the Admiral's lifetime, is now known as the *Lettera Rarissima*, a name that has been often incorrectly applied to references made to extracts from the Salamanca Manuscript. There are important textual differences between the Salamanca scribal copy and the *Lettera Rarissima*.

Hernando had a copy of the *Lettera Rarissima* in his library. In the *Historie* he said that his father had written "a report that the reader can know, because it is in print."[1] In 1810 a facsimile of the *Lettera Rarissima* was published by Cavalieria Morelli, the librarian of St. Marks in Venice. In 1903 Thacher provided a facsimile of the *Lettera Rarissima*, together with an English translation.[2] A more exact transcription of the Salamanca Manuscript than Fernández de Navarrete's was provided by César de Lollis at the end of the nineteenth century in the *Raccolta*.

Another copy of this letter is found in *El libro copiador*, which also has three previously unknown letters that were written at this time. This copy is unique in many ways, including the fact that it is the only one of the two known manuscript copies to be signed with Columbus's pyramidal cryptogram, in this case undersigned with "Christo Ferens," a possible indication that it was copied from at least a near-original. Besides the many textual differences, this copy also contains a previously unknown postscript in which Columbus summarized some of his views. Antonio Rumeu de Armas made a comparative study of the Salamanca Manuscript and the copy of the report in *El libro copiador* together with similar data provided in the *Historie*.[3] Gil designated in italics in his transcription of the letter in *El libro copiador* the many phrases and paragraphs that are not to be found in the Salamanca Manuscript.[4]

It must be kept in mind that Hernando, although only thirteen years old at the time, went on this voyage with his father. He dedicated nineteen chapters of his *Historie* to his account of this voyage. Columbus's retainer Diego Méndez also sailed on the flagship. Many years later, on June 26, 1536, Méndez gave, in his will, his own account of what took place at the time that he sought help on Española for Columbus and his crews, who were then stranded on

Jamaica.[5] The original of Méndez's testament, located in the archives of the duke of Veragua, was first printed by Fernández de Navarrete in 1825.

The official report of the fourth voyage was written by the official scribe, Diego de Porras. A copy is in the Salamanca archives.[6] Although Columbus had said earlier that it was King Ferdinand who had burdened him with the troublesome Porras brothers, he seems to have been confused. In a letter written in 1504 he said, "I took from here two brothers, who are called Porras, at the request of the Treasurer Morales."[7] Alonso Morales, treasurer of Castile, was said by Hernando to have been the lover of a sister of the Porras brothers. The brothers rebelled against Columbus while they were all marooned on Jamaica. Their rebellion lasted from January 2, 1504, until they were brought back to obedience by Bartolomé Colón on May 20. Columbus arrested Francisco Porras, who had captained one of the ships, but when they returned to Española the governor, Nicolás de Ovando, released him, and much later Francisco was given an important government post on Jamaica.

Bernáldez dedicated only a dozen or so lines to the fourth voyage. He said that Diego Rodriguez Cómitre of Triana captained the ship that brought Columbus back to Spain from Española at the end of the voyage, a fact confirmed by Columbus in a payment order dated September 7, 1504.[8] Bernáldez apparently did not know that it was Méndez who had gone by canoe to Española to get help for Columbus; he wrote that some Indians notified Ovando of the Admiral's plight.[9]

Fernández de Oviedo wrote extensively about this voyage. He appears to have been guided by Hernando's version, yet Hernando's account was not published until some forty years after his own. At the time of his writing, Fernández de Oviedo and Diego Méndez were both living in Santo Domingo.

There are many differences between the versions of Columbus's letter in *El libro copiador*, in the Salamanca Manuscript, and in the Italian translation *Lettera Rarissima*. As noted, many of these differences have been identified and studied by Rumeu and Gil. In this chapter no examination will be made of the versions of the fourth voyage given by the biographers under review; none of them used contemporay accounts, which are the sole basis for this chapter.

The Return to Española

The dates for the departure from Cádiz were reported differently by all participants. Columbus gave May 9, 1502, in *El libro copiador,* although no date was given in the the *Lettera*. The *Historie* said May 6, and the *Relación* of Diego de Porras gave May 11. We know that he was on Gran Canaria between May 20 and May 25 because he wrote a letter to Father Gaspar Gorricio on those dates.[10] There are similar problems with most of the dates for the rest of the journey. As to the crossing, Columbus limited himself to saying that it took him four days to reach the Canary Islands and sixteen days to reach Dominica, where he wrote a letter to the monarchs telling them his plans for the voyage. This letter is not known today. Hernando, Porras, and Juan de Quexo (testifying in the *Pleitos*) said they sailed directly to Matininó (Martinique). Martire reported Dominica. Hernando was the only one to tell of their having stopped off in Algeria at the beginning of the journey in order to lend support to the Portuguese, who were under attack from the Moors.[11]

The Spanish monarchs had expressly forbidden Columbus to land on Española and so instructed Nicolás de Ovando, the island's new governor, who had arrived there on April 15. Hernando wrote that his father's fleet reached Santo Domingo on June 24. Claiming that he wanted only to purchase a vessel to replace one of his that he found unseaworthy, Columbus attempted to land anyway. Since the ship that Columbus claimed was unseaworthy was later one of the two ships (out of the four in his fleet) that survived as far as Jamaica on the return trip from Veragua, perhaps Columbus exaggerated its unseaworthiness as an excuse to come into the harbor despite the monarchs' express prohibition. Hernando added that Columbus also sought safe haven in the port due to an impending storm. Permission was denied. According to Porras, two crew members (not three, as often reported) deserted in Santo Domingo.[12]

While at anchor in the Santo Domingo roadstead, Columbus is said to have warned Ovando that a severe storm was coming. His warning was supposedly ignored, and a fleet commanded by Luis Torres set sail and was destroyed. This fleet of twenty-eight ships was carrying Francisco Roldán, Francisco de Bobadilla, and the cacique Guarionex. The loss of the Torres fleet was not reported in either the *Lettera* or Porras's *Relación* but was in both the *Historie* and Las Casas's *Historia*.[13] Hernando is the sole source for the tale that only one vessel in the Torres fleet made it through to Spain and that this was the ship carrying the Admiral's gold, originally confiscated by Bobadilla but returned to him by Ovando on orders of the monarchs. The three hundred Indian slaves who had been given to Roldán and his followers and who who did reach Spain presumably sailed at this time.

Columbus's ships were dispersed by the same storm but were soon reunited near Azua on the southern coast of Española. His companions said that he sailed from there to Jamaica. He wrote that he made his crossing to the mainland from the Jardines de la Reina (July 24) off the Cuban shore. He wrote: "From there, when I could, I navigated to the mainland where the wind and terrible current were against me: I fought them for sixty days, and finally could only make seventy leagues. In all of this time I didn't and couldn't enter any port . . . it seemed like the end of the world. . . . I arrived at Cape Gracia á Dios . . . this was on the twelfth of September. It was eighty eight days that I hadn't been without fearsome storms, so much so that I didn't see sun or stars for the sea."[14]

This tale of woe is obviously greatly exaggerated. To begin with, from the time he left Santo Domingo on June 29 until his arrival off Honduras on September 12 was only seventy-six days. He wrote earlier that he was becalmed for eight days, and he did not report bad weather until he left Cuba to cross to the mainland on July 27. All contemporary accounts reported that Bartolomé landed on the island of Guanaja off the Central American coast on July 30. Columbus was obviously in error to claim that he was caught in a storm for sixty days when in fact he took only forty-three days to sail to Guanaca and Cape Gracias á Dios.

Columbus on the Central American Coast

Columbus's exploration of the eastern shore of the mesoamerican coast was his most difficult feat of discovery. The weather was constantly against him, and he met with the first real Indian opposition, as well as losing two of his four ships. He recognized that this area was an extension of the coast that he had discovered on his second voyage and that Pero Alonso Niño and others had since cruised as far as Darién. Porras and Hernando both noted that the farther south they traveled, the poorer the quantity and quality of the gold. To each of them this was conclusive evidence that they were approaching the previously discovered area.

At the beginning of the voyage the first Indians to approach the Spanish ships sprinkled powders and burned incense, blowing the smoke toward the ships. This was the first report of incense in the Americas. The first and probably only time that Columbus went ashore on the isthmus, he was shown mummified bodies, another first in the Americas.

It is evident from his own statements at this time that Columbus was seeking a way through the isthmus, a strait that would let him reach Ptolemy's Asia. He was convinced that it lay below the Chinese mainland, which he had earlier identified as Cuba. Porras confirmed this, noting Columbus's actions after the fleet left Cape Gracias: "He went seeking ports and bays, thinking to find the strait."[15] Columbus wrote that in Cariay (today's Costa Rica)[16] he understood the Indians to tell him of the riches to be found in Ciguare to the west of Veragua:

> They say that there is [an] infinite [amount] of gold and that they wear crowns on their heads, very thick bracelets on their feet and hands; and they adorn and cover the chairs, chests and tables with it. . . . In Ciguare they trade in fairs and goods. . . . They say besides that the ships carry cannon, bows and arrows and swords and cuirasses, and on land they have horses and use them in war. . . . They say also that the sea touches Çiguare, and from there the Ganges is ten days away; it appears that these lands are to Veragua as is Tortosa [on the Mediterranean] to Fuenterravia [on the Bay of Biscay], or Pisa [near the Ligurian Sea] to Venice [on the Adriatic].[17]

All the known copies of Columbus's own report on the fourth voyage include the above passage, one that indicates that the Indians from Guanahaní and those from the isthmus could understand each other. It has convinced some that Columbus not only knew that he had not yet reached the Asian mainland but also was fully aware that another sea had to be crossed to reach it. He indicated that he had a clear idea as to where he was on the isthmus. His comparisons of the relative geographical positions of cities in Spain and Italy is roughly equivalent to the relative positions of Veragua and Ciguare on the Caribbean and Pacific coasts. Thus, he believed that by traveling, as he said earlier, for nine days to the west, he would reach the shores of another sea that could be crossed in ten days to reach the Ganges River.

Hernando went into considerable detail about the search for the strait, noting that Columbus did not tarry at any one place on the coast because he persisted in his search "to discover the strait in the mainland, in order to open up to navigation the Sea of the Mediodía [South Sea] of which he had need in order to discover the lands of the spices. For this he determined to continue his trip to the east, towards Veragua and Nombre de Dios, where he imagined and believed the referred to strait was, as in effect it was; but he deceived himself in imagining it, because he did not know that it was a land strait."[18]

Fernández de Oviedo offered a remarkably similar explanation: Columbus had set out "to seek the strait which he said had to be found to pass to the southern sea; in which he deceived himself, because the strait that he thought to be of the sea, is of land."[19] It is perhaps for this reason that in April 1503 Columbus founded Santa María de Belén on the banks of the river Yebra, probably as a base for the exploitation of the vast gold mines he believed were nearby, as well as for future efforts to find the strait. Hernando wrote of this settlement, "Besides the houses, which were of wood, covered with palm leaves, a large house was made to serve as a storeroom and granary, in which [there was] much powder, artillery, provisions and other things for the support of the settlers, the most necessary ones such as wine, bread, oil, vinegar, cheese and many vegetables."[20]

Columbus said that he had established good relations with the local chieftain, but he added, "I knew well that this harmony could not last; they being very rustic and our people very inopportune."[21] He managed to capture but then lose the chief, who then drove the

Spaniards out of the settlement and burned it down. The loss of these supplies for seventy to eighty men is probably the reason for Columbus's complaint that he now had to head back for Spain because his ships were in bad condition and there was insufficient food for the men. After having fruitlessly cruised the coast from September to April, during which time he had lost two of his vessels and a number of his men, Columbus headed back for Española. On the way, however, it became clear that his remaining two ships were simply not seaworthy, forcing him to beach them on the coast of Jamaica.

Stranding and Rescue on Jamaica

Columbus wrote of his continuing ill luck in this attempt to sail back to Española. He complained of storms, loss of sails and anchors, and near collisions. He commented that by the time he reached Jamaica, his men were "frightened and lost" and his ships eaten by shipworms—they had "more holes than a honeycomb." Having lost all his ships' boats, he lacked the means to send for help from Española. In his letter to the king he asked for rescue by a seventy-tun vessel that should bring two hundred quintals of bread (ship's biscuit) as well as other supplies. He also made a strange comment: "I would not have gone to Española even if my ships had been able. I already said that I was ordered by Your Majesty that I should not go there. If I have taken advantage of this order, God knows."[22] Yet earlier, in the same letter, he said: "I arrived on May 13 in the province of Mango, that joins with that of Catayo, and from there I left for Española. . . . I took the route in order to bring me as close as possible to Española."[23] The first comment would seem to support the crews' complaint that he had no intention of going back to Spain, but his earlier statement indicates that he was headed for Española. Columbus's statements on this matter are contradictory, yet there is little question: he was indeed headed for Española.

He apparently intended to send Indians for help after he became stranded on Jamaica. He wrote: "This letter I send by way and hand of Indians. [It will be] a great marvel if it arrives there."[24] Actually, Columbus's retainer Diego Méndez failed in one attempt to reach

Española in a canoe but was successful on his next try. Hernando said that his father sent two canoes, the second commanded by a fellow Genoan Bartolomé Fiesco, who was to return to Jamaica and report if they had safely reached their destination. Fernández de Oviedo told only of Méndez and the one canoe.

The version that should be reliable is the account given by Méndez himself. He did not mention Fiesco by name, reporting only that he had prepared one canoe with a keel, decking, and sails "and the supplies necessary for me and one Christian and for six Indians." After the initial failure, he set out again a few days later.

> I navigated for five days and four nights without leaving hold of the oar, steering the canoe while my companions rowed . . . at the end of five days, I should reach the island of Española at cape San Miguel, there having been two days during which we had neither eaten nor drunk . . . I beached my canoe . . . there I remained two days resting. I took six Indians from there. . . . It was a hundred and thirty leagues from there to the city of Santo Domingo . . . I reached the province of Azua . . . I left my canoe and made my way by land to Xaragua, where I found the governor. . . . He detained me there for seven months, until he had burned and hanged eighty-four caciques [Las Casas said eighty, Francisco López de Gómara forty], lords of vassals, and with them Nacaona [sic] . . . I went on foot to the district of Santo Domingo, and I remained there expecting ships to come from Castile, since it was more than a year since any had come . . . three ships [came] I bought one . . . and sent her to where the admiral was . . . I myself went forward in the other two ships to give an account to the king and queen of all that had occured on that voyage.[25]

This account presents some problems. Ostensibly the delay in sending aid immediately was due to the fact that there were no ships available. Yet it is known, as Fernández de Oviedo wrote, that when "the Commendor Mayor [Nicolás de Ovando] saw the letters of the admiral he then sent a caravel to see if it was true, and to see how the Admiral was, and feel out the thing, and not to bring him."[26] He also said that there was only one vessel finally sent to rescue Columbus. Hernando wrote a somewhat different version; he said that Ovando sent a boat (bajel) commanded by Diego de Escobar, who landed and explained that Ovando could not send right away a ship large enough to take all of the men. He brought Columbus a present of a barrel of wine and half a roast pig, returned to his boat without accepting any letter, and left that same evening.[27] Hernando and Fernández de Oviedo agreed that only the one ship sent by Méndez finally came to the rescue. If, as Méndez wrote, only three ships came from Spain and, as he also wrote, he returned to Spain with two of them, then there was only the one ship available for the rescue.

Columbus's return was delayed by bad weather. Waiting on Beata while going from Jamaica to Santo Domingo, he wrote a letter to Ovando in which he said, "Diego de Salzedo [*sic*] arrived with the help of the ships (*los navíos*) that Your Worship sent to me where I was."[28] Thus two of those who participated in these events told of only one ship, and Columbus, their leader, said there were two. There are three surviving payment orders that relate to this journey and that were written in the hand of Columbus; they refer only to Diego Salcedo and his caravel. Columbus's relative Andrea Colón (there were five Genoans on this voyage, not counting Columbus, his brother Bartolomé, and his son Hernando) wrote of only one ship having come to the rescue.[29] Barring proof to the contrary, one must assume either that Columbus was mistaken or that he linked in this sentence the earlier vessel sent by Ovando with the rescue vessel sent by Méndez.

During the interval between the departure of Méndez and the arrival of the rescue ship, Columbus faced problems with the Indians on Jamaica as well as with some members of his crews. It was left to his brother Bartolomé to cope with these problems because Columbus kept to his bed due to an attack of gout. The Porras brothers with 48 men (according to Hernando) out of the 110 survivors rebelled and for a period of over four months lived apart from the Columbus camp. The revolt was claimed to have been caused by the rebels' fear that Columbus had never intended to return to Spain because of his problems with the monarchs. Yet, a few months earlier, when he had taken what appeared to be an unusual route to return to Española when he left the mainland coast for the return voyage, they accused him of attempting to sail directly for Spain, a voyage they feared in the unseaworthy ships. The payroll submitted by Porras showed that thirty-two men died on this voyage.

Of these, eight died in 1504, one of whom died in February, another in March, and two in May, one of these on the seventeenth and the other on the twentieth; the rest died after the surrender of the Porras group. Both Porras and Hernando reported the last two as having died, although they did not coincide on the dates or the manner of the deaths. With only four reported deaths, causes unknown, this does not appear to have been a particularly bloody rebellion. Las Casas described the confrontation that occurred on May 20 as the first battle in the Indies between Spaniards.

In a curious passage referring to the Porras brothers, Columbus wrote that he had taken them with him at the request of the monarchs, contradicting his later claim that it was at the request of Morales. He went on to complain, "The service that these did with Christobal Guerra with the pearls, and my old age and with the experience of the intention (*yntinçión*) it was not necessary that the Porros came to order me, nor their knowledge, nor quality of persons."[30] The reference to Guerra is to his voyage to the Pearl Coast in 1500–1501 during which at least one of the Porras brothers participated as overseer. On the return to Spain, the claim was made that they had hidden pearls from the monarchs. Columbus apparently believed that the Porras brothers were sent to spy on him. Was this paranoia or another example of King Ferdinand's hands-on approach to Columbus and his voyages? In the postscript to the letter in *El libro copiador* on this voyage, Columbus clearly laid the blame for his failure to reach India on the shoulders of the Porrases: "They disgraced the voyage [so that] I didn't enter the Glory (*Aurea*) or the mines through the Gate of the Pardon."[31] The "Gate of the Pardon" is the door into the cathedral of Seville through which the Spanish kings always entered. Interestingly, this postscript was written five months before the brothers openly rebelled against him.

Columbus and Santo Stefano

Another important paragraph in the copy in *El libro* copiador does not appear in the Salamanca Manuscript. It refers to the voyage of Santo Stefano and his relations with Columbus. Santo Stefano and Gerolamo Adorno, fellow Genoans, set out in 1491 to cross by sea and land into India. According to Rumeu de Armas, they went half way up the Nile, crossed over to the Red Sea and the Indian Ocean, and journeyed on to Calcutta. From Ceylon they traveled to the mouth of the Ganges River and reached the port of Pegú on the Gulf of Bengal. Adorno died, and Stefano returned via Sumatra, the Persian Gulf, and Aleppo, ending his travels at Tripoli in today's Lebanon, where on September 1, 1499, he wrote a report on his journey. It was first published in 1901.

In the Salamanca Manuscript, while referring to Stefano, Columbus wrote: "As to the other that I did not say (*dexo de dezir*) I now say because I am encircled; I don't say it that way nor do I affirm with the double three in all that I have ever said and written, and that I am now at the source."[32] Taken out of context, this passage was simply incomprehensible before *El libro copiador* provided the data on Stefano. Columbus was apparently trying to say that he had known but not told how to circle the globe by passing through the Chersonese to India. It is interesting to note that even at this late stage in his travels, he was still holding back information that he believed useful for finding the route to the Indies. Columbus now wrote:

> Xeronimo de Sant Esteban [*sic*] navigated in the year 98 east to Colocati [*sic*] for 58 days; he arrived at the port of Pegú which is in the kingdom of Prigo and wanted to go on ahead to where the metals (*rrobins*) [*sic*] grow . . . in his letter he writes me this at length, and he says that the ships of Your Highnesses are in the best [part] of India . . . and he says that in all extremes that he went, he found that gold was held in as high esteem as in Italy. . . . He considers that who knows how much he went from this cape of the river Ganges towards Veragua, and [to] make a hole (*punto*) in [to] ours.[33]

Gil provided a somewhat different transcription: Stefano arrived "at the kingdom of Pego [*sic*]," with no mention of Prigo.[34] Columbus's apparent intent here was to demonstrate that there was a passage that would link up the farthest point in Santo Stefano's travels with his own westernmost point in Veragua. What makes this paragraph of particular interest is that two months before sailing, Columbus had written to his friend Nicolás Oderigo: "If

Gerónimo de Santiesteban [*sic*] comes, he should wait for me and not engage (*enbaraçar*) with anything (*con nada*) [anyone?] because they would take from him what they could and afterward leave him in blank (*desarán en blanco*). [That] he come here. and the King and Queen will receive him until I arrive."[35]

These references indicate that Columbus and Santo Stefano had exchanged correspondence and apparently had planned to embark together on Columbus's fourth voyage. This is a totally unexplored aspect of Columbus's plans for what turned out to be his final voyage. He was also seemingly afraid that unscrupulous discoverers might try to get the help of Santo Stefano, who should therefore go to the court to await Columbus's return. This would seem to imply that the Catholic Kings were privy to Columbus's plans to find a passage, the *punto* previously referred to. This opinion also fits well with Columbus's remarks above about Guerra and the Porras brothers. Columbus attached sufficient importance to this letter to Oderigo that he preserved a copy for himself.

Treatment of the Indians

In another passage that was suppressed in the Salamanca Manuscript, Columbus, after a long list of complaints, wrote, "All of the coasts of the land of Paria and the islands of the region, that are so many, have been robbed, and a great number of people killed: for the days that those who are alive [now] live, they will not be friends of ours."[36] In this passage he recognized, as he had before, the difficulties that could arise from excessive use of force against the Indians. It is curious that earlier he told how he had kept the secret of the route to Veragua (a claim confirmed by Diego Porras)[37] and that he was close to the source of the gold that King Solomon had sent to buy in this region. He went on, however, to say that the monarchs could have the gold for the taking. Yet later in this same letter he said that he had not taken gold at this time so as not to antagonize the natives. Thus, as with slavery, Columbus showed his ambivalence on such matters. When Columbus had experienced problems with the natives on Jamaica, he had pacified them by predicting an eclipse that he said would be caused by their behavior toward him and his men. Columbus claimed that by the time the Spaniards left Jamaica, the Indians did not want them to leave, believing they were gods.

In another previously unknown passage, Columbus told how, during the time he was in command on Española, the island was heavily populated with useful people and how he could send a man from one end of the island to the other without the man's being interfered with. He went on to say that he had always told the monarchs how the richness of the island was its Indians but that the Spaniards had acted as though they were the descendents of King Priam of Troy and wanted to be so treated. Then he commented, "Lost the Indians, lost the land." He said: "The Emperor of Catayo had already had the seignieury of all of this island, he lost it because of the governors. . . . The eye of the owner fattens the horse." Inferentially, the Spanish monarchs were likely to lose the islands, as had the kings of Catayo. In this letter Columbus also railed against the captains of the Andalusian voyages, the governors Bobadilla and Ovando, and the Spanish settlers. Incidentally, in this passage, he forgot that in 1495 he had sent Indians to Spain to be sold as slaves; he now said, "If I sent them to Castile it was for [them] to return to the Indies."[38] The earlier use of the Spanish adage of the horse and its owner referred to himself: he could be the owner who would remedy matters on Española if given the opportunity. None of the quotations given in this paragraph appear in the Salamanca Manuscript or in the *Lettera Rarissima.*

In a final and perplexing paragraph, Columbus wrote, according to the Samanca Manuscript, "I humbly beg Your Highnesses that, if it please God, to take me out of here." The version in *El libro copiador* added: "I beg Your Highnesses that if I have said anything against Your Royal wishes that I be pardoned; I am in such anguish and to such an extreme, that it is a marvel that I am alive and not going crazy. Throwing stones at a thousand papers would not write my miseries. My blood is turned to puss. I also beg Your Highnesses, if it please God, to take me out of here."[39]

In the letter written in Jamaica toward the end of his last voyage, Columbus showed all of his many, and often mutually contradictory, personality characteristics. This complex man believed that the

Indians were good but also stupid and vicious. Gold was not to be taken without recompense yet could be taken by force. Throughout, he remained convinced that he, and he alone, could find the way around Catayo through the Chersonese to India. And, as he had done so often before, he again admitted on the fourth voyage to holding back some of the information as to how this enterprise could be accomplished. There is an undertone of complaint bordering on paranoia. He was tired, suffering from gout, and frustrated.

Cecil Jane, while discussing this last journey, commented: "He was fully convinced that he had by his discovery of Veragua placed King Solomon's Mines in the possession of the Crown of Spain. The picture which the Admiral draws of himself, trembling and weeping, but consoled by a heavenly vision, shows that dissapointment and hardship had gone far to transform his religious fervour into fanaticism, and his belief in his destiny into an *idée fixe* from which he could not escape."[40]

Return to Española and Spain

Columbus left Jamaica on June 28, 1504; crossing over to Española without incident, he arrived in Santo Domingo on August 13. Ovando received him with courtesy, and he sailed for Spain a month later, arriving at Sanlúcar on November 7. In a holograph dated September 7, he ordered payment to Diego Rodriguez of "eighty gold pesos" for "the passage from here to Castile for twenty five persons" who were to go with Columbus. Porras's payroll indicated that six of the crew members stayed on Española. The rest of them returned to Spain on the caravel that Méndez had sent to Jamaica. This caravel required an extensive overhaul, including new sails and a new mast, which accounts for the delay in sailing for Spain. All contemporary reports agree that Columbus paid for the ships, the food for the men, and all other expenses.

In retrospect it seems strange that no one before the discovery of *El libro copiador* attached importance to Columbus's known correspondence with his fellow Ligurian the explorer Santo Stefano. While on Jamaica, he showed himself to be knowledgeable about the depredations committed by the Andalusian voyagers but was wrong in his belief that misgovernment would deprive Spain, at least in the short term, of the Indies. He was very near to understanding the existence of two great oceans between Europe and Asia. He had discovered his islands in the Indies but was unprepared and unable to manage them. He knew that he had reached a mainland but was unable to determine that it was a new and previously unknown continent. He had come so near to reshaping the known and unknown continents into one world, and yet he was still so far from the ultimate reality. He remained blocked by the very lands he had discovered. There is an underlying tone of a bitter and very disturbed man in his last letters. He had had a brilliant conception but, when the opportunity came, was unable to fulfill his dream. He had been imprisoned, shipwrecked, and left abandoned by Ovando for over a year. He was perhaps not exaggerating when he wrote that it was a marvel he had not gone crazy.

On November 26, a few days after Columbus's return, Queen Isabel died. His letters reveal that he had hoped, fruitlessly, that she had mentioned him in her will. In 1503, while he was on his fourth voyage, the Crown had established the Casa de Contratación, which was charged with the full control of all shipping and commercial affairs in the Indies. At this time all of those administrative responsibilities were taken away from him. During his last years he wrote many letters, most of them concerned with his reclamations and recriminations. He continued to try to enlist first the church and then the city officials of Genoa on his behalf. The fact should not be overlooked that at the time Columbus first sought support from Pope Alexander VI, the Catholic Kings were joined in an effort to replace Alexander, claiming that he had been elected pope illegally. The pope, in turn, declared that they were illegally wed and had usurped the throne of Castile. This claim was made despite the fact that as papal legate to Spain in 1472, he had personally given dispensation to Ferdinand and Isabel for their marriage, which, until so dispensed, was invalid due to consanguinity.

At the time of Columbus's return from his last voyage, important events were occurring in Spain. First were the queen's illness and death. In 1504 King Ferdinand finally succeeded in outwitting the French in Naples, thereby incorporating Naples with Sardinia,

Majorca, and Sicily under Aragonese rule. In the last year of Columbus's life the king was engaged in renewing Aragón's ties with France, actions that culminated in Ferdinand's marrying Germaine de Foix of Navarre, the eighteen-year-old niece of the French king. Columbus foolishly tried at this time to ingratiate himself with Ferdinand's daughter Juana and her husband, Philip, who had returned to Spain from France to assume their positions as queen and prince consort of Castile. Ferdinand was irreconcilably opposed to the two of them.

Thus during his last years, Columbus sought support from Genoa, a city opposed to Ferdinand's Italian ambitions; from Alexander VI, who had his own problems with the Catholic Kings; and finally from Philip and Juana, a foreign prince and his mentally incapacitated wife. Columbus was obviously a better discoverer than courtier.

There is a surviving fragment of a letter that Columbus wrote to his old friend Diego de Deza shortly before he died. In it he wrote: "And it seems that His Highness [Ferdinand] does not intend to comply with what he has promised together with the Queen, of saintly glory, by word and writing. I believe that for me to struggle to the contrary, as I am a plower, would be to whip the wind; and it would be well that I now let God our Master do [it], since I have done what I could."[41] He was in Seville in February 1505 and in Segovia in May; from there he went in October to Salamanca as he followed the court on its customary peregrinations. When the court moved to Valladolid in March 1506, Columbus followed it there. He died in that city in May 1506.

Today there is no way of knowing exactly where Columbus died or where his remains are. At the time of his death, he was following the court. Customarily when the court came into a city, it requisitioned quarters for its followers. In the case of towns such as Valladolid, this meant that half of the dwelling places in the city were requisitioned, accomplished by taking one floor of two-story houses, for example. Columbus was probably housed in one such place. This may be the reason that some historians claim he died in a tavern. Whatever the circumstances, he had already fallen into such a state of oblivion that no note was made in court or municipal records of his death. Only the Carthusian monastery records listed his death and burial.

As far as Spain was concerned, he left the world as he had entered it, unnoticed.

As in life, mystery attended Columbus's death. There is no question that he wanted to be buried in Concepción de la Vega on Española. For an unknown time after his death, his remains were in the Carthusian monastery at Las Cuevas, outside of Seville. According to one school of thought, the remains are still there, possibly in a crypt discovered in 1949.[42] Other evidence indicates that at some undeterminable time his remains were transfered to Santo Domingo, where they were buried, as far as we know without ceremony, in the cathedral. A manuscript written by Esteban de Garibay in 1571 indicated that Columbus's daughter-in-law María de Toledo brought Columbus's and Diego's remains to Santo Domingo, which would have occurred in either 1538 or 1544.[43] The Cathedral of Santo Domingo was finished in 1540. Las Casas sailed on the voyage that brought María de Toledo to Santo Domingo in 1544, yet he made no mention of either man's remains being on board.

At the time that the Spanish colony of Santo Domingo was ceded to France, remains assumed to be Columbus's were removed to Havana. Years later, when that colony attained its independence, they were again removed, this time to Seville, where these remains are today. Late in the nineteenth century, however, a crypt was opened in the Cathedral of Santo Domingo. It contained a lead box holding skeletal remains and was inscribed with the name of Columbus. The inscriptions are definitely post–sixteenth century. Ever since, the Dominicans have claimed to hold his final remains. According to another theory, Columbus's remains are now scattered between the cathedrals in Seville and Santo Domingo.[44] Each of these cathedrals claimed to be the sole repository for the remains until 1992, when the Dominicans moved theirs into a monstrous monument erected for this purpose near the site of the first Spanish settlement in Santo Domingo.

In 1878 Harrisse made the first independent study of the question as to the whereabouts of the remains of Christopher Columbus. He concluded that there was no way of determining where they were.[45] Generally speaking, Dominican, French, Italian, and U.S. authors place them in Santo Domingo.[46] Spaniards insist on Seville. Many studies have been done, but there has never been a study of either set of remains by a forensic pathologist. Neither claimant has provided a detailed list of the osteal remnants in its possession. In the often heated debate on the subject, generally motivated as much by nationalism as by tourism interests, neither side can claim victory. The question of the Admiral's burial place remains the final enigma in the Columbus story.

Demonstration fails to change established opinion.
Herbert Spencer (1820–1903)

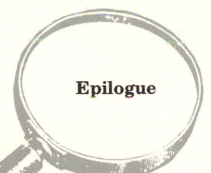

Epilogue

The author of this biographical critique is neither biographer nor historian. As a writer and a collector of Columbiana, I am disturbed by the general lack of use, and the occasional misuse, of the primary and secondary sources for a life of Columbus. The information is there; one has only to adequately research the available materials. Accordingly, an attempt has been made in this text to determine the basic outlines for a Columbus biography, based as nearly as possible on contemporary documentation, preferably facsimiles. This objective approach must on occasion take note of some of the disparate interpretations that have contributed so much to the Columbian myth. However, although it is normally the duty of the subjective biographer, not of his reviewer, to furnish corroborative documentation, in the present case the positions have been reversed—the critic provides the archival data with which to judge the biographer.

Thus, rather than approach the task as one of demythologizing, I have attempted to instead re-create a life of Columbus from what documentation is available. This is not a Columbus biography but an accumulation, for comparative purposes, of known facts of his life.

During the process, I could not follow in the footsteps of those being critiqued who chose to ignore the invaluable data now available in Columbus's recently found *El libro copiador*. Although I have provided much information from these letters, I have taken care at the same time not to fault the authors for not knowing about information that is available only in these letters. The same does not apply to those who failed to avail themselves of readily available sources such as Simón Verde's letters, Pietro Martire d'Anghiera's correspondence, the *Lettera Rarissima,* and the *Memorial de la Mejorada.*

I have also made extensive use of the postils in the books in the Columbine Library. These Columbus holographs were available to the authors being critiqued, all of whom opted not to fully avail themselves of these sources. Although most of the authors referred frequently to Marco Polo's book, such references were not always taken from Columbus's own much-annotated copy of the 1485 Pipino Latin edition of this work, the only source for Columbus's knowledge of Marco Polo's text. Both text and annotations of these books were available to them in the *Raccolta*, which most of them listed as a source. At the same time, the Columbus holograph of the Toscanelli letter has been known for over a century, yet all of these biographers used the textully different copies provided by Bartolomé de Las Casas and Hernando Colón.

In most cases I worked from facsimiles of contemporary books and manuscripts, providing my own transcriptions. These do not always agree with transcriptions made by others. Similarly, translators do not always coincide in their translations of the sometimes difficult texts. Again, I provided my own translations.

Some differences reflect interpretations based on inadequate documentation, whereas others reflect changing biographical criteria. It must be kept in mind that both Columbus and his contemporaries were writing at a time when many values were viewed differently than they are today. At the time, the art of biography was a recent innovation in Italy and was as yet barely known in most European countries. Biographical data that would be considered essential today may have appeared insignificant to those writing in the fifteenth and sixteenth centuries. For example, only three of his many contemporary biographers provided a physical description of the Admiral.[1]

In Columbus's day the Spanish language was much more simple than today. Some translators offer their readers more modern linguistic usages in their translations of what might be termed rustic documents. These changes can, and often do, provide a different sense than the one intended by the author, giving a false sense of reality. As has been noted, some postmoderns attach great importance to their "reading of Columbus." Yet they attach too little importance to the study of word usages whose connotations in the fifteenth and sixteenth centuries may differ from the meanings today. To accentuate the importance of Columbus's frequent use of the word "marvelous" is to ignore the possibility that this use may have been due as much to his limited vocabulary as to allegorical intent. A comparison with his frequent use of such words in his postils is revealing as to his intent. A judicious employment of Ockham's Razor is often indicated.

In some instances the paucity of contemporary documentation has led to a mixture of biographical data with historical background materials filled out with speculation, which sometimes makes it difficult to say whether a given work is biography, history, or legend. There is legitimate scope for disagreement as to the point at which possible or probable truth leaves off and legend begins. Perhaps the best gauge available is to be found in the fact that myth and legend alike are—as defined by Samuel Schoenbaum—indifferent to fact.[2]

Much of the life of Columbus has become so stylized over the centuries that the modern biographer seeks to reinterpret this corpus rather than revalue its component parts. Most, if not all, of the authors whose works are reviewed in this study have worked from a combination of the Lascasian and Hernandine versions of Columbus's life. Las Casas, in his *Historia*, was concerned primarily with the history of the conquest and administration of the Spanish colonies as it affected the indigenous population. What information he does provide for Columbus and his voyages is derived mainly from Columbus's own writings and the *Historie* attributed to his son Hernando, both of which works are notoriously inexact. Modern-day Spanish scholars do not believe that Hernando wrote the biographical sections of the *Historie,* yet much of the biographical data in this attributed work was used uncritically by many of these authors.

Las Casas made a habit of repeating all rumors as though they were facts, but he did generally clarify them, pages or even chapters later. This has led to many selective and misleading citations by Columbus's often subjective biographers. In some cases, both Las Casas and Hernando gave accounts that differed from those given by eyewitnesses, yet the authors under review generally neglected to mention the contradictions. One example is that of the date of the first finding of land in the Americas: October 11 or 12?

There are numerous cases of silent emendation—for example, the wording of the *Capitulaciones*—as well as of selective editing of Columbus's own reports. A close reading of the *Diario* entries for December 24–26 reveals conflicting descriptions by Columbus of what supposedly happened after the *Santa María* went aground. These biographers, without exception, relied only on the version given in the journal entry for December 24. Later, on the twenty-sixth, Columbus made it clear that the vessel was in as good a condition as the day he had left Spain, yet all but one of these authors reported the ship as wrecked. The many other inconsistencies in the story were simply ignored in favor of the conventional version that the vessel was wrecked while sailing toward an Indian village; in one case the ship even broke up and sank. Yet Columbus wrote that his intent had been to bypass the village, a not irrelevant fact but one ignored by these biographers.

There is the occasional interlinear reading that leaves one unconvinced. Examples are found in the treatment of the Garcí Hernández testimony in the *Pleitos* and in the interpretations given to Miguel de Cuneo's reference to the supposedly merry widow of Gomera.

The Columbus letters in *El libro copiador* now provide important new information, as is the case with the letter of the first voyage. Felipe Fernández-Armesto and Stephen Greenblatt were aware of the letters but opted not to use them. In a separate publication, Margarita Zamora provided a translation of Columbus's March 4 letter but did not incorporate the information given in the letter in her study. Perhaps of equal importance is the fact that these letters provide confirmation for some of the information given by Columbus contemporaries such as Gonzalo Fernández de Oviedo, Andrés Bernáldez, and Martire, who did work from copies of some of the letters. One of the letters shows that at least in the case of the Lascasian copy of the letter on the third voyage, the previously suspected editorial voice of Las Casas did not intervene. Another shows that Bernáldez copied one passage verbatim but that it was he, not Columbus, who went on to relate the given information to that found in the work of Sir John Mandeville.

As noted earlier, none of these authors appeared to have personally researched the many postils in the books in the Columbine Library. I found these invaluable for evaluating Columbus's pre- and post-discovery cosmographic concepts. A perhaps key year, 1491, for Columbus's reading of the *Ymago mundi* is provided in a postil in his papers bound in with his copy of this important book, yet none of these authors noted its presence. There are over twenty-one hundred postils in the four most important of these books. They are essential to the proper understanding of Columbus regardless of when or by whom these notations were written. It is a tricky business to sort them out, but a necessary one.

In writing about Columbus, the biographer is basically dealing with a man who came from a humble background and who left little information about his early life. He virtually burst on the world scene with his monumental discovery of the Indies. His early biographers concentrated, naturally, on this great achievement, not on the man or his antecedents. These came into play only later, through the need to explain how a man of his humble background conceived his "Great Enterprise."

In the search for answers, one must go beyond the written record and seek explanation in what Henri-Louis Bergson termed the élan vital. Columbus was an Italian from Genoa. His formative years were spent in an atmosphere vastly different from that of the Spain in which he resided during the years that most interest us today. As an adult, he sought out friends and business associates from Florence, the leading city of the Renaissance. Much thought has been given to the strange mixture of medieval man and Renaissance man so evident in Columbus. Genoa took almost no part in the Renaissance. Jacob Burckhardt observed, "The inhabitant of the

Riviera was proverbial among the Italians for his contempt of higher culture." The Spain to which Columbus moved was as backward culturally, in relation to Genoa, as Genoa was to Florence. Genoa, like Spain, enjoyed wealth, commerce, and distant colonies but was also the scene of constant internal disorders. Columbus lived between two worlds.

Columbus was influenced by the people he dealt with. In Portugal this was with the king and fellow Italian merchants. In Spain this was with the monarchs and their advisers, clerical and lay, most of whom were conversos. Two vital movements were occurring simultaneously during his years in Spain. First was the virtual unification of Spain, which necessarily included the defeat of the Moors, and second was the spread of the Inquisition, with its concomitant expulsion of the Jews. The first movement delayed the acceptance of his project, whereas the second provided the funding for it. Hardly less important to the later affairs of Columbus were the Aragonese wars with France, which occupied so much of the time and money of the Spanish monarchs.

The Berardis and the Bardis of Florence were among Columbus's supporters. Members of the latter family were major players in international finance. A century and a half earlier, they and their associates had been able to sustain the very substantial loss of 1,350,000 gold florins that they had misguidedly lent to England. This was at a time when the public income of their native city was only 300,000 florins per year. The city had a post-plague population of 90,000 yet listed at that time more than 8,000 children learning reading, 1,000 or more in six schools studying arithmetic, and 600 in four schools learning Latin and logic. Already in the fourteenth century, Florence had made attendance at the university compulsory for natives of the city. The citizen of Florence was by definition an educated man. Columbus may have benefited more than economically by his close association with Florentins.

By the fifteenth century, every town in Italy had a Latin school because reading, writing, arithmetic, and Latin were considered necessities. Unlike the few schools in Spain, the numerous Italian schools depended more on the municipality than the church. Italy was a land of many dialects, with Latin being the lingua franca. In such an educational and cultural climate, it is not surprising that Columbus and his brother Bartolomé could read and write in Latin. There is no need to postulate an imaginary attendance at the University of Padua.

Much has been made of Columbus's declared interest in the financing for a new crusade to recover the Holy City. The Crusades had opened up for western Europe vistas of a far greater world than had been known since the fall of the Roman Empire. The Italians were the most interested of the Europeans, due not only to the fact that Italy was a region of naval powers, with the fleets of Venice and of Columbus's hometown of Genoa, but also to the fact that these, and other major Italian cities, already had commercial interests in the Near East.

With the humanism of the thirteenth through the early sixteenth centuries came the revival of antiquity. When united to what has been termed the genius of the Italian people, they achieved the intellectual conquest of Europe. Burckhardt proposed, "In geography, as in other matters, it is vain to attempt to distinguish how much is to be attributed to the study of the ancients, and how much to the special genius of the Italians." He found the Italians to be "strikingly superior" to the other Western nations in the development of the geographical and allied sciences.[3] Regardless of whether Columbus acquired his cosmographic skills while living in Spain, Portugal, or Italy, the study of the ancients, perhaps one key to his venture, was made possible for him by this revival of antiquity by the Italian humanists.

John Hale drew attention to what he termed the "repossession" of antiquity by the humanists. At the same time, "its popularization through translations and paraphrases, had acquired critical mass which produced unstoppable chain reactions. There was hardly a branch of inquiry, from jurisprudence to mathematics, military science and the arts, that was unaltered by the stimulus of a relevant text, artifact or record of historical experience."[4] Columbus's numerous references to the classics was "politically correct" for the times. A written life of Columbus must go beyond the artisan background of his family and consider the cultural, political, and mercantile climates in which he lived.

The Italy of Columbus's day differed from Spain not only culturally but also politically. Italy was a land of individualists; the Italian
princes were not as dependent on the society of an aristocracy as
were the kings of Castile and, even more so, the Aragonese princes.
The monarchs of Spain maintained the most rigorous court protocol
of Europe, and their civil institutions were rigidly segregated. In
Italy, social mobility had been traditionally acceptable for centuries.
Largely due to the humanists, Renaissance Italy provided a home
for the all-sided man (*l'uomo universal*). The fifteenth century has
been seen as being, above all, that of the many-sided man. In this
sense Columbus was an Italian modern.

To be able to get the rewards that he wanted for providing Spain
with the lands in the western seas, Columbus had to have the
backing of a magnate. Even in Italy a commoner would not make
demands of princes in anticipation of success. Columbus had to deal
with men who were successful, not only militarily but also politically, with men who were practical, like King Ferdinand of Aragón,
who at one time allied himself with the Moorish Prince Boabdil
against the latter's father, at the time the king of Granada. Later
Ferdinand negotiated with then King Boabdil for the peaceful
surrender of Granada and then paid for his and many of his
followers' return to North Africa.

Earlier in the century Ferdinand's grandfather, Alfonso V of
Aragón, had been captured by the Milanese, who released him after
he convinced them that their support of the House of Anjou in its
claim for the throne of Naples would make the French the masters
of Italy. Genoa, unlike Milan, backed Count René in his fight to
regain the throne. King Ferdinand has been quoted as saying, "The
King of France complains that I have twice deceived him. He lies,
the fool; I have deceived him ten times and more."[5] Columbus too
claimed involvement in the affairs of René, as well as having his own
troubles with Ferdinand. He was to learn, to his regret, the sometimes bitter fact, which he never accepted as fair, that the affairs of
the state took precedence over the affairs of the individual, even
those of a Spanish admiral.

The maxim, so often repeated, that Spain gave Italy Alexander VI
and Italy gave Spain Columbus is not simple metaphor. The Borgia

Pope Alexander was Spanish in every way: he spoke Spanish in public, his daughter Lucrezia wore Spanish costume, and his son's army was made up mainly of Spaniards. He and his family brought papal corruption to its highest point, although it had existed long before the Borgias. Columbus sought his support against what he viewed as the usurpations of the Catholic Kings at a time when Alexander had his own problems with the Spanish monarchs. In the small world of the fifteenth century, the affairs of the mighty in such distant places as Anjou, Naples, Rome, and Granada were on occasion intertwined with the affairs of the plebeian sailor from Genoa.

Pope Pius II, whose *Historia rerum* Columbus studied so assiduously, was the last pope to seriously sponsor a crusade against the Turks. Yet even he recognized the futility of the venture, saying: "I do not hope for what I want. Christianity has no longer a head: neither Pope nor Emperor is adequately esteemed or obeyed: they are treated as fictitious names and painted figures."[6] Columbus dreamed late in life of regaining the Holy City. Could his interest be attributed to a medieval hangover, to ignorance of the political realities (Pius's frustrated objective was to regain Constantinople, not Jerusalem), to his quixotic nature, or, perhaps, to the affectation of a parvenu hoping to impress the Catholic queen with his religious fervor?

Over the years many historians have wondered about the motivating force behind Columbus's lofty ambition to found a new dynasty in lands that he presumably only surmised to exist. The Portuguese established a precedent by awarding hereditary governorships in the Madeira Islands. Perhaps Columbus took his project to Portugal first because the Portuguese not only were the foremost discoverers of the times but also recognized the need to reward the individual. During the Reconquest of Moorish Spain, favored officials were named *adelantados* (governors of a forward territory), a title awarded only after the particular area had been occupied. Yet Columbus asked for more, much more, and he sought recognition in advance. This puzzled people then, as it still does today. By what right did he claim for himself so much? Perhaps he had taken to heart what Pius II wrote: "In our change-loving Italy, where nothing stands firm, and where no ancient dynasty exists, a servant can easily become king."[7]

Columbus the plebeian individualist and the aspirant to vice-regal honors was in these senses a true son of Italy.

Much has been made of the claim that Columbus was mocked at the Spanish court. This has been taken as indicative of the ignorance of Spanish court officials. Yet this unwarranted criticism overlooks the fact that in the fifteenth century and the first half of the sixteenth century and up until the time of the Spanish-led Counter-Reformation, ridicule was the tool commonly used to control those whose sense of highly developed individuality led them to seek personal fame. In the Middle Ages, such control had been exercised by symbolic insult. During the Renaissance, the method used was personal ridicule, as epitomized in Rome by the scandalous pasquinade and throughout Italy by the venomous barbs of Pietro Aretino. Perhaps Columbus was fortunate in that, being geographically far from the center of the savage insults of Rome, his attackers in Spain expressed their fear of this presumptuous foreigner merely by making fun of his project.

Once Columbus had achieved his goal, by crossing the Atlantic and revealing a new world (the phrase by which he too once referred to it), people naturally wanted to know how it was that this unknown had done the seemingly impossible. Columbus was the first to offer cosmographic explanations derived from mythology, biblical passages, Greek and Roman classics, Arabian theorists, and fifteenth-century humanists—in short, every conceivable source for his "Great Enterprise." As a demonstrably able propagandist, he used recognized names indiscriminately and inferred study of works that he probably knew only through compendia. He helped to fabricate his own legend.

The study of his claims and the sources he offered was taken up by biographers and chroniclers alike; these claims were debated, accepted by some, and rejected by others. For one and all, there simply had to be a reason behind the accomplishment of what no man had been known to have done before. Chroniclers naturally looked back to the myths and legends that over the ages had spoken to the subject. Some simply could not accept the possibility that an itinerant sailor, coming out of the unknown, could have conceived the idea without some empirical knowledge, picked up perhaps from

mariners' tales or even from an unknown pilot who may have preceded him across the ocean to the Indies and back (though others did
speculate that Columbus was himself the "unknown pilot"). Las
Casas, not alone among his contemporaries, found a more satisfactory explanation in the mysterious ways of God.

Contemporary sources for the study of Columbus require the same
critical study as is needed for any other form of historiography. In
his recent work *Inventing America*, José Rabasa quoted Hayden
White: "The historical narrative endows sets of real events with the
kinds of meaning found only in myth and literature." It is the task
of the biographer to interpret these meanings, not to add to the
myth. Biography is an important form of interpretative literature,
but it must leave fiction to the writers of fiction. One more quotation
from Rabasa perhaps applies here: "The production of the real in
contemporary historiography has been likened by Michel de Certeau
to the *trompe l'oeil* of the baroque, but as de Certeau quickly added,
this is profoundly different 'from the *trompe l'oeil* of old in that it no
longer furnishes any visible signs of its theatrical nature or of the
code whereby it is fabricated.'"[8] Identifying the "real" in the life of
Columbus has always provided the greatest challenge to his biographers, and the requisite "visible signs" are, more often than not,
lacking in their works.

The early writers on Columbus lived at the time when the medieval age had given way to the Renaissance. The humanists were in
turn supplanted by traditionalists in the early sixteenth century as
a result of the Counter-Reformation. Shortly after the death of
Columbus, interest shifted from discovery per se to the legal and
moral ethics of subjugation and of the exploitation of the Americas.
Even greater worlds than the one Columbus had discovered had by
then been opened up—Mexico, Peru, and Chile, as well as the
mysterious lands in the Pacific. By the beginning of the seventeenth
century, all of the chroniclers' works in which Columbus appeared
were known in either manuscripts or publications. These are among
the works studied comparatively in this critique.

In the nineteenth century the new age of skepticism and ration-
alism, opened by the Encyclopedists a century before, was in full
bloom. This brought about a renewed interest in the historical past,

which in turn fostered research into both official and private archives. In the case of Columbus, the inquiries carried out by Juan Bautista Muñoz and Martín Fernández de Navarrete resulted in vast amounts of contemporary data being collected, collated, transcribed, and ultimately published. This mass of newly available data provided much of the raw material out of which writers and scholars alike attempted to make an intelligible whole. Washington Irving and Henry Harrisse were preeminent among the first Americans to become so engaged.

At this point the whole nature of the inquiry into Columbus and the discovery reached a fork in the road. Irving took the path of fictionalized subjective biography, whereas Harrisse and others chose the route of the analytical objective study. Each method acquired a school of followers. Those who tried to reconcile the two approaches created a hybrid, a curious blend of fact and fiction, pseudo-biography. Today, many Spanish scholars continue the work of Muñoz and Fernández de Navarrete, devoting themselves to meticulous archival research and study. Columbus's Italian biographers generally prefer the route of compromise; they tend to blend cautiously the legendary with the factual. In the United States, the tendency has been to follow in the footsteps of Irving in the biographical context while occasionally following Harrisse in developing new insight into valid data gleaned from the study of the purely historical context of the times.

There is no point in repeating in detail the individual cases given in the text where silent emendation, unsupported supposition, and unbridled speculation posing as fact have marred the works under review. Suffice it to say that these authors, without exception, engaged in one or more of these unacceptable practices. Many patent inaccuracies have been revealed in the course of this study; even though a number of them have been minor, they are symptomatic and, as such, stir unease.

Consistently reaffirmed inaccuracies lead to mythology, harmless in itself but dangerous when mistaken for history. This has led to what Schoenbaum described as "a process inevitable in rehashes, what was tentative or qualified hardens into positive assertion. . . . In such a way do traditions flourish and take on the particularities of truth."[9] The result is most evident in the works of the social historians, who based their theories on what they assumed to be historically confirmed facts that as often as not were at best unproven assumptions. A case in point is the group of works that relied heavily on the supposition that Columbus had read Marco Polo and Mandeville before he set sail for the Indies.

There is a consensus that Columbus was a great navigator and ship's captain. The first claim is relative: great compared with whom? Columbus has become so central to discovery thinking in the United States that those who preceded him, as well as those who followed, are paid relatively scant attention. Certainly his contemporaries Bartolomeu Dias, Vasco da Gama, Amerigo Vespucci, and Ferdinand Magellan played critical parts in opening up the routes to the Americas and Asia. The second claim, concerning Columbus's presumed role as a ship's captain, is unsupported by any contemporary evidence. The only time that he is said to have sailed as a captain was on the voyage for René of Anjou, a voyage that doubtfully ever took place. On his four transatlantic voyages he was captain-general of fleets in which each vessel carried its own captain, *maestre*, and pilot. He said that he had sailed all of the known seas, but he never said in what capacity. In two of his known prediscovery voyages, he sailed as a merchant, not as a ship's officer.

Any analysis of Columbus's character must take care to avoid the customary one-sided attention paid to his religious fervor. As pointed out in the text, this grew incrementally as his political fortunes faded. His oftimes blatant religiosity is generally ignored.

By his own testimony, he was a very cautious man; he repeatedly withheld information from his sponsors and associates. He was almost paranoid in his constant fear of being mistreated. In his correspondence with the Spanish monarchs he was at once arrogant and groveling. His treatment of the indigenous population of the Indies fluctuated constantly between his naive admiration for societal attributes that he failed to understand and his outright barbarity in treatment of the natives.

The works reviewed here reveal a marked tendency to accept contemporary gossip as factual reporting when it involved Columbus's relations with his companions Fray Bernardo Buil, Pedro Margarite,

Bernal Díaz de Pisa, Alonso de Ojeda, Juan de la Cosa, and Juan Aguado. What is not noted is that all of these men were later rewarded by the Crown with important appointments. Did the Crown simply ignore the complaints against these men, complaints that we know of only through secondary sources, or were their differences with Columbus less serious than is generally believed? The same question applies to the captains of his vessels; several had supposedly disobeyed him, yet he used them again on later voyages.

Regardless of how Columbus devised his plan for crossing the ocean, scientifically or empirically, what finally made it possible was his stubbornness. When he first went to the Spanish court he had probably already developed his plan. This is made apparent by the very fact that the stranger from Portugal was personally received and financially subsidized by the Spanish monarchs. Yet he had to wait six years for the necessary authorization to set sail. During that long delay he never revealed the full details of his plan, unless perhaps at the very end of his wait. Columbus was a very patient man. He was also duplicitous, first with his sponsors, then with his crews, and later with the Indian caciques. His was a far more complex personality than the one portrayed by his hagiographers.

Columbus has been traditionally faulted as a poor administrator. Sufficient consideration has not been given to the complexities he faced. From the beginning there was a conflict of interests—Columbus's personal ambition versus the state's interests. Centuries-old legal customs were introduced into an inhospitable environment, one in which new concepts were required. Initial colonizing efforts were made with a motley mixture of court officials and individuals seeking their fortune in a far-off land that had been grossly oversold. Disease and near-starvation appeared almost immediately. The gold that they sought was not found until almost a decade had passed. Only days after arriving at Navidad, Buil and some of the court-appointed officials sought royal permission to leave the land that they had come to colonize. Columbus's successors Francisco de Bobadilla and Nicolás de Ovando were no more successful than he was at administering the colony. At the same time, the much-vaunted evangelization of the Indians was an equal failure; Father

Ramón Pane baptized the first Indian on Española after the death of Columbus. By then there were few natives left to baptize.

The study of the many incongruities in the life of Columbus—such as relating to the romantic story of his activities as a corsair, the little-known prediscovery voyages, his marriage, his arrival in Spain, La Rábida, the Khan, the double entries in the *Diario*, the mutiny, Guanahaní, and the sinking of the *Santa María*, to name but a few—requires informed choices among often incompatible alternatives. These subjects should be treated with neither naive credulity nor excessive skepticism but with critical balance. Unfortunately, the authors reviewed here share in a common fault: they too often offer versions with unwarranted certainty. Expressions of certitude in the life of Columbus can be misleading.

The biographies reviewed in this critique sometimes show an ingenuous acceptance of legend, whereas, paradoxically, many of them do present unquestionable evidence of solid research in the individual author's own field of specialized interest. For John Noble Wilford, the field is geography; William and Carla Rahn Phillips, history; Kirkpatrick Sale, ethnological-cum-ecological. Fernández-Armesto, a Spaniard writing in English, provides a less legendary biography than most while offering insight into the historical-geographical, one might say the geopolitical.

Samuel Eliot Morison was a case unto himself. He had obviously carried out a great deal of research over the years. He delved most deeply into nautical matters. In matters of biographical import he took a few known facts and enhanced them with suppositions of his own and of others to produce a work that makes for fascinating reading but is often seriously flawed historically. According to some, the general acceptance of his work was perhaps due as much to respect for its author, the "American Admiral," as to respect for its content. He had become a part of the Harvard legend, a person not to be lightly disputed in midcentury academia. Sadly, none of his confrères took the trouble to correct him during his lifetime; if they had, he may have been able to apply his undoubted gifts to a critical revision of his own works. Regrettably, as matters have been left to stand, Morison cannot be taken for an authority on the life of

Columbus. Yet, as has been shown, the authors reviewed tended to follow him uncritically.

The biographer's lot is never an easy one. On the writing of biography, Schoenbaum quoted Desmond McCarthy, who "said somewhere that trying to work out Shakespeare's personality was like looking at a very dark glazed picture in the National Portrait Gallery: at first you see nothing, then you begin to recognize features, and then you realize that they are your own."[10] In most of these biographies, one sees too often the authors' own images.

The rationale behind Columbus's discovery derives from either one or a combination of two basic sources. The first is empirical, including either prior discovery or maritime lore and experience, and the other is "scientific," based on the study of the classical Greek, Roman, and Arab cosmographical writings gleaned from his readings of the *Ymago mundi*. As far as the historical record is concerned, there are equally valid reasons to accept either hypothesis. What is not acceptable historiographically is to present a presumption in favor of the one or the other as a given truth. How Columbus came by his certainty that he would find what he did where he said he would will probably never be known. What cannot be taken away from Columbus is the indisputable fact that he, unlike the man who first chances to stumble onto something, was the true discoverer as defined by Burckhardt: "a man who finds what he has sought." What he found was a new world—America.

Notes

The particular editions used (see the bibliography) are those in the Davidson Reference Library. Exceptions are indicated with an asterisk. In references to limited early editions, chapter numbers are given so that the reader can locate the references in later editions.

Introduction

1. Nowell, 802.
2. Boorstin, 21.
3. Certeau, vii, 64, 70.
4. Zamora, 3.
5. Rabasa, 9.
6. Quoted in Boorstin, 53.
7. Tuchman, 22.
8. Bowen, introduction.
9. Haile, 359.

10. Bowen, 360–61.
11. Gould, 81.
12. Haile, 361.
13. Tuchman, 33.
14. Gardner, 4.
15. Hamilton, 32.
16. Haile, 337.
17. Tuchman, 20.
18. Jackson, 85.

Sources

1. Facsimiles of Lascasian manuscripts in the Biblioteca Nacional, Madrid, Spain; Sanz, *Relación*; Sanz, *Diario*. Transcriptions: Spain, Fernández de Navarrete; United States, Dunn and Kelley. Free translations: Fuson; Cummins. Studies: Jane; Rumeu, *El Diario de a bordo de Cristóbal Colón*; Henige, *In Search of Columbus*. Colón, *Historie*, was first published in Italy as *Historie del S. D. Fernando Colombo*, 1571.* Translations: French, Cotlendy, 1681 (until 1932, French translations were the best available); English, Churchill, 1704; Spanish, González de Barcia, 1749* (a poor translation, reprinted without corrections in the *Biblioteca de Autores Españoles*, 1928), and Serrano y Sanz, 1932 (this definitive Spanish edition—*Historia del Almirante*—is cited throughout the notes below); United States, Belknap, 1792 (a condensed version), Keen, 1959 and 1992.

2. Rumeu, *El libro copiador.*

3. Henige, *Finding Columbus.*

4. Gil, "Las nuevas cartas," in Varela, *Textos.*

5. Ibid., 76–79.

6. Zamora, "Letter to the Sovereigns," 3–9.

7. Ibid., introduction, 24–43.

8. Study: Henige, "Samuel Eliot Morison."

9. Dunn and Kelley.

10. Sanz, *La carta de Colón.*

11. *Biblioteca Colombina* (in seven volumes published over the years 1888–1948 by the Spanish Royal Academy); also available as a facsimile edition (illegible), published by Archer Huntington* in 1905). The definitive study is Marín.

12. For disputed postils written in bastard Latin about Dias's rounding of the Cape of Good Hope, see the Quintana edition of Las Casas's *Historia*,

chap. LXXVII, p. 146; Asensio, 1:221, who attributed it to Bartolomé Colón; Varela, *Textos*, 12, attributed it to Cristóbal.

13. D'Ailly; Piccolómini; Gil, *El libro de Marco Polo*. Some of these appeared originally over the years 1987–90.

14. Las Casas's *Historia* was first published edited by Marqués de la Fuensanta del Valle in Madrid 1875. A modern edition by Agustín Millares Carlo, with a study by Lewis Hanke, was published in Mexico City in 1951. Manuel José Quintana's transcription was reproduced in Santo Domingo 1985 (since this is the edition most often used by contemporary Spanish historians, it is used in this study in order to facilitate checking page numbers cited by these historians). An edition of the Quintana version was edited by Juan Perez de Tudela with Emilio López Oto and published in Madrid in 1961. Herrera, *Historia general de los hechos*. Herrera acknowledged his access to the manuscript of Las Casas's *Historia de las Indias*. Bernáldez, first Cronista de Indias, probably also had access to this document for his *Historia de los Reyes Católicos* (first full edition published in Seville in 1869–70).

15. Las Casas, *Brevissima relacion*. A modern version in facsimile, with notes and introduction by Ballesteros Gaibrois, was published in Madrid in 1977.

16. Broome.

17. Hanke and Jímenez Fernández, *Bartolomé de Las Casas*.

18. Colón, *Historia del Almirante Don Cristobal Colón*.

19. Colón, *The History of the Life and Actions of Adm. Christopher Columbus*.

20. Rumeu, *Hernando Colón*.

21. Harrisse, *L'histoire de Christophe Colomb*, 58.

22. Studies: Fernández Duro, *Nebulosa de Colón*; Colón, *Historia del Almirante Don Cristobal Colón*, introduction; Rumeu, *Hernando Colón*; Jos Pérez.

23. First proposed: Sanguinetti in his *Vita de Cristoforo Colombo* in 1846. Best-known: Roselly de Lorgues (1878–90). Amended and condensed version: Barry (1870). Roselly de Lorgues's work was critiqued by Sanguinetti, *Intorno alla seconda edizione*, in 1881. Study: Clarke (1893). See: Paolini (1938). Most recently: Granzotto (1984).

24. Henige, "Samuel Eliot Morison," 69–88.

25. Irving's work was translated into many languages. Lamartine, basing his work largely on Irving's book, wrote an equally popular novelistic life of Columbus in French. Also see Wasserman for a revisionist psychological study.

Chapter 1

1. Cittá di Genova.

2. Ibid., xii. First published by Assereto, titled "La data della nascita di Colombo accertata de un documento nuovo."*

3. *Colección de documentos inéditos*. Also see Muñoz, *Historia del Nuevo Mundo*, and Muñoz, *Santo Domingo en los manuscritos* (1981). The first Muñoz work was the basis on which Fernández de Navarrete built his own monumental work, his *Colección de los viajes y descubrimientos que hicieron por mar los españoles*, a basic source for most of the biographies known today. It was the basis for Irving's biography of Columbus, *A History of the Life and Voyages of Christopher Columbus*. See also Fernández Duro, *Bibliografía Colombina*. The *Bibliografía*, though in very many instances unreliable, does provide some archival data not readily available elsewhere in print. It was published as a quadricentennial commemorative work by the Spanish Royal Academy. Harrisse published his *Christophe Colomb et les Académiciens espagnols* in 1894, a devastating critique of this earlier work.

4. *Raccolta di documenti e studi publicatti della R. Commissione Colombiana per quatro centenario della scoperta dell'America*, 18 vols. (Rome, 1892–94).* These volumes were recently reprinted in Rome.

5. William Robertson's *History of America* (1777)* was the first documented British study of the discovery; considered unacceptable by the Spanish authorities, it was banned in Spain, and Juan Bautista Muñoz was commissioned to document a refutation of Robertson's work. Later, better-documented British works include Helps, which is especially important for documentation on slavery in the Americas and on early Spanish colonial administration. Also see Young.

6. Harrisse devoted his scholastic life to the study of Columbus. For a bibliography of his works, see Sanz, *Indice general: Henry Harrisse (1829–1910)*. Vignaud, an American diplomatist stationed in Paris, was a serious student of both Columbus and Vespucci. He published in Paris and London. His major works were *Toscanelli and Columbus*, his study of the disputed relationship between Toscanelli and Columbus, a limited edition of 365 pages that provoked much dispute, and his equally well-documented *Histoire critique de la Grande Entreprise de Christophe Colomb*, a limited edition in two volumes. His major works were written in French, like the works by Harrisse, who wrote in French and Spanish, they have never been translated into English. See also Thacher. This is one of the most valuable collections of documents on Columbus available in English. Due to its small edition, as well as perhaps academic disdain for a nonprofessional historian

(a criticism also leveled against Vignaud), it has not been used as much as warranted by later American biographers. Thacher's study, together with the massive *Narrative and Critical History of America*, in eight volumes, edited by Harvard Professor Justin Winsor, and Winsor's later one-volume *Christopher Columbus* are among the most important sources in English for contemporary documentation on Columbus and his times.

Columbus's Origins and Birthplace

7. Città di Genova, 124: "Dei gratia Januensium Dux, elegit ad custodiam turris et porte Olivele dilectum suum Dominicum de Columbo."

8. Ibid., 132: "vinorum eidem Christofforo et dicto Dominico vendotorum."

9. Ibid., 104.

10. A few of the more recent ones: Beltrán, *Cristóbal Colón y Cristóforo Colombo* and *Cristóbal Colón*; Calzada, *La Patria de Colón*; Otero Sánchez, *España, Patria de Colón*. Galician-converso: Andre, *Columbus*. Catalan-Sephardic: Madariaga, *Christopher Columbus, Being the Life of the Very Magnificent Lord Don Cristobal Colón*, and the Spanish-language edition of Madariaga, *Vida del Muy Magnífico Señor Don Cristóbal Colón*. Perhaps because Madariaga is a Spaniard, he is one of the few major biographers to use Columbus's name correctly when writing in English.

11. Rumeu, *El "Portugues."*

12. Cesarini.

13. Malloy.*

14. Winsor, *Narrative and Critical History*, 1:76, 129. This is a study of the confusion of the Danish explorer Scocius—Scolvus, Skorno—with Columbus.

15. Cateras is one of the most recent efforts in this direction, a strictly minor work retelling a fable that has been around for centuries. Its origin probably lies in the facts that Chios was a Genoese colony and that Columbus wrote that he had sailed there where he first saw mastic as well his son's claim that they were related to the Greek corsair Georgi Bissipat.

16. Beltrán, *Cristóbal Colón y Cristóforo Colombo*.

17. Napione. Also noted in Città di Genova, chap. 9.

18. Spotorno, *Della origine e della patria di Cristoforo Colombo*. This valuable work by the editor of the *Codice diplomatico* (1823), in which first appeared in print the famous letter to the nurse of Prince Juan, has not been translated. It is not readily available, having been published in a very limited edition; Harrisse complained that he was unable to locate a copy. See also Desimoni.

19. Genealogical studies are provided by Asensio, Cittá di Genova, Thacher, and Winsor. References on some of these are in Fernández Duro, *Bibliografía Colombina*. See his listings under Colón. One of the complications lies in the fact that descendants of all three female companions of grandson Christopher have at one time or another claimed a right to the title with its lucrative pensions and privileges.

20. Harrisse, *Bibliotheca Americana Vetustissima* (1866).

21. Fernández Duro, *Bibliografía Colombina*.

22. Davidson, *A Columbus Handbook*, 293–95.

23. Bernáldez, chap. I, p. 357: "hombre de tierra de genova."

24. Brunet y Bellet, French historian, in his *Colón. ¿Fue el verdadero descubridor de américa? ¿Donde nació?* (1892), based his support for Cogoreo on Interiano's *Ristretto delle Historie Genovesi*, 227: "Genuense . . . d'una villa discosta XX. Miglia dalla Citta nostra. Cogoreo." Also given in Fernández Duro, *Bibliografía Colombina*, 412.

25. Augustini Giustiniani, *Salterio Ebreo, Greco, Arabico e Caldeo*, facsimile in Cittá di Genova, 66.

26. Martire, *Oceaneae decadis: De rebus oceanicis*, 455.

27. Santa Cruz.

28. Alessandro Geraldini, 138: "el genovés Colón." This was partially translated into Spanish in 1892, fully by Sociedad Dominicans de Bibliófilos in 1977. A facsimile of passages referring to Columbus is in Cittá di Genova, 38.

29. Muro Orejón, *Pleitos Colombinos* (1964, 1967).

30. Uhagon: "Oyo decir que hera ginoves."

31. Ibid. Also in Cittá di Genova, 185. Testimony of Rodrigo Barreda: "oyo decir que hera de la senioria de Genova de la cibdad de Saona."

32. Uhagon.

33. Cittá di Genova, 146: "Cristoforo Colombo laniere di Genova."

34. Ibid., 137: "Christofforus Columbus civis Janae."

35. Wiesenthal (1973) and, more recently, Amler (1991).

36. Cittá di Genova, 65: "Christoforo Colombo Genovese . . . fu de parenti plebei, como che il padre fussi testore de panni di lanna et lui fussi testatore di seta." Ibid. in Giustiniani, *Psalterium*, 47, facsimile in Cittá di Genova, 66: "nato de umili genitori."

37. Gallo in Cittá di Genova, 63: "Christoforus & Bartholomoæus [*sic*] Colombi fratres, natione Ligures, ac Genuæ plebieii [*sic*]." A later edition (1773) cited another Gallo version: "I fratelli Cristoforo e Bartolomeo Colombo, di origine Liguri, nati in Genova da genitori plebei e che vivevano dell'arte di lavore la lana (perchè il padre era tessitore e i figli erano stati un giorno scardassieri)."

38. Fernández Duro, *Bibliografía Colombina*, 412: "con la destrezza solo dell'ingegno (como che poco literato fusse)."

39. Colón, *Historia del Almirante*, chap. II, p. 24: "La señoría de génova, ha puesto pena a aquellos que la tuvieron o leyeron."

40. Columbus. Also Cittá di Genova, xix. This letter was first published in Spanish by Spotorno, *Codice diplomatico* (1823).

41. Colón, *Historia del Almirante*, chap. II, p. 17: "por ocasión de las guerras y parcialidades de la Lombardia reducidos a necesidad y pobreza."

42. Ibid., chap. III, p. 28.

Hernando Colón and the Historie

43. Harrisse, *L'histoire de Christophe Colomb*; Barry.

44. Rumeu, *Hernando Colón*.

45. Jos Peréz.

46. Colón, *Historia del Almirante*, chap. I, p. 11.

47. Ibid., introduction, cxxx.

The Columbine Library

48. Real Academia de la Historia, *Biblioteca Colombina*.

49. Marín.

50. Varela, *Textos*, 9–13.

51. Gil, *El libro de Marco Polo*, xl–lix.

Columbus and the French Corsairs

52. Las Casas, *Historia*, chap. CLXXXII, p. 198.

53. Spotorno, *Codice diplomatico*, 298.

54. Columbus.

55. Colón, *Historia del Almirante*, chap. V, pp. 37–38.

56. Ibid., chap. V, p. 39.

57. Cittá di Genova, ix.

The Family Name

58. The first published edition of Las Casas's *Historia de las Indias*, Madrid 1875, is not reliable. Two excellent editions are those edited by Agustín Millares Carlo, with a study by Lewis Hanke, and the Madrid edition edited by Juan Pérez de Tudela and Emilio López Oto. These were the fourth and fifth printings respectively of this work. The listed 1875

edition was the first, although Las Casas is believed to have finished writing his history sometime after 1552. He started it while he was living in the Dominican monastery in Puerto Plata on the northern coast of Española.

59. Phillips and Phillips, 9.

Chapter 2

Columbus's Birthdate

1. Vignaud, *The Real Birth-Date of Columbus.*
2. Spanish translation: Charlevoix.
3. Cittá di Genova, 104.
4. Ibid., 144: "testor pannorum et tabernarius."
5. Ibid., 132: "in presentia, auctoritate, consilio et consensu dicti"; "Domenico eius patris presentis et auctorizante"; "major annis decemnovem."
6. Ibid., 132: "respondit quod sit etatis annorum viginti septem vel circa."
7. Morison, *Southern Voyages*, 6: "was born . . . some time between 25 August and the end of October 1451."
8. Varela, *Textos*, 318: "poco me ha aprovechado veinte años que yo he servido."
9. Ibid., 329: "Yo vine a servir de veinteocho años."

Early Maritime Experience

10. Ibid., 318.
11. D'Ailly, #490, p. 149.
12. Varela, *Textos* (*Raccolta* #490), 90; d'Ailly, #490, p. 149.
13. Ibid. (*Raccolta* #23), 91.
14. Cittá di Genova, 136–37.
15. Ibid., 110, 135, 148: "Dominicus Columbus, habitator Saone, et Christoforus eius filius."
16. Morison, *Admiral*, 12.

Voyage to Chios

17. Dunn and Kelley, fol. 23r:3, p. 144.
18. Ibid., fol. 35v:5–8, p. 216.
19. D'Ailly, #342, p. 105: "la isla de Quio [sic] donde nace el mástix"; Piccolómini, #762, p. 196: "Aqui se da la almáciga."

20. Morison, *Admiral*, 13.
21. Phillips and Phillips, 93.
22. Wilford, *The Mysterious*, 64.

Ultima Thule (Iceland)

23. Varela, *Textos*, 167.
24. Morison, *Admiral*, 14–15.
25. Varela, *Textos*, 167.
26. Taviani, 403: "sulla base di ulteriore documentazione—che egli avrebbe viaggiato con i marinai di Bristol fin dal 1489 e poi nel 1494."
27. Gil and Varela, *Cartas*, 266–69.
28. Ibid.

England and Ireland

29. Dunn and Kelley, fol. 41v:13–17, p. 252: "yo e andado veynte y tres años en la mar sin salir della t(iem)po q(ue) se aya de contar; y vido el leva(n)te y poniente q(ue) diz por yr al camino de septentrion q(ue) es inglaterra: y e andado la guinea."
30. Colón, *Historia del Almirante*, chap. I, p. 36.
31. Varela, *Textos* (*Raccolta* #20), 9: (Homine)s de Catayo uersus oriens uenierunt. (N)os uidi[mi]mus multa notablia et (spe)cialiter in Galuei Ibernie uirum et (ux)orem in duobus lignis arreptis ex mirabili (for)ma."
32. Piccolómini, #10, p. 7: "un hombre y una mujer en dos leños arrastrados, de extraña catadura."
33. Morison, *Admiral*, 16.
34. Phillips and Phillips, 105.

African Voyages

35. Varela, *Textos* (*Raccolta* #16), 89: "sub linea equinoxialis est castrum Mine serenissimi regis Portugalie, quem uidimus"; d'Ailly, #16b, p. 40: "que hemos visto"; ibid., #234, p. 85: "el rey serenisimo de Portugal tiene alli una fortaleza en la que estuve."
36. Varela, *Textos*, 11: "Quis omnia adinpeuit et renunciauit dito serenissimo regi, me presente."
37. Ibid., 285.
38. Ibid., #23, p. 92, and Las Casas, *Historia*, chap. XXVII, p. 146, are in Latin. A Spanish version is in d'Ailly, #23b, p. 43.

39. Las Casas, *Historia*, chap. XXVII, p. 146: "Estas son palabras escritas de la mano de Bartolomé Colón, no sé si las escribió de si o de su letra por su hermano Cristóbal Colón, [la letra yo lo conozco ser de Bartolomé Colón, porque tuve muchas suyas]. Algœn mal latín parece que hay [e todo lo es malo], pero pongolo a la letra como lo hallé de la dicho mano escrita."

40. Ibid.

41. Asensio, 1:221.

42. Ibid: "Este libro era del adelantado my tio. Esta registrado. 3361."

43. Las Casas, *Historia*, chap. XXVII, p. 146, quoting Bartolomé Colón that Dias returned from discovering the Cape of Good Hope in 1488: "pude ser verdad todo desta manera y es, que algunos comienzan a contar el año siguiente desde el día de Navidad, que es así lo debía de contar Bartolomé Colón . . . y otros desde enero . . . y así . . . refirió el coronista que el año de 87 llegaron a Lisboa."

44. Taviani, 59: "nel 1487, Bartolomeo Diaz raggiunge e doppia l'estremo capo meridionale"; Fernández-Armesto, *Columbus*, 41: "reference to Bartolomeu Dias . . . must date from at least 1488"; Wilford, *The Mysterious*, 15: "discovered the Cape of Good Hope in 1488." This comment was made in connection with the voyage by "maestre Josephe" to the equator in 1485. Las Casas, *Historia*, chap. XXVII, p. 145, went on to discuss the voyage of Días in 1488, on which, according to Las Casas, "aunque D. bartolomé Colón, hermano del Almirante, que se halló en este descubrimiento," and later, "en este del cabo de Buena Esperanza se halló Bartolomé Colón."

Count René of Anjou

45. Varela, *Textos*, 285.

46. Las Casas, *Historia*, chap. III, p. 48.

47. Colón, *Historia del Almirante*, chap. III, p. 33.

48. Asensio, 1:24; Morison, *Admiral*, 21.

49. Asensio, 1:25.

50. Colón, *Life of the Admiral*, note 1 to chap. 4, 288.

51. Morison, *Admiral*, 13.

52. Sale, 52.

53. Phillips and Phillips, 94.

54. Fernández-Armesto, *Columbus*, 16.

Arrival in Portugal

55. Colón, *Historia del Almirante*, chap. I, pp. 38–40; Keen, in Colón, *Life of the Admiral*, 12–15, offered a literary translation.

56. Las Casas, *Historia*, chap. IV, p. 35: "de la mucha humedad del agua y de los trabajos que había pasado, y curado también por ventura de algunas heridas que en la batalla había recibido, fuese a Lisboa."

57. Morison, *Admiral*, 24.

58. Wilford, *The Mysterious*, 64.

59. Morison, *Southern Voyages*, 13.

60. Colón, *Historia del Almirante*, introduction, cxxxv–viii.

Trips to Madeira

61. Cittá di Genova.

62. Varela, *Textos*, 167.

63. D'Ailly, #409, p. 149: "navegando a menudo desde Lisboa al sur hacia Guinea observé con cuidado la derrota como es usual entre capitanes y marineros."

Chapter 3

Two Visits to Portugal

1. Morison, *Admiral*, 13.

2. Colón, *Historia del Almirante*, introduction, cxxxix.

3. Bernáldez, chap. CXVIII, p. 357: "un hombre de tierra de Génova, mercader de libros."

4. Las Casas, *Historia*, chap. III, p. 33: "Agustín Justiniano se contradice en la dicha colección del *Psalterio* diciendo estas palabras: . . 'pasó a Lisboa, en Portugal, donde aprendió las cosas de cosmografía, etc.'"

5. Colón, *Historia del Almirante*, chap. V, p. 41: "tomó tanta plática y amistad con él, que se casaron."

6. Las Casas, *Historia*, chap. XXVII, p. 146: "porque Cristóbal Colón y su hermano Bartolomé Colón en aquellos tiempos vivían en Portugal."

7. Asensio, bk. I, chap. VIII, p. 134 and in *Colección de documentos inéditos*, 33:9, March 20, Juan II of Portugal: "Vimos á carta que nos escribestes: é á boa vontade é afeiçaon que por ella mostrades tenerdes á nosso servicio. . . . E quanto á vossa vinda cá, certo, assi por lo que apontaes. . . . E porque por ventura tenerdes algum reçeo de nossas justiças, por raçon d'algunas covsas á que dejades obrigado . . . vos seguramos . . . que non dejades presso, retenudo, acusado, Citado nem demandado por nemhuna causa ora seja civil, ora crime de qualquer cualidade."

8. Colón, *Historia del Almirante*, chap. XII, p. 107.

9. Wilford, *The Mysterious*, 90.

10. Fernández-Armesto, *Columbus*, 33, 200.

11. Colón, *Historia del Almirante*, chap. XI, p. 101 n.

12. Ibid., chap. XII, p. 107: "Y así, con toda brevedad y secreto aramda una carabela, fingiendo enviarla con vituallas y socorro a los que estaban en las islas de Cabo Verde, le mandó hacia donde el Almirante se había ofrecido a ir."

13. Ibid., chap. XI, p. 99: "le parecía que no estaba obligado a tan gran premio como Colón pedía por su hallazgo."

14. See Colón, *Historia del Almirante*, vol. 1, p. 100 n, 100 for a copy of the Dulmo exploration contract.

Bartolomé in England and France

15. Las Casas, *Historia*, chap. XXIX, p. 153.

16. Ibid., chap. XXIX, p. 154, gave the date as "decimaque die mensis Februarii." Hernando Colón, Colón, *Historia del Almirante*, chap. XI, p. 104, dated it February 13: "Bartholomeus Columbus de Terra Rubra, opus editit istud Londoniis, anno Domini 1480, atque insuper anno Octavo, decimaque die cum tertis mensis februarii."

17. Colón, *Historia del Almirante*, chap XI, pp. 102–3.

18. Fernández de Oviedo, *Historia general*, chap. IV, p. 18: "aunque ya era Colom casado en aquel reyno, é se habia hecho natural vasallo de aquella tierra por su matrimonio."

19. Ibid., pp. 18–19: "su hermano con el rey Enrique VII . . . vido que alli no era acogido su servicio . . . començó a mover é tractar . . . con el rey Don Juan."

20. Varela, *Colón y los florentinos*, 48.

21. Ibid., 49.

22. Morison, *Admiral*, 39.

23. Phillips and Phillips, 129.

24. Wilford, *The Mysterious*, 90.

25. Taviani, 64.

26. Sale, 251.

Marriage

27. Colón, *Historia del Almirante*, chap. V, pp. 41–42.

28. Las Casas, *Historia*, chap. IV, pp. 35–36.

29. Morison, *Admiral*, 16.

30. Phillips and Phillips, 99.

31. Asensio, 1:52.

32. Ibid., 1:55: "à outra persona que não fosse geragáo de Gil Ayres Mogniz."

33. Winsor, *Narrative and Critical History*, 2:90. Winsor quotes Harrisse to the effect that Columbus's wife's name was Philippa Moniz and that she was a daughter of Vasco Gil Moniz, not of Bartholomeu Perestrello, while coincidentally Vasco's sister Isabel was married to Perestrello.

34. López de Gómara, 165.

35. Asensio, 1:55.

Wife and Children

36. Dunn and Kelley, fol. 62r:21–24, p. 370: "[February 14] Dize mas q(ue) tambie(n) le dava gran pena dos hijos q(ue) tenia en cordova al estudio q(ue) los dexava guerfanos de padre y madre en tierra estraña."

37. Varela, *Textos*, 272: "vine a servir estos Prínçipes de tan leixos y desé mujer y fijos, que jamás vi por ello."

38. Ibid., 177.

39. Las Casas, *Historia*, chap. IV, p. 36: "por ventura por sola esta causa de querer navigar, dejar allí su mujer."

40. Fernández-Armesto, *Columbus*, 17.

41. Phillips and Phillips, 114.

Briolanja Muñiz

42. Varela, *Colón y los florentinos*, 46.

43. Fernández Duro, *Bibliografía Colombina*, sec. I:15: "Real cédula [May 30, 1493] de los Reyes Católicos á los inquisidores de Sevilla, mandando que los bienes muebles y raices que están secuestrados á Bartolomé de Sevilla, vecino de Huelva, se pongan en poder de Miguel Muliarte, vecino de Sevilla, y de su mujer Violante [*sic*] Muñiz hasta la causa se determine."

44. Varela, *Colón y los florentinos*, 103, 101 n.

The Toscanelli Letters

45. Gil and Varela, *Cartas*, 129.

46. Las Casas, *Historia*, chap. XII, p. 63: "Rescibida la carta de Cristóbal Colón, el dicho maestro Paulo respondióle una carta en latin, la cual yo vide y tuve en mi mano, vuelta de latin en romance."

47. Piccolómini, xxi.

48. *Biblioteca Colombina.* Hernando's registry does not show the customary provence of the work; however, the library registry number 3123 does follow entry number 3122 for Bartolomé's copy of the *Imago mundi.* Also see Asensio 1:232.

49. Vignaud, *Toscanelli and Columbus.*

50. Sumien.

51. Piccolómini, #854, p. 261.

52. Colón, *Historia del Almirante*, chap. VIII, pp. 57–65. In a footnote (p. 65), Serrano y Sanz, the editor, wrote, "We have copied these letters from the MS holograph of Father Las Casas' *Historia de las Indias* in the National Library."

53. Bentley, 157–58.

54. Wilford, *The Mapmakers*, 58.

55. Polo, *Most Noble and Famous Travels*, 19: "The Pope . . . straighte way gave them two Friers, of the order of Sainct Dominike, being great Clerkes, to go with them to the great Cane . . . they came to a towne called Giaza . . . fearing to passe anye further, the two Friers taryed there."

56. Chaliand, 465–74. For the reports of John and his companion, "Friar Benedict the Pole," see Rubruck, 1–40. Comment on this voyage is in Yule, 1:156.

57. Bentley, 157.

58. For further information, see Rubruck, 282.

59. Bentley, 157.

60. Yule, 3:45–59.

61. Ibid., 177–269.

62. Ibid., 2:96–278.

63. Greenblatt, *New World Encounters*, 10.

64. Polo, *Most Noble and Famous Travels*, 126–36.

65. Bentley, 156–63.

66. Ibid., 216.

67. Wilford, *The Mysterious*, 77.

68. Colón, *Historia del Almirante*, chap. VIII, p. 55: "llego esto a noticia del Almirante, que era curiosísimo de estas cosas, y al instante por medio de Lorenzo Giraldo, Florentin, que se hallaba en Lisboa."

69. Las Casas, *Historia*, chap. XII, p. 62.

70. Varela, *Colón y los florentinos*, 35: "Nacido en 1457 hubo Giannetto [Columbus's agent Berardi, known later in Spain as Juanoto] de emigrar muy joven a la Peninsula Ibérica, quizá llamado por su padre Lorenzo quien en Lisboa, muy vinculado a la pesqueria de coral y al comercio africano en general, ocupaba una posición de cierta revelancia."

71. Taviani, 383.

72. Varela, *Colón y los florentinos*, 48.

73. Colón, *Historia del Almirante*, chap. XI, pp. 100–101.

74. Varela, *Colón y los florentinos*, 22.

75. Fernández de Oviedo, *Historia general*, chap. IV, p. 19.

Chapter 4

Cosmographic Concepts and Postils

1. Ramos, *Memorial de Zamora*.

2. Thacher believed that postils #490 and #460 were written in the same hand as #860, in which the writer says he was in Portugal when Master Joseph's expedition returned, which would put Columbus in Portugal late in 1485 if he wrote this. Vignaud, *Histoire*, 1:354, and *Biblioteca Colombina* attribute it to Bartolomé. Vignaud, *Histoire*, 1:406.

3. Las Casas, *Historia*, chap. XXVII, p. 146: "La letra yo lo conozco ser de Bartolomé Colón, porque tuve muchas suyas."

4. Varela, *Textos*, introduction, lvii: "Desde entonces los historiadores manejaron las anotaciones como mejor convenía a sus intereses investigadores."

5. Piccolómini, #858c, p. 264. Also in West and Kling: "(Y desde el comienço fasta esta era de 1481 son 5241 años."

6. D'Ailly, #621, p. 338.

7. Fernández-Armesto, *Columbus*, 29.

8. Winsor, *Narrative and Critical History*, 1:3, 4.

9. Dawson, 475.

10. Most recently by Cummins, 40.

11. Piccolómini, chap. I, p. 5: "Sobre la forma del Mundo casi todos están de acuerdo en que es redonda."

12. D'Ailly, #5, p. 29.

13. Sanz, *Relación*, fol. 6, unnumbered pages 11, 12: "Yo siempre leí que el mundo, tierra y agua, era esférico e las auctoridades y experiençias que Ptolomeo y todos los otros que escrivieron de este sitio, daban e amostraban para ello"; "Mas este otro digo que es como sería la mitad de la pera bien redonda, la cual toviese el pezón alto, como yo dije, o como una teta de mujer en una pelota redonda."

14. Piccolómini, chap. I, p. 6: "Su figura unos consideran esférica, otros alargada. Con esto está de acuerdo Claudio Ptolomeo y parece la opinión más conveniente."

15. D'Ailly, #23c, p. 43.

16. Winsor, *Narrative and Critical History*, 1:34.

17. D'Ailly, chap. 4, p. 223.

18. Dawson, 505.

19. Winsor, *Narrative and Critical History*, 2:28.

20. D'Ailly, 23c-g, 43–44.

21. Sanz, *Relación*, fol. 8, unnumbered page 16: "Plinio escrive . . . El Maestro [Peter Comestor] . . . dize que las aguas son muy pocas . . . El Aristotel dize que este mundo es pequeño y es el agua muy poca y que fácilmente se puede pasar de España a las Indias, y esto confirma el Avenrouyz [Averröes] y le alega el Cardenal Pedro de Aliaco [d'Ailly] autorizando este decir y aquel de Séneca, el cual conforma con éstos diziendo que Aristóteles pudo saber muchos secretos del mundo a causa de Alexandre Magno, y Séneca a causa de Cesar Nero y Plinio por repecto de los romanos. El cual Cardenl da a éstos autoridad más que a Ptolomeo ni a otros griegos ni árabes, y a confirmación de decir que el agua sea poca, al respecto de lo que se decía por autoridad de Ptolomeo y de sus secuaces; a este trae una autoridad de Esdras . . . adonde dice que de siete partes del mundo las seis son descubiertas y la una cubierta de agua. La cual autoridad es aprobada por santos . . . así como es Sant Agustín e San Ambrosio."

22. Eratosthenes (c.276–c.196 B.C.). Cleomedes, a second-century Greek astronomer who was first published in Paris in 1539, preserved Eratosthenes' method for measuring the circumference of the earth.

23. Piccolómini, #28, p. 11.

24. D'Ailly, #28, p. 47.

25. Ibid., 222–24.

26. Fernández de Navarrete, 2:117: "El compartimiento de los stadios . . . que pone Tolomeo, segun lo que ponen los suso dichos Doctores Strabo, Alragano, Macrobi, Teodosi et Euristhenes in essencia todo acude a un, porque Tolomeo pone los stadios mas grandes, de manera que los suyos ciento y ochenta mil stadios son los de los dichos Doctores doscientos cincuenta y dos mil por la linea equinoccial como suso dicho es."

27. Dawson, 506.

28. Wilford, *The Mapmakers*, 22.

29. Fernández-Armesto, *Columbus*, 27.

30. Dunn and Kelley, fol. 34v:47–48, p. 212: "Este puerto tiene en la boca mil passos que es un quarto de legua." For a study of the Spanish maritime league as given by Columbus, Martire, Magellan, Vasco da Gama, and others, see Etayo, appendix 1, 243–47.

31. Rumeu, *El libro copiador*, 1:451–52; Varelo, *Textos*, 239–40.

The Degree

32. D'Ailly, #490, p. 149: "Navegando a menudo desde Lisboa al sur hacia Guinea . . . tomé la altura del sol . . . y hallé que concordaba con Alfragano, es decir que a cada grado corresponde 56 millas y ⅔. . . . Eso mismo fue lo que halló José, fisico y astrólogo." This postil is cited here as a Columbus holograph, although there is considerable dispute on the matter, with some scholars believing that it was written by Bartolomé.

33. Fernández-Armesto, *Columbus*, 31.

34. Etayo, 250.

The Antipodes

35. Las Casas, *Historia*, chap. VIII, p. 53: "Refiere también Solino en su *Polistor*, capitulo 56, que Alexandre Magno envió un capitán que se llamó Onesicritus con una flota para descubrir la isla de la Taprobana, adonde navegando perdieron el norte y nunca vieron las Cabrillas, por manera que muchos de aquellos tiempos sospecha tenían que hubiese tierras y poblaciones de hombres en el mar Oceano."

36. Sanz, *Relación*, fol. 1, p. 2: "Salomón, que enbió desde Hierusalén en fin de Oriente, a ver el monte Sopora, en que se detovieron los navíos tres años, el cual tienen Vuestras Altezas agora en la isla Española; ni de Alejandre que envió a ver el regimento de la isla de Trapobana en India." II Chronicles 9:21, cited by Columbus: "Once every three years the king's [Solomon's] fleet would sail to Tharsis, with the servants of Hiram, and from there they would bring back gold, and silver, and ivory, and apes, and peacocks." I Kings 9, 25, also cited by Columbus: "And three times a year did Solomon offer burnt offerings . . . so he finished the house." I Kings, 10, 22, goes on to say that the king built a fleet and that it went from the "shore of the Red Sea" to Ophir and brought back gold; in the following chapter "The king had at sea a navy of Tharshish with the navy of Hiram: once in three years came the navy of Tharshish, bringing gold and silver and ivory, and apes and peacocks."

37. Vignaud, *Histoire*, 1:98: "Les auteurs anciens qu'il [d'Ailly] cite le plus souvent sont Aristotle, Pline, Sénèque et Ptolémée [ses ouvrages de mathématique et d'astronomie]; puis viennent les auteurs ecclsiastiques, saint Jérome et Isidore de Séville, particulièrement, et les auteurs arabes, comme Avveroës [*sic*], Alfragan et Hali, auxquels il fait de fréquents emprunts."

38. Las Casas, *Historia*, chap. VIII, p. 53: "Alexandre Magno envió un

capitán que se llamó Onesicritus con una flota para descubrir la isla de la Taprobana."

39. Ramos, *Memorial de Zamora*, 13: Cisneros: "el Rey Alixandre fue señor del mundo. E por su mandado Onosicrito, Capitán de su flota, descubrio todas las yslas de Yndia . . . E la mayor dellas es la Ysla Taprobana."

40. Colón, *Historia del Almirante*, chap. VII, p. 53: "Plinio en la Historia Natural, dice que el Océano rodea toda la tierra . . . el mismo . . . y Solino en el capítulo 68 *De las cosas memorables del mundo* dicen de Cabo Verde, hay cuarenta días . . . por el mar Atlántico, hasta las islas Hespérides." Fernández de Oviedo, *Historia general*, vol. I, bk. II, chap. III, p. 17: "que señalen Seboso é Solino, é Plinio é Isodoro." Ramos, *Memorial de Zamora*, 8, 13: Cisneros: "Vna dellas me paresçe que los auctores ponen por muy rica. E dista quarenta jornadas de tierra firme segund escriue Plinio."

41. Winsor, *Narrative and Critical History*, 1:27: Seneca, *Naturalium Quaest. Praefatio*: "The earth . . . is a point, a mere point, in the universe. . . . How far is it from the utmost shores of Spain to those of India? But a very few days sail with a favoring wind." Colón, *Historia del Almirante*, chap. VII, p. 54: "Pedro de Aliaco [Pierre d'Ailly] . . . en el capítulo 19 de su *Cosmografía* dice estas palabras: 'Según los filósofos y Plinio, el Océano, que se extiende entre los fines de España y del Africa Occidental, y entre el principio de la India, hacia Oriente, no tiene muy largo intervalo, ya se tiene por muy cierto, que se puede navigar de una parte a otra, en pocos días, con viento próspero, por lo cual el principio de la India por Oriente no puede distar mucho del fin de Africa, por Occidente.'" Las Casas, *Historia*, chap. XI, p. 61: "Trae también el filósofo [Pliny] en el fin del segundo libro *De caelo et mundo*, que dice que de las Indias se pude pasar a Cáliz en pocos días, y lo mismo afirma su conmentador allí, Averroiz [Averroës]. Alega eso mismo a Séneca en el primero de los *Naturales*, donde dice que de los fines últimos de España se puede navegar en pocos días con viento conveniente hasta las Indias . . . dice que India es grande . . . porque, según Plinio en el VI libro de su *Natural historia*, ella sola es la tercera parte de la tierra habitable . . . la frente della merediana llega al tropico de Capricornio." Winsor, *Narrative and Critical History*, 1:27: "Some, such as Eratosthenes, even said that the antipodes were in a temperate zone and that people could live there . . . he [Eratosthenes] says that if the extent of the Atlantic Ocean was not an obstacle, we might easily pass by sea from Iberia to India, still keeping in the same parallel, the remaining portion of which parallel . . . occupies more than a third of the whole circle . . . but it is quite possible that in the temperate zone there may be two or even more habitable earths, especially near the circle of latitude which is drawn through Athens and the Atlantic

Ocean (*Georgics*, i, 4, §6)." Avicenna, Ibn Sina (A.D. 980–1037): most renowned philosopher of medieval Islam; most influential name in European medicine from 1100 to 1500; interpreter of Aristotle; cited three times in postils written by Columbus, twice in *Imago mundi,* first in chapter 7 and second in his *Compendium.* D'Ailly quoted Avicenna as saying that the lands below the equator are temperate. In his copy of *Historia rerum,* citing the same by Eratosthenes, Columbus added the postil "Avicenna also." Columbus knew of Eratosthenes through d'Ailly.

Passage to the East and Mythical Islands

42. D'Ailly, #23c, p. 44: "Esdras: seis partes están pobladas y la séptima está cubierta de agua." Sanz, *Relación,* fol. 8, unnumbered page 16: Columbus: "a esto trae una autoridad de Esdras del tercero libro suyo, adonde dice que de siete partes del mundo las seis son descubiertas y la una cubierta de agua." Copy also in West and Kling, 88–89. Columbus also referred to Esdras in postil #856 in *Historia rerum.*

43. D'Ailly, #228, p. 84: "lo que hay entre Hispania y Africa no era en un tiempo agua que corria, sino tierra continua.

44. Las Casas, *Historia,* chap. VIII, p. 52: "Según dice Pedro de Aliaco [d'Ailly] en el tratado *De Mappa mundi* ser opinion antigua que España y Africa por la parte de Mauritania o por allí cerca era toda tierra y se contaba hasta allí Africa." Ibid., chap. XI, p. 61: "Dice, pues, Pedro de Aliaco en el tractado *De imagine mundi,* en el VII . . . de su *Cosmografía,* alegando a Aristóteles, que no es mucha mar del fin de España, por la parte Occidente, al principio de India por la parte de Oriente; y llama el fin de España al fin de Africa, porque lo que agora se llama Africa se llamaba y era España. La razón de esto da el mismo Aliaco en el XXXI *De imagine mundi* donde describe a España y sus partes, porque antiguamente no había estrecho de agua entre lo que agora se llama Gibraltar y lo que Africa se llama . . . y desta España dice Aliaco hablan Plinio y Osorio e Isidoro . . . dice Aliaco más en el XIX de su *Cosmografía,* que según los filósofos y Plinio, el mar Oceano . . . no es gran latitud, porque experiencia, dice él, hay que aquel mar sea navegable en muy pocos días, si viento fuese tal cual conviniese." Colón, *Historia del Almirante,* chap. VII, p. 52. "Estrabón en el primer libro de su *Cosmografía* dice que el Océano circunda toda la tierra y qual Oriente baña la India y al Occidente, España y Mauritania, y que no lo impidiese la grandeza del Atlántico, pudiera navegarse de un sitio a otro por el mismo paralelo, y lo vuelve a decir en el libro 2." Estrabón, (Strabo c.63 B.C.–A.D.24), was the most important source for classical Greek geography and geogra-

phers. His *Geographia* (first published in Latin in 1469) is based on Homer, Eratosthenes, Polybius, and Posidonius. The first Latin edition of his *De situ orbis* was published in 1472; the first printed edition in the original Greek was published in 1516. He taught the spherical theory and held that the then known world was something more than one-third of the actual circumference of the whole, or 129 degrees. He also pointed to an unknown and habitable part of the world to the west.

45. Fernández-Armesto, *Columbus*, 123.

46. Ramos, *Memorial de Zamora*, 8, 13: Cisneros: "E las yslas que agora nueuamente son falladas sabra vuestra alteza que no son de Indya sinon en el mar oçeano atlantico Ethiopico. E son llamadas Hesperidas y Hesperienteras."

47. Colón, *Historia del Almirante*, chap. VII, p. 53: "las islas Hespérides, las cuales tuvo por cierto el Almirante que fuesen las de las Indias."

48. Fernández de Oviedo, *Historia general*, chap. III, p. 17: "assi las islas que se diçen Hespéridas, é que señalen Seboso é Solino, é Plinio é Isodoro segund está dicho, se deben tener indubitadamente por estas Indias."

49. Colón, *Historia del Almirante*, chap. X, pp. 79–82: "Oviedo... aduciendo como prueba de su intento lo que Aristoteles dice de la isla de Atlanta, y Beroso, de las Hespéridas... Aristoteles diciese que en el mar Atlántico, más allá de las Columnas de Hércules, fue antiguamente hallada cierta isla... no entendiendo Gonzalo Fernández de Oviedo la lengua latina, por fuerza se acogió a la declaración que alguno lo hizo."

50. Morison, *Southern Voyages*, 20.

51. Wilford, *The Mysterious*, 45.

52. Colón, *Historia del Almirante*, chap. VI, p. 45.

53. Las Casas, *Historia*, chap. V, p. 39: "Todo lo en este capítulo contenido es a la letra, con algunas palabras añididas mías, de D. Hernando Colón, hijo del mismo egregio varón D. Cristobal Colón."

The Toscanelli Letters

54. Thacher, 1:354.

55. Vignaud, *Histoire*, 1:103–4: "Beragua et Puerto de Retrete (Nombre de Dios), dans le voisinage de la Cattigara de Ptolémée. Vers le centre le groupe des Antilles, oú Española tient la place de Cipangu. Cette feuille est divisée en espaces de 10 degrés chacun, et il y en a 13 entre le méridien de Lisbonne et celui de Cattigara, soit 130 degrés... La seconde feuille... D'Aprés Marin et Colomb il y a du cap Saint-Vincent à Cattigara 225 degrés ou quinze heures. D'aprés Ptolémée il y a jusqu'à Cattigara 180 degrés ou douze heures.

On sait que cette carte est de Barthélemy, parce qu'il alla à Rome en 1506 . . . il y vit un religeux de l'ordre de Saint-Jean de Latran auquel il laissa une description et une carte de Veragua . . . qui paraît d'ailleurs avoir fait une autre carte de Veragua mentionée par Oviedo (II:467)."

56. Wilford, *The Mapmakers*, 61.

57. Ibid., 32–33, "Ocean Section" of Martin Behaim's globe of 1492.

58. Dunn and Kelley, fol. 4v:3–6, p. 34.

59. Ibid., fol. 5v:19–40, p. 40.

60. Morison, *Southern Voyages*, 27.

61. Vignaud, *Histoire*, 1:280: "Toscanelli se résume dans l'idée erronée d'une reduction à 130° degrés de l'espace s'entendant à l'ouest du vieux monde, avec une extension corrélative de l'Asie vers l'est, et que cette idée venait des auteurs grecs anciens, notamment Marin de Tyr, qui lui donna une forme systématique en avançant les limites orientales de l'Asie jusqu'au 225° méridien . . . cette vielle erreur n'avait jamais obtenu créance au moyen âge; qu'elle ne fut connue qu'au XV° siècle par la publication de la géographie de Ptolémée, qu l'avait rectifiée, en partie, en ramenent la mesure du monde à 180 degrés."

62. D'Ailly, 161: "Ptolomeo, quien en el capitulo duodécimo de su primer libro sobre *Cosmografía* enmendó lo dicho por Marino sobre la longitud de nuestra tierra habitable y mostró que la longitud de la misma no se extende más allá de 180 grados."

63. Piccolómini, postil #16, p. 9.

64. C'Ailly, #23b, p. 43.

65. Sanz, *Relación*, fol. 8, unnumbered page 16: "Alexandre Magno, y Séneca a causa de Cesar Nero, y Plinio . . . el cual Cardenal da a éstos grande auctoridad, más que a Ptolomeo ni a otros griegos ni árabes."

66. Fernández-Armesto, *Columbus*, 30.

67. Phillips and Phillips, 108.

68. Sale, 357.

69. Morison, *Southern Voyages*, 27.

Influence of Marco Polo and Mandeville

70. Asencio, 2:250–51.

71. Gil and Varela, *Cartas*, 267. The Fortunati work is referred to by both Hernando and Las Casas but in neither case in connection with John Day.

72. Sanz, *Relación*, fol. 1:18–24, p. 3.

73. Las Casas, *Historia*, chap. CXLVIII, p. 67: "Aquí torna a exortar a los reyes que tengan este negocio en mucho, pues . . . que llevó a Sus Altezas . . .

perlas finísimas y perlas bermejas, de que dize Marco Paulo que valen más que las blancas . . . Todas estas son sus palabras."

74. Gil, *El libro de Marco Polo*, #267, p. 137.

75. Ibid., #239, p. 123.

76. Ibid., #319, p. 157.

77. Ibid., #243, p. 124.

78. Piccolómini, #662, p. 182.

79. Gil, *El libro de Marco Polo*, #272a, p. 140.

80. Ibid., #277, p. 142.

81. Dunn and Kelley, fol. 25r:17–18, p. 156: "Hallaro(n) los marineros vn animal q(ue) parecia taso/o taxo."

82. Gil, *El libro de Marco Polo*, #359, p. 172.

83. Dunn and Kelley, fol. 25r:37–39, p. 158: "hallo nueces gra(n)des dlas de yndia creo q(ue) dize / y ratones grandes slos de yndia tabien."

84. Ochse et al., 2:1127–28.

85. Dunn and Kelley, fol. 16v:19, p. 108: "y segu(n) yo fallare recaudo de oro /o espeçeria determinare lo q(ue) e de fazer /. mas todavia tengo determinado de yr a la t(ie)rra firme y a la çiudad de quisay y las [?] dar las c[ar]tas de v(uest)ras altezas al gra(n) Can y pedir repuesta y venir con ella."

86. Ibid., fol. 19r:47–51, p. 124: "y dize q(ue) avia de trabajar de yr al gra(n) Can q(ue) pensava q(ue)stava por alli /o a la çiudad de Cathay q(ue)s del gran Can / q(ue) dize es m(u)y gra(n)de segu(n) le fue dicho [   ] [?] antes q(ue) p[ar]tiese despaña."

87. Gil, *El libro de Marco Polo*, 73.

88. Fernández de Navarrete, 2:7.

89. Gil, *Mitos y utopías*, 23.

90. Piccolómini, #110–117, pp. 27–28.

91. For Conti, see Polo, *Most Noble and Famous Travels*, 125–49, and Yule, vol. 1.

92. "Cambayta, ginger, gold, 'Synamon,' Ilande named Taprobana, Ilande of Golde . . . no strangers go there . . . those barbrous people hewe them to pieces, and eate them; pepper much Brasill; there be Canes of suche a marvellous breadth; pearles, redde Ants as bigge as a crabbe; unicorne; there is another Province . . . Cataya, and he is Lord of it that is named the great CANE, whyche is as muche to say in their tongue, as Emperoure . . . City royall . . . Cymbalecheya; Zeitano; all India lacketh Vines and Wine; Laua; nutmegges, Masticke, parrets; certaine men from Ethiopia . . . with whom I had communication; a King, which is entituled King of Kings." See Polo, *Most Noble and Famous Travels*.

93. Dunn and Kelley, fol. 28r:31–35, p. 176: "los quales diz q(ue) dspues q(ue) le viero(n) tomar la [   ] [?] buelta desta t(ie)rra no podian hablar ~~ni les podia quitar el medio~~ temiendo q(ue) los [   ] [?] avian de comer / y no les podia quitar el temor /. y dezia(n) q(ue) no tenian sino vn ojo y cara de perro."

94. Mandeville, probably a pseudonym for a fourteenth-century writer who concocted a compilation of Marco Polo, Ordoric, and William of Boldensele. This work was completed as a travel romance in 1356 and was first printed in French in 1480. Fernández de Oviedo, Hernando, and Las Casas refer to Mandeville's extravagant travel tales.

95. Yule, *Ibn Batuta*, 5–166.

96. Ibn Khaldûn, 146.

97. Ibid., 36.

98. Ibid., introduction, viii.

99. Bernáldez, vol. I, chap. CXVIII, p. 358: "y sintió como este mundo y firmamiento de tierra y agua, segun cuenta Juan de Mandavilla."

100. Greenblatt, *Marvelous Possessions*, 26.

101. Todorov, *The Conquest*, 13.

102. Gil, *El libro de Marco Polo*, 11; Garin, 153.

103. Todorov, *The Conquest*, 31.

104. Greenblatt, *Marvelous Possessions*, 36.

105. Greenblatt, *New World Encounters*, 10.

106. Rabasa, 15.

107. Ibid., 196

108. Ibid., 55.

109. Ibid., 59.

110. Ibid., 227 n. 25.

111. Gil, *Mitos y utopías*, 123–24.

112. Gil, *El libro de Marco Polo*, #23, p. 183: "Del ambra es çierto nasçere in India soto tierra, he yo ne ho fato cavare in molti monti in la isola de Feyti . . . a la quale habio posto nome Spagnola." This is clearly postdiscovery.

113. Gil, *Mitos y utopías*, 125.

114. D'Ailly, #167, p. 73, #782, p. 289.

115. Todorov, *The Conquest*, 121.

116. Fernández-Armesto, *Columbus*, 37.

117. Morison, *Admiral*, 71.

118. Las Casas, *Historia*, chap. XXVIII, p. 150: "dice la dicha Historia portuguesa, que porque el Cristóbal Colón era hombre más hablador y glorioso en mostrar sus habilidades, y más fantástico de sus imaginaciones

con su isla de Cipango, que cierto en lo que decía, dábale poco crédito . . . dice que tuvieron por vanidad las palabras de Cristóbal Colón, por ser fundadas en imaginaciones y cosas de la isla de Cipango."

119. Phillips and Phillips, 46.

120. Wilford, *The Mysterious*, 77.

121. Ibid., 66.

122. Ibid., 79.

123. Colón, *Historia del Almirante*, chap. VII, p. 53.

124. Sale, 108.

125. Dunn and Kelley, 24r:46–15v:1, p. 152: "estas Islas son aq(ue)llas Innumerables q(ue) en los mapamu(n)dos mapamumundos [?] en fin de orie(n)te se ponen /."

126. Gil, *Mitos y utopías*, 22: "Colón, por confesión propia, ha visto y consultado 'esperas . . . e mapamundos' (24 de octubre) [p. 44], que contaban maravillas del Cipango, gracias a los cuales puede deducir el 14 de noviembre que el archipiélago de las Antillas forma parte de <<aquellas innumerables [islas] que en fin de oriente se ponen>> [p. 58]. Efectivamente, Marco Polo había encarecido la multitud sin cuento de las islas de la India, y en el mapa catalán de 1375 se había fijado su numero en 7,548, siguiendo la pauta del viajero veneciano."

127. Gil, *El libro de Marco Polo*, #345, p. 166: "Según se sabe por la carta de marear y la observación de los compases del mar de la India, hay en este mar islas en numero de mccclxxviii."

128. Ramos, *Memorial de Zamora*, 13. "E por esto dezia Platon en el libro de la *República* que tales eran los vasallos qual era su prinçipe, y desta causa, siendo sabidor el rey Alexandre fue señor del mundo. E por su mandado Onosicrito, Capitán de su flota, descubrio todas las yslas de Yndia e falló que eran mill e trezientas e setenta e ocho, segund escriue Tolomeo. E la mayor dellas es la ysla Taprobana."

129. Wilford, *The Mysterious*, 77.

D'Ailly, Pliny, and Ptolemy

130. Sanz, *Relación*, fol. 1:15–26, p. 1.

131. D'Ailly, #398, p. 123.

132. Ibid., #48, p. 53, #90, p. 148.

133. Piccolómini, #23–25, p. 10.

134. Ibid., #190–226, pp. 40–45.

135. Ibid., #53, 56, p. 17, #84, p. 23.

136. Varela, *Textos*, 135, 381.

137. Thacher, 3:405.

138. Gil, *El libro de Marco Polo*, introduction, ix.

139. Dawson, 504.

140. Colón, *Historia del Almirante*, chap. VII, p. 51: "El segundo fundamento que dió animo al Almirante para la empresa . . . como afirma Aristóteles en el libro 2, *Del Cielo y del Mundo*."

141. Las Casas, *Historia*, chap. VIII, p. 53: "Ser la dicha Atlantica mayor que Asia y Africa parece no ser dificil de creer, por lo que dice Aristóteles."

142. Vignaud, *Histoire*, 1:102.

143. Morison, *Southern Voyages*, 27.

144. Fernández-Armesto, *Columbus*, 28.

145. Phillips and Phillips, 109.

Chapter 5

The Unknown Pilot

1. Fernández de Oviedo, *Historia general*, chap. II, p. 13, chap. III, p. 14.

2. Fernández Duro, in his *Nebulosa de Colón*, included a copy of Esteban de Garibay, *Los quarenta libros del compendio historial de las Cronicas y universal historia de todos los reinos de España*, (Anvers, 1571)* (Garibay's memorandum "De Don Cristobal Colon").

3. Fernández de Oviedo, *Historia general*, chap. I, pp. 13–14.

4. Travers.

5. Benzoni.

6. Thacher, 1:328; López de Gómara.

7. Suárez de Peralta, 56–57.

8. Colón, *Historia del Almirante*, chap. IX, pp. 76–77.

9. Las Casas, *Historia*, chap. XIV, pp. 70–71.

10. Ibid., p. 72.

11. Acosta, bk. 1, chap. 19.

12. Castellanos, Elegia I, canto i:

> Otros quieren decir que este camino
> Que del piloto dicho se recuenta,
> A Cristobal Colon le sobrevino
> Y él fué quien padecio la tormenta.
>
> Para confirmacion de lo contado.
> Algunos dan razon algo fundada,
> Y entre ellos el varon Adelantado,
> D. Gonzalo Jimenez de Quesada.

13. Jos Pérez, 46.
14. Las Casas, *Historia*, chap. XXXIX, p. 197.
15. Herrera, *Historia general*, preface.
16. Thacher, 1:328.
17. Manzano, *Colón y su secreto*; also in his *Colón descubrió*.
18. Solórzano, bk. 4, chap. 5; Pizzaro, *Varones ilustres del Nuevo-Mundo*.

Alonso Sánchez of Huelva, Pero Vásquez, and Diego de Teive

19. Thacher, 1:328–31 (Spanish version with English translation).
20. Ibid., 1:329; Jos Pérez, 98: "Yo quise añadir este poco que falto de la relación de aquel antiguo historiador [López de Gómara], que como escrivio lexos de donde acaecieron estas cosas . . . y yo las oy en mi tierra de mi padre y sus contemporaneos."
21. Colón, *Historia del Almirante*, chap. IX, p. 77, footnote by Serrano y Sanz: "Casas extractó este capítulo en su Historia, I, I, c. XIII, algunas veces literalmente."
22. Ibid., chap. IX, p. 74: "Aún fué a buscar esta isla cierto Diego de Tiene, cuyo piloto, llamado Diego de Velasco, natural de Palos de Moguer, en Portugal [sic] dijo al Almirante."
23. Muro Orejón, *Pleitos Colombinos: Rollo del proceso*, 339. "El dicho Alonso Gallego . . . este testigo oyo dezir a vn Pedro Vásquez de la Frontera vino a querer ir el dicho viaje quel dicho Colon venia a tomar lengua y aviso del dicho Pedro Vásquez de la Frontera como persona que avia sido criado del Rey de Portugal y tenia notiçia de la tierra de las dichas Yndias."
24. Cortesão, 9–29.
25. Colón, *Historia del Almirante*, chap. IX, p. 75: "un marinero tuerto . . . en un viaje suyo a Irlanda vió dicha tierra . . . la cual debe de ser la misma que ahora llamamos tierra de Bacallaos."
26. Morison, *Admiral*, 62.
27. Ibid., 63.
28. Suárez de Peralta, 56.
29. Wilford, *The Mysterious*, 82.
30. Ibid., 4.

Vicente Díaz

31. Ibid., 115–16.
32. Ibid., 46.
33. Colón, *Historia del Almirante*, chap. IX, p. 76.

34. Las Casas, *Historia*, chap. XIII, p. 69.

35. Wilford, *The Mysterious*, 81. Manzano, *Colón y su secreto*. In his bibliographical notes, Wilford cited John Larner, *The Certainty of Columbus*, as his source for Manzano (p. 289).

36. Ibid., 82.

37. Vignaud, *Histoire*.

38. Fernández-Armesto, *Columbus*, 186.

39. Phillips and Phillips, 104.

40. Morison, *Admiral*, 58, 62.

41. Phillips and Phillips, 140.

42. Muro Orejón, *Pleitos Colombinos: Rollo del proceso*, 258. Alonso Velez, mayor of the village of Palos, testified that Martín Alonso took with him information about the route, information that he gained from Pedro Vásquez de la Frontera, who had sailed for the King of Portugal. Ibid., 301. Fernando Valiente testified in the same proceedings, saying that Columbus consulted with Vásquez before going to the court to seek approval for his voyage.

43. Ibid., 256.: "que avia ydo a descubrir esta tierra con vn ynfante de Portogal y dezia que por cortos la avian errado y se avian engañado por las yervas queavian hallado en el golfo de la mar y dixo al dicho Martin Alonso que quando llegasen a las dichas yervas y quel dicho Almirante quisiera bolverse de alli quel no lo consintiese salvo que siguiesen la via derecha porque hera ynposible no dar en la tierra ... y despues de venidos el dicho Martin Alonso y el dicho Colon del viaje se dixo por cosa çierta quel dicho Almirante quando llego a las dichas yervas se quisiera bolver y el dicho Marin Alonso por razon del aviso que llevava no lo consintio."

44. Ibid., 341: "Pinçon avia dicho entonçes al dicho Colon señor acuerdese vuestro señoria que en casa de Pedro Vasquez de la Frontera os prometi por la corona rreal [sic] que yo ni ninguno de mis parientes no aviamos de bolver a Palos hasta descubrir tierra en tanto que la gente fuese sana y oviese mantenamientos."

45. Vignaud, *Histoire*, 1:75.

Hearsay, Rumors of Lands to the West, and Flotsam and Jetsam

46. Las Casas, *Historia*, chap. XIII, p. 67.

47. Colón, *Historia del Almirante*, chap. IX, p. 71: "Séneca ... dice que son de piedra tan fofa y ligera, que nadan en el agua las que forman en la India. De modo que, aunque resultase verdad que el dicho Antonio de Leme había visto alguna isla, creía el Almirante que no podía ser otra que alguna de las mencionadas"

48. Las Casas, *Historia*, chap. XIII, p. 67.

49. Dunn and Kelley, fol. 2v:31–42, pp. 25–26: "q(ue) cada año vian tierra al vveste dlas Canarias q(ue) es al poniente; y otros co(mo) jurame(n)to / Dize aqui el almi(rant)e q(ue) se acuerda q(ue)stando ~~en la Isla de la madera~~ en portugal el año de 1484. vino vno dla madera al rey a le pedir vna caravela p[ar]a yr a esta t(ie)rra q(ue) via el qual jurava q(ue) cada año la via y siempre de vna ma(ne)ra; y tambien dize q(ue) se acuerda q(ue) lo mismo dezia(n) en las Islas dlos açores y todos estos en vna derrota y en vna ma(ne)ra de señal y vna gra(n)deza /."

50. Vignaud, *Histoire*, 1:72.

51. Colón, *Historia del Almirante*, chap. IX, p. 68: "Noticias que, por cuadrar algo a su propósito, las retenía en su memoria."

52. Ibid., chap. IX, p. 69; Las Casas, *Historia*, chap. XIII, p. 66: "Pedro Correa, casado con una hermana del Almirante, le dijo que él había visto en la isla de Puerto-Santo otro madero, llevado por los mismos vientos, bien labrado, como al anterior; y que igualmente habían llegado cañas tan gruesas que de un nudo u otro cabían nueve garrafas de vino. Dice que afirmaba lo mismo el Rey de Portugal, y que hablando con éste de tales cosas, se las mostró; y no habiendo parajes en estas partes, donde nazcan semejantes cañas, era cierto que los vientos los habían llevado de algunas islas vecinas, o acaso de las Indias; pues Ptolomeo, lib. primero de su *Cosmografía*, capítulo 17, dice que en las parte orientales de las Indias hay de estas cañas."

53. Las Casas, *Historia*, chap. IX, p. 68: "Conviene saberse que un Martín Vicente, piloto del Rey de Portugal, le dijo que hallándose, en un viaje, a 450 leguas al Poniente del cabo de San Vicente, había cogido del agua un madero ingeniosamente labrado, y no con hiero, de lo cual, y por haber soplado muchos días el viento del oeste, conoció que dicho leño venía de algunas islas que estaban al Poniente."

54. Morison, *Admiral*, 60.

55. Ibid. Colón, *Historia del Almirante*, chap. IX, p. 70, gave it quite differently: "en la isla de Flores hallaron en la orilla dos hombres muertos, cuya cara y traza era diferente de los de sus costas."

Chapter 6

Departure from Portugal and Arrival in Spain

1. Colón, *Historia del Almirante*, chap. XI, pp. 101–2: "siéndole ya muerta su mujer, tomó tanto odio a aquella ciudad y nación, que acordó irse a Castilla con un niño quele dejó su mujer, llamado Diego Colón."

2. Las Casas, *Historia*, chap. XXXVIII, pp. 150–52.

3. Ibid., chap. XXXVIII, p. 151: "porque convenía estar desocupado del cuidado y obligación de la mujer."

4. Pina* (copy in Jos Pérez, 114): "Especialmente acusava El-Rei de negligente por se escusar de ele por mingua de crédito e autoridade, acerca deste descubrimiento para que primeiro o viera requerer."

5. Vignaud, *Histoire*, 1:357.

6. Fernández de Oviedo, *Historia general*, chap. IV, pp. 18–19: "De manera que determinó de irse en Castilla; y llegado á Sevilla, tuvo sus inteligençias con el ilustre y valeroso don Enrique de Guzman, duque de Medina-Sidonia; y tampoco halló en él lo que buscaba. E movió despues el negocio mas largamente con el muy ilustre don Luis de la Cerda, primero duque de Medina Celi . . . quieren decir algunos que el duque de Medina Celi, ya queria venir en armar al dicho Colom en su villa de Puerto de Sancta Maria, y que no le quisieron dar liçencia el Rey y Reyna Cathólicos para ello."

7. Bernáldez, chap. CXVIII, p. 358: "bien fundados marineros, que no lo estimaron, y presumian en el mundo no haber otros mayores descubridores que ellos."

8. Las Casas, *Historia*, chap. XXXI, p. 165: "salió un padre, que había nombre fray Juan Peréz, que debía ser el guardián del monasterio, y comenzó a hablar con él en cosas de la corte . . . hizo llamar a un médico o fisico, que se llamaba Garci Hernandez, su amigo, que, como filósofo, de aquellas proposiciones más que él entendía."

9. Morison, *Admiral*, 79.

10. Vignaud, *Histoire*, 1:600–601: "dixo que sabe este testigo . . . que sabe que el dicho Almirante Don Cristóbal Colon viniendo a la Rábyda con su hijo Don Diego, que agora Almirante, a pié, se vino a la Rábida, ques monasterio de frayles de esta villa, el qual demandó á la portería que le diesen para aquel niñico que era niño pan, y agua que beviese, y que stando allí ende este testigo, un frayle que se llamaba frey Juan Perez, ques ya dyfunto, quiso fablar con el dicho Don Cristóbal Colon e viéndole despusycion de otra tyerra o reino ageno de su lengua, le preguntó que quién era e dónde venia, e aquel dicho Cristóbal Colon le dixo que venia de la corte de su Alteza e le quiso dar parte de su embaxada a qué fue a la corte e cómo venya, e que dixo el dicho Cristóbal Colon al dicho fray Juan Perez como avia puesto en plática a descobryr ante su Alteza e que se obligava a darle tierre fyrme . . . le bolaron su palabra, e qué no fué acogydo, mas que antes fazian burla de su razon . . . el se vino de la Corte e yba derecho de esta villa a la villa de Huelva, para fablar y veerse con un su cuñado, casado con hermana de

su muger, e que a la sazón estaba, e que avia nombre Mulyer . . . una carta a la Reyna . . . del dicho fray Juan Perez que era su confesor . . . ende a catorze día, la Reyna nuestra Señora escrivió al dicho fray Juan Pérez . . . e manadava que luego, vista la presente, paresciese en la corte ante Su Alteza."

11. Irving, 1:96.

12. Morison, *Admiral*, 79.

13. Wilford, *The Mysterious*, 84.

14. Colón, *Historia del Almirante*, chap. XII, p. 107.

15. Las Casas, *Historia*, chap. XXIX, p. 155.

Briolanja Muñiz and Miguel Muliart

16. Fernández de Navarrete, 1:253–54: "Envío allá a tu hermano, que bien él sea niño en días, no es ainsí en el entendimiento." Arranz, 36.

17. Las Casas, *Historia*, chap. CLIX, p. 103: "su hijo D. Diego Colón, que ésta en la corte, crescía en fuerza, haciéndose hombre para acá servirles."

18. Phillips and Phillips, 114.

19. Ibid.

20. Valera, *Colón y los florentinos*, 99.

Santa María de la Rábida

21. Wilford, *The Mysterious*, 114–15.

22. Fernández-Armesto, *Columbus*, 60.

23. Phillips and Phillips, 114, 137.

24. Fernández-Armesto, *Columbus*, 47.

25. Sale, 54.

26. Colón, *Historia del Almirante*, chap. XII, p. 108; Las Casas, *Historia*, chap. XXIX, p. 155.

27. Varela, *Colón y los florentinos*, 47.

28. Las Casas, *Historia*, chap. XXXI, p. 165.

29. Dunn and Kelley, fol. 62r:21–23, p. 370: "Dize mas q(ue) tambie(n) le dava gran pena dos hijos q(ue) tenia en cordova al estudio q(ue) los dexava guerfanos."

At the Spanish Court

30. Ibid., fol. 56v:35–37, p. 336: "yo vine a los servir q(ue) son siete años agora a veynte dias de henero este mismo mes."

31. Sanz, *Relación*, fol. 1, unnumbered page 1: "Puso en esto seis o siete años de grave pena."

32. Ibid.: "a .xx. de enero año de 1489 entro en la corte el almi[e] a proponer su descubrimiento /."

33. Varela, *Textos*, 197 n.

34. Fernández de Navarrete, 3:8, 9.

35. Rumeu, *El "Portugues,"* 17.

36. Fernández de Oviedo, *Historia general*, chap. IV, p. 20: "En aquel tiempo que Colom, como dixe, andaba en la corte, llegábase a casa de Alonso de Quintanilla, contador mayor de los reyes Cathólicos . . . y mandábale dar de comer y lo nesçessario por una compasibildad de su pobreça. Y en este caballero halló mas parte é acogimiento Colom que en hombre de toda España, é por su respecto é interçession fué conosçido del reverendissimo é ilustre cardenal de España, arçobispo de Toledo don Pedro Gonçalez de Mendoça."

37. Fernández de Navarrete, 2:20, doc. XIV (copy also in Thacher, 1:412): "tove en mi casa mucho tiempo a Cristóval Colomo, que se venía de Portugal y se quería ir al rey de Francia . . . e yo lo quisiera probar y enviar desde este puerto . . . con tres ó cuatro carabelas . . . escribilo a su Alteza desde Rota, y respondióme que gelo enviasse . . . Su Alteza lo recibió, y lo dió en cargo á Alonso de Quintanilla . . . merced . . . por yo detenerle en mi casa dos años."

38. Wilford, *The Mysterious*, 90.

39. Vignaud, *Histoire*, 1:603: "le dió a Don Diego su hijo, en guarda, a este testigo, e a Martyn Sánchez, clérigo . . . e les mostró el dicho Almyrante carátulas de oro que traya de las dichas Yndias e sys o siete Yndios que traya de allá e con un cuchillo quytó el dicho Almyrante un poco de oro a un Yndio e se lo dió a este testigo . . . dixo . . . que avia descubierto muchas yslas en que avia mucho oro en las dichas Yndias."

The Dukes of Medina-Sidonia and Medina Celi

40. Fernández de Oviedo, *Historia general*, chap. IV:19: "E movió despues el negoçio mas largamente con el muy ilustre don Luis de la Cerda, primero duque de Medina Celi . . . quieren deçir algunos que el Duque . . . ya queria venir en armar al dicho Colom . . . y que no quisieron dar liçençia el rey é Reina Cathólicos para ello."

41. Morison, *Admiral*, 82.

42. Wilford, *The Mysterious*, 86–87.

Fray Juan Pérez

43. Muro Orejón, *Pleitos Colombinos: Rollo del proceso*, 257: "Colon estuvo en la villa de Palos muncho tiempo . . . e poso en el monesterio de la Rabida."

44. Taviani, 309. Francisco de Gonzaga, *De Origine seraphicæ, religionis Franciscanæ* (Rome, 1587). The matter is dealt with extensively by Coll.

45. Thacher, 3:185: "Digo que al tiempo que él vino a Sus Altezas con la impresa de las Indias, que él demandaba por un memorial muchas cosas, y fray Juan Pérez y Mosen Coloma, los cuales entendían en esto por mandado de Sus Altezas, le concertaron que le fiezen su Almirante de las islas y tierra firme que descobriesen en la mar Oceana."

46. Varela, *Textos*, 441: "Ainsí mismo de las cosas que son menester para curar los enfermos al padre fray Juan enformará a Vuestras Alteças de lo que será menester."

47. Rumeu, *El libro copiador*, vol. 1, fol. 33v:9–13, p. 571.

48. Varela, *Textos*, 471: "Fray Johan Perez lo diría y el ama [the nurse of Prince Juan], y ainsi me estoy más firme de continuo."

49. Ibid., 521: "Yo espero en Nuestro Señor de reçebir esta semana que viene repuesta del Ofiçio de San Georgi, al cual atribuía el diezmo de mi renta . . . . Padre Juan diz que los de San Georgi son muy nobles señores y que complirán conmigo."

50. Sanz, *Relación*, fol. 1:23–25: "todos los que habián entendido en ello, y oidó esta pláctica, todos a una mano lo tenían a burla, salvo dos frailes [blank space in the manuscript] que siempre fueron constantes." There are two errors in Sanz's transcription. He gave 'o' instead of 'lo' and, more seriously, erred in stating that there was a blank in the manuscript between the words "frailes" and "que siempre," a space not shown on the facsimile.

51. Muro Orejón, *Pleitos Colombinos: Rollo del proceso*, 257: "vido este testigo quel dicho almirante Colon estuvo en la villa de Palos muncho tiempo publicando el descubrymiento de las Yndias e poso en el monasterio de la Rábida e comunicava la negoçiaçion del descubrir con frayle estrologo que ende estava en el convento por guardian e ainsi mismo con fray Juan que avia servido siendo moço a la rreyna doña Ysabel Catolica siendo moço en oficio de contadores el que sabida la negoçiaçion fue al rreal de Granada donde estavan entonçes los Reyes Catolicos e alli comunico la cosa con sus Altezas en tal manera que mandaron llamar al Almirante e alli se dio asiento como fuese el dicho Almirante a descubrir las dichas Yndias."

52. Rubin, 231.

53. Muro Orejón, *Pleitos Colombinos: Rollo del proceso*, 609: "el dicho

Martin Alonço le dio al dicho Almirante dinero e le fizo yr a la corte a el y a un frayle que se dezia fray Juan Peres, los cuales fueron, e que lo sabe este testigo por que se falló a todo."

54. Colón, *Historia del Almirante*, chap. XIII, p. 116: "fué a la Rábida, para llevar su niño Diego, que le había dejado allí, a Córdoba, y despues continuar su camino. Pero Dios, a fin de que no quedase sin efecto lo que había dispuesto, inspiró al guardián de aquella casa. llamado fray Juan Pérez, para que trabase mucha amistad con el Almirante. . . . Partido el Almirante de la Rábida, que está cerca de Palos, juntamente con fray Juan Pérez, al campamento de Santa Fe."

Rodríguez Cabezudo and Andrés del Corral

55. Vignaud, *Histoire*, 1:603: Rodríguez Cabezudo: "dixo que lo que sabe es que puede aver veynte e dos años pocos más o menos queste testigo vido el dicho Almyrante viejo en esta villa de Moguer andando negociando de yr a descubrir las Indias con un frayle de Sant Francisco que andava con el."

56. Ibid., 1:605: "Este testigo estando en la corte en madrid [*sic*] con el dicho Almyrante al tiempo que negociava con sus Altezas la venyda a descobrir, el dicho almirante viendo como los del consejo e muchos otros eran contrarios, dixera a Sus Altezas que, pues no le creyan a él, qel darya persona a quien creyesen, e entonces llego un flayre [*sic*] de la horden de San Francisco, cuyo nombre no sabe, el qual dixo a Sus Altezas que hera verdad lo que aquel Almyrante dezia, e entonces lo despacharon, e vino a estas partes descobryr."

57. Las Casas, *Historia*, chap. XXXI, p. 165: "salió un padre, que había nombre fray Juan Pérez, que debía ser el guardián del monasterio y comenxó a hablar con él en cosas de la corte como supiese que della venía, y Cristóbal Colón le dió larga cuenta de todo lo que con los reyes y con los duques le había occurido . . . hizo llamar a un médico o fisico, que se llamaba Garci Hernández, que como filósofo, de aquellas proposiciones más que él entendía."

58. Fernández de Oviedo, *Historia general*, chap. V, p. 21: "Antes que Colom entrasse en la mar algunos dias, tuvo muy largas consultaciones con un religioso llamado fray Juan Perez, de la order de sanct Françisco, su confessor; el cual estaba en el monasterio de la Rábida (que es media legua de Palos hácia la mar). Y este frayle fué la persona sola de aquesta vida, á quien Colom mas comunicó sus secretos; é aun del qual é de su sçiençia se diçe hasta hoy que él resçibió mucha ayuda é buena obra, porque este religioso era gran cosmógrapho."

Fray Antonio de Marchena

59. Varela, *Textos*, 407: "Ya saben Vuestras Altezas que anduve siete años en su corte importunándoles por esto. Nunca en todo este tiempo se halló piloto ni marinero ni philósofo ni de otra sçiençia que todos no dixessen que mi empresa era falsa; que nunca yo hallé ayuda de nadie, salvo de fray Antoño de Marchena, despúes de aquella de Dios eterno."

60. Las Casas, *Historia*, chap. XXXII, p. 171: "Aqui también ocurre más que notar, que, según parece, por algunas cartas de Cristóbal Colón, escritas de su misma mano, para los reyes, desde esta isla Española, que yo he tenido en mis manos, un religioso que había nombre fray Antonio de Marchena, no dice de qué orden, ni en qué, ni cuando, fué el que mucho le ayudó a que la reina se persuadiese y aceptase la petición, el cual dice así: 'Ya saben Vuestras Altezas . . . y abajo dice otra vez que no halló persona que no tuviese burla, salvo aquel padre fray Antonio de Marchena . . . nunca pude hallar de qué orden fuese, aunque creo que fuese de Sant Francisco, por cognoscer que Cristóbal Colón, despúes de Almirante, siempre fué devoto de aquella orden. Tampoco pude saber cuándo, ni en qué, ni cómo le favoreciese. o qué entrada tuviese en los reyes el ya dicho padre fray Antonio de Marchena.'"

61. Fernández Duro, *Bibliografía Colombina*, sec. I:2: "Carta de los reyes á D, Cristobal Colón. Llegaron los mensajeros del rey de Portugal y dicen que la carabela que salió de la isla de Madera lo hizo sin licencia, y que el rey ha enviado otras tres en su busca. Encárganle que impida traten de descubrir en la partes que les pertenecen y en caso de pasar los límites covenidos las castigue tomando navíos y personas. Encargan no toque en el cabo de San Vicente ni se acerque á la costa de Portugal. Para poder entender bien su libro han menester saber los grados en que estan las islas y tierras. Paréceles será bien lleve consigo un astrólogo y que sea Fr. Antonio de Marchena ú otro que le parezca; mas no se detenga una hora de partir."

62. Fernández de Navarrete, 2:123–25: "y siempre nos parecio que se conformaba con vuestro parecer."

Allesandro Geraldini and Francisco López de Gómara

63. Allesandro Geraldini, 148: "Pero sobreviviendo la muerte de mi hermano, destituto de todo apoyo humano, acosándole la desconfianza de sus familiares y la pobreza, se vió en tanta penuria que tuvo que acogerse a un monasterio de San Francisco que se halla en la regíon de Andalucía y

término de Marchena, humildemente suplicando le suministraran los alimentos necesarios para vivir. Allí Fray Juan de Marchena, varón bien probado por su vida, religión y santidad, viendo en Colón a un hombre en todo culto, movido de miesricordia, se fué al Rey Fernando y a la Reina Isabel, etc."

64. Belisario Geraldini.

65. López de Gómara, 14: "Fray Juan Perez de Marchena, frayle franciscano en la Rabida cosmographo y humanista, a quien en puridad descubrio su coraçon."

66. Rumeu, *La Rábida.*

67. Milhou.

Modern Versions of Marchena's Role

68. Morison, *Admiral*, 80–81.

69. Ibid., 398.

70. Morison, *Southern Voyages*, 34.

71. Wilford, *The Mysterious*, 85.

72. Ibid., 117.

73. Fernández-Armesto, *Columbus*, 55, 59, 62.

74. Phillips and Phillips, 117.

75. Sale, 8.

76. Rubin, 230.

Columbus at Court

77. Fernández de Navarrete, 3:8, 9. Fernández Duro, *Bibliografía Colombina*, sec. I:4: July 3: "Son siete mil mrs. con tres mil que se le mandaron dar para ayuda de su costa por otra parte en 3 julio." Fernández Navarrete, 3:8, 9, 2:4 (doc II): August 27: "Di á Cristobal Colomo cuatro mil mrs. para ir al Real [de Málaga] por mandado de SS. AA. por cedula del Obispo. Son siete mil maravedis, con tres mil que se mandaron, para ayuda de costa, por otra partida de 3 de julio." Rumeu, *El "Portugues,"* 19, offers a facsimile of an account book with this entry. May 7 to August 18 siege of Málaga: Fernández de Navarrete, 3:8, 9: October 15, 1487: "Di á Cristobal Colomo cuatro mil mrs. que SS. AA. le mandaron dar para ayuda á su costa por cedula del Obispo." Fernández Duro, *Bibliografía Colombina*, sec. I:4: June 16, 1488, 3000 maravedis.

78. Colón, *Historia del Almirante*, chap. XII, pp. 109–13.

79. Ibid., p. 113.

80. Las Casas, *Historia*, chap. XXIX, pp. 155–61.

81. Fernández de Navarrete, 3:315: "Que fué causa principal de que se emprendiese la empresa de las Indias y seconquistasen, y si por él no fuera, no hobiera Indias, á lo menos para provecho de Castilla."

82. Thacher, 1:414: "Es de trabajar de saber si la Reina, que Dios tiene, dejo dicho algo en su testamento, de mí, y es dar prisas al Sr. Obispo de Palencia [Diego de Deza] el que fue causa que sus Altezas hobiesen las Indias, y que yo, quedase en Castilla, que ya estaba yo de camino para fuera y ainsí al Señor Camarero de su Alteza."

83. Las Casas, *Historia*, chap. XXIX, p. 158.

84. Amler, Thacher, Madariaga, and Wiesenthal, among others, studied these relationships.

85. Las Casas, *Historia*, chap. XXIX, p. 158.

86. Ibid., chap. XXX, p. 162.

87. Fernández de Oviedo, *Historia general*, chap. IV, p. 19.

Talavera Commission

88. Vignaud, *Histoire*, I:570.

89. Ibid., 2:556 n. 124.

90. Jos Pérez, 13.

91. Colón, *Historia del Almirante*, chap. XII, p. 110, chap. XIII, p. 115.

92. Bernáldez, chap. CXVIII, p. 359.

93. Las Casas, *Historia*, chap. XXIX, pp. 155–61.

94. Morison, *Admiral*, 88, 98.

95. Morison, *Southern Voyages*, 35, 38.

96. Morison, *Admiral*, 89.

97. Phillips and Phillips, 122.

98. Bernáldez, chap. LXXXII, p. 229.

Columbus at Málaga and Baza

99. Fernández de Navarrete, 3:8, 9: "5 de mayo 1487, dí a Cristobal Colombo, extranjero que está aqui faciendo algunas cosas complideras á servicio de SS. AA. por cedula de Alonso de Quintanilla con mandamiento del Obispo, tres mil mrs."

100. Ibid., 3:8, 9, 2:4 (doc II): "Di á Cristobal Colomo cuatro mil mrs. para ir al Real por mandado de SS. AA. por cedula del Obispo. Son siete mil maravedis, con tres mil que se mandaron, para ayuda de costa, por otra partida de 3 de julio."

101. Bernáldez, chap. LXXXIII, p. 233.

102. Phillips and Phillips, 122.

103. Bernáldez, chap. XCII, p. 271.

104. Vignaud, *Histoire*, 1:672. The only known copy of the king's reply is dated March 20, 1488, and is addressed "To Cristovam Colon our special Friend, in Sevilha." Earlier copies of this letter, such as those in Fernández de Navarrete and the *Raccolta*, are inexact. This was due to the fact that the editors of these works were refused permission to copy this letter in the archives of the duke of Alba. Vignaud was the first to receive such permission.

Beatriz Enríquez de Arana

105. Varela, *Textos*, 477.

106. Ibid., 535.

107. Las Casas, *Historia*, chap. XXXIX, pp. 198–99: "Vido la tierra primero un marinero que se llamaba Rodrigo de Triana, pero los 10,000 maravedís de juro, sentenciaron los reyes que los llevase Cristóbal Colón . . . Estos 10,000 maravedís de juro llevó siempre por todo su vida . . . la virreina de las Indias . . . me dijo habérsele librado en las carnicerías de la ciudad de Sevilla, donde siempre lo pagaron.

108. Morison, *Admiral*, 85.

109. Thacher, 3:629–30.

110. Morison, *Admiral*, 85.

111. Ibid., 83.

112. Wilford, *The Mysterious*, 89.

113. Phillips and Phillips, 126–7.

114. Fernández-Armesto, *Columbus*, 52.

115. Varela, *Textos*, 342: October 31, 1497, letter appointing guardian for his "hijos legítimos," Diego and Hernando, before Columbus embarked on the third voyage.

116. Fernández Duro, *Bibliografia Colombina*, sec. #921, p. 431.

117. Vignaud, *Histoire*, 1:605.

118. Paolini.

Chapter 7

1. Morison, *Southern Voyages*, 40.

2. Colón, *Historia del Almirante*, chap. XIII, pp. 116–17: "fué a la Rábida, para llevar su niño Diego, que le había dejado allí . . . Pero Dios . . .

inspiró al guardián de aquella casa. llamado fray Juan Peréz ... pues él iría a ver a la Reina, de la que esperaba que, por ser como era, su confesor ... se acomodó al deseo y a los ruegos del fraile, pues le parecía ser ya natural de España ... y por haber tenido hijos en ella."

3. Las Casas, *Historia*, chap. XXXI, p. 165: "saliese descontento sobre el descontento que trujo de la corte Cristóbal Colón, según los que dijeron que fué a la villa de Palos con su hijo, o a tomar su hijo, Diego Colón, niño, lo cual creo yo."

Columbus at Santa Fé

4. Dunn and Kelley, fol. 1r:16–23, p. 16: "ado(n)de este presente año a dos dias del mes de enero por fuerça de armas vide poner las vanderas reales de .v .al. en las torres dla alfambra: q(ue) es la fortaleza dla d)ic)ha çiudad: y vide salir al re moro a las puertas dla çiudad y besar las reales manos de v(uest)ras altezas y dl principe mi señor."

5. Colón, *Historia del Almirante*, chap. XV, pp. 124–26: "Siendo ya entrado el mes de Enero de 1492, el mismo día que el Almirante salió de Santa Fe."

6. Fernández de Navarrete, 3:600: "y los dió con una carta á este testigo, á fin de que lo diese á Colón para que se vistiese honestamente é comprase una bestezuela, é pareciese ante S. A."

7. Ibid. This scenario is taken from the testimony of García Fernández and Juan Rodríguez Cabezudo.

8. Las Casas, *Historia*, chap. XXXI, p. 165.

9. Morison, *Southern Voyages*, 42.

10. Wilford, *The Mysterious*, 90–92.

11. Phillips and Phillips, 131.

12. Fernández-Armesto, *Columbus*, 65.

13. Fernández de Oviedo, *Historia general*, chap. IV, p. 21: "Antes que Colom entrasse en la mar algunos dias, tuvo muy largas consultaciones con un religioso llamado Juan Perez, de la orden de sanct Francisco, su confessor; el que estaba en el monesterio de la Rábida (que es media legua de Palos hácia la mar). Y este frayle fué la persona sola de aquesta vida, á quien Colom mas comunicó de sus secretos; é aun del qual é de su sçiençia se diçe hasta hoy que él resçibió mucha ayuda é buena obra, porque este religioso era grande cosmógrapho."

14. Las Casas, *Historia*, chap. XXXI, p. 165: "Fuese al monasterio ... salió un padre, que había nombre fray Juan Perez, que debía ser el guardián

del monasterio . . . al dicho guardián, el cual diz que, o era confesor de la serenissima reina, o lo había sido."

15. Muro Orejón, *Pleitos Colombinos: Rollo del proceso*, fol. 65; Fernández de Navarrete, 3:257: Alonso Veles: "vido este testigo quel dicho almirante Colón estuvo en la villa de Palos muncho tiempo publicando el descubrymiento de las Yndias e poso en el monesterio de la Rábida e comunicava la negoçiaçion del descubrir con fraile estrolago que ende estava en el convento por guardian e ainsi mismo con fray ('le' crossed out) Juan que avia servido siendo moço a la reyna doña Ysabel Catolica siendo moço en ofiçio de contadores."

16. Fernández de Navarrete, 2:599.

Finances for the First Voyage

17. Colón, *Historia del Almirante*, chap. XV, pp. 124–26: "Luis de Santángel . . . se presentó a la Reina . . . para persuadirla . . . la Reina . . . respondió . . . diciendo que era gustosa de aceptarlo . . . y también . . . se hallaba pronta a que con las joyas de su Cámara se buscase algún empréstito por la cantidad de dinero necesaria para hacer tal armada . . . Pero Santángel . . . respondió que no era menester empeñar las joyas, porque él haría un pequeño servicio a Su Alteza prestándole de su dinero."

18. Herrera, *Historia general*, 1:I3.

19. Martínez y Martínez.

20. Jos Pérez, 26 (also in Fernández de Navarrete and Vignaud, *Histoire*): "que dio e pago mas el dicho Alonso de cabeças, por otro libramiento del dicho arçobispo de granada, fecho V de mayo de XCII Annos, A luys de santangel escribano de Raçion del Rey nuestro sennior, E por el a alonso de Angulo, por virtud de un poder que del dicho escribano mostro en el cual estava ynserto el dicho libramiento, dozientos mill maravedis a quenta de CCCC mill que enel e en vasco de quiroga, le libro el dicho arçobispo, por el dicho libramiento de II quentos DCXC mill, que ovo de aver en esta manera: I quento d mill para pagar A don ysaque Abrauanel por otro tanto que presto A sus Altezas para los gastos del la guerra, E el I quento CXC mill restantes para pagar al dicho escribano de Raçion, en quenta de otro tanto que presto para la paga de las tres caravelas que sus Altezas mandaron yr de Armada A las yndias, E para pagar A xristoual colon que va en la dicha armada. (mostro carta de pago del dicho Alonso de Angulo)." There is a marginal notation saying, "Transfer (copy, transcript, notification) of the warrant (draft) and power (authorization, proxy) and

payment . . . collated. to the clerk of the *Ración*. Charge them." Jos Pérez found this last notation questionable.

21. Varela, *Colón y los florentinos*, 49–50; Vignaud, *Histoire*, 2:117: " a Luis de Santángel, escrivano del rey . . . por virtud de un poder que del dicho escrivano mostró . . . e el I cuento CXC mill restantes para pagar al dicho escrivano de ración, en cuenta de otro tanto que prestó para la paga de las tres caravelas que Sus Altezas mandaron ir de armada a las Yndias, e para pagar a Cristóbal Colon que va en dicha armada"

22. Rumeu, *El "Portugues,"* 33.

23. Las Casas, *Historia*, chap. XXXVII.

24. Fernández de Navarrete, 3:497.

25. Fernández Duro, *Bibliografía Colombina*, sec. I:5: "Recibense en cuenta al dicho escribano de racion e Francisco Pinelo por cedula del rey e de la Reyna nuestros Sres. fha. en 2 de mayo de 1492, un cuento, ciento cuarenta mil mrs. que prestó a sus altezas para el despacho de Cristobal Colom Almirante." Fernández Duro introduces this receipt with the following: "In the accounts of Luis de Sant Angel and of Francisco Pinelo, treasurers of the Hermandad from 1491 á 1493 there is this entry." This can be interpreted as saying that the two men named were treasurers of the Hermandad over those years or that this is taken from the account book for those years. This dating by Fernández Duro is probably an error. Vignaud and Varela give it as May 5.

26. Thacher, 3:314. Pinelo provided a guarantee that "assured the return of the said bier to the church in safety."

27. Varela, *Colón y los florentinos*, 69.

28. Ibid., 115.

29. Varela, *Textos*, 467.

30. Manzano, *La incorporación*, 324.

31. Varela, *Colón y los florentinos*, 51.

32. Ibid.: "Berardi . . . Afirma . . . que lleva sirviendo a Colón desde 'tres años ha' . . . Declaró . . . que Colón le adeudaba 'por su cuenta corriente' cientos ochenta mil maravedies." Columbus factor Juanoto Berardi died on December 15 (Gil and Varela, *Cartas*, 227). Vespucci, given as Amerigo Vespuchi, was the executor of his will as well as designated with Jerónimo Rufaldi to receive payment of this debt. Also in Vignaud, *Histoire*, 1:125, and in Berwick y Alba, 7–9.

33. Fernández Duro, *Bibliografía Colombina*, sec. I:6.

34. Las Casas, *Historia*, chap. XXXIV, p. 176.

35. Herrera, *Historia general*, 1:13.

36. Dunn and Kelley, fol. 1v:19–22, p. 18: "Y partí yo de la ciudad de Granada a doze días del mes de mayo . . . y vine a la villa de Palos."

Modern Versions of the Financing of the First Voyage

37. Morison, *Admiral*, 104.
38. Wilford, *The Mysterious*, 94.
39. Varela, *Colón y los florentinos*, 51–55.
40. Phillips and Phillips, 136.
41. Fernández-Armesto, *Columbus*, 62 63.
42. Sale, 92 n.
43. Amler, 134.

The First Documents in the Genesis of America

44. Ramos, *La carta de Colón*. He concluded that the letters were apocryphal and were probably written by King Ferdinand. Varnhagen believed there was only one letter. The basic bibliography is Carlos Sanz, *Bibliografía general de la carta de Colón*. A recent study, with facsimile, is Antequera.

45. Arranz, 46.

46. Morales, 49. For study and copy of the confirmation see, Zavala.

47. Fernández de Navarrete, 1:32: "Las cosas suplicadas, e que Vuestras Altezas dan e otorgan a don Cristoval Colon, en alguna satisfaçion de lo que ha descubierto en las mares Oçeanas, e del viaje que agora, con la ayuda de Dios, ha de faxer por ellas en serviçio de Vuestras Altezas, son las que se siguen."

48. Las Casas, *Historia*, chap. XXXIII, p. 172: "de lo que ha de descubrir"; in the first paragraph: "en todas aquellas islas y tierras firmes que . . . se descubrieran o ganaren." Las Casas also used "descubriere o ganare."

49. Davenport, 746–76.

50. Colón, *Historia del Almirante*, chap. XIV, p. 121: "(Q)ue los cargos de adminstración y justicia en todas dichas islas y tierra firme fuesen en absoluto provistos, o removidos a su voluntad y arbitrio." This was not in the merced.

51. Fernández de Navarrete, 2:11: "(Testimonio auténtico existente en el Archivo del Exceléntisimo Sr. Duque de Veraguas. Registrado en el Sello de Corte en Simancas.) 1492 17 de Abril."

52. Ibid., 2:12: "Las cosas suplicadas é que vuestras Altezas dan y otorgan á Don Cristóbal Colon, en alguna satsfacion de lo que ha de descubrir en las mares Océanas."

53. Irving.

54. Madariaga, *Christopher Columbus*, 187.

55. Morison, *Admiral*, 104–5.

56. Wilford, *The Mysterious*, 95.

57. Fernández-Armesto, *Columbus*, 70: "The use in the commission [capitulation] of the title of viceroy, unprecedented in Castilian usage [Fernández-Armesto failed at this time to mention that this was an Aragonese title, although later he does refer to it as such], tends to confirm the impression that the royal chancery adopted a draft submitted by Columbus without detailed editing and perhaps without much thought or scrutiny. This alone helps to explain the insecurity Columbus evinced in writing his own summary record in the prologue to *The First Voyage*."

58. Sale, 431.

59. Fernández de Oviedo, *Historia general*, chap. IV, p. 20.

60. Colón, *Historia del Almirante*, chap. XIV, pp. 120–21.

61. Spotorno, *Codice diplomatico*.

62. Udina Martorell.

63. Pérez-Bustamante.

64. Levene, 14–15.

65. Morison, *Admiral*, 104.

66. Berwick y Alba, 17–20.

67. Fernández Martínez, *La enigma de Colón*.

68. Alvarez Pedroso, 93.

69. Morison, *Admiral*, 93. Also see Duff.

70. Fernández Martínez.

Meaning in the Capitulaciónes

71. Hanke, *Las teorías políticas*, 9.

72. Juan Ginez de Sepulveda (1490–1573), a theologian, was appointed historiographer of King Charles V. Justin Winsor, *Narrative and Critical History*, 2:315 n, said Sepulveda was "vehement, intollerant and dogmatic." His debate with Las Casas over the rights of conquest took place in 1550.

73. Vitoria.

74. Córdoba.

75. López de Palacios Rubios.

76. Las Casas, *De imperatoria seu regia potestate*.

77. Solórzano, 1:90.

78. Morales, 217.

79. Ibid., for study and copy of the treaty, see chap. 8, pp. 187–212.

80. Manzano, *Colón y su secreto*, 19 n.

81. Ibid., 25.

82. Manzano, *La incorporación de las indias.*
83. Zavala. Also in Morales, 160.
84. Gottschalk. Also Morales, 157–86.
85. Archivo General de Simancas, 45.
86. Studies: Harrisse, *The Diplomatic History of America*; Dawson.
87. Manzano, *Colón y su secreto*, 16–17.
88. Fernández de Navarrete, 1:235.

Use of the Conjunction "Or"

89. Las Casas, *Historia*, chap. XXXIII, p. 172.
90. Herrera, *Historia general*, vol I, chap. IX, p. 14.
91. Rabasa, 57.
92. Greenblatt, *Marvelous Possessions*, 53–54.
93. Pérez-Bustamante, 32.
94. Morison, *Southern Voyages*, 43.
95. Sale, 12.
96. Ibid., 25.
97. Manzano, *Colón y su secreto.*

The Capitulaciónes *and Prior Discovery*

98. Travers. Bibliography: Nowell, 802–22. Cortesão, 9–29.
99. Fernández de Oviedo, *Historia general*, chap. II, p. 13.
100. Cronau, *America.*
101. Muro Orejón, *Pleitos Colombinos: Rollo del proceso*, 209: "las cosas suplicadas que a vuestras Altezas dan e otorgan a don Christoual Colon en alguna sastifiçion de lo que a descubierto en las mares oçeanas y del viaje que agora con el ayuda de Dios a de hazer . . . prymeramente . . . hazen desde agora el dicho don Christoual Colon su almirante en todas aquellas yslas e tierra firmes que por su mano o yndustrya se descubryran e ganaran."
102. Ibid., 210–12: "E agora por quanto vos . . . nos suplicastes e pedistes . . . vos fuese guardada la dicha carta merced . . . por quanto vos don Christoval Colon vades por nuestro mandado a descubrir e ganar . . . e ansi es cosa justa e rrazonable que pues os poneys al dicho peligro por nuestro serviçio seades dello rrenumerado . . . es nuestra merçed e voluntad que vos el dicho Christoval Colon despues que ayas descubierto e ganado las dichas yslas e tierra firme . . . seades nuestro Almirante de las dichas yslas e tierra firme que ainsi descubrierdes e ganardes e seades nuestro almirante e

visorrey e governador en ellas e vos podades dende en adelante llamar e yntitular don ... vos mandamos dar esta dicha nuestra carta de privillegio ... en esta nuestra confirmaçion contenidas queremos y es nuestra voluntad que se guardan e cumplan dada en la çibdad de Burgos a veynte e tres dias del mes de abril ... Yo Hernand Alvares de Toledo, seçretario ... en las espaldas de la dicha carta de privillegio estava escryto lo siguiente (the letter of 30 April)."

103. Berwick y Alba, 13.

104. Columbus, *Christopher Columbus*, introduction (Harrisse), xiv.

105. Pérez-Bustamante: "En las Cortes de Toledo de 1480 ... ≪Todos los derechos aborrescieron la perpetuydad del officio público en una persona ... convertida en ley por los propios Reyes al decretar que ninguno de los oficios públicos que tengan cargo de administración de justicia e de regimiento e governación de pueblo o provincia puede enajenarse ... todas e cuales quier mercedes e facultades que de aqui adelante fueron fechas e dadas contra el tenor desta ley e contra lo en ella contenido sean en sí ningunas e de ningun valor, aunque cintengan en sí cuales quier cláusula deregatoria e no obstancias. ≫" Berwick y Alba, 13: "Y aun suponiendo que a pesar de esta disposición pudieron hacer estas concesiones los Reyes, por tratarse de bienes de ganancia y no de herencia de la Corona, todavía quedaba otra mucho más prohibitiva, contenida en el Ordenamiento de Alcalá y alegada por el fiscal en el pleito de los Colones: Si la donación o enaxenación se fysciere en persona non natural nin vecino del Reyno."

106. Colón, *Historia del Almirante*, chap. XIV, p. 121: "(Q)ue los cargos de adminstración y justicia en todas dichas islas y tierra firme fuesen en absoluto provistos, o removidos a su voluntad y arbitrio."

Preparations for the First Voyage

107. Fernández de Navarrete, 2:17–18: "vecinos de la Villa de Palos ... Bien sabedes como por algunas cosas fechas é cometidas por vosotros en deservicio nuestro, por los del Consejo, fuisteis condenados á que fuésedes obligados á Nos sevir doce meses con dos carabelas armadas á vuestras propias costas é espensas ... é agora por cuanto Nos habemos mandado á Cristóbal Colon que vaya con tres carabelas, para ciertas pares del mar Oceana, sobre algunas cosas que cumplen á nustro servicio ... que Nos le mandamos que vos pague luego sueldo por cuatro meses para la gente que fuere con las dichas carabelas al precios que pagaren á las otras gentes que fueren en las dichas tres carabelas, é en la otra carabela que Nos le mandamos llevar." At the bottom of the document: "En miercoles veinte é

tres de Mayo . . . estando en la Iglesia de san Jorge desta Villa de Palos, estando ende presente Fr. Juan Perez é Cristóbal Colon . . . luego el dicho Cristóbal Colon dió é presentó á los sobredichos esta Carta de sus Altezas . . . E luego los dichos Acaldes é Regidores dijeron que obedecian la dicha Carta con la reverencia debida."

108. Muro Orejón, *Pleitos Colombinos: Rollo del proceso*, 129: "en miercoles veynte y tres de mayo . . . estando en la iglesia de sant Gorge desta villa de Palos estando ende presente frey Juan Peres y Christoual Colon e asimismo estando ende presentes . . . alcaldes mayores . . . e rregidoes luego el dicho Christoual Colon dio y presento a los sobre dichos esta carta de sus Altezas."

109. Fernández de Navarrete, 2:19. "Carta . . . noticiando á las Justicias haber mandado á Cristóbal Colón que con tres carabelas armadas vaya á ciertas partes de la mar Oceana y ordenando le facilite, si lo hubiera menester, madera, carpinteros, mantenimientos, pólvora, pertrechos ú otras cosas, pagando su valor á precios razonables.

110. Ibid., 2:23.

111. Ibid., 2:22.

112. Las Casas, *Historia*, chap. XXXIV, p. 178.

113. Colón, *Historia del Almirante*, 130 n.

114. Rumeu, *El libro copiador*; Varela, *Textos*, 414–18: "Jhesus a 1498 a XVI dias de Noviembre . . . mis señores . . . acordaron que yo fuese a descobrir las Indias . . . porque pareçiese lo que yo gastase, quise que fuese ante escrivano público en la villa de Palos, adonde armé por mandado de sus Altezas tres navíos, una nao y dos caravelas . . . agora este año de 98 que yo estaba en su real Corte me ficieron merced que non fuese obligado a la pago del gasto pasado fasta llegar aquí, que fué el dicho año de 98 a 31 de Agosto . . . alí [*sic*] se está la cuenta . . . los cuales pagaron esta gente en la buelta de las Indias lo que se le debía, demás d'esto que se emprestó ante que fuesen, y el resto que ganaron recebieron en Barcelona en Mayo de <Sua Altezas>. . . . En la villa de Palos, sábado veinte e tres días de Junio . . . En este día sobredicho puso tabla el Señor Cristóbal Colón, capitán de sus Altezas . . . para dar sueldo a los marineros grumetes e gente que en la dicha armada van."

115. Rumeu, *El libro copiador*, 1:439.

116. Ibid., 436.

117. Colón, *Historia del Almirante*, chap. XVI, p. 130.

118. Las Casas, *Historia*, chap. XXXIV, p. 179.

119. Fernández de Oviedo, *Historia general*, chap. V, p. 22: "Todos estos tres capitanes eran hermanos é pilotos naturales de Palos, é la mayor parte de

los que yban en esta armada eran assi mismo de Palos. Y serian por todos hasta çiento y veynte hombres."

120. "An Unusual Diary Entry: A Converso with Christopher Columbus— 5283/1523," *Chai Today*, March 1992, pp. 18, 19.

121. Varela, *Textos*, 548.

122. Wilford, *The Mysterious*, 121–23.

123. Phillips and Phillips, 143.

124. Sale, 14.

125. Fuson, 224.

Chapter 8

The Diario de Colón

1. Henige, *In Search of Columbus*, 11.

2. Ibid., 19.

3. Ibid., 11.

4. Ibid., 100–101.

5. Ibid., 18.

6. Morison, *Southern Voyages*, 63.

7. Fuson, 8.

The Santángel/Sánchez Letters and El libro copiador

8. See Harrisse, *Bibliotheca Americana Vetustissima* (1866, 1872), and Sanz: *Bibliografía; Indice general; El gran secreto de la carta de Colón.*

9. Eames; Robbins; Major, *Bibliography*; Varnhagen; Ramos, *La carta de Colón*; Antequera. In Seville in 1892, the first facsimile and full version of the Dati versification was published in *Curiosidades Bibliográficas y Documentos Inéditos.* Morison published a Spanish-language edition and an English translation, which he claimed, incorrectly, was the first new one "since 1891": *Christopher Columbus, Mariner,* and *Cristóbal Colón, Marino.*

10. Fernández de Navarrete, 2:281.

11. Colón, *Historia del Almirante*, chap. XI, p. 283.

12. Facsimile in Sanz, *La carta de Colón*, 12, and transcription in Fernández de Navarrete, 1:175.

13. Las Casas, *Historia*, chap. LXXVII, p. 331.

14. Rumeu, *El libro copiador*, 1:34.

15. Asensio, 1:449.

16. Dunn and Kelley, fol. 62r:34–44, p. 370: "Porq(ue) ... los reyes oviesen noticia de su viaje: tomo vn pargamino scrivio en el todo lo q(ue) pudo de todo lo q(ue) avia hallado paga(n)do mucho a que(n) lo hallase q(ue) lo llevase a los reyes / . Este pargamino metio enbolvio en vn paño ençerado atado m(u)y bien: y ma(n)do traer vn gra(n) barril de madera y pusolo en el sin q(ue) ningu(n)a persona supiese q(ue) era; sino q(ue) pensaro(n) q(ue) era alguna devoçion y asi lo ma(n)do echar en la mar."

17. Colón, *Historia del Almirante*, chap. XXXVII, p. 265.

18. Morison, *Admiral*, 328.

19. Wilford, *The Mysterious*, 12.

20. Morison, *Admiral*, 376.

21. Dunn and Kelley, fol. 65v:35–36, p. 392.

22. Ibid., fol. 66r:25–28, p. 394.

23. Phillips and Phillips, 182.

24. Varela, *Textos*, 226.

25. Morison, *Admiral*, 320–28.

26. Fernández-Armesto, *Columbus*, 92.

27. Sale, 123.

28. Sale gave the Dunn and Kelley transcription of the *Diario*: "supplemented by Morison, JAOD (which I generally have used for page citations, since it is most accessible) Cecil Jane ... Robert Fuson ... Thacher, vol. I." None of these authors cited by Sale gave incorrectly the date for the letter written at sea.

29. Eames, 12.

30. Ibid., introduction, viii–ix.

31. Robbins, 7.

32. Sanz, *Indice general*.

33. Eames, viii.

Proposed Destination

34. Las Casas, *Historia*, chap. XXXV, p. 180.

35. Dunn and Kelley, fol. 16v:16–20, p. 108.

36. Jos Pérez, 28: "nobilem virum xpoforum colon, cum tribus caravelis armatis per maria oceana ad partes Indie."

37. Transcription of the Barcelona letter in Varela, *Textos*, 224.

38. Morison, *Southern Voyages*, 43.

39. Wilford, *The Mysterious*, 9.

40. Phillips and Phillips, 124.

41. Ibid., 134.

42. Fernández-Armesto, *Columbus*, 69.
43. Dunn and Kelley, fol. 1r:24–26, p.16: "por la informaçion q(ue) yo avia dado a .v.al. dlas t(ie)rras de yndia y de vn principe q(ue) es llamado gra(n) Can."
44. Varela, *Textos*, 234.

Columbus's Navigational Methods

45. Morison, *Admiral*, 187–89.
46. Wilford, *The Mysterious*, 134–35.
47. Todorov, *The Conquest*, 19.
48. Dunn and Kelley, 31 n. 2.
49. Ibid., f. 26r:9–12, p. 162.
50. Colón, *Historia del Almirante*, chap. LXIV, p. 102.
51. Sanz, *Relación*, fol. 6v:485–87.
52. Ibid., fol. 60r:6–9, p. 356.
53. Ibid., fol. 9v:29–33, p. 68.
54. Phillips and Phillips, 74.
55. Fernández-Armesto, *Columbus*, 75.
56. Rubin, 231–38.

Double Entries in the Diario

57. Dunn and Kelley, fol. r:26–30, p. 28: "anduvo aq(ue)l dia .15. leguas y acordo contar menos dlas q(ue) andava porq(ue) si el viaje fuese lue(n)go no se espantase y desmayase la gente."
58. Colón, *Historia del Almirante*, chap. XVIII, p. 140.
59. Morison, *Southern Voyages*, 57.
60. Henige, *In Search of Columbus*, 128.
61. Herrera, *Historia general*, vol. I, chap. XI, p. 19.
62. Las Casas, *Historia*, chap. XXXVIII, p. 193.
63. Rabasa, 58.
64. Henige, *In Search of Columbus*, 139.

Shipboard Morale and Mutiny or Near-Mutiny

65. Dunn and Kelley, fol. 2r:21–28, p. 22: "Se le quebro Salto /o desencasose el goVrnrio a la Caravela pinta donde yva martin alo(n)so pinçon a lo q(ue) se creyo / o sospecho por industria de vn gomez [R]ascon[?] y x(ris)poual quintero cuya era la Caravela porq(ue) le pesava yr aq(ue)l

viaje /. y dize el almi(rant)e q(ue) antes q(ue) partiesen avian hallado en çiertos reveses y grisquetas como dize(n) a los d(ic)hos /."

66. Ibid., 31:33, p. 22: "y dize q(ue) algu(n)a pena p[er]dia con saber q(ue) martin alo(n)so pinçon era p[er]sona esforçada y de bue(n) ingenio."

67. Colón, *Historia del Almirante*, chap. XII, p. 134.

68. Dunn and Kelley, fol. 4r:26–28, p. 32: "y temian los marineros y estava(n) penados y no dezia(n) de que."

69. Ibid., fol. 4r:39–41, p. 34.

70. Ibid., fol. 5r:27–31, p. 38.

71. Ibid. Las Casas used here the word *murmurar.* This sometimes translated as "grumble," or "complain." The more literal translation is "gossip," as in "discuss."

72. Ibid., fol. 5r:42–44, fol. 5v:1–5, p. 40. Alternative meanings for *asombrar* are (1) "darken," (2) "frighten, terrify," (3) "astonish, amaze." In the latter sense, it is usually used with *con* or *de*. Dunn and Kelley preferred in this case "astonish."

73. Ibid., fol. 4v:43, p. 40.

74. Herrera, *Historia general*, chap. X, p. 17: September 25: "Vicente Yañez dixò a voces: Tierra, Tierra." Here he adds a novel remark: "esta que fe juzgò por invencion, concertada entre los dos."

75. Dunn and Kelley, fol. 7v:22–25, p. 54: "por esto el almi(rant)e acordo dexar el camino del gueeste: y pone la proa hazia guesueste con deter-minaçion de andar dos dias por aq(ue)lla via."

76. Ibid., fol. 8r:9–14, p. 56.

77. Henige, "The Mutinies," 29.

78. Dunn and Kelley, fol. 62r:6–12, p. 368: "+qua(n)do tenia mayor razo(n) de temer" (in the right margin).

79. Ibid., fol. 62r:8–14, p. 368: "devia creer q(ue) le daria co(m)plimi(ent)o d(e)lo come(n)çado y le llevaria en saluame(n)to / . mayorme(n)te q(ue) pues le avia libra/do a la yda + [*qua(n)do tenia mayor razo(n) de temer* in the right margin] de los trabajos q(ue) con los marine/ros y gente q(ue) llevava: los quales todos a vna voz estavan determinados de se bolver a alçar se contra el haziendo protestaçiones."

80. Henige, *In Search of Columbus*, 45–47. See also his comments in "The Mutinies," 31.

81. Las Casas, *Historia*, chap. XXXIX, pp. 195–97.

82. Colón, *Historia del Almirante*, chap. XIX, pp. 147–49.

83. Ibid., chap. XX, pp. 151–52.

84. Bernáldez, chap. CXVIII, pp. 359–60: "viendo que habian andado más de mil leguas y no se descubria, las opiniones de los marineros eran muchas,

que de ellos decian, que ya no era razon de andar más, que iban sin remedio perdidos, y que seria maravilla acertar á volver; y de esta opinion eran los más; y Colon y los otros capitanes, con dulces palabras, los convenceron que anduviesen más, y que fuesen certos, que con la ayuda de Dios fallarian tierra."

85. Gil, *Tres notas colombinas*, 15–16: "la gente dexía al dicho Almirante que se devían bolver, e el dicho Almirante les respondía que tomarían el consejo del dicho Martín Alonso para ver lo que devían hazer . . . le respondió que su paresçer hera lo mismo e que devía seguir su derrota."

86. Gil and Varela, *Cartas*, 41 (Spanish translation of Martire's *Decadas*).

87. Fernández de Oviedo, *Historia general*, chap. V, p. 22.

88. Interiano, 67: "doppo molti contrasti, & dispareri del la gente fua, laquale votea tornar adietro."

89. Morison, *Admiral*, 215.

90. Ibid., 210.

91. Phillips and Phillips, 152.

92. Ibid.

93. Fernández-Armesto, *Columbus*, 76.

94. Fuson, 11.

95. Ibid., 11–12.

96. Cummins.

Chapter 9

1. Dunn and Kelley, fol. 10r:22, p. 70: "Esta isa es bien gra(n)dey m(u)y llana y de arboles m(u)y verdes y muchas aguas y una laguna en medio muy gra(n)de." Dunn and Kelley translate this as "quite big."

2. One of the early and more influential studies is Jal, reproduced in Asensio, 1:188. See G. V. Fox, 1880, a U.S. coastal survey in Winsor, *Narrative and Critical History*, 2:56.

3. Cronau, *The Discovery of America*.

4. Marden, 572–601.

Columbus and Pinzón

5. Muro Orejón, *Pleitos Colombinos: Rollo del proceso*, 113–14.

6. Ibid., 172.

7. Ibid., 180.

8. Morison, *Admiral*, 138.

9. Wilford, *The Mysterious*, 118, 224.

10. Phillips and Phillips, 138–39.

11. Fernández-Armesto, *Columbus*, 72.

12. Colón, *Historia del Almirante*, chap. XXXIII, p. 249: "El Almirante, aunque sabía bien lo contrario y mala intención de aquel hombre, y se acordaba de la mucha insolencia que contra él se había tomado en muchas cosas de aquel viaje, sin embargo, disimuló con él, y todo lo soportó, por no deshacer el proyecto de su empresa, lo que fácilmente acontecería, porque la mayor parte de la gente que llevaba consigo, era de la patria de Martín Alonso, y aún, muchos parientes déste."

13. Dunn and Kelley, fol. 52v:1–14, pp. 311–12: "vino martin alonso pinçon a la Caravela dl almirante niña donde yva el almir(an)te a se escusar diziendo q(ue) avia p[ar]tido dl co(n)tra su volu(n)tad dando razones p[ar]a ello / p[er]o el almi(rant)e dize q(ue) era falsas todas y q(ue) con mucha sobervia y cudiçia se avia ap[ar]tado aq(ue)lla noche q(ue) se aparto dl/ y q(ue) no sabia (dize el almi(rant)e) de donde le oviese venido las sobervias y deshonestidad q(ue) avia vsado con el aq(ue)l viaje /. las quales quiso el almi(rant)e dissimular; por no dar lugar a las malas obras de Sathanas."

14. Ibid., fol. 52v:14–15, p. 312: "q(ue) deseava impedir aq(ue)l viaje como hasta esto(n)çes avia hecho."

15. Ibid., fol. 51r:14–19, p. 304.

16. Ibid., fol. 52v:14–15, p. 312: "despues q(ue) martin alonso fue a la Isla baneque diz q(ue) y no hallo nada de oro; se vino a la costa dla española; por informaçion de otros yndios q(ue) le dixero(n) aver en aq(ue)lla isla española q(ue) los indios llamava(n) bohio mucha Cantidad de oro y muchas minas; y por esta causa llego çerca dla villa dla navidad obra de quinze veynte leguas y avía entonces mas de veynte dias: por lo qual pareçe q(ue) fiero(n) Verdad las nuevas q(ue) los yndios davan."

17. Las Casas, *Historia*, chap. LXV, pp. 300–301: "Supo el Almirante de la gente de la carabela que Martín Alonso quisiera que toda la gente jurara que no había estado en el dicho río sino seis días."

18. Ibid.: "estado diez y seis días Martin Alonso rescatando mucho oro que allí hobo, al cual puso nombre Río de Gracia."

19. Fernández de Oviedo, *Historia general*, chap. VI, pp. 26–27.

20. Ibid., 26: "Mas como de la quedada de aquesta gente no le plugo al capitan de la otra carabela Pinta, llamado Martin Alonso Pinçon, hermano de estos otros, contradíxolo todo quanto él pudo; é deçia que era mal hecho que aquellos chripstianos quedassen tan lexos de España, seyendo tan pocos, é porque no se podrian proveer ni sostener y se perderian. Y á este propósito dixo otras palabras, de que el quisiera prender; y el Martín Alonso, con

temor que ovo desta sospecha, se saleó a la mar con su caravela Pinta é fuése al puerto de Gracia."

21. Dyson, 173.

22. Dunn and Kelley, fol. 59r:5–13, p. 350.

23. Colón, *Historia del Almirante*, chap. XLII, p. 292.

24. Fernández de Oviedo, *Historia general*, chap. VI, p. 27.

25. Morison, *Admiral*, 352.

26. Morison, *Southern Voyages*, 90.

Juan de la Cosa

27. Channing, 2:206.

28. Vascano.

29. Andresco.

30. Ibid., 80.

31. Ibid. Alonso de Ojeda named him "piloto major" of his first expedition. Letter from Isabel to bishop of Badajoz "Juan de la Cosa, vecino del Puerto de Santoñia" (August 25, 1496). In 1507 he was given command of two caravels sent out to intercept a boat reported to be planning to waylay a Spanish vessel returning from the Indies with gold. *Cédula* issued in 1508 by Doña Juana confirming Isabel's naming of Juan de la Cosa Alguacil Mayor of Urabá.

32. Dunn and Kelley, fol. 46v:2–3, p. 278.

33. Las Casas, *Historia*, chap. LIX, p. 277.

34. Dunn and Kelley, fol. 21r:37, p. 134.

35. Ibid., fol. 48v:5, p. 288.

36. Ibid., fol. 65v:45, fol. 66r:2, p. 392: "oy dspues q(ue)l patron dla nao gra(n)de dl rey de portugal . . . vino el patron dlla q(ue) se llamava bartolome diaz de lisboa."

37. Morison, *Admiral*, 119, 144–45, 300–302.

38. Ibid., 396.

39. Vascano, 82.

40. Herrera, *Historia general*, vol. I, bk. 4, chap, p. 11.

The Loss of the Santa María.

41. Dunn and Kelley, fols. 46r:15–45, 46v:1–27, pp. 276, 278. For this purpose, I have used both the Sanz facsimile and the Dunn and Kelley transcription. For the convenience of the reader, the appropriate passages in the Dunn and Kelley transcription will be the only ones indicated in the footnotes, although the actual transcription cited is my own.

42. Colón, *Historia del Almirante*, chap. XXXIII, pp. 235–36.

43. Bernáldez, chap. CXVIII, p. 367.

44. Fernández de Oviedo, *Historia general*, bk. II, chap. VI, p. 25.

45. Thacher, 1:8.

46. Martire, *Décades*, 5:42, 6:43, in Gil and Varela, *Cartas*: "De la nave, que dijimos que había encallado en el escollo [reef], sacaron a nuestros hombres y cuanto en ella iba en sus almadías, que llaman canoas, con tanta rapidez y disposición de ánimo, que ningun vecino entre nosotros sociorrería a otro movido a mayor compasión."

47. Morison, *Admiral*, 300–301.

48. Dunn and Kelley, fol. 46v:20, p. 278: "y entonçes se abriero(n) los conventos y no la nao."

49. Sale, 116.

50. Wilford, *The Mysterious*, 164.

51. Phillips and Phillips, 172.

52. Dunn and Kelley, fol. 48v:21–23, p. 290: "porq(ue) ella quedo sana como qua(n)do salie partio: saluo q(ue) se corto y rajo algo p[ar]a sacar la vasija y todas las mercaderias."

53. Fernández-Armesto, *Columbus*, 88.

54. Dunn and Kelley, fol. 46r:6–10, p. 274.

55. Ibid., fol. 46v:26–27, p. 278.

56. Ibid., fol. 48r:22, p. 186.

57. Sale, 116

58. Fuson, 151.

Sank or Scuttled?

59. Bernáldez, 2:63: "se hallaron embarazados entre muchas islas, y en muy poco fondo, de manera que no hallaban canal que lo consintiense pasar adelante, é á cabo de un dia y medio por una canal muy angusta é baja por fuerza de ánclas y cabestral pudieron de pasar los navios casi una braza por la tierra en seco, hasta haber andado bien dos leguas."

60. Colón, *Historia del Almirante*, chap. LVIII, p. 402: "navegó hasta llegar a Cuba; de donde, siguiendo la vía de Levante, con escasísimos vientos, y por canales y bajos de arena, el 30 de Junio, mientras escribía la relación de aquel viaje, dió en el fondo su navío tan fuertemente, que, no pudiendo sacarlo afuera con las áncoras, ni con otros ingenios, quiso Dios que fuera sacado por la proa, si bien con bastante daño, por los golpes que había dado en el suelo." Las Casas, *Historia*, chap. XCVI, p. 391: "a 30 de Junio, encalló su nao, la cual, no pudiéndola sacar con anclas y cables por

popa, sacáronla por proa, y por los golpes que dió en la arena, con harto daño."

61. D'Ailly, 222: "la milla tiene 4,000 codos." This would make a codo 1.25 feet.

62. Gil, "El libro copiador"; Varela, *Textos*, 292.

The Founding of Navidad

63. Wilford, *The Mysterious*, 164.

64. Phillips and Phillips, 172–73.

65. Colón, *Historia del Almirante*, chap. XXXIV, pp. 242–44: "resolvió el Almirante fabricar un fuerte con la madera de la nave perdida, de la que ninguna cosa dejó que no sacase fuera, y no llevara todo lo útil."

66. Muro Orejón, *Pleitos Colombinos: Rollo del proceso*, 175.

67. Fernández de Oviedo, *Historia general*, vol. I, bk. II, chap. V, p. 22: "Y serian por todos hasta çiento y veynte hombres."

68. Interiano, 67: "con CXX huomini."

69. Colón, *Historia del Almirante*, chap. LXIII, p. 92.

70. Thacher, 2:450 n.

71. Muro Orejón, *Pleitos Colombinos: Rollo del proceso*, 182.

72. Thacher, 1:8.

73. Dunn and Kelley, fol. 48r:44–45, pp. 288, 303.

74. Bernáldez, chap. CXVIII, p. 367.

75. Martire, *Décades*, in Gil and Varela, *Cartas*, 46: "Dejó treinta y ocho hombres . . . para reconocer la naturaleza del lugar y de la zona hasta que volviese él en persona."

Return Voyage

76. Dunn and Kelley, fol. 52v:23–32, p. 312: "despues q(ue) martin alonso fue a la Isla baneque diz q(ue) y no hallo nada de oro; se vino a la costa dla española; por informaçion de otros yndios llamava(n) bohio mucha cantidad de oro y muchas minas; y por esta causa llego çerca dla villa dla navidad obra de quinze ~~veynte~~ leguas y avía entonces mas de veynte dias: por lo qual pareçe q(ue) fiero(n) Verdad las nuevas q(ue) los yndios davan."

77. Ibid., fol. 56r:7–25, p. 332.

78. Colón, *Historia del Almirante*, chap. XXXVI, pp. 254–55.

79. Las Casas, *Historia*, chap. LXV, pp. 304–5: "Y esta fué la primera pelea que hobo en todas las Indias, y donde hobo derramada sangre de

indios, y es de creer que murió el de la saetada, y aun el de las nalgas desgarradas no quedaría muy sano."

80. Morison, *Admiral*, 312.

81. Phillips and Phillips, 175.

82. Sale, 120–21.

83. Dunn and Kelley, fol. 55v:30–34, p. 330.

84. Ibid., fol. 57v:1–37, p. 342: "nu(n)ca esto despues se averiguo q(ue) oviese tales mugeres."

85. Ibid., fol. 57r:40–48, p. 340.

86. Ibid., 57v:30–41, p. 342.

87. Morison, *Admiral*, 315.

88. Dunn and Kelley, f 58r:28–34, p. 346: "por vn pescado q(ue) se llama rabiforcado q(ue) anduvo alrededor dla caravela y despues se fue la via dl sursueste q(ue) ya[?] creyo el almi(rant)e q(ue) avia por alli algunas Islas / y al lessueste dla Isla española dixo q(ue) quedava la Isla Carib y la de matinino y otras mas."

89. Morison, *Admiral*, 317.

90. Wilford, *The Mysterious*, 162.

91. Morison, *Southern Voyages*, 88.

92. Dunn and Kelley, fol. 66v:15, p. 396.

93. Morison, *Admiral*, 349.

Chapter 10

1. Greenblatt, *Marvelous Possessions*, 54.

The Objective of the Journey

2. *Chai Today*, March 1992, 19.

3. Greenblatt, *Marvelous Possessions*, 54.

4. Rubruck, 52.

The Discovery of America

5. Fernández de Oviedo, *Historia general*, bk. II, chap. V, p. 24: "segund yo oy decir á Viçente Yañez Pinçon y á Hernan Perez Matheos, que se hallaron en este primero descubrimiento, era de Lepe, como he dicho."

6. Dunn and Kelley, fol. 8r:38, 8v:8, p. 58.

7. Fernández de Navarrete, 3:612.

8. Morison, *Admiral*, 225.

9. Las Casas, *Historia*, chap. XXXIX, p. 198.

10. Fernández de Oviedo, *Historia general*, vol. I, bk. II, chap. V, p. 24: "E como sobrevino la noche, mandó apocar las velas y que corriesen con solo los trinquetes baxos; é andando assi, un marinero de los que yban en la capitana, natural de Lepe, dixo: lumbre! . . . tierra! . . . E luego un criado de Colom, llamado Salçedo, replico diciendo: Esso ya lo ha dicho el almirante, mi señor y encontinente Colom dixo: Rato que yo lo he dicho y he visto aquella lumbre que está en tierra. Y assi fué: que un jueves, á las dos horas despues de media noche . . . y el que vido primero la tierra, quando ya fué de dia, se llamaba Rodrigo de Triana, á onçe dias de octubre . . . Y de aver salido tan verdadero el almirante, en ver la tierra en el tiempo que avia dicho, se tuvo mas sospecha que él estaba çertificado del piloto que se dixo que murió en su casa, segund se tocó de suso . . . aquel marinero que dixo primero que veia lumbre en la tierra, tornado despues en España, porque no se lo dieron las albriçias, despechado de aquesto, se pasó en Africa y renegó de la fé. Este hombre, segund yo oy deçir á Viçente Yañez Pinçon y á Hernan Perez Matheos, que se hallaron en este primero descubrimiento, era de Lepe, como he dicho."

11. Colón, *Historia del Almirante*, chap. XXII, pp. 169–73.

12. Gil, *Tres notas colombinas*, 74.

13. *Chai Today*, March 1992, 19.

Taking Possession

14. Morison, *Admiral*, 228–29.

15. Greenblatt, *Marvelous Possessions*, 55.

16. Varela, *Textos*, 228.

17. Todorov, *The Conquest*, 28.

18. Las Casas, *Historia*, chap. XL, p. 201.

19. Greenblatt, *Marvelous Possessions*, 59.

Gold in Relation to the Discovery

20. Dunn and Kelley, fol. 10r:9, p. 70.

21. Ibid., fol. 10v:41, p. 74.

22. Rumeu, *El libro copiador*, line 142:440.

23. Todorov, *The Conquest*, 8.

24. Ibid., 42.

25. Rumeu, *El libro copiador*, fol. 1v:52, p. 437.

26. Ibid., fol. 2r:80–82, p. 428.

27. Ibid., fol. 2v:135–39, p. 439.

28. Varela, *Textos*, 234.

Columbus's Religious Motivation

29. Dunn and Kelley, fol. 1r:24–31, p. 16.

30. Varela, *Textos*, 233.

31. Ibid.

32. Plaïdy, 36.

33. Greenblatt, *Marvelous Possessions*, 72.

34. Dunn and Kelley, fol. 48v:24–35, p. 290.

35. Varela, *Textos*, 232.

36. Ibid., 360.

37. West and Kling, 66.

38. Zamora, *Reading Columbus*, 137.

39. Quoted in Hale, 372.

40. Todorov, *The Conquest*, 12.

Reaction in Spain to the Discovery

41. Varela, *Textos*, 219.

42. Fernández Navarrete, 2:54–55: May 23: "prometimos al dicho Almirante ó á otra cualquier persona que viese ó descubriese primero las dichas Islas, ó algunas de ellas, de le faser merced de diez mil marevedis de merced de por vida: é porque el dicho Almirante D. Cristóbal Colon ha descubierto primero que otro alguno la tierra de las dichas Islas, y somos ciertos y certificados que él fue el primero que vió é decubrió las dichas Islas ... D. Cristóbal Colon haya y tenga de Nos los dichos diez mil maravedis de por vida ... situadas señalamente en cualsquier rentas de alcabalas é tercias é almojarifazgo é otras rentas de la ciudad de Córdoba" postscript dated November "las alcalabas de las carnecerías de la ciudad de Córdoba."

43. Martire, *Epistolario*, 9:242–43: September 13, Martire letter to Tendilla and Fray Hernando de Talavera: "Colón, el de Liguria, estuvo en los campamentos [de Santa Fé tratando con los Reyes acerca del recorrido por los antipodas occidentales de un nuevo hemisferio de la tierra. . . . Este ha regresado sano y salvo; dice que ha encontrado cosas admirables; ostenta el oro como prueba de las minas de aquellas regiones."

44. Morison, *Admiral*, 382.

45. Martire, *Epistolario*, 9:243–45: September 13, letter to Sforza: "es cosa admirable que de toda la redondez de la tierra, a la que el sol da la vuelta en el escpacio de veintecuatro horas, no haya sido conocida ni recorrida hasta nuestros tiempos—lo que tú bien sabes—sino la mitad desde el dorado Quersoneso hasta nuestra Caliz española. El resto lo dejaron los cosmógrafos por desconocido; y si alguna mención se hizo de ello, es liger y dudisa. Mas ahora—¡oh feliz hazaña!—, bajo los auspicios de mis Reyes, ha comenzado a conocerse lo que desde el principio de la creación hasta el presente estuvo oculto."

46. Ibid., 9:245: October 1, Martire to Braga: "Cierto Colón navegó hacia Occidente hasta llegar a las costas de las Indias —según él cree—, en los antipodas. Encontró muchas islas, y piensan que son las mencionadas por los cosmógrafos más allá del Oceano Oriental, y adyacentes a la India. Yo no lo niego por completo, aunque la magnitud de la esfera parece indicar lo contrario; pues no faltan quienes opinan que el litoral índico dist [de ser admitido lo supuesto] muy poca de las playas españolas."

47. Jos Pérez, 81–90.

48. Ramos, *Memorial de Zamora*, fol. 4, unnumbered; also in Martire, *Epistolario*, 9:250.

49. Martire, *Decadas*, book 1 of the first decade.

50. Ramos, *Memorial de Zamora*, fol. 5.

51. Colón, *Historia del Almirante*, chap. VI, p. 48.

Chapter 11

Note: In this chapter, several passages are copied in extenso in the text because many are rarely, if ever, cited in the critiqued biographies.

1. Dunn and Kelley, fol. 67r:5–8, p. 400.

2. Ibid., 401.

Proposed Colonization of Española

3. Las Casas, *Historia*, chap. LXXVII, pp. 331–32 (also a copy in Fernández de Navarrete, 2:27–28).

4. Ibid.

5. Thacher, 3:98–113, with a facsimile of the holograph: "lo que me ocure para la poblaçion y negoçiaçion asy de la ysla española ... Primeramente ... que vayan hasta en numero de dos mil veçinos ... porque mejor y mas presto se puebla la dicha isla ninguno tenga facultad para cojer

oro en ella, salvo los que tomren veçindad e hiçieren casas . . . que haya
iglesia y abades o frayles . . . que ninguno de los veçinos pueda yr a coger
oro salvo con liçencia del gobernador o alcalde del lugar donde biviere [this
is followed by five paragraphs dealing exclusively with the control of gold]
. . . que en la dicha ysla haya thesorero que reciva todo el oro pereteneciente
a vuestras altezas y tenga un escrivano que lo asçiente."

6. Fernández de Navarrete, 2:44; Thacher, 3:95.

Columbus in Seville and Barcelona in 1493

7. Bernáldez, chap. CXVIII, p. 369.
8. Fernández de Oviedo, *Historia general*, chap. VII, p. 28.
9. Martire, *Epistolario*, 9:236–37.
10. Martire, *Décades*, 1:12, in Gil and Varela, *Cartas*, 4.
11. Fernández Duro, *Nebulosa de Colón*, 74–75 (undated): Fray Antonio
de Aspa, Jeronymite from the convent of la Mejorada: "Los Reyes estaban
á la sazón en Barcelona, que fué el año que dieron la cuchillada al dicho Rey
D. Fernando, y el dicho Colón llegó ya quel dicho Rey era curado y estaba
bueno, porque dende poco quel Colón llegó se partieron los dichos Reyes de
Barcelona, y ansí con el alegría que entonces tenían por haber sanado el
dicho Rey de la dicha cuchillada, como con las buenas nuevas e ciertas
señales que traía de las tierras que había ido á buscar el dicho Colón, fué
muy bien rescebido y con mucho placer y alegría de todos los cortesanos, que
no se hartaban los Reyes y ellos, y los unos y los otros, de le preguntar de
las cosas y gentes de aquellas islas. El dicho D. Fernando e la reina doña
Isabel, oidas tantas y tan nuevas cosas de aquellas tierras, como sus
pensamientos fuesen siempre firmados en cómo ensalzarían y aumentarían
nuestra Santa Fee [*sic*] Catholica, esperando que fácilmente se covertirían
y traerían á la Fee tantas y tan simples gentes y naciones, comviéronse á
tratar bien al dicho Colón y á lo hablar y hacer mercedes, como por tales
servicios lo merecía, y hiciéronle sentar delanta públicamente, lo cual es
señal de grande amor y agradecimiento cuando esto hacen los Reyes de
España con alguno, y señal de algún gran sercicio, y hiciéronle Almirante
de aquellas tierras y mares occidentales, y ansí mandaron que de así
adelante le llamasen."

12. Asensio, bk. II, chap. XII, pp. 460–61.
13. Colón, *Historia del Almirante*, chap. XLII, p. 293.
14. Herrera, *Historia general*, vol. I, bk. II, pp. 38–39.
15. Morison, *Admiral*, 358.

16. Bisson, 160–61.
17. Morison, *Admiral*, 361.
18. Wilford, *The Mysterious*, 22–25.
19. Rubin, 331–32.
20. Martínez, 6, 12.
21. Phillips and Phillips, 189–90.
22. Sale, 63.

Portuguese Reaction to the Discovery

23. Manzano, *Colón y su secreto*, 21 n.
24. Asensio, bk. II, chap. XII, p. 466: Bernardino de Carvajal: "recibió de los Reyes . . . el encargo . . . de poner en noticia de Alejandro VI el viaje de Cristóbal Colón . . . su oración . . . dijo 'Plugo a N.S. Jesucristo sujetar á su imperio (el de los Reyes Católicos) las Indias afortunadas, cuya admirable fertilidad es tan notoria. Y ahora mismo les ha dado otras muchas hacia la India, hasta aqui desconocidas, que se juzga no los hay más presciosas y ricas en todo lo que del mundo se conoce.'"
25. Earliest copy in Solórzano, bk. 1 lib. 1°, chap, X; facsimiles of all four bulls with transcriptions in Gottschalk; first bull in Fernández de Navarrete, 2:29–43.

Papal Bulls

26. Gottschalk, 4.
27. Morales, 160.
28. Ibid., 167–80.
29. Ibid., transcription, 184.
30. Dawson.
31. Gottschalk, 29.
32. Morison, *Admiral*, 367.
33. Gottschalk, 15.
34. Thacher, 2:16.
35. Ibid.

The Individual Bulls

36. Harrisse, *The Diplomatic History of America*, 26.
37. Dunn and Kelley, fol. 4r:26, 37–39, pp. 32, 34.

Negotiations between Spain and Portugal: The Treaty of Tordesillas

38. Harrisse, *The Diplomatic History of America*, 22 n.

39. Fernández de Oviedo, *Historia general*, chap. VIII, p. 32: "Pero porque estas cosas estan aprobadas por el vicario de Dios é de la sagrada Iglesia, no es neçessario deçir otra cosa, sino que yo he visto un treslado, auctorizado y signado, de la Bula apostólica, la data de la qual diçe: *Datis Romæ apud sanctum Petrum, anno Incarnationis Domini millessimo quadrigentessimo nonagessimo tertio, quarto nonas maii, pontificatus nostri anno primo.*"

40. Fernández de Navarrete, 2:12: September 25, carta mensajera de la Reina: "Con este correo vos envio un traslado del libro que acá dejastes, el cual ha tardado tiempo porque se escribiese secretamente, para que estos que estan aqui de Portugal, ni otro alguno non supiese dello, y a cabsa desto, porque mas presto se ficiese, va de dos letras segund vereis ... La Carta del marear que habiades de faser, si es acabada, me enviad luego."

41. Ibid., 2:174: "queriamos si ser pudiese que vos os hallasedes en ello, y la hiciesedes con otros que por parte del rey de Portugal en ello han de entender, y si hay mucha dificultad en vuestra ida á esto ó podría traer algun inconvniente en o que ende estais, ved si vuestro hermano ó otro alguno tenende que lo sepa, é informadlos por escripto, y por palabra y aun por pintura y por todas las maneras que mejor pudieren ser informados, é inviadnoslos acá luego con las primeras carabelas que vinisen ... y quier hyais vos de ir á esto ó no, escribidnos muy largamente todo lo que en esto supiéredes y á vos pareciere que se debe hacer para nuestra informacion; y faced de manera que vuestras carta y las que habeis de enviar vengan presto, porque puedan volver adonde se ha de hacer la raya antes que se cumpla el tiempo que tenemos asentado con el rey de Portugal."

42. Ibid., 2:111: August 26, letter from Cardinal Mendoza to Jaime Ferrer ordering him to Barcelona with "el Mapamundi y otros instrumentos si teneis tocantes á cosmografia."

43. Harrisse, *The Diplomatic History of America*, 96–97.

44. Fernández de Navarrete, 2:155.

45. Ibid., 2:171.

46. Gil, *Mitos y utopías*, 101.

47. Harrisse, *The Diplomatic History of America*, 83.

48. Ibid., 176 n.

49. A full-scale facsimile by sections is in Gottschalk.

Memorial de la Mejorada

50. Thacher, 2:429. Thacher was the first to point out that the Muñoz/ Navarrete copies of the nurse's letter had important omissions and obscure transcriptions. The word "colucuti" was transcribed by them as "polo artico" from an illegible entry in the Genoa Codex that Spotorno had transcribed as "colo arti." Thacher and, more recently, Rumeu de Armas each used the Paris Codex in which the word is clearly written as "Colucuti." Unfortunately, Varela's translation is apparently from Las Casas's copy. As Thacher pointed out, the copy made for Columbus's personal use takes precedence over one copied more than half a century later. In 1893 Stevens published the first facsimile of the Paris Codex. In 1951 Ciriaco Pérez-Bustamante published the first Spanish translation of the Genoa Codex, providing a new transcription and comparative analysis with the Spotorno, Lollis, and Stevens versions.

51. Varela, *Textos*, 430.

52. Fernández-Armesto, *Columbus*, 99.

53. Fernández de Navarrete, 1:222.

54. Rumeu, *Un escrito*, 33.

55. Ibid.

56. Ibid., 81: "ha mandado nauegar a sus naos grandissimo numero de leguas al oriente, atrauesando Arabia, Persia e Yndia, fata llegar casy adonde auian llegado las naos de los sobredichos rrey y rreyna."

57. Ibid., transcription, 82, facsimile MS fol. 3v:7–8: "el mar Oçeano es entre Africa, España y las tierras de Yndias; el tiene de la parte del poniente las Indias y de la parte de levante Africa y España, hasta el poniente."

58. Ibid., 77–78.

59. Ibid., 82.

60. Ramos, *Memorial de Zamora*, fol. 8.

61. Fernández de Navarrete, 2:28: May 2, in carta mensajera to the duke of Medinasidonia, the sovereigns wrote: "nos fesistes [*sic*] saber lo que habiades sabido del armada que el Rey de Portugal ha fecho para enviar á la parte del mar Oceano á lo que agora decubrió por nuestro mandado el Almirante D. Cristóbal Colon . . . vos rogamos y encargamos que esten prestas y aparejadas todas las carabelas de vuestra tierra, porque nos podamos servir dellas en lo que menester fuere."

62. Ibid., 2:84: "Vimos vuestra letra, y cuanto á lo que nos escribistes que supistes de dos navios que el rey de Porugal envió, aquello es conforme con lo que acá sabiamos, Y cuanto á lo que habeis menester el libro que acá dejastes, y que se trasladase y se vos enviase, así se hará."

63. Ibid., 2:88.

Consequences of the First Voyage

64. Michael Mallet has studied this question.
65. Wilford, *The Mysterious*, 28–29.

Chapter 12

1. Colón, *Historia del Almirante*, chap. LI, p. 351.
2. Bernáldez, chap. CXXIII, p. 44.
3. Thacher, 2:223–63.
4. Varela, *Colón y los florentinos*, 83–93.
5. Gil and Varela, *Cartas*, 213.

Preparations

6. Fernández de Oviedo, *Historia general*, chap. XX, p. 22, 44 (also in *Colección de documentos inéditos*, and in Muñoz): May 20, *provision real* issued by "D. Fernando é Doña Isabel" in which Columbus was granted coat of arms: "de mas de vuestras armas encima dellas un Castillo é un Leon, que Nos vos damos por armas . . . unas islas doradas en ondas de mar." Ibid., II:22: May 8, Diego named page to Don Juan. Ibid., VII:31: "les dieron las mismas armas reales de Castilla é de Leon, mezcladas y repartidas con otras que assi mesmo le conçedieron de nuevo; . . . é por defuera del escudo una letra en un rótulo blanco, con unas letras de sable, que diçen: *Por Castilla é por Leon nuevo mundo halló Colom.*"

7. Ibid., chap. XXXIII, p. 57 (also in Muñoz, *Catálogo de la colección*, vol. 1, par. 438, p. 278. Muñoz, *Santo Domingo en los manuscritos*, 127: royal *cédula*: "A Vos Cristobal Colon nuestro Almirante de las nuestras islas e tierra firme que por nuestro mandado se ha descubierto e ha de descubrir en el mar Oceano e en la parte de las Indias e a Vos Don Juan de Fonseca Arcediano de Sevilla del nuestro Consejo . . . Sepades que nos avemos acordado de mandar que se haga cierta armada de algunos navios e fustas para embiar a dichas Indias, asi para señorear las (tierras) . . . Para hacer e pertrechar dicha armada . . . ireis a Sevilla i Cadiz i sus Diocesis, i donde quiera comprareis o embargareis navios i mantenimientos pagando sus precios regulares . . . Barcelona 23. de Mayo de 1493."

8. Asensio, bk. III, chap. I, pp. 602–3: May 23, *cédula*: "es menester que todo el dinero é oro é plata é joyas é otras cosas que . . . vuestros criados tomaron que lo pasava de judios para Portugal, se traiga ante nos." *Colección de documentos inéditos*, 33:13: May 24: "*Despacho-treslado* que

llevó Garcia de Herrera, Contino de la Casa del Rey e de la Reyna, para Búrgos, sobre el dinero e otras cosas que alli se ha de proveer para el Armada que vá a las Indias; el cual partió de Barcelona el 24 de Mayo de 1493; e otros despachos para los Corregidores de Soria e Búrgos, sobretenga del dinero de los xudios."

9. Fernández de Navarrete, 2:46.

10. Ibid., 2:49 (also in Varela, *Colón y los florentinos*, 52); Muñoz, *Santo Domingo en los manuscritos*, 128.

11. Muñoz, *Catálogo de la colección*, vol. 1, par. 438, p. 278: May 23: "Al dicho Fernando de Zafra que ademas de las 20 lanzas, busque i embie a Sevilla para ir con l'armada 20 labradores habiles del Reino de Granada, i uno que sepa hacer azequias." Muñoz, *Santo Domingo en los manuscritos*, 128; Fernández Duro, *Bibliografía Colombina*, sec. I:10, notes referring the canal builder "(que sepa hacer azequias) que no sea moro."

12. Fernández de Navarrete, 2:63.

13. Pérez-Bustamante, 107: May 28: "Sepades que nos avemos mandado a don Christoual Colom [*sic*] . . . con çiertas naos e caravelas e otras fustas . . . mandamos a todos e a cada uno de vos los dichos maestres e capitanes e patrones . . . que tengan por capitan general de las dichas . . . al dicho don Christoual Colom [*sic*]." Ibid., 110. Also, Asensio, bk. II, chap. XVI, pp. 594–95: May 28: "vos ayays de nonbrar tres personas para cada ofiçio, é que nos nonbremos é probeamos al uno dellos del tal ofiçio, y al presente no se puede guardar el dicho asyento por la brebedad de vuestra partida para las dichas ysas; confiando de vos . . . por la presente vos damos poder . . . podays probeher de los dichos ofiçios de governaçion . . . á las personas . . . que á vos bien visto fuere." Ibid., 109. Asensio, bk. II, chap. XVI, p. 595: May 28: "por la presente damos poder é facultad á la persona que en vuestra ausençia vos nombraredes para quedar en las dichas islas é tierra firme para que pueda librar é espedyr los negoçios e causas que ally ocurrieren."

14. Muñoz, *Santo Domingo en los manuscritos*, 3: May 29: "Acerca de la conversion de los Indios, para lo que va el P. Fray Buil con otros religiosos. Que los Indios sean bien tratados, i se castigue mucho a quien los ofendiere."

15. Fernández Duro, *Bibliografía Colombina*, sec. I:16: June7: "Carta de los reyes á los obispos de Cartagena y de Badajoz, sus procuradores en Roma, enviando propuesta para delegado pontificio en Indias en favor de Fr. Bernal Buyl, *ordinis fratrum minimorum heremitarum fratris Francisci de Paula, et in Hispaniis dicto fratris Francisci vicarium generalem, cundem ordinem expresse professum, in presbiteratus ordine constitutum.*"

16. Ibid., sec. 1:21: August 4: "Carta de los Reyes al P. Buil, agradeciendo les haya informado lo ocurrido y encargando lo siga haciendo, lo mismo antes la partida que depués allá. Han tenido enojo de las cosas que escribe porque quieren que el Almirante de las Indias sea muy honrado; esperan que todo será remediado. Encárganle atienda á todo lo de su cargo."

17. Fernández de Oviedo, *Historia general*, bk. II, chap. VII, p. 32.

18. Asensio, bk. III, chap. VIII, p. 730: June 25: "la Bula de Alejandro VI fecha 25 de junio de 1493 en que se hizo el nombramiento de Fray Buil." Fernández Duro, *Bibliografía Colombina*, sec. I:17: June 25: "Bula de Alejandro VI acordando sus privilegios para Indias á Bernardo Boil, *fratri ordinis minorum, vicario dicti ordinis in Hispaniarum Regnis.*"

19. Rumeu, *El libro copiador*, 128.

20. Morison, *Admiral*, 396–97.

21. Phillips and Phillips, 192.

22. *Colección de documentos inéditos*, 33:20: June 1: "*Real Cédula a Xoanoto Berardi, sobrel facer vizcocho para el Armada.*" Ibid., 33:28. Fernandez Duro, *Bibliografía Colombina*, sec. I:15.

23. Fernandez Duro, *Bibliografía Colombina*, bk. II, sec. LI:89: June 30, letter: "Juan Aguado, mi Repostero, va alá á me servir en esa armada que llevais . . . Yo vos mando é encargo que le hagais dar en esa dicha armada algun cargo bueno en que me sirva."

24. Varela, *Textos*, 263.

Departure and the Armada

25. Fernández de Oviedo, *Historia general*, bk. II, chap. VIII, p. 33.

26. Comas, *Relación*, in Gil and Varela, *Cartas*, 182.

27. Bernáldez, chap. CXIX, p. 5.

28. Martire, *Décades*, in Gil and Varela, *Cartas*, 47–48.

29. Rumeu, *El libro copiador*, 447; Varela, *Textos*, 35.

30. Colón, *Historia del Almirante*, chap. XLV, p. 316.

31. Ibid., chap. XLVI, p. 319.

32. Las Casas, *Historia*, chap. LXXXIII, p. 351.

The Crossing

33. For the rest of this chapter, references made to a letter from Columbus, unless otherwise identified, will be to one of his letters on the second voyage as found in *El libro copiador*. The text transcriptions used for

these letters will be primarily Gil's, compared when necessary with those by Rumeu. Much of the information given by Martire in the third chapter of the first decade of his *Decadas* and by Bernáldez in chapters 119–131 of his *Historia de los Reyes Católicos* corresponds to information given in the fourth letter in *El libro copiador*. No comparisons will be made between the information given in these letters and the versions of these events as provided in the biographies under review, due to the fact that none of these authors availed themselves of this new information supplied by their protagonist himself. Zamora did consult one of these letters in her collected essays *Reading Columbus*.

34. Coma, *Relación*, in Gil and Varela, *Cartas*, 183–85.
35. Chanca, *Carta*, in ibid., 155–56; Fernández de Navarrete, 1:198.
36. Cuneo, *Relación*, in Gil and Varela, *Cartas*, 239–40.
37. Ibid.
38. Piccolómini, #543, p. 135.
39. Morison, *Admiral*, 164–65.
40. Wilford, *The Mysterious*, 92.
41. Fernández-Armesto, *Columbus*, 53.

Landfall and the Leeward Islands

42. Gil and Varela, *Cartas*, 156.
43. Rumeu, *El libro copiador*, fol. 3v:21, 2:447; Varela, *Textos*, 236.
44. Rumeu, *El libro copiador*, 1:116.
45. Cuneo, in Gil and Varela, *Cartas*, 240; Coma, in ibid., 188.
46. Varela, *Textos*, 236.
47. Ibid., 237.
48. Ibid., 238.
49. Colón, *Historia del Almirante*, chap. XLVII, p. 326.
50. Manzano, *Colón y su secreto*, 431–36.
51. Morison, *Admiral*, 408–9.
52. Varela, *Textos*, 238.
53. Phillips and Phillips, 197.
54. Sale, 131–35.
55. Chanca, in Gil and Varela, *Cartas*, 158.
56. Coma, in ibid., 190–91.
57. Varela, *Textos*, 238.
58. Varela, *Retrato de un hombre*, 86–7.
59. Varela, *Textos*, 238.

60. Morison, *Admiral*, 397.
61. Cuneo, *Relación*, in Gil and Varela, *Cartas*, 241.

His Map of the Islands

62. Varela, *Textos*, 240.
63. Wilford, *The Mapmakers*, 29.
64. Varela, *Textos*, 249.
65. Martire, in Gil and Varela, *Cartas*, 64.
66. Varela, *Textos*, 315: "esta çiudad dista de su linea equinoçial veinte y cinco grados, y la parte más austr[u]al de la isla diez y ocho grados se faze hazia el polo ártico fuera."
67. West and Kling, 227.
68. Varela, *Textos*, 479.
69. Las Casas, *Historia*, chap. XCVI, p. 390.
70. Sale, 207, 305.

Columbus's Treatment of the Carib Indians

71. Cuneo, in Gil and Varela, *Cartas*, 242.
72. Wilford, *The Mysterious*, 179.

Chapter 13

1. Varela, *Textos*, 242.
2. Ibid., 242–43.
3. Ibid., 245: "Pedro y a Escobedo . . . qu'ellos se determinaron para ir a otro rey a quien llaman Caonaboa [*sic*] . . . qu'él les rogó que no se fusen que les daria pan y pescado y mujeres . . . tomaron sus mugeres, y un fijico que tenia Pedro, y se fueron."
4. Ibid., 246.
5. Las Casas, *Historia*, chap. LXXXVII, pp. 358–59.
6. Chanca, in Gil and Varela, *Cartas*, 167–69.
7. Cuneo, in ibid., 243.
8. Morison, *Admiral*, 426.
9. Fernández-Armesto, *Columbus*, 104.
10. Wilford, *The Mysterious*, 166.
11. Varela, *Textos*, 247: "como yo escrivo más largo a V. Al. [a] por otra carta del Diurnal que yo escrivi."

Isabela

12. Varela, *Textos*, 249: "Vuestras Altezas que después de diziembre hasta oy acá a fecho grandes frios . . . una noche me partí de la villa de la navidad con las barcas a ver un puerto, . . . y un rato que al sueño di parte me atormentó todo el lado derecho, de la planta del pie hasta la cabeza, en manera de perlesía, de que no poco e çofrido pena."

13. Ibid., 247.

14. Las Casas, *Historia*, chap. LXXXVIII, pp. 362–63: "buscaba para poblar; pero su instinción principalmente iba enderezada al Monte de Plata . . . Fueronlé los vientos muy contrarios . . . que con muy gran trabajo y de muchas días y con todo la armada, se vido en gran pena y conflicto . . . por estas dificultades no pudo pasar del puerto de Gracia, en el cual arriba dijimos que había estado Martín Alonso Pinzón, cuando en el primer viaje se apartó del Almirante . . . y está cinco o seis leguas del Puerto de Plata . . . puesto que dice aquí el Almirante que está once pero entonces no se sabía la tierra como agora . . . hobo de tornar atrás tres leguas de allí . . . donde sale a la mar un río grande y hay un buen puerto; aunque descubierto para el viento Norueste, pero por los demás bueno donde acordó saltar en tierra, en un pueblo de indios que allí había, y vido por el río arriba una vega muy graciosa, y que el río se podía sacar por acequias que pasasen por dentro del pueblo, y para hacer también en él aceñas y otras comodidades convenientes para edificar . . . comenzó a fundar un pueblo o villa . . . cuyo nombre quiso que fuese la Isabela . . . puso suma diligencia en edificar luego casa para los bastimentos y municiones del armada, e iglesia y hospital, y para su morada una casa fuerte . . . las casas publicas se hicieron de piedra; las demás cada uno hacía de madera y paja."

15. Thacher, 2:277–78 (the Chanca letter in English translation). Asensio, bk. III, chap. XII, p. 104: "mayor pena nos fué tornar 30 leguas atrás que venir desde castilla, que con el tiempo contrario é a la larguez del camino ya eran tres meses pasados cuando descendimos en tierra."

16. Fernández de Navarrete, 1:198. See Thacher, 2:278, and Asensio, bk. 3, p. 106: "El día que yo sali á dormir en tierra fué el primero día del Señor; el poco tiempo que habemos gastado en tierra ha sido mas en hacer donde nos metamos, é buscar las cosas necesarias que en saber las cosas que hay en tierra."

17. Gil and Varela, *Cartas*, 174.

18. Varela, *Diego Alvarez Chanca*, 43.

19. Coma, facsimile, in Thacher, 2:236: "Yn littore octo diebus a natali salvatoris."

20. Varela, *Textos*, 249: "Oy son treinta y un dia que yo llegué en este puerto."

21. Muñoz, *Catálogo de la colección*, vol. 1, par. 438, p. 1: "Lo que voz, Antonio de Torres, Capitán de la nao *Marigalante* e Alcaide de la ciudad Isabela habéis de decir y suplicar de mi parte al Rey y la Reina, Isabela, 30 de enero de 1494. Con notas marginales correspondientes a minuta de repuesta real. De Cristóbal Colón, F° 172 v-189."

22. Rumeu, *El libro copiador*, 1:451.

23. Varela, *Textos*, 287.

24. Las Casas, *Historia*, chap. LXXXIX, p. 366, chap. CIII, p. 409: "al susdicho Antonio de Torres ... entregó el oro y todos sus despachos ... Hiciéronse a la vela a 2 días de febrero del año de 1494."

25. Bernáldez, chap. CXXI, p. 38: "los navios ... los cuales vinieron debajo de la capitania de Antonio de Torres ... partieron de la dicha ciudad Isabela a 3 de febrero del año 1494."

26. Morison, *Admiral*, 428.

The Settlement at Isabela

27. In Thacher, 2:278.

28. Ibid., 2:495 (facsimile with translation of the *Libretto De Tutta La Nauigatione*).

29. Cuneo, in Gil and Varela, *Cartas*, 241.

30. See Palm for the most complete study of the town.

31. Varela, *Textos*, 287.

32. Martire, *Oceaneae decadis*, bk. II, chap. I, p. 124.

First Mass at Isabela

33. Fernández de Oviedo, *Historia general*, bk. II, chap. XIII, p. 49: "Aveis de saber que como luego que se pobló aquella cibdad y el almirante repartió los solares para que los españoles fiçiessen, como hiçieron, sus casas, é les señaló las caballerias y tierras para sus heredamientos; viendo los indios que esta veçindad les avia de durar, pesóles de ver el propóssito de los chripstianos. E para escusar esto é darles ocasion que se fuessen desta tierra, pensaron un mal ardid, con que murieron mas de los dos partes ó la mitad de los españoles, é de los propios indios murieron tantos que no se pudieron contar ... Acordaron todos los indios de aquella provincia de no sembrar ... los chripstianos comieronse sus bastimentos; é aquellos acabados ... desta manera se caían los hombres muertos de hambre; y en

la fortaleza de Sancto Thomás, do estaba el comendador Mossen Pedro Margarite, tambien por la misma nesçessidad se le murió la mitad de la gente."

34. Martire, in Gil and Varela, *Cartas*, 61: "El Prefecto eligió un lugar elevado y cercano al puerto para fundar la ciudad y allí, una vez que llevantó, en breve plazo ... unas casas y una capilla, en el día en que celebramos la fiesta de los Tres Reyes fue cantada por trece sacerdotes concelebrantes la sagrada misa."

35. Colón, *Historia del Almirante*, chap. LVIII, p. 403.

36. Varela, *Textos*, 305.

37. Colón, *Historia del Almirante*, chap. LXIII, pp. 93–94.

38. Muro Orejón, *Pleitos Colombinos: Rollo del proceso*, 531: "hyzieron vna horca [forked prop] e con las velas de los nabios hyzieron toldos (awnings) en senal de iglesia y alli se dixo misa por vn frayle francisco que alli yva e por Juan Martinelo clérigo natural de esta villa [Palos] que fue en la dicha armada."

39. Colón, *Historia del Almirante*, chap. XC, p. 288.

40. Lunardi. Also Llaverias.

41. Coll, for a Franciscan at Guanahaní on the first voyage. He included Menendez's account, written in 1681, claiming a Dominican celebrated the first mass at Navidad.

Exploration of Española

42. Dunn and Kelley, fol. 45r:1–3, p. 270.

43. Varela, *Textos*, 463–64; Gil and Varela, *Cartas*, 250–51.

44. Coma, *Relación*, in Gil and Varela, *Cartas*, 199.

45. Thacher, 223–41.

46. Yule, 1:188 (extracts from the *Geography* of Ptolemy circa A.D. 150).

47. Ibid., 1:303 n. 1.

48. Polo, *Most Noble and Famous Travels*, 32–33.

49. Varela, *Textos*, 258.

50. Gil and Varela, *Cartas*, 252.

51. Chanca, *Relación*, in Gil and Varela, *Cartas*, 175.

52. Varela, *Textos*, 287.

53. Fernández de Navarrete, 3:485: "Carta de los reyes a D. Juan de Fonseca, dandole gracias por la alegre noticia de la llegada de las carabelas de Indias, y al contino Torres, que las vino mandando, que se dé priesa en ir personalmente á inormar á sus Altezas." Also in Fernandez Duro,

Bibliografía Colombina, sec. I:25. There is another *carta* of the same date directed to Torres, thanking him and ordering him to come to court.

54. Fernández de Navarrete, 3:500.

55. Las Casas, *Historia*, chap. XC, p. 367.

56. Asensio, bk. III, chap. X, p. 34.

57. Muro Orejón, *Pleitos Colombinos: Proceso hasta la sentencia*, 161–62.

58. Las Casas, *Historia*, chap. CIII, p. 410.

59. Varela, *Textos*, 287.

60. Las Casas, *Historia*, chap. LXXXIX, p. 365.

61. Colón, *Historia del Almirante*, chap. LI, p. 351.

62. Manzano, *Colón decubrío*, 15–57, and his *Colón y su secreto*, 445–52.

63. Varela, *Textos*, 467.

First Trip into the Interior and Pacification

64. Ibid., 274.

65. Cuneo, *Relación*, in Gil and Varela, *Cartas*, 244.

66. Varela, *Textos*, 276.

67. Colón, *Historia del Almirante*, chap. LII, pp. 362–65.

68. Las Casas, *Historia*, chap. XCII, p. 376.

69. Ibid., chap. XCII, p. 378.

70. Varela, *Textos*, 278–79.

71. Fernández de Navarrete, 2:177.

72. Varela, *Textos*, 280.

73. Ibid.

74. Morison, *Admiral*, 484; Phillips and Phillips, 205; Wilford, *The Mysterious*, 174; Sale, 146.

75. Varela, *Textos*, 290.

76. Fernández de Oviedo, *Historia general*, bk. II, chap. XII, p. 48.

77. Varela, *Textos*, 281.

78. Fernández de Navarrete, 2:125–30; Asensio, bk. 3, chap. XII, pp. 121–23 (manuscript in Archivo de Indias, copy in *Colección de documentos inéditos*, 38:249).

79. Las Casas, *Historia*, chap. CII, p. 406.

Pedro Margarite and Fray Bernardo Buil

80. Ramos, *El conflicto de las lanzas*, 16.

81. Fernández de Oviedo, *Historia general*, bk. II, chap. XIV, p. 55.

82. Morison, *Admiral*, 484.

83. Wilford, *The Mysterious*, 172.

84. Fernández de Oviedo, *Historia general*, bk. II, chap. XIII, p. 51.

85. Las Casas, *Historia*, chap. C, pp. 398–99.

86. Martire, *Décades*, in Gil and Varela, *Cartas*, 78.

87. Las Casas, *Historia*, chap. CLX, p. 428.

88. Ibid., chap. CLX, p. 428: "porque dice Oviedo que llegó el Adelantado D. Bartolomé Colón a este puerto día de Sancto Domingo, a 5 de agosto del año 1494, y este parece manefiesto ser falso, porque él llegó a esta isla en catorce días de abril del mismo año 94, antes que el Almirante viniese de descubrir a Cuba . . . y no había de volar luego a este puerto a tres meses, sin ver al Almirante ni sin tener cargo alguno." Asensio, 151–52. Asensio discussed these differences in dating by Las Casas (April 14) and Fernández de Oviedo (August 5).

89. Fernández de Oviedo, *Historia general*, bk. II, chap. XIII, p. 52.

90. Utrera.

91. Asensio, bk. III, chap. IX, p. 10; *Colección de documentos inéditos*, 30:299; Fernández Duro, *Bibliografía Colombina*, sec. I:26.

92. Las Casas, *Historia*, chap. CLX, p. 427.

93. Ibid., chap. CVII, p. 421.

94. Asensio, bk. III, chap. VIII, p. 720.

95. Manzano, *Colón y su secret*, 584.

96. Asensio, bk. III, chap. VIII, p. 723; Muñoz, *Catálogo de la colección*, vol. 1, par. 439, p. 5.

97. Fernández de Oviedo, *Historia general*, bk. II, chap. XIII, pp. 53–54.

98. Las Casas, *Historia*, chap. CIX, p. 427.

99. Ibid.

100. Asensio, bk. III, chap. VIII, p. 731: August 16: "Vimos vuestra letra (fray Buil) que con Torres nos enviastes . . . Y quanto á lo que nos escrivistes que pensais que vuestra estada allá no aprovecha tanto como pensabades por falta de lengua, que no hay para faser yntérpretes con los yndios, y que por esto vos queriades venir, por servicio nuestro, que esto no se faga por ahora en manera alguna . . . sabemos que vuestro estada allá es muy necesario y provechosa por ahora."

101. Varela, *Textos*, 277.

102. Ibid., 325–26: "Fuera muy bueno que fray Buil truxera muy debotos religiosos así por este remedio como por todos los otros en qu'estamos, pues V. Al. le avia probeído por manos del Papa. Mucho serviçio hará V. Al. a Dios a enbiar acá algunos frailes debotos y fuera de cobdiçia de cosas del mundo, porque nos den buenos exemplos que, çierto, bien nos falta, y dolesrse de

cosas malignas . . . Dévelo fazer V. Al., porque nosotros emos más menester quien nos reforme la fee que no los indios tomarla."

103. Morison, *Admiral*, 484.

104. Fernández-Armesto, *Columbus*, 108.

105. Ibid., 138.

106. Fernandez Duro, *Bibliografía Colombina*, sec. I:32: February 16, 1495: "Carta de los Reyes á Garcilaso de la Vega, su embajador en Roma, noticiando que Fr. Bernal Buil vino doliente de Indias, y por qué no puede volver, suplique á Su Santidad otorgue á otra persona que propondrán, las facultades que aquel tenía."

107. Varela, *Textos*, 276.

108. Wilford, *The Mysterious*, 175.

109. Morison, *Admiral*, 484.

110. Deive, 15.

111. Pane (first published in the *Historie*).

Discontent on Española

112. Las Casas, *Historia*, chap. CVII, p. 421.

113. Ibid., chap. XCII, pp. 376–77, chap. LXXXVIII, pp. 362–63: "[M]andó luego desembarcar toda la gente, que venia muy cansada y fatigada y los caballos muy perdidos, bastimentos y todas las otras cosas de la armada, lo cual todo mandó poner en un llano, que estaba junto a una peña bien apare-jada, para edeficar en ella su fortaleza . . . por este aparejo dióse grandisima priesa y puso sumo diligencia en edificar luego casa para los bastimentos y munciones del armada, e iglesia y hospital, y para su morada una casa fuerte . . . y avecínanse las personas principales y manda que cada uno haga su casa como mejor pudiera; las casas públicas se hicieron de piedra; las demás cada uno hacía de madera y paja y como hacerse podía. Mas como la gente venía fatigada de tan largo viaje y no acostumbrada de la mar, y luego, mayormente la trabajadora y oficiales mecánicos, fueron puestos en los grandes trabajos corporales de hacer las obras y edificios susodichos y materiales para ellos . . . comenzó la gente tan de golpe a caer enferma, y por lo poco refrigerio que había para los enfermos, a morir también muchos dellos, que apenas quedaba hombre de los hidalgos y pleybeyos por muy robusto que fuese, que de calenturas terribles enfermo no cayese . . . Sobreveníales a sus males la gran angustia y tristeza que concebían de verse tan alongadas de sus tierras y tan sin esperanza de haber presto remedio y verse defraudados también del oro y riqueza que se prometió a sí mismo."

114. Fernández de Oviedo, *Historia general*, bk. II, chap. XIII, p. 53.

115. Wilford, *The Mysterious*, 173.
116. Bernáldez, chap. CXX, pp. 37–38.
117. Varela, *Textos*, 274.
118. Colón, *Historia del Almirante*, chap. LIII, p. 369.

The "Revolt of the Lancers"

119. Inchaustegui Cabral.
120. Varela, *Textos*, 262.
121. Ibid., 264.
122. Ibid., 270.
123. Ramos, *El conficto de las lanzas*, 92.

Trip to Cuba and Jamaica

124. Cuneo, *Relación*, in Gil and Varela, *Cartas*, 252.
125. Las Casas, *Historia*, chap. XCIV, p. 383.
126. Varela, *Textos*, 289.
127. Nagy.
128. Varela, *Textos*, 291.
129. Ibid.
130. Ibid., 296.
131. Ibid., 299.
132. Morison, *Admiral*, 458.
133. Zamora, *Reading Columbus*, 145.
134. Rabasa, 196.
135. Hale, 62.
136. Varela, *Textos*, 301.
137. Colón, *Historia del Almirante*, chap. LVII, p. 395.
138. Las Casas, *Historia*, chap. XCV, p. 388.
139. Bernáldez, chap. CXXVIII, p. 58.
140. Morison, *Admiral*, 461.
141. Varela, *Textos*, 302.
142. Colón, *Historia del Almirante*, 302.
143. Manzano, *Colón y su secreto*, 512.
144. Bernáldez, chap. CXXIII, p. 43.
145. Varela, *Textos*, 313.
146. Diego de Peñalosa, in Gil and Varela, *Cartas*, 217–19.
147. Ibid.
148. Morison, *Admiral*, 466.

Return to Española from Cuba

149. Martire, *Décades*, vol. 3, in Gil and Varela, *Cartas*, 49.

150. Ibid., 67: "Allí residía la Corte, cuando en torno al día noveno antes de las calendas de abril [24 de marzo] de este año noventa y cuatro unos correos enviados al Rey y a la Reina anunciaron que habían llegado de las islas doce navios."

151. Martire, *De Orbe Novo*, lib. II, I:124.

152. Fernández de Navarrete, 3:485 (also listed in chronological sequence 3:633).

153. Gil, *Mitos y utopías*, 83.

154. Varela, *Colón y los florentinos*, 54.

155. Phillips and Phillips, 202.

Resupply Fleets in 1494 and 1495

156. *Colección de documentos inéditos*, 33:32.

157. Asensio, bk. III, chap. IX, p. 10 (also in *Colección de documentos inéditos*, 30:299). Fernandez Duro, *Bibliografía Colombina*, sec. I:26: "las caravelas que nos mandamos ir á las islas . . . nuestro capitan de las dichas caravelas á don Bartolomé Colón . . . é fagadas é cumplades todas las cosas que voz él dixere é mandare . . . fasta ser llegados á las dichas islas donde está el dicho Almirante, porque dende en adelante aveis de obedecer al dicho Almirante."

158. Thacher, 2:345: "I served as Captain from April 14, '94, to March 12, '96, when the Admiral left for Castile."

159. Asensio, bk. III, chap. VIII, p. 720: April 28: "Bartolomé (Colón) . . . recibió de mano de Juan de Fonseca 50,000 maravedis."

160. Ibid.: "Su desembarco en Isabela se verificó en el día de San Juan, 24 de Junio."

161. Gil and Varela, *Cartas*, 67 n.

162. Fernández de Navarrete, 3:501, copy of a letter thanking Fonseca for news of their arrival. Asensio, bk. III: "3 de Diciembre . . . ya los Reyes habían recibido la noticia del desembarco 'Placer por ser venidas carabelas de Indias, y venga al punto Fray Buil.'"

163. *Colección de documentos inéditos*, 30:35: September 11: "*Real Cédula al Padre Fray Bruyl*, sobre haber rescebido con Torres, cuanto se le tiene en servicio; e se le ruega continue en aquellas partes, sin embargo de que se quexa de no tener interprete."

164. Cuneo, *Relación*, in Gil and Varela, *Cartas*, 256: "El día ultimo de

septiembre, con el nombre de Dios, entramos en salvamiento en la Isabela
. . . al cabo de pocas días plugo a Dios que arribaron cuatro carabelas de
España."

165. Las Casas, *Historia*, chap. CIII, pp. 410–11.

166. Fernández de Navarrete, 3:497–99.

167. Morison, *Admiral*, 485.

168. Cuneo, *Relación*, in Gil and Varela, *Cartas*, 256: "pero a cabo de pocas
días plugo a Dios que arribaron cuatro carabelas de españa cargadas de
bastimientos."

169. Gil, *Mitos y utopías*, 98.

170. Fernández de Navarrete, 2:196.

171. Ibid., 2:186.

172. Ibid.

173. For a study of the matter, see Gil, *Tres notas colombinas*, 75–80.

174. Gil, *Mitos y utopías*, 96.

175. Fernández de Navarrete, 2:178.

176. Rumeu, *El libro copiador*, 1:272: letter of April 9, 1495, Archivo de
Indias: "Vimos vuestra letra que con Alonso [Sánchez] de Carvajal nos
escribistes, i oímos lo que de vuestra parte nos habló."

177. *Colección de documentos inéditos*, 33:38: "Relación del oro e joyas e
otras cosas que el señor almirante ha resçebido después que el reçebdor
Sebastián d'Olano partió desta isla para Castilla el X de março de XCV
años."

Columbus's Treatment of the Indians on Española

178. Varela, *Textos*, 316.

179. Las Casas, *Historia*, chap. CV, p. 416: "Anduvo el almirante . . . nueve
o diex meses, y como él mismo en cartas diversas que escribió a los reyes y
a otras personas dice."

180. Ibid., chap. CII, pp. 405–6: "Por ventura, poco antes de lo dicho, fué
Alonso de Hojeda . . . enviado disimulamente con nueve cristianos él solo, a
caballo, para visitar de su parte al rey Caonabo . . . a rogarle que le fuese
a ver a la Isabela, y si pudiese prenderlo con un ardid."

181. Varela, *Textos*, 317: "Y estando en esto, ove cartas de una compañia
de nuestro gente, la cual, avía enbiado a ver todas las sierras . . . y me dezía
como avía venido a parar donde vivía Cahonaboa y le avían movido y fecho
determinar a benir a la Ysavela, diziéndole que yo lo faría grandes fiestas
y daría grandes dádivas."

182. Bernáldez, chap. CXX, p. 37.

183. Las Casas, *Historia*, chap. CII, p. 405: "envió a vender a Castilla más de 500 esclavos en los cuatro navíos que trujo Antonio de Torres, y se partió con ellos para Castilla, en 24 de febrero de 1495."

184. Ibid., chap. CII, p. 408.

185. Varela, *Textos*, 318.

186. Rumeu, *El libro copiador*, 2:526: "Temía yo, y por esto proveydo con *tiempo*, que hize firmar a un yndio dellos que llevé a Castilla, aunquél no sea d'esta *tierra*, hize que Guarionex casó con él a Cora, su hermana, y este le asentó mui mucho."

187. Varela, *Textos*, 317: "Tenía yo [y] por esto proveído con tiempo, que hize formar a un indio de [l]los que llevé a Castilla <e>, auqu'él no sea d'esta tierra, hize que Guarionex casara con él a una su hermana, y éste le asentó muy mucho."

188. Martire, *Décades*, in Gil and Varela, *Cartas*, 79.

189. Varela, *Textos*, 318: "avían estado diez y seis días que no comieron salvo frutas y yervas . . . y él (Guarionex) proveyó muy bien y a toda nuestra gente."

190. Martire, *Décades*, in Gil and Varela, *Cartas*, 80: "durante dieciséis días no habían comido otra cosa que raíces de plantas y de palmitos y otras frutas naturales del monte . . . Guarionexio [*sic*] . . . repartió algo de alimento entre los nuestros."

191. Varela, *Textos*, 319: "Este hedifiçio y el desfazer de las naos, las cuales heran ya viejas e innabegables, avía quitado a los indios la opinión de me ir a Castilla; con todo no çesan de preguntar a los nuestros por ello. . . . Determiné de imbiar algunas cuadrilla con [d]el pan que allé en la Conçebçion, para acavar de andar e esplorar toda la provinçia de çibao."

192. Ibid.: "disimulé con ellos . . . les dixe que yo me dexaría de cavar las minas, si me querían dar en nombre de V. Al. cada cuatro lunas llenas la mitad de un caxcavel lleno de oro cada cabeza; y ellos dixeron que los plazía. . . . Yo hize experimentar si hera posible si en tres días lo pudieron cojer; y fallé que algunas personas que vien savían cogello, cogen lleno un caxcavel en que avía de ocho castellanos; verdad es que hay lugares y caciques donde no tienen tan buenos rios y tan (buen) aparejo [preparation] como otros."

193. Ibid., 320.

194. Ibid.: "algodón y pimienta y cosas que baldrán oro."

195. Ibid., 321: "La estraña hambre, que en toda la isla y en espeçial en çibao a sido y continúa, me ha fecho mudar la esperança, porque en la provinçia tenía yo conçierto con tantos caciques que bien (a)llegavan cincuenta mill 'naborías', a que vasallos llamamos, y escripto la mayor parte d'ellos . . .

mas la neçesidad y hambre a sido la causa de la muerte de más de los dos terçios d'ellos, y no es acavado ni (se save) cuándo se puede esperar el fin."

196. Ibid., 322: "Guarionex y otros d'estos caçiques ya truxeron el tributo, mas no el caxcavel lleno y no salvo poquita cossa. Reçebíselo y les hize tan buena cara como si todo le dieron por entero. Hízeles dezir después que lo remediasen porque no avían cumplido . . . dixeron que no sería ainsí en lo benidero, y que la hambre avía sido causa d'ello . . . Dulçemente es de tratarlos a benibolençia y no con agruras, porque no despueblan y se bayan de la provinçia; antes es de procurar de llegar allí gentes de otras partes."

197. Martire, *Décades*, in Gil and Varela, *Cartas*, 82.

198. Varela, *Textos*, 323.

199. Ibid., 317: "porqu'es cierto que ay aquí tanta gente que, en nombre de dezir, que sólo con el soplo, si ellos asasen, nos hechasen sin tocar los pies hasta Castilla, ni son de poco ingenio ni fuerza ni rudos en pelea."

200. Bernáldez, chap. CXXXI, p. 78: "al gran Cacique Caonaboa [*sic*] y á un su hermano, é á un su fijo de fásta diez años, no en pelea salvo desque los aseguró y depues diz que dijo que los traia á ver al Rey y á la Reina para despues volverles en su honra y estado . . . y murióse el Caonaboa en la mar ó de dolencia ó poco plazer."

201. Rumeu, *El libro copiador*, 275: "reçibió tres carátula con XIX pieças de hoja de oro e dos espejos, las lunbres de hoja de oro, e dos torteruelas de hoja de oro, que truxo un hermano de Cahonabo [*sic*], en el dicho día."

202. Ibid., 279.

203. Varela, *Textos*, 323: "sería bien de ir allá por temoriçar todas aquellas tierras y las otras provinçias, porque no le paresçiese que dexávamos de pasar a ellas por alguna cosa, (e) porque en esto conoçiera mucho toda la isla. Y ainsí enbié allá a *** Hojeda con setenta personas, a los cuales un hermano de cahonaboa luego allí los puso çerco."

204. Martire, *Décades*, in Gil and Varela, *Cartas*, 83.

205. Fernández de Oviedo, *Historia general*, bk. II, chap. I, p. 59.

206. Las Casas, *Historia*, chap. CIV, p. 414.

207. Martire, *Décades*, in Gil and Varela, *Cartas*, 79.

208. Fernández de Oviedo, *Historia general*, bk. III, chap. I, p. 59.

Juan Aguado

209. Fernández de Navarrete, 2:30: June 1493: "*Carta* al Almirante recomendando a Xoan de Aguado (su repostero) para que se le dé un buen cargo en al Armada." Also in *Colección de documentos inéditos*, 33:23.

210. Varela, *Textos*, 263: "en lo de Juan Aguado Sus Altezas avrán memoria de él, pues acá está."

211. Fernández-Armesto, *Columbus*, 114.

212. Fernández de Navarrete, 2:183: April 9: *cédula* referring to Carillo voyage, being sent "porque temiendo que algo ha Dios dispuesto del Almirante de las Indias en el camino que fue, pues que ha tanto tiempo que dél no sabemos, tenemos acordado de enviar allá al Comendador Diego Carrillo, é á otra persona principal de recaudo para que en ausencia del Almirante provea en todo lo de allá, y aun en su presencia remedie en las cosas que conveniere remediarse, segund la informacion que hobimos de los que de allá vinieron."

213. Ibid., 2:183, 179.

214. Ibid., 2:190.

215. Varela, *Textos*, 433.

216. Ibid., 435.

217. Fernández de Oviedo, *Historia general*, bk. II, chap. XIII, p. 53: "A estas passiones respondian diversas opiniones, aunque no se publicaban; pero cada parte tuvo manera de escribir lo que sentia en ellas a España, por lo qual informados en differente manera los Reyes cathólicos de lo que acá passaba, enviaron á esta isla á Juan Aguado, su criado (que agora vive en Sevilla). E assi se partió con cuatro caravelas . . . como paresçe en una cédula que yo he visto . . . hecho en Madrid á çinco de mayo."

218. Las Casas, *Historia*, chap. CVII, p. 422.

219. Ibid., 425.

220. Fernández de Navarrete, 2:197–98.

221. Berwick y Alba, 1.

222. Jane, 2:9 n.

223. Morison, *Admiral*, 493.

224. Phillips and Phillips, 210.

225. Wilford, *The Mysterious*, 175.

226. Phillips and Phillips, 211.

227. Fernández-Armesto, *Columbus*, 114.

Return from the Second Voyage

228. Varela, *Textos*, 327.

229. Ibid.

230. Gil and Varela, *Cartas*, 84 n. 123.

231. Las Casas, *Historia*, chap. CVIII, p. 425.

232. Ibid., 408–9.

233. Martire, *Décades*, in Gil and Varela, *Cartas*, 84.

234. Fernández de Oviedo, *Historia general*, bk. II, chap. XIII, p. 54.

235. Martire, *Décades*, in Gil and Varela, *Cartas*, 85.

236. Colón, *Historia del Almirante*, chap. LXIII, p. 92: "Por lo que, con doscientos veinticinco cristianos y treinta indios, el jueves, a 10 de Marzo del año 1496, se embarcó . . . navegó por la costa arriba con dos carabellas llamadas Santa Cruz y la Niña, que eran las mismas con las que habia ido a descubrir la isla de Cuba."

237. Bernáldez, chap. CXXXI, p. 78: "vino en Castilla en el mes de Junio de 1496 años, vestido de unas ropas de color de hábito de San Francisco, de la observancia, y en la hechura poco menos que hábito, é un cordon de San Francisco por devocion, y trujo consigo algunos indios que antes que el de alli partiese él habido prendido, al gran Cacique Caonaboa, é á un su hermano, é á un su fijo de fásta diez años, no en pelea, salvo desque los aseguró . . . murióse el Caonaboa en la mar ó de dolencia ó de poco placer."

238. Fernández de Navarrete, 2:201.

Chapter 14

1. Daelli.

2. Sanz, *Relación*, 9 fol.:xiii.

3. Rumeu, *El libro copiador*, fol. 31v:345–71, p. 558.

4. Zamora, *Reading Columbus*, 69.

5. Sanz, *Relación*, fol. 7r:39–42.

6. Rumeu, *El libro copiador*; Sanz, *Relación*, fol. 31v, 32r:360–68, p. 559. Also in Varela, *Textos*, 380.

7. D'Ailly, 126–27: "Por ello Jerónimo (*Sit. et nom.* 202) sostiene que el origen de los ríos del paraíso hay que entenderlo de otra forms, pues estos ríos nacen del paraiso de modo que, absorbidos después por la tierra, salen por fin en diferentes lugares."

8. Polo, *Most Noble and Famous Travels*, 16: "The River . . . Tygis, whiche is one of the foure that cometh out of Paradise terrenal."

9. Sanz, *Relación*, fol. 8v:674–77.

10. Rumeu, *El libro copiador*, fol. 32r:384–85, p. 560.

11. Harrisse, *Bibliotheca*, 470–71.

12. Varela, *Colón y los florentinos*, 84.

13. Fernández de Navarrete, 1:242–64.

14. Spotorno, *Codice diplomatico*.

15. Thacher, 2:424.

Simón Verde

16. Vespucci, *Lettera di Amerigo* (the Soderini letter 1504 in facimile); Northrup.
17. Vigneras, 63–64.
18. Gil and Varela, *Cartas*, 283.
19. Rumeu, *El libro copiador*, fol. 1. (MS 28v:25–28), lines 57–61, p. 546.
20. Gil and Varela, *Cartas*, 283.
21. Vigneras, 15.
22. Rumeu, *El libro copiador*, fol. 30r:202, p. 553.
23. Gil and Varela, *Cartas*, 284.

Martire, Trivigiano, Montalboddo

24. Trivigiano, *Libretto de Tutta la nauigatione* (1930).
25. Ibid., 1.
26. Ibid., 3.
27. Thacher, 2:457–514.
28. Trivigiano, *Libretto de Tutta la nauigatione* (1930), 1.
29. Thacher, 2:444.
30. Ibid., 446.
31. Ibid., 452.
32. Trivigiano, *Libretto de Tutta la nauigatione* (1930), 6.
33. Thacher, 2:451; Wagner, 15 n. 36.
34. Trivigiano, *Libretto de Tutta la nauigatione* (1930), 8.
35. Thacher, 2:444.
36. Ibid., 449.
37. Vespucci, *Paessi nouamente retrovati*.
38. Vigneras, 6 (from AGI, *Contratación* 3249, fol. 144v).
39. Gil and Varela, *Cartas*, 97 n.
40. Varela, *Textos*, 369 n.
41. Gil, *El rol del Tercer Viaje*, 85.
42. Martire, *Epistolario*, 9:132.
43. Winsor, *Narrative and Critical History*, 1:xxi.
44. Vespucci, *The Mundus Novus Letter*.
45. Vespucci, *Lettera di Amerigo*.
46. Rabasa, 130.
47. Sale, 222–25.
48. Wagner, 34.

The Religious and Mercantile Motivations of Columbus

49. Todorov, *The Conquest*, 15.

50. Ibid., 17.

51. Greenblatt, *Marvelous Possessions*, 78–79.

52. Gil, *Mitos y utopías*, 131.

53. Sanz, *Relación*, fol. 18–21: "Y si de allí del paraiso no sale, parece aun mayor maravilla, porque no creo que se sepa en el mundo de río tan grande y tan fondo."

54. D'Ailly, #19, p. 41: "el paraiso terrenal está allí."

55. Zamora, *Reading Columbus*, 144.

56. Greenblatt, *Marvelous Possessions*, 73.

57. Hale, 534.

58. Piccolómini, #59, p. 19, #67, p. 20, #105, p. 27.

59. Zamora, *Reading Columbus*, 135.

The 1498 Letter on the Third Voyage

60. See Thacher, 2:362, for a study of this particular application.

61. Zamora, *Reading Columbus*, 47.

62. Bloch, 1:80.

63. Haile, 73.

64. West and Kling, 3, 5.

65. Zamora, *Voyage to Paradise*, 150, in Greenblatt, *New World Encounters*.

66. Rabasa, 51.

67. Ibid., 54.

68. Sanz, *Relación*, fol. 1, line 1: "esta de acá es otro mundo."

69. Ibid., fol. 1, lines 1–3.

70. Ibid., fol. 1, lines 82–85.

71. Ibid., fol. 1, lines 85–98.

72. Varela, *Textos*, 368 n. 15.

The Naming of the New Lands

73. Rumeu, *El libro copiador*, carta VI, fol. 29, lines 91–100.

74. Las Casas, *Historia*, chap. CXXXI, p. 8.

75. Morison, *Admiral*, 529.

76. Jane, 2:12.

77. Las Casas, *Historia*, chap. CXXXII, p. 10.

78. Thacher, 2:384.

79. Sanz, *Relación*, fol. 3, line 2.

80. Wilford, *The Mysterious*, 204.
81. Fernández-Armesto, *Columbus*, 126.
82. Las Casas, *Historia*, chap. CXXXIII, pp. 14–16.
83. Zamora, *Reading Columbus*, 145.
84. Ibid., 175.

Religious Symbolism in the 1498 Letter on the Third Voyage

85. Ibid., 145
86. Rabasa, 51.
87. Todorov, *The Conquest*, 20; Las Casas, *Historia*, chap. XLIV.
88. Varela, *Textos*, 436.
89. West and Kling, 101.
90. Gardner, 140.

Preparations for the Third Voyage

91. Morison, *Admiral*, 512.
92. Gil, *El rol del Tercer Viaje*, 102.
93. Ibid., 85.
94. Colón, *Historia del Almirante*, chap. LXIX, p. 157.
95. Gil and Varela, *Cartas*, 96–97 n. 147; Morison, *Admiral*, 513.
96. Sale, 170.
97. Città di Genova, 81.
98. Morison, *Admiral*, 378.
99. Gil and Varela, *Cartas*, 267–69.
100. Fernández-Armesto, *Columbus*, 120.
101. Phillips and Phillips, 212.
102. Sale, 169.
103. Williamson,
104. Las Casas, *Historia*, chap. CXII, p. 437.

Columbus's Return to Española in 1498

105. Thacher, 2:423–24.
106. Varela, *Textos*, (1992), 431.
107. Thacher, 2:425.
108. Varela, *Textos* (1992), 431.
109. Thacher, 2:425.
110. Wilford, *The Mysterious*, 215.
111. Rumeu, *El libro copiador* 1:326.

112. Vigneras, 56.
113. Berwick y Alba, 25–38.
114. Thacher, 2:425.
115. Las Casas, *Historia*, chap. CLXXVII, p. 175.
116. Morison, *Admiral*, 570.
117. Gil and Varela, *Cartas*, 285.
118. Varela, *Textos*, 432.
119. Morison, *Admiral*, 567.
120. Ots Capdequi, 42–43.
121. For an in-depth study of the origins and development of the *encomienda* system, see Bloch, beginning with chapter 11, "Vassal Homage."
122. Hale, 475–78.

Chapter 15

1. Colón, *Historia del Almirante*, chap. II, p. 328. Winsor, *Narrative and Critical History*, 2:62 n. 2: "It is usually said that Ferdinand Columbus asserts it was printed; but Harrisse says that he can find no such statement in Ferdinand's book."
2. Thacher, 2:669–99.
3. Rumeu, *El libro copiador*, 2:377–430.
4. Varela, *Textos*, 485–502.
5. Gil and Varela, *Cartas*, 333–45.
6. Ibid., 301–17.
7. Valera, *Textos*, 509.
8. Ibid., 506.
9. Bernáldez, chap. CXXXI, p. 82.

The Return to Española

10. Varela, *Textos*, 484.
11. Colón, *Historia del Almirante*, chap. LXXXVIII, pp. 267–68.
12. Gil and Varela, *Cartas*, 315–16.
13. Colón, *Historia del Almirante*, chap. LXXXVIII, pp. 270–74; Las Casas, *Historia*, chap. V, p. 222.
14. Varela, *Textos*, 486.

Columbus on the Central American Coast

15. Ibid., 302.
16. *Colección de Documentos para la historia de Costa Rica*.

17. Rumeu, *El libro copiador*, fol. 34v:63–75.
18. Colón, *Historia del Almirante*, chap. CX, p. 286.
19. Fernández de Oviedo, *Historia general*, bk. III, chap. IX, p. 77.
20. Colón, *Historia del Almirante*, chap. XCVI, p. 340.
21. Rumeu, *El libro copiador*, fol. 35v:158–60.

Stranding and Rescue on Jamaica

22. Varela, *Textos*, 464.
23. Ibid., 493.
24. Ibid., 494.
25. Jane, 134.
26. Fernández de Oviedo, *Historia general*, chap. II, p. 79.
27. Colón, *Historia del Almirante*, chap. CIV, pp. 402–3.
28. Varela, *Textos*, 505.
29. Gil and Varela, *Cartas*, 320.
30. Rumeu, *El libro copiador*, fol. 38v:475–80.
31. Varela, *Textos*, 502.

Columbus and Santo Stefano

32. Ibid., 497.
33. Rumeu, *El libro copiador*, fol. 37r:323–30.
34. Varela, *Textos*, 497.
35. Ibid., 482.

Treatment of the Indians

36. Rumeu, *El libro copiador*, fol. 37v:400–404.
37. Gil and Varela, *Cartas*, 304.
38. Varela, *Textos*, 501.
39. Rumeu, *El libro copiador*, fol. 38v:464–69.
40. Jane, lxxxvii.

Return to Española and Spain

41. Varela, *Textos*, 531.
42. Jímenez Fernández.
43. Fernández Duro, *Nebulosa de Colón*; also Granzotto.
44. Peña Camara.
45. Harrisse, *Los restos de Don Cristóval Colón*.

46. The Davidson Reference Library, Santo Domingo, contains fifty-two works dealing with this controversial question. The principal ones are Colmeiro, Cocchia, and Tejera y Penson, *Los dos restos de Cristóbal Colón.*

Epilogue

1. See Ponce de León for the most thorough study of Columbus's appearance. Two of these descriptions are those by Trivigiano copied by F. Montalboddo: "homo de alta & provera statura roso de grande ingegno & faza longa."
2. Schoenbaum, 36, 75.
3. Burckhardt, 173.
4. Hale, 102.
5. Durant and Durant, 206.
6. Hale, 102.
7. Burckhardt, 15.
8. Rabasa, 30.
9. Schoenbaum, 90.
10. Ibid., viii.

Bibliography

This bibliography lists only those works that are cited in the text and notes or that directly relate to the argument. In selecting the particular editions to be used in this book, I chose those for which copies can be found in the Davidson Reference Library, Santo Domingo, Dominican Republic.

Acosta, José (de). *Histoire naturelle et moralle des indes.* Paris: Chéz Marc Orry, 1600.

Airoli, G. F. *Gli ultimi viaggi di Cristoforo Colombo.* Firenze: Tip. Succ. Vestri, 1900.

Alegria, Ricardo. *La biblioteca erasmista de Diego Méndez.* Ciudad Trujillo: Editora Montalvo, 1945.

Altoaguirre y Duvale, Angel (de). *¿Colón Español? Estudio histórico-crítico.* Madrid: Imprenta del Patronato de Huérfanos de Intendencia é Intervención Militares, 1928.

Alvarez Pedroso, Armando. *Nueva revisión de algunos de los que fueron "Problemas Colombinos."* Limited ed. Ciudad Trujillo: Pol Hermanos, 1946.

———. *Cristóbal Colón: Biografía del descubridor.* Havana: Cultura S.A., 1944.

Amler, J. Frances. *Christopher Columbus's Jewish Roots.* Northvale, N.Y.: Jason Aranson, 1991.

Andre, Marius. *Columbus.* Translated by Eloïse Parkhurst Huguenin. New York: Alfred A. Knopf, 1928.

Andresco, Victor. *Juan de la Cosa: Autor del primer mapa de América.* Madrid: Editorial "Gran Capitán," 1949.

Antequera Luengo, Juan José. *La carta de Colón anunciando el descubrimiento.* Madrid: Alianza Editorial, 1992. Facsimile of the "Posa Letter." Includes comparative analysis of transcriptions by Antonio Rumeu de Armas (*El libro copiador*), Carlos Sanz, and Consuelo Varela.

Anzoategui, Ignacio B., ed. *Los cuatro viajes del Almirante y su testamento.* Madrid: Colección Austral, 1982.

Archivo General de Simancas. *Testamento de Isabel la Católica.* Valladolid: Alfrodisión Aguado S.A., 1944. Facsimile.

Arciniegas, Germán. *Amerigo and the New World: The Life and Times of Amerigo Vespucci.* New York: Alfred Knopf, 1955.

———. *Caribbean: Sea of the New World.* New York: Alfred Knopf, 1946.

Arranz Marquéz, Luis. *Don Diego Colón: Almirante, Virrey y Gobernador de las Indias.* Madrid: CSIC, 1982.

Asensio y Toledo, José María. *Cristóbal Colón. Su vida, sus viajes—sus descubrimientos.* 2 vols. Barcelona: Espasas y Ca., 1892.

Assereto, Ugo. "La data della nascita di Colombo accertata de un documento nuovo." *Giornale storico e litterario della Liguria* (Genova) Fasc. 1–2 (1904).

Ballesteros Gaibrois, Manuel. "Fernando el Católico y América." *Anales de la Universidad de Santo Domingo* (Ciudad Trujillo) 71–72 (1954): 353–69.

———. *Historia de América.* Madrid: Ediciones Pegaso, 1954.

———, ed. *Brevissima relacion dela destrucion de indias.* Madrid: Fundación Universitaria Española, 1977.

———, ed. *Gonzálo Fernández de Oviedo: Sumario de la natural historia de las indias.* Madrid: Historia 15, 1986.

Barrero-Meiro, Roberto. *Guanahani.* Madrid: Instituto Histórico de la Marina, 1967.

————. *Guanahani de Ponce de León.* Madrid: Instituto Histórico de la Marina, 1967.

————. *Más sobre la Isla de Guanahani.* Madrid: Instituto Histórico de la Marina, 1967.

Barry, J. J. *The Life of Christopher Columbus from authentic Spanish and Italian Documents.* Boston: Patrick Donahoe, 1870.

Bataillon, Marcel. *Estudios sobre Bartolomé de Las Casas.* Barcelona: Ediciones Peninsula, 1976.

Baudizzone, Luis M. *Relación del primer viaje de D. Cristùbal Colùn.* Buenos Aires: Imprenta patagonia, 1942.

Bayle, Constantino, S. J. *El clero secular y la evangelización de américa.* Madrid: Instituto Santo Toribio de Mogrovejo, 1950.

Beltrán y Rozpide, Ricardo. *Cristóbal Colón ¿genovés? Los testamentos de Colón. El linaje verdadero de los llamados de Colón. Las razones de la duda sobre la patria de Colón. Estudio crítico.* Madrid: Patronato de Huérfanos de Intendencia é Intervención Militares, 1925.

————. *Cristóbal Colón y Cristóforo Columbo: Estudio crítico documental.* Madrid: Imprenta del Patronato de Huérfanos de Intendencia é Intervención Militares, 1918.

Bentley, Jerry H. *Old World Encounters: Cross-Cultural Contacts and Exchanges in Pre-Modern Times.* New York: Oxford University Press, 1993.

Benzoni, M. Girolamo. *La historia del mundo nuevo.* 1567; Caracas: Biblioteca de la Academia Nacional de la Historia, 1967. Study by León Croizat.

Bernáldez, Andrés. *Historia de los Reyes Católicos Dn. Fernando y Dª Isabel. Escrita por El Bachiller Andrés Bernaldez Cura de los Palacios, y Capellan del Arzobispo de Sevilla D. Diego Deza.* 2 vols. Sevilla: Bibliófilos Andaluces, Imprenta que fué de D. José María Geofrin, 1869–70.

Berwick y Alba, Duquesa de. *Autógrafos de Colon.* Madrid: Mariano Murillo, 1892. Facsimiles.

Biblioteca Colombina. *Catálogo de sus libros impresos publicado por primera vez . . . con notas bibliográficas del Dr. Simón de la Rosa y López.* 7 vols. Holland and Spain: various publishers, 1948–71. Authorized facsimiles of the first edition, 1888–91. Volume 7 was first published in 1948.

Bisson, T. N. *The Medieval Crown of Aragon.* New York: Clarendon, 1991.

Bloch, Marc. *Feudal Society.* 2 vols. Chicago: University of Chicago Press, 1961.

Boorstin, Daniel J. *The Discoverer: A History of Man's Search to Know His World and Himself.* New York: Vintage Books, 1985.

———. *Hidden History.* New York: Vintage Books, 1989.

Bowen, Catherine Drinker. *John Adams and the American Revolution.* Boston: Little, Brown, 1950.

Broome, William, trans. *The Spanish Colonie, or Briefe Chronicle of the Acts and gestes of the Spaniards in the West Indies, called the newe world.* London: Imprinted for William Broome, Readex Microprint, 1966. Facsimile. The first English edition of Las Casas's *Brevissima relación.* Translated in 1583 for William Broome from the Jacques de Miggrode French translation.

Brunet y Bellet, J. *Colón. ¿Fue el verdadero descubridor de américa? ¿Donde nació?* Barcelona: Libreria y Tipografía de L'Avenç, 1892.

Burckhardt, Jacob. *The Civilization of the Renaissance in Italy.* New York: Barnes and Noble, 1992.

Caddeo, Rinaldo. *Grandi Ritorni, relazioni di viaggio e lettere di Cristoforo Colombo.* Milano: Valentino Bompiani, 1941.

Calzada, Rafael. *La patria de Colón.* Buenos Aires: Libreria "La Facultad," 1920.

Camusso, Lorenzo. *The Voyages of Columbus, 1492–1504.* Translated by Elizebeth Leister. New York: Dorset Press, 1991.

Carbia, Rómulo D. *La patria de Cristóbal Colón. Examen crítico de las fuentes históricas en que descansan las aseveraciones Itálicas e Hispánicas, acerca del origen y lugar de nacimiento del descubridor de América.* Buenos Aires: Talleres S.A., 1923.

Carpentier, Alejo. *El arpa y la sombra.* Bogotá: Siglo xxi editores, 1987.

Castelar y Ripoll, Emilio. *Historia del descubrimiento de América.* Madrid: Establecimiento Tipográfico Succesores de Rivadeneyra, 1892.

Castellanos, Juan (de). *Elegías de varones ilustres de Indias.* 1589; Madrid: Biblioteca de Autores Españoles, 1914. Introduction and notes by Isaac Pardo.

Catálogo de la colección de Juan Bautista Muñoz. 3 vols. Madrid: Imprenta y Editorial Maestre, 1954, 1955, 1956.

Cateras, Spyros. *Christopher Columbus Was a Greek Prince: His Real Name Was Nikolaos Ypshilantis from the Greek Island of Chios.* Manchester, N.H.: privately published, 1937.

Certeau, Michel (de). *The Writing of History.* Translated by Tom Conley. New York: Columbia University Press, 1988.

Cesarini, A. Eduine (épouse Paoli). *Cristóbal Colón Nació en Corcega en la Ciudad de Calvi el año 1441.* Montevideo: Morales and Risero, 1924.

(See also the French edition: *Christophe Colomb Identifié Corse.* Nice: Imprimerie de "L'Eclaireur," 1932).

Chaliand, Gérard. *The Art of War in World History.* Berkeley: University of California Press, 1994.

Channing, Edward. "The Companions of Columbus." In Winsor, *Narrative and Critical History,* vol. 2.

Chardon, Roland, "The Elusive Spanish League: A Problem of Measurement in Sixteenth-Century Spain." *Hispanic American Historical Review* (May 1980): 294–302.

Charlevoix, Pierre-François Xavier. *Historia de la Isla Española o de Santo Domingo.* 2 vols. Santo Domingo: Sociedad Dominicana de Bibliófilos, 1977.

Cittá di Genova. *Cristoforo Colombo. Documenti e prove della sua apparenza a Genova.* Bergamo: Istituto D'Arti Grafiche di Bergamo, 1931. Facsimiles.

Clarke, Richard H. *Old and New Lights on Columbus. With Observations on Controverted Points and Criticisms.* New York: privately pubished, 1893.

Cocchia, Roque (Mons.). *Los restos de Cristóbal Colón en la Catedral de Santo Domingo. Contestación al informe de la Real Academia de la Historia al Gobierno de S. M. el Rey de España por Monseñor Roque Cocchia de la Orden de Capuchinos, Arzobispo de Siarce, Vicario Apostólico de la Arquidiócesis de Santo Domingo.* Santo Domingo: Imp. García Hermanos, 1879.

Colección de documentos inéditos relativos al descubrimiento, conquista y organización de las antiguas posesiones españolas de América y Océania sacados de los archivos del reino y muy especialmente del de Indias. Vol. 33. Madrid: Imp. de Manuel G. Hernández, 1880.

Colección de documentos para la historia de Costa Rica relativos al Cuarto y Ultimo Viaje de Cristóbal Colón. San José: Impr. y Libreria Atenea, 1952.

Colección Documental Colombina. Madrid: Inst. "Gonzalo Fernández de Oviedo," 1957. Copies of seven documents dating from 1479–1504.

Coll, José. *Colón y la Rábida con un estudio acerca de los franciscanos en el Nuevo Mundo, por M. R. P. Fr. José Coll, Definidor de la Orden de San Francisco.* Madrid: Librería Católica de Gregorio del Almo, 1891.

Colmeiro, Manuel. *Los restos de Colón. Informe de la Real Academia de la Historia al Gobierno de S. M. sobre el supuesto hallazgo de los verdaderos restos de Cristóval Colon en la Iglesia Catedral de Santo Domingo.* Madrid: Imprenta y Fundición de M. Tello, 1879.

Colón, Hernando. *A Discourse, Intended to Commemorate the Discovery of America by Christopher Columbus, Delivered at the Request of the Historical Society of Massachusetts, on the 23rd Day of October, 1792, Being the Completion of the Third Century since That Memorable Event, to Which Are Added Four Dissertations.* Edited and translated by Rev. Jeremy Belknap. Boston: Apollo Press, 1792. A condensed version of the *Historie.*

———. *Historia del Almirante Don Cristobal Colón por su hijo Hernando: Traducido nuevamente del Italiano (Alfonso Ulloa).* Edited and translated by Manuel Serrano y Sanz. 2 vols. Madrid: Libreria General de Victoriano Suárez, 1932. The definitive Spanish edition of the *Historie.*

———. *Historia del Sr. don Hernando Colón.* Edited by González de Barcia. Madrid: Biblioteca de Autores Españoles, 1928. Reprinted without corrections from the 1749 translation.

———. *The History of the Life and Actions of Adm. Christopher Columbus, and of his discovery of the West-Indies, call'd the New World, now in Possession of his Catholick Majesty, Written by his own Son D. Ferdinand Columbus.* Vol. 2 (of 4), *Collection of Voyages and Travels.* London: Churchill, Awnsham and J., 1704.

———. *The Life of the Admiral Christopher Columbus by His Son Ferdinand.* Translated, annotated, and with a new introduction by Benjamin Keen. 2d ed. Westport, Conn.: Greenwood Press, 1992. (1st ed., New Brunswick, N.J.: Rutgers University Press, 1959.)

———. *La Vie de Cristofle Colomb et la découverte qu'il a faite des Indes Occidentales, vulgairement appellés Le Nouveau Monde, composée par Fernand Colomb son Fils & traduite en Français par Cotlendy.* Paris: Chez Claude Barbin et Chez Christophe Ballard, 1681.

Columbus, Christopher, comp. *Christopher Columbus: His Own Book of Privileges, 1502.* Introduction by Henry Harrisse. Transcriptions and translations by George F. Barwick. London: B. F. Stevens, 1893. Facsimiles. (See Pérez-Bustamante, *Libro de los privilegios,* for a Spanish study and translation.)

———. *Relaciones y cartas de Cristóbal Colón.* Madrid: Librería de Perlado, Páez y Cia., 1914. Copies of several documents not previously published.

Coma, Guglielmo. *Concerning the Islands Recently Discovered.* [Pavia?: N.p., 1497?]. Facsimile and English translation of the Lenox Library copy (one of five known copies) in Thacher, *Christopher Columbus*. (See Gil and Varela, *Cartas de particulares*, for a Spanish translation. Sometimes listed under the name of the original translator, Niccolò Syllacio.)

Cordier, Henri. *Mélanges Américains*. Paris: Jean Maisonneuve and Fils, 1913.

Córdoba, Fray Pedro (de). *Doctrina Cristiana para instrucción y información de los indios, por manera de historia*. Vol. 38 Universidad de Santo Domingo. Ciudad Trujillo: Universidad de Santo Domingo, 1945. Facsimile and translation of the 1544 edition.

Cortesão, Jaime. *El viaje de Diego de Tieve y Pero Vásquez de la Frontera al banco de Terranova*. Cuadernos Colombinos #5. Valladolid: Cuadernos Colombinos, 1975.

Cozza Luzi, Giuseppe. *Cristoforo Colombo e L'Umbria*. Rome: Tipografia Sociale, 1893.

Cronau, Rudolph. *America. Historia de su descubrimiento desde los tiempos primitivos hasta los modernos*. Barcelona: Montaner y Simon, 1892.

———. *The Discovery of America and the Landfall of Columbus: The Last Resting Place of Columbus*. New York: privately published, 1921.

Cuartero y Huerta, Baltasár. *La prueba plena. Documentos inéditos, demostrativos de la autenticidad de los restos de Cristóbal Colón. Revisión Histórica*. Madrid: Instituto "Gonzalo Fernández de Oviedo," 1963.

Cummins, John. *The Voyage of Christopher Columbus: Columbus' Own Journal of Discovery, Newly Restored and Translated*. New York: St. Martin's Press, 1992.

Daelli, G., ed. *Lettere autografe edite ed inedite di Cristoforo Colombo; e fra l'altre quella sulle isole de lui scoperte, tratta da una stampa rarissima. Con un discorso di Cesare Correnti su Colombo; nove tavole illustrative; ed una avertenza degli Editori*. Milan: G. Daelli e Comp. Editori, 1863. First publication of the "Ambrosian Letter." Facsimile with woodcuts of the Basle (1493) edition with both Spanish and Italian translations.

D'Ailly, Pierre. *Ymago Mundi y otros opúsculos*. Translated by Antonio Ramírez de Verger. Sevilla: Alianza Editorial, 1992.

D'Albertis, E. A. *Citazioni giustificative per la Ricostituzione del modelli delle cravelle Niña e della nave Santa Maria*. Genova: Tipografia del R. Istituto Sordomuti, 1892.

Dati, Juliano. *Curiosidades Bibliográficas y Documentos Inéditos. Homenaje del Archivo Hispalense al Cuarto Centenario del descubrimiento del Nuevo Mundo*. Sevilla: En la Oficina de E. Rasco, 1892. Simón de la

Rosa y López, first editor of the *Biblioteca Colombina*, reported in volume 2 this previously unknown versification of the "first letter," which he had found in the library of Hernando Colón. The Hispalense copy with facsimiles and with Spanish translations is of this only known copy of the Rome edition dated June 15, 1493 (the two later copies published in Florence are dated October). The frontispiece is the only known print of the woodcut (facsimile provided) depicting Columbus in his caravel receiving instructions from Ferdinand. Carlos Sanz provided facsimiles with transcriptions of the first letter in its Latin, German, and Dati versions. (See Sanz, *Indice general*.)

Davenport, Francis G. "Text of Columbus' Privileges." *American Historical Review* 14, no. 4 (July 1909).

Davidson, Miles H. *A Columbus Handbook: An Annotated Bibliography of Works in the Davidson Reference Library That Relate to Christopher Columbus and His Family and Their Connections with the Island of Hispaniola.* Santo Domingo: privately published, 1991.

Dawson, Samuel Edward. *The Lines of Demarcation of Pope Alexander VI. And the Treaty of Tordesillas* A.D. *1493 and 1494.* Ottowa: J. Hope and Sons, 1899.

Deagan, Kathleen A. "Europe's First Foothold in the New World La Isabela." *National Geographic Magazine*, January 1992, pp. 41–53.

De Gandia, Enrique. *Historia crítica de los mitos de la conquista americana.* Madrid: Sociedad General Española de Librería, 1929.

Deive, Carlos Esteban. *Heterodoxia é Inquisición en Santo Domingo, 1492–1822.* Santo Domingo: Taller, 1983.

Desimoni, Cornelio. *Di alcuni recenti giudizi intorno alla patria di Cristofro Colombo.* Genoa: Tipografia del R. Istituto Sordo-Muti, 1890.

Didiez Burgos, Ramón A. *Análisis del Diario de Colón, Guanahani y Mayaguain, las primeras isletas descubiertas en el Nuevo Mundo.* Santo Domingo: Editora Cultural Dominicana, 1974.

———. "El Dia de la Fundación de la Ysabela." *Boletín de la Sociedad Dominicana de Geografía* (Santo Domingo) 3 (1973): 115–37.

———. *El milagro en el Fuerte de Santo Tomás.* Santo Domingo: privately published, 1971.

Dobal, Carlos. *La Isabela: Jerusalem Americana. La primera misa en América.* Santiago, Dominican Republic: Universidad Católica Madre y Maestra, 1987.

Duff, Charles. *La verdad acerca de Cristóbal Colón y del descubrimiento de América.* Madrid: Espasa-Calpe, 1938.

Dunn, Oliver, and James E. Kelley Jr., trans. and eds. *The Diario of Christopher Columbus's First Voyage to America, 1492–1493.* Norman: University of Oklahoma Press, 1989. Spanish transcription with English translation.

Durant, Will, and Ariel Durant. *The Reformation: A History of European Civilization from Wyclif to Calvin, 1300–1364.* New York: Simon and Schuster, 1957

Dyson, John. *Columbus: For Gold, God, and Glory.* New York: Simon and Schuster, 1991.

Eames, Wilberforce, ed. *The Letter of Columbus on the Discovery of America. From the originals in the Lenox Library. A Facsimile of the Pictorial Edition, with a New and Literal Translation, and a Complete Reprint of the Oldest Four Editions in Latin.* New York: Trustees of the Lenox Library, 1892.

Echeberri, José Manuel (de). *¿Do existen las cenizas de Cristóbal Colón?* Santo Domingo: J. R. Vda. Garcia, 1879.

Eliot, J. H. *El viejo mundo y el nuevo 1492–1650.* Madrid: Alianza Editorial, 1984.

Enguita Qtrilla, José María. "El oro e las Indias. Datos léxicos en la 'Historia general y natural' de Fernández de Oviedo." *América y la España en el siglo XVI* (Madrid) 1 (1982): 273–94.

Ezquerra Abadia, Ramón. "Los primeros contactos entre Colón y Vespucio." *Revista de Indias* 143–44:19–47.

Etayo, Carlos. *Naos y carabelas de los descubrimientos y las naves de Colón.* Madrid: Industrial Gráfica Aralar, 1971.

Fernández-Armesto, Felipe. *Columbus.* New York: Oxford University Press, 1991.

———. "Columbus: Hero or Villain?" *History Today* 42 (1992): 4–9.

Fernández de Navarrete, Martín. *Colección de los viajes y descubrimientos que hilcieron por mar los españoles desde fines del siglo XV.* 5 vols. Madrid: La Imprenta Nacional, 1829–37.

Fernández de Oviedo y Valdéz, Gonzalo. *Historia general y natural de las Indias, Islas y Tierra-Firme del Mar Oceano.* 4 vols. 1531; Madrid: Imprenta de la Real Academia de la Historia, 1851–53.

———. *Sumario de la natural historia de las Indias.* Introduction by José Miranda. 1526; Mexico City: Fondo de Cultura Económico, 1950.

Fernández Duro, Césario. *Nebulosa de Colón según observaciones hechas en ambos mundos: Indicación de algunos errores que se comprueban con documentos inéditos.* Madrid: Estabecimiento Tipográfico Sucesores de Rivadeneyra, 1890.

————. *Primer viaje de Colón*. Madrid: Ateneo de Madrid, 1892.

————, ed. *Bibliografía Colombina. Enumeración de libros y documentos concernientes a Cristobal Colón y sus viajes. Obra que publica la Real Academia de la Historia por encargo de la Junta Directiva del cuarto centenario del descubrimiento de América*. Madrid: Establecimiento Tipográfico de Fortanet, 1892.

Fernández Martínez, José. *La enigma de Colón (La otra historia del descubrimiento de América)*. Granada: Litografía Anel, 1962.

Fournier, A. *Histoire de la Vie et des Voyages de l'amiral Christophe Colomb d'aprés les documents de l'époque et nottament suivant l'histoire véridique de l'amiral écrite par son fils Don Fernando Colon*. Paris: Librairie de Fermin-Diderot, 1894.

Fuson, Robert H., trans. *The Log of Christopher Columbus. His own account of the voyage that changed the world, in the acclaimed new translation by Robert H. Fuson*. Camden, Maine: International Marine Publishing, 1987.

Gavano, Antonio. *The Discoveries of the World from their first originall unto the yeere of our Lord 1555*. New York: World Publishing Company, 1966. A facsimile of the first English edition of this Portuguese history published in 1601. Translated by Richard Hakluyt.

Garcilaso de la Vega. *Comentarios Reales de los Incas*. Prologue by Nuria Nuiry. 1607; Havana: Casa de las Américas, 1973. This work was named *Comentarios* because it had, for example, twenty-seven quotations from Acosta and eleven from López de Gómara, as well as from other authors.

Gardner, John. *The Life and Times of Chaucer*. New York: Vintage Books, 1977.

Garibay, Esteban de. *Los quarenta libros del compendio historial de las cronicas y universal historia de todos los reinos de España*. Anvers, 1571. A copy of his chapter "Cristobal Colon" is in Fernández Duro, *Nebulosa de Colón*.

Garin, Eugenio, ed. *Renaissance Characters*. Translated by Lydia G. Cochrane. Chicago: University of Chicago Press, 1991.

Geraldini, Alessandro. *Itinerario por los regiones subequinocciales*. Santo Domingo: Editora del Caribe, 1977. Cittá di Genova, *Cristoforo Colombo*, 38, contains a facsimile of the page in the Rome 1631 edition with passages referring to Columbus.

Geraldini, Belisario. *Cristoforo Colombo ed su primo vescovo di S. Domingo Mons. Alessandro Geraldini d'Amelia*. Amelia, Italy: Tip. A. Petrignani, 1892.

Gerson, Jean. *Treinta proposiciones de astrologia teologizada.* Also *Opusculo de astrologia teologizada, Opusculo contra la observancia supersticiosa de los dias,* and *Contra la doctrina de un médico de Montpellier.* Edited by Antonio Ramírez de Verger. Madrid: Alianza Editorial, 1992. Translation of Columbus's excerpts with postils in the *Biblioteca Colombina* copy.

Gil, Juan. "El rol del tercer viaje Colombino." *Historia y Bibliografía Americanistas (CSIC)* (Sevilla) 29 (1985): 35–82.

——. "El libro copiador." Transcription by Gil in Varela, *Textos* (1992).

——. *Mitos y utopías del Descubrimiento.* Vol. 1, *Colón y su tiempo.* Vol. 2, *El Pacífico.* Vol 3, *El Dorado.* Madrid: Alianza Editorial, 1989.

——. "Tres notas colombinas." *Historia y Bibliografía Americanistas (CSIC)* (Sevilla) 28 (1984): 73–91.

——, ed. *El libro de Marco Polo: Las Apostillas a la Historia Natural de Plinio el Viejo.* Madrid: Alianza Editorial, 1992.

Gil, Juan, and Consuelo Varela, eds. *Cartas de particulares a Colón y Relaciones coetáneas.* Madrid: Alianza Universidad, 1984.

Giustiniani, Augustini. "Polyglot Psalter" (1516). Study and facsimile in Thacher, 1:202–12.

——. *Psalterium Hebraeum, Arabicum, et Chaldaeum cum tribus latinis interpretationibus et glossis.* Genova, 1516. In Cittá di Genova, *Cristoforo Colombo,* 66.

——. *Castigatissimi Annali . . . della Eccelsa et Illustrissima Republ. di Genoa.* Genoa, 1537. In Cittá di Genova, *Cristoforo Colombo,* 65. Facsimile in Harrisse, *Bibliotheca Americana Vetustissima* (1866).

Gonzalez de la Fuente, Sebastián. "Informe Oficial. Presentado por el Coronel Don Sebastián Gonzalez de la Fuente al Gobernador de Cuba." *El Faro a Colún* (Ciudad Trujillo) 7 (1952): 26–56.

Gottschalk, Paul. *The Earliest Diplomatic Documents of America: The Papal Bulls of 1493 and the Treaty of Tordesillas Reproduced and Translated.* Berlin: privately pubished, 1927. Full-scale facsimiles of manuscripts and maps.

Gould, Stephen J. *Wonderful Life.* New York: W. W. Norton, 1989.

Granzotto, Gianni. *Cristoforo Colombo.* Milan: Arnoldo Mondadori, 1984. (English translation: Norman: University of Oklahoma Press, 1987.)

Greenblatt, Stephen. *Marvelous Possessions: The Wonder of the New World.* Chicago: University of Chicago Press, 1991.

——, ed. *New World Encounters.* Berkeley: University of California Press, 1993.

Gutierrez, Carlos. *Fray Bartolomé de Las Casas. Sus tiempos y su apostolado*. Prologue by Emilio Castelar. Madrid: Imprenta de Fortanet, 1878.

Haile, H. G. *Luther: An Experiment in Biography*. New York: Doubleday and Company, 1980.

Hale, John. *The Civilization of Europe in the Renaissance*. New York: Touchstone Press, 1995.

Hamilton, Edith. *The Greek Way*. New York: W. W. Norton, 1930.

Hanke, Lewis. *The First Social Experiments in America*. Cambridge: Harvard University Press, 1935.

———. *El prejuicio racial en el Nuevo Mundo: Aristóteles y los indios de Hispanoamérica*. Santiago de Chile: Editorial Universitaria, 1958.

———. *The Spanish Struggle for Justice in the Conquest of America*. Philadelphia: University of Pennsylvania Press, 1949.

———. *Las teorías políticas de Bartolomé de Las Casas*. Publ. del Instituto de Investigaciones Históricos Número LXVII. Buenos Aires: Instituto de Investigaciones Históricos, 1935.

Hanke, Lewis, and Manuel Jímenez Fernández. *Bartolomé de Las Casas, 1474–1566: Bibliografía crítica y cuerpo de materiales para el estudio de su vida, escritos, actuación y polémicas que suscitaron durante cuatro siglos*. Santiago de Chile: Fondo Histórico y Bibliográfico José Toribio Medina, 1954. Facsimiles.

Haring, C. H. *The Spanish Empire in America*. New York: Harcourt Brace Jovanovich, 1952. Reprinted with corrections and a new bibliography.

Harrisse, Henry. *Bibliotheca Americana Vetustissima: A Description of the Works Relating to America Published between the Years 1492 and 1551*. New York: George P. Philes, 1866.

———. *Bibliotheca Americana Vetustissima: A Description of the Works Relating to America Published between the Years 1492 and 1551, with Additions*. Paris: Librairie Tross, 1872. Over the years 1958–60, Carlos Sanz reproduced, updated, and added five new volumes to his reproductions of the Harrisse originals.

———. *Christophe Colomb et la Corse: Observations sur un decrét du gouvernement français*. Paris: Ernest Leroux, 1883.

———. *Christophe Colomb et les Académiciens espagnols: Notes pour servir à l'histoire de la science en Espagne au XIXieme siècle par l'auteur de la Bibliotheca Americana Vetustissima*. Paris: H. Welter, 1894.

———. *The Diplomatic History of America: Its First Chapter, 1452–1493–1494*. London: B. F. Stevens, 1897.

————. *L'histoire de Christophe Colomb attribuée à son fils Fernand: Examen critique du memoire lu par M. D'Avesac... aout 1873.* Paris: Imprimerie de E. Martinet, 1875. Facsimiles.

————. *Los restos de Don Cristoval Colón: Disquisición por el autor de la Bibliotheca Americana Vetustissima.* Sevilla: Francisco Alvarez y Ca., 1878. Facsimiles.

Helps, Arthur (Sir). *The Spanish Conquest in America and Its Relation to the History of Slavery and the Government of the Colonies.* 6 vols. London: John W. Parker and Son, 1855–61.

Henige, David. "Edited ... and Not Precipitated: Three Recent Editions of Columbus' *diario.*" *Terrae Incognitae* 22 (1990): 93–104.

————. "Finding Columbus: Implications of a Newly Discovered Text." In *European Outthrust and Encounter: The First Phase, 1400–c.1700, Essays in Tribute to David Bears Quinn on His Eighty-Fifth Birthday,* edited by Cecil Clough and P. E. H. Hair, 141–65. Liverpool, 1994.

————. *In Search of Columbus: The Sources for the First Voyage.* Tucson: University of Arizona Press, 1991.

————. "The Mutinies on Columbus' First Voyage: Fact or Fiction?" *Terrae Incognitae* 23 (1991): 29–38.

————. "Samuel Eliot Morison as Translator and Interpreter of Columbus' *diario de abordo.*" *Terrae Incognitae* 20 (1988): 69–88.

Henriquez y Castro, Abad. *Acerca de los dos Juan de la Cosa.* Ciudad Trujillo: Editora Montalvo, 1958.

Herrera y Tordesillas, Antonio. *Histoire generale des voyages et conquestes des castillans, dans les Isles & Terre ferme des Indes occidentales.* Paris: Chez Nicolas and Jean de la Coste, 1659.

————. *Historia general de los hechos de los Castellanos en las islas y Tierrafirme de el Mar Océano.* 4 vols. 1601–15; Madrid: Oficina Real de Nicolas Rodríguez Franco, 1726–30.

Ibn Batuta. *Travels in Bengal and China.* Edited by Sir Henry Yule. Revised by Henri Cordier. London: Hakluyt Society, 1916; Kraus reprint, Millwood, N.Y., 1967.

Ibn Khaldûn. *The Muqaddimah: An Introduction to History.* Translated from the Arabic by Franz Rosenthal. Abridged and Edited by N. J. Dawood. Bollingen Series. Princeton: Princeton University Press, 1989.

Inchaustegui Cabral, and Joaquín Marino. *Francisco de Bobadilla: Tres homónimos, y un enigma colombino decifrado.* Madrid: Ediciones Cultura Hispánica, 1964.

Interiano, Paolo. *Ristretto delle historie Genovesi di Paolo Interiano: Lucca 1551.* (See Brunet y Bellet, *¿Fue el verdadero descubridor de américa?* for translation. Facsimile of Italian text in Cittá di Genoa, *Cristoforo Colombo,* and copy in Fernández Duro, *Bibliografía Colombina,* sec. 4, p. 783.)

Irving, Washington. *A History of the Life and Voyages of Christopher Columbus.* 3 vols. New York: G. and C. Carvill, 1828.

Jackson, Donald Dale. *Smithsonian* (September 1991).

Jane, Cecil. *The Journal of Columbus.* New York: Jackson N. Potter, 1960.

Jímenez Fernández, Manuel. *Dos ensayos polémicos sobre los restos de Cristóbal Colón en Sevilla.* Sevilla: Imprenta de la Escuela de Estudios Hispano-Americanos, 1954.

————. *Fr. Bartolomé de las Casas: Tradado de Indias y el Doctor Sepulveda.* Caracas: Academia Nacional de la Historia, 1962. Transcription.

John of Plano of Carpini (Friar). *The Journey of Friar John of Plan de Carpine to the Court of Kuyuk Khan, 1245–1247, as Narrated by Himself.* Translated and edited by William Woodville Rockhill. London: Hakluyt Society, 1900; Kraus reprint, Millwood, N.Y., 1967.

————. *A Narrative of Friar John of Pian de Carpine's Mission, Derived from an Oral Statement of His Companion, Friar Benedict the Pole.* Translated and edited by William Woodville Rockhill. London: Hakluyt Society, 1900; Kraus reprint, Millwood, N.Y., 1967.

Jones, Mary Ellen, ed. *Christopher Columbus and His Legacy: Opposing Viewpoints.* San Diego, Calif.: Greenhaven Press, 1992.

Jos Pérez, Emiliano. *El plan y la genesis del descubrimiento Colombino.* Valladolid: Serie Cuadernos Colombinos, 1979–80.

Lamartine, Alonso (de). *Cristóbal Colón: Descubrimiento de las Américas.* Edited by Orbano Manini. 4 vols. Madrid: Imp. de Santos Larxe, 1867.

Las Casas, Fray Bartolomé (de). *Apologética Historia Sumaria.* Preface and preliminary study by Edmundo O'Gorman. Mexico City: Universidad Nacional Autónoma, 1967.

————. *Brevissima relación de la destruycion de las Indias: Colegida por el Obispo dõ fray Bartolome de las Casas /o Casaus de la ozden de Sacto Domingo, 1552.* Sevilla: Sebastian Trujillo, 1552. (See also a modern version with facsimile, notes, and introduction by Manuel Ballesteros Gaibrois. Madrid: Fundación Universitaria Española, 1977.)

————. *De imperatoria seu regia potestate.* Madrid: C.S.I.C., 1984. Spanish and Latin edition. Reprint with corrections of first edition.

————. *Historia de las Indias*. 5 vols. Edited by Marqués de la Fuensanta del Valle and D. José Sancho Rayon. Madrid: Imprenta de Miguel Ginesta, 1875.

————. *Historia de las Indias*. 3 vols. Edited by Agustín Millares Carlo, with a study by Lewis Hanke. Mexico City: Fondo de Cultura Económico, 1951.

————. *Historia de las Indias*. 2 vols. An edition of Quintana edited by Juan Pérez de Tudela y Bueso, with Emilio López Oto. Madrid: Biblioteca de Autores Españoles, 1961.

————. *Historia de las Indias*. 3 vols. Transcribed by Manuel José Quintana. Reprint. Santo Domingo: Ediciones del Continente, 1985.

————. *Opusculos, cartas y memoriales*. Edited by Juan Pérez de Tudela y Bueso. Madrid: Biblioteca de Autores Españoles, 1958.

————. *Il supplice Schiauo Indiano di Monsig. Reverendiss. D. Bartolomeo dalle Case ò Casaus, Siuigliano, dell'Ordine de' Predicatori, & Vescuo di Chiapa, Città Regale dell'Indie. Conforme suo vero Originale Spagnuolo gija stampato en Siuglia. Tradotto in Italiano per opera Marco Ginammi*. Venice: Marco Ginammi, 1636.

————. *Tratados de Fray Bartolomé de las Casas*. Prologues by Lewis Hanke and Manuel Jímenez Fernández. Transcription by Juan Pérez de Tudela y Bueso. Translations by Agustín Millares Carlo and Rafael Moreno. Mexico City: Fondo de Cultura Economico, 1965. Facsimiles of the nine tracts.

Le Goff, Jacques, ed. *Medieval Callings*. Chicago: University of Chicago Press, 1990.

Levene, Ricardo. *Las indias no eran colonias*. Madrid: Colección Austral, 1973.

Llaverias, Federico. *La primera misa en América*. Ciudad Trujillo: Imprenta J. R. Vda. Garcia Sucs., 1936.

López de Gómara, Francisco. *Hispañia vitrix: Primera y segunda parte de la historia general de las Indias con todo el descubrimiento, y cosas notables que han acaecido desde que ganaron hasta el año de 1551; con la conquista de Méjico y de la Nueva España*. Madrid: Biblioteca de Autores Españoles, 1931.

López de Palacios Rubios, Juan. *De las islas del mar Océano*. 1514[?]; Mexico City, Fondo de Cultura Economica, 1954. Introduction by Silvio Zavala, translation and notes by Augustín Millares Carlo.

Lunardi, Federico (Mons.). *A primeira missa na america*. Rio de Janéiro: Imprenta Nacional, 1936.

Lyon, Eugene. "Fifteenth-Century Manuscript Yields First Look at Niña." *National Geographic Magazine*, November 1986, pp. 601–5.

———. "Search for Columbus." *National Geographic Magazine*, January 1992, pp. 4–26.

Madariaga, Salvador (de). *Christopher Columbus, Being the Life of the Very Magnificent Lord Don Cristobal Colón.* London: Hollis and Carter, 1949.

———. *Vida del Muy Magnífico Señor Don Cristóbal Colón.* Buenos Aires: Editorial Sudamericana, 1942.

Magnaghi, Alberto. *Prescursori di Colombo? Il tentativo di viaggio trans-oceanico del genovesi fratelli Vivaldi nel 1291.* Rome: Societá Anonima Italiana Arti Grafiche, 1935.

Maguidovich, I. P. *Historia del descubrimiento y exploración de latino-america.* Moscow: Editorial Progresso, 1965.

Major, R. H. *Bibliography of the "First Letter" of Christopher Columbus Describing His Discovery of the New World.* London: Ellis and White, 1872. This copy belonged to John Russel Bartlett, librarian of the John Carter Brown Library. It has extensive postils written by Bartlett.

———, trans. and ed. *Select Letters of Christopher Columbus, with Other Original Documents, Relating to His Four Voyages to the New World.* London: Hakluyt Society, 1847. Facsimiles.

Mallet, Michael. *The Borgias: The Rise and Fall of the Most Infamous Family in History.* Chicago: Academy Publishers, 1987.

———. "The Condotiere." In Garin, *Renaissance Characters.*

Manzano Manzano, Juan. *Colón descubrió américa del sur en 1494.* Caracas: Biblioteca de la Academia Nacional de la Historia, 1972.

———. *Colón y su secreto.* Madrid: Ediciones Cultura Hispánica, 1976.

———. *La incorporación de las indias a la corona de castilla.* Madrid: Ediciones Cultura Hispánica, 1948.

Marcone, Angelo. *Della relazioni di Cristoforo Colombo con S. Caterina da Genova. Questione preliminare seguita da parrechie altre riguardanti la vita dell'eroe nonché da due documenti pontificii di omma importanza sull'unita della chiesa fondata ga Gesú Cristo.* Siena: Tip. Editrice s. Bernardino, 1895.

Marden, Luis. "Tracking Columbus across the Atlantic." *National Geographic* 170, no. 5 (November 1986): 572–601.

Marignolli, John (de). *Recollections of Travel in the East.* Translated and edited by Sir Henry Yule. Revised by Henri Cordier. London: Hakluyt Society, 1914; Kraus reprint, Millwood, N.Y., 1967.

Marín Martínez, Tomás. *Obras y libros de Hernando Colón.* "Memoria de las obras y libros de Hernando Colón" del Bachiler Juan Pérez. Sevilla: Imprenta de la CSIC, 1970.

Martínez, Manuel M., O. P. *Fray Bartolomé de Las Casas, "Padre de América": Estudio biográfico-crítico.* Madrid: Imp. La Rafa, 1958.

Martínez-Vigil, Ramón (Padre). *La orden de predicadores, sus glorias en santidad, apostolado, ciencias y artes y gobierno de los pueblos.* Madrid: Librería de D. Gregorio del Amo, 1884.

Martínez y Martínez, Francisco. *El descubrimiento de América y las joyas de la reina Da. Isabel.* Valencia: Imprenta hijos de Francisco Vives, 1916.

Martire d'Anghiera, Pietro. *Decadas del Nuevo Mundo.* Appendices by Edmundo O'Gorman. Translations by Agustín Millares Carlo. Bibliography by Joseph H. Sinclair. Santo Domingo: Sociedad Dominicana de Bibliófilos, 1989.

———. *Documentos para la historia de España: Epistolario de Pedro Mártir de Anglería.* Translated by José López de Toro. 4 vols. Madrid: Imprenta Góngora, 1955–57.

———. *Oceaneae decadis I–III.* 1516. *De rebus oceanicis et nove orbe, decada tres, Petri Martyris ab Angleria mediolanensis.* Bound together with *De Babylonica legatione* and *Hispanicis* by Damiani da Goes, Equitis Lusitani. Cologne: Gerruinum Calenium, 1574. The Hispania decade (1541) is the epitome to the fourth decade.

———. *Primera décade oceanica de Pedro Martir de Angleria in Cartas de particulares a Colón.* In Gil and Varela, *Cartas,* 39–124.

Menéndez Pidal, Ramón. *El padre Las Casas. Su doble personalidad.* Madrid: Espasa-Calpe, 1963.

———. "El Padre Las Casas y la leyenda negra." *Cuadernos Hispanoamericanos* (Madrid) 157 (January 1963).

———. "Una norma anormal del Padre Las Casas." *Cuadernos Hispanoamericanos* (Madrid) 88 (April 1957).

Milhou, Alain. *Colón y su mentalidad mesianica en el ambiente franciscanista español.* Valladolid: Casa-Museo de Colón, 1983.

Montecorvino, John (of). *First Letter of John of Montecorvino.* Translated and edited by Sir Henry Yule. Revised by Henri Cordier. London: Hakluyt Society, 1914; Kraus reprint, Millwood, N.Y., 1967.

Montojo, D. Patricio. *Las primeras tierras descubiertas por Colón. Ensayo crætico.* Madrid: Estabecimiento Tipográfico Sucesores de Rivadeneyra, 1892.

Morales Padrón, Francisco. *Teoría y Leyes de la Conquista.* Madrid: Ediciones Cultura Hispanica, 1979.

Morison, Samuel Eliot. *Christopher Columbus: Admiral of the Ocean Sea.* London: Oxford University Press, 1942.

———. *Christopher Columbus, Mariner.* Boston: Little, Brown and Company, 1955. (See also the Spanish-language edition: *Cristóbal Colón, Marino.* Translated by Haroldo Dies. Mexico City: Editorial Diana, 1966.)

———. *The European Discovery of America: The Northern Voyages,* A.D. *500–1600.* New York: University of Oxford Press, 1971.

———. *The European Discovery of America: The Southern Voyages, 1492–1616.* New York: Oxford University Press, 1974.

Muñoz, Juan Bautista. *Catálogo de la colección de Don Juan Bautista Muñoz.* 3 vols. Madrid: Real Academia de la Historia, 1954.

———. "Historia del Nuevo Mundo (parte inédita relativa a Santo Domingo)." *Boletín del Archivo General Nacional* (Ciudad Trujillo) 11 (1940): 169–222.

———. *Santo Domingo en los manuscritos de Juan Bautista Muñoz: Transcripción y glosas.* Edited by Roberto Marte. Santo Domingo: Fundación García-Arevalo, 1981.

Muntaner, Ramón. *The Chronicle of Muntaner, Translated from the Catalan by Lady Goodenough.* London: Hakluyt Society, 1921; Kraus Reprint Lichtenstein, 1967.

Muro Orejón, Antonio, ed. *Pleitos Colombinos: Proceso hasta la sentencia de Sevilla (1511).* Sevilla: Escuela de Estudios Hispano-americanos, 1967.

———. *Pleitos Colombinos: Rollo del proceso sobre la Apelación de la Sentencia de Dueñas y probanzas del fiscal y del almirante (1534–1536).* Sevilla: Escuela de Estudios Hispano-americanos, 1964.

Nagy, Adam Szaszdi. *Un mundo que descubrió Colón: Las rutas del comercio prehispánico de los metales.* Valladolid: Publicaciones Casa-Museo de Colón, 1984.

Napione, Gianfrancesco. *Della patria di Cristoforo Colombo: Stampata del tomo XXVII delle memorie dell'Accademia Reale delle cienze di Torino a pagina 73.* Turin: Accademia Reale, 1820.

Northrup, George Tyler, ed. *The Mundus Novus Letter to Lorenzo Pietro di Medici in Translation.* Princeton: Princeton University Press 1916. Facsimile.

Nowell, Charles E. "The Columbus Question." *American Historical Review,* 1939.

Ober, Frederick A. *In the Wake of Columbus.* Boston: D. Lathrop, 1893.

Ochse, J. J., with M. J. Soule Jr., M. J. Dijkman, and C. Wehlburg. *Cultivo y mejoramiento de plantas tropicales y subtropicales.* 2 vols. Mexico City: Editorial LIMUSA, 1976.

Odoric of Pordenone. *The Eastern Parts of the World Described.* Translated and edited in Yule *Cathay and the Way Thither,* vol. 2.

Otero Sánchez, Prudencio. *España: Patria de Colón.* Madrid: Biblioteca Nueva, 1922.

Ots Capdequí, José María. *El estado español en las Indias.* Mexico City: Fondo de Cutura Economica, 1946.

———. "Los intereses privados y la intervención del Estado en la obra de descubrimiento, conquista y colonización de América." *Anales de la Universidad de Santo Domingo* (Ciudad Trujillo) 31–32 (1944): 332–44.

———. *El régimen de la tierra en la América Española durante el período colonial.* Ciudad Trujillo: Editora Montalvo, 1946.

Palm, Erwin Walter. *Los monumentos arquitectónicos de la Española.* Barcelona: Industrias Gráficas Seix y Barral Hnos., 1955.

Pane, Román. "Relación de fray Román de las antiguedades de los indios, los cuales con diligencia, como hombre que sabe el idioma de estos, recogio por mandato del Almirante." *Anales de la Universidad Autonoma de Santo Domingo* (Ciudad Trujillo) 41–44 (1947): 108–38.

Paolini, P. Fr. M^a. *Cristoforo Colombo nella sua vita morale.* Livorno: Officine Grafiche G. Chiappini, 1938.

Peña Camara, José (de la). "Los restos de Colón divididos entre Sevilla y Santo Domingo." *CLIO* (Santo Domingo) 141 (1984): 84–94.

Pereda, Setembrino E. *Colón y América . . . Contiene además una réplica a las inexatitude histórica en que incurre D. Fernando Uriarte, que habló por los Españoles.* Montevideo: Tipografía Goyena, 1893.

Pérez-Bustamante, Ciriaco. *Libro de los privilegios del Almirante Don Cristóbal Colón (1498): Estudio preliminar, edición y notas por el Excmo. Señor Don Ciriaco Pérez-Bustamante de la Real Academia de la Historia.* Madrid: Editorial Maestre, 1951. Facsimiles.

Peréz de Tudela y Bueso, Juan. *Obras escogidas de Fray Bartolomé de las Casas.* Vol. 1, *Historia de las Indias.* Madrid: Biblioteca de Autores Españoles, 1957. Vol. 5, *Opúsculos, Cartas y Memoriales.* Madrid: Biblioteca de Autores Españoles, 1958.

———. *Rasgos del semblante espiritual de Gonzalo Fernández de Oviedo: La hidalguía caballeresca ante el Nuevo Mundo.* Madrid: CSIC, 1957.

Phillips, William D., Jr., and Carla Rahn Phillips. *The Worlds of Christopher Columbus.* New York: Cambridge University Press, 1992.

Piccolómini, Eneas Silvio (de') (Pope Pius II). *Descripción de Asia*. The first part of *Historia rerum ubique gestarum*. Edited and translated by Francisco Socas, from Columbus's copy. Madrid: Alianza Editorial, 1992.

Pina, Rui (da). *Crónica del Rei D. João II*. (First published in Lisbon in 1792; see Jos Pérez, *El plan*, for pertinent excerpts.)

Plaïdy, Jean. *The Spanish Inquisition: Its Rise, Growth, and End*. 3 vols. Vol. 1, *The Rise of the Spanish Inquisition*. Vol. 2., *The Growth of the Spanish Inquisition*. Vol. 3, *The End of the Spanish Inquisition*. New York: Barnes and Noble, 1994.

Pliny the Elder. *Historia Natural*. Translated by Juan Gil. Madrid: Alianza Editorial, 1992. Excerpts with postils by Columbus in the *Biblioteca Colombina* copy of *Historia natural*.

Polo, Marco. *El Iibro de Marco Polo*. Translated by Juan Gil. Sevilla: Alianza Editorial, 1992. From the Pipino 1487 Latin edition owned by Columbus; includes all postils.

———. *The Most Noble and Famous Travels of Marcus Paulus Together with the Travels of Nicolò De' Conti, Edited from the Elizebethan Translation of John Frampton (1579)*. Edited by N. M. Penzer. London: Argonaut Press, 1929. An English translation of Rodrigo Fernández de Santaella y Córdoba's 1503 Spanish edition.

———. *The Travels of Marco Polo the Venetian*. Translated by John Masefield. London: J. M. Dent and Sons, 1907.

Ponce de León, Néstor. *The Columbus Gallery: The "Discoverer of the New World" as Represented in Portraits, Monuments, Statues, Medals, and Paintings. Historical Description*. New York: privately published, 1893.

Prescott, William Hickling. *History of the Reign of Ferdinand and Isabella*. Rev. 3d ed. New York: Burt, 1838.

Rabasa, José. *Inventing America: Spanish Historiography and the Formation of Eurocentrism*. Norman: University of Oklahoma Press, 1993.

Ramos Pérez, Demetrio. *La carta de Colón sobre el descubrimiento*. Valladolid: La Casa–Museo de Colón, 1981. Study by Ramos Pérez with a facsimile of the Simancas manuscript.

———. *El conflicto de las lanzas jinetas: El primer alzamiento en tierra americana, durante el segundo viaje colombino*. Valladolid: La Casa–Museo de Colón, 1982.

———. *Memorial de Zamora sobre las Indias*. Zamora: Fundación Ramos de Castro, 1981. Study with transcription. Facsimile.

————. *Testamento de Cristóbal Colón otorgado en Valladolid a 19 de mayo de 1506 ante el escribano Pedro de Hinojeda.* Valladolid: La Casa-Museo de Colón, 1980. Facsimile with transcription.

————. *Variaciones ideológicas en torno al descubrimiento de América: Pedro Martir de Angleria y su mentalidad.* Valladolid: Publicaciones de la Casa-Museo de Colón 1982.

Raynal, Gme. T.mas. *Histoire philosophique et politique des Etablissements & du Commerce des Européens dans les deux indes.* Geneve: Chez les Librairies Associés, 1775. First published in Amsterdam in 1770; the author issued this revised edition to correct errors in the first.

Real Academia de la Historia. *Bibliografía Colombina: Enumeración de libros y documentos concernientes a Cristobal Colón y sus viajes.* Edited by Cesareo Fernández Duro. Madrid: Establecimiento Tipográfico de Fortanet, 1892.

————. *Biblioteca Colombina: Catálogo de sus libros impresos publicado por primera vez . . . con notas bibliográficas del Dr. Simón de la Rosa y López.* 7 vols. Seville: various publishers, 1888–1948.

Revelli, Paolo. *Il Genoese.* Genova: Istituto Grafico Bertello, 1951.

Robbins, Frank E., trans. *The Columbus Letter of 1493: A Facsimile of the Copy in the William L. Clements Library with a New Translation into English.* Ann Arbor, Mich.: Clements Library Associates, 1952.

Roselly de Lorgues, Antoine (Conde de). *Monumento a Colón: Historia de la vida y viajes de Cristóbal Colón.* 3 vols. Madrid: Jaime Seix, 1878–90.

Royo Guardia, Fernando. "Don Cristóbal Colón, la insularidad de Cuba y el mapa de Juan de la Cosa." *Revista de Indias* (Madrid) 113–14 (1968): 433–76.

Rubin, Nancy. *Isabella of Castile: The First Renaissance Queen.* New York: St. Martin's Press, 1991.

Rubruck, William (of). *The Journey to the Eastern Parts of the World of William of Rubruck, of the Order of Minor Friars, in the Year of Grace MCCLIII, as Narrated by Himself.* Translated and edited by William Woodville Rockhill. London: Hakluyt Society, 1900; Kraus reprint, Millwood, N.Y., 1967.

Ruiz Martinez, Cándido. *Gobierno de Frey Nicolás de Ovando en la española.* Madrid: Establecimiento Tipográfico Sucesores de Rivadeneyra, 1892.

Rumeu de Armas, Antonio. "El Diario de a bordo de Cristóbal Colón: El problema de la paternidad del extracto." *Revista de Indias* (Madrid) 24, nos. 143–44 (1976): 7–18.

——. *Un escrito desconocido de Cristobal Colón: El memorial de La Mejorada.* Madrid: Ediciones Cultura Hispánica, 1972. Facsimile with transcription.

——. *Hernando Colón, historiador del descubrimiento de América.* Madrid: Ediciones Cultura Hispánica, 1973.

——. *El libro copiador de Cristóbal Colón.* 2 vols. Madrid: Colección Tabula Americae, 1988, 1989. Transcription and study.

——. *El "Portugues" Cristóbal Colón en Castilla.* Madrid: Ediciones Cultura Hispánica, 1987.

——. *La Rábida y el descubrimiento de América: Colón, Marchena, y Fray Juan Pérez.* Madrid: Ediciones Cultura Hispánica, 1968.

Sale, Kirkpatrick. *The Conquest of Paradise: Christopher Columbus and the Columbian Legacy.* New York: Plume, 1991.

Sales Ferre, Manuel. *El descubrimiento de América según las últimas investigaciones.* Sevilla: Tipografía de Díaz y Carballo, 1893.

Sanguinetti, Angelo. *Delle sigle usate da Cristoforo Colombo nella sua firma.* Genoa: Tipogr. Sordo-Muti, 1876.

——. *Disquisiioni Colombine No. 4: La favola di Alonso Sanchez, precursore e maestro di Cristoforo Colombo. Parte prima, studi storico-critici.* Lisboa: Tipografia della Reale Academia delle Scienze, 1896.

——. *Intorno alla seconda edizione della storia di Cristoforo Colombo del Conte Roselly de Lorgues (Parigi 1879).* Genova: Tipografia de Gaetano Schenone, 1881.

——. *Se Cristoforo Colombo abbia studiato all'universita di Padua.* Genova: Tipografia de Gaetano Schenone, 1881.

——. *Vita de Cristoforo Colombo.* Genova: Presso Antonio Bettolo Libraio, 1846.

Santa Cruz, Alonso (de). *Crónica de los Reyes Católicos.* Sevilla: Edición Carriazo, 1951.

Sanz, Carlos. *Bibliografía general de la carta de Colón.* Madrid: Librería General Victoriano Suarez, 1958.

——. *La carta de Colón anunciando el descubrimiento del Nuevo Mundo, 15 Febrero–14 Marzo 1493: Reprodución del texto original español impreso en Barcelona (Pedro Posa 1493).* Madrid: Gráficas Yagües, 1961. Facsimile.

——. *Concepto histórico-geográfico de la Creación: Mundo, Otro Mundo, Nuevo Mundo y Plus Ultra (con ilustraciones documentadas).* Madrid: Librería Victoriano Suarez, 1960.

——. *Descubrimiento del Continente Americano: Relación del tercer viaje por Don Cristóbal Colón.* Madrid: Gráficas Yagües, 1962. Facsimile.

————. *Diario de Colón: Libro de la primera navegación y descubrimiento de las indias.* Madrid: Gráficas Yagües, 1962. Facsimile.

————. *El gran secreto de la carta de Colón: (Crítica histórica) y Otras adiciones a la Bibliotheca Americana Vetustissima.* Madrid: Librería General Victoriano Suarez, 1959. Facsimiles.

————. *Indice general: Henry Harrisse (1829–1910), "Principe de los Americanistas," su vida—su obra con nuevas adiciones a la Biliotheca Americana Vetustissima.* Madrid: Libreria General Victoriano Suarez, 1958. Facsimiles.

Sauer, Carl Ortwin. *The Early Spanish Main.* Berkeley: University of California Press, 1969.

Saunders, Frederick. *The Story of the Discovery of the New World by Columbus, Compiled from Accepted Authorities.* New York: Thomas Whittaker, 1892.

Schama, Simon. "They All Laughed at Christopher Columbus." *New Republic*, January 3 and 13 1992, pp. 30–40.

Schoenbaum, S. *Shakespeare's Lives.* Oxford: Clarendon Press, 1991.

Sepúlveda, Juan Ginés (de). *De rebus Hispanorum ad novum terrarum Orbem, Mexicumque: Gestis.* 1521. Edited by Demetrio Ramos. Valladolid: Graficas 66, 1976.

————. *Historia del Nuevo Mundo.* Edited by Antonio Ramírez de Verger, from the Trujillo or Torrepalma Codex. Madrid: Alianza Editorial, 1987.

Simpson, Lesley Byrd. *Los conquistadores y el indio americano.* Barcelona: Gráficas Saturno, 1970.

Sociedad del Archivo Hispalense. *Curiosidades Bibliográficas y Documentos Inéditos. Homenje del Archivo Hispalesne al Cuatro Centenario del descubrimiento del Nuevo Mundo.* Sevilla: En la Oficina de E. Rasco, 1892. Facimiles of the Dati versification of the "first letter" and other documents.

Solórzano Pereira, Juan (de). *Política Indiana.* 2 vols. 1648; Madrid: Matheo Sacristan, 1736, 1739.

Spotorno, Gio. Battista. *Della origine e della patria di Cristoforo Colombo.* Genova: Presso Andrea Frugoni, 1819.

————. *Codice diplomatico Colombo-Americano ofsia Raccolta di Documenti Originali e Inediti, spettanti a Cristoforo Colombo alla scoperta ed al Governo dell'America Publicato per ordine degl'Ill.mi Decurioni della Città di' Genova.* Genova: Dalla Stamperia e Fonderia Ponthenier, 1823.

Suárez de Peralta, Juan. *Tratado del descubrimiento de las Yndias y su conquísta (transcripción del manuscrito de 1589)*. Edited by Giorgio Perissinotto. Madrid: Alianza Editorial, 1990.

Sumien, N. *La Correspondance du savant florentin Paolo dal Pozzo Toscanelli avec Christophe Colomb*. Paris: Societé d'Editions Geographiques, Maritimes at Coloniales, 1927.

Taviani, Paolo Emilio. *I viaggio di Colombo: La grande scoperta*. Novara, Italy: Istituto Geografico de Agostini, 1986.

Tejera y Penson, Emiliano. *Los dos restos de Cristóbal Colón exhumados de la catedral de Santo Domingo en 1795 i 1877*. Santo Domingo: Imprenta de Garcia Hermanos, 1878.

———. *Los Restos de Colón en Santo Domingo*. Santo Domingo: Imprenta de J. R. Vda. Garcia, 1879.

Thacher, John Boyd. *Christopher Columbus: His Life, His Works, His Remains as Revealed by Original Printed and Manuscript Records, Together with an Essay on Peter Martyr of Anghera, and Bartolomé Las Casas, the First Historians of America*. 3 vols. New York: G. P. Putnam's Sons, 1903–4. Facsimiles.

Tillinghast, William H. "The Geographical Knowledge of the Ancients in Relation to the Discovery of America." In Winsor, *Narrative and Critical History*, 1:33–58.

Todorov, Zvetan. *The Conquest of America: The Question of the Other*. Translated by Richard Howard. New York: Harper Perennial, 1992.

———. "Voyagers and Natives." In Garin, *Renaissance Characters*.

Travers, Emile. *Alonso Sanchez de Huelva et la tradition qui lui attribue la découverte du Nouveau Monde*. Caen, France: Henri Desleques, 1892.

Trivigiano, Angelo. *Libretto De Tutta La Nauigatione De Re De Spagna De Le Isole Et Terreni Nouamente Trovati*. Venice: Albertino Vercelle, 1504. (See Thacher, *Christopher Columbus*, for the first facsimile as well as an English translation of the copy in Venice's San Marco Library.)

———. *Libretto de Tutta la nauigatione de re de Spagna de le isole et terreni nuouamente trouati*. Introduction by Lawrence C. Wroth. Paris: Librairie Ancienne Honoré Champion, 1930. Facsimile of the copy in the John Carter Brown Library.

Trucchi, Francesco. *Del primi scopritori del nuovo continente americano*. Forence: Tipografia Gran Ducale, 1842.

Tuchman, Barbara. *Practicing History*. New York: Alfred A. Knopf, 1981.

Udina Martorell, Federico. *Capitulaciones del Almirante Don Cristóbal Colón y salvaconductos para el descubrimiento del Nuevo Mundo*.

Transcription by Rafael Conde and Delgado de Molina. Maracena, Spain: Excma. Diputación de Granada, 1983. Facsimiles.

Uhagon, Francisco de. *La Patria de Colón según los documentos de las ordenes militares.* Madrid: Libreria de Fernado Fé, 1892.

Utrera, Fray Cipriano (de). *Isabel la Católica Fundadora de la Ciudad de Santo Domingo.* Ciudad Trujillo: Tipografía Franciscana, 1951. Also in *El Faro á Colón* 4 (1951): 27–76 and *CLIO* 91 (1950): 116–32.

———. "Rodán e ingrato." *El Faro á Colón* 5 (1952): 56–76.

Varela, Consuelo. *Colón y los florentinos.* Madrid: Alianza América, 1988.

———. *Cristóbal Colón: Los cuatro viajes. Testamento.* Madrid: Alianza Editorial, 1986.

———. *Cristóbal Colón: Retrato de un hombre.* 3d ed. Madrid: Alianza Editorial, 1992.

———. "Diego Alvarez Chanca, cronista del Segundo Viaje Colombino." *Historia y Bibliografía Americanistas* (Sevilla) 29 (1985): 35–82.

———, ed. *Cristóbal Colón: Textos y documentos completos.* 3d ed., revised and including the *nuevas cartas* from "El libro copiador" edited by Juan Gil. Madrid: Alianza Universidad, 1992. (1st ed., 1982.)

Varnhagen, Francisco Adolfo (de). *Carta de Colón enviada de Lisboa a Barcelona en marzo de 1493.* Limited ed. Vienna: Tipografía T. y R. del E. de la Corte, 1869.

Vascano, Antonio. *Ensayo biográfico del celebre navegante e consumado cosmógrafo Juan de la Cosa y descripción é historia de su famosa carta geográfica.* Madrid: Tipo-Litografía de V. Faure, 1882.

Verlinden, Charles. *Christophe Colomb et Barthelemy Díaz.* Lisbon: Academia de Ciencias, 1979.

Verlinden, Charles, and Florentino Pérez-Embid. *Cristóbal Colón. El descubrimiento de América.* Pamplona, Spain: Rialp Navarra, 1967.

Vespucci, Amerigo. *Lettera di Amerigo Vespucci delle isole nuouamente trovati in quattro suoi viagi.* Princeton: Princeton University Press, 1916. The "Soderini Letter" (1504) in facsimile.

———. *The Mundus Novus Letter to Lorenzo Pietro di Medici in Translation.* Princeton: Princeton University Press, 1916. Facsimile.

———. *Paesi nouamente retrovati et novo mondo da Alberico Vesputio Florentino intitulati (1508).* Princeton: Princeton University Press, 1916. Facsimile of the Vicenza edition. (Facsimile of passages in the 1512 edition referring to Columbus is in Cittá de Genova, *Cristoforo Colombo*, 93.)

Vignaud, Henry. *Americ Vespuce, 1451–1512, son bibliographie, sa vie ses voyages, ses Découvertes: L'attribution de son nom a l'Amérique,* ses relations authentiques et contestés. Paris: Ernest Leroux Editeur, 1917.

———. *Histoire critique de la Grande Entreprise de Christophe Colomb, Comment il aurait conçu et formé son projet. Sa présentation a différentes cours. Son acceptation finale. Sa mise en exécution—son véritable caractère.* Limited ed. 2 vols. Paris: H. Welter, 1911.

———. *The Real Birth-Date of Columbus, 1451: A Critical Study of the Various Dates Assigned to the Birth of Christopher Columbus, the Real Date 1451 with a Bibliography of the Question.* London: Henry Stevens, Son and Stiles, 1903.

———. *Toscanelli and Columbus: The Letter and Chart of Toscanelli on the Route to the Indies by Way of the West, Sent in 1474 to the Portuguese Fernam Martins and Later on to Christopher Columbus—A Critical Study on the Authenticity and Value of These Documents and the Sources of Cosmographical Ideas of Columbus, Followed by the Various Texts of the Letter, with Translations, Annotations, Several Facsimiles, and Also a Map.* London: Sands and Company, 1902.

Vigneras, Louis-André. *The Discovery of South America and the Andalusian Voyages.* Chicago: University of Chicago Press, 1976.

Vitoria, Francisco (de). *Grandes figuras de la evangelización de America. Fray Francisco de Vitoria.* Santo Domingo: Amigo del Hogar, 1992.

———. *Reflecciones sobre los indios y el derecho de guerra.* Edited by Armando D. Pirotto. Madrid: Espasa-Calpe, 1975.

Wagner, Henry R. *Peter Martyr and His Works.* Separatum: American Antiquarian Society, 1947.

Wasserman, Jakob. *Cristóbal Colón: El Quijote del Océano.* Madrid: Ediciones Ulíses, 1930.

West, Delno C., and August Kling. *The Libro de las profecías of Christopher Columbus: An en face edition.* Gainesville: University of Florida Press, 1991. Transcription, translation, and commentary. Facsimile.

Wiesenthal, Simon. *Operación Nuevo Mundo (La misión secreta de Cristóbal Colón).* Barcelona: AYMA S.A., 1973.

Wilford, John Noble. *The Mapmakers: The Story of the Great Pioneers in Cartography, from Antiquity to the Space Age.* New York: Alfred A. Knopf, 1981.

———. *The Mysterious History of Columbus: An Exploration of the Man, the Myth, the Legacy.* New York: Alfred A. Knopf, 1991.

Williamson, James A. *The Cabot Voyages and Bristol Discovery under Henry VII, with the Cartography of the Voyages by R. A. Skelton.* London: Hakluyt Society, 1962; Kraus reprint, Millwood, N.Y., 1986.

Winsor, Justin. *Christopher Columbus and How He Received and Imparted the Spirit of Discovery.* Boston: Houghton, Mifflin and Company, 1892.

————, ed. *Narrative and Critical History of America.* 8 vols. Boston: Houghton, Mifflin and Company, 1884–89.

Ximenez de Sandoval, Felipe. *Cristóbal Colón. Evocación del Almirante de la mar Océanea.* Madrid: Ediciones Cultura Hispánica, 1968.

Young, Filson. *Christopher Columbus and the New World of His Discovery.* 2 vols. London: E. Grant Richards, 1906.

Yule, Henry (Sir), trans. and ed. *Cathay and the Way Thither. Being a Collection of Medieval Notices of China.* Revised edition by Henri Cordier. 4 vols. London: Hakluyt Society, 1913–16; Kraus reprint, Millwood, N.Y., 1967.

Zamora, Margarita. "Christopher Columbus's 'Letter to the Sovereigns': Announcing the Discovery." In Greenblatt, *New World Encounters.*

————. *Reading Columbus.* Berkeley: University of California Press, 1993.

Zas, Enrique. *Si . . . ¡Colón Español! Refutación al folleto ¿Colón Español? publicado por Don Angel Altoaguirre y Duvale, individuo de numero de la Real Academia de la Historia.* Havana: Imprenta y Papeleria de Rambla, Bouza y Ca., 1924.

Zavala, Silvio A. *Las instituciones jurídicas en la conquista de américa.* Mexico City: Editora Porrua, 1971.

Zeri, Augusto. *Tre lettere di Cristoforo Colombo ed Amerigo Vespucci. Pubblicate per le prima volta dal monistero del Fomento in ispagna. Recate in lingua italiana col testo spagnuolo a fronte.* Rome: Tipografia della Pace, 1881.

Index